THE

ENTERTAINMENT

2011-2012

SOURCEBOOK

Authored and edited
by the
**ASSOCIATION OF THEATRICAL
ARTISTS AND CRAFTSPEOPLE**

APPLAUSE
THEATRE & CINEMA BOOKS

W9-BJG-390

Copyright © 2010 by Association of Theatrical Artists and Craftspeople

All rights reserved. No part of this book may be reproduced in any form, without written permission, except by a newspaper or magazine reviewer who wishes to quote brief passages in connection with a review.

Published in 2010 by Applause Theatre & Cinema Books
An Imprint of Hal Leonard Corporation
7777 West Bluemound Road
Milwaukee, WI 53213

Trade Book Division Editorial Offices
33 Plymouth St., Montclair, NJ 07042

Printed in the United States of America

Book design by members of ATAC

ISBN 978-1-4234-9274-0

ISSN 1545-4037

www.applausepub.com

The Entertainment Sourcebook
New Listings Information Sheet

If you know of a company that you feel is such a great resource that you would like to see them included in the next edition of our book, please submit their information below for consideration. The Association of Theatrical Artists and Craftspeople (ATAC) will review and/or visit the company to consider listing them in the next edition of the Entertainment Sourcebook.

Company / Last, First Name:_____

Contact Name:_____

Address:_____

Cross Streets:_____

City, State, Zip:_____

Business Phone:_____

Fax Phone:_____

Other Phones:_____

Business Hours:_____

E-mail:_____

Web Address:_____

Business Description:_____

_____

Accept Credit Cards?_____Rentals?_____

Suggested Categories_____

_____

***Annotation (25 words or less)_____

_____

Please Send, Fax or E-mail to:
The Association of Theatrical Artists and Craftspeople (ATAC)
48 Fairway St.
Bloomfield, NJ 07003-5515
(973) 320-4493
E-mail: ATACSourcebook@aol.com, or visit our website at www.entertainmentsourcebook.com

*** To be sure this company is included in the *2013-2014 Entertainment Sourcebook*, you must write the annotation. The listing will not be accepted without the annotation written. Please refer to the current sourcebook for typical content and style.

ATAC

THE ASSOCIATION OF THEATRICAL ARTISTS AND CRAFTSPEOPLE

ATAC is a professional trade association for artists and craftspeople working in theatre, film, television and advertising. Members are able to meet their peers, make new contacts, increase their exposure in the industry and discuss professional concerns. ATAC creates a professional network through quarterly meetings, a membership directory and articles in the ATAC Quarterly.

Our members are some of the most experienced and sought after artists and craftspeople in the industry. Their work can be seen on and Off-Broadway, at Radio City Music Hall, the Metropolitan Opera, feature films, major television programs, print work and other various productions all over the world.

For more information about ATAC contact us at:

THE ASSOCIATION OF THEATRICAL
ARTISTS AND CRAFTSPEOPLE (ATAC)
48 Fairway St.
Bloomfield, NJ 07003-5515
E-mail: info@ATACBIZ.com
www.ATACBIZ.com
For more information about The Entertainment
Sourcebook contact us at:
E-mail: ATACSourcebook@aol.com

ATAC EDITORIAL STAFF 2010-2011
Cindy Anita Fain, Chairperson, Database Manager
Nadine Charlsen, Computer Layout Manager
Arnold S. Levine, Deborah Glassberg, Editing Committee
Anne-Marie Wright, Corrie Griffin,
Stanley Sherman, Sarah Timberlake, Member Verifiers
and Josh Schnetzer, Kean University Student Verifier

Also thank you to our honorary ATAC members, Marty Vreeland, Mike Huffman, Sharon McCardell, Rolande Duprey, Jenifer Shenker-Greene, Richard Storm and Julie Heneghan

Table of Contents

CONTENTS

By the Association of Theatrical Artists and Craftspeople

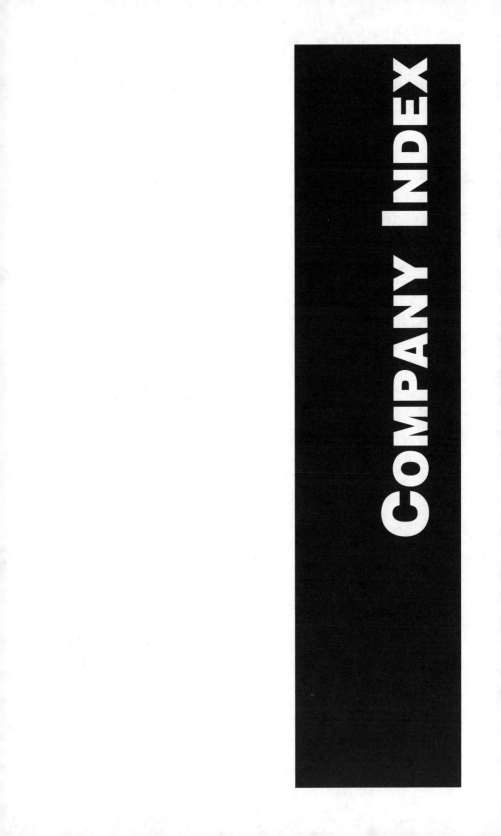

COMPANY INDEX

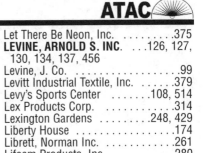

M

P

www.entertainmentsourcebook.com

**COMPANIES LISTED IN BOLD CAPITALS
ARE MEMBERS OF ATAC.**

**THEY ARE ALSO SHOWN IN BOLD IN THE
INDIVIDUAL CATEGORIES THROUGHOUT
THE BOOK.**

**The professional trade association for artists and craftspeople
working in theatre, film, television and advertising**

ATAC Membership 2010-11

Sharlot Battin	Marian Jean "Killer" Hose	Adele Recklies
Montana Leatherworks	J. Michelle Hill	Monona Rossol
Chris Bobin	Louise Hunnicutt	Arts, Crafts, & Theatre
Sharon Braunstein	John Jerard	Safety (A.C.T.S.)
Randy Carfagno	Jerard Studio	Bill Rybak
Nadine Charlsen	Joni Johns	Jody Schoffner
Eileen Connor	Jan Kastendieck	James R. Seffens
Mary Creede	Rachel Keebler	Lisa Shaftel
Margaret Cusack	Cobalt Studios	Shaftel S2DO
Cindy Anita Fain	Amanda Klein	Stanley Allen Sherman
CINAF Designs	Arnold S. Levine	Mask Arts Company
James Feng	Arnold S. Levine, Inc.	Linda Skipper
Keen Gat	Janet Linville	Michael Smanko
Deborah R. Glassberg	Jeanne Marino	Prism Prips
Rodney Gordon	Moonboots Productions	Sarah Timberlake
Joseph Gourley	Jerry Marshall	Timberlake Studios
Corrinna Griffin	Betsey McKearnan	Mari Tobita
Jung K. Griffin	Gene Mignola	US Institute for Theatre
Denise Grillo	Gene Mignola, Inc.	Tech. (USITT)
Offstage Design	Mary Mulder	Monique Walker
Stockton Hall	Mulder / Martin, Inc.	Anne-Marie Wright
Karen Hart	Susan Pitocchi	John Yavroyan
Suzanne Hayden	Elizabeth Popeil	Yavroyan & Nelsen, LTD

For membership information visit our website at
www.ATACBIZ.com
Email: info@ATACBIZ.com
Or drop us a line at:

ATAC Membership Application
Anne-Marie Wright
280 Third St. Apt # 1
Jersey City, NJ 07302-2759

ADHESIVES & GLUES

3M Company ....(product info) 651-737-6501
3M Center 800-364-3577
St. Paul, MN 55144 FAX 800-713-6329
Hours: 7-6 Mon-Fri
www.3m.com
Distributors of 3M glues and respirators. Some minimums required.

Adhesive Products Co. 323-589-5516
4727 E 48th St. FAX 323-589-6460
Los Angeles, CA 90058
Hours: 8-4:30 Mon-Fri E-mail: sales@api-la.com
www.adhesiveproductsinc.com
Adhesives and label printers. CREDIT CARDS.

Adhesives Tech., Inc. ....(orders) 800-458-3486
3 Merrill Industrial Dr. 603-926-1616
Hampton, NH 03842 FAX 603-926-1780
Hours: 8-5 Mon-Fri E-mail: marketing@adhesivetech.com
www.adhesivetech.com
Glitter glues, glue gun with flat wide to small round interchangeable tips,
glue pads. Literature package available. CREDIT CARDS.

Basic Adhesives, Inc. 973-614-9000
60 Webro Rd. 800-394-9310
Clifton, NJ 07012 FAX 973-614-9099
Hours: 9-5 Mon-Fri E-mail: myrna@basicadhesives.com
www.basicadhesives.com
Gripstix and a variety of adhesives for many applications.

Beacon Adhesives 914-699-3405
125 MacQuesten Pkwy. South FAX 914-699-2783
Mt. Vernon, NY 10550
Hours: 8:30-4:30 Mon-Fri E-mail: davidmesh@cs.com
www.beacon1.com
Manufacturers of millinery adhesives and lacquers. $50 minimum.

Bostik, Inc. 414-774-2250
11320 Watertown Plank Rd. 800-558-4302
Wauwatosa, WI 53226 FAX 414-774-8075
Hours: 8-4:30 Mon-Fri
www.bostik-us.com
Adhesives and textile coatings and caulks.

The Compleat Sculptor, Inc. 212-243-6074
90 Vandam St. (Hudson-Greenwich) 800-9-SCULPT
NY, NY 10013 FAX 212-243-6374
Hours: 9-6 Mon, Thurs-Sat / 9-8 Tue-Wed E-mail: tcs@sculpt.com
www.sculpt.com
Carries complete line of sculpture materials including; clay, wood, wax,
sculpting tools, alabaster, marble, mold-making and casting materials, books,
videos, pedestals and bases. Friendly and knowledgeable help. Catalog.
Technical support line (212) 367-7561. CREDIT CARDS.

Delta Creative, Inc. 562-943-0003
2690 Pellissier Pl.   800-423-4135
City of Industry, CA 90601   FAX 562-695-4227
Hours: 8-5 Mon-Fri   E-mail: advisor@deltacreative.com
www.deltacreative.com
Manufacturer of Sobo, Velverette, Quik and Tacky in quantity; phone for info.
Distributors. Tax ID or resale number required. $100 minimum order, ships
COD.

Ellsworths Adhesive 800-888-0698
W129 N10825 Washington Dr.   262-253-8600
Germantown, WI 53022   FAX 262-253-8619
Hours: 8-5 Mon-Fri   E-mail: webcsrs@ellsworth.com
www.ellsworth.com
Good source of adhesives and glues, glue guns. Helpful service. View
website for other locations. CREDIT CARDS.

Hollywood Rentals Production Services 800-233-7830
19731 Nordhoff St.   FAX 818-407-7875
Northridge, CA 91324
Hours: 8-6 Mon-Fri / mobile car for 24-hr. service
www.hollywoodrentals.com
Fulleri̇s earth, glue, tape and other studio supplies. Will deliver. CREDIT
CARDS.

Jurgen Industries, Inc. 800-735-7248
17461 147th St,. SE, Ste. 13   360-794-7886
Monroe, WA 98272   FAX 360-794-9825
Hours: 9-4 Mon-Thurs / 9-3 Fri   E-mail: sales@jurgeninc.com
www.jurgenindustries.com (Wholesale) www.glassgiftsforless.com (retail)
Glass stain color designed for simulated i̇tiffanyi̇ glass. Also have synthetic
non-toxic product for stained glass production. First order $75 minimum.
CREDIT CARDS.

Loctite Corp. . . . .(Consumer Div.) 440-937-7000
1001 Trout Brook Crossing   (Industrial Div.) 860-571-5100
Rocky Hill, CT 06067   FAX 860-571-5465
Hours: 8-5 Mon-Fri (office) / 8-8 Mon-Fri (tech & sales)
www.loctite.com
Distributors of industrial glues. Customer and technical assistance. Catalog
available. Some minimums required. (Technical) 800-562-8483. No credit
cards.

Louis Birns & Sons, Ltd. 518-690-7141
6 Charles Blvd.   800-533-3023
Guilderland, NY 12084   FAX 518-690-7142
Hours: 8-5 Mon-Fri   E-mail: lbssons@vuno.com
Wholesale to the shoe and leather repair trades. Pre-cut leather soles, half
soles and heels. Lacings, leather dyes and glues, shoemaker supplies.
CREDIT CARDS.

McGinley Adhesive Distribution Svc., Inc. 201-493-9330
   80 Greenwood Ave. Unit 8   FAX 201-670-7789
   Midland Park, NJ 07432
   Hours: 9-5 Mon-Fri
   Carries dextrin paste; will locate sources for hard-to-find adhesives. Hot
   melts, white glues, and contact adhesives. CREDIT CARDS.

Numax, Inc. 800-842-4230
   1073 Rte 94, Unit 11   845-674-9060
   New Windsor, NY 12553   FAX 845-562-1145
   Hours: 8-5 Mon-Fri (Close at 4:30 on Fridays in summer)
   www.numax.com
   East Coast distributor of Duo-Fast products. Staplers, nailers, tackers (air and
   electric); tapes and adhesives; hot melt glue guns. Phone orders. No
   minimum. CREDIT CARDS.

Rosco Laboratories, Inc. 203-708-8900
   52 Harbor View Ave.   800-ROSCONY
   Stamford, CT 06902   FAX 203-708-8919
   Hours: 9-5 Mon-Fri   E-mail: info@rosco.com
   www.rosco.com
   Flexbond, Foamcoate, Roscobond. Adhesives and coatings formulated for
   scenic needs.

Sculptural Arts Coating, Inc. 800-743-0379
   2912 Baltic Ave.   336-379-7652
   Greensboro, NC 27406   FAX 336-379-7653
   Hours: 9-5 Mon-Fri
   www.sculpturalarts.com
   Creators of Sculpt or Coat; foam coat, clearcoating, adhesive. Plastic Varnish;
   sealer, binder, extender. Tough 'N White primers and high quality scenic
   brushes. CREDIT CARDS.

Smooth-On, Inc. 610-252-5800
   2000 St. John's St.   800-762-0744
   Easton, PA 18042   FAX 610-252-6200
   Hours: 8:30-5:30 Mon-Fri   E-mail: smoothon@smooth-on.com
   www.smooth-on.com
   Industrial strength epoxies for set construction, all applications. Free
   samples, literature and technical help available. $20.00 minimum order.
   Phone orders. CREDIT CARDS.

Sprotzer Tools & Hardware Co., Inc. 718-349-2580
   2743 Jackson Ave.
   Long Island City, NY 11101
   Hours: 8-5 Mon-Fri
   Hot glue guns and medium quantity cartons of pellets. Wholesale hand tools
   and cutting tools. Phone orders accepted. No credit cards.

ATAC

Supply One 718-392-7400
58-51 Maspeth Ave.   FAX 718-361-2733
Maspeth, NY 11378
Hours: 8-5 Mon-Fri   E-mail: info-newyork@supplyone.com
www.supplyone.com
Hot glue by 25lb. carton or more; phone and fax orders delivered. Kraft paper.
Packing materials and janitorial supplies. Adhesives and glues, staples and
staple guns. Contact Katie Singh @ X230. CREDIT CARDS.

Technical Library Services, Inc./ TALAS 212-219-0770
330 Morgan Ave.   FAX 212-219-0735
Brooklyn, NY 11211
Hours: 9-5:30 Mon-Fri
www.talasonline.com
Acid-free adhesives and glues, conservation supplies and bookbinding
supplies.

Tomar Industries 732-780-2200
300 Commerce Dr.   FAX 732-780-4123
Freehold, NJ 07728
Hours: 9-5 Mon-Fri   E-mail: tfieldjr@tomarind.com
www.tomarind.com
Gaffers, duct, many types of pressure-sensitive tapes. Honeycomb paper
products. Janitorial supplies, safety equipment and adhesives. A 3-M dealer.
CREDIT CARDS.

Worthen Industries 800-967-8436
3 E Spit Brook Rd.   603-888-5443
Nashua, NH 03060   FAX 603-888-7945
Hours: 8-5 Mon-Fri
www.worthenind.com
Manufacturers of UPACO 1812, a non-toxic water-based contact cement for
foams, fabrics, leathers and most materials used in theater productions.
Minimum order 5 gallons. CREDIT CARDS.

AMUSEMENT PARK & CIRCUS EQUIPMENT
See also: ARCADE & AMUSEMENT DEVICES
    TOYS & GAMES

Brian Dube, Inc. 212-941-0060
520 Broadway, 3rd Fl. (Spring-Broome)   800-763-0909
NY, NY 10012   FAX 212-941-0793
Hours: 10-6 Mon-Fri   E-mail: info@dube.com
www.dube.com
Manufacturer of juggling equipment. Catalog available. CREDIT CARDS.

Frankies Carnival Time 877-937-2652
3437 E Tremont Ave. (Bruckner Blvd)   718-823-3033
Bronx, NY 10465   FAX 718-824-2979
Hours: 9-6 Mon-Sat / until 7 Fri / 9-3 Sun   E-mail: frankiebe@aol.com
www.frankiescarnival.com
Carnival games, booths, carts, fun house mirrors, inflatable rides, dunk tanks
and bingo supplies. Hot dog carts, Cotton Candy and Popcorn machines.
Tents, chairs, tables, etc. RENTALS. CREDIT CARDS.

Jukebox Classics & Vintage Slot Machines 718-833-8455
36 72nd St.   FAX 718-833-0560
Brooklyn, NY 11209
Hours: by appt. only
Carousel animals, coin operated antiques, arcade games, slot machines. Will help locate unusual items. Speak to John. RENTALS. CREDIT CARDS.

Paladin Amusements, Inc. 908-464-0826
9 Maple Ave.   800-699-8552
Berkeley Heights, NJ 07922   FAX 908-464-3661
www.paladinamusements.com   E-mail: paladin@paladinamusements.com
Rental of Carnival games, trailers, tents, rides, speedball, hi-striker and other carnival and amusement equipment. Sales of carnival and boardwalk-type prizes and merchandise. RENTALS.

PM Amusements 914-937-1188
36 Bush Ave.   FAX 914-939-8189
Port Chester, NY 10573
Hours: 9-5 Mon-Fri / 10-3 Sat
www.pmamusements.com
All types of amusement park and circus games, food booths. Including the popular Sumo Wrestlers, dunk machines, casino equipment, props and decor. RENTALS. CREDIT CARDS.

ANIMAL RENTAL
For stuffed animal rental, see TAXIDERMISTS & TAXIDERMY SUPPLIES

All Creatures Great And Small 914-232-3623
3 Little Ln.   914-682-8870
White Plains, NY 10605   FAX 914-328-3331
Hours: 24-hour phone service and by appt.   E-mail: cat@animalagent.com
www.animalagent.com
Professional animal talent and handlers. Over 40 years of experience in the business. Exotic and domestic animals handled by professionals. Speak to Cathryn or Ruth.

All-Tame Animals, Inc. 212-873-5000
440 West End Ave. (81st St)   FAX 212-873-5000
NY, NY 10024
Hours: by appt.   E-mail: alltameanimals@aol.com
www.alltameanimals.com
Trained animals for film, theatre, fashion, parties and advertising. Many references. Dogs, ponies, carriage horses, donkeys and birds.

Animal Actors 908-537-7800
4 American Way   FAX 908-537-7801
Glen Gardner, NJ 08826
Hours: 24-hour phone service   E-mail: mcauliff@eclipse.net
www.animalactorsinc.com
Speak to Steve or Carol.

Animals for Advertising 212-245-2590
310 W 55th St., Ste. 6H (8-9th Ave)   FAX 212-262-2531
NY, NY 10019
Hours: by appt.   E-mail: animals4advertising@gmail.com
All types; speak to Linda Hanrahan.

William Berloni Theatrical Animals, Inc. 860-345-8734
181 Little City Rd.   Cell 860-478-3935
Higganum, CT 06441   FAX 860-345-3184
Hours: by appt.   E-mail: wberloni@sbcglobal.net
www.theatricalanimals.com
*Humanely trained animals for all media. Animal rental. Contact William
Berloni.*

Chateau Theatrical Animals & Chateau Stable 212-246-0520
608 W 48th St. (11-12th Ave)   FAX 718-828-4636
NY, NY 10036
Hours: 10-6 Mon-Fri (office) / stables always open
                                   E-mail: trackergirl99@yahoo.com
www.chateauweddingcarriages.com
*Horses and horse-drawn vehicles, carriages, wagons, carts. Catalog of props
and brochure available. CREDIT CARDS.*

Dawn Animal Agency 212-575-9396
413 W 47th St. (46th St)   FAX 212-575-9726
NY, NY 10036
Hours: 10-6 Mon-Fri / on call 24 hours   E-mail: dawnanimalagcy@aol.com
www.dawnanimalagency.com
*Exotic and domestic animals with handlers; also carriages, wagons. 300 acre
farm available for location shoots. RENTALS.*

Exotics Unlimited 718-720-4677
16 Sunset Ave.
Staten Island, NY 10314
Hours: 8-7 seven days a week   E-mail: exoticsunlimated@aol.com
www.exoticanimalsunlimited.com
*Animal talent agency; mostly exotics; snakes, birds, large cats. Will train.
RENTALS.*

Frank J. Zitz & Company, Inc. 845-876-4896
479 Schultz Hill Rd.   FAX 845-876-5541
Rhinebeck, NY 12572
Hours: 7:30-5:30 Mon-Fri   E-mail: zitzf@valstar.net
www.taxidermymuseum.com
*Taxidermy rentals mounted animals, birds etc. Cleaning, repair and
restoration services available. Located about 1 1/2 hours from Manhattan.
RENTALS. CREDIT CARDS.*

God of Insects 914-318-6814
P.O. Box 343
Hastings on Hudson, NY 10706
Hours: 24-hr. website　　　　　　　E-mail: contact@godofinsects.com
www.godofinsects.com

God Of Insects grants you access to thousands of insects and their kin. Whether you need them for a photo shoot or display, they have just about anything you could be looking for. Offers bug wrangling services as well as displays of various framed and under glass insects. Be sure to check out website. RENTALS. PayPal, Checks or Money Orders.

ANTIQUE TRADES

William Cahill / Roof Thatching & Bamboo 513-772-4974
PO Box 62054　　　　　　　　　　　　　　　FAX 513-772-6313
Cincinnati, OH 45262
Hours: by appt.　　　　　　　　　　E-mail: info@roofthatch.com
www.roofthatch.com

Specializing in custom roof thatching for interior and exterior themes and displays. Bamboo and Eucalyptus poles.

Angela Scott 202-547-7945
414 Seventh St. SE
Washington, DC 20003
Hours: by appt.

Custom bookbinding, portfolios, restorations, new bindings, cases, gold stamping. Will design for customers. No credit cards.

Victor Trading Company & Manufacturing Works 719-689-2346
114 S Third St. / P.O. Box 53
Victor, CO 80860
Hours: 10-5 Daily　　　　　　　　　e-mail: mail@victortradingco.com
www.victortradingco.com

A dozen styles of brooms made ithe old-fashioned way," on a foot powered broom winder, circa 1900. Good selection and reasonable prices. Also carry nice variety of hand-dipped candles, etc. Call for literature.

ANTIQUES: EUROPEAN & AMERICAN

ABC Carpet & Home Co., Inc. 212-473-3000
888 Broadway(19th St)　　　　　　　　　　　　212-473-3000
NY, NY 10003　　　　　　　　　　　　　　FAX 212-777-3713
Hours: 10-8 Mon - Fri / 10-7 Sat / 11-6:30 Sun

1055 Bronx River Ave.(Bruckner Blvd) Outlet　　　　　718-842-8772
NY, NY 10472　　　　　　　　　　　　　　FAX 718-812-6905
Hours: 10-7 Mon - Fri / 10-7 Sat / 11-6 Sun
www.abccarpet.com

Large stock of antiques and reproductions. Sales and rental. CREDIT CARDS.

Antiek 518-766-3445
Rt. 20, 1-5 Church St.(near Rt. 203)

Nassau, NY 12123
Hours: 11-4:30 Wed-Mon
FAX 518-766-9826
E-mail: info@antiekllc.com

274 River St.
Troy, NY 12180
Hours: 11-4:30 Wed-Mon
www.livingroomantiques.com
518-266-9344

Full line of formal and country antiques. RENTALS. CREDIT CARDS.

Antiques Plus 201-392-1828
100 Dorigo Ln. (Cortelyou Rd)
Secaucus, NJ 07094
Hours: 10-6 Mon-Sat
FAX 201-392-1715

Rugs, tapestries, glassware, china, silver, furniture. Speak with Joel Stern.

Barton Sharpe, Ltd. 646-935-1500
200 Lexington Ave. Ste. 914 (32-33rd St)
NY, NY 10012
Hours: 9-5 Mon-Sat
www.bartonsharpe.com
FAX 646-935-1555

E-mail: info@bartonsharpe.com

Quality Reproduction 18th-early 19th American furniture. Windsor chairs, American Empire sofas, glass fronted bookcases, drop leaf tables. Also hand-blown glass in period forms. Ask for Marcos Delgado. RENTALS. CREDIT CARDS.

Belvedere Antiques 212-979-8548
(B'way-University)
NY 10003
Hours: 10-5:30 Mon-Fri / 12-5 Sat by appt. only
www.belvedereantiques.com   E-mail: info@belvedereantiques.com
Eclectic mix of antiques ranging from Venetian Rococo to Empire to Art Deco. Inventory on website. Call for appt. to go to warehouse. RENTALS. No credit cards.

Bijan Royal, Inc. 212-228-3757
60 E 11th St. (B'way-Univ Pl)
NY, NY 10003
Hours: 9-5 Mon-Fri
212-533-6390
FAX 212-982-5022
E-mail: royalant@aol.com

Five floors of French, English, Italian and Spanish antique furniture and bronzes; expensive. Contact Debbie. RENTALS. No credit cards.

Evergreen Antiques 212-744-5664
1249 Third Ave. (72nd St)
NY, NY 10021
Hours: 11-7 Mon-Fri / 1-5 Sat
www.evergreenantiques.com
FAX 212-744-5666

19th century Scandinavian and European furniture and accessories. Biedermeier, Empire and Neoclassical as well as Scandinavian Provincial antiques. RENTALS. CREDIT CARDS.

George Glazer Gallery 212-535-5706
28 E 72nd St., Ste. 3A (Park-Madison Ave)
FAX 212-658-9512

NY, NY 10021
Hours: by appt. only   E-mail: worldglobe@georgeglazer.com
www.georgeglazer.com
A fine and extensive collection of antique terrestrial and celestial globes; floor-standing, table and miniature. Armillary spheres and orreries. Also atlases, maps, antique prints and photographs. Free catalog upon request. Part of inventory on website. Contact for use of web images. RENTALS.

Global Fine Reproductions 212-533-8500
801 Broadway (11th St)   212-533-5810
NY, NY 21045   FAX 212-955-2832
Hours: 9:30-5:30 Mon-Fri   E-mail: globalfine@aol.com
18th and 19th century French and English reproduction furniture. RENTALS. CREDIT CARDS.

Golden Oldies 718-445-4400
132-29 33rd Ave. (College Pt)   FAX 718-445-4986
Flushing, NY 11354
Hours: 9-6 Mon-Sat / 11-6 Sun
www.goldenoldiesltd.com
Large collection of armoires. Small dressing items such as sporting equipment, suitcases and books for sale or rent. Visit web address for other locations and offerings. Visual merchandising and store fixtures. RENTAL. CREDIT CARDS.

Granny's Attic Antiques 201-529-5516
142 Franklin Turnpike
Mahwah, NJ 07430   FAX 201-632-0107
Hours: 11-5 Wed-Sat

619 N. Maple Ave. (Rear)(Bergen County Antiques & Auction)   201-632-0102
Ho-Ho-Kus, NJ 07423
Hours: 10-6 daily   E-mail: arial165@aol.com
www.grannysattic.com
Everything old in a diverse selection of periods and styles. 29 mins. from Manhattan. Ho-Ho-Kus location has over 30,000 sq. feet of retail space. RENTALS. CREDIT CARDS.

Howard Kaplan Designs 646-443-7170
240 E 60th St. (2nd-3rd Ave)   FAX 646-443-7174
NY, NY 10022
Hours: 10-5:30 Mon-Fri   E-mail: hkaplandesigns@aol.com
www.howardkaplandesigns.com
French and English formal and country antiques and reproductions; also lighting fixtures and vintage telephones. RENTALS. CREDIT CARDS.

Johnson & Johnson 518-789-3848
Route 22 N   FAX (same)
Millerton, NY 21045
Hours: 10-5 Fri-Sun
Large selection of antiques and used furniture; inexpensive. 2 hours from Manhattan. See Russ, Gary or Chris Johnson. No rentals. No credit cards.

A-B

Eileen Lane Antiques 212-475-2988
   150 Thompson St. (Houston-Prince St)   FAX 212-673-8669
   NY, NY 11232
   Hours: 10-5 Mon-Fri by appt. only
   www.eileenlaneantiques.com
   Swedish and Austrian, Biedermeier through Art Deco furniture. Original
   alabaster light fixtures. RENTALS. CREDIT CARDS.

Les Pierre Antiques 212-243-7740
   369 Bleecker St. (Charles St)   FAX 212-675-8273
   NY, NY 10014
   Hours: 10-6 Mon-Fri / 11-5 Sat / others by appt. E-mail: info@lespierreinc.com
   www.lespierreinc.com
   Fine selection of French country antiques. RENTALS. CREDIT CARDS.

Lillian August Designs, Inc. 203-847-3314
   32 Knight St. (North Ave-Park St)   FAX 203-852-0524
   Norwalk, CT 06851
   Hours: 10-7 Mon-Sat / 11-6 Sun   E-mail: kcavalier@lillianaugust.com
   www.lillianaugust.com
   100,000 sf of contemporary, antique and imported furnishings and
   accessories. Home and garden. Contact Kim at X 3019. RENTALS. CREDIT
   CARDS.

The Metropolitan Prop House 646-421-5128
   44-01 Eleventh St. (44th Rd)   FAX 718-392-8435
   Long Island City, NY 11101
   Hours: 9-6 Mon-Fri   E-mail: rental@metropolitanprops.com
   www.metropolitanprops.com
   European classic & modern furniture. Carpets, objects, distressed furniture,
   antiques, fabric, curtains, pillows, lamps, chandeliers, bikes and wooden
   ladders. RENTALS.

Ann Morris Antiques 212-755-3308
   239 E 60th St. (2nd-3rd Ave)   FAX 212-838-4955
   NY, NY 10022
   Hours: 9-6 Mon-Fri
   English Country; eclectic selection. Open to the trade only.

Newel Art Gallery 212-758-1970
   425 E 53rd St. (Sutton-1st Ave)   FAX 212-371-0166
   NY, NY 10022
   Hours: 8:30-5 Mon-Fri / Sat by appt.   E-mail: info@newel.com
   www.newel.com
   Extraordinary selection of antique furniture, art, architectural pieces, lamps;
   all periods. Expensive. Sales and RENTALS. No credit cards.

Paramount Antiques, Inc. 718-707-9977
   47-61 Pearson Place (University-B'way)   FAX 718-707-9976
   Long Island City, NY 11101
   Hours: 9-6 Mon-Fri   E-mail: sales@paramount-antiques.com
   www.paramount-antiques.com
   18th century period repro furniture; chairs, tables, sideboards, secretaries.
   Very reasonable.

Roland Antiques Gallery, Inc. 212-260-2000
74 E 11th St. (University-Broadway)   FAX 212-260-2778
NY, NY 10003
Hours: 10-5 Mon-Fri   E-mail: info@rolandantiques.com
www.rolandantiques.com
*18th,19th and early 20th century furniture, paintings, early antique lighting,
bric-a-brac; wholesaler. RENTALS. CREDIT CARDS.*

John Rosselli International 212-750-0060
306 E 61st St., Ground Floor   212-750-0060
NY, NY 10065   FAX 212-750-0076
Hours: 9:30-5:30 Mon-Fri

1515 Wisconsin Ave. NW   202-337-7676
Washington, DC 20007   FAX 202- 337-4443
Hours: 9:30-5:30 Mon-Fri   E-mail: info@johnroselliantiques.com
www.johnroselliantiques.com
*Beautiful selection of antique decorative items: Chinese vases, crystal, silver.
Visit website for other locations in the USA. RENTALS.*

Spencertown Arts & Antiques Co. 518-392-4445
806 State Road 203   518-392-4442
Spencertown, NY 21045
Hours: by appt.
*Unusual American colonial items; 19th and 20th century American paintings;
2 1/2 hours from Manhattan. Contact Martin Parker. AMEX.*

T & K French Antiques 212-213-2470
200 Lexington Ave., Ste. 410 (32-33rd St.)   FAX 212-213-2464
NY, NY 10016
Hours: 9-5 Mon-Fri
www.tkcollections.com
*18th and 19th century furniture and unusual decorative accessories from
France. Drucker cafe chairs. CREDIT CARDS.*

ANTIQUES: MALLS

Another Period in Time 410-675-4776
1708 Fleet St.   FAX 410-675-2777
Baltimore, MD 21231
Hours: 9-5 Mon-Thurs / 10-6 Fri-Sat / 12-5 Sun   E-mail: joe@anotherperiod.com
www.anotherperiod.com
*15 dealers under one roof! Watches, jewelry, furniture, clocks, dolls, toys,
linens, fine china, decoys, coins, pottery, advertising and many other items.
CREDIT CARDS.*

Antique Center 413-584-3600
9 1/2 Market St. (Bridge St)
Northampton, MA 01060
Hours: 10-5 Mon, Tue, Thurs-Sat. / 12-5 Sun / Closed Wed.
*Wide and varied selection of vintage and antique furnishings, decorative
accessories.*

A-B

The Antique Center of Red Bank 732-842-4336
226 W Front St. (exit 109 off Garden State Pkwy)
Red Bank, NJ 07701
Hours: 11-5 Mon-Sat / 12-5 Sun   E-mail: info@redbankantiques.com
www.redbankantiques.com
150 dealers in three buildings. 1 hour from Manhattan. RENTALS. CREDIT CARDS.

Glenwood Manor Antiques 518 798-4747
60 Glenwood Ave. (Rt. 87, exit 19E, one mile on Hwy 254)
Queensbury, NY 12824
Hours: 10-5 Mon-Sat / 12-5 Sun   E-mail: glenwood@aldelphia.net
35 dealers; will locate specific items. 3 1/2 hours from Manhattan.

The Millbrook Antiques Center 845-677-3921
3283 Franklin Ave. Rt 44
Millbrook, NY 12545
Hours: 11-5 Mon-Sat / 11:30-5:30 Sun
www.millbrooknyonline.com
44 Antique dealers under one roof. Malcom Mokotoff, owner. Some RENTALS. CREDIT CARDS.

Somerville Center Antiques 908-595-1887
34 W Main St.   908-595-1294
Somerville, NJ 08876
Hours: 11-6 Mon, Wed-Sat / 12-5 Sun
www.somervilleantiques.net
30,000 square feet of fun. Deco to pop. Everything from the 50s thru the 70s. Other shops down the street and around the corner on Difision Street. Spend a day . . . not a fortune.

ANTIQUES: VICTORIAN & 20TH CENTURY

Abeís Antiques, Inc. 212-260-6424
815 Broadway (11-12th St)
NY, NY 10003
Hours: 9:30-5:30 Mon-Fri
19th century furniture, chandeliers, objets díart and accessories. Speak to Abe. RENTALS. CREDIT CARDS.

Alice-Aliya, Inc. 905-886-1172
92 Springbrook Dr.   FAX 905-707-1549
Richmond Hill, Ontario, Canada L4B 3P9
Hours: 24-hr web   E-mail: info@alicealiya.com
www.perfumeatomizersking.com
One of the largest manufacturers of perfume atomizers in the world. This company offers art glass, antique, modern atomizers as well as replacement parts for just about any bottle you can imagine. You must visit the website to appreciate the wide selections available. Fast and efficient service. Very reasonable prices for any budget. CREDIT CARDS.

Another Period in Time 410-675-4776
1708 Fleet St.   FAX 410-675-2777
Baltimore, MD 21231
Hours: 9-5 Mon-Thurs / 10-6 Fri-Sat / 12-5 Sun   E-mail: joe@anotherperiod.com
www.anotherperiod.com
15 dealers under one roof! Watches, jewelry, furniture, clocks, dolls, toys,
linens, fine china, decoys, coins, pottery, advertising and many other items.
CREDIT CARDS.

Art & Industrial Design 212-477-0116
50 Great Jones St. (4th Ave)   FAX 212-477-1420
NY, NY 10012
Hours: 10-5 Mon-Fri / 10-1 Sat   E-mail: info@aid20c.com
www.aid20c.com
20th-century and Art Deco furniture, furnishings, art and objects. Many
original high-style works. Also collectibles, clocks and lighting fixtures.
RENTALS. CREDIT CARDS.

E. J. Audi 212-337-0700
207 W 25th St. (7-8th Ave)   FAX 212-229-2189
NY, NY 10010
Hours: 10-6 Mon-Sat / Thurs until 8 / 12-5 Sun
www.stickley.com
Mission oak reproduction.18th century cherry and mahogany reproduction
furniture. 8-12 weeks for catalog purchases. CREDIT CARDS.

Authentiques 212-675-2179
255 W 18th St. (7-8th Ave)
NY, NY 10011
Hours: 12-6 Wed-Sat / 1-6 Sun or by appt.   E-mail: fab.stuff@verizon.net
www.fab-stuff.com
1950s to 70s small props and lamps. Wonderful selection of lighting fixtures
and antique Christmas decorations.

Bikini Bar 212-571-6737
148 Duane St. (Church-W B'way)
NY, NY 10013
Hours: 12-7 Tue-Sat   E-mail: surf@bikinibar.com
www.bikinibar.com
Vintage Hawaiian rattan furniture, surfboards, travel posters and collectibles.
Surf Attire. Contact Aileen Oser or Stuart Smith. RENTALS.

Braswell Galleries 203-327-5101
1 Muller Ave.   203-357-0753
Norwalk, CT 06851   FAX 203-846-0617
Hours: 10:30-5 Mon-Sat / 11-5 Sun   E-mail: kathy@braswellgalleries.com
www.braswellgalleries.com
Wide range of furniture and furnishings, paintings, chandeliers, lighting,
artwork, glassware and china. Rugs from many time periods and also unique
items such as a x-ray machine from 1930-50. Animal heads, rowing scull and
more. Rentals as well as sales at very reasonable prices. RENTALS.

A-B

Chatsworth Auction Room & Furniture Studios 914-698-1001
151 Mamaroneck Ave. (near Boston Post Rd)   FAX 914-698-1028
Mamaroneck, NY 10543
Hours: 8-6 Tue-Sat   E-mail: john@chatsworthauctions.com
www.chatsworthstudios.com
Four floors of antique and used furniture. Desks, chairs, fireplace accessories, rugs, more. 25 mins. from Manhattan. See Sam Lightbody. RENTALS. CREDIT CARDS.

W. Chorney Antiques 203-387-9707
42 Morris St. (Westville Section)   FAX 203-387-9707
Hamden, CT 06515
Hours: call for information   E-mail: w.chorney@juno.com
Antique jukeboxes, including diner remotes; period cigarette, pinball, gumball, vending and soda fountains; radios, kitchen equipment and bar items. Antique office furniture and accessories. 90 mins. from Manhattan. Will search for items; speak to Wayne. RENTALS. AMEX.

Circa Antiques, Ltd. 718-596-1866
374 Atlantic Ave. (Hoyt-Bond St)
Brooklyn, NY 11217
Hours: 11-6 Tue-Fri / 11-6 Sat / 12-6 Sun   E-mail: circa@circaantiquesltd.com
www.circaantiquesltd.com
Mostly 19th century American furniture, paintings, lighting, accessories, also architectural salvage. See Rachel or David. RENTALS. CREDIT CARDS.

City Barn Antiques 718-855-8566
145 Front St. (Jay-Pearl St)
Brooklyn, NY 11201
Hours: 12-6 Daily   E-mail: citybarn@aol.com
1930-1960 modern furniture, lighting accessories. Specializing in vintage Heywood-Wakefield. Also Herman Miller, Knoll. RENTALS.

DeLorenzo 1950 212-995-1950
440 Lafayette St. (Astor Pl)   FAX 212-614-0610
NY, NY 10003
Hours: 10-6 Mon-Fri / 12-5 Sat   E-mail: alberto@delorenzo1950.com
www.delorenzo1950.com
Unique collection of 50s and 60s French furniture. Contact Alberto Aquilino. RENTALS.

Donzella 212-965-8919
17 White St. (6th Ave-W B'way)   FAX 212-965-0727
NY, NY 10013
Hours: 11-6 Mon-Sat   E-mail: info@donzella.com
www.donzella.com
Mid-century furniture and decorative arts. Modernist furniture designers from 40-50s. Also has ceramic and glass objects from the same period. RENTALS. AMEX.

Eclectic / Encore Properties, Inc. 212-645-8880
620 W 26th St., 4th Fl. (11-12th Ave)   FAX 212-243-6508
NY, NY 10001
Hours: 9-5 Mon-Fri / or by appt.   E-mail: props@eclecticprops.com
www.eclecticprops.com
Prop rental house with antique and reproduction furniture and furnishings.
Can request rental items thru online catalog. RENTALS. CREDIT CARDS.

Elan Antiques 212-529-2724
51 Bleeker St. (Lafayette-Mulberry)
NY, NY 10012
Hours: 1-6 Daily   E-mail: elannyc1@aol.com
Art Deco, 50s furniture, lighting accessories. RENTALS. CREDIT CARDS.

The Family Jewels 212-633-6020
130 W 23rd St. (6-7th Ave)   FAX (same)
NY, NY 10011
Hours: 11-7 Sun-Tue / 11-8 Wed-Sat   E-mail: chelseagirl@familyjewelsnyc.com
www.familyjewelsnyc.com
Victorian to 1980s clothing, textiles, accessories and bric-a-brac. Sales and
RENTALS.   CREDIT CARDS.

Farm River Antiques 203-248-2434
27 Marne St.   FAX 203-248-2433
Hamden, CT 06514
Hours: by appt only
www.farmriver.com
Large stock of original American high-style Victorian furniture. 90 mins. from
Manhattan.

Fifty-50 718-779-5050
95-11 37th Ave.   FAX 718-779-5050
Jackson Heights, NY 11372
Hours: 11-7 Mon-Sat / 11-6 Sun
50s furniture and accessories. RENTALS. CREDIT CARDS.

Gallery 532 203-858-1432
50 John St. (John Street Antiques) (Manhattan-Market)   203-324-4677
Stamford, CT 06902
Hours: 10:30-5:30 Daily   E-mail: gallery532@aol.com
Early 20th century (1900-1920) furniture, lighting fixtures and other decorative
arts. Currently selling at John St. Antiques. Very helpful. RENTALS. CREDIT
CARDS.

Hudson City Antiques & Books 212-675-8855
150 & 154 Ninth Ave. (19-20th St)
NY, NY 10011
Hours: 12-7 Wed-Sat / 12-6 Sun
Victorian to Art Deco lighting fixtures. Leatherbound books, art/crafts
furniture, wall sconces and desk lamps. CREDIT CARDS.

John Koch Antiques 212-799-2167
201 W 84th St. (B-way-Amst)
NY, NY 10024
Hours: 12-6 Mon / 11-7 Tue-Sat / 12-5 Sun   E-mail: jochantiques@mac.com
www.kochantiques.com
Eclectic collection of vintage and modern furniture, decorative accessories,
rugs, lamps, fine art, porcelain and silver. Can see some of their colletion on
the website. Also they have a booth at Hidden Gallery in Stamford, CT.
RENTALS. CREDIT CARDS.

Eileen Lane Antiques 212-475-2988
150 Thompson St. (Houston-Prince St)   FAX 212-673-8669
NY, NY 11232
Hours: 10-5 Mon-Fri by appt. only
www.eileenlaneantiques.com
Swedish and Austrian, Biedermeier through Art Deco furniture. Original
alabaster light fixtures. RENTALS. CREDIT CARDS.

Lehman's 330-857-5757
One Leham Cr. / P.O. Box 270   888-438-5346
Kidron, OH 44636   FAX 888-780-4975
Hours; 8-5:30 Mon-Sat / Thurs til 8   E-mail: GetLehmans@aol.com
www.lehmans.com
Housewares, oil lamps, cast-iron cookery, wood cook stoves, homestead
tools. Rustic old-fashioned stuff. Non-electric Amish products. Plus, all
those old-fashioned health and beauty products, canning supplies, food and
laundry supplies. Great catalog ($10 including shipping) or shop online.
CREDIT CARDS.

The Lively Set 212-807-8417
33 Bedford St. (Carmine-Downing St)
NY, NY 10014
Hours: 11-7 Mon-Fri / 12-6 Sat-Sun   E-mail: m2525@erols.com
www.thelivelyset.com
An interesting mix of decorative accessories, etc. Contact Steven. RENTALS.
CREDIT CARDS.

Lost City Arts 212-375-0500
18 Cooper Sq. (5th St)   FAX 212-375-9342
NY, NY 10012
Hours: 10-6 Mon,-Fri / 12-6 Sat-Sun   E-mail: lostcityarts@yahoo.com
www.lostcityarts.com
Architectural antiques, antique advertising, Art Deco furniture and lighting;
19th century-50ís. RENTALS. CREDIT CARDS.

Mantiques Modern, Ltd. 212-206-1494
146 W 22nd St. (6-7th Ave)   FAX 212-355-4403
NY, NY 10022
Hours: 10:30-6:30 Mon-Fri / 11-7 Sat-Sun   E-mail: info@mantiquesmodern.com
www.mantiquesmodern.com
Fine antique smoking accessories, furniture, desk dressing, sporting goods
and canes. Visit website. RENTALS. CREDIT CARDS.

McErlain Antiques 908-598-7300
456 Springfield Ave.   FAX 908-598-7444
Summit, NJ 07901
Hours: 10-5:30 Mon-Sat   E-mail: mcerlainantiques@aol.com
www.kmantiques.com
Eclectic furniture and objects. RENTALS. CREDIT CARDS.

Judith & James Milne, Inc. 212-472-0107
506 E 74th St., 2nd Fl. (York Ave)   FAX 212-472-1481
NY, NY 10021
Hours: 9:30-5:30 Mon-Fri / and by appt.   E-mail: milneinc@aol.com
www.milneantiques.com
Specializing in American country antiques, folk art, weathervanes,
architecturals, garden furniture, quilts and rugs. Many quilts. RENTALS.
CREDIT CARDS.

Monmouth Antique Shoppes 732-842-7377
217 W Front St.
Red Bank, NJ 07707
Hours: 11-5 daily
Enormous selection of American antiques and collectibles. 50 mins. from
Manhattan; see John. CREDIT CARDS.

Alan Moss Studios 212-473-1310
436 Lafayette St. (Astor Pl)   FAX 212- 387-9493
NY, NY 10003
Hours: 11-6 Mon-Fri / 12-5 Sat   E-mail: alanmossny@aol.com
www.alanmossny.com
20th century decorative arts, lamps and furniture. RENTALS.

Oldies, Goldies & Moldies Ltd. 212-737-3935
1609 Second Ave. (83-84th St)
NY, NY 10028
Hours: by appt.
Two levels of furniture, fixtures, clocks, jewelry, clothing. Turn of the century
to 1950s. Contact Lior Grinberg. RENTALS. CREDIT CARDS.

Palumbo 212-734-7630
972 Lexington Ave. (70-71st St)   FAX 212-734-6590
NY, NY 10021
Hours: 11-6 Mon-Fri   E-mail: mail@palumbogallery.com
www.palumbogallery.com
Mid-20th-century furniture. Custom post-war designers like Tommi Parzinger,
Edward Wormley & William Paklmann. Contact Pat Palumbo or Don Silvey.
RENTALS.

The Prop Company / Kaplan and Associates 212-691-7767
111 W 19th St., 8th Fl. (6-7th Ave)   FAX 212-727-3055
NY, NY 10011
Hours: 9-5 Mon-Fri   E-mail: propcompany@yahoo.com
Prop rental house with a unique collection of antique and contemporary
furniture and furnishings, all in excellent condition. RENTAL only. CREDIT
CARDS.

A-B

Props for Today 212-244-9600
330 W 34th St. (8-9th Ave)   FAX 212-244-1053
NY, NY 10001
Hours: 8:30-5 Mon-Fri   E-mail: info@propsfortoday.com
www.propsfortoday.com
Full-service prop house offering sales and rentals on antique to ultra-modern
furniture. Long term rental packages and custom orders available. RENTALS.
CREDIT CARDS.

Recycling the Past 609-660-9790
381 N. Main St.   FAX 609-660-0878
Barnegat, NJ 08005
Hours: 10-5 Tue-Sun / by appt.   E-mail: contact@gmail.com
www.recyclingthepast.com
Architectural salvage and antiques. Vintage tile, statuary, iron fencing, doors,
garden items and other funky finds. Inventory changes, check website for
new items daily. RENTALS. CREDIT CARDS.

Remains Lighting 212-675-8051
130 W 28th St. (6-7th Ave)   FAX 212-675-8052
NY, NY 10001
Hours: 9-6 Mon-Fri   E-mail: mail@remains.com
www.remains.com
Vintage and antique lighting fixtures, sconces, etc. RENTALS. CREDIT
CARDS.

Rent A Thing 845-628-9298
Rt 6, Box 337   FAX 845-628-0390
Baldwin Place, NY 10505
Hours: 24 hours / leave message, will return call
Good selection of antiques; over 5000 unusual items. Also many sites for
location filming. Will help locate items. RENTALS.

A Repeat Performance 212-529-0832
156 First Ave. (9-10th St)
NY, NY 10009
Hours: 12-8 Mon-Sun   E-mail: bevbronson@yahoo.com
www.repeatperformancenyc.com
Wide assortment of European lamp shades, brocade curtains, furniture, hats,
shoes, bric-a-brac from the 30s - 60s, typewriters. Ask for Beverly Bronson.
RENTALS. CREDIT CARDS.

Reprodepot Fabrics 413-527-4047
115 Pleasant St.   FAX 413-527-6407
East Hampton, MA 01027
Hours: Web 24-hrs.   E-mail: help@reprodepotfabrics.com
www.reprodepotfabrics.com
Largest selection of reproduction vintage fabrics on the Internet. Hard-to-
find prints and barkcloth. Swatching available. Very friendly. Great website.
CREDIT CARDS.

A-B

Paula Rubenstein Ltd. 212-966-8954
65 Prince St. (B'way-Lafayette St)
NY, NY 10292
Hours: 12-6 Mon-Sat　　　　　　　　　E-mail: paularubinsteinltd.com
Mostly American textiles and furnishings. Vintage and antique drapery and upholstery fabric. Speak to Paula Rubenstein. Retail and to the trade. RENTALS. CREDIT CARDS.

Scottie's Gallery & Antiques 718-851-8325
624 Coney Island Ave. (Beverly-Ave C)
Brooklyn, NY 11218
Hours: 11-5 Mon-Fri / 132-3 Sat-Sun
Oak and Victorian furniture; Tiffany lamps.

Secondhand Rose 212-393-9002
230 Fifth Ave. (W B'way-Church St)　　　　　FAX 212-393-9084
NY, NY 10001
Hours: 10-6 Mon-Fri /Weekends by appt.　　　E-mail: shroseltd@aol.com
www.secondhandrose.com
19th century furniture, accessories, period wallpaper and linoleum. Many unusual pieces, 1850s-1940s. Contact Suzanne Lipschutz. RENTALS. CREDIT CARDS.

Sentimento Antiques 212-750-3111
306 E 61st St., 6rd Fl. (1st-2nd Ave)　　　　FAX 212-750-3839
NY, NY 10021
Hours: 10-6 Mon-Fri　　　　　　E-mail: info@sentimentoantiques.com
www.sentimentoantiques.com
Wholesale decorative accessories, furniture, small items and jewelry. RENTALS.

Fred Silberman & Co. 212-924-6330
36 W 25th St. (B'way-6th Ave)　　　　　　FAX 212-924-6360
NY, NY 10010
Hours: 11-5:30 Tue-Fri / 12-5:30 Sat　　　E-mail: silbermanf@aol.com
www.fredsilberman.com
Art Deco furniture and accessories. RENTALS. CREDIT CARDS.

Time & Again 800-290-5401
1416 Linden Ave.　　　　　　　　　　　　　908-862-0200
Lindon, NJ 07036　　　　　　　　　　　FAX 908-862-3438
Hours: 10-6 Mon-Sat　　　　　　E-mail: tandagain@aol.com
www.timeandagainantiques.com
Furniture, paintings, china, bric-a-brac, silver, pianos, jewelry, bronzes, tapestries. RENTALS.

Toaster Central 212-744-3773
1427 York Ave. (76th St)
NY, NY 10021
Hours: by appt.　　　　　　　　　E-mail: pop@toastercentral.com
www.toastercentral.com
Working vintage toasters, small appliances, coffee pots, etc. from 1920 to present day. Great website, very helpful. Speak to Michael Sheafe. RENTALS. AMEX.

Ugly Luggage 718-384-0724
214 Bedford Ave.
Brooklyn, NY 11211
Hours: 1-8 Mon-Fri / 12-7 Sat-Sun (Call first, hours can vary)
www.uglyluggage.com
Antiques, furniture, collectibles and clothing. Ask for Jim Lanning. **RENTALS.**
CREDIT CARDS.

Waves 212-273-9616
40 W 25th St., Gallery 107 (in the Antiques Showplace)   FAX 201-461-7121
NY, NY 10001
Hours: 11-5 Wed-Sun   E-mail: wavesllc@gmail.com
www.wavesllc.com
Good collection of antique radios, phonographs, microphones and
televisions. **RENTALS. CREDIT CARDS.**

White Trash 212-598-5956
304 E Fifth St. (1st-2nd Ave)
NY, NY 10003
Hours: 2-8:30 Tue-Sat / 1-8 Sun
www.whitetrashnyc.com
Fun, kitschy 50s-60s furniture, lighting fixtures and decorative accessories.
RENTALS.

Wooster Gallery 212-219-2190
440 Lafayette St., 2nd Fl   FAX 212-941-6678
NY, NY 10003
Hours: 11-5 Mon-Fri   E-mail: woostergallery@verizon.net
www.woostergallery.1stdibs.com
Art Deco. Speak to Ralph. **RENTALS.**

Zero to Sixties 212-925-0932
354 Broadway (Franklin)
NY, NY 10013
Hours: 11-6 Mon-Fri   E-mail: genie354@bellatlantic.net
19th-and 20th-century furniture, furnishings, art, lighting and accessories.
Unusual items. **RENTALS. CREDIT CARDS.**

APPLIANCES

J. Eis & Sons Appliances 212-475-2325
105 First Ave., 2nd Fl. (6-7th St)   FAX 212-388-0392
NY, NY 10003
Hours: 9-5 Mon-Thurs / 9-2 Fri
Ranges, refrigerators, washers, dryers, air conditioners. **RENTALS. CREDIT**
CARDS.

ATAC

Everything Goes 718-273-0568
17 Brook St.   FAX 718-448-6842
Staten Island, NY 10301
Hours: 10:30-6:30 Tue-Sat   E-mail: ganas@well.com
www.etgstores.com
*Convenient to the ferry; 4 locations with a constantly changing stock of
estate sale furniture, furnishings and some antiques. Contact Ellen
Oppenheim. See website for other locations. RENTALS. CREDIT CARDS.*

Gringer & Sons 212-475-0600
29 First Ave. (1st-2nd St)   FAX 212-982-1935
NY, NY 10003
Hours: 8:30-5:30 Mon-Fri / 8:30-4:30 Sat E-mail: gringerandsons@aol.com
www.gringerandsons.com
Large appliances and microwaves. RENTALS. CREDIT CARDS.

J & R Television & Air Conditioning 718-638-3040
108 Seventh Ave. (President-Union St)   FAX 718-638-6655
Brooklyn, NY 11215
Hours: 10-7:30 Mon-Fri / 10-6 Sat / 11:30-5 Sun E-mail: dturbos@aol.com
*Large and small appliances; televisions and refrigerators; great prices.
CREDIT CARDS.*

The Prop Company / Kaplan and Associates 212-691-7767
111 W 19th St., 8th Fl. (6-7th Ave)   FAX 212-727-3055
NY, NY 10011
Hours: 9-5 Mon-Fri   E-mail: propcompany@yahoo.com
*Vintage ranges. Large and small electrical appliances, contemporary and
vintage. All in fine condition. RENTAL only. CREDIT CARDS.*

R.C.I. Radio Clinic, Inc. 212-864-6000
2599 Broadway (98th St)   FAX 212-316-6933
NY, NY 10025
Hours: 9-7 Mon-Fri / 9-6 Sat / 12-5 Sun E-mail: rciappl@verizon.net
www.rciappl.com
*Refrigerators, washers, dryers, air-conditioners, humidifiers and small
appliances for the home. CREDIT CARDS.*

Toaster Central 212-744-3773
1427 York Ave. (76th St)
NY, NY 10021
Hours: by appt.   E-mail: pop@toastercentral.com
www.toastercentral.com
*Working vintage toasters, small appliances, coffee pots, etc. from 1920 to
present day. Great website, very helpful. Speak to Michael Sheafe.
RENTALS. AMEX.*

ARCADE & AMUSEMENT DEVICES
See also: VENDING MACHINES
            AMUSEMENT PARK & CIRCUS EQUIPMENT

W. Chorney Antiques 203-387-9707
42 Morris St. (Westville Section)   FAX 203-387-9707
Hamden, CT 06515
Hours: call for information   E-mail: w.chorney@juno.com
Antique jukeboxes, including diner remotes; period cigarette, pinball,
gumball, vending and soda fountains; radios, kitchen equipment and bar
items. Antique office furniture and accessories. 90 mins. from Manhattan.
Will search for items; speak to Wayne.   RENTALS. AMEX.

Jukebox Classics & Vintage Slot Machines 718-833-8455
36 72nd St.   FAX 718-833-0560
Brooklyn, NY 11209
Hours: by appt. only
Arcade games, slot machines, nickelodeons, carousel animals, neon lights;
will help locate unusual items; buy, sell, repair. Speak to John. RENTALS.
CREDIT CARDS.

New York Pinball 516-735-5756
3550 Sarah Dr.
Wantagh, NY 11793
Hours: 8-6 daily   E-mail: info@nypinball.com
www.nypinnball.com
Pinball machines, video games sales and service. Restorations. CREDIT
CARDS.

ARCHITECTURAL ELEMENTS

A Beautiful Bar 212-431-0600
49 E Houston St.   (warehouse) 718-730-5427
NY, NY FAX 212-625-0980
Hours: by appt.   E-mail: info@abeautifulbar.com
www.abeautifulbar.com
Barroom architectural pieces and accessories. Nice online catalog. Speak to
Steve. RENTALS.

American Wood Column Corp. 718-782-3163
913 Grand St. (Bushwick-Morgan Ave)   FAX 718-387-9099
Brooklyn, NY 11211
Hours: 8-4:30 Mon-Fri
www.americanwoodcolumn.com
All types of wood turnings, columns, pedestals and mouldings. Brochure. Will
ship worldwide. Speak with Tom Lupo.

Architectural Antiques Exchange 215-922-3669
715 N Second St. (Brown-Fairmont)   FAX 215-922-3680
Philadelphia, PA 19123
Hours: 10-5 Mon-Sat   E-mail: AAExchange@aol.com
www.architecturalantiques.com
Architectural artifacts, mostly Victorian; street lights, plumbing and bars.
Brochure. Ask for Dedrick Hervas. RENTALS. CREDIT CARDS.

A-B

Architectural Artifacts, Inc. 773-348-0622
4325 N. Ravenswood   FAX 773-348-6118
Chicago, IL 60613
Hours: 10-5 Mon-Sun   E-mail: sales@architecturalartifacts.com
www.architecturalartifacts.com
80,000 sq. feet of Architectural elements. One of the best finds in Chicago.
Stained Glass, fireplace mantels, period lighting, garden furnishings,
decorative, cast & wrought iron. Must see to believe the stock. Some
RENTALS.

Architectural Sculpture & Restoration, Inc. 212-431-5873
1818 Atlantic Ave. (@ Utica Ave)   718-467-2013
Brooklyn, NY 11233   FAX 212-334-4230
Hours: 9:30-5:30 Mon-Fri / 12-5 Sat   E-mail: info@asyrnyc.com
www.asrnyc.com
Plaster architectural detail; all pieces made to order. Shipping available.
Catalog. RENTALS.

Art & Industrial Design 212-477-0116
50 Great Jones St. (4th Ave)   FAX 212-477-1420
NY, NY 10012
Hours: 10-5 Mon-Fri / 10-1 Sat   E-mail: info@aid20c.com
www.aid20c.com
20th-century and art deco furniture, furnishings, art and objects. Many
original works. Also collectibles, clocks and lighting fixtures. RENTALS.
CREDIT CARDS.

Julius Blum & Co., Inc. 201-438-4600
PO Box 816   800-526-6293
Carlstadt, NJ 07072   FAX 201-438-6003
Hours: 8:30-5 Mon-Fri   E-mail: bluminfo@juliusblum.com
www.juliusblum.com
Ornamental metalwork (stock components) in a variety of metals. Speak to
Joanne Blum. Catalog. Will ship.

Build it Green! 718-777-0132
3-17 26th Ave. (4th St)   FAX same
Astoria, NY 11102
Hours: 10-6 Tue-Fri / 10-5 Sat   E-mail: greeninfo@bignyc.org
www.bignyc.org
An 18,000 sq. ft. warehouse filled with salvaged building materials, bathroom
and lighting fixtures. Also recycled staging, signage and set pieces from film
and commercial shoots. Drop-off and pickup donations are by appointment
only.

Chelsea Decorative Metal Co. 713-721-9200
8212 Braewick Dr.   FAX 713-776-8661
Houston, TX 77074
Hours: 8-4 Mon-Fri   E-mail: tinman83@earthlink.net
www.thetinman.com
Tin ceilings, walls and backdrops. Catalog available at no charge. Contact
Glenn Aldridge. Will ship. CREDIT CARDS.

A-B

Circa Antiques, Ltd. 718-596-1866
374 Atlantic Ave. (Hoyt-Bond St)
Brooklyn, NY 11217
Hours: 11-6 Tue-Fri / 11-6 Sat / 12-6 Sun   E-mail: circa@circaantiquesltd.com
www.circaantiquesltd.com
Mostly 19th century American furniture, paintings, lighting, accessories, also architectural salvage. See Rachel or David. RENTALS. CREDIT CARDS.

The Decorators Supply Co. 773-847-6300
3610 S Morgan St.   FAX 773-847-6357
Chicago, IL 60609
Hours: 7:45-4 Mon-Fri CST   E-mail: info@decoratorssupply.com
www.decoratorssupply.com
Capitals and brackets in composition ornament. Min. order $40. No credit cards.

Demolition Depot / Irreplaceable Artifacts 212-860-1138
216 E 125th St.(2nd-3rd Ave)
NY, NY 10035
Hours: 10-6 Mon-Sat / 12-5 Sun   FAX 212-860-1560

428 Main St.   860-344-8576
Middletown, CT 06457   FAX 860-638-0834
Hours: by appt. only call 212-860-1138   E-mail: info@demolitiondepot.com
www.demolitiondepot.com
Architectural ornamentation from demolished buildings; fireplaces, panelled rooms, bars, urns, garden furniture, etc. Will ship worldwide. RENTALS.

Dennis Miller Assoc., Inc. 212-684-0070
200 Lexington Ave # 1510 (32nd-33rd St)   FAX 212-684-0776
NY, NY 10016
Hours: 9-5 Mon-Fri or by appt.
www.dennismiller.com
Contemporary furniture.

Eclectic / Encore Properties, Inc. 212-645-8880
620 W 26th St., 4th Fl. (11-12th Ave)   FAX 212-243-6508
NY, NY 10001
Hours: 9-5 Mon-Fri / or by appt.   E-mail: props@eclecticprops.com
www.eclecticprops.com
Prop rental house; antique and reproduction furniture and furnishings. Can request rental items thru online catalog. RENTALS. CREDIT CARDS.

Elizabeth Street Gallery, Inc. 212-941-4800
209 Elizabeth St. (Spring-Prince)   FAX 212-274-0057
NY, NY 10012
Hours: 10-5 Mon-Fri call for appt.   E-mail: info@elizabethstreetgallery.com
www.elizabethstreetgallery.com
French, English and American stone and marble fireplaces. 17th-19th century garden statuary and furniture; columns, pilasters and keystones. Also studio collection of reproductions based on historical designs. RENTALS. CREDIT CARDS.

The Iron Shop 610-544-7100
    400 Reed Rd. / P.O. Box 547   800-523-7427
    Broomall, PA 19008   FAX 610-544-7297
    Hours: 8-4:30 Mon-Fri / 8-11:30 Sat
    www.theironshop.com
    Spiral stairs and do-it-yourself kits. Website has interactive explanation of
    assembly process. Many styles and sizes. Very nice staff. Speak to Steve.
    Other national locations listed on website.

Lost City Arts 212-375-0500
    18 Cooper Sq. (5th St)   FAX 212-375-9342
    NY, NY 10012
    Hours: 10-6 Mon,-Fri / 12-6 Sat-Sun   E-mail: lostcityarts@yahoo.com
    www.lostcityarts.com
    Interesting and eclectic collection of fixtures, architectural items and urban
    antiques. RENTALS. CREDIT CARDS.

Newel Art Gallery 212-758-1970
    425 E 53rd St. (Sutton-1st Ave)   FAX 212-371-0166
    NY, NY 10022
    Hours: 8:30-5 Mon-Fri / Sat by appt.   E-mail: info@newel.com
    www.newel.com
    Columns, doors, mantels and other interesting interior fittings in addition to
    their incredible collection of exotica. RENTALS. No credit cards.

W.F. Norman Corp. 417-667-5552
    PO Box 323, 214 N Cedar St.   800-641-4038
    Nevada, MO 64772   FAX 417-667-2708
    Hours: 8-4 Mon-Fri
    www.wfnorman.com
    Molded zinc architectural detail; tin ceilings; ornamental stampings, catalog
    available. Will ship. CREDIT CARDS.

Olde Good Things 212-989-8814
    5 E 15th St. (5th-Mad)   888-551-7333
    NY, NY 10003   FAX 212-337-9959
    Hours: 10-7 Mon-Sun   E-mail: mail@oldegoodthings.com
    www.ogtstore.com
    Large architectural salvage company specializing in stones, terra-cotta, iron
    work, interior / exterior lighting, doors and hardware. Eclectic handmade
    furnishing, green-minded. National warehose located in Scranton, PA.
    CREDIT CARDS.

Plaster Galaxy 718-769-8500
    2756 Coney Island Ave. (Ave Y)   917-353-5754
    Brooklyn, NY 11235   FAX 718-368-3430
    Hours: 11-7 daily   E-mail: plastergalaxy@yahoo.com
    www.jimmyplastercreations.com
    Stock and custom columns, pedestals, etc. in plaster; also plaster statuary
    and figurines. CREDIT CARDS.

The Prop Company / Kaplan and Associates 212-691-7767
111 W 19th St., 8th Fl. (6-7th Ave)   FAX 212-727-3055
NY, NY 10011
Hours: 9-5 Mon-Fri   E-mail: propcompany@yahoo.com
Contemporary tabletop, decorative accessories, antiques, ephemera and
furniture. A nice collection of linens. RENTALS.

Props for Today 212-244-9600
330 W 34th St. (8-9th Ave)   FAX 212-244-1053
NY, NY 10001
Hours: 8:30-5 Mon-Fri   E-mail: info@propsfortoday.com
www.propsfortoday.com
Good selection of shutters, windows, barn board and other patina surfaces.
RENTALS. CREDIT CARDS.

Recycling the Past 609-660-9790
381 N. Main St.   FAX 609-660-0878
Barnegat, NJ 08005
Hours: 10-5 Tue-Sun / by appt.   E-mail: contact@gmail.com
www.recyclingthepast.com
Architectural salvage and antiques. Vintage tile, statuary, iron fencing, doors,
garden items and other funky finds. Inventory changes, check web-site for
new items daily. RENTALS. CREDIT CARDS.

Shanker Industries 877-742-6516
1979 Marcus Ave., Ste. 203   FAX 516-437-8866
Lake Success, NY 11042
Hours: 8-4 Mon-Fri
www.shanko.com
Tin ceilings, tin walls and kitchen back spashes. Formerly AA Abbingdon
Affiliates, Inc. Items available for purchase at new website. CREDIT CARDS.

United House Wrecking 203-348-5371
535 Hope St.   FAX 203-961-9472
Stamford, CT 06906
Hours: 9:30-5:30 Mon-Sat / 12-5 Sun   E-mail: info@unitedhousewrecking.com
www.unitedhousewrecking.com
Antique and repro doors, mantels, beveled and stained glass, Victorian
gingerbread and more. Brochure. RENTALS. CREDIT CARDS.

Urban Archeology, Co. 212-431-4646
143 Franklin St., 2nd Fl.(Hudson-Varick St)
NY, NY 10013   FAX 212-343-9312
Hours: 8-6 Mon-Thurs / 8-5 Fri   E-mail: nydowntown@urbanarchaeology.com

239 E 58th St.(3rd-2nd Ave)   212-371-4646
NY, NY 10022   FAX 212-371-1601
Hours: 9-5 Tue-Sat   E-mail: nyuptown@urbanarchaeology.com

2231 Montauk Hwy.(Butter Ln)   631-537-0124
Bridgehampton, NY 11932   FAX 631-537-7123
Hours: 9-5 Mon, Wed-Sat / 11-3 Sun
                        E-mail: bridgehampton@urbanarchaeology.com
www.urbanarchaeology.com
Nice interior and exterior architectural pieces; quality reproductions;
reasonable; also does restoration. See web address for Boston and Chicago
locations. RENTALS. CREDIT CARDS.

Vintage Wood Works 903-356-2158
PO Box 39, Highway 34 S   FAX 903-356-3023
Quinlan, TX 75474
Hours: 8-4:30 Mon-Fri   E-mail: mail@vintagewoodworks.com
www.vintagewoodworks.com
Supplier of Victorian gingerbread, porch parts and architectural detail.
Catalog. Visit website for online shopping. CREDIT CARDS.

J. P. Weaver Co. 818-500-1740
941 Air Way   FAX 818-500-1798
Glendale, CA 91201
Hours: 8:30-4 Mon-Fri by appt. only   E-mail: info@jpweaver.com
www.jpweaver.com
Composition ornament capitals and brackets. Catalog is clear and in scale.
Technical help over the phone. Contact Mayra Gomez. CREDIT CARDS.

ARMOR
See also: FIREARMS & WEAPONRY
                    COSTUME RENTAL

Chainmaille Fashions 800-729-4094
1706 Norris Dr.   512-447-6040
Austin, TX 78704
Hours: by appt.   E-mail: randolph @Chainmail.com
www.chainmail.com
Armor and clothing items made of chain mail. Catalog available on website.
Contact Lord Randolph. CREDIT CARDS.

Costume Armour, Inc. 845-534-9120
PO Box 85, 2 Mill St.   FAX 845-534-8602
Cornwall, NY 12518
Hours: 8-4 Mon-Fri   E-mail: info@costumearmour.com
www.costumearmour.com
Replica weapons, arms, armor. Also custom work. Catalog. RENTALS.

Euro Co. Costumes, Inc. 212-629-9665
254 W 35th St., 15th Fl (7-8th Ave)   FAX 212-629-9608
NY, NY 10001
Hours: 9-6 Mon-Fri / or by appt.   E-mail: euroconyc@aol.com
Chain-mail suits, garments and pieces for purchase or rental. Custom work
available, call for sample. Contact Janet Bloor. RENTALS.

Global Effects, Inc. 818-503-9273
7115 Laurel Canyon Blvd.   FAX 818-503-9459
N. Hollywood, CA 91605
Hours: by appt.   E-mail: chris@globaleffects.com
www.globaleffects.com
Higy quality replicas of NASA space suits and fabrication of armour,
vacuumforming, etc. Leather masks, creature suits, ventilated walk-around
costumes. Medieval: armour, weapons, jewelry. Very pleasant to deal with.
RENTALS. CREDIT CARDS.

ARMOR

Historic Arms & Armor 760-789-2299
17228 Voorhes Ln.   FAX 760-789-6644
Ramona, CA 92065
Hours: 9-6 Mon-Fri, by appt.   E-mail: info@historicenterprises.com
www.historicenterprises.com
Ancient Greek to vacuumform sci-fi armor. Specializes in medieval and
renaissance. RENTALS.

The Noble Collection 800-866-2538
PO Box 1476
Sterling, VA 20167
Hours: 9-5 Mon-Fri (customer service)
www.noblecollection.com   E-mail: customerservice@noblecollection.com
Historic and fantasy reproduction armor and sword. Life-size reproductions of
15th century armor and Samurai armor. Mail order only, call for catalog.
Layaway plan available. CREDIT CARDS.

Sword and the Stone 818-562-6548
723 N Victory Blvd.   FAX 818-562-6549
Burbank, CA 91502
Hours: Mon-Fri by appt only / 12-6 Sat   E-mail: tony@swordandstone.com
www.swordandstone.com
Armor, chain mail, Medieval masks, custom jewelry, leather work. Custom
shoes and weapons.

ART RENTAL

Art & Industrial Design 212-477-0116
50 Great Jones St. (4th Ave)   FAX 212-477-1420
NY, NY 10012
Hours: 10-5 Mon-Fri / 10-1 Sat   E-mail: info@aid20c.com
www.aid20c.com
20th-century and art deco furniture, furnishings, art and objects. Many
original works. Also collectibles, clocks and lighting fixtures. RENTALS.
CREDIT CARDS.

Art for Media 212-431-0607
84 Walker St. (B'way-Lafayette St)   212-431-3828
NY, NY 10013   FAX 212-219-0183
Hours: by appt.   E-mail: media4art@att.net
Rents art for film, TV, photography and corporations. We specialize in
contempory paintings, drawings, sculpture and photography. Sale and
fabrication available. RENTALS.

Art:asap 212-956-0805
7 W 39th St. (5-6th Ave)   800-821-4717
NY, NY 10019   FAX 212-956-0796
Hours: 10-7 Mon-Fri / 11-5 Sat   E-mail: info@artasap.com
www.artaddictioninc.com
Largest selection of cleared artwork, framed and unframed, in NY. For rental
and sale. Custom framing as needed. RENTALS. CREDIT CARDS.

Available Art 917-279-4686
204 Dean St.
Brooklyn, NY 11217
Hours: by appt. daily   E-mail: alex@availableart.com
www.availableart.com
Cleared art for film, television and commercials. Photography, drawing,
painting and sculpture. Speak to Alex. RENTALS.

Carol J. Phipps 812-265-2124
2246 Shawnee Dr. #1
Madison, IN 47250
Hours: by appt.   E-mail: cjphipps_servo@msn.com
www.caroljphipps.com
Original artwork and photography designed and produced celebrating the
arts and the Creator. RENTALS.

Corporate Art Associates Ltd. 212-941-9685
568 Broadway, Ste. 501 (Prince-Houston)   FAX 212-925-3449
NY, NY 10012
Hours: 11-6 Mon-Fri / or by appt.   E-mail: caanyc@yahoo.com
Provide contemporary, impressionist and modern art for film and theatre.
RENTALS. CREDIT CARDS.

Eclectic / Encore Properties, Inc. 212-645-8880
620 W 26th St., 4th Fl. (11-12th Ave)   FAX 212-243-6508
NY, NY 10001
Hours: 9-5 Mon-Fri / or by appt.   E-mail: props@eclecticprops.com
www.eclecticprops.com
Prop rental house with 18th, 19th and 20th century furniture, accessories and
art. Can request rental items thru online catalog. RENTALS. CREDIT CARDS.

Film Art 323-461-4900
5241 Melrose Ave.   888-858-7107
Hollywood, CA 90038   FAX 323-461-4959
Hours: 9-5 Mon-Fri   E-mail: info@filmartla.com
www.filmartla.com
Film Art is your answer to finding painting, sculpture, posters, prints and
photography. Rents and sells the artwork of over 300 established artists. All
artwork comes with a copyright license. Online art research available.

Andrew Kolb & Son Ltd. 718-292-1486
728 E. 136th St. (27-28th St)   FAX 718-402-6360
Bronx, NY 10454
Hours: 9-5 Mon-Fri   E-mail: sales@andrewkolbart.com
www.andrewkolbart.com
Original and reproduction paintings, posters, prints and framed mirrors, all
wall decor. Speak to Claude. RENTALS. CREDIT CARDS.

Newel Art Gallery 212-758-1970
425 E 53rd St. (Sutton-1st Ave)   FAX 212-371-0166
NY, NY 10022
Hours: 8:30-5 Mon-Fri / Sat by appt.   E-mail: info@newel.com
www.newel.com
Extraordinary selection of antique furniture, art, architectural pieces, lamps;
all periods. Expensive. Sales and RENTALS. No credit cards.

A-B

Prop Art Studios / Prop Art New York 917-804-4543
267 Wyckoff St. (Nevins-3rd Ave)
Brooklyn, NY 11217
Hours: by appt.   E-mail: lilia@propartnewyork.com
www.propartnewyork.com
*On-line rental resource serving the New York film and photography
communities. All work is original, cleared and available for rental. View
website for art. RENTALS. CREDIT CARDS.*

The Prop Company / Kaplan and Associates 212-691-7767
111 W 19th St., 8th Fl. (6-7th Ave)   FAX 212-727-3055
NY, NY 10011
Hours: 9-5 Mon-Fri   E-mail: propcompany@yahoo.com
*Prop rental house. Artwork ranging from antique to contemporary. Contact
Maxine Kaplan. Rental only. CREDIT CARDS.*

Props for Today 212-244-9600
330 W 34th St. (8-9th Ave)   FAX 212-244-1053
NY, NY 10001
Hours: 8:30-5 Mon-Fri   E-mail: info@propsfortoday.com
www.propsfortoday.com
*Good selection of paintings, prints and posters covering broad spectrum of
periods and styles. RENTALS. CREDIT CARDS.*

Savacou Gallery 212-473-6904
240 E 13th St. (2nd-3rd Ave)
NY, NY 10003
Hours: by appt.   E-mail: savaca@webspan.net
www.savacougallery.com
*Original African, African-American and Caribbean artwork and batiks. Also
custom framing. RENTALS. CREDIT CARDS.*

Troubetzkoy Paintings Ltd. 212-688-6544
425 E 53rd St. (1st-York)   Gallery 212-758-1970
NY, NY 10022   FAX 212-371-0166
Hours: 9-4 Mon-Fri   E-mail: christopher@troubetzkoypaintints.com
www.troubetzkoypaintings.com
*Custom artwork specifically for the entertainment and photography
industries. RENTALS.*

ART SUPPLIES
See also: PAINTS & DYES: ALL HEADINGS
            CASTING & MODELING SUPPLIES

7th Avenue Stationers 212-695-4900
210 W 35th St., 2nd Fl. (7-8th Ave)   800-320-5735
NY, NY 10001   FAX 212-643-0480
Hours: 9-5:30 Mon-Fri   E-mail: info@7thavenuecollector.com
www.pensandgifts.com
Art, drafting, graphics, office supplies and stationery. CREDIT CARDS.

A.C. Moore 201-902-0377
400 Mill Creek Dr. (Mill Creek Mall Area)
Secaucus, NJ 07094
Hours: 99 Mon-Fri / 9-8 Sat-Sun
www.acmoore.com
Chain based craft supply store. General crafts, art materials & framing, yarn and needlecrafts, wedding supplies and more. Visit website for other 95 locations across the USA. CREDIT CARDS.

American Foam Technologies, Inc. 304-497-3000
Box 317 H   (Plant) 304-647-5439
Lewisburg, WV 24901   FAX 304-497-3001
Hours: 8-5 Mon-Fri   E-mail: don@americanfoamtech.com
www.americanfoamtech.com
Sells balsa-foam, a plastic product that carves like butter and paints like wood. Comes in a variety of sizes. Also has floral foam.

Art Station, Ltd. 212-807-8000
144 W 27th St. (6-7th Ave)
NY, NY 10001
Hours: 8:30-6:30 Mon-Fri / 11-6 Sat (closed Sat June-Aug)
                                              E-mail: artstationltd@aol.com
Full line of quality art supplies in stock at great prices. Craft supplies and drafting materials. CREDIT CARDS.

Arthur Brown International Pen Shop .212-575-5555
2 W 45th St. (5-6th Ave)   800-772-PENS
NY, NY 10036   FAX 212-575-5825
Hours: 9-6:15 Mon-Fri / 10-6 Sat   E-mail: penshop@artbrown.com
www.artbrown.com
Framing supplies, custom framing available; art supplies. CREDIT CARDS.

Artists Medium Supply 802-879-1236
300 Cornerstone Drive   FAX 802-879-2778
Williston, VT 05495
Hours: 9-6 Mon-Fri / 10-5 Sat
www.artistsmedium.com
Airbrush parts and supplies. Pasche & Holbein brands, mail orders, $25 min. CREDIT CARDS.

BioShield Healthy Living 505-438-3448
3005 S. St. Francis Ste. 2A   800-621-2591
Santa Fe, NM 87505   FAX 505-438-0199
Hours: 9-5 Mon-Fri / 10-3 Sat   E-mail: info@bioshieldpaint.com
www.bioshieldpaint.com
Carries environmentally friendly paints, wood finishes, pigments, hand cleaners. Catalog. CREDIT CARDS.

Blick Art Materials 212-533-2444
1-5 Bond St. (B'way-Lafayette St)   800-828-4548
NY, NY 10012   FAX 212-677-6955
Hours: 9-8 Mon-Fri / 10-7 Sat / 11-6 Sun
www.dickblick.com
A supermarket of art supplies. Has several hard-to-find items like Golden acrylics and Lascaux oils. Visit website for other locations. CREDIT CARDS.

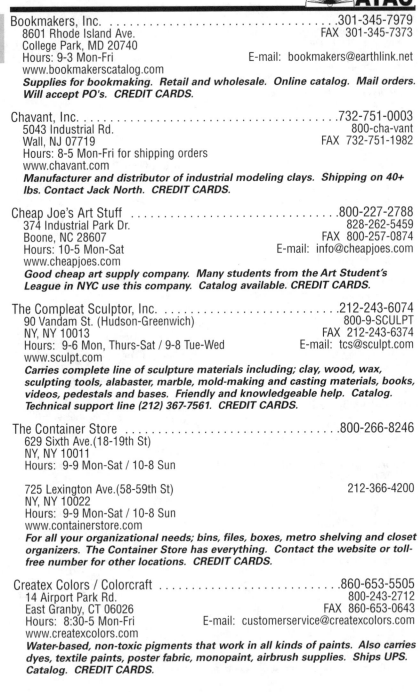

Bookmakers, Inc. 301-345-7979
8601 Rhode Island Ave.   FAX 301-345-7373
College Park, MD 20740
Hours: 9-3 Mon-Fri   E-mail: bookmakers@earthlink.net
www.bookmakerscatalog.com
Supplies for bookmaking. Retail and wholesale. Online catalog. Mail orders.
Will accept PO's. CREDIT CARDS.

Chavant, Inc. 732-751-0003
5043 Industrial Rd.   800-cha-vant
Wall, NJ 07719   FAX 732-751-1982
Hours: 8-5 Mon-Fri for shipping orders
www.chavant.com
Manufacturer and distributor of industrial modeling clays. Shipping on 40+
lbs. Contact Jack North. CREDIT CARDS.

Cheap Joe's Art Stuff 800-227-2788
374 Industrial Park Dr.   828-262-5459
Boone, NC 28607   FAX 800-257-0874
Hours: 10-5 Mon-Sat   E-mail: info@cheapjoes.com
www.cheapjoes.com
Good cheap art supply company. Many students from the Art Student's
League in NYC use this company. Catalog available. CREDIT CARDS.

The Compleat Sculptor, Inc. 212-243-6074
90 Vandam St. (Hudson-Greenwich)   800-9-SCULPT
NY, NY 10013   FAX 212-243-6374
Hours: 9-6 Mon, Thurs-Sat / 9-8 Tue-Wed   E-mail: tcs@sculpt.com
www.sculpt.com
Carries complete line of sculpture materials including; clay, wood, wax,
sculpting tools, alabaster, marble, mold-making and casting materials, books,
videos, pedestals and bases. Friendly and knowledgeable help. Catalog.
Technical support line (212) 367-7561. CREDIT CARDS.

The Container Store 800-266-8246
629 Sixth Ave.(18-19th St)
NY, NY 10011
Hours: 9-9 Mon-Sat / 10-8 Sun

725 Lexington Ave.(58-59th St)   212-366-4200
NY, NY 10022
Hours: 9-9 Mon-Sat / 10-8 Sun
www.containerstore.com
For all your organizational needs; bins, files, boxes, metro shelving and closet
organizers. The Container Store has everything. Contact the website or toll-
free number for other locations. CREDIT CARDS.

Createx Colors / Colorcraft 860-653-5505
14 Airport Park Rd.   800-243-2712
East Granby, CT 06026   FAX 860-653-0643
Hours: 8:30-5 Mon-Fri   E-mail: customerservice@createxcolors.com
www.createxcolors.com
Water-based, non-toxic pigments that work in all kinds of paints. Also carries
dyes, textile paints, poster fabric, monopaint, airbrush supplies. Ships UPS.
Catalog. CREDIT CARDS.

Crystal Productions 800-255-8629
PO Box 2159, 1812 Johns Drive   FAX 800-657-8149
Glenview, IL 60025
Hours: 8:30-4:30 Mon-Fri   E-mail custserv@crystalproductions.com
www.crystalproductions.com
Good art supply company. Catalog available. CREDIT CARDS.

David Davis Artist Materials and Services 718-222-1090
499 Van Brunt St. #6A   800-965-6554
Brooklyn, NY 11231
Hours: 8:30-4:30 Mon-Fri   E-mail: ddavisart@aol.com
www.daviddavisart.com
Easels, custom brushes, fabric dye, paints; all types of art supplies. Will ship.
Catalog. CREDIT CARDS.

Dymalon, Inc. 410-686-7711
9100 Yellow Brick Rd., Ste D   FAX 410-686-7743
Baltimore, MD 21237
Hours: 8:30-5:30 Mon-Fri   E-mail: rjnee@verizon.net
www.dymalon.com
Excellent selection of wood grain contact papers, mattes, enamels, marbles,
frosts, transparents, metallics and more. 17.5" wide, some up to 35". Foam
tapes and all kinds of Velcro, including dual lock. Quick and friendly service.
CREDIT CARDS.

Elmers Products, Inc. 800-848-9400
2020 W Front St.
Statesville, NC 28677
Hours: 8-5:30 Mon-Fri
www.elmersbrands.com
Manufacturers of foam board in colors, exacto tools and krazy glue. Visit
website for other products. Limited purchasing on-line.

A. I. Friedman, Inc. 212-243-9000
44 W 18th St. (5-6th Ave)   800-204-6352
NY, NY 10011   FAX 212-929-7320
Hours: 9-7 Mon-Fri / 10-7 Sat / 11-6 Sun
www.aifriedman.com
Art supplies, drafting, paints, etc. Monthly sales with low prices. Catalog
and shopping available online. See website for other locations. CREDIT
CARDS.

N. Glantz & Son 718-439-7707
218 57th St. (2nd-3rd Ave)   866-645-2689
Brooklyn, NY 11220   FAX 718-492-5463
Hours: 8-4:30 Mon-Fri   E-mail: brooklyn@nglantz.com
www.nglantz.com
Distributer of vinyl neon, electrical sign supplies. Paints and boards.
Locations across US - see website. Wholesale. Phone orders and deliveries.
Catalog available. CREDIT CARDS.

A-B

Gordon Brush Manufacturing 800-950-7950
6247 Randolph St.   323-724-7777
Commerce, CA 90040   FAX 323-724-1111
Hours: 7:30-4:30 Mon-Fri   E-mail: web@gordonbrush.com
www.gordonbrush.com
Commercial and artist brushes for all applications. Good prices.
Comprehensive online catalog. CREDIT CARDS.

Guerra Paint & Pigment 212-529-0628
510 E 13th St. (Ave A-B)   FAX 212-529-0787
NY, NY 10009
Hours: 12-7 Mon-Sat
www.guerrapaint.com
Excellent selection of pigments: dry and in dispersion for oil, acrylic and
alkyd bases. Also an extremely useful selection of additives and related
materials; hard-to-find colors; expensive. Catalog. CREDIT CARDS.

Hyatt's 800-234-9288
910 Main St. (Allen-Virginia)   716-884-8900
Buffalo, NY 14202   FAX 716-884-3943
Hours: 9-6 Mon-Fri / 10-5 Sat   E-mail: mail@hyatts.com
www.hyatts.com
Wide range of art supplies, graphic supplies and equipment. Catalog
available. See website for addtional locations. CREDIT CARDS.

Lee's Art Shop & Studio 212-247-0110
220 W 57th St. (B'way-7th Ave)   FAX 212-581-7023
NY, NY 10019
Hours: 9-7:30 Mon-Fri / 10-7 Sat / 11-6 Sun   E-mail: info@leesartshop.com
www.leesartshop.com
Large stock artists materials, seamless paper, drafting furniture, framing;
catalog. No phone orders. CREDIT CARDS.

New York Central Art Supply, Inc. 212-473-7705
62 Third Ave. (10-11th St)   800-950-6111
NY, NY 10003   FAX 212-475-2513
Hours: 8:30-6:15 Mon-Sat   E-mail: sales@nycentralart.com
www.nycentralart.com
Large, well-stocked general art papers and art supplies. Always crowded!
Catalog. CREDIT CARDS.

Pearl Paint / World's Largest Creative Resource 800-451-7327
308 Canal St.(B'way-Church St)   212-431-7932
NY, NY 10013   (mail order) 800-221-6845
Hours: 9-7 Mon-Fri / 10-7 Sat / 10-6 Sun   FAX 212-431-6798

42 Lispenard St. (Craft & Home Center)(B'way-Church St)   212-226-3717
NY, NY 10013   800-221-6845
Hours: 9-7 Mon-Fri / 10-7 Sat / 10-6 Sun

776 Rt. 17 N   201-447-0300
Paramus, NJ 07652   FAX 201-447-4012
Hours: 10-9 Mon-Sat

A-B

Pearl Paint / World's Largest Creative Resource (cont.) 954-567-9678
1033 E Oakland Park Blvd.(Corp. Office)
Ft. Lauderdale, FL 33334
www.pearlpaint.com
Four floors of art supplies, large crafts section. Phone orders over $50.
Catalog. Online shopping available. CREDIT CARDS.

Plaid Enterprises 678-291-8100
3225 Westech Dr.   FAX 678-291-8383
Norcross, GA 30092
Hours: 8-5 Mon-Fri
www.plaidonline.com
Pre-mixed paints, stencils, patterns, brushes, glass stain, glues and paints,
specialty products. No credit cards.

Sam Flax Art Supplies 212-620-3000
3 W 20th St.   FAX 212-620-3060
NY, NY 10011
Hours: 9:30-7 Mon-Fri / 10:30-6 Sat   E-mail: 20st@samfalx.com
www.samflax.com
Art, drafting, graphics and photo supplies; drafting tables, presentation
portfolios; casting rubber and moulage. Will ship anywhere. CREDIT CARDS.

Sax Arts & Crafts 800-558-6696
2725 S Moorland Rd., Ste. 101   262-784-6880
New Berlin, WI 53151   FAX 800-328-4729
Hours: 8:30-5 Mon-Fri   E-mail: info@saxarts.com
www.saxarts.com
Art supply company. Catalog available, 530 pages, $5 refundable with first
order. CREDIT CARDS.

School Specialty 920-734-2756
6316 Design Dr.   888-388-3224
Greenville, WI 54942   FAX 888-388-6344
Hours: 7:30-5 Mon-Fri
www.schoolspecialty.com
Complete art supply company. Wonderful catalog. Will ship anywhere.
CREDIT CARDS.

Superior Giftwrap 812-949-2477
P.O. Box 458   812-949-2479
Floyd-Knobs, IN 47119
Hours: 8-5 Mon-Fri   E-mail: info@superiorgiftwrap.com
www.superiorgiftwrap.com
All your giftwrapping needs available at their website. Ribbon, giftwrap
paper, tissue, bags, apparel boxes, gift tying yarns, bows and industrial paper
cutters. Quick and courteous service. CREDIT CARDS.

Utrecht Art & Drafting Supplies 212-777-5353
111 Fourth Ave. (11-12th St)   FAX 212-420-9632
NY, NY 10003
Hours: 9-7 Mon-Sat / 11-5 Sun
www.utrechtart.com
Specializes in house brand paints and canvas, as well as other art supplies;
excellent prices; catalog. Accepts phone orders. CREDIT CARDS.

Village Supplies, Ltd. 708-824-1402
P.O. Box 605   FAX 708-824-1410
Oak Lawn, IL 60803
Hours: website 24-hrs.
www.artstuff.net
Art supplies, drafting and graphic supplies, modeling and casting, Pantone
products, imaging, industrial lettering and laminating. Presentation papers,
business furnishings and office supplies. Great website. $15 minimum order.
CREDIT CARDS.

Wilma's Egg Art 765-284-6327
5100 Southwest St.
Muncie, IN 47307
Hours: 10-6 Mon-Fri / Web 24-hrs.   E-mail: wilmaseggart@yahoo.com
www.wilmaseggart.com
This company has many varieties of art supplies for crafts as well as anything
you would need for egg art. Miniature figurines, metal findings, paper cuts,
pens, tools, adhesives and instructional videos and books. CREDIT CARDS.

ARTIFICIAL FLOWERS, PLANTS & FOOD
See also: TRIMMINGS: FEATHERS & FLOWERS
                     DISPLAY HOUSES & MATERIALS

American Foliage & Design Group 212-741-5555
122 W 22nd St. (6-7th Ave)   FAX 212-741-9499
NY, NY 10011
Hours: 8-5 Mon-Fri   E-mail: afdesigngr@aol.com
www.americanfoliagedesign.com
Silk and live flowers for TV, commercials, special events. RENTALS.

Center of Floral Design and Supply, Inc. 212-279-5044
145 W 28th St. (6-7th Ave)   FAX 212-563-5489
New York, NY 10001
Hours: 9-5 Mon-Sat   E-mail: info@cfdnewyork.com
www.cfdnewyork.com
Well-priced silk flowers and plants. Large selection. Also artificial produce
and fruits. CREDIT CARDS.

Dry Nature Designs 212-695-8911
245 W 29th St. (7-8th Ave)   FAX 212-695-4104
NY, NY 10001
Hours: 8:30-5 Mon-Fri / 9:30-5:30 Sat   E-mail: drynaturedesigns@aol.com
www.drynature.com
Great selection of natural earth & nature products. Branches, corals,
porcupine quills, ostrich & emu eggs, dry fruits & flowers, gourds, grasses,
grains & fall leaves, driftwood and more. Designer arrangements. A must see
located in the Floral District of NYC. Visit website for really cool photos of
shop. CREDIT CARDS.

Hillcrest Gardens 201-599-3030
95 W Century Rd.   FAX 201-599-3064
Paramus, NJ 07652
Hours: 6-5 Mon-Fri / 6-12 Sat / 8-11 Sun
Complete line of silk flowers and greenery, also fruit. Helpful and friendly
service. Contact Tom x234.

A-B

Humphrey's Farm, Inc. / Display Fake Foods 786-955-6584
PO Box 5800 (Mail Order)   FAX 305-749-8099
Miami Lakes, FL 33014
Hours: 9:30-5:30 Mon-Fri   E-mail: sales@displayfackfoods.com
www.displayfake foods.com
Large selection of display foods, mixed drinks, seafood, etc. CREDIT CARDS.

Josline Display 978-284-6660
10 Upton Dr. Ste 8   800-325-1030
Willmington, MA 01887   FAX 978-658-4263
Hours: 8:30-5 Mon-Fri
www.joslindisplays.net
Seasonal and decorative dried flowers, grass mats, natural funeral grass.
Phone and web orders. CREDIT CARDS.

Charles Lubin Co. 914-968-5700
145 Saw Mill River Rd.   FAX 914-968-5723
Yonkers, NY 10701
Hours: 7:30-4:30 Mon-Fri
www.lubinflowers.com
Silk flowers for decoration, home and store display, fashion and packaging.

Metropolitan Artificial 718-246-2130
63 Flushing Ave. Bldg 5 Rm 601   FAX 718-403-0583
Brooklyn, NY 11205
Hours: 8-5 Mon-Fri   E-mail: mekatmet@aol.com
Provides artificial trees, plants and flowers to many of NYC's daytime dramas.
Artificial rocks, gazebos, urns, trellises. Phone orders. Location work.
RENTALS. CREDIT CARDS.

Mill Studios / Philadelphia Botanical .215-482-2100
123 Leverington Ave.   FAX 215-483-2324
Philadelphia, PA 19127
Hours: 8:30-5 Mon-Fri
Silk and cloth flowers, foliage; floral accessories. Phone orders. Contact
Scott Gresen. CREDIT CARDS.

Pany's Silk Flowers 212-645-9526
146 W 28th St. (6-7th Ave)   FAX (same)
NY, NY 10001
Hours: 8-5:30 Mon-Fri / Sat 9-4
Beautifully crafted silk flowers. Great selection. Wholesale prices. MC/VISA.

Silk Gardens & Trees 212-629-0600
113 W 28th St. (6th Ave)   FAX 212-629-0612
NY, NY 10001
Hours: 8:30-6 Mon-Fri / 10-5 Sat
Manufacturer-distributor of artificial trees and plants. Good work. RENTAL.
CREDIT CARDS.

Teins Decoratives 516-227-1184
3 North Ave.   FAX 516-227-1183
Garden City, NY 11530
Hours: 10:30-6 Mon-Sat / Sat call first   E-mail: info@telesilk.com
www.telesilk.com
Large selection of permanent flowers, plants and trees. Also decorative
accessories such as urns, pedestals and paintings. CREDIT CARDS.

Tinsel Trading 212-730-1030
1 W 37th St. (5-6th Ave)   FAX 212-768-8823
NY, NY 10018
Hours: 9:45-5:30 Mon-Fri / 11-5 some Sat (call first)
www.tinseltrading.com   E-mail: sales@tinseltrading.com
Gold mesh fabrics, metallic and antique trims, vintage flowers, fruit stamens,
buttons, fringes, cords, tassels, horsehair, ribbons, etc. Also upholstery gimps
and trims. $75 minimum order for shipping. CREDIT CARDS.

Trengove Studios, Inc. 212-268-0020
60 W 22nd St., 2nd Fl (7-8th Ave)   800-366-2857
NY, NY 10010   FAX 212-268-0030
Hours: call for appt. 9-5 Mon-Fri   E-mail: info@trengovestudios.com
www.trengovestudios.com
Realistic looking artificial foods, ice cubes and crushed ice. Brochure
available.

AUDIO & VIDEO EQUIPMENT

Audio Visual Workshop 212-643-0040
500 W 37th St., 3rd FL (10-11th Ave)   FAX 212-564-5277
NY, NY 10018
Hours: 9-5 Mon-Fri   E-mail: sales@avworkshop.com
www.avworkshop.com
Audio and video equipment. Speak to Dennis Troy or Tim Roache. RENTALS.
CREDIT CARDS.

Bentley Meeker Lighting & Staging, Inc. 212-722-3349
465 10th Ave. 2nd Fl   FAX: 212-722-8803
NY, NY 10018
Hours: 10-6 Mon-Fri   E-mail: mail@bentleymeeker.com
www.bentleymeeker.com
Full-service lighting, staging and audio firm specializing in live events,
parties, fashion shows, etc.

BTL Productions 201-943-4190
815 Fairview Ave., Unit 11 (Tracey Ave)   FAX 201-943-4191
Fairview, NJ 07022
Hours: 9-5 Mon-Fri
www.bltprod.com
Full service production company providing project management, design
(scenic, lighting and sound.) Fabrication and installation. Extensive
experience in fashion shows and special / corporate events as well as theatre
and television. the will help you design or realize your design. Custom logos
and backdrops. RENTALS.

A-B

Coleman Audio 516-334-7109
81 Pilgrim Ln.
Westbury, NY 11590
Hours: 9-5 Mon-Fri or by appt.　　　E-mail: coley@colemanaudio.com
www.colemanaudio.com
Manufacturer of audio gear.

Computer Rent, Inc. 212-619-6363
225 Broadway (Barclay St)　　　　　　　　　　800-872-2983
NY, NY 10007　　　　　　　　　　　　　FAX　212-619-6844
Hours: 9-6 Mon-Fri　　　　　　　　E-mail: rentapcnow@aol.com
Computers, printers in all shapes and sizes; working or props. Can do
custom configurations from large inventory. Rental of LCD panels, plasma
screens, projectors. Willing to work with customers. RENTALS. CREDIT
CARDS.

Harvey Home Entertainment 212-575-5000
2 W 45th St.(5th Ave)　　　　　　　　　　　212-575-5000
NY, NY 10036　　　　　　　　　　　　　FAX　212-768-8114
Hours: 9:30-6 Mon-Fri / 10-6 Sat / 12-5 Sun

888 Broadway, inside ABC Carpet & Home(19th St)　　212-228-5354
NY, NY 10003　　　　　　　　　　　　　FAX　212-260-4454
Hours: 10-8 Mon-Fri / 10-7 Sat / 12-6 Sun
www.harveyonline.com
Stereo, home theater, audio and video equipment. Ask for Evan Press. See
website for additional locations in NY, NJ and CT. CREDIT CARDS.

Hello World Communications 212-243-8800
118 W 22nd St. (6-7th Ave)　　　　　　FAX　212-691-6961
NY, NY 10011
Hours: 8-7 Mon-Fri / 9-6 Sat　　　　　E-mail: elronyo@msn.com
www.hwc.tv
Hello World Communications offers audio/digital video production tools and
postproduction services. Rentals include; audio-video-lighting-
computer/video projector-office equipment-cellular phone and two-way radio
(walkie-talkie). RENTALS. CREDIT CARDS.

J & R Music & Computer World 212-238-9000
15-23 Park Row (Beekman-Ann St)　　　　　　800-221-3191
NY, NY 10038　　　　　　　　　　　　　FAX　212-238-9191
Hours: 9-7:30 Mon-Sat / 10:30-6:30 Sun
www.jr.com
Extensive selection of stereo and video equipment from inexpensive to high
end. Catalog. CREDIT CARDS.

K-Mart 212-760-1188
250 W 34th St.(7-8th Ave)　　　　　　　　　212-760-1188
NY, NY 10019
Hours: 8-10 Mon-Thurs / 9-10 Fri-Sun

770 Broadway(8th St)　　　　　　　　　　　212-673-1540
NY, NY 10003-9535
Hours: 8-10 Daily
www.kmart.com
Audio and video equipment. Purchase Orders. CREDIT CARDS.

Kadan Productions, Inc. 212-674-7080
3200 Liberty Ave., Bldg 3 (Paterson Plank Rd)   FAX 212-674-7244
North Bergen, NJ 07047
Hours: 9-6 Mon-Fri
www.kadaninc.com
Full-service staging, lighting, audio/video, set construction and design company. Extensive experience in fashion, corporate conventions and special events. Can provide video graphics and slide projection. Will design or make any part of your design happen.

Ken Logert Productions 718-292-1257
2680 Park Ave. (141st St)   FAX 718-742-2461
Bronx, NY 10451
Hours: 9-5 Mon-Fri / call for appt.   E-mail: info@klprods.com
www.klprods.com
One-stop, full-service equipment provider of lighting, audio/video and projection equipment for concerts, special events, promotions and environmental production services. RENTALS. CREDIT CARDS.

Media Services Worldwide 201-770-9950
3200 Liberty Ave. Unit 2C (Hudson-Greenwich St)   FAX 201-770-9956
North Bergen, NJ 07047
Hours: 9-5 Mon-Fri
Audio/Visual staging and events. Installations and rentals. RENTALS.

MSI Security Systems, Inc. 201-955-1200
62-70 Second Ave.   800-333-1013
Kearny, NJ 07032   FAX 973-758-0800
Hours: 9-5 Mon-Fri   E-mail: theboss@msisecurity.com
www.msisecurity.com
Design/installation of CCTV security systems. Speak to Marvin Schnapper. RENTALS. CREDIT CARDS.

Park Avenue Audio 212-685-8101
425 Park Ave. South (29th St)   FAX 212-689-0468
NY, NY 10016
Hours: 10-6:30 Mon-Wed, Fri / 10-6 Thurs / 10:30-6 Sat-Sun
www.parkavenueaudio.com   E-mail: info@parkavenueaudio.com
Audio and video equipment; custom installations. CREDIT CARDS.

PLS Staging 973-857-7242
371 Little Falls Road   800-783-4757
Cedar Grove, NJ 07009   FAX 973-857-8867
Hours: 9-5 Mon-Fri / 24-hr. paging service
www.plsstaging.com
Full-service audio-visual company. Rentals speak to Scott. RENTALS. CREDIT CARDS.

PRG 201-758-4000
539 Temple Hill Rd.   845-567-5700
New Windsor, NY 12553   FAX 845-567-5800
Hours: 8-6 Mon-Fri

7777 West Side Ave.   201-758-4000
North Bergen, NJ 07047   FAX 201-758-4312
Hours: 8-6 Mon-Fri

PRG (cont.) 201-758-4000
   250 E Sandford Blvd.   914-662-3540
   Mt. Vernon, NY 10550   FAX 914-668-6844
   Hours: 8-6 Mon-Fri

   9111 Sunland Blvd.   818-252-2600
   Sun Valley, CA 91352   818-262-3983
   Hours: 8-6 Mon- Fri   FAX 818-252-2620

   6050 S Valley View Blvd.   702-942-4774
   Las Vegas, NV 89118   702-942-4774
   Hours: 8-6 Mon-Fri   FAX 702-942-4772

   2480 Tedlo St.   905-270-9050
   Mississauga, ON L5A 3V3   FAX 905-270-2590
   Hours: 8-6 Mon-Fri

   1902 Cypress Lake Dr., Ste 100   407-855-8060
   Orlando, FL 32837   FAX 407-855-8059
   Hours: 8-6 Mon-Fri

   8351 Eastgate Blvd.   615-834-3190
   Mount Juliette, TN 37122   FAX 615-834-3192
   Hours: 8-6 Mon-Fri

   8617 Ambassador Row Ste. 120   214-630-1963
   Dallas, TX 75247   FAX 214-630-5867
   Hours: 8-6 Mon-Fri

   11801 E. 33rd Ave., Ste. D   303-341-4848
   Aurora, CO 80010   FAX 702-942-4623
   Hours: 8-6 Mon-Fri   E-mail: prg.com
   www.prg.com
   A premier audio reinforcement company known for innovation, reliability and
   service. Experienced in the Broadway market, theatrical touring, corporate
   theatre and special events. RENTALS.

ProMix, Inc. / PRG 914-662-3540
   250 E Sandford Blvd.   FAX 914-662-3731
   Mt. Vernon, NY 10550
   Hours: 9-5 Mon-Fri
   www.prg.com
   Provider of sound equipment rentals, design and consulting services for
   theatrical, industrial and private functions. Tour packages available.
   RENTALS. CREDIT CARDS.

Scharff Weisberg, Inc. 212-582-2345
   36-36 33rd St.   800-477-SHOW
   Long Island City, NY 11106   FAX 718-610-1750
   Hours: 9-5:30 Mon-Fri / 24 hr Tech Support
   www.swinyc.com   E-mail: scharffweisberg@swinyc.com
   Rents, sells, stages and installs a full line of audio, video and multimedia
   equipment. Specializes in video projection, image magnification, computer
   data display, sound and video walls. Developing a full-service lighting
   division. RENTALS.

AUDIO & VIDEO EQUIPMENT

Uncle Steve's 212-925-5185
334 Canal St. (Wooster-Greene St)   FX 212-925-8600
NY, NY 10013
Hours: 10-7:30 Daily
www.unclestevecarstero.net
Large selection; a real NYC experience. Speak to Saff. CREDIT CARDS.

AUDIO & VIDEO EQUIPMENT: ANTIQUE & DUMMY

Ace Video & Props 718-392-1100
37-24 24th St., Ste. 106 (Houston & West St)   212-206-1475
Long Island City, NY 11101   FAX 718-392-1155
Hours: 10-6 Mon-Fri / 10-2 Sat by appt.
E-mail: acevideorentals@gmail.com / acepropsnyc@gmail.com
www.aceprops.com
*Wide variety of sound, A/V and video equipment - consumer and
professional, period and contemporary. Installation and technical support
available. RENTALS. CREDIT CARDS.*

Harry Poster - Vintage TVs 201-794-9606
1310 Second St.
Fairlawn, NJ 07410
Hours: 24 hours 7 days a week by appt.   E-mail: tvs@harryposter.com
www.harryposter.com
*Vintage televisions; props and 24 frame. Signs, radios, tubes, TV-shop items.
Very helpful website. Sales and RENTALS.*

Waves 212-273-9616
40 W 25th St., Gallery 107 (in the Antiques Showplace)   FAX 201-461-7121
NY, NY 10001
Hours: 11-5 Wed-Sun   E-mail: wavesllc@gmail.com
www.wavesllc.com
*Interesting collection of 78s, Victrolas, radios, telephones. RENTALS. CREDIT
CARDS.*

AUTOMOBILE & MOTORCYCLE RENTAL

AAA Movie Time Cars 201-955-0934
90 Porete Ave.   877-CARS4FILM
North Argington, NJ 07031   FAX 201-955-0935
Hours: 24-hrs. daily   E-mail: movietimecars@me.com
www.movietimecars.com
*Good selection of picture cars in stock; vintage, limousines, exotic,
motorcycles, police cars and ambulances with NJ and NY markings. Speak
to Ron or Joe. RENTALS. CREDIT CARDS.*

All Star Rentals, Inc. 973-591-1333
61 Willett St. A Bldg. Ste. 7   800-479-8368
Passaic, NJ 07055   FAX 973-591-1336
Hours: 9-5 Mon-Fri
*Vintage Harley-Davidson Motorcycles for production rentals or special events.
Delivery available. RENTALS.*

Auto Film Club 718-447-2255
   10 Cross St. (Bay St)   FAX 718-447-2289
   Staten Island, NY 10304
   Hours: 9-5 Mon-Fri   E-mail: autofilm@aol.com
   www.autofilmclub.com
Automobile and motorcycle rental to the film industry. P.O.s accepted.
RENTALS.

Auto Props 973-470-9354
   8 Lexington Ave.   FAX 973-591-1835
   Wallington, NJ 07057
   Hours: by appt.   E-mail: 57gasser@comcast.net
   www.autoprops-waterworks.com
Automobiles and trucks of all types and periods, including Harley Davidson
motorcycles. Stunt rigging; wet downs, water effects, water trucks, scuba;
garage facilities. Ask about other effects. Talk to Ken Maletsky. RENTALS.
CREDIT CARDS.

Cars of Yesterday Rentals 201-784-0030
   PO Box 43, State Hwy. 9W   201-707-6619
   Alpine, NJ 07620   FAX 201-784-0015
   Hours: 9-5 Mon-Fri or by appt.
               E-mail: jerrymcspirit@carsofyesterdayrentals.com
   www.carsofyesterdayrentals.com
Antique to present autos, police cars and taxi cabs including Checkers. Speak
to Jerry McSpirit. RENTALS.

Chrome Everything, Inc. 718-325-4840
   3530 Noell Ave (Boston Rd-Hollers Ave)   347-255-7101
   Bronx, NY 10475   FAX 718-325-6510
   Hours: 10-6 Mon-Fri   E-mail: racerx1200ccW@aol.com
   www.chromeverything.com
Spray chrome any solid materials including leather, vinyl and all foams.

Cooper Classic, Ltd. 212-929-3909
   137 Perry St. (Washington-Greenwich St)   800-719-3909
   NY, NY 10014   FAX 212-633-6952
   Hours: 9-5:30 Mon-Fri / 10-4 Sat   E-mail: info@cooperclassiccars.com
   www.cooperclassiccars.com
Any car, any period. Studio available for car shoots. RENTALS. CREDIT
CARDS.

Cycle Tenders / NY Motorcycles 718-479-2929
   222-02 Jamaica Ave.   718-479-7777
   Queens Village, NY 11428   FAX 718-740-4887
   Hours: 9-6 Mon-Sat / Wed-Fri till 8pm   E-mail: questions@newyorkmc.com
   www.newyorkmotorcycle.com
Motorcycles and film cars; 24-hr. pick-up and delivery. Speak to Whitey.
RENTALS. CREDIT CARDS.

Lost Soul Entertainment . . . . Matt 973-979-1503
3 Melissa Dr.   Bryan 201-982-5255
N. Haledon, NJ 07508
Hours: 24 hrs by appt.   E-mail: LShollywood@aol.com
www.lostsoulent.com
Supplier of modern and vintage prop vehicles for the film and commercial industry. The vehicles can be modified (paint, decals, etc.) and are delivered to your location, any time, any place, any where. RENTALS.

Metro Film Cars 973-450-1692
114 Brighton Ave.   973-699-7707
Belleville, NJ 07109   FAX 973-751-8320
Hours: open 7 days, call first   E-mail: metro4film@aol.com
Not just cars! This company will rent you anything that moves: tractors, planes, boats, trains, trailers, helicopters, etc. International clientele. Friendly service. Speak to Tom. RENTALS.

modprop 212-628-7582
1044 Madison Ave. (79-80th St)
NY, NY 10021
Hours: 9-5 Mon-Fri   E-mail: info@modprop.com
www.modprop.com
Modern funiture prop rental house. Specializing in contemporary furniture, they rent anything from vintage automobiles, shooting locations to plates and glasses. Wide selections in superior condition. Speak to Stephen. RENTALS. CREDIT CARDS.

New York Motorcycle 718-479-7777
222-02 Jamaica Ave. (22-24th St)   800-527-2727
Queens Village, NY 11428   FAX 718-740-4887
Hours: 9-6 Mon-Tue, Sat / 9-8 Wed-Fri   E-mail: questions@newyorkmc.com
www.newyorkmotorcycle.com
Motorcycles form the 40s and up. Ducatis, Harleys, exotics, scooters, vespa, segways, boats, jetskiis, atvs plus a waterfront marina to shoot from. Over 1000 different pieces. RENTALS. CREDIT CARDS.

Obsolete Fleet 212-255-6068
45 Christopher St. (7th Ave)
NY, NY 10014
Hours: by appt.
Antique and classic vehicles; see Daniel List. RENTALS.

Picture Cars East, Inc. 718-852-2300
72 Huntington St. (Henry-Hicks St)   800-319-3388
Brooklyn, NY 11231   FAX 718-858-1583
Hours: 9-5 Mon-Fri   E-mail: info@pixxcars.com
www.pixxcars.com
Prop cars, wagons, cabs, all kinds of vehicles. RENTALS.

Vogel's EuroCars, Inc. 914-968-8200
365 Mclean Ave.   203-265-2226
Yonkers, NY 10705   FAX 914-968-5506
Hours: 8-8 Mon-Sun
www.eurocars.com
Mercedes Benz cars; front door delivery and pick-up available. RENTALS. CREDIT CARDS.

AUTOMOBILE & TAXICAB ACCESSORIES & SUPPLIES

American Taximeter 718-937-4600
21-46 44th Dr.   800-882-0280
Long Island City, NY 11101   FAX 718-937-4805
Hours: 8-5 Mon-Fri   E-mail: info@at-c.com
www.at-c.com
Taxi stickers, license holders, motorola radios, old taxi meters and accessories. Speak to Tony Martinez. CREDIT CARDS.

Cybert Tire Corp. 212-265-1177
726 Eleventh Ave. (51st-52nd St)   FAX 212-265-1181
NY, NY 10019
Hours: 7-6 Mon-Fri / 7-3 Sat / 10-3 Sun   E-mail: cyberttire@aol.com
Tires; also batteries. Automotive repair. RENTALS. CREDIT CARDS.

Lost Soul Entertainment ....Matt 973-979-1503
3 Melissa Dr.   Bryan 201-982-5255
N. Haledon, NJ 07508
Hours: 24 hrs by appt.   E-mail: LShollywood@aol.com
www.lostsoulent.com
Supplier of modern and vintage prop vehicles for the film and commercial industry. The vehicles can be modified (paint, decals, etc.) and are delivered to your location, any time, any place, any where. RENTALS.

Herman Sticht Co. 800-221-3203
45 Main St. (Fulton St)   718-852-7602
Brooklyn, NY 11201   FAX 718-852-7915
Hours: 9-5 Mon-Fri   E-mail: stichtco@aol.com
www.stichtco.com
Static electricity eliminators, conductivity test kit, insulation testers and meters. CREDIT CARDS.

The Traffic Safety Store 800-429-9030
P.O. Box 1449   FAX: 610-701-9369
West Chester, PA 19380
Hours: 24-hr website   E-mail: contact@trafficsafetystore.com
www.trafficsafetystore.com
Traffic cones, barricades, barricade flashers, and parking lot blocks, reflective tapes, traffic and construction signs, just to name a few, are ready for immediate, same-day shipment. Speak to Kevin. CREDIT CARDS.

NOTES

BACKDROPS

See also: SCENIC SHOPS
                PROP & SCENIC CRAFTSPEOPLE: Scenic Painters
For soft goods, see CURTAINS & DRAPERIES, THEATRICAL

A-B

Ace Banner, Flag & Graphics Co. 212-620-9111
107 W 27th St. (6th Ave)   800-675-9112
NY, NY 10011   FAX 212-463-9128
Hours: 7:30-4 Mon-Fri   E-mail: service@acebanner.com
www.acebanner.com / www.acebannershop.com
Custom four-color printed backdrops, any size. CREDIT CARDS.

Adirondack Studio 518-638-8000
439 County Rt 45   FAX 518-761-3362
Argyle, NY 12809
Hours: 9-5 Mon-Fri
www.adirondackscenic.com
Sets, props, soft goods, lighting equipment. RENTALS.

Broderson Backdrops 212-925-9392
873 Broadway Studio 603 (18th St)   FAX 212-473-6464
NY, NY 10003
Hours: 9-5 Mon-Fri   E-mail: info@brodersonbackdrops.com
www.brodersonbackdrops.com
Backdrops; will deliver, ship nationwide. RENTALS.

BTL Productions 201-943-4190
815 Fairview Ave., Unit 11 (Tracey Ave)   FAX 201-943-4191
Fairview, NJ 07022
Hours: 9-5 Mon-Fri
www.bltprod.com
*Full service production company providing project management, design
(scenic, lighting and sound.) Fabrication and installation. Extensive
experience in fashion shows and special / corporate events as well as theatre
and television. the will help you design or realize your design. Custom logos
and backdrops. RENTALS.*

Chalkline Studios 954-454-8336
7015 River Club Dr. (3rd Ave)   Cell 305-546-9998
Bradenton, FL 34202   FAX (same)
Hours: by appt.   E-mail: info@chalklinestudios.com
www.chalklinestudios.com
*Non-union paint shop. Custom drops, scenery, murals and props. Rental
space available daily or weekly.*

COBALT STUDIOS 845-583-7025
134 Royce Rd.   FAX 845-583-7025
White Lake, NY 12786
Hours: 8-5 Mon-Fri   E-mail: mail@colbaltstudios.net
www.cobaltstudios.net
*Cobalt Studios paints custom backdrops and rents backdrops to the
entertainment and exhibit industries. Scenic art training and seminars
available. RENTALS. CREDIT CARDS. Member ATAC.*

A-B

Betsy Davis Backdrops 212-645-4197
601 W 26th St. # 308 (11-12th Aves)   917-445-2114
NY, NY 10014   FAX 212-645-4197
Hours: 10-6 Mon-Fri   E-mail: info@betsydavisbackdrops.com
www.betsydavisbackdrops.com
Custom-made props and backdrops, specializing in photoshoots. Also
teaches Yoga at her studio. See web address for class schedules. RENTALS.

Martin Izquierdo Studio 212-807-9757
118 W 22nd St., 9th Fl. (6-7th Ave)   FAX 212-366-5249
NY, NY 10011
Hours: 9-7 Mon-Fri   E-mail: izquierdostudio@gmail.com
www.izquierdostudio.com
Custom fabrication of all types of soft goods, including backdrops. Fabric,
costume and prop painting/dyeing techniques for theatre, film, commercials,
display and video. No rentals.

J.C. Backings Corp. 310-244-5830
10202 W Washington Blvd. (Overland Ave)   FAX 310-244-7949
Culver City, CA 90232
Hours: 8-4:30 Mon-Fri   E-mail: info@jcbackings.com
www.jcbackings.com
Over 3500 scenic backdrops, primarily for film and TV; fully equipped union
scenic shop for custom work. Will ship. Catalog. RENTALS.

JERARD STUDIO, INC. 718-852-4128
481 Van Brunt St., Ste. 11D (Beard St)   FAX 718-852-2408
Brooklyn, NY 11231
Hours: 9-6 Mon-Fri   E-mail: mary@jerardstudio.com
www.jerardstudio.com
Custom backdrops, scenic painting, murals, decorative and faux finishes,
trompe l'oeil. Backpainted glass. Member ATAC.

National Flag & Display Co., Inc. 212-462-4000
22 W 21st St., 7th Fl. (5-6th St)   FAX 212-462-2624
NY, NY 10010
Hours: 9-5:30 Mon-Fri / eves. & weekends by appt.
www.nationalflag.com   E-mail: hsiegel@nationalflag.com
Manufacturers of banners, flags, backdrops and wall murals. Applique,
silkscreen, inkjet, dye-sublimation and electrostatic full-color printing. Rush
orders. RENTALS. CREDIT CARDS.

Jane Nelson Studios 212-431-4642
21 Howard St. (B'way-Lafayette St)
NY, NY 10013
Hours: by appt.   E-mail: janeynel@gmail.com
Custom painted backdrops, murals and sets. Rental stock available.
Member USA Local 829. RENTALS.

Oliphant Backdrops 212-741-1233
20 W 20th St., 6th Fl. (5-6th Ave)   FAX 212-366-6772
NY, NY 10011
Hours: 9-5 Mon-Fri   E-mail: rentals@osstudio.com
www.osstudio.com
Large stock of rental drops; custom work. Will deliver/ship. Catalog
available. RENTALS. CREDIT CARDS.

Pacific Studios, Inc. 323-653-3093
8315 Melrose Ave.   rentals 323-653-3093 Ext 2
West Hollywood, CA 90069   FAX 323-653-9509
Hours: 7-5 Mon-Fri   E-mail: pacstudios@sbcglobal.net
*Photographic backgrounds and chromatrons. Custom orders available.
Catalog. RENTALS.*

Provost Displays, Inc. 800-555-3772
501 W Washington St., 2nd Fl.   610-279-3970
Norristown, PA 19401   FAX 610-279-3968
Hours: 8-5:30 Mon-Thurs   E-mail: toprovost@verizon.net
www.provostdisplays.com
*Vacuumformed architectural & scenic panels. Manufacturers of
GIANTFORMES; flame and weatherproof vacuumformed plastic decorative
panels up to 4' x 12'. Custom molds made to order. Free shipping to NY and
NJ areas. Catalog of stock designs available. CREDIT CARDS.*

Rosco Laboratories, Inc. 203-708-8900
52 Harbor View Ave.   800-ROSCONY
Stamford, CT 06902   FAX 203-708-8919
Hours: 9-5 Mon-Fri   E-mail: info@rosco.com
www.rosco.com
*Transparencies or opaque art into large textile drops. Beautiful results.
Shipping available.*

Showman Fabricators 718-935-9899
47-22 Pearson Place (Hamilton Ave-Bowne St)   FAX 718-855-9823
Long Island City, NY 11101
Hours: 7-5:30 Mon-Fri   E-mail: info@showfab.com
www.showfab.com
*Showman backdrops have been used by many commercials and television
productions. Visit website to view large selection.*

Surface Studio 212-244-6107
242 W 30th St., Ste. 1203 (7-8th Ave)   FAX 212-244-8522
NY, NY 10001
Hours: 9-5 Mon-Thurs / 9-3:30 Fri
www.surfacestudio.com
*Solid backgrounds: wood, metal, stucco, tile, rustic, modern. A large
selection and variety in formats up to 6' x 6', with finished edges, all in
perfect condition.*

BAKERIES

Birthday Bakers / Party Makers 212-288-7112
195 E 76th St. (3rd-Lex Ave)   888-321-PARTY
NY, NY 10021   FAX 212-628-3084
Hours: 10-5:30 Mon-Fri   E-mail: lindakaye@partymakers.com
www.partymakers.com
*Cakes in all sizes and shapes for events and personal celebrations. 4-foot
pop-out cake with optional edible layer serves up to 100. Expensive. Contact
Linda Kaye. CREDIT CARDS.*

Creative Cakes 212-794-9811
400 E 74th St. (1st Ave)   FAX 212-794-9811
NY, NY 10021
Hours: 8-4:30 Mon-Fri / 9-11am Sat   E-mail: cakeman2357@aol.com
www.creativecakesny.com
Cakes made to order; very helpful. Speak to Bill. No credit cards.

Gail Watson Custom Cakes 212-967-9167
335 W 38th St. #11 (8-9th Ave)   FAX 646-619-4364
New York, NY 10018
Hours: by appt.   E-mail: gail@gailwatsoncake.com
www.gailwatsoncake.com / www.asimplecake.com
*Making great cakes and original wedding favors since 1988 using only the
finest ingredients available. Wedding cake kits available for various cakes.
View website for photos. RENTALS. CREDIT CARDS.*

La Delice Pastry Shop 212-532-4409
372 Third Ave. (27th St)
NY, NY 10016
Hours: 7-9 Mon-Sat / 7-9 Sun
Will make cakes to order in one day; very helpful.

Mazur's Bakery 201-438-8500
323 Ridge Rd.   FAX 201-438-0048
Lyndhurst, NJ 07071
Hours: 6-9 Mon-Sat / 6-8 Sun
*Custom cakes for all occasions including film needs and weddings. Also
breads, pastries, rolls, cookies.*

Orwasher's 212-288-6569
308 E 78th St. (1st-2nd Ave)   FAX 212-570-2706
NY, NY 10021
Hours: 8-7 Mon-Sat / 9-4 Sun
www.orwashersbakery.com
Fabulous breads of all kinds. CREDIT CARDS.

Poseidon Bakery 212-757-6173
629 Ninth Ave. (44-45th St)
NY, NY 10036
Hours: 9-7 Tue-Sat   E-mail: paul@poseidonbakery.com
Greek pastries. Strudel, spinach pies, meat pies. CREDIT CARDS.

BAKERY AND CANDY SUPPLIES

New York Cake & Baking Distributors 212-675-CAKE
56 W 22nd St. (5-6th Ave)   800-942-2539
NY, NY 10010   FAX 212-675-7099
Hours: 10-6 Mon-Sat
www.nycake.com
*All kinds of cake decorating supplies. Specialty pans, novelty cake decor and
items for the professional. Wilton dealer. CREDIT CARDS.*

Streichs Cake and Candy Supply 814-723-0784
RR # 1 Box 1320   FAX 814-732-7294
Clarendon, PA 16313
Hours: 24 on website   E-mail: sales@streichs.com
www.streichs.com
One of the largest selections of cake and candy supplies on the web. Over
500 chocolate and candy molds. Very helpful staff. Speak with Steve.
CREDIT CARDS.

BALLOONS & HELIUM

Balloon Bouquets of New York 212-265-5252
457 W 43rd St. (9-10th Ave)   FAX 212-586-8364
NY, NY 10036
Hours: 9-5 Mon-Fri   E-mail: balloonnyc@aol.com
www.balloonbouquetsnyc.com
Balloon sculpture and special effects; exploding weather balloons, balloon
drops, meetings, corporate functions. $40 minimum. Helium tank rentals.
CREDIT CARDS.

Balloons to Go 212-989-9338
212 W 17st St. (7-8th Ave)   FAX 212-633-9193
NY, NY 10011
Hours: 10-5 Mon-Fri / 10-3 Sat / Sun pre-orders only E-mail: btg989@aol.com
www.balloonstogo.com
Custom balloons. CREDIT CARDS.

Mayflower Distributing Co. 800-678-4892
1155 Medallion Dr.   651-452-4892
Mendota Hts, MN 55120   FAX 888-655-0921
Hours: 8-5 Mon-Fri   E-mail: info@mayflowerdistributing.com
www.mayflowerdistributing.com
Mylar balloons, mylar ribbon; wholesale. Catalog. CREDIT CARDS.

McKinney Welding Supply 212-246-4390
535 W 52nd St. (10-11th Ave)   FAX 212-582-3105
NY, NY 10019
Hours: 7-4:30 Mon-Fri   E-mail: sales@mckinneynyc.com
www.mckinneynyc.com
Helium; industrial, medical and specialty gases. Will rent and deliver helium
tanks. RENTALS. CREDIT CARDS.

Remember our Balloons 973-316-8200
623 Eagle Rock Ave.   973-296-0872
West Orange, NJ 07052
Hours: by appt. 7 days a week   E-mail: robbie@balloonsbyrobbie.com
www.balloonsbyrobbie.com
One-stop shopping for all your decorating needs. From the very quirky to
regular balloon columns, Robbie is the most unique balloon artist. Visit
website to see all the fun fantastical shapes he has dreamed up for film and
TV. CREDIT CARDS.

T.W. Smith Welding Supply 718-388-7417
885 Meeker Ave. (Bridgewater-Varick St)   FAX 718-388-8943
Brooklyn, NY 11222
Hours: 7:30-4:30 Mon-Fri   E-mail: info@twsmith.com
www.twsmith.com
Helium, balloon attachments; deposit required.

T-Shirt Express 212-874-4464
209 W 80th St. (B'way-Amst Ave)   800-292-1562
NY, NY 10024   FAX 212-874-3740
Hours: 8-5 Mon-Fri / 9:30-3:30 Sat   E-mail: hp2@nyc.rr.com
www.tshirtexpress.com; www.printballoons.com
*Custom screen printing, embroidery, heat transfers on all apparel. Latex and
mylar balloons. No minimum. Speak to Harvey. CREDIT CARDS.*

Toy Balloon Corp. 212-682-3803
5 Tudor City Place (1st-2nd Ave)   FAX 212-682-0122
NY, NY 10017
Hours: by appt.
*Novelty, plain or printed balloons to order (minimum on printed balloons);
helium.   Wholesale and retail.*

U.S. Balloon Mfg. Co. 718-492-9700
140 58th St. (Bklyn Army Terminal)   800-285-4000
Brooklyn, NY 11220   FAX 718-492-8711
Hours: 8:30-7 Mon-Fri   E-mail: sales@usballoon.com
www.usballoon.com
*Large selection of mylar and latex balloons and balloon accessories; carries
animal shapes; wholesale. Catalog. CREDIT CARDS.*

BARRELS

Adelphia Container Corp. 718-388-5202
125 Division Pl. (Vandervort)   FAX 718-388-0967
Brooklyn, NY 11211
Hours: 7-3:30 Mon-Fri
*Cardboard barrels, steel and plastic drums. Small and large orders. CREDIT
CARDS.*

Bradbury Barrel Co. 207-429-8141
479 US Highway 1   800-332-6021
Bridgewater, ME 04735   FAX 207-429-8188
Hours: 8-5 Mon-Fri   E-mail: sales@bradburybarrel.com
www.bradburybarrel.com
*Handmade cedar barrels and tubs. Display units, barrel liners. Catalog.
CREDIT CARDS.*

A-B

Greif Brothers Corporation 740-484-4020
425 Winter Rd.   800-625-7971
Delaware, OH 43015   FAX 251-679-9945
Hours: 8-5 Mon-Fri   E-mail: tammy.drumheller@greif.com
www.greif.com
Good source for cardboard barrels, shipping containers, large 35 gal,
plastic/fiber containers and steel containers. Website offers full listings.
Manufacturer minimums accordingly.

R & P Trading 903-613-2012
203 Pack Saddle
Holly Lake Ranch, TX 75765
Hours: 24-hrs. by website   E-mail: sales@rptrading.biz
www.rptrading.biz
Wooden wagons, butter churns, porch swings, Old West and Civil War historic
merchandise, hay, barrels and Amish products. Very nice and helpful staff.
CREDIT CARDS.

James Townsend & Son 800-338-1665
PO Box 415, 133 N First St.   574-594-5852
Pierceton, IN 46562   FAX 574-594-5580
Hours: 9-5 Mon-Fri   E-mail: jastown@jastown.com
www.jastown.com
18th and 19th century military uniforms, clothing, hats, patterns, guns,
pistols, knives, axes, barrels, kegs, baskets, blankets, lanterns; repro colonial
household goods; catalog. CREDIT CARDS.

BASKETS & WICKER ITEMS
See also: ETHNIC GOODS: ALL HEADINGS
                 PROP RENTAL HOUSES
For supplies see RATTAN, REED, RAFFIA & WILLOW

Basketville 802-387-5509
8 Bellows Falls Rd.   800-258-4553
Putney, VT 05346   FAX 802-387-5235
Hours: 9-6 Mon-Fri
www.basketville.com
Wide selection of oak and ash weave baskets, wooden buckets; wholesale.
Catalog. Also retail internet sales. CREDIT CARDS.

Bikini Bar 212-571-6737
148 Duane St. (Church-W B'way)
NY, NY 10013
Hours: 12-7 Tue-Sat   E-mail: surf@bikinibar.com
www.bikinibar.com
Vintage Hawaiian rattan furniture, surfboards, travel posters and collectibles.
Surf Attire. Contact Aileen Oser or Stuart Smith. RENTALS

Bill's Flower Market, Inc. 212-889-8154
816 Sixth Ave. (28th St)   FAX 212-889-2352
NY, NY 10001
Hours: 8-6 Mon-Fri / 9-5 Sat   E-mail: bfm816@aol.com
www.billsflowermarket.com
Live flowers, baskets, floral supplies and large selection of feathers, artificial
birds. CREDIT CARDS.

Corner House Antiques 413-229-6627
599 Sheffield Plain Rd., Rt 7   FAX 413-229-6627
Sheffield, MA 01257
Hours: open most days 10-5 (call first)
www.americanantiquewicker.com   E-mail: tetro@americanantiquewicker.com
*Specializes in antique wicker furniture. Also general selection of antiques
and country accessories including bamboo. See Kathleen or Thomas Tetro.
RENTALS.*

Fran's Wicker & Rattan Furniture 800-372-6799
295 Rt. 10 East   FAX 973-584-7446
Succasunna, NJ 07876
Hours: 9-5:30 Mon-Fri (Wed & Thurs until 8:30) / 9:30-6 Sat / 12-5 Sun
www.franswicker.com   E-mail: inquiry@franswicker.com
*Large selection wicker baskets, outdoor rugs, rattan, wicker, teak and cast
aluminum furniture 1 hour from NYC. Ask for Fran Gruber. CREDIT CARDS.*

The Gazebo 770-632-7756
1427 Barberry Lane   800-998-7077
Peachtree City , GA 30269
Hours: 10-6 Mon-Sat   E-mail: response@thegazebo.com
www.thegazebo.com
*Quilts, wicker furniture, rag rugs, pillows and country home furnishings;
Expensive. Customized handcrafted quilts. CREDIT CARDS.*

Pier 1 Imports 800-245-4595
1550 Third Ave.(87th St)   212-987-1746
NY, NY 10128
Hours: 10-9 Mon-Sat / 11-7 Sun

71 Fifth Ave.(14-15th St)   212-206-1911
NY, NY 10003
Hours: 10-9 Mon-Sat / 11-7 Sun
www.pier1.com
*Popular chain of stores carries baskets; wicker furniture and decorative items
for the home. Some lighting, clothing, frames. See website for over 800
locations nationally. Some rentals. CREDIT CARDS.*

The Prop Company / Kaplan and Associates 212-691-7767
111 W 19th St., 8th Fl. (6-7th Ave)   FAX 212-727-3055
NY, NY 10011
Hours: 9-5 Mon-Fri   E-mail: propcompany@yahoo.com
*Antique and contemporary baskets and containers of all types. Picnic
baskets. All in fine condition. RENTAL only. CREDIT CARDS.*

Tabwa 212-924-8444
66 Greenwich Ave. (Perry-7th Ave)   FAX 212-924-8444
NY, NY 10011
Hours: 12-8 Mon-Fri / 12-7 Sat   E-mail: tabwa.com@verizon.net
www.tabwa.com
*Wonderful selection of baskets, as well as small rugs, decorative accessories,
vintage fabrics, ikats and block print Indian fabrics. Contact Carl. CREDIT
CARDS.*

A-B

Walter's Wicker, Inc. 201-567-2000
   120 North St. (58-59th St)   FAX 201-567-8668
   Teterboro, NJ 07608
   Hours: 9-5 Mon-Fri   E-mail: info@walterswicker.com
   www.walterswicker.com
   Wicker furniture and furnishings. 60 years in the business. Catalog. Speak to
   Kenneth Schindler. RENTALS.

Wicker Garden 212-410-7000
   1300 Madison Ave. (93-94th St)   FAX 212-410-6609
   NY, NY 10128
   Hours: 10-6 Tue-Sat
   Wicker and antique hand-painted furniture. RENTALS. CREDIT CARDS.

Wicker Outlet 732-356-5820
   135 Darren Dr.   877-942-5374
   Basking Ridge, NJ 07920   FAX 732-356-5822
   Hours: 9-5 Mon-Fri   E-mail: info@wickeroutlet.com
   www.wickeroutlet.com
   Wicker and rattan furniture and accessories. Discounts to the trade; delivery
   available. Speak to Kathy Malloy. CREDIT CARDS.

Wicker Warehouse, Inc. 201-342-6709
   195 South River St.   800-274-8602
   Hackensack, NJ 07601   FAX 201-342-1495
   Hours: 9-5 Mon-Sat   E-mail: sales@wickerwarehouse.com
   www.wickerwarehouse.com
   Wicker and rattan furniture, accessories, baskets. Catalog. CREDIT CARDS.

BATHROOM ACCESSORIES
See also: HARDWARE, DECORATIVE
              LINENS

Bed, Bath and Beyond . . . . .1-800-Go Beyond
   620 Sixth Ave.(18th St)   212-255-3550
   NY, NY 10011   FAX 212-229-1040
   Hours: 8-9 Daily

   410 E 61st St.(1st Ave)   646-215-4702
   NY, NY 10010   FAX 646-215-4713
   Hours: 9-9 Daily

   1932 Broadway(64-65th St)   917-441-9391
   NY, NY 10023
   Hours: 9-10 Daily   www.bedbathandbeyond.com
   A department store for bedroom, bathroom and kitchen: as well as seasonal.
   Visit the website for other locations across the USA. CREDIT CARDS.

Build it Green! 718-777-0132
3-17 26th Ave. (4th St)   FAX same
Astoria, NY 11102
Hours: 10-6 Tue-Fri / 10-5 Sat   E-mail: greeninfo@bignyc.org
www.bignyc.org
An 18,000 sq. ft. warehouse filled with salvaged building materials, bathroom
and lighting fixtures. Also recycled staging, signage and set pieces from film
and commercial shoots. Drop-off and pickup donations are by appointment
only.

Eldridge Textile Co. 732-544-4500
22 Meridian Rd. # 3   800-635-4399
Eatontown, NJ 07724   FAX 732-544-4555
Hours: 9:30-6 Mon-Fri   E-mail: custserv@eldridgetextile.com
www.eldridgetextile.com
Sheets, bedding, towels, tablecloths and custom window treatments. $3
refundable charge for catalog. Will ship. Catalog available online. CREDIT
CARDS.

Gracious Home 212-988-8990
1220, 1217, 1201 Third Ave.(70th-71st St)
NY, NY 10021   212-517-6300
Hours: 8-7 Mon-Fri / 9-7 Sat / 10-6 Sun   FAX 212-249-1534

1992 Broadway(67th St)   212-231-7800
NY, NY 10023   800-237-3404
Hours: 9-9 Mon-Sat / 10-7 Sun   FAX 212-875-9976
www.gracioushome.com   E-mail: info@gracioushome.com
Good selection of bath accessories, faucets, hampers, towel bars, decorative
hardware, lighting fixtures, bed linens and decorative items. CREDIT CARDS.

Howard Kaplan Designs 646-443-7170
240 E 60th St. (2nd-3rd St)   FAX 646-443-7174
NY, NY 10022
Hours: 10-5:30 Mon-Fri   E-mail: hkaplandesigns@aol.com
www.howardkaplandesigns.com
Antique bathroom accessories and fixtures; formal & informal French and
English country furniture; expensive. RENTALS. CREDIT CARDS.

The Jar Store 860-826-1881
221 South Street, Bldg F-5   FAX 860-826-1880
New Britain, CT 06051
Hours: 9-5:30 Mon-Fri
www.jarstore.com
Wholesale jar company and candle supply company. Apothecary, storage and
many other styles. Excellent selection on website. CREDIT CARDS.

Laytner's Linen & Home 800-690-7200
2270 Broadway(82nd-83rd St)   212-724-0180
NY, NY 10024   FAX 212-769-0620
Hours: 10-8 Mon-Sat / 11-7 Sun

237 E 86th St.(2nd-3rd Ave)   212-996-4439
NY, NY 10028
Hours: 10-8 Mon-Sat / 11-7 Sun

A-B

Laytner's Linen & Home (cont.) 800-690-7200
72-10 Austin St.   718-793-0003
Forest Hills, NY 11375
Hours: 10:30-7:30 Mon-Sat / 11-6 Sun

794 Union St.   718-622-0300
Park Slope, NY 11215
Hours: 10-7:30 Mon-Sat / 11-7 Sun   E-mail: sales@laytners.com
www.laytners.com
*Nice selection of bedding, towels, bath rugs, shower curtains, accessories;
will ship. Catalog. Online shopping. CREDIT CARDS.*

Paradise & Co. 530-872-5020
2902 Neal Rd.   FAX 530-872-5052
Paradise, CA 95969
www.paradise-co.com   E-mail: paradise@sunset.net
*Old-fashioned perfume bottles, atomizers etc. Company also restores
antique equipment and replacement parts. Catalog available or visit website
for complete selection. Very helpful. Paypal and CREDIT CARDS.*

The Prop Company / Kaplan and Associates 212-691-7767
111 W 19th St., 8th Fl. (6-7th Ave)   FAX 212-727-3055
NY, NY 10011
Hours: 9-5 Mon-Fri   E-mail: propcompany@yahoo.com
*Vintage & contemporary bathroom accessories, all in fine condition.
RENTAL. CREDIT CARDS.*

The Terrence Conran Shop 212-755-9079
888 Broadway Lower Level (18-19th St)   FAX 212-755-3989
NY, NY 10003
Hours: 11-8 Mon-Fri / 10-7 Sat / 12-6 Sun
www.conranusa.com   E-mail: terenceconranshop@conranusa.com
*Designer furniture, household, bedding and bath, textiles and hardware. Very
nice people. Will do rentals to film and television. CREDIT CARDS.*

Waterworks 212-371-9266
225 E 57th St. (2nd & 3rd Ave)   800-899-6757
NY, NY 10022   FAX 212-371-9263
Hours: 9-6 Mon-Fri / 11-5 Sat   E-mail: info@waterworks.com
www.waterworks.com
*Huge selection of bathroom fixtures, tubs and accessories; towels, robes,
bath soaps, oils and beads. Check website for additional locations. CREDIT
CARDS.*

ATAC

BEADS AND BEADING SUPPLIERS

See also: ETHNIC GOODS: All Headings
JEWELRY
TRIMMINGS: General

A.C. Moore 201-902-0377
400 Mill Creek Dr. (Mill Creek Mall Area)
Secaucus, NJ 07094
Hours: 99 Mon-Fri / 9-8 Sat-Sun
www.acmoore.com
*Chain based craft supply store. General crafts, art materials & framing, yarn
and needlecrafts, wedding supplies and more. Visit website for other 95
locations across the USA. CREDIT CARDS.*

S. Axelrod Co., Inc. 212-594-3022
7 W 30th St., 2nd Fl. (5th-B'way)   FAX 212-947-3787
NY, NY 10001
Hours: 9-5 Mon-Fri   E-mail: sales@axelrodco.com
www.axelrodco.com
*Wholesaler of google eyes, decorative trims, rhinestones, metal findings.
Contact Harvey Axelrod. CREDIT CARDS.*

Beads World, Inc. 212-302-1199
1384 Broadway (37-38th St)   FAX 212-302-2330
NY, NY 10018
Hours: 9-7 Mon-Fri / 10-6 Sat-Sun   E-mail: beadsworld@aol.com
www.beadsworldusa.com
Beads, trimmings, chains and findings. Wholesale and retail. CREDIT CARDS.

Bruce Frank Beads 212-595-3746
215 W 83rd St. (Amst & B'way)   877-232-3775
New York, NY 10024   FAX 212-873-6069
Hours: 11-7:30 Mon-Sat / 11-6 Sun   E-mail: info@brucefrandbeads.com
www.brucefrankbeads.com
*Unique selection of unusual antique and contemporary beads for creating
distinctive necklaces, earrings, bracelets, beaded apparel and other
accessories. Online catalog and print catalog available. Beading classes and
advice. CREDIT CARDS.*

Daytona Trimmings Co. 212-354-1713
251 W 39th St. (7-8th Ave)   FAX 212-391-0716
NY, NY 10018
Hours: 9-6:30 Mon-Fri / 9:30-5:20 Sat   E-mail: daytrim@worldnet.att.net
*Ric-rac, braids, laces, scarves, emblems, shoulder pads; wholesale. CREDIT
CARDS.*

Fire Mountain Gems . . . .(orders) 800-355-2137
One Fire Mountain Way   800-423-2319
Grants Pass, OR 97526   FAX 800-292-3473
Hours: 6-6 Mon,Tue,Thurs,Fri / 9-6 Wed / 7-3 Sat
www.firemountaingems.com   E-mail: questions@firemtn.com
*Mail order supplies for jewelry making. Their stock includes beads,
cabochons, crystal, wire and findings. Fast, friendly service. Online catalog
and shopping available. CREDIT CARDS.*

Grey Owl Indian Crafts 732-389-4626
15 Meridian Rd.   (orders) 800-487-2376
Eatontown, NJ 07724   FAX 732-389-4629
Hours: 9-5 Mon-Fri   E-mail: sales@greyowlcrafts.com
www.greyowlcrafts.com
Kits for American Indian headdresses and crafts; catalog. CREDIT CARDS.

Hai's Trimming Co. 212-764-2166
242 W 38th St. (7-8th Ave)   FAX (same)
NY, NY 10018
Hours: 10-6 Mon-Fri / 10-5 Sat
*All kinds of trims; bridal accessories. Good stock of heat fix and glue on
rhinestones, ribbons, buttons, etc. Beaded trims and feathers. Vinyl repair
glues and adhesives that stick vinyl to vinyl. CREDIT CARDS.*

Har-Man Importing Corp. 800-BEADSNY
95 B County Blvd.   631-756-9800
Farmingdale, NY 11735   FAX 631-756-9845
Hours: 9-4:30 Mon-Fri

16 W 37th St., 2nd Fl(5-6th Ave)   212-239-0772
NY, NY 10018   FAX 212-239-0350
Hours: by appt. only   E-mail: info@harmanbeads.com
www.harmanbeads.com
Jewels, findings.

Joyce Trimming, Inc. 212-719-3110
109 W 38th St. (Bway-7th Ave)   800-719-7133
NY, NY 10018   FAX 212-719-3091
Hours: 9-6 Mon-Fri   E-mail: info@ejoyce.com
www.ejoyce.com
*Broad selection of rhinestones, bandings, buttons, beads, trimmings and
accessories. Heat transfer motifs in crystal and metal studs. Visit website to
view selections. CREDIT CARDS.*

M & J Trimmings . . . . .1-800-9MJ TRIM
1008 Sixth Ave. (37-38th St)   212-204-9595
NY, NY 10018   FAX 212-704-8090
Hours: 9-8 Mon-Fri / 10-6 Sat / 12-6 Sun   E-mail: info@mjtrim.com
www.mjtrim.com
*Pricey; ribbons, buttons, buckles, frogs, beads, rhinestones, handbag handles
and Swarovski heatsets. CREDIT CARDS.*

Margola Import Corp 212-695-1115
48 W 37th St. (5-6th Ave)   FAX 212-594-0071
NY, NY 10018
Hours: 8:30-6 Mon-Fri / 10-4 Sat
www.margola.com
*Rhinestones, beads, rosemontees, pearls, beaded and embroidered trims.
View catalog online. Contact them for minimum ordering requirements.
CREDIT CARDS.*

Mayer Import Co., Inc. 212-391-3831
25 W 37th St. (5-6th Ave)   FAX 212-768-9183
NY, NY 10018
Hours: 8:30-4:30 Mon-Fri   E-mail: store@mayerimport.com
www.mayerimport.com
Jewels, pearls, cameos, trade beads, faceted plastic domes, etc. Catalog
available.

Mode Int'l, Inc. 718-765-0124
5111 Fourth Ave.   800-MODE 527
Brooklyn, NY 11220   FAX 718-765-0126
Hours: 9-5 Mon-Thurs / 9-1 Fri   E-mail: mode@modebeads.com
www.modebeads.com
Bohemian glass, beads, buttons, pearls & rhinestones. Manufacturer of
beaded straps. Visit their website.

New York Beads, Inc. 212-382-2994
1026 Sixth Ave. (38-39th St)   212-382-2986
NY, NY 10018   FAX 212-382-1060
Hours: 9-6:30 Mon-Fri / 10-5:30 Sat-Sun
Fine selection of beads, chains, findings and jewelery supplies. Wholesale and
retail. CREDIT CARDS.

Ornamental Beads 303-567-2222
5712 W. 38th Ave.   800-876-6762
Wheat Ridge, CO 80212   FAX 303-567-4245
Hours: 10-6 Mon-Sat / 12/4 Sun   E-mail: orna@ornabead.com
www.ornabead.com
Beads, findings and trims. Fabulous finds.

Rehka International 212-631-0220
218 W 37th St. (7-8th Ave)   FAX 212-714-1915
NY, NY 10018
Hours: 9:30-5 Mon-Fri
Carries chain beads, rhinestones, sew-on stones, beaded fringe. P.O.s. CREDIT
CARDS.

Toho Shoji, Inc. 212-868-7465
990 Sixth Ave. (36-37th St)   212-868-7466
NY, NY 10018   FAX 212-868-7464
Hours: 9-7 Mon-Fri / 10-6 Sat / 10-5 Sun   E-mail: toho@tohoshoji-ny.com
www.tohoshoji-ny.com
Large selection of beads, buttons, chains, jewelry components and findings
in a well-lighted shop. Wholesale and retail. CREDIT CARDS.

Top Trimmings 212-302-2999
228 W 39th St. (7-8th Ave)
NY, NY 10018
Hours: 9-7 Mon-Fri / 10-6 Sat / 11-5 Sun   E-mail: toptrimming@yahoo.com
www.toptrimming.com
Wholesale and retail. Custom productions. Sequins, beads, feathers,
ribbons, stones, buckles, chains novelties, findings and more. Sewing
supplies, thread, yarn and tools. CREDIT CARDS.

Wooden Buttons 212 354-7591
260 West 39th St., 3rd Fl. (7-8th Ave)   FAX 212 354-8291

NY, NY 10018
Hours: 9-5 Mon-Fri   E-mail: info@woodbuttons.com
www.woodbuttons.com
Wooden beads, buttons, buckles; wholesale. Catalog available online.
CREDIT CARDS.

World Beads and Trimmings, Inc. 212-730-1228
   25 W 38th St. (5-6th Ave)   800-244-3526
   NY, NY 10018   FAX 212-730-1399
   Hours: 8:30-6:30 Mon-Sat   E-mail: info@rhinestoneny.com
   www.rhinestoneny.com
   Asian imported beads, acrylic stones and findings. CREDIT CARDS.

BEAUTY SALON EQUIPMENT
For beauty supplies, see HAIR SUPPLIES & WIGS
                MAKE-UP SUPPLIES

425 Enterprises Ltd. 516-223-4030
   200 E Sunrise Hwy. (Meadowbrook Pkwy)   516-223-0772
   Freeport, NY 11520   FAX 516-223-0348
   Hours: 9-5:30 Mon-Fri / 11-3:30 Sun   E-mail: info@beautyprops.com
   www.beautyprops.com
   Creators of beauty, barber, skin care, facial and nail salons. Large retail
   showroom and warehouse. New, used and period salon equipment. Over 30
   years in the business. See Scot. RENTALS. CREDIT CARDS.

Alice-Aliya, Inc. 905-886-1172
   92 Springbrook Dr.   FAX 905-707-1549
   Richmond Hill, Ontario, Canada L4B 3P9
   Hours: 24-hr web   E-mail: info@alicealiya.com
   www.perfumeatomizersking.com
   One of the largest manufacturers of perfume atomizers in the world. This
   company offers art glass, antique, modern atomizers as well as replacement
   parts for just about any bottle you can imagine. You must visit the website
   to appreciate the wide selections available. Fast and efficient service. Very
   reasonable prices for any budget. CREDIT CARDS.

The Art of Shaving 800-696-4999
   19501 Biscayne Blvd.(Aventura Mall)   305-937-1877
   Miami, FL 33180
   Hours: 10-9:30 Mon-Sat / 12-8 Sun   Barber Services by appt. only

   141 E 62nd St.(Park & Lex Ave)   212-317-8436
   NY, NY 10021
   Hours: 10-6 Mon-Fri / 10-5 Sat   No barber services

   373 Madison Ave.(45-46th St)   212-986-2905
   NY, NY 10017
   Hours: 9:30-7 Mon-Fri / 9:30-6 Sat / 12-6 Sun   Shaving services by appt. only

The Art of Shaving (cont.) 702-632-9356
   3930 Las Vegas Blvd. S(Mandalay Pl)

Las Vegas, NV 89119
Hours: 10-6 Mon-Sat
www.theartofshaving.com
FAX 702-632-9357
E-mail: info@theartofshaving.com

A unique shop with grooming items designed specifically for men. Rated the world's leading experts on shaving. Great selection of oils, razors and antique items. Barber and shaving services offered at various locations. See hours to make appts. Visit web address for other locations. CREDIT CARDS.

Prestige Beauty Supply 845-623-8079
191 W Rt. 59
Nanuet, NY 10954
Hours: 9:30-7 Mon & Sat / 9:30-8 Tue-Fri / 10-6 Sun
FAX 845-623-5978

Beauty salon supply house, some equipment. CREDIT CARDS.

Ray Beauty Supply Co., Inc. 212-757-0175
721 Eighth Ave. (45-46th St)
NY, NY 10036
Hours: 8:30-6 Mon-Wed / 8:30-7 Thurs-Fri / 9-5:15 Sat
www.raybeauty.com
800-253-0993
FAX 212-459-8918
E-mail: ray.beauty@verizon.net

Wide variety hair supplies and make-up; beauty salon equipment rental; see Bobby. Phone orders and shipping available. CREDIT CARDS.

Salon Interiors 201-488-7888
62 Leaning St.
South Hackensack, NJ 07606
Hours: 9-5 Mon-Fri (Mon until 6)
www.saloninteriors.com
800-642-4205
FAX 201-488-0058
E-mail: info@saloninteriors.com

Beauty/barber salon furniture and equipment new and used; sinks, hair dryers, reception desks, seating. Not far from the G.W. Bridge. RENTALS. CREDIT CARDS.

Takara Belmont USA, Inc. 212-541-6660
17 W 56th St. (4-6th Ave)
NY, NY 10019
Hours: 9-5 Mon-Fri or by appt.
www.takarabelmont.com
212-541-6661
FAX 212-315-4598
E-mail: award@takarabelmont.com

Manufacturer of salon equipment.

BICYCLES & ACCESSORIES

Dixon's Bicycle Shop 718-636-0067
792 Union St. (7th Ave)
Brooklyn, NY 11215
Hours: 9:30-7 Mon-Sat / 11-6 Sun
FAX 718-398-7919

New bikes, adult and children. Repairs.

Frank's Bike Shop 212-533-6332
553 Grand St. (Jackson St)
NY, NY 10002
Hours: 9-7 Thurs-Tues
www.franksbikes.com
FAX 212-475-1584

Sales, repairs and rentals; also has exercise bikes. Speak to Frank. RENTALS. CREDIT CARDS.

Larry & Jeff's Bicycles Plus 212-794-2929
   1400 Third Ave. (79-80th St)   FAX 212-202-4617
NY, NY 10021
Hours: 10-7 daily   E-mail: info@bicyclesnyc.com
www.bicyclesnyc.com
   Sales, service, repair of bicycles; fitness equipment. RENTALS. CREDIT
CARDS.

Metro Bicycle Store 212-427-4450
   1311 Lexington Ave.(88th St)   212-427-4450
NY, NY 10128   FAX 212-427-4451
Hours: 10-6:30 Mon-Fri / 9:30-6 Sat / 10-6 Sun

   231 W 96th St.(B'way-Amst)   212-663-7531
NY, NY 10025   FAX 212-663-7511
Hours: 10:30-6:30 Mon-Fri / 9:30-6 Sat-Sun

   332 E 14th St.(1st Ave)   212-228-4344
NY, NY 10003   FAX 212-228-4750
Hours: 10-6 Daily

   360 W 47th St.(9th Ave)   212-581-4500
NY, NY 10036   FAX 212-581-4503
Hours: 9:30-6:30 Mon-Fri / 9:30-6 Sat / 10-6 Sun

   1 Hudson St.(Varick-Watts St)   212-334-8000
NY, NY 10013   FAX 212-334-8132
Hours: 10:30-6 Mon-Sat / 10-5 Sun

   546 Sixth Ave.(15th St)   212-255-5100
NY, NY 10011   FAX 212-255-5255
Hours: 9:30-6 Mon-Sat / 10-6 Sun

   396 Main St. (New Rock City)   914-633-6336
New Rochelle, NY 10801
Hours: 10-6:30 Mon-Fri / 9:30-5 Sat / 11-5 Sun
www.metrobicycles.com   E-mail: ride@metrobicycles.com
   Adult and children's. New only. Very helpful with bike accessories. Catalog.
RENTALS. CREDIT CARDS.

The Prop Company / Kaplan and Associates 212-691-7767
   111 W 19th St., 8th Fl. (6-7th Ave)   FAX 212-727-3055
NY, NY 10011
Hours: 9-5 Mon-Fri   E-mail: propcompany@yahoo.com
   Small selection of children's and adult bikes in fine condition. Vintage and
contemporary. RENTAL only. CREDIT CARDS.

Rideable Bicycle Replicas, Inc. 510-769-0980
   2329 Eagle Ave.   FAX 510-521-7145
Alameda, CA 94501
Hours: 9-6 Mon-Fri   E-mail: info@hiwheel.com
www.hiwheel.com
   Rideable full-size replicas of bicycles from 1860-1950; hi-wheels, 2, 3 and 4
wheel in wood or steel. Catalog and price list available. Contact Greg Barron.
Ship worldwide. RENTALS. CREDIT CARDS.

BLACKBOARDS & BULLETIN BOARDS
See also: OFFICE SUPPLIES & STATIONERY

Aywon Chalkboard, Inc., DBA The Cork Store 718-853-2300
P.O. Box 280088 (Ocean Pkwy-Coney Island Ave)   FAX 718-238-0684
Brooklyn, NY 11228
Hours: 8-4 Mon-Thurs / 8-12 Fri
www.aywon.com
Custom work. Also rolls of cork and cork tiles. Speak to Mr. Pine. CREDIT CARDS.

Bulletin Boards & Directory Products, Inc. 914-248-8008
2986 Navajo St.   FAX 914-248-5150
Yorktown Heights, NY 10598
Hours: 9-4:30 Mon-Fri
Bulletin, chalk, directory and menu display boards. Catalog; contact Charles Kranz.

Green Mountain Graphics 718-472-3377
21-10 44th Dr. (21st & 23rd St)   FAX 718-472-4040
Long Island City, NY 11101
Hours: 8:30-5 Mon-Fri   E-mail: sales@gm-graphics.com
www.gm-graphics.com
In-house manufacturers of engraved and silkscreened signs and promotional products awards; also vinyl graphics. Suppliers of all kinds of signs including cast bronze, faux cast bronze, etched, banners, etc. Also, blackboards and bulletin boards. Convenient location to all L.I.C. soundstages. Catalogs and rush service available. CREDIT CARDS.

New York Blackboard of New Jersey, Inc. 973-926-1600
83 Rt. 22 West   800-652-6273
Hillside, NJ 07205   FAX 973-926-3440
Hours: 8-4:30 Mon-Fri   E-mail: info@nyblackboard.com
www.nyblackboard.com
Chalkboards, marker boards, corkboards, directory boards and vinyl letters. Also custom work. Next day delivery on stock items. 7-10 for custom work. Catalog. CREDIT CARDS.

BLADE & SCISSOR SHARPENING

Edge Grinding Shop 201-943-4109
388 Fairview Ave.
Fairview, NJ 07022
Hours: 8-5 Mon-Fri / 9-1 Sat
Scissors, knives, chisels, and saw blades sharpened. RENTALS.

Gracious Home 212-988-8990
  1220, 1217, 1201 Third Ave.(70th-71st St)   212-988-8990
  NY, NY 10021   212-517-6300
  Hours: 8-7 Mon-Fri / 9-7 Sat / 10-6 Sun   FAX 212-249-1534

  1992 Broadway(67th St)   212-231-7800
  NY, NY 10023   800-237-3404
  Hours: 9-9 Mon-Sat / 10-7 Sun   FAX 212-875-9976
  www.gracioushome.com   E-mail: info@gracioushome.com
  Knife and scissor sharpening while you wait. CREDIT CARDS.

Henry Westpfal & Co. 212-563-5990
  115 W 25th St. (6-7th Ave)   FAX 212-563-5068
  NY, NY 10001
  Hours: 9:30-6 Mon-Fri
  Scissors, cutlery and blades sharpened; also leather working tools and
  sewing supplies. Distributors of Swiss Army knives. Sells scissors, knives.
  Business checks and CREDIT CARDS.

BLEACHERS, GRANDSTANDS & TENTS

All Star Rentals, Inc. 973-591-1333
  61 Willett St. A Bldg. Ste. 7   800-479-8368
  Passaic, NJ 07055   FAX 973-591-1336
  Hours: 9-5 Mon-Fri
  Tents, stages, tables, chairs. Pipe/drape. Also motorcycle rentals. Delivery
  available. Corporate checks or cash on delivery. RENTALS.

Chair Hire Co. 973-345-8007
  173 Gould Ave.
  Paterson, NJ 07503
  Hours: 8-4:30 Mon-Fri
  Bleachers, grandstands, platforms, staging, tables, chairs, podiums. Delivery
  available. RENTALS only. AMEX Only.

Four Seasons Tentmasters 517-436-6245
  4221 Livesay Rd. (Sand Creek Hwy)   Cell 517-903-1441
  Sand Creek, MI 49279   FAX 517-436-3425
  Hours: 8-5 Mon-Fri   E-mail: infofourseasons-tentmasters.com
  www.fourseasonstent-masters.com
  Canvas tipis, wall tents, marquees, lean-tos and wedge tents. Historical styles
  and specs available. Over 20 years in the business. Money orders, cashier
  checks or COD. CREDIT CARDS.

Ken Logert Productions 718-292-1257
  2680 Park Ave. (141st St)   FAX 718-742-2461
  Bronx, NY 10451
  Hours: 9-5 Mon-Fri / call for appt.   E-mail: info@klprods.com
  www.klprods.com
  One-stop, full-service equipment provider of lighting, audio/video and
  projection equipment for concerts, special events, promotions and
  environmental production services. RENTALS. CREDIT CARDS.

Main Attractions 732-225-3500
  85 Newfield Ave. (Raritan Ctr Pkwy)   800-394-3500

Edison, NJ 08837
Hours: 9:30-5 Mon-Fri
www.mainattractions.com
732-225-2110
E-mail: events@mainattractions.com

Special events contractors; specializing in custom tent rentals, restroom trailers, decor, portable staging, lighting and the production of displays and signage. Visit website to see the full spectrum of their products. RENTALS. CREDIT CARDS.

P.J. McBride, Inc. 631-643-2848
8 LaMar St.
West Babylon, NY 11704
Hours: 9-5:30 Mon-Fri
www.pjmcbride.com

Tents and flooring; long-and-short term rental for functional and scenic use. Delivery available. Contact Kevin McBride. RENTALS. CREDIT CARDS.

My Perfect Awning 973-992-2333
236 Margaret King Ave.   973-464-8335
Ringwood, NJ 07456
Hours: 9-6 Mon-Fri   E-mail: dana@breslow.com
www.myperfectawning.com

Retractable awnings, canopies made to your specifications in record speed. Great company to deal with and great prices. CREDIT CARDS.

Safway Services, Inc. 718-383-8400
31-31 123rd St.   800-640-8778
Flushing, NY 11354   FAX 718-321-8106
Hours: 6:30-3 Mon-Fri   E-mail: jamie.kelly@safway.com
www.safway.com

Bleachers, ladders, lifts and scaffolding; delivery available. Catalog. RENTALS. CREDIT CARDS.

Western Canvas, LLC 800-587-6707
86 McNeil Lane   307-587-6707
Cody, WY 82414   FAX 307-587-8186
Hours: 9-12, 1-5 Mon-Fri   E-mail: info@westerncanvas.com
www.westerncanvas.com

Authenic handmade tipis. Various styles. Mail order and online shopping. CREDIT CARDS.

BLUEPRINTING MACHINERY & SUPPLIES

General Reproduction Products 201-934-0027
23 McKee Dr.   800-GRP-8402
Mahwah, NJ 07430   FAX 201-934-8368
Hours: 9-5 Mon-Fri
www.grprod.com

Lease and sell Diazit machines and HP plotters; provide maintenance and supplies. Catalog. Product list online. RENTALS. CREDIT CARDS.

BOOKBINDING SERVICES & SUPPLIES

John Gailer 212-243-5662
   37-18 Northern Blvd., FL 3   FAX 212-242-5132
   Long Island City, NY 11101
   Hours: 8-6 Mon-Fri   E-mail: estimate@gailer.com
   www.gailer.com
   Gold-leaf stamping of books, portfolios; dye cutting, mounting, film lamination and hand assembly. Special orders.

Angela Scott 202-547-7945
   414 Seventh St. SE
   Washington, DC 20003
   Hours: by appt.
   Custom bookbinding, portfolios, restorations, new bindings, cases, gold stamping. Will design for customers. No credit cards.

Technical Library Services, Inc./ TALAS 212-219-0770
   330 Morgan Ave.   FAX 212-219-0735
   Brooklyn, NY 11211
   Hours: 9-5:30 Mon-Fri
   www.talasonline.com
   Bookbinding and conservation supplies; acid-free papers and adhesives.

BOOKS: FAKE & RENTAL

Pageant Book & Print Shop 212-674-5296
   PO Box 1081, Canal St. Station / 69 E 4th St.
   NY, NY 10013
   Hours: 12-8 Tue-Sat / 1-7 Sun   E-mail: info@pageantbooks.com
   www.pageantbooks.com
   Rents books by subject area, by the foot. See Shirley Solomon. RENTALS.

The Prop Company / Kaplan and Associates 212-691-7767
   111 W 19th St., 8th Fl. (6-7th Ave)   FAX 212-727-3055
   NY, NY 10011
   Hours: 9-5 Mon-Fri   E-mail: propcompany@yahoo.com
   Specialty subject or by the foot rental. Beautiful leather bound editions. CREDIT CARDS.

Strand Book Store 212-473-1452
   828 Broadway (12th St)   FAX 212-473-2591
   NY, NY 10003
   Hours: 9:30-10:30 Mon-Sat / 11-10:30 Sun   E-mail: strand@strandbooks.com
   www.strandbooks.com
   Main store. New, used and remaindered books, all greatly discounted. Will help find out-of-print art books. Large selection of art books. Rare book room has excellent prices on antiquarian books, however it closes daily at 6:20 pm. See Nancy Bass. RENTALS. CREDIT CARDS.

BOOKSTORES

A-B

Argosy Book Stores, Inc. 212-753-4455
116 E 59th St. (Park-Lex Ave)   FAX 212-593-4784
NY, NY 10022
Hours: 10-6 Mon-Fri / 10-5 Sat (Sept-April)   E-mail: argosy@argosybooks.com
www.argosybooks.com
Out-of-print books, maps, posters, prints. CREDIT CARDS.

Backstage, Inc. 202-544-5744
545 Eighth St. SE   FAX 202-544-7025
Washington, DC 20003
Hours: 11-7 Mon-Sat   E-mail: backstagebooks@aol.com
http://backstagebooks.com
Theatre books and scripts; quarterly newsletter on new releases; mail orders.
Also dancewear, masks, makeup and some costumes for rent. RENTALS
CREDIT CARDS.

Barnes & Noble Bookstores, Inc. 800-883-8895
675 Sixth Ave.(21st-22nd St)   212-727-1227
NY, NY 10010   FAX 212-727-1672
Hours: 9-10 Mon-Sat / 10-10 Sun

105 5th Ave.(18th St)   212-807-0099
NY, NY 10003   FAX 212-633-2522
Hours: 9-8:30 Mon-Fri / 9:30-7:30 Sat / 11-7 Sun

1972 Broadway(66th St at Lincoln Center)   212-595-6859
NY, NY 10023   FAX 212-595-8946
Hours: 9-midnight Daily

33 E 17th St.(Union Square)   212-253-0810
NY, NY 10003   FAX 212-253-0820
Hours: 10-10 Daily

4 Astor Pl.(B'way-Lafayette St)   212-420-1322
NY, NY 10003   FAX 212-420-1652
Hours: 10-11 Mon-Sat / 10-10 Sun

160 E 54th St.(Lex-3rd Ave)   212-750-8033
NY, NY 10022   FAX 212-750-8038
Hours: 7-9 Mon-Fri / 10-9 Sat / 11-6 Sun

Barnes & Noble Bookstores, Inc.(cont.) 212-362-8835
2289 Broadway(82nd-83rd St)
NY, NY 10024   FAX 212-362-6908
Hours: 9-11 Sun-Thurs / 9-Midnight Fri & Sat

396 Sixth Ave.(8th St)   212-674-8780
NY, NY 10011   FAX 212-475-9082
Hours: 10-10 Mon-Sat / 12-7 Sun

267 Seventh Ave.(6th St-7th Ave)   718-832-9066
Brooklyn, NY 11215   FAX 718-832-9077
Hours: 9-11 Daily

1280 Lexington Ave.(86-87th St)   212-423-9900
NY, NY 10028
Hours: 9-10 Mon-Sat / 10-9 Sun

106 Court St.(State-Schenmerhorn)   718-246-4996
Brooklyn, NY 11201
Hours: 9-11 Mon-Sat / 10-10 Sun

555 Fifth Ave.   212-697-3048
NY, NY 10017
Hours: 8-9 Mon-Fri / 9-8 Sat / 10-8 Sun
www.bn.com
They've made buying and reading books fashionable again. Visit website for other locations nationwide. CREDIT CARDS.

Books of Wonder 212-989-3270
18 W 18th St. (5-6th Ave)   800-835-4315
NY, NY 10011   FAX 212-989-1203
Hours: 10-7 Mon-Sat / 11-6 Sun   E-mail: info@booksofwonder.com
www.booksofwonder.com
New and antique children's books; no rental. CREDIT CARDS.

Builders Booksource 800-843-2028
1817 Fourth St. (near Hearst)   510-845-6874
Berkeley, CA 94710   FAX 510-845-7051
Hours: 8:30-7 Mon-Sat / 10-7 Sun   E-mail: service@buildersbooksource.com
www.buildersbooksource.com
A dream bookstore for architects and designers alike. This store offers books, reference materials and software (they have in-store software demos) for home builders, architects, contractors, do-it-yourselfers, and consumers. Whatever you want to build, they have the book for it. Great website. CREDIT CARDS.

Choices: The Recovery Bookshop 212-794-3858
220 E 78th St. (2nd-3rd Ave)   866-245-4818
NY, NY 10075
Hours: 11-7 Mon-Fri / 11-6 Sat-Sun
www.choices-nyc.com
Bookstore specializing in 12-step programs (Alcoholics Anonymous, Overeaters Anonymous, etc.). Literature, gifts, posters, tapes. CREDIT CARDS.

The Complete Traveller Antiquarian .212-685-9007
199 Madison Ave. (35th St)   FAX 212-481-3253
NY, NY 10016
Hours: 9:30-6:30 Mon-Fri / 10-6 Sat / 12-5 Sun   E-mail: info@ctrarebooks.com
www.ctrarebooks.com
Antique maps, childrens collectible, out-of-print and rare collectible books and accessories. CREDIT CARDS.

Digital Manga Distribution 310-817-8010
1487 W 178th St., Ste. 300   FAX 310-817-8018
Gardena, CA 90248
Hours: 9-6 Mon-Fri   E-mail: ericr@dmd-sales.com
www.dmd-sales.com
Japanese and Oriental books, design and graphic arts books, CDs, videos,
gifts. Source for calligraphy and painting supplies. See our catalog online.
Wholesale only. CREDIT CARDS.

Dover Publications, Inc. 516-294-7000
31 E 2nd St.   FAX 516-742-6953
Mineola, NY 11501
Hours: 9-4:30 Mon-Fri   E-mail: rights@doverpublications.com
www.doverpublications.com
Mail order catalogs with a thorough collection of paperback books on fine
arts and crafts with many facsimile reproductions and excellent pictorial
archives. Order online or view web address for retail locations.

The Drama Book Shop 212-944-0595
250 W 40th St. (7-8th Ave)   800-322-0595
NY, NY 10018   FAX 212-730-8739
Hours: 10-8 Mon-Sat / 12-6 Sun   E-mail: info@dramabookshop.com
www.dramabookshop.com
Huge selection of books on every aspect of the performing arts. CREDIT
CARDS.

Forbidden Planet 212-473-1576
840 Broadway (13th St)   (office) 212-475-6161
NY, NY 10003
Hours: 10-10 Sun-Tue / 9-12am Wed, 10-12am Thur-Sat
www.fpnyc.com   E-mail: jeff@fpnyc.com
Science fiction, fantasy, comic books, magazines on special effects. CREDIT
CARDS.

French & European Publications, Inc. 212-581-8810
1562 First Ave., Box 227   FAX 212-202-4356
NY, NY 10028
Hours: online orders only   E-mail: frenchbookstore@aol.com
www.Frencheuropean.com
French and Spanish books; dictionaries and language learning aids for over
100 foreign languages. Online orders only. CREDIT CARDS.

Samuel French, Inc. 212-206-8990
45 W 25th St., 2nd Fl.(B'way-6th Ave)
NY, NY 10010   FAX 212-206-1429
Hours: 9-5 Mon-Fri / Summer Hours 9-4 Mon-Fri

Samuel French, Inc. (cont.) 323-876-0570
7623 Sunset Blvd.
Hollywood, CA 90046   FAX 323-876-6822
Hours: 10-6 Mon-Fri / 10-4 Sat (Bookstore only)
www.samuelfrench.com   E-mail: info@samuelfrench.com
Comprehensive theatrical and film bookstore. Mostly scripts; catalog
available. See website for additional locations. CREDIT CARDS.

 **ATAC**

A-B

Harper House 630-837-0926
2100 Green Bridge Lane
Hanover Park, IL 60133
Hours: 8:30-4:30 Mon-Fri, 24-hr. fax and voice mail.
www.longago.com   E-mail: mjak88@comcast.net
Costume history books, period and ethnic patterns from 650 AD to 1950.
Chatelaine pins, sewing and needlework accessories, hoop skirts. Catalog $7.

Harry N. Abrams 212-206-7715
115 W 18th St. (6-7th Ave)   800-345-1359
NY, NY 10011   FAX 212-519-1210
Hours: 9-5 Mon-Fri
www.hnabooks.com
Publisher for craft art books, fashion, jewelry, fabric. Catalog available.

Kinokuniya Bookstore 212-869-1700
1073 Ave. of the Americas (40-41st St)   FAX 212-869-1703
NY, NY 10018
Hours: 10-8 Mon-Sat / 11:30-7:30 Sun   E-mail: kinokuniya@kinokuniya.nyinfo
www.kinokuniya.com
Books from and about Japan. Also carries magazines from Japan including a
large fashion section. CREDIT CARDS.

Law Book Exchange Ltd. 800-422-6686
33 Terminal Ave.   732-382-1800
Clark, NJ 07066   FAX 732-382-1887
Hours: 9-5 Mon-Fri (call first)   E-mail: law@lawbookexchange.com
www.lawbookexchange.com
Law books by the foot for sale. CREDIT CARDS.

Pageant Book & Print Shop 212-674-5296
PO Box 1081, Canal St. Station / 69 E 4th St.
NY, NY 10013
Hours: 12-8 Tue-Sat / 1-7 Sun   E-mail: info@pageantbooks.com
www.pageantbooks.com
Rents books by subject area, by the foot; see Shirley Solomon. RENTALS.
CREDIT CARDS.

Quite Specific Media Group 323-851-5797
7373 Pyramid Place   FAX 323-851-5798
Hollywood, CA 90046
Hours: 10-3 Mon-Fri   E-mail: info@quitespecificmedia.com
www.quitespecificmedia.com
Publishers of theatrical books, British publications; good costume, fashion
and make-up books; stage lighting design and special effects books; catalog.
Not a retail store. CREDIT CARDS.

Red Wheel Weiser & Conari Press .800-423-7087
65 Parker St., Ste. 7 (Mail Order)   978-465-0504
Newburyport, MA 01950   FAX 978-465-0243
Hours: 9-5 Mon-Fri   E-mail: info@redwheelweiser.com
www.redwheelweiser.com
Publisher of spunky self-help, women's, inspirational and esoteric books.
Also large selections of religion, oriental philosophy and Egyptology books.
CREDIT CARDS.

Rizzoli Bookstore 212-759-2424
31 W 57th St. (5-6th Ave)   FAX 212-826-9754
NY, NY 10019
Hours: 10-7:30 Mon-Fri / 10:30-7 Sat / 11-7 Sun
www.rizzoliusa.com
Art, architecture, design, international music, photography books; magazines.
CREDIT CARDS.

Shakespeare & Co. Booksellers 212-529-1330
716 Broadway (Washington Pl-W 4th St)   FAX 212-979-5711
NY, NY 10003
Hours: 10am-11pm MonSat/ 11-9 Sun   E-mail: genifo@shakespeare-nyc.com
www.shakeandco.com
Well stocked "general" bookstore; carries some books for all the performing
arts. CREDIT CARDS.

R.L. Shep Publications 707-964-8662
PO Box 2706   FAX 707-964-8662
Fort Bragg, CA 95437
Hours: 9:30-5 Mon-Sat   E-mail: fsbks@mcn.org
www.rlshep.com
Publisher of books from the Regency Period to 1920s tailoring, costume and
patterns. Mail order only. Free brochure on request. Contact Fred Struthers.
CREDIT CARDS.

Richard Stoddard Performing Arts Books 212-598-9421
43 E 10th St. # 6D
NY, NY 10003
Hours: by appt.   E-mail: rs@richardstoddard.com
www.richardstoddard.com
Playbills; specializes in out-of-print theatre books with special interest in
scenic and costume design. Carries original scenic and costume sketches.
CREDIT CARDS.

Strand Book Annex 212-732-6070
95 Fulton St. (William - Gold)   FAX 212-406-1654
NY, NY 10038
Hours: 9:30-9 Mon-Fri / 11-8 Sat-Sun   E-mail: strand@strandbooks.com
www.strandbooks.com
Remainders, used and discounted current titles. Jazz and opera CDs. CREDIT
CARDS.

Strand Book Store 212-473-1452
828 Broadway (12th St)   FAX 212-473-2591
NY, NY 10003
Hours: 9:30-10:30 Mon-Sat / 11-10:30 Sun   E-mail: strand@strandbooks.com
www.strandbooks.com
Main store. New, used and remaindered books, all greatly discounted. Will
help find out-of-print art books. Large selection of art books. Rare book room
has excellent prices on antiquarian books, however it closes daily at 6:20 pm.
See Nancy Bass. RENTALS. CREDIT CARDS.

A-B

Theatrebooks Ltd. 416-922-7175
   11 Saint Thomas St.   800-361-3414
   Toronto, Ontario, CAN M5S2B7   FAX 416-922-0739
   Hours: 10-7 Mon-Fri / 10-6 Sat / 12-5 Sun   E-mail: action@theatrebooks.com
   www.theatrebooks.com
   The theatre, film and performing arts bookstore of Canada. Most British
   publications available here earlier than in U.S. Catalog available. Will ship
   worldwide. CREDIT CARDS.

Three Lives & Company Ltd. 212-741-2069
   154 W 10th St. (Waverly Pl)   FAX (call first) 212-741-2073
   NY, NY 10014
   Hours: 12-8 Mon-Tues / 11-8:30 Wed-Sat / 12-7 Sun
   www.threelives.com   E-mail: contact@threelives.com
   Interesting art, architecture, garden/landscape, travel and photography
   sections along with literature, new fiction and non-fiction. Will special order.
   CREDIT CARDS.

Verizon Directory Store 888-266-5765
   125 Fulton St. SW   330-394-2509
   Warren, OH 44483   FAX 877-814-6850
   Hours: 8-8 Mon-Fri
   Domestic and international phone books. FEDEX overnight on USA books
   only. Ten-day regular mail delivery on all other in-stock books. Business to
   business, street address, fax, 800 numbers and national directory of
   addresses. Don't be surprised if they answer "Evergreen Teleservices."
   CREDIT CARDS.

Wonder Book / Booksbythefoot.com 301-694-0350
   2421-A Monocacy Blvd.   FAX 301-694-5910
   Frederick, MD 21701
   Hours: 7:30-4:30 Mon-Fri   E-mail: chuck@wonderbk.com
   www.wonderbk.com
   Millions of old and new books in stock as low as 50 cents per book. Quick
   shipments. They have supplied books to broadway, major hotel chains and
   all levels of interior designers. See their website for over 30 sample designs.
   They can customize to any specs. CREDIT CARDS.

BRASS ITEMS
See also: ANTIQUES: All Headings
               PROP RENTAL HOUSES

A-B

Decorative Crafts, Inc. 203-531-1500
50 Chestnut St.   800-431-4455
Greenwich, CT 06830   FAX 203-531-1590
Hours: 9-4:30 Mon-Fri   E-mail: info@decorativecrafts.com
www.decorativecrafts.com
To trade only. Imported brassware, Oriental screens and furniture; catalog.
CREDIT CARDS.

Humphrey's Farm, Inc. / Display Fake Foods 786-955-6584
PO Box 5800 (Mail Order)   FAX 305-749-8099
Miami Lakes, FL 33014
Hours: 9:30-5:30 Mon-Fri   E-mail: sales@displayfackfoods.com
www.displayfakefoods.com
Decorative accessories. Brass, silver plate, wood, iron, glass, ceramic trays,
bowls and aluminum. CREDIT CARDS.

Majestic Reproductions Co., Inc. 718-782-6155
65 N. 7th Ave.   FAX 718-782-7578
Brooklyn, NY 11211
Hours: 9-5 Mon-Fri   E-mail: info@majesticrepro.com
www.majesticrepro.com
Reproduction brass, wrought iron and steel items. Visit website to see
extensive line of products. Also offering repair and restoration services.
Contact Mark, Wally or Sid. Catalog. RENTALS.

BREAKAWAYS

Alfonso's Breakaway Glass 818-768-7402
8070 San Fernando Rd.   866-768-7402
Sun Valley, CA 91352   FAX 818-767-6969
Hours: 7-5:30 Mon-Fri   E-mail: info@alfonsosbreakawayglass.com
www.alfonsosbreakawayglass.com
Great selection of breakaways. Just about anything you can think of, they
have it. Catalog. CREDIT CARDS.

EFEX Rentals 718-505-9465
5805 52nd Ave. (43rd Ave)   FAX 718-505-9631
Woodside, NY 11377
Hours: 8:30-5:30 Mon-Fri   E-mail: efexrentals@verizon.net
www.efexrentals.com
Distributors of many types of fog machines and fog juice; also special effects
materials; snow, breakaways, turntables and rigging. Catalog available. P.O.s
accepted. RENTALS.

J&M Special Effects 718-875-0140
524 Sackett St.   FAX 718-596-8329
Brooklyn, NY 11217
Hours: 9-4 Mon-Fri by appt.   E-mail: info@jmfx.net
www.jmfx.net
Full-service special effects shop; design, construction, rental, sales of
equipment and supplies. Speak to Greg Meeh. RENTALS.

SFX Design, Inc. 817-599-0800
2500 I-20 E   FAX 817-599-0496
Weatherford, TX 76087

Hours: 8-4 Mon-Fri   E-mail: info@sfxdesignninc.com
www.sfxdesignninc.com

Stock and custom gobos. Decorative and fighting swords, handguns, rifles, machine guns; any period, able to fire blanks. Breakaway resin to mold your own bottles, glass, panes, etc. Fog-Master machines and Aquafog component; also cobweb system. Pyrotechnics and miniature pneumatics, blood effects, atmospherics; custom projects. Great website. Catalog. No credit cards.

Trengove Studios, Inc. 212-268-0020
60 W 22nd St., 2nd FL (7-8th Ave)   800-366-2857
NY, NY 10010   FAX 212-268-0030
Hours: call for appt. 9-5 Mon-Fri   E-mail: info@trengovestudios.com
www.trengovestudios.com

Breakaway bottles and glasses in stock. CREDIT CARDS.

Zeller International, Ltd. 607-363-7792
15261 Highway 30   FAX 607-363-2071
Downsville, NY 13755
Hours: 9-5 Mon-Fri   E-mail: contact@zeller-int.com
www.zeller-int.com

Casting materials, flameproofing, fog, make-up supplies, breakaways and atmospherics. Some minimums apply. Contact Carla Zelaschi. Catalog. CREDIT CARDS.

A-B

The professional trade association for artists and craftspeople working in theatre, film, television and advertising

ATAC Membership 2010-11

Sharlot Battin
 Montana Leatherworks
Chris Bobin
Sharon Braunstein
Randy Carfagno
Nadine Charlsen
Eileen Connor
Mary Creede
Margaret Cusack
Cindy Anita Fain
 CINAF Designs
James Feng
Keen Gat
Deborah R. Glassberg
Rodney Gordon
Joseph Gourley
Corrinna Griffin
Jung K. Griffin
Denise Grillo
 Offstage Design
Stockton Hall
Karen Hart
Suzanne Hayden

Marian Jean "Killer" Hose
J. Michelle Hill
Louise Hunnicutt
John Jerard
 Jerard Studio
Joni Johns
Jan Kastendieck
Rachel Keebler
 Cobalt Studios
Amanda Klein
Arnold S. Levine
 Arnold S. Levine, Inc.
Janet Linville
Jeanne Marino
 Moonboots Productions
Jerry Marshall
Betsey McKearnan
Gene Mignola
 Gene Mignola, Inc.
Mary Mulder
 Mulder / Martin, Inc.
Susan Pitocchi
Elizabeth Popeil

Adele Recklies
Monona Rossol
 Arts, Crafts, & Theatre
 Safety (A.C.T.S.)
Bill Rybak
Jody Schoffner
James R. Seffens
Lisa Shaftel
 Shaftel S2DO
Stanley Allen Sherman
 Mask Arts Company
Linda Skipper
Michael Smanko
 Prism Prips
Sarah Timberlake
 Timberlake Studios
Mari Tobita
US Institute for Theatre
 Tech. (USITT)
Monique Walker
Anne-Marie Wright
John Yavroyan
 Yavroyan & Nelsen, LTD

For membership information visit our website at
www.ATACBIZ.com
Email: info@ATACBIZ.com
Or drop us a line at:
ATAC Membership Application
Anne-Marie Wright
280 Third St. Apt # 1
Jersey City, NJ 07302-2759

CANDLES

Chace Candles, Inc. 800-225-2250
   4208 Balloon Park Rd. NE   505-344-3413
   Albuquerque, NM 87109   FAX   505-344-3590
   Hours: 8-4:30 Mon-Thurs / 8-12 Fri   E-mail: info@chacecandles.com
   www.chacecandles.com
   Dripless insert mechanical candles in five heights and 20 colors. Friendly.
   CREDIT CARDS.

Paramold Manufacturing, Ltd. 631-589-5454
   90 Bourne Blvd. (Smithtown Ave)   877-527-4461
   Sayville, NY 11782   FAX   631-589-1232
   Hours: 8:30-4:30 Mon-Fri   E-mail: info@paramold.com
   www.paramold.com
   Variety of candles, sold only by the case. Manufacturer. No credit cards.

Pier 1 Imports 800-245-4595
   1550 Third Ave.(87th St)   212-987-1746
   NY, NY 10128
   Hours: 10-9 Mon-Sat / 11-7 Sun

   71 Fifth Ave.(14-15th St)   212-206-1911
   NY, NY 10003
   Hours: 10-9 Mon-Sat / 11-7 Sun
   www.pier1.com
   Popular chain of stores carries baskets; wicker furniture and decorative items
   for the home. Some lighting, clothing, frames. See website for over 800
   locations nationally. Some rentals. CREDIT CARDS.

CANDY

Economy Candy Corp. 212-254-1531
   108 Rivington St. (Essex-Ludlow St)   800-352-4544
   NY, NY 10002   FAX   212-254-2606
   Hours: 9-6 Sun-Fri / 10-5 Sat
   www.economycandy.com
   All types of candy, chocolate, nuts, dried fruit, and hard to find old time
   favorites, wholesale or retail. Free catalog, $25 minimum for shipping. CREDIT
   CARDS.

Lazar's Chocolates 516-829-5785
   72 Middleneck Rd.(Bay Terrace Shopping Center)   516-829-5785
   Great Neck, NY 11021   FAX   516-829-1333
   Hours: 10-6 Mon-Sat

   212-67A 26th Ave.   718-428-3032
   Bayside, NY 11360   FAX   718-428-3021
   Hours: 10-6 Mon-Sat / 12-5 Sun

Lazar's Chocolates (cont.) 516-484-1987
340 Wheatley Plaza Ste. A
Greenvale, NY 11548
Hours: 10-6 Mon-Sat / 12-5 Sun   E-mail: marc@lazarschocolate.com
www.lazarschocolate.com
Wonderful assortment of chocolates. Has boxed candies (Valentine's Day)
any day of the year. Will ship. CREDIT CARDS.

Oriental Trading Company, Inc. 800-875-8480
4206 S. 108th St.   402-331-6800
Omaha, NE 68137   FAX 402-331-3873
Hours: 24-hr. online catalog service
www.orientaltrading.com
Thousands of small toys, novelties and party supplies for every occasion.
Catalog available. CREDIT CARDS thru Paypal.

The Sweet Life 212-598-0092
63 Hester St. (Ludlow St)   FAX 212-598-0092
NY, NY 10002
Hours: 11-6 Sun-Fri / 11-5 Sat   E-mail: info@sweetlife.com
www.sweetlife.com
Candies, dried fruits, nuts, coffees; sells large lollipops, holiday items, old-
fashioned, hard-to-find items. Will ship or use local courier. Speak to Teri.
CREDIT CARDS.

CARRYING CASES

Anvil Cases 800-359-2684
15730 Salt Lake Ave.   626-968-4100
City of Industry, CA 91745   FAX 626-968-1703
Hours: 8-4 Mon-Fri   E-mail: anvil@anvilcase.com
www.anvilcase.com
Reusable transit cases designed to transport light sources, control consoles,
sound, video and film production equipment. Measuring, designing and
quoting available at no charge. CREDIT CARDS.

Bragley Manufacturing Co., Inc. 718-622-7469
924 Bergen St. (Classon-Franklin Ave)   800-314-4066
Brooklyn, NY 11238   FAX 718-857-3557
Hours: 9-5 Mon-Fri
www.bragleycases.com
Fiber cases made to order. Ask for Neil. Helpful and friendly. P.O.s accepted.
CREDIT CARDS.

Calzone Case Company 800-243-5152
225 Black Rock Ave.   203-367-5766
Bridgeport, CT 06605   FAX 203-336-4406
Hours: 9-5:30 Mon-Fri   E-mail: info@calzonecase.com
www.calzonecase.com
Manufacturer of reusable shipping cases, standard and custom. Musical
instrument and road cases. CREDIT CARDS.

Case Design 215-703-0130
    333 School Ln.   (outside NY) 800-847-4176
    Telford, PA 18969   FAX 215-703-0139
    Hours: 9-5 Mon-Fri   E-mail: sales@casedesigncorp.com
    www.casedesigncorp.com
    Fiber storage and shipping cases; custom work. P.O.s accepted. CREDIT CARDS.

Fibre Case Corp. 212-566-2720
    160 Broadway Ste 1105   800-394-6871
    NY, NY 10038   FAX 212-566-2726
    Hours: 9-5 Mon-Fri   E-mail: info@fibrecase.com
    www.fibrecase.com
    Specialized shipping cases from lightweight poly tuff. Quick delivery and affordable prices. Custom cases available. CREDIT CARDS.

Oasis/Stage Werks 801-363-0364
    249 Rio Grande St.   FAX 801-575-7121
    Salt Lake City, UT 84101
    Hours: 9-6 Mon-Fri
    www.oasis-stage.com
    Custom-built cases to your needs, dimensions, hardware, compartments, foam and colors. Meets ATA 300 spec. Professional workmanship. CREDIT CARDS.

CASKETS & FUNERAL SUPPLIES

Bay Ridge Funeral Home, Inc. 718-630-5500
    1275 65th St. (76-77th St)   718-939-4515
    Brooklyn, NY 11219   FAX 732-817-0283
    Hours: 24 hours, 7 days a week
    Caskets, funeral cars, chapel decor. Contact Alex Marchak, Jr. RENTALS. No credit cards.

CASTING & MODELING SUPPLIES
See also: MAKE-UP SUPPLIES
For alginate & plaster bandages see MEDICAL & SCIENTIFIC SUPPLIES: DENTAL

Aqua Resins, R.L. Lucas, Inc. 212-226-1208
    224 Pegasus Ave   FAX 212-226-2068
    Northvale, NY 07647
    Hours: 10-6 Mon-Fri   E-mail: info@rllucas.com
    www.aquaresin.com
    Manufacturer of AQUA RESINS. $500 minimum, smaller orders through distributors. Accelerator, thickener and mold release also available. Samples. CREDIT CARDS.

BJB Enterprises 714-734-8450
14791 Franklin Ave.   FAX 714-734-8929
Tustin, CA 92780
Hours: 7:30-4 Mon-Fri   E-mail: info@bjbenterprises.com
www.bjbenterprises.com
Flexible, castable plastics; flexible urethane foams, various colors and clear; Skin-Flex (for artificial skin and foods). Catalog and phone orders. CREDIT CARDS.

Burman Industries 818-782-9833
13536 Saticoy St.   FAX 818-782-2863
Van Nuys, CA 91402
Hours: 8:30-5 Mon-Fri / 10-3 Sat   E-mail: info@burmanindustries.com
www.burmanfoam.com
Complete line of casting and moldmaking supplies specifically geared to SPFX industries; distributor of BJB products, latex, foam latex, flexible paint, gypsum products, adhesives for latex. Online catalog. CREDIT CARDS.

Ceramic Supply, Inc. 973-340-3005
7 Rt. 46 W   800-723-7264
Lodi, NJ 07644   FAX 973-340-0089
Hours: 9-5 Mon-Fri   E-mail: orders@eceramicsupply.com
www.7ceramic.com
Casting plaster, potter's plaster, ceramic materials and supplies. Use the 800 number for deliveries. CREDIT CARDS.

Chavant, Inc. 732-751-0003
5043 Industrial Rd.   800-CHA-VANT
Wall, NJ 07719   FAX 732-751-1982
Hours: 8-5 Mon-Fri for shipping orders   www.chavant.com
Manufacturer and distributor of industrial modeling clay. CREDIT CARDS.

City Chemical 800-248-2436
139 Allings Crossing Rd.   203-932-2489
West Haven, CT 06516   FAX 203-937-8400
Hours: 8-5 Mon-Fri   E-mail: sales@citychemical.com
www.citychemical.com
Stearic acid. Catalog. CREDIT CARDS.

The Compleat Sculptor, Inc. 212-243-6074
90 Vandam St. (Hudson-Greenwich)   800-9-SCULPT
NY, NY 10013   FAX 212-243-6374
Hours: 9-6 Mon, Thurs-Sat / 9-8 Tue-Wed   E-mail: tcs@sculpt.com
www.sculpt.com
Carries complete line of sculpture materials including; clay, wood, wax, sculpting tools, alabaster, marble, mold-making and casting materials, books, videos, pedestals and bases. Friendly and knowledgeable help. Catalog. Technical support line (212) 367-7561. CREDIT CARDS.

Critical Coatings 888-802-7349
Twin Pine Dr.
Louisville, MI 39339
Hours: 8-5 Mon-Fri   E-mail: sales@criticalcoatings.com
www.criticalcoatings.com
Neoprene latex available in 51 oz, 1 and 5 gallon pails. Discounts for quantity orders and educational institutions. Custom mixes available. Excellent quality of materials. CREDIT CARDS.

Defender Industries, Inc. 800-628-8225
42 Great Neck Rd.   860-701-3420
Waterford, CT 06385   FAX 800-654-1616
Hours: 8-6 Mon-Fri / 9-5 Sat / 9-3 Sun (June-Aug)
www.defender.com   E-mail: orders@defender.com
Fiberglass cloth, mat, polyester and epoxy resins; marine supplies. $25 minimum. Phone orders accepted. CREDIT CARDS.

Douglas and Sturgess / Artstuf.com .888-278-7883
730 Bryant St.   510-235-8411
San Francisco, CA 94107   FAX 510-235-4211
Hours: 8:30-5 Mon-Wed, Fri / 8:30-8 Thurs
www.artstuf.com
Thermoplastics in mesh, solid, perforated sheets, even a putty material you can mold. Safe non-toxic, fast setting, recyclable and biodegradable. Excellent substitute for Celastic. Also coatings for foam and latex. Urethane foam systems; hand mixable, flexible, rigid, self-skinning; castable latex.

ETI / Environmental Technologies, Inc. 707-443-9323
PO Box 365, South Bay Depot Rd.   800-368-9323
Fields Landing, CA 95537   FAX 707-443-7962
Hours: 8-4:30 Mon-Fri   E-mail: eti@northcoast.com
www.eti-usa.com
Manufacturer of natural latex, polyester casting resin, molds and mold making, epoxy finishes, adhesives, pigments and dyes. Brochures; call for local distributors. CREDIT CARDS.

The Hammer / Robin David Ludwig .845-679-7335
PO Box 115 (mailing address)   845-532-5724
Bearsville, NY 12409
Hours: by appt.   E-mail: rth@fivepointsband.com
www.sweetbryar.com/hammer/
Fine model making, mold-making, casting in small lots, gold, silver and bronze. Quick service.

Hapco, Inc. 781-826-8801
353 Circuit St.   877-729-4272
Hanover, MA 02339   FAX 781-826-9544
Hours: 8:30-5 Mon-Thur / 8:30-3 Fri.   E-mail: info@hapcoweb.com
www.hapcoweb.com
Casting materials, broad selection, primarily urethane, also Synwood (stable solid surface material). Catalog available. CREDIT CARDS.

Holden's Latex 212-741-1770
   121 Varick St. (Dominick-Broome St)   FAX 212-627-2770
   NY, NY 10013
   Hours: 8-5 Mon-Fri   E-mail: info@holdenslatex.com
   www.holdenslatex.com
   Good selection of coating, casting and molding supplies. Online catalog and
   phone orders. CREDIT CARDS.

Industrial Arts Supply Co. 952-920-7393
   5724 W 36th St. (near Hwy 100)   FAX 952-920-2947
   Minneapolis, MN 55416
   Hours: 8:30-5 Mon-Fri   E-mail: info@iasco-tesco.com
   www.iasco-tesco.com
   Distributor of Water-extended polyester: fires with hydrogen peroxide, briefly
   flexible. Brochures, phone orders. No credit cards.

Kindt-Collins Co. 800-321-3170
   12651 Elmwood Ave.   216-252-4122
   Cleveland, OH 44111   FAX 216-252-5639
   Hours: 8-5:30 Mon-Fri   E-mail: info@kindt-collins.com
   www.kindt-collins.com
   Rubber, silicone, adhesives, injection wax and wax for investment casting.
   Catalog available. CREDIT CARDS.

Mutual Hardware Corp. 718-361-2480
   36-27 Vernon Blvd. (Vernon Blvd)   866-361-2480
   Long Island City, NY 11106   FAX 718-786-9591
   Hours: 8:30-4:30 Mon-Fri
   www.mutualhardware.com
   Complete stage hardware, rigging supplies, casters, catalog. Contact John or
   Sal.

North American Composites 651-481-6860
   1225 Willow Lake Blvd.   FAX 651-481-9834
   St Paul, MN 55110
   Hours: 8-5 Mon-Fri
   www.interplastic.com
   Flexible and rigid urethane foam, fiberglass, casting resins, color pastes;
   catalog. No minimum. No credit cards.

Pink House Studios 802-524-7191
   35 Bank St.   FAX (same)
   St. Albans, VT 05478
   Hours: 9-5 Mon-Sat   E-mail: pinkhousestudios.pinkhouse@myfairpoint.net
   www.pinkhouse.com
   Supplies for life mold-making, catalog and instructional DVD's available.
   CREDIT CARDS.

Plastic Coatings Corporation 304-755-9151
   4904 Teays Valley Rd.   800-279-9151
   Scott Depot, WV 25560   FAX 304-755-0229
   Hours: 8-4:30 Mon-Fri   E-mail: jaxsan@verizon.net
   www.jaxsancoatings.com
   Manufacturers of Jaxsan 600, a fibrous acrylic latex coating that is weather
   resistant and fire retardant. Friendly technical assistance over the phone.
   CREDIT CARDS.

Polymer Tooling Systems 800-327-8787
303 Commerce Dr.   610-363-5440
Exton, PA 19341   FAX 610-524-1004
Hours: 8:30-4 Mon-Thurs   E-mail: sales@polymertooling.com
www.polymertooling.com
*Silicones (GI 1000), epoxy, urethane, adhesive, fiberglass cloth, Kevlar, carbon
fiber, U.S. Gypsum products, Renshape 450 (solid surface material), supplies.
Catalog available upon request. Contact John Flint. CREDIT CARDS.*

Polytek Development Corp. 610-559-8620
55 Hilton St.   800-858-5990
Easton, PA 18042   FAX 610-559-8626
Hours: 8:30-4:30 Mon-Fri   E-mail: sales@polytek.com
www.polytek.com
*Manufacturer of rubber mold products, plastic tooling compounds; contact
Robert LeCompte. Brochure available; no minimum. CREDIT CARDS.*

Rose Brand 800-223-1624
                                                           FAX 800-594-7424

4 Emerson Lane(15-16th St)   800-223-1624
Secaucus, NJ 07094   201-809-1730
Hours: 8-5 Mon-Fri   FAX 201-809-1851

10616 Lanark St.   800-360-5056
Sun City, CA 91352   818-505-6290
Hours: 8-5 Mon-Fri   FAX 818-505-6293
www.rosebrand.com   E-mail: sales@rosebrand.com
*Specialty coatings and adhesives including Sculpt or Coat, Aqua Resins,
Rosco Bond, Clear Acrylics. Call or fax for catalog. CREDIT CARDS.*

Rudolph Brothers & Co. 614-833-0707
6550 Oley Speaks Way   Fax Orders 800-600-9508
Canal Winchester, OH 43110   FAX 614-833-0456
Hours: 8-5 Mon-Fri   E-mail: rbcsupport@rudbro.com
www.rudolphbros.com
*Distributors of specially formulated chemical resins and adhesives for casting
and mold-making. 14 National sales offices. CREDIT CARDS.*

Sam Flax Art Supplies 212-620-3000
3 W 20th St.   FAX 212-620-3060
NY, NY 10011
Hours: 9:30-7 Mon-Fri / 10:30-6 Sat   E-mail: 20st@samfalx.com
www.samflax.com
Casting rubber, moulage, art supplies. CREDIT CARDS.

Sammons Preston 800-323-5547
1000 Remington Blvd., Ste. 210   630-378-6000
Bolingbrook, IL 60440   FAX 630-378-6010
Hours: WEB 24-hrs.   E-mail: sp@patterson-medical.com
www.sammonspreston.com
Thermoplastic (Roylan), Velcros and miscellaneous post-op therapy items.

ATAC

Sculptor's Supplies Co., Inc. 914-665-3989
221 N. Macquesten Pkwy.
Mt. Vernon, NY 10550
Hours: 9-6 Mon-Fri / 10-3 Sat
Tools, materials, bases; will mount sculpture. CREDIT CARDS.

Sculpture House Casting 212-645-9430
155 W 26th St. (6-7th Ave)   888-374-8665
NY, NY 10001   FAX 212-645-3717
Hours: 8-5:30 Mon-Fri / 10-3 Sat / call for Summer hours
www.sculptshop.com   E-mail: orders@sculptshop.com
Plaster and metal statuary including busts, casting and sculpting tools,
supplies and materials. CREDIT CARDS.

Seal Reinforced Fiberglass 631-842-2230
23 Bethpage Rd.   FAX 631-842-2276
Copiague, NY 11726
Hours: 8-5 Mon-Fri   E-mail: sealrf@aol.com
www.sealfiberglass.com
Hand-held polyester spray and pour equipment; speak to Tom Kaler. No credit
cards.

Sealoflex, Inc. 843-554-6466
2520 Oscar Johnson Dr.   800-770-6466
Charleston, SC 29405   FAX 843-554-6458
Hours: 8-5 Mon-Fri   E-mail: info@sealoflex.com
www.sealoflex.com
Manufacturer and distributor of water-base products that are hard and
paintable. No minimum; brochure available. CREDIT CARDS.

Silicones, Inc. 800-533-8709
211 Woodbine St.   336-886-5018
High Point, NC 27261   FAX 336-886-7122
Hours: 8:30-5 Mon-Fri   E-mail: info@silicones-inc.com
www.silicones-inc.com
Manufacturer of GI 1000 and other silicones. Catalog available. CREDIT
CARDS.

Slide Products 847-541-7220
PO Box 156, 430 S Wheeling Rd.   800-323-6433
Wheeling, IL 60090   FAX 800-756-7986
Hours: 8-4:30 Mon-Fri   E-mail: info@slideproducts.com
www.slideproducts.com
Many types of mold releases, even one for foods. Minimum order: 12 can
box. Catalog. CREDIT CARDS.

Smooth-On, Inc. 610-252-5800
2000 St. John's St.   800-762-0744
Easton, PA 18042   FAX 610-252-6200
Hours: 8:30-5:30 Mon-Fri   E-mail: smoothon@smooth-on.com
www.smooth-on.com
Industrial strength epoxies for set construction, all applications. Free
samples, literature and technical help available. $20.00 minimum order.
Phone orders. CREDIT CARDS.

Solutia 800-325-4330
575 Merryville Ctr.   314-674-1000
St. Louis, MO 63141   FAX 314-674-1585
Hours: 8:30-5 Mon-Fri
www.solutia.com
Manufacturer of raw materials. Call for product information. No credit cards.

Stepan Chemical Co., Urethane Dept. 847-446-7500
22 W Frontage Rd.   800-457-7673
Northfield, IL 60093   FAX 847-501-2100
Hours: 7-5:30 Mon-Fri
www.stepan.com
Manufacturer of rigid and flexible urethane foam; 55 gal. drums. No credit cards.

VanDyke's 605-796-4425
39771 SD Hwy 34   800-787-3355
Woonsocket, SD 57385   FAX 605-796-4085
Hours: 8-6 Mon-Fri / 9-3 Sat   E-mail: restoration@cabelas.com
www.vandykes.com
Taxidermy supplies. 24-hr. order with live operators. Great catalog. Very pleasant to deal with. CREDIT CARDS.

Zeller International, Ltd. 607-363-7792
15261 Highway 30   FAX 607-363-2071
Downsville, NY 13755
Hours: 9-5 Mon-Fri   E-mail: contact@zeller-int.com
www.zeller-int.com
Special effects consultation and services. Non-toxic environmental chemistry. Some minimums apply. Contact Carla Zelaschi. Catalog. CREDIT CARDS.

CASTING, CUSTOM

Architectural Fiberglass Corp. 631-842-4772
1395 Marconi Blvd.   800-439-2000
Copiague, NY 11726   FAX 631-842-4790
Hours: 9-5:30 Mon-Fri   E-mail: info@afcornice.com
www.afcornice.com
Fiberglass custom molded scenery, props, special and stock shapes; architectural reproductions; Contact Charles Wittman.

Architectural Molded Composites 718-937-1977
10-06 38th Ave.   FAX 718-937-7237
Long Island City, NY 11101
Hours: 8-5 Mon-Fri   E-mail: info@architecturalmolded.com
www.architecturalmolded.com
Sculpture casting, fiberglass, mold-making (large), bronze casting, also fairly large acrylic casting. No credit cards.

ATAC

Argos Art Casting Foundry 845-278-2454
397 Rt 312   FAX   845-278-6769
Brewster, NY 10509
Hours: 8-4:30 Mon-Fri   E-mail: roger@argosart.com
www.argosart.com
Fine quality art casting in bronze, aluminum, silver, pewter, stainless and
regular steel. No credit cards.

FiberArtz 914-939-5543
51 Purdy Ave.   FAX 914-934-1939
Port Chester, NY 10573
Hours: 9-6 Mon-Sat   E-mail: sales@fiberartz.com
www.fiberartz.com
Fiberglass ornament, custom casting; ask for Don or Dawn.

Saldarini & Pucci, Inc. 718-852-1656
219 Westminister Rd. (Beverly Blvd)   FAX 718-852-1656
Brooklyn, NY 11218
Hours: 9-6 Mon-Fri   E-mail: paylessplastering@netscape.net
Casting, mold-making, Established in 1925. Flexible resins. Also Plastic
contracting and sculpting. No credit cards.

Seal Reinforced Fiberglass 631-842-2230
23 Bethpage Rd.   FAX 631-842-2276
Copiague, NY 11726
Hours: 8-5 Mon-Fri   E-mail: sealrf@aol.com
www.sealfiberglass.com
Custom fiberglass casting; architectural and scenic work; speak to Tom Kaler.
No credit cards.

CHINA, CRYSTAL & GLASSWARE
See also: ANTIQUES: All Headings
            KITCHEN EQUIPMENT: HOUSEHOLD
            PARTY GOODS
            PROP RENTAL HOUSES

Baccarat, Inc. 212-826-4100
625 Madison Ave. (59th St)   FAX 212-826-5043
NY, NY 10022
Hours: 10-6 Mon-Fri / 11-6 Sat
www.baccarat-us.com
Crystal, china. Expensive. Catalog. CREDIT CARDS.

Bloomingdales 212-705-2000
1000 Third Ave. (59th St)   (Studio Services) 212-705-3673
NY, NY 10022   FAX 212-705-3939
Hours: 10-6 Mon-Fri
www.bloomingdales.com
Extensive selection from traditional to contemporary.
Contact Barbara D-Arsanel.

The End of History 212-647-7598
548 1/2 Hudson St. (Perry-Charles St)
NY, NY 10014
Hours: 12-7 Mon-Fri / 1-6 Sat-sun
Collection of vintage glassware, ceramics and lighting. Mostly 50s-60s from Italy, Scandinavia and America. Has furniture from the same period. RENTALS. CREDIT CARDS.

Michael C. Fina Co. 212-557-2500
545 Fifth Ave. (45th St)   800-289-3462
NY, NY 10017   FAX 212-557-3862
Hours: 11-8 Mon-Thurs / 10-7 Fri / 10-6 Sat / 11-6 Sun
www.michaelcfina.com
Silver, silverware, china, crystal and jewelry. Good prices. Catalog and online shopping available. CREDIT CARDS.

Fishs Eddy 212-420-9020
889 Broadway (19th St)   (web sales) 201-420-8828
NY, NY 10003   FAX 212-353-1454
Hours: 10-9 Sun-Mon / 9-9 Tue-Sat   E-mail: info@fisheseddy.com
www.fishseddy.com
A selection of china and glassware including restaurant dishes. See website for additional locations. RENTALS. CREDIT CARDS.

La Terrine 877-837-7463
1024 Lexington Ave.(73rd St)   212-988-3366
NY, NY 10021   FAX 212-249-5846
Hours: 10-5:30 Mon-Sat

280 Columbus Ave.   212-362-2122
NY, NY 10023
Hours: 11-7 Mon-Sat / 12-6 Sun   E-mail: info@laterrinedirect.com
www.laterrinedirect.com
Tabletop ceramics, linens, glassware. RENTALS. CREDIT CARDS.

Pottery Barn 888-779-5176
                                                 FAX 702-363-2541

1965 Broadway(66-67th St)   212-579-8477
NY, NY 10023
Hours: 10-9 Mon-Sat / 11-7 Sun

127 E 59th St.(Lexington)   917-369-0050
NY, NY 10022
Hours: 10-9 Mon-Sat / 11-7 Sun
www.potterybarn.com
China, glassware, cookware, utensils, etc. Catalog. RENTALS (M-W 10-12, with credit card deposit). Over 160 stores in USA and Canada. CREDIT CARDS.

The Prop Company / Kaplan and Associates 212-691-7767
111 W 19th St., 8th Fl. (6-7th Ave)   FAX 212-727-3055
NY, NY 10011
Hours: 9-5 Mon-Fri   E-mail: propcompany@yahoo.com
Fine china, crystal, candlesticks, tableware, decorative accessories. Antique,
contemporary, ethnic. Nice collection of antique kitchenware. Very good for
styling and table top. Contact Maxine Kaplan. RENTALS. CREDIT CARDS.

Props for Today 212-244-9600
330 W 34th St. (8-9th Ave)   FAX 212-244-1053
NY, NY 10001
Hours: 8:30-5 Mon-Fri   E-mail: info@propsfortoday.com
www.propsfortoday.com
Full-service prop rental house. Large selection of china and glassware, some
period. Sells floor samples and custom furniture. RENTALS. CREDIT CARDS.

Carole Stupell Ltd. 212-260-3100
29 E 22nd St. (B'way-Park)   FAX 212-260-3100
NY, NY 10010
Hours: 10:30-6 Mon-Sat   E-mail: keith@carolestupell.com
www.carolestupell.com
Fine china and crystal; decorative accessories. Good service. See Cory.
RENTALS. CREDIT CARDS.

The Terrence Conran Shop 212-755-9079
888 Broadway Lower Level (18-19th St)   FAX 212-755-3989
NY, NY 10003
Hours: 11-8 Mon-Fri / 10-7 Sat / 12-6 Sun
www.conranusa.com   E-mail: terenceconranshop@conranusa.com
Designer furniture, household, bedding and bath, textiles and hardware. Very
nice people. Will do rentals to film and television. CREDIT CARDS.

Tiffany & Co. 212-755-8000
727 Fifth Ave. (57th St)   800-843-3269
NY, NY 10022   FAX 212-605-4465
Hours: 10-7 Mon-Sat / 12-6 Sun
www.tiffany.com
Fine china, crystal, silver, clocks, watches, jewelry; the very best. CREDIT
CARDS.

Williams-Sonoma 877-812-6235
110 Seventh Ave.(at 17th St)   212-633-2203
NY, NY 10011   FAX 212-206-0826
Hours: 10-8 Mon-Fri / 10-7 Sat / 12-6 Sun

1175 Madison Ave.(86th St)   212-289-6832
NY, NY 10028
Hours: 10-7 Mon-Fri / 10-6 Sat / 12-6 Sun

121 E 59th St.(Park & Lex)   917-369-1131
NY, NY 10022
Hours: 10-8 Mon-Sat / 11/7 Sun

Williams-Sonoma (cont.) 212-823-9750
  10 Columbus Circle Time Warner Building(Columbus Circle)
  NY, NY 10022
  Hours: 10-7 Mon-Fri / 10-6 Sat / 10-6 Sun
  www.williams-sonoma.com
  Kitchenware store; china, glassware, cookware, utensils, etc. Catalog. Studio
  services available thru corporate offices 415-421-7900. See website for other
  locations. CREDIT CARDS.

Yellow Shed Antiques 845-628-0362
  PO Box 706, 571 Rt 6   FAX 845-628-2777
  Mahopac, NY 10541
  Hours: 10-5 Wed-Sun
  China, crystal, silver items, memorabilia, quilts, jewelry, posters and prints.
  1 hr. from Manhattan. 8,000 sq. ft. of decorative accessories. Contact Mark or
  Patty. RENTALS. CREDIT CARDS.

CLEANERS: CARPET, DRAPERY & UPHOLSTERY

Adler Rug Cleaning 718-328-4433
  644 Whittier St. (off Hunts Pt)   FAX 718-328-4434
  Bronx, NY 10474
  Hours: 8-5 Mon-Fri
  Carpet cleaners repair, refringing and binding. CREDIT CARDS.

Reynolds Drapery Service, Inc. 315-845-8632
  7440 Main St.   FAX 315-845-8645
  Newport, NY 13416
  Hours: 8-4 Mon-Fri   E-mail: rynldpry@ntc.net.com
  Cleans, repairs and fireproofs theatrical drapery. P.O.s accepted. No credit
  cards.

CLOCKS

Art & Industrial Design 212-477-0116
  50 Great Jones St. (4th Ave)   FAX 212-477-1420
  NY, NY 10012
  Hours: 10-5 Mon-Fri / 10-1 Sat   E-mail: info@aid20c.com
  www.aid20c.com
  20th-century and Art Deco furniture, furnishings, art and objects. Many
  original high-style works. Also collectibles, clocks and lighting fixtures.
  RENTALS. CREDIT CARDS.

Central Time Clock, Inc. 718-784-4900
  5-23 50th Ave.   800-556-3504
  Long Island City, NY 11101   FAX 718-742-9491
  Hours: 8-5 Mon-Fri   E-mail: info@centraltimeclock.com
  www.centraltimeclock.com
  Timeclocks, supplies, sales and service. All makes and models; digital,
  biometric hand readers and stock broker timestamps. Timecards and racks.
  Contact Hal. RENTALS. CREDIT CARDS.

Centuryhurst Berkshire Antiques Gallery 413-229-8131
173 Main St. (Rt. 7)   413-229-3277
Sheffield, MA 01257
Hours: 9-5 Daily (10-4 in winter)
Specializes in antique clocks. See Ron or Judith Timm. CREDIT CARDS.

Clock Hutt 718-428-8531
42-11 Corporal Kennedy St.
Bayside, NY 11361
Hours: 10-4 Thur - Fri   E-mail: davidthehook@aol.com
Antique clocks; repairs.

Fanelli Antique Timepieces Ltd. 212-517-2300
790 Madison Ave., Ste. 202 (66-67th St)   FAX 212-737-4774
NY, NY 10021
Hours: 11-6 Mon-Fri / Sat by appt. only   E-mail: cindyclocks@verizon.net
Antique clocks, wristwatches, pocket watches, jewelry repairs; ask for Cindy.
RENTALS. CREDIT CARDS.

Klockit 262-248-1150
N 3211 County Road H / PO Box 636   800-556-2548
Lake Geneva, WI 53147   FAX 262-248-9899
Hours: 9-5 Wed-Fri / 8:30-4 Sat   E-mail: klockit@klockit.com
www.klockit.com
Clock parts and reparis, movements, kits. Free catalog available or shop
online. CREDIT CARDS.

Merritts Clocks 800-345-4101
PO Box 277 / 1860 Weavertown Rd.   610-689-9541
Douglassville, PA 19518   FAX 610-689-4538
Hours: 8-4:30 Mon-Fri / 9-2 Sat   E-mail: info@merritts.com
www.merritts.com
Antique clocks and clock parts. Country, 19th and 20th century. Call for
directions. 45 miles NW of Philadelphia.

The Prop Company / Kaplan and Associates 212-691-7767
111 W 19th St., 8th Fl. (6-7th Ave)   FAX 212-727-3055
NY, NY 10011
Hours: 9-5 Mon-Fri   E-mail: propcompany@yahoo.com
Many unique antique & contemporary clocks; travel, alarm, mantel, etc.
RENTAL only. CREDIT CARDS.

Sutton Clock Shop 212-758-2260
139 E 61st St., 2nd Fl. (Lexington Ave)
NY, NY 10065
Hours: 11-4 Tue-Fri by appt.   E-mail: info@suttonclocks.com
www.suttonclocks.com
Antique clocks and barometers. RENTALS.

Tiffany & Co. 212-755-8000
727 Fifth Ave. (57th St)   800-843-3269
NY, NY 10022   FAX 212-605-4465
Hours: 10-7 Mon-Sat / 12-6 Sun
www.tiffany.com
Fine china, crystal, silver, clocks, watches, jewelry; the very best. CREDIT
CARDS.

Zero to Sixties 212-925-0932
354 Broadway (Franklin)
NY, NY 10013
Hours: 11-6 Mon-Fri   E-mail: genie354@bellatlantic.net
19th-and 20th-century furniture, furnishings, art, lighting and accessories.
Unusual items. RENTALS. CREDIT CARDS.

CLOTHING: ACCESSORIES
See also: CLOTHING: All Headings   EYEGLASSES   GLOVES
            HATS   JEWELRY   LUGGAGE & HANDBAGS
            SHOES & BOOTS   UMBRELLAS & CANES

Ambassador Spat Co. 610-532-7840
900 Ashland Ave.   FAX 610-534-3777
Folcroft, PA 19032
Hours: 8-4:30 Mon-Fri   E-mail: spatsco@aol.com
Spats in many styles. CREDIT CARDS.

Crystal Crown, Inc. 601-947-8074
183 Webb Davis Rd.   888-278-9531
Lucedale, MS 39452   FAX: 601-947-1860
Hours: 7:30-5 Mon-Thurs   E-mail: crystal@datasync.com
www.crystalcrown.com
USA manufacturer of crowns, tiaras, scepters, jewelry, and embroidered
Sashes for beauty pageants and weddings. Very reasonable prices and quick
service. CREDIT CARDS.

Full Line Accessories 212-967-5327
67 W 36th St. (6th Ave)   212-216-9253
NY, NY 10018   FAX 212-967-5176
Hours: 9-7 Mon-Sat / 10-6:30 Sun
Inexpensive costume jewelry with an extensive selection of fancy rhinestone
pieces. CREDIT CARDS.

Medals of America 864-862-6425
114 S Chase Blvd.   800-308-0849
Fountain Inn, SC 29644   FAX 864-862-7495
Hours: 9-7 Mon-Fri   E-mail: tom@usmedals.com
www.usmedals.com
Complete Military Award Service; medals, ribbons, lapel and hat pins, badges
and patches. Books and Manuals. All periods. Mail order and catalog. CREDIT
CARDS.

Rawhides Custom Leatherware 201-333-2571
P.O. Box 2146
Secaucus, NJ 07096
Hours: by appt.   E-mail: hidemaster@rawhides.com
www.rawhides.com
Custom leather clothing, theatrical costumes, garments or accessories. Visit
website for ordering information. CREDIT CARDS.

Screaming Mimi's 212-677-6464
382 Lafayette St. (E 4th St)   FAX 212-677-6523
NY, NY 10003
Hours: 12-8 Mon-Sat / 1-7 Sun   E-mail: sales@screamingmimis.com
www.screamingmimis.com
Men's and women's vintage clothing from 1950-1980. Large selection of
shoes and accessories. The Home Department has vintage bar ware and gifts.
RENTALS. CREDIT CARDS.

Tiecrafters, Inc. 212-629-5800
252 W 29th St. (7-8th Ave)   FAX 212-629-0115
NY, NY 10001
Hours: 9-5 Mon-Fri / 10-2 Sat   E-mail: info@tiecrafters.com
www.tiecrafters.com
Custom neckware, tie cleaning service available, contact Andrew Tarshis.
Accepts personal checks.

Unique Boutique NYC 917-686-8017
Box 1164, Cooper Station
NY, NY 10276
Hours: 10-8 Mon-Fri or by appt.   E-mail: style@ubnyc.com
www.ubnyc.com
Website offers large colletion of vintage and designer clothing of very high
quality. Willing to work with film, TV and theatrical companies on rentals.
Clothing, hats, furs, shoes and accessories for women from the 40s thru 60s.
RENTALS. CREDIT CARDS or PayPal.

CLOTHING: ANTIQUE & VINTAGE
See also: CLOTHING UNIFORMS
              THRIFT SHOPS

Alias Costume Rental 212-564-1530
231 W 29th St. # 608 (6-7th Ave)   FAX 212-564-1534
NY, NY 10001
Hours: 9-6 Mon-Fri / Sat and after hours by Appt.
www.aliascostumesnyc.com   E-mail: info@aliascostumesnyc.com
Alias is open to serve the needs of the film, theatre, commercial and print
community. Large stock of men's and women's vintage clothing, uniforms
(police, firemen, medical, security, hospitality), work wear, theatrical
costumes, accessories and shoes. RENTALS.

Andy's Chee-Pees 212-420-5980
18 W 8th St. (5th-McDougal)   FAX 212-254-3610
NY, NY 10003
Hours: 11-8 Mon-Thurs / 11-9 Fri-Sat / 12-8 Sun
www.andyscheepees.com   E-mail: info@andyscheepees.com
Wholesale, retail antique clothing and jeans, army surplus. No shipping.
CREDIT CARDS.

Cheap Jack's Vintage Clothing 212-777-9564
303 Fifth Ave. (31st St)   212-995-0403
NY, NY 10016   FAX 914-238-5733
Hours: 11-8 Mon-Sat / 12-7 Sun   E-mail: info@cheapjacks.com
www.cheapjacks.com
Good selection of vintage clothing 1920-1970. Phone orders. RENTALS.
CREDIT CARDS.

Early Halloween 212-691-2933
130 W 25th St., 11th Fl. (6-7th Ave)   FAX 212-243-1499
NY, NY 10001
Hours: by appt. only   E-mail: earlyhalloween@aol.com
www.earlyhalloween.com
Vintage clothing, hats, shoes and accessories. Also vintage luggage and
memorabilia. RENTAL only.

The Family Jewels 212-633-6020
130 W 23rd St. (6-7th Ave)   FAX (same)
NY, NY 10011
Hours: 11-7 Sun-Tue / 11-8 Wed-Sat   E-mail: chelseagirl@familyjewelsnyc.com
www.familyjewelsnyc.com
Victorian to 1980s clothing, textiles, accessories and bric-a-brac. Sales and
RENTALS. CREDIT CARDS.

Frock 212-594-5380
170 Elizabeth St. (Spring-Kenmare)   FAX 212-594-5684
NY, NY 10012
Hours: 12-7 Mon-Sat / 12-5 Sun   E-mail: info@frocknyc.dom
www.frocknyc.com
Sale and rental of vintage women's designer and couture clothing and
accessories. Lesser known labels available also. Late 60s to late 90s.
Website has photos of many items. RENTALS. CREDIT CARDS.

Gothic Renaissance 212-780-9558
110 Fourth Ave. (11-12th St)   FAX 212-780-9560
NY, NY 10003
Hours: 11-8 Mon-Sat / 12-7 Sun   E-mail: gothicrenaissance@gmail.com
www.gothicrenaissance.com
Everything from the Gothic / Renaissance era. Modern with a Goth bend,
Victorian costumes. Wonderful selection of Goth and glam corsets and
masks. Small occult section. CREDIT CARDS.

Hero Wardrobe 212-929-4376
1 W 21st St., Street Level (5-6th Ave)   FAX 212-929-4333
NY, NY 1010
Hours: 9-6 Mon-Fri   E-mail: lani@herowardrobe.com
www.HEROwardrobe.com
Uniforms, vintage (men's, women's, & children's), footwear, big & tall,
accessories and novelty items. RENTALS. CREDIT CARDS.

JANET LINVILLE 917-952-4713
575 Main St. Apt 808
NY, NY 10044
Hours: by appt.   E-mail: jlinvillehats@aol.com
Millinery for theatre, film, fashion and all other media. Member ATAC.

Love Saves the Day 215-862-1399
1 South Main St. (7th St)
New Hope, PA 18938
Hours: 11-7 Daily
Vintage clothing, toys, props. Phone orders. **CREDIT CARDS.**

Poppet 718-789-7890
121 St. Johns Place
Brooklyn, NY 11217
Hours: by appt.   E-mail: info@poppetnyc.com
www.poppetnyc.com
*Men and Women's vintage clothing and accessories specializing from 1940s
to early 1980s. RENTALS. CREDIT CARDS.*

Rags-A-Gogo 646-486-4011
218 W 14th St. (7-8th Aves)   212-254-6115
NY, NY 10011
Hours: 11-8 Mon-Fri   E-mail: joshuasuzzane@gmail.com
www.rags-a-gogo.com
Vintage clothing for men and women. CREDIT CARDS. RENTALS.

Right to the Moon Alice 607-498-5750
240 Cooks Falls Rd.   FAX: SAME
Roscoe, NY 12776
Hours: by appt.   E-mail: righttothemoonalice@yahoo.com
www.righttothemoonalice.com
*Located in a 30,000 sq. foot warehouse, this company has a wide collection
of vintage clothing for men, women and children, from the 1940s-1980s.
Hats, shoes, ties, gloves, purses, belts, scarves and fabric. You may have seen
many of their items in many of your favorite films. Their inventory is worth
the 2 hour drive. View web-site for visual reference. RENTALS. CREDIT
CARDS.*

Screaming Mimi's 212-677-6464
382 Lafayette St. (E 4th St)   FAX 212-677-6523
NY, NY 10003
Hours: 12-8 Mon-Sat / 1-7 Sun   E-mail: sales@screamingmimis.com
www.screamingmimis.com
*Men's and women's vintage clothing from 1950-1980. Large selection of
shoes and accessories. The Home Department has vintage bar ware and gifts.
RENTALS. CREDIT CARDS.*

Jana Starr Antiques 212-861-8256
236 E 80th St. (2nd-3rd Ave)   FAX 212-861-8256
NY, NY 10075
Hours: 12-6 Mon-Sat / Sun by appt.   E-mail: jana@janastarr.com
www.janastarr.com
*1890-1950's clothing, lace, jewelry, collectibles, textiles and props. CREDIT
CARDS.*

Stock Vintage 212-505-2505
143 E 13th St. (3rd-4th Ave)
NY, NY 10003
Hours: 11-7 Mon-Fri / 12-7 Sat / 12-6 Sun
*Vintage clothing specializing in men's fashions pre 1960s. Shoes, boots
accessories, jewelry etc. Some women's clothing. CREDIT CARDS.*

Timbuktu 212-473-4955
45 2nd Ave. (2nd-3rd st)   FAX 212-473-9376
NY, NY 10003
Hours: 1-8 Daily   E-mail: timbuktu-ny@hotmail.com
Good selection of men's and women's clothing, hats, shoes and formal wear.
Pre 70s. Also textiles, tribal jewelry and serber rugs. RENTALS. CREDIT
CARDS.

Trash & Vaudeville, Inc. 212-982-3590
4 Saint Marks Pl. (2nd-3rd Ave)   FAX 212-260-2393
NY, NY 10003
Hours: 12-8 Mon-Thurs / 11:30-8:30 Fri / 11:30-9 Sat / 1-7:30 Sun
Punk and rock and roll; wholesale or retail. CREDIT CARDS.

Helen Uffner Vintage Clothing .212-594-7440
30-10 41st Ave., 3rd FL (8-9th Ave)   718-937-0220
Long Island City, NY 11101   FAX 718-937-0227
Hours: 10-6 Mon-Fri   E-mail: uffnervintage@aol.com
Men's, women's, children's vintage clothing and accessories 1860-1960; also
period fabric, lace and trim. RENTALS.

Unique Boutique NYC 917-686-8017
Box 1164, Cooper Station
NY, NY 10276
Hours: 10-8 Mon-Fri or by appt.   E-mail: style@ubnyc.com
www.ubnyc.com
Website offers large colletion of vintage and designer clothing of very high
quality. Willing to work with film, TV and theatrical companies on rentals.
Clothing, hats, furs, shoes and accessories for women from the 40s thru 60s.
RENTALS. CREDIT CARDS or PayPal.

Vintage by Stacey Lee 914-328-0788
305 Central Ave., Ste. 4   FAX 914-741-2461
White Plains, NY 10606
Hours: by appt only
Men's and women's vintage clothing in pristine condition, costume jewelry,
handbags and millinery from 1900 to 1970. Will ship, some RENTALS.

CLOTHING: CHILDREN'S
See also: CLOTHING: Antique & Vintage
                UNIFORMS
                STUDIO SERVICES

Conway Stores 212-967-3460
1345 Broadway(35-36th St)
NY, NY 10018
Hours: 8-8 Mon-Fri / 9:30-8 Sat / 10:30-7 Sun

450 Seventh Ave.(34-35th St)   212-967-1371
NY, NY 10001
Hours: 8-8 Mon-Sun

ATAC

Conway Stores (cont.) 212-868-0002
245 W 34th St.(7-8th Ave)
NY, NY 10001
Hours: 8-8 Mon-Fri / 9:30-8 Sat / 10:30-7 Sun
Reasonably priced clothing, footwear and accessories and various housewares. Call 212-967-5300 for info on all locations. CREDIT CARDS.

Little Folks Shop 212-982-9669
123 E 23rd St. (Park-Lexington Ave)   800-675-9669
NY, NY 10010   FAX 212-228-7889
Hours: 9:30-7 Mon-Thurs / 9:30-3 Fri / 12-5 Sun
www.littlefolksnyc.com
Clothing from newborn to 14 yrs; toys, books, baby furniture. Phone orders. RENTALS. CREDIT CARDS.

Western Spirit 800-976-9287
395 Broadway (Walker)   212-343-1476
NY, NY 10013   FAX 212-343-0257
Hours: 10:30-7:30 Mon-Fri / 11-8 Sat-Sun   E-mail: iwesternspiritj@yahoo.com
www.westernspiritny.com
Largest Western shop in NYC. Native American art, crafts, jewelry, pottery, leathercraft and headdresses. Western clothing in men's, women's and children's sizes. Toys. CREDIT CARDS.

CLOTHING: DANCEWEAR

B.T. Industries / Baltogs Dancewear 201-866-0201
6605 Smith Ave. # 09   800-992-6629
North Bergen, NJ 07047   FAX 201-866-9433
Hours: 8:30-5 Mon-Fri   E-mail: customerservice@baltogs.com
www.baltogs.com
Men's, women's and children's leotards, unitards, tights, lycra, cotton dancewear. See website for links to online retailers. No rentals.

Backstage Dancewear / ADA Discount Dancewear 800-882-9882
P.O. Box 50073   FAX 541-341-1470
Eugene, OR 97405
Hours: 8-8 Mon-Sat or by appt.   E-mail: service @adadance.com
www.adadance.com / backstagedance.net
Large selection of dance and theatrical supplies for dance. Online, mail or fax ordering. CREDIT CARDS.

Backstage, Inc. 202-544-5744
545 Eighth St. SE   FAX 202-544-7025
Washington, DC 20003
Hours: 11-7 Mon-Sat   E-mail: backstagebooks@aol.com
http://backstagebooks.com
Theatre books and scripts; quarterly newsletter on new releases; mail orders. Also dancewear, masks, makeup and some costumes for rent. RENTALS CREDIT CARDS.

Ballroom Dance Shoppe 952-476-0058
3403 Kilmer Lane N.   877-888-9436
Plymouth, MN 55441   FAX 763-541-7448
Hours: 11-3 Mon-Fri   E-mail: mconstantine@celebritydanceshoes.com
www.celebritydanceshoes.com
Custom made dance and street shoes and boots. Will work from your
designs. Contact Chrysana Constantine.

Capezio Dance-Theatre Shop 212-245-2130
1650 Broadway, 2nd Fl. (B-way-7th Ave)   FAX 212-245-2235
NY, NY 10019
Hours: 10-7 Mon-Sat / 12-5 Sun   E-mail: store1@balletmakers.com
www.capeziodance.com
Dancewear, shoes, lingerie, large selection; call ahead for large orders. Pete
Ktenas on premises for all your custom shoes. Account service available to
designers and stylists. Phone orders. Will ship. No rentals. CREDIT CARDS.

Capezio at 69th 212-586-5140
201 Amsterdam Ave. (69th St)   FAX 212-262-1747
NY, NY 10019
Hours: 10-7 Mon-Fri / 10-6 Sat / 12-5 Sun
www.capeziodance.com   www.capezio57stnyc@balletmakers.com
Outfitters for dance, fitness and special events; dance footwear, bodywear
and accessories. Also videos, records, books and teaching materials. Catalogs
available. CREDIT CARDS.

Capezio East 212-758-8833
136 E 61st St. (Lexington Ave)   FAX 212-980-1013
NY, NY 10021
Hours: 10-6 Mon-Sat   E-mail: capezio61stnyc@balletmakers.com
www.capeziodanceshop.com
Dancewear; large selection for students. No rentals. CREDIT CARDS.

Capezio Theatricals 212-245-2152
1650 Broadway, 2nd FL (B'way-7th Ave)   FAX 212-245-1699
NY, NY 10019
Hours: 10-6 Mon-Fri   E-mail: kcollins@balletmakers.com
www.capeziodance.com
This location only outfits professional, broadway and opera companies.
Custom footwear and repairs.

The Costume Collection 212-989-5855
601 W 26th St., 3rd Fl. (11-12th Ave)   FAX 212-206-0922
NY, NY 10001
Hours: 9-5:30 Mon-Fri by appt.   E-mail: costume@tdf.org
www.tdf.org
Rental for non-profit organizations only. TDF Costume Collection. RENTALS.

The Dance Store 310-271-3664
1446 South Robertson Blvd.   FAX 310-271-3647
Los Angeles, CA 90035
Hours: 9-6 Mon-Fri
The Dance Store offers a wide range of dance wear products: pointe shoes,
ballet shoes, tap shoes, dance wear and more. We specialize in fitting pointe
shoes as well as a wide range of dance wear. CREDIT CARDS.

ATAC

Danskin, Inc. 800-288-6749
530 Seventh Ave., M1 (38-39th St)
NY, NY 10018
Hours: 9-5 Mon-Fri   E-mail: contact_us@danskin.com
www.danskin.com
Showroom for buyers. Wholesale. Catalog. CREDIT CARDS.

Grishko 800-474-7454
241 King Manor Dr., Ste. D   FAX 610-239-6441
King of Prussia, PA 19406
Hours: 10-6 Mon-Fri   E-mail: info@grishko.com
www.grishko.com
High quality custom designed shoes and boots for men, women and dance.
Also nice selection of dancewear and gifts. Good website. CREDIT CARDS.

Stephanie Handler 212-268-9817
555 Eighth Ave., Ste. 2009 (37-38th St)
NY, NY 10018
Hours: By appt., please call   E-mail: shandler1@verizon.net
Specializing in design and construction of theatrical costumes, skating
competition garments and other athletic clothing. CREDIT CARDS.

On Stage Dancewear of New York 212-725-1174
197 Madison Ave. (34-35th St)   866-725-1174
NY, NY 10016   FAX 212-725-4524
Hours: 10-7 Mon-Fri / 11-7 Sat
www.onstagedancewear.com
Large selection of leotards, tights, unitards and accessories; will special
order. Catalog available; will do mail order. Phone orders. CREDIT CARDS.

T-O-Dey Custom Made Shoes 212-683-6300
9 E 38th St., 7th Fl. (5th Ave & Madison)   FAX 212-683-3445
NY, NY 10016
Hours: by appt.   E-mail: todeyco@aol.com
www.todeyshoes.com
Custom-made shoes for theatre and dance.

Tutus by Christine 440-949-7996
3962 Colorado Ave.   FAX: 440-949-7996
Sheffield Village, OH 44054
Hours: 9-5 Mon-Fri   E-mail: pie545@aol.com
Custom professional tutus. Performance quality.

Worldtone Dance 212-691-1934
230 Seventh Ave., 2nd Fl. (23rd-24th St)   866-WTD-SHOES
NY, NY 10011   FAX 212-691-2554
Hours: 11-7 Mon-Wed / 11-8 Thurs-Sat / 12-6 Sun   E-mail: info@wtdance.com
www.worldtonedance.com
Specialize in the sale of dance materials including shoes, recordings, videos,
books, castanets. CREDIT CARDS.

CLOTHING: ECCLESIASTICAL

C.M. Almy & Son, Inc. 203-531-7600
3 American Ln. / PO Box 2644   800-225-2569
Greenwich, CT 06836   FAX 800-426-2569
Hours: 9-6 Mon-Fri / 24-hr. website   E-mail: almyaccess@almy.com
www.almy.com
Vestments, sacred vessels, choir robes, clerical clothing. Catalog. Great website. CREDIT CARDS.

Duffy & Quinn 212-725-0213
247 W 37th St. 17th FL   800-425-3466
NY, NY 10018   FAX 212-685-3503
Hours: 9:30-5 Mon-Fri / 9:30-1 Sat   E-mail: info@duffyandquinn.com
www.duffyandquinn.com
Bishop's robes and furnishings, pulpit robes, choir robes, judicial robes, graduation caps and gowns. Also custom tailoring. RENTALS. CREDIT CARDS.

Holy Land Art Co., Inc. 201-666-6604
12 Sullivan St.   800-334-3621
Westwood, NJ 07675   FAX: 201-666-6069
Hours: 8-5:30 Mon-Fri   E-mail: info@holylandartcompany.com
www.holylandartcompany.com
Clerical clothing, vestment materials. Church furnishings, altar furniture, pews, benches, statues, candlesticks, etc. Shop online. CREDIT CARDS.

J. Levine Co. 212-695-6888
5 W 30th St. (B'way-5th Ave)   800-553-9474
NY, NY 10001   FAX 212-643-1044
Hours: 9-6 Mon-Wed / 9-7 Thurs / 9-2 Fri / 10-5 Sun
www.levinejudaica.com
Prayer shawls, great selection of yarmulkes, lots of books and other religious items. Phone orders, catalog or shop online. CREDIT CARDS.

Oak Hall Cap & Gown 800-223-0429
840 Union St. (4th St)   540-387-0000
Salem, VA 24153   FAX 540-387-2034
Hours: 8:15-5 Mon-Fri
www.oakhalli.com
Custom ecclesiastical clothing, choir, academic and judicial robes. Catalog. Contact Donna or Kathy. CREDIT CARDS.

CLOTHING: FORMAL WEAR

ADORNMENTS BY SHARON 404-877-4469
393 Fifth St. #2   FAX 404-874-8452
Atlanta, GA 30308
Hours: by appt.   E-mail: sharon@adornmentsbysharon.com
www.adornmentsbysharon.com
Unique handcrafted bridal headpieces, jewelry and accessories. Custom work created for clients throughout the country. Call or e-mail for a free consultation. Member ATAC.

Baldwin Formal Wear 800-427-0072
1156 Ave. of the Americas, 2nd Fl. (45th St)   FAX 212-956-5831
NY, NY 10036
Hours: 9-7 Mon-Fri / 10-5 Sat   E-mail: info@nyctuxedos.com
www.nyctuxedos.com
*Anything formal, from top hats to capes and canes to white tie attire. Small
orders to large groups. Same day service, tailor on premise. Sell new and
used merchandise. RENTALS. CREDIT CARDS.*

Michael's 212-737-7273
1041 Madison Ave. (79th St)   FAX 212-737-7211
NY, NY 10075
Hours: 9:30-6 Mon-Sat / Thurs til 8   E-mail: info@michaelsconsignment.com
www.michaelsconsignment.com
*Delicately worn designer dresses. Stocks an impressive collection of more
than 100 dresses. No rentals. CREDIT CARDS.*

Off-Broadway Boutique 212-724-6713
139 W 72nd St. (B'way-Columbus)   FAX 212-873-3825
NY, NY 10023
Hours: 10:30-8 Mon-Fri / 10:30-7 Sat / 1-7 Sun   E-mail: alixcohen@aol.com
www.boutiqueoffbroadway.com
*Women's tuxedos, gowns, jewelry and accessories. Gently worn star's
clothes available. Phone orders. Will ship. CREDIT CARDS.*

R K Bridal 212-947-1155
318 W 39th St. (8-9th Ave)   800-929-9512
NY, NY 10018
Hours: 11-7 Mon-Fri / 9:30-3:30 Sat / 11-3 Sun   E-mail: bridalinfo@rkbridal.com
www.rkbridal.com
*Extra large selection of bridal gowns and bridesmaids dresses. Limited
assistance and alterations available. All dresses must be ordered. Be sure to
leave plenty of time for shipping. CREDIT CARDS.*

Jack Silver Formal Wear 212-582-0202
250 W 49th St., FL 8 (57-58th St)   FAX 212-765-6933
NY, NY 10019
Hours: 9-7 Mon, Thurs / 9-6 Tue, Wed, Fri / 10-3 Sat
                              E-mail: info@jacksilverformalwear.com
www.jacksilverformalwear.com
*Men's and women's tuxes and tails, children's tuxedos. RENTALS. CREDIT
CARDS.*

Ted's Formal Wear 212-966-2029
155 Orchard St. (Rivington-Stanton)
NY, NY 10002
Hours: 10-6 Mon-Sun
Reasonable prices. Shipping. Phone orders. RENTALS. CREDIT CARDS.

The Tuxedo Wholesaler 623-979-2331
7622 W Olive   800-828-2802
Peoria, AZ 85345   FAX 888-456-2233
Hours: 8-4 Mon-Fri   E-mail: questions@tuexedowholesaler.com
www.tuxedowholesaler.com
*New and used formal wear, standard and period, catalog. Phone orders.
RENTALS. CREDIT CARDS.*

CLOTHING: FURS

Fabulous-Furs 800-848-4650
20 W Eleventh St.   859-291-3300
Covington, KY 41011   FAX 859-291-9687
Hours: 9-5 Mon-Fri / 10-3 Sat / 24-7 Catalog
www.fabulousfurs.com   E-mail: custserv@fabulousfurs.com
*Finest faux furs, European and domestic, in coats, jackets, accessories,
throws and pillows. Used throughout the entertainment industry in movies,
on Broadway, and TV; yardage also available. Order from online catalog.
CREDIT CARDS.*

Fur & Furgery, Inc. 212-244-7601
211 W 37th St. (7-8th Ave)   FAX 212-244-7603
NY, NY 10018
Hours: 9:30-6 Mon-Fri / 10-4 Sat
www.furgery.com
*Furs; real and fake. Will work with designers and do custom work for theatre.
CREDIT CARDS.*

Henry Cowit, Inc. 212-594-5744
151 W 29th St. (6-7th Ave)   212-594-5824
New York, NY 10001   FAX 212-947-9436
Hours: 8-5 Mon-Fri / 10-4 Sat   E-mail: hcfurmatcher@msn.com
www.cowitfurs.com
*Wholesaler and retailer of new and used furs. Fur remodel experts. Over
2000 used and new furs in inventory all year round. Period furs included.
Rental to the entertainment industry for over 30 years. RENTALS. CREDIT
CARDS.*

Steven Corn Furs 212-695-1635
337 Seventh Ave. (28-29th St)   FAX 646-473-1380
NY, NY 10001
Hours: 10-6 Mon-Sat / Summer weekend hrs July-Aug.
www.stevencorn.com
New and secondhand furs; sales. CREDIT CARDS.

Unique Boutique NYC 917-686-8017
Box 1164, Cooper Station
NY, NY 10276
Hours: 10-8 Mon-Fri or by appt.   E-mail: style@ubnyc.com
www.ubnyc.com
*Website offers large collection of vintage and designer clothing of very high
quality. Willing to work with film, TV and theatrical companies on rentals.
Clothing, hats, furs, shoes and accessories for women from the 40s thru 60s.
RENTALS. CREDIT CARDS or PayPal.*

CLOTHING: HOSIERY & LINGERIE

AW Kaufman Lingerie 212-226-1629
   73 Orchard St. (Broome)   FAX 212-226-1787
   NY, NY 10002
   Hours: 11-5 Sun-Thurs / 12-2 Fri
   www.awkaufman.com
   Huge selection of bras, girdles, long lines, etc. They have every size available,
   if it's out there they will have it. Carrying all European brands, mens and
   womens. CREDIT CARDS.

Bra Tenders 212-957-7000
   630 Ninth Ave., Ste. 601 (44-45th St) Film Center Building   888-GET-ABRA
   NY, NY 10036   FAX 212-957-7010
   Hours: 10-6 Mon-Fri / or by appt.   E-mail: info@bratenders.com
   www.bratenders.com
   Theatrical and personal underwear for men and women. Very helpful with
   many years experience in the industry. If it is still available, Lori will order it
   for you. Supporter of Broadway Cares. CREDIT CARDS.

Louis Chock, Inc. 718-252-4340
   3011 Avenue J   800-222-0020
   Brooklyn, NY 11210   FAX 718-252-4360
   Hours: 9-5 Sun-Thurs / 9-3 Fri   E-mail: questions@chockcatalog.com
   www.chockcatalog.com
   Hosiery, underwear and sleepwear for the whole family. Catalog available.
   Phone orders. CREDIT CARDS.

Frederick's of Hollywood 800-323-9525
   6608 Hollywood Blvd.   FAX 602-760-2181
   Hollywood, CA 90028
   Hours: 8:30-8 Mon-Fri
   www.fredericks.com
   Sexy lingerie for women and men; bathing suits, hooker shoes and wigs.
   Catalog and shopping online. Over 200 stores, check the website for a store
   near you. CREDIT CARDS.

Gothic Renaissance 212-780-9558
   110 Fourth Ave. (11-12th St)   FAX 212-780-9560
   NY, NY 10003
   Hours: 11-8 Mon-Sat / 12-7 Sun   E-mail: gothicrenaissance@gmail.com
   www.gothicrenaissance.com
   Everything from the Gothic / Renaissance era. Modern with a Goth bend,
   Victorian costumes. Wonderful selection of Goth and glam corsets and
   masks. Small occult section. CREDIT CARDS.

Lismore Hosiery Company 212-674-3440
   334 Grand St. (Orchard-Ludlow St)   FAX 212-674-3974
   NY, NY 10002
   Hours: 12-6 Sun-Thurs / 10-2:45 Fri
   Complete line of hosiery for men, women, children; including tights, leotards,
   seamed stockings and pantyhose in all sizes. Will ship. CREDIT CARDS.

My Secret 212-877-8860
   145 W 71st St. (Columbus)   800-579-5389
   NY, NY 10023   FAX 212-799-8356
   Hours: 9:30-5:30 Mon-Thurs   E-mail: mysecret@verizon.net
   Breast Prostheses in natural and ethnic colors. All shapes and sizes. Also bras and wigs. Make an appointment for a fitting.

Period Corsets 206-264-0997
   PMB 5584 10002 Aurora Ave N # 36   877-226-7738
   Seattle, WA 98133   FAX 206-264-1657
   Hours: 9-6 Mon-Fri   E-mail: sales@periodcorsets.com
   www.periodcorsets.com
   Corsets for film and stage. Many styles and sizes available and other historic undergarments. Custom orders welcome.

Isaac Sultan & Sons 212-979-1645
   330 Grand St. (Ludlow-Orchard St)   (outside NYS) 800-999-1645
   NY, NY 10002   FAX 212-677-4215
   Hours: 9-5 Mon-Thurs / 9-2 Fri
   www.isaacsultan.com
   Discount lingerie and girdles. Phone orders. CREDIT CARDS.

CLOTHING: MEN'S & WOMEN'S
See also: CLOTHING: Antique & Vintage
               COSTUME RENTAL & CONSTRUCTION
               ETHNIC GOODS: All Headings
               SPORTING GOODS
               STUDIO SERVICES

Brooks Brothers 212-682-8800
   346 Madison Ave. (44th St)   800-274-1815
   NY, NY 10017   FAX 800-274-1010
   Hours: 8-8 Mon-Fri / 9-7 Sat / 11-7 Sun
   www.brooksbrothers.com
   The best in Ivy League menswear. Catalog available. Phone orders. CREDIT CARDS.

Canal Jean Co., Inc. 212-226-3663
   2236 Nostrand Ave. (Ave H-I)   718-421-7590
   Brooklyn, NY 11210   FAX 212-353-0261
   Hours: 10:30-7:30 Mon-Sat / 12-6 Sun
   Large vintage collection; casual clothing; good prices. Phone orders. CREDIT CARDS.

Chipp 2 212-687-0850
   11 E 44th St. (Madison-5th Ave)   FAX 973-706-7765
   NY, NY 10017
   Hours: 8-4 Mon-Fri / 9-3 Sat (except summers)   E-mail pwinstan@chipp2.com
   www.chipp2.com
   Carries kennel club collections of dog related products for humans. Cuff links, watches, belts, suspenders, pillows. CREDIT CARDS.

Conway Stores 212-967-3460
1345 Broadway(35-36th St)
NY, NY 10018
Hours: 8-8 Mon-Fri / 9:30-8 Sat / 10:30-7 Sun

450 Seventh Ave.(34-35th St)   212-967-1371
NY, NY 10001
Hours: 8-8 Mon-Sun

245 W 34th St.(7-8th Ave)   212-868-0002
NY, NY 10001
Hours: 8-8 Mon-Fri / 9:30-8 Sat / 10:30-7 Sun
Reasonably priced clothing, footwear and accessories and various housewares. Call 212-967-5300 for info on all locations. CREDIT CARDS.

Eisner Brothers 212-475-6868
75 Essex St. (Delancey-Broome St)   (outside NY) 800-426-7700
NY, NY 10002   FAX 212-475-6824
Hours: 8:30-6 Mon-Thurs / 8:30-1 Fri / 8:30-4:30 Sun
www.eisnerbros.com   E-mail: eisnerbros@yahoo.com
Caps, t-shirts, sweatshirts, jackets for football, baseball teams, etc.; catalog. No rentals. CREDIT CARDS.

Everything Goes 718-273-0568
17 Brook St.   FAX 718-448-6842
Staten Island, NY 10301
Hours: 10:30-6:30 Tue-Sat   E-mail: ganas@well.com
www.etgstores.com
Convenient to the ferry; 4 locations with a constantly changing stock of estate sale furniture, furnishings and some antiques. Contact Ellen Oppenheim. See web address for other locations. RENTALS. CREDIT CARDS.

Michael Salem Boutique 212-697-0644
300 E 46th St., 2nd Fl. (2nd Ave)   917-412-9739
NY, NY 10017
Hours: by appt only 24/7   E-mail: msaleminc@msn.com
www.michaelsalem.com
Complete line of ladies' clothing for men, including shoes and wigs. CREDIT CARDS.

Paul Stuart, Inc. 212-682-0320
Madison Ave. & 45th St.   800-678-8278
NY, NY 10017   FAX 212-983-2742
Hours: 8-6:30 Mon-Fri (Thurs until 7) / 9-6 Sat / 12-5 Sun
www.paulstuart.com   E-mail: service@paulstuart.com
Fashionable mens and womenswear. Phone orders. RENTALS. CREDIT CARDS.

Poppet 718-789-7890
121 St. Johns Place
Brooklyn, NY 11217
Hours: by appt.   E-mail: info@poppetnyc.com
www.poppetnyc.com
Men and Women's vintage clothing and accessories specializing from 1940s to early 1980s. RENTALS. CREDIT CARDS.

ATAC

Shirt Store, Inc. 212-557-8040
   51 E 44th St. (Vanderbilt-Mad Ave)   800-289-2744
   NY, NY 10017   FAX 212-557-1628
   Hours: 8-6:30 Mon-Fri / 10-5 Sat   E-mail: carol@shirtstore.com
   www.shirtstore.com
   Stock and custom men's shirts. Contact Matthew. Phone orders. CREDIT
   CARDS.

Syms Clothing 201-902-9600
   42 Trinity Pl.(Wall St)   212-797-1199
   NY, NY 10004
   Hours: 8-8 Mon-Fri / 10-6:30 Sat / 12-5:30 Sun

   400 Park Ave.(50-51st St)   212-317-8200
   NY, NY 10022
   Hours: 8-7:30 Mon-Fri / 10-6:30 Sat / 12-5:30 Sun
   www.syms.com   E-mail: customerservice@syms.com
   Great selection of men's and women's name-brand clothing; great prices.
   Check website for locations outside NYC. CREDIT CARDS.

Western Spirit 800-976-9287
   395 Broadway (Walker)   212-343-1476
   NY, NY 10013   FAX 212-343-0257
   Hours: 10:30-7:30 Mon-Fri / 11-8 Sat-Sun   E-mail: iwesternspiritj@yahoo.com
   www.westernspiritny.com
   Largest Western shop in NYC. Native American art, crafts, jewelry, pottery,
   leathercraft and headdresses. Western clothing in men's, women's and
   children's sizes. Toys. CREDIT CARDS.

CLOTHING: STUDIO SERVICES

Albright 212-977-7350
   62 Cooper Sq. (6-7th Ave)   212-375-1465
   NY, NY 10003
   Hours: By appt. only
   www.albrightnyc.com
   Over 4000 sq. ft. of top designer collections shoes and accessories. As the
   name implies, especially strong in shoes. Contact Irene Albright. RENTALS.
   CREDIT CARDS.

Banana Republic 212-751-5570
   130 E 59th St. (Lexington Ave)   FAX 212-751-8547
   NY, NY 10022
   Hours: 9-9 Mon-Sat / 11-7 Sun
   www.bananarepublic.com
   No cash accepted for studio services. Check your telephone directory or the
   website for locations of stores in your area. CREDIT CARDS.

Barney's New York 212-826-8900
660 Madison Ave.(60th-61st St)   (studio services) 212-833-2086
NY, NY 10021   FAX 212-833-2593
Hours: 10-8 Mon-Fri / 10-7 Sat / 11-6 Sun (Studio Services 10-7 Mon-Fri)
                                E-mail: info-madison@barneys.com

9570 Wilshire Blvd.   310-276-4400
Beverly Hills, CA 90212   FAX 310-777-5742
Hours: 10-7 Mon-Fri / 12-6 Sun   E-mail: info-beverlyhills@barneys.com
www.barneys.com
*Gorgeous and expensive men's and women's clothing and accessories.
Watch for great warehouse sales. Contact Joyce Villareal. See website for
other locations nationwide. CREDIT CARDS.*

Henri Bendel 212-247-1100
712 Fifth Ave. (55-56th St)
NY, NY 10019
Hours: 10-8 Mon-Sat / 12-7 Sun   E-mail: concierge@henribendel.com
www.henribendel.com
Personal Shopper Service. CREDIT CARDS.

Bergdorf Goodman 212-753-7300
754 Fifth Ave. (57-58th St)   (studio services) 212-872-8772
NY, NY 10019
Hours: 10-8 Mon-Sat (Sat until 7) / 12-6 Sun
www.bergdorfgoodman.com
*High-fashion clothing department store. Contact Betty Halbreich for both
men's and women's studio services, by appt. only. CREDIT CARDS.*

Bloomingdales 212-705-2000
1000 Third Ave. (59th St)   (Studio Services) 212-705-3673
NY, NY 10022   FAX 212-705-3939
Hours: 10-6 Mon-Fri
www.bloomingdales.com
*Men's, women's and plus-size fashions. Helpful and pleasant. Will need to
set up account. Contact Barbara D-Arsanel.*

Bra Tenders 212-957-7000
630 Ninth Ave., Ste. 601 (44-45th St) Film Center Building   888-GET-ABRA
NY, NY 10036   FAX 212-957-7010
Hours: 10-6 Mon-Fri / or by appt.   E-mail: info@bratenders.com
www.bratenders.com
*Theatrical and personal underwear for men and women. Very helpful with
many years experience in the industry. If it is still available, Lori will order it
for you. Supporter of Broadway Cares. CREDIT CARDS.*

The Gap, Inc. - Studio Services 818-762-9192
12169 Ventura Blvd.   FAX 818-762-9194
Studio City, CA 91604
Hours: by appt.
*Studio Service program available. Check your telephone directory for regular
retail stores in your area. No cash accepted for studio services. CREDIT
CARDS.*

Guess?, Inc. 212-730-7200
　　1385 Broadway (37-38th St)
　　NY, NY 10018
　　Hours: 8-5:30 Mon-Fri
　　www.guess.com
　　Fashion conscious clothing for young adults. Corporate office.

Lord & Taylor 212-391-3344
　　424 Fifth Ave. (38-39th St)　　　　　　(studio services) 212-391-3519
　　NY, NY 10018
　　Hours: 10-8:30 Mon-Tue, Thur-Fri / 9-8:30 Wed / 10-7 Sat / 11-7 Sun
　　www.lordandtaylor.com
　　Red Rose Shopping Service. Men's and women's clothing, accessories.
　　Traditional and well priced. CREDIT CARDS.

Saks Fifth Ave. Studio Service . . . .(studio services) 212-940-4560
　　611 Fifth Ave.(49-50th St)　　　　　　　　(store) 212-753-4000
　　NY, NY 10022
　　Hours: 10-6 Mon-Fri

　　9600 Wilshire Blvd.　　　　　　　　　　　(store) 310-275-4211
　　Beverly Hills, CA 90212
　　Hours: 10-6 Mon-Fri (10-8:30 Thurs) / 10-7 Sat / 12-6 Sun
　　www.sacksfifthavenue.com
　　Fashionable clothing and accessories for men, women, children. Great memo
　　service for stylists and costume designers. Also linens and home furnishings.
　　CREDIT CARDS.

Showroom Seven 212-643-4810
　　263 Eleventh Ave.　　　　　　　　　　　FAX 212-971-6066
　　NY, NY 10018
　　Hours: 9-6 Mon-Fri
　　Extensive selection of designer fashions; shoes, handbags, hats, gloves, belts
　　and scarves. List of designers they carry available upon request. CREDIT
　　CARDS.

CLOTHING: UNIFORMS - ATHLETIC & SCHOOL

BQ Sports, Inc. 718-349-3528
　　601 Manhattan Ave. (Nassau - Driggs)　　　FAX 718-389-0143
　　Brooklyn, NY 11040
　　Hours: 10:30-7:30 Mon-Sat　　　　　E-mail: gmax907@msn.com
　　Custom logo design, embroidery, screen printing, chenille work. CREDIT
　　CARDS.

Gerry Cosby & Co., Inc. 212-563-6464
　　1110 Penn Plaza (31st St Between 6-7th Ave)　　　877-563-6464
　　NY, NY 10001　　　　　　　　　　　　FAX 212-967-0876
　　Hours: 9:30-6 Mon-Fri　　　　　　　E-mail: gemsg@aol.com
　　www.cosbysports.com
　　Athletic outfitters for official sports uniforms. Sell and apply iron on
　　numbers and letters. Some vintage uniform pieces. Sales only. Phone
　　orders. CREDIT CARDS.

Craft Clothes 800-425-3466
   247 W 37th St., 17th Fl. (7-8th Ave)   FAX 212-685-3503
   NY, NY 10018
   Hours: 9:30-5:30 Mon-Fri / 9:30-1 Sat   E-mail: info@duffyandquinn.com
   www.duffyandquinn.com
   School uniforms, caps and gowns, judicial robes; also clerical apparel. Phone orders. Will ship. RENTALS. CREDIT CARDS.

Frank Bee Enterprises, Inc. 718-823-9475
   3439 E Tremont Ave. (off I-95/Bruckner)   800-372-6523
   Bronx, NY 10465   FAX 718-823-9812
   Hours: 9-6 Mon-Sat / 10-4 Sun   E-mail: uniforms@msn.com
   www.frankbee.com
   School, cheerleading, Scout uniforms and accessories. Caps and gowns, choir robes, judicial robes and clerical vestments. All military uniforms; dress, camouflage and parade. RENTALS. CREDIT CARDS.

Frank's Sport Shop . . . .(Store) 718-299-9628
   430 E Tremont Ave. (Park Ave)   (Office) 212-945-0020
   Bronx, NY 10457   FAX 718-583-1652
   Hours: 9-8 Mon-Fri / 9-6 Sat   E-mail: info@frankssports.com
   www.frankssports.com
   Baseball, football uniforms and equipment; sporting goods. Catalog available online. RENTALS. CREDIT CARDS.

Ideal 718-252-5090
   1816 Flatbush Ave.(Avenue K)   FAX 718-692-0492
   Brooklyn, NY 11210
   Hours: 9-7:30 Mon-Fri / 10-7 Sat / 11-6 Sun

   1575 Unionport Rd.   718-239-4010
   Bronx, NY 10462
   Hours: 10-7 Mon-Sat / 10:30-5:30 Sun
   www.idealuniform.com
   School, camp, scout and cheerleading uniforms; caps and gowns, teen's clothing. Will ship. No rentals. CREDIT CARDS.

Levy's Sports Center 201-861-7100
   6116 Bergenline Ave., 2nd Fl.   FAX 201-861-8836
   West New York, NJ 07093
   Hours: 10-6 Mon-Fri / 10-3 Sat   E-mail: levysports@verizon.net
   Sports uniforms, t-shirts, jackets, etc. Retail and custom. Also custom pads and matting. Will ship. CREDIT CARDS.

Peacock's Marching World 928-692-2263
   4755 Olympic Dr.   800-733-2263
   Kingman, AZ 86401   FAX 928-692-2270
   Hours: 9-5:30 Mon-Fri / Call on Saturdays   E-mail: sales@marchingworld.com
   www.marchingworld.com
   Marching props and accessories for bands and colorguards including hats, gloves, marching shoes and prop rifles. CREDIT CARDS.

The Queensboro Shirt Co. 910-251-1251
1400 Marstellar St.   800-847-4478
Wilmington, NC 28401   FAX 910-251-7771
Hours: 8-6 Mon-Fri   E-mail: service@queensboro.com
www.queensboro.com

Quantity purchase of cotton polos, sweatshirts, jackets and golf towels; many sizes and several colors; will embroider your logo; catalog. CREDIT CARDS.

CLOTHING: UNIFORMS - LAW ENFORCEMENT & SERVICE INDUSTRIES

Allan Uniform Rental 212-529-4655
121 E 24th St., 7th Fl. (Lexington-Park Ave)   FAX 212-505-7781
NY, NY 10010
Hours: 9-5 Mon-Fri   E-mail: ibussuniform@aol.com
www.ibuss-allan.com

Police and doorman uniforms. RENTALS. CREDIT CARDS.

Brigade Quartermasters, Ltd. / Ira Green, Inc. 800-663-7487
177 Georga Ave.   800-228-7344
Providence, RI 02905   FAX 800-738-8522
Hours: 8-4:30 Mon-Sat   E-mail: critter @iragreen.com
www.brigadequartermasters.com

Combat, SWAT uniforms and accessories; survival, camping, climbing, hunting and expedition gear, outdoor action gear. Online catalog. No rentals. CREDIT CARDS.

Costume Rentals Corp. 800-400-7444
11149 Vanowen St.   818-753-3700
N. Hollywood, CA 91605   FAX 818-753-3737
Hours: 8 - 6 M-F   E-mail: crcresearch@hughes.net
www.costumerentalscorp.com

All types of uniforms for rent only. Will ship. Only RENTALS. CREDIT CARDS.

Dornan Uniforms 516-536-8800
265 Sunrise Hwy, Ste. 1-313   800-223-0363
Rockville Centre, NY 11570   FAX 516-536-9455
Hours: 8:30-4 Mon-Fri (Thurs until 6)   E-mail: sales@dornanuniforms.com
www.dornanuniforms.com

Complete line of uniforms and accessories, in stock and custom; chauffeur, butler, maid, doormen, janitorial, police, security, fire, medical, etc. Will ship. No rentals. CREDIT CARDS (with phone orders).

Ideal 718-252-5090
1816 Flatbush Ave.(Avenue K)   FAX 718-692-0492
Brooklyn, NY 11210
Hours: 9-7:30 Mon-Fri / 10-7 Sat / 11-6 Sun

1575 Unionport Rd.   718-239-4010
Bronx, NY 10462
Hours: 10-7 Mon-Sat / 10:30-5:30 Sun
www.idealuniform.com

Full line of medical apparel including scrubs, lab coats, nurses uniforms, etc. CREDIT CARDS.

O.K. Uniforms Co. 212-791-9789
253 Church St. (Franklin-Leonard)   FAX 212-791-9795
NY, NY 10013
Hours: 9:45-5:45 Mon-Thurs / 9:45-2 Fri / 12-4 Sun
www.okuniform.com   E-mail: okuniform@gmail.com
Complete selection of uniforms and accessories for all service industries.
Name and logo emblems available. Sales only. CREDIT CARDS.

Scafati Uniforms, Inc. 212-695-4944
417A W 44th St. (9-10th Ave)   FAX: 212-695-4944
NY, NY 10036
Hours: 11-7 Mon-Sat
Doorman, bellboy, waiter outfits to purchase; also custom orders. Top quality,
pleasant service, reasonable rates. CREDIT CARDS.

B. Schlesinger & Sons, Inc. 212-206-8022
249 W 18th St. (7-8th Ave)   FAX 212-206-8559
NY, NY 10011
Hours: 9:30-6 Mon-Thurs / 9:30-5 Fri   E-mail: schlesingeruniforms@verizon.net
www.schlesingeruniforms.com
Police, security guard, emergency medical service and postal uniforms;
workclothes; accessories. Phone orders. No rentals. CREDIT CARDS.

Uniforms by Park Coats, Inc. 718-499-1182
790 Third Ave., # 718 (27th St)   718-499-8016
Brooklyn, NY 11232   FAX 718-499-1646
Hours: 9-5 Mon-Fri / 9-1 Sat
www.uniformsbypark.com
Manufacturer of police, fire and law enforcement uniforms-all styles-shoes
and accessories. No rentals. CREDIT CARDS.

Yankee Linen Service 973-278-1225
63 2nd Ave.   FAX 973-278-5145
Paterson, NJ 07514
Hours: 8-5:30 Mon-Fri
www.yankeelinen.com
Yankee Linen can provide you with many different services from table linens,
uniforms, floor mats, restroom supplies, and much more. Delivery.
RENTALS. CREDIT CARDS.

CLOTHING: UNIFORMS - MILITARY

Battlezone Exchange 203-795-8387
371 Boston Post Rd.   FAX 203-795-1158
Orange, CT 06477
Hours: 10-6 Mon-Sat / 11-4 Sun   E-mail: daysdudley@yahoo.com
Military dress uniforms, battle fatigues, boots, medals, ribbons, military
surplus and accessories; mostly Vietnam items, some WWII items also. Phone
orders. CREDIT CARDS.

Church St. Surplus 212-226-5280
327 Church St. (Canal-Lispinard St)
NY, NY 10013
Hours: 10:30-6 Mon-Sat (closed in July / No Sat in Aug)
A good supply of Army/Navy surplus, all antique military. CREDIT CARDS.

The Duffle Bag 845-878-7106
1270 Rte. 311   FAX 845-878-7106
Patterson, NY 12563
Hours: 10-7 Mon-Sat / 10-5 Sun   E-mail: info@dufflebaginc.com
www.dufflebaginc.com
Military uniforms: USA and foreign, WW1-1991. Also vehicles, equipment,
props, etc. Technical advising, all wars. Sales and RENTALS. CREDIT CARDS.

Frank's Sport Shop . . . .(Store) 718-299-9628
430 E Tremont Ave. (Park Ave)   (Office) 212-945-0020
Bronx, NY 10457   FAX 718-583-1652
Hours: 9-8 Mon-Fri / 9-6 Sat   E-mail: info@frankssports.com
www.frankssports.com
Military uniforms and insignia; postal, police, sanitation, parks dept., traffic,
corrections, baseball, football uniforms and equipment; sporting goods,
hunting and archery equipment. Catalog available online. RENTALS. CREDIT
CARDS.

G. Gedney Godwin, Inc. 610-783-0670
P.O. Box 100   FAX 610-783-6083
Valley Forge, PA 19481
Hours: 9:30-4:30 Mon-Fri   E-mail: sales@gggodwin.com
www.gggodwin.com
18th century military gear and accessories; catalog. See Tina Perkins. Catalog.
CREDIT CARDS.

Government Surplus Sales, Inc. 860-247-7787
69 Francis Ave.   FAX 860-586-8020
Hartford, CT 06106
Hours: 10-5:30 Mon-Fri / Sat by appt.   E-mail: government@snet.net
www.aviationhelmets.com
Manufacturers and sell all types of helmets. New and used government issue
military uniforms (WWI through present), military surplus, flight equipment,
etc. See David Schweitzer. CREDIT CARDS.

Iceberg of Soho Army-Navy 212-226-8485
452 Broadway (Grand-Canal St)   FAX 212-274-1816
NY, NY 10013-2575
Hours: 10-7 Mon-Fri / 11-7 Sat-Sun
www.icebergarmynavy.com
Good selection of Army/Navy surplus clothes, boots, etc. RENTALS. CREDIT
CARDS.

Kaufman's Army & Navy 212-757-5670
    319 W 42nd St. (8-9th Ave)   FAX 212-757-9686
    NY, NY 10036
    Hours: 11-6 Mon-Wed / 11-7 Thurs / 12-6 Sat
    www.kaufmansarmynavy.com
    RENTALS and SALES of military uniforms and equipment. Also, related props,
    work clothes, Levi's and boots. Popular among costumers and stylists.
    Contact Jim for special orders. Very informative website.

Quartermaster 800-444-8643
    750 Long Beach Blvd.   562-436-6247
    Long Beach, CA 90813
    Hours: 9-6 Mon-Fri / 9-5:30 Sat

    2543 W 6th St.   213-351-9632
    Los Angeles, CA 90057
    Hours: 9-6 Mon-Fri / 9-5:30 Sat

    623 W 17th St.   714-285-0300
    Santa Ana, CA 92706
    Hours: 9-6 Mon-Fri / 9-5:30 Sat

    3879 Spring Mountain Rd.   702-364-1500
    Las Vegas, NV 98102
    Hours: 9-6 Mon-Fri / 9-5:30 Sat   E-mail: help@qmuniforms.com
    www.qmuniforms.com
    Law enforcement and medical uniforms. CREDIT CARDS.

The Sentry Post 610-520-1283
    222 Ashwood Rd. (office)   610-842-2609
    Villanova, PA 19085   FAX 610-520-1284
    Hours: 9:15-5:30 Mon-Fri by appt.
    Authentic historic or military wardrobe, made to order or rental. Very
    knowledgeable and helpful over the phone; also historic and military props
    (accoutrements and swords).

Some's Uniforms 201-843-1199
    314 Main St. (East Berry St)   FAX 201-843-3014
    Hackensack, NJ 07601
    Hours: 9-5 Mon-Fri / 9-1 Sat   E-mail: someunif@somes.com
    www.somes.com
    Uniforms, accessories and related items for the military, law enforcement,
    firemen and service industries. Catalog. Phone orders. CREDIT CARDS.

Strand Surplus Center 409-762-7397
    2202 Strand   800-231-6005
    Galveston, TX 77550   FAX 409-762-7396
    Hours: 10-4 Tue- Sat   E-mail: emailrequest@colbubbie.com
    www.colbubbie.com
    Military uniforms from the Revolutionary War through Iraqi Freedom. CREDIT
    CARDS.

James Townsend & Son 800-338-1665
   PO Box 415, 133 N First St.   574-594-5852
   Pierceton, IN 46562   FAX 574-594-5580
   Hours: 9-5 Mon-Fri   E-mail: jastown@jastown.com
   www.jastown.com
   18th and 19th century military uniforms, clothing, hats, patterns, guns,
   pistols, knives, axes, barrels, kegs, baskets, blankets, lanterns; repro colonial
   household goods; catalog. CREDIT CARDS.

Weiss & Mahoney 212-675-1915
   142 Fifth Ave. (19th St)   FAX 212-633-8573
   NY, NY 10011
   Hours: 9-6:30 Mon-Fri / 9-5 Sat
   www.weissmahoney.com
   Inexpensive military clothing and surplus goods; shoes, medals, camping
   attire and equipment. No rentals. CREDIT CARDS.

COINS & CURRENCIES

Brigandi Coin Co. 212-869-5350
   60 W 44th St. (5-6th Ave)   FAX 212-869-5359
   NY, NY 10036
   Hours: 9-5 Mon-Fri   E-mail: info@brigandicoin.com
   www.brigandicoin.com
   Coin and paper money, including foreign; also baseball cards. RENTALS.
   CREDIT CARDS.

Dory Development 518-854-7613
   PO Box 546 / 408 Carney Cassidy Road   FAX 518-854-7613
   Salem, NY 12865
   Hours: 8:-3 Mon-Fri   E-mail: info@dorydevelopment.com
   www.dorydevelopment.com
   Coin reproductions; including Greek, Roman, U.S., foreign, civil war, biblical,
   pirate. Catalog.

Historical Document Co. 215-533-4500
   2555 Orthodox St.   888-700-7265
   Philadelphia, PA 19137   FAX 215-533-9319
   Hours: 8:30-4:30 Mon-Fri   E-mail: info@histdocs.com
   www.histdocs.com
   Replicas of historical documents and currency. Quill pens. Good friendly and
   helpful people.

Jules J. Karp Coins & Bullion, Inc. .212-943-5770
   125 Maiden Ln.   FAX 212-785-4675
   NY, NY 10038
   Hours: 9-5 Mon-Fri   E-mail: juleskarp2@aol.com
   www.juelskarpcoinsandbullioninc.com
   Rare coins and bullion, currency and jewelry. Buy backs possible. RENTALS.

Stack's 212-582-2580
123 W 57th St. (6-7th Ave)   800-566-2580
NY, NY 10019   FAX 212-245-5018
Hours: 10-5 Mon-Fri   E-mail: info@stacks.com
www.stacks.com
Foreign and U.S. coins and currency. Also books and some publications.
Catalog.

COMPUTERS & BUSINESS MACHINES

Ace Video & Props 718-392-1100
37-24 24th St., Ste. 106 (Houston & West St)   212-206-1475
Long Island City, NY 11101   FAX 718-392-1155
Hours: 10-6 Mon-Fri / 10-2 Sat by appt.
                E-mail: acevideorentals@gmail.com / acepropsnyc@gmail.com
www.aceprops.com
Practical & dummy credit card terminals, time clocks, laptop/desktop
computers. RENTALS. CREDIT CARDS.

All Care Business Machine, Inc. 212-431-3200
184 Bowery (Spring-Delancey St)   866-431-3200
NY, NY 10012   FAX 212-219-1744
Hours: 8-5 Mon-Fri / 9-4 Sat   E-mail: info@acbm-inc.com
www.acbm-inc.com
New and used cash registers, restaurant equipment and safes. RENTAL.
CREDIT CARDS.

American Copy Machines, Inc. 212-244-2727
141 W 28th St., 10th Fl. (6-7th Ave)   888-992-2666
New York, NY 10001   FAX 212-244-2739
Hours: 9-5 Mon-Fri   E-mail: mf@americancopymachines.com
www.americancopymachines.com
Rental, leasing and sales of copiers, printers and fax machines. Offering sales,
service and supplies in a moments notice. RENTALS.

Computer Rent, Inc. 212-619-6363
225 Broadway (Barclay St)   800-872-2983
NY, NY 10007   FAX 212-619-6844
Hours: 9-6 Mon-Fri   E-mail: rentapcnow@aol.com
Computers, printers in all shapes and sizes; working or props. Can do
custom configurations from large inventory. Rental of LCD panels, plasma
screens, projectors. Willing to work with customers. RENTALS. CREDIT
CARDS.

J & R Music & Computer World 212-238-9000
15-23 Park Row (Beekman-Ann St)   800-221-3191
NY, NY 10038   FAX 212-238-9191
Hours: 9-7:30 Mon-Sat / 10:30-6:30 Sun
www.jr.com
Computers and home office outlet. Good selection of software. Large
Macintosh showroom. Catalog. CREDIT CARDS.

Smart Source 201-5568-6555
 600 Sylvan Ave.   800-888-8686
 Englewood Cliffs, NJ 07632   FAX 201-568-4448
 Hours: 8:30-6 Mon-Fri / deliveries available on weekends
                                    E-mail: info@smartsourcerentals.com
 www.rentapcny.com
 *Desktop computers, monitors, printers, notebook computers, fax machines,
 desktop copiers and other business equipment. Check website for over 22
 additional locations in USA. RENTALS. CREDIT CARDS.*

Tekserve 212-929-3645
 119 W 23rd St. (6-7th Ave)   FAX 212-463-9280
 NY, NY 10011
 Hours: 9-8 Mon-Fri / 10-6 Sat / 12-6 Sun   E-mail: sales@tekserve.com
 www.tekserve.com
 Mac repair. Very helpful, fair prices.

Wetkeys.com 866-938-5397
 44 25th St. NW   FAX 866-938-5397
 Atlanta, GA 30309
 Hours: 9-6 Mon-Fri   E-mail: sales@wetkeys.com
 www.wetkeys.com
 *World's largest source and lowest prices for waterproof computer keyboards,
 touchpads, flexible travel keyboards and accessories. Great for field use and
 location shoots. CREDIT CARDS.*

COPY, BLUEPRINTING & OUTPUT CENTERS

57th St. Copy Center 212-581-8046
 119 W 57th St. Rm1010 (6-7th Ave)   FAX 212-246-7095
 NY, NY 10019
 Hours: 9-5:30 Mon-Thurs / 8:30-1 Fri / call for Sun hours
                                          E-mail: copy57@aol.com
 Full-service photocopying, color copies from slides. No credit cards.

Atlantic Blue Print Co., Inc. 212-755-3388
 575 Madison Ave. (57th St)   FAX 212-751-5598
 NY, NY 10022
 Hours: 8:30-5 Mon-Fri (machines stop at 4:30)
 www.atlanticblueprint.com
 *Blueprinting, offset, photocopies, including color Xerox. PC-based AutoCad
 along with printing and plotting. Pick-up and delivery if you have a charge
 account.*

BPI Reprographics 212-686-2436
 295 Madison Ave.(41st St)   FAX 212-532-8397
 NY, NY 10017
 Hours: 7:30-6 Mon-Fri

 11 Broadway, 9th FL(Morris-Beaver)   212-514-8010
 NY, NY 10006   FAX 212-514-0838
 Hours: 9-8 Mon-Fri

BPI Reprographics (cont.) 212-686-2436
853 Broadway, 5th FL (Administrative Offices)   212-777-1110
NY, NY 10003   FAX 212-777-0880
Hours: Administrative Offices Only   E-mail: info@bpirepro.com
www.bpirepro.com
Blue prints, B&W and color copying, photo stats, etc. Mac and IBM plotting.
CREDIT CARDS.

Coloredge Visual 212-594-4800
127 W 30th St.   800-321-8864
NY, NY 10011   FAX 212-594-4488
Hours: 24-hrs.   E-mail: sales@coloredgevisual.com
www.coloredgevisual.com
Transfers, bubble, duplicating chromes, photo CDs and Mac and PC output.

Copy 4less / Sir Speedy 212-564-9320
234 W 35th St. (7-8th Ave)   FAX 212-564-9336
NY, NY 10001
Hours: 8-7:30 Mon-Fri   E-mail: sirspeedynyc@earthlink.net
B&W and color copying, Mac output, giant photocopies. Contact Pete or
Shabir. CREDIT CARDS.

Copy Access DBA East Side Copy 212-807-0465
15 E 13th St. (5th-Univ Pl)   800-959-COPY
NY, NY 10003   FAX 212-463-0232
Hours: 8-10 pm Mon-Fri / 10-8 Sat / 12-8 Sun   E-mail: print@eastsidecopy.com
www.eastsidecopy.com
B&W and color copying, Kodak Ektaprint and Mac output. CREDIT CARDS.

A. Esteban & Co. 212-989-7000
136 W 21st St., 3rd Fl.(6-7th Ave)   FAX 212-989-6087
NY, NY 10011
Hours: 9-5:30 Mon-Fri   E-mail: plotting21@esteban.com

132 W 36th St.(6-7th Ave)   212-714-2227
NY, NY 10018   FAX 212-714-1387
Hours: 9-5:30 Mon-Fri

701 W Broad St.   703-532-6090
Falls Church, VA 22046   FAX 703-532-7548
Hours: 9-5:30 Mon-Fri
www.esteban.com
Blueprints, sepias, giant photocopies to 24" and color copies. Pick-up and
delivery service available with account. CREDIT CARDS.

Ever Ready Blue Print 212-228-3131
200 Park Ave. S, 13th Fl. (17th St)   212-228-3132
NY, NY 10003   FAX 212-505-8083
Hours: 8:30-6:30 Mon-Fri / 10-5 Sat   E-mail: submit@everreadyblueprint.com
www.everreadyblueprint.com
The best and quickest service in town. Bluelines, sepias, mylar prints; color
copies, photostats; giant photocopies to 36" wide (variable
enlargement/reduction) on bond, vellum and mylar film, plotting service, also
computer-based services. Flier. CREDIT CARDS.

FedEx Kinko's 800-254-6567
800-GO-FEDEX

1211 Sixth Ave.(47th St) 212-391-2679
NY, NY 10020 FAX 212-391-0263
Hours: 24 Mon-Fri / 9-12 Sun E-mail: usa0264@fedexkinkos.com

21 Astor Pl.(Lafayette-B'way) 212-228-9511
NY, NY 10003 FAX 212-228-9281
Hours: 7-12am Mon-Fri / 8-12am Sat-Sun E-mail: usa0230@fedexkinkos.com

191 Madison Ave.(34-35th St) 212-685-3449
NY, NY 10016 FAX 212-685-3831
Hours: 7-11 Daily E-mail: usa0202@fedexkinkos.com

1122 Lexington Ave.(78th St) 212-628-5500
NY, NY 10021 FAX 212-628-6703
Hours: 24 hours daily E-mail: usa0219@fedexkinkos.com

100 Wall St.(Water St) 212-269-0024
NY, NY 10005 FAX 212-269-1225
Hours: 7-10 Mon-Fri E-mail: usa0346@fedexkinkos.com

600 Third Ave.(39th St) 212-599-2679
NY, NY 10016 FAX 212-599-1733
Hours: 7-11pm Mon-Fri / 8-11pm Sat-Sun E-mail: usa0268@fedexkinkos.com

250 E Houston St.(Avenue A-B) 212-253-9020
NY, NY 10002 FAX 212-253-9029
Hours: 7-11 Mon-Fri / 8-8 Sat-Sun E-mail: usa0267@fedexkinkos.com

105 Duane St.(B'way-Church St) 212-406-1220
NY, NY 10007 FAX 212-406-1216
Hours: 7-11 Daily E-mail: usa0231@fedexkinkos.com

16 E 52nd St.(Madison Ave) 212-308-2679
NY, NY 10022 FAX 212-838-8065
Hours: 24 Hrs. E-mail: usa0212@fedexkinkos.com

245 Seventh Ave.(24th St) 212-929-0623
NY, NY 10001 FAX 212-929-1560
Hours: 12am-11pm Mon-Thurs / 12am-7pm Fri / 24 hrs Sat-Sun
E-mail: usa0203@fedexkinkos.com

221 W 72nd St.(B'way-West End Ave) 212-362-5288
NY, NY 10023 FAX 212-362-3546
Hours: 24 hours daily E-mail: usa0812@fedexkinkos.com

240 Central Park S(Columbus Circle) 212-258-3750
NY, NY 10019 FAX 212-258-3381
Hours: 24 hours daily E-mail: usa0763@fedexkinkos.com
www.kinkos.com

Part of the huge international chain. Full-service. B&W and color copies, FAX service, business cards, self-service copiers and desktop publishing. To find the location nearest you anywhere in the USA call 800-2-KINKOS of visit the website. CREDIT CARDS.

C

Hart Multi-Copy, Inc. 212-704-0556
555 Eighth Ave (37-38th St)   FAX 212-704-0003
NY, NY 10018
Hours: 9-5 Mon-Fri   E-mail: brett@hartrepro.com
www.hartrepro.com
Photocopying, offset printing, typesetting. Plotting from Mac-based.

National Reprographics, Inc. 212-366-7250
44 W 18th St.(5-6th Ave)   FAX 212-691-1264
NY, NY 10011
Hours: 8-5 Mon-Sat   E-mail: csr.18@nrinet.com

1064 Jackson Ave.(49-50th)   718-784-1792
Long Island City, NY 11101
Hours: 8-4:30 Mon-Fri   E-mail: csr.queens@nrinet.com

193 Joralemon St.(Court-Clinton)   718-875-0696
Brooklyn, NY 11201
Hours: 8-5 Mon-Fri   E-mail: csr.brooklyn@nrinet.com
www.nrinet.com
*Blueprinting, photostats, photocopies-color, B&W and color acetate. See
web address for other locations. CREDIT CARDS.*

Park Heights Stationers Copy Center 718-398-0202
164 Park Pl. (Flatbush-7th Ave)   FAX 718-622-3860
Brooklyn, NY 11217
Hours: 9-7:30 Mon-Fri / 10-7:30 Sat / 12-5 Sun
Copy service, color, B&W; commercial stationer, stationery supplies.

Park Slope Typing & Copy Center 718-783-0268
123 Seventh Ave. (President-Carroll St)   FAX 718-622-8373
Brooklyn, NY 11215
Hours: 8:30-7 Mon-Fri / 10-6 Sat / 11:30-5 Sun   E-mail: pscc@nyc.rr.com
*Typing, word processing, color and B&W copies, printing. Mac and PC output,
engineer and shipping. CREDIT CARDS.*

Pro Print Copy Center 212-354-0400
260 W. 36th St., 5th FL (7-8th Ave)   FAX 212-768-3550
NY, NY 10018
Hours: 8:30-5:30 Mon-Fri   E-mail: 18W45@pro-print.com
www.pro-print.com
*Printing, photocopying, color photocopies, typesetting, binding and
layout/design.*

The Village Copier 212-666-0600
2872 Broadway(111-112th St)   FAX 212-666-0691
NY, NY 10003
Hours: 8-11 Mon-Thrus / 8-9pm Fri / 9-10 Sat-Sun
                            E-mail: broadway@villagegroup.com

25 W 43rd St.(5-6th Ave)   212-220-6143
NY, NY 10036   FAX 212-666-0691
Hours: 8:30-6:30 Mon-Fri   E-mail: digital@villagecopier.com

The Village Copier (cont.) 212-869-9665
   10 East 39th St. (main office)(5th-Mad Ave)   FAX 212-655-4322
   NY, NY 10036
   Hours: 24 hours Daily
   www.villagecopier.com
   Copies, Canon color, laser copies, FAX service and resumes. Mac and PC
   based. CREDIT CARDS.

CORK

American Star Cork Co., Inc. 718-335-3000
   33-53 62nd St. (34th Ave)   800-338-3581
   Woodside, NY 11377   FAX 718-335-3037
   Hours: 8-4:45 Mon-Fri   E-mail: info@amstarcork.com
   www.amstarcork.com
   Cork for bottles and fishing poles. Cork sheets. Can order stamping or
   custom shapes. $50 minimum. No credit cards.

Aywon Chalkboard, Inc., DBA The Cork Store 718-853-2300
   P.O. Box 280088 (Ocean Pkwy-Coney Island Ave)   FAX 718-238-0684
   Brooklyn, NY 11228
   Hours: 8-4 Mon-Thurs / 8-12 Fri
   www.aywon.com
   Rolls of cork, bottle cork, laminate thicknesses. Custom orders. CREDIT
   CARDS.

Sommer Cork Company 800-242-0808
   259 W 61st St.   630-852-8500
   Westmont, IL 60559   FAX 630-852-8502
   Hours: 9-4:30 Mon-Fri   E-mail: info@sommercork.com
   www.sommercork.com
   Cork stoppers and bulletin board cork. No credit cards.

Wolf-Gordon Wallcovering, Inc. 800-347-0550
   33-00 47th Ave.(33-34th St) offices   718-391-4800
   Long Island City, NY 11101   FAX 718-361-1090
   Hours: 8:30-7 Mon-Fri

   979 Third Ave., Rm 413(58-59th St) Showroom   212-319-6800
   NY, NY 10022
   Hours: 9:30-4:30 Mon-Fri

   8687 Melrose Ave., Ste BM5(N Sweetzer & N Harper Ave)   310-652-1914
   Los Angeles, CA 90069
   Hours: 9-4 Mon-Fri

   200 World Trade Ctr.(Merchandise Mart # 10-61)   312-755-1892
   Chicago, IL 60654
   Hours: 9-5 Mon-Fri   E-mail: info@wolf-gordon.com
   www.wolf-gordon.com
   Wallcoverings: vinyl, cork, acoustical, wood veneers, paperbacked fabric; at
   showroom. To the trade, account required. CREDIT CARDS.

COSTUME CONSTRUCTION SHOPS

ADELE RECKLIES CO. 718-768-9036
420 Fourth Ave. #1 (7-8th St)   FAX (same)
Brooklyn, NY 11215
Hours: by appt.   E-mail: knitter718@earthlink.net
www.beadcrochetsnakes.com
Custom knitwear for theater and film; crocheting and beading. Member ATAC.

Behrle NYC 212-279-5626
440 W 34th St # 4B (9-10th Aves)
NY, NY 10001
Hours: by appt. only   E-mail: behryenyc@gmail.com
www.behrlenyc.com
Custom leather clothing ranging from corsetry, cordovan lacing, applique etc. Original designs for the home including curtains, upholstery and pillows. Member IATSE USA Local 829. RENTALS. CREDIT CARDS.

Carelli Costumes, Inc. 212-765-6166
109 W 26th St., 2nd Fl. (6-7th Ave)   Fax: 212-765-6168
NY, NY 10001
Hours: By appt.
Custom costume construction for theater, dance, film and TV. Custom millinery.

Costumes and Creatures 612-378-2561
504 Malcolm Ave. SE, Ste. 200   FAX 612-378-2635
Minneapolis, MN 55414
Hours: 8-4:45 CST   E-mail: info@vee.com
www.vee.com
A division of VEE Corp., producer of Sesame Street Live Tours; specializing in full body character and animal costumes; period garments, accessories, soft props. Custom design and construction.

Donna Langman Costumes 212-382-2558
520 W 27th St., #301 (10-11th Ave)   FAX 212-382-0937
NY, NY 10001
Hours: 10-6 Mon-Fri / or by appt.   E-mail: donna@donnalangman.com
A full-service costume shop; exquisite work.

Eric Winterling, Inc. 212-629-7686
20 W 20th St., 5th Fl (5-6th Ave)   FAX 212-629-7543
NY, NY 10011
Hours: by appt.   E-mail: ewinter216@aol.com
Custom work for theatre, film, opera and dance. Specializing in all aspects of costume construction. No RENTALS.

Euro Co. Costumes, Inc. 212-629-9665
254 W 35th St., 15th Fl (7-8th Ave)   FAX 212-629-9608
NY, NY 10001
Hours: 9-6 Mon-Fri / or by appt.   E-mail: euroconyc@aol.com
Costume construction for film, theatre and TV. Chain-mail rentals only.

Stephanie Handler 212-268-9817
555 Eighth Ave., Ste. 2009 (37-38th St)
NY, NY 10018
Hours: By appt., please call   E-mail: shandler1@verizon.net
*Specializing in design and construction of theatrical costumes, skating
competition garments and other athletic clothing. CREDIT CARDS.*

Yvette Helin Studio 718-389-8797
1205 Manhattan Ave., Unit 136 (New Town Creek)   Cell 917-617-5935
Brooklyn, NY 11222
Hours: 9-5 Mon-Fri, or by appt.   E-mail: yvette@yvettehelinstudio.com
www.yvettehelinstudio.com
Entertainment costume designer, maker. Specialty costumes.

Imagination Costumes 702-362-3096
4350 Arville St., Ste. 15B   FAX 702-362-2028
Las Vegas, NV 89103
Hours: 9-5 Mon-Fri   E-mail: generalinfo@imaginationcostume.com
www.imaginationcostume.com
*Costume designing, draping, patternmaking, various dyeing techniques. Mask
making, prop construction. No rentals. P.O.s and CREDIT CARDS.*

Irene Corey Design Associates 214-821-9633
5304 Junius St.
Dallas, TX 75214
Hours: 9-5 Mon-Fri   E-mail: info@irenecoreydesign.com
www.irenecoreydesign.com
*Designer and fabricator of the original character costume of Barney. Custom
props, body puppets and specialty costumes. Contact Suzanne Lockridge.*

Martin Izquierdo Studio 212-807-9757
118 W 22nd St., 9th Fl. (6-7th Ave)   FAX 212-366-5249
NY, NY 10011
Hours: 9-7 Mon-Fri   E-mail: izquierdostudio@gmail.com
www.izquierdostudio.com
*Construction of costume crafts and props for theatre, film, commercials,
display and video; full-service shop. Shop and dye facilities for long-or-short
term rental. No rental stock.*

Jennifer Love Costumes 212-367-9114
37 W 37th St., 11th Fl. (5-6th Ave)   FAX 212-367-9201
NY, NY 10018
Hours: by appt.   E-mail: jlovecostumes@aol.com
Costume construction and alteration.

Linda LaBelle / The Yarn Tree 718-384-3793
347 Bedford Ave.   718-384-8030
Brooklyn, NY 11211   FAX (same)
Hours: 4-8 Mon-Thurs / 12-7 Sat-Sun / or by appt.
www.theyarntree.com   E-mail: info@theyarntree.com
*Costume design and construction, design and construction of soft props.
Custom handwoven fabrics, handknits and fabric painting.*

Barbara Matera Ltd. 212-475-5006
890 Broadway, 5th Fl. (19-20th St)   FAX 212-254-4550
NY, NY 10003
Hours: by appt.
Costumes made to order in all areas: Broadway, film, opera, ballet and dance. Wonderful tutus, beading and tailoring onsite. No Rentals.

Menkes 212-541-8401
250 W 54th St., 8th Fl. (B'way-8th Ave)   877-227-5460
NY, NY 10019   FAX 212-541-7409
Hours: 11-6 Mon-Sat   E-mail: menkesny@verizon.net
www.menkes.es
Flamenco shoes, clothing and accessories. Spanish combs, bullfighter apparel. Castanets.

MULDER / MARTIN, INC. 610-807-9887
1606 Woodfield Dr.
Bethlehem, PA 18015
Hours: 8-6 Mon-Fri   E-mail: foam@rcn.com
Speciality costumes for theatre, opera, TV, industrials, sports and promotional events. The same reasonable and reliable service you have known for over 20 years. No rentals. Member ATAC.

Parsons-Meares, Ltd. 212-967-1663
519 8th Ave., 11th Fl. (Corner 36th)   FAX 212-741-1869
NY, NY 10018
Hours: by appt.   E-mail: costumes@parsons-meares.com
www.parsons-meares.com
Custom draping, tailoring; dyeing and painting services available.

Period Corsets 206-264-0997
PMB 5584 10002 Aurora Ave N # 36   877-226-7738
Seattle, WA 98133   FAX 206-264-1657
Hours: 9-6 Mon-Fri   E-mail: sales@periodcorsets.com
www.periodcorsets.com
Costume construction & tailoring. Clients include: NY City Opera, Seattle Opera.

Pierre of Paris, Ltd. 212-947-0316
450 Seventh Ave., Ste. 2105   FAX 212-947-0322
NY, NY 10123
Hours: 10-9 Mon-Sat   E-mail: pierreofparisltd@aol.com
Custom tailoring and alterations for men and women for all production needs.

Rawhides Custom Leatherware 201-333-2571
P.O. Box 2146
Secaucus, NJ 07096
Hours: by appt.   E-mail: hidemaster@rawhides.com
www.rawhides.com
Custom leather clothing, theatrical costumes, garments or accessories. Visit website for ordering information. CREDIT CARDS.

Saint Laurie Merchant Tailors 212-643-1916
22 W 32nd St., 5th Fl. (32nd St)
NY, NY 10001
Hours: 9-6 Mon-Fri / 9-4 Sat   E-mail: tailor@saintlaurie.com
www.saintlaurie.com
Tailors for theatre and film, specializing in custom-built men's suits, sport coats, trousers and overcoats from the 1900 to present. One week turnarounds possible. Large selection of fabrics on hand. No rentals. CREDIT CARDS.

Seamless Costumes / Monica Viani 416-533-3434
754 Bathurst St., 2nd FL   FAX 416-533-5743
Toronto, Ontario, Canada M5S 2R6
Hours: by appt.   E-mail: info@seamlesscostumes.com
www.seamlesscostumes.com
Costume construction.

Singer Clothing Co. 718-384-6200
116 Lee Ave.   FAX (same)
Brooklyn, NY 11211
Hours: 10:30-7:30 Sun-Thurs / 10:30-2 Fri
Large stock; custom-made clothing worn by Russian and Polish nobles; other period suits. CREDIT CARDS.

Spotlight Costumes, LLC 412-381-7733
1503 E Carson St. (S 16th St)   800-256-8645
Pittsburgh, PA 15203   FAX 412-381-0260
Hours: 10-6 Mon-Sat / 12-9 (October)   E-mail: info@spotlightcostumes.com
www.spotlightcostumes.com
Costume rental and construction. In-house design services available. Also wigs, masks and make-up. RENTALS. CREDIT CARDS.

Frankie Steinz Costumes 212-925-1373
580 Broadway Ste 309
New York, NY 10012
Hours: by Appt.   E-mail: info@frankiesteinz.com
www.frankiesteinz.com
Halloween rentals, rentals for children and custom costumes for music videos, TV shows and advertising. RENTALS.

Studio Rouge 212-989-8363
152 W 25th St., 7th Fl. (6-7th Ave)   FAX 212-989-5575
NY, NY 10001
Hours: 9-5 Mon-Fri   E-mail: rosi@studiorouge.com
www.studiorouge.com
Tailoring (men's and women's), costume construction, alterations for film, theatre and television. Contact Rosi Zingales.

Sword in the Stone Crafts 905-299-5550
152 Commercial St.
Milton, Ontario, Canada L9T 2J2
Hours: 9-5 Mon-Fri   E-mail: spike@ica.net
www.swordinthestone.ca
Skilled artisans working primarily in leather, specializing in custom-made gunleather and holsters, armour, belts, bags, pouches and cases, scabbards and sheaths, custom leather carving and more. RENTALS. CREDIT CARDS.

COSTUME CONSTRUCTION SHOPS

Sally Thomas 718-797-4028
Brooklyn, NY 11201
Hours: by appt.   E-mail: sally@softworkstudio.com
www.softworkstudio.com
On-set sewing, costume construction and design. Miniature costumes for
stop-motion, puppets and toys. Props and soft furnishings.

TIMBERLAKE STUDIOS 212-967-4736
322 Seventh Ave. # 2-F (28-29th St)   917-407-7688
NY, NY 10001   FAX 212-967-4737
Hours: by appt.   E-mail: timberlakestudios@gmail.com
www.timberlakestudios.com
Originally established in 1964, Timberlake studios provides costume
construction and alterations in all areas of entertainment (stage, promotion,
and fashion), our specialty is in the area of stretch and/or dancewear.
Member ATAC.

Tricorne 212-216-9229
555 Eighth Ave., 6th Fl. (37-38th St)   FAX 212-216-9696
NY, NY 10018
Hours: 9-6 Mon-Fri
Custom-made costumes for theatre and the entertainment fields.

Tutus by Christine 440-949-7996
3962 Colorado Ave.   FAX: 440-949-7996
Sheffield Village, OH 44054
Hours: 9-5 Mon-Fri   E-mail: pie545@aol.com
Custom professional tutus. Performance quality.

Warner Bros. Studios Costume Design Center 818-954-5693
4000 Warner Blvd. Bldg #153   Rentals 818-954-1297
Burbank, CA 91522   FAX 818-954-2667
Hours: 8-6 Mon-Fri   E-mail: wbsfcostumedesk@warnerbros.com
www.warnerbros.com/home.html
Full-service costume construction facility. RENTALS. CREDIT CARDS.

COSTUME CRAFTSPEOPLE

Anney Fresh Productions 917-838-3519
27 Olive St., # 8
Brooklyn, NY 11211
Hours: by appt.   E-mail: anney@anneyfresh.com
www.anneyfresh.com
Design and construction of puppets, costume characters, and props. Union
and non-union performer staffing and puppet wrangling.

Association of Theatrical Artists and Craftspeople (ATAC) 212-501-9090
555 Eighth Ave. #2009 (mailing address) c/o Arnold S. Levine
NY, NY 10018
Hours: by appt.   E-mail: atacbiz@aol.com
www.atacbiz.com
*Professional trade association for artists and craftspeople working in theater,
film, television and advertising. ATAC creates a professional network through
quarterly meetings, a membership directory and articles in the ATAC
Quarterly. Compilers and editors of The Entertainment Sourcebook.*

CINDY ANITA FAIN 212-501-9090
48 Fairway St.   917-796-4641
Bloomfield, NJ 07003   FAX 973-320-4493
Hours: by appt.   E-mail: cinaf@aol.com
www.cinafdesigns.com
*Costume crafts, costume painting and distressing. Drapery and upholstery.
Model building, props for puppets and speciality prop and crafts. Set
decoration, prop shopping and photo styling. Member IATSE Locals 1
Stagehands, 52 Motion Pictures and 829 United Scenic Artists. Member ATAC.*

CHRIS BOBIN 646-742-0630
347 Fifth Ave., Rm 1102 (34-35th St)   917-683-5239
NY, NY 10016
Hours: by appt.   E-mail: chris@chrisbobin.com
www.chrisbobin.com
*Sewn solutions for props, costumes and illustrations; miniature and oversize-
quilting, applique and embroidery. Member ATAC.*

CORRINNA GRIFFIN 917-544-1287
1040 Bushwick Ave.
Brooklyn, NY 11211
Hours: by appt.   E-mail: corgriffin@gmail.com
Millinery, costume crafts and event planning. Member ATAC.

Euro Co. Costumes, Inc. 212-629-9665
254 W 35th St., 15th FL (7-8th Ave)   FAX 212-629-9608
NY, NY 10001
Hours: 9-6 Mon-Fri / or by appt.   E-mail: euroconyc@aol.com
*Specializing in custom pieces of textured stretch fabrics, chain-mail and other
hard to find fabric effects. Janet Bloor, craftsperson.*

Yvette Helin Studio 718-389-8797
1205 Manhattan Ave., Unit 136 (New Town Creek)   Cell 917-617-5935
Brooklyn, NY 11222
Hours: 9-5 Mon-Fri, or by appt.   E-mail: yvette@yvettehelinstudio.com
www.yvettehelinstudio.com
Entertainment costume designer, maker. Specialty costumes.

MARIAN JEAN 'KILLER' HOSE, LLC 212-594-0990
307 W 38th St., Ste 1110 (8-9th Ave)   917-596-6405
NY, NY 10018   Fax 212-594-0990
Hours: by appt.   E-mail: oxoxkill@nyc.rr.com
www.myspace.com/oxoxkill
*Custom costume crafts; sculptural wire framework, foam work, masks,
millinery, wings, character costumes and soft goods. Member ATAC.*

ARNOLD S. LEVINE, INC. 212-563-5830
555 Eighth Ave., Ste. # 2009 (37-38th St) FAX 212-563-5838
NY, NY 10018
Hours: 10-5:30 Mon-Fri / or by appt. E-mail: aslevine@nyc.rr.com
www.asltheatricalmillinery.com
Custom millinery, masks and costume crafts for all areas of performance.
Member ATAC.

JANET LINVILLE 917-952-4713
575 Main St. Apt 808
NY, NY 10044
Hours: by appt. E-mail: jlinvillehats@aol.com
Millinery for theatre, film, fashion and all other media. Member ATAC.

David Samuel Menkes 212-989-3706
144 Fifth Ave., 3rd Fl. (19-20th St)
NY, NY 10011
Hours: by appt. E-mail: dsm@davidmenkesleather.com
www.davidmenkesleather.com
Custom leatherwork, theatrical and personal. No credit cards.

MULDER / MARTIN, INC. 610-807-9887
1606 Woodfield Dr.
Bethlehem, PA 18015
Hours: 8-6 Mon-Fri E-mail: foam@rcn.com
Speciality costumes for theatre, opera, TV, industrials, sports and promotional
events. The same reasonable and reliable service you have known for over 20
years. No rentals. Member ATAC.

Carolie Tarble 650-349-1060
1500 S Claremont St. #G
San Mateo, CA 94402
Hours: by appt. E-mail: my.arts@rcn.com
Costume construction. Specialties include folk dance costumes and cross-
gender evening gowns.

Sally Thomas 718-797-4028
Brooklyn, NY 11201
Hours: by appt. E-mail: sally@softworkstudio.com
www.softworkstudio.com
On-set sewing, costume construction and design. Miniature costumes for
stop-motion, puppets and toys. Props and soft furnishings.

COSTUME CRAFTSPEOPLE: ACCESSORIES

Anne Guay, Inc. 917-225-6550
689 Myrtle Ave. # 5-H (Spencer) FAX 718-852-7589
Brooklyn, NY 11205
Hours: By Appt. E-mail: info@anneguay.com
www.anneguay.com
Custom millinery, fashion accessories, costume crafts, soft goods for display,
stage, print, TV and film. High-end draperies and fabric treatments. CREDIT
CARDS.

Eia Millinery Design 773-975-5959
1620 W Nelson St.
Chicago, IL 60657
Hours: by appt.   E-mail: info@eiahatart.com
www.eiahatart.com
Custom millinery and headpieces for fashion, theatre, film and advertising.
RENTALS. CREDIT CARDS.

RODNEY GORDON, INC. 212-594-6658
519 Eighth Ave., 11th Fl. (35-36th St)   FAX 212-594-6693
NY, NY 10018
Hours: 10-6 Mon-Fri   E-mail: rodneygordoninc@hotmail.com
Custom-made theatrical jewelry, armor, masks and millinery. Member ATAC.

Louise Grafton 609-921-1919
229 Hartly Ave.
Princeton, NJ 08540
Hours: by appt.   E-mail: legraft@hotmail.com
Props, set and costume pieces, soft goods, circus and clown props. Also
upholstery done in her studio.

ARNOLD S. LEVINE, INC. 212-563-5830
555 Eighth Ave., Ste. # 2009 (37-38th St)   FAX 212-563-5838
NY, NY 10018
Hours: 10-5:30 Mon-Fri / or by appt.   E-mail: aslevine@nyc.rr.com
www.asltheatricalmillinery.com
Custom millinery, masks and costume crafts for all areas of performance.
Member ATAC.

Zoe Morsette 718-784-8894
43-01 21st St., Studio 224A   917-733-1731
Long Island City, NY 11101
Hours: by appt.
Costume construction in foam, fabric and fake fur. Masks, millinery, costume
accessories.

Sword in the Stone Crafts 905-299-5550
152 Commercial St.
Milton, Ontario, Canada L9T 2J2
Hours: 9-5 Mon-Fri   E-mail: spike@ica.net
www.swordinthestone.ca
Skilled artisans working primarily in leather, specializing in custom-made
gunleather and holsters, armour, belts, bags, pouches and cases, scabbards
and sheaths, custom leather carving and more. RENTALS. CREDIT CARDS.

Wigboys Theatrical Wigs 707-763-1978
170 Rainsville Rd.   FAX (Same)
Petaluma, CA 94952
Hours: 9-5 Mon-Fri   E-mail: information@wigboys.com
www.wigboys.com
Wonderful selection of theatrical wigs. Wigs are styled according to your
research. Visit their website to view their stock. Nice folks to deal with.
RENTALS.

COSTUME CRAFTSPEOPLE: CRAFTS

ABS Art Effects LLC 315-422-5825
110 Dorset Road
Syracuse, NY 13210
Hours: by appt.   E-mail: andrewbenepe@gmail.com
Body puppets, masks, full animal and monster costumes in a wide range of
materials.

Association of Theatrical Artists and Craftspeople (ATAC) 212-501-9090
555 Eighth Ave. #2009 (mailing address) c/o Arnold S. Levine
NY, NY 10018
Hours: by appt.   E-mail: atacbiz@aol.com
www.atacbiz.com
Professional trade association for artists and craftspeople working in theater,
film, television and advertising. ATAC creates a professional network through
quarterly meetings, a membership directory and articles in the ATAC
Quarterly. Compilers and editors of The Entertainment Sourcebook.

CINDY ANITA FAIN 212-501-9090
48 Fairway St.   917-796-4641
Bloomfield, NJ 07003   FAX 973-320-4493
Hours: by appt.   E-mail: cinaf@aol.com
www.cinafdesigns.com
Costume crafts, costume painting and distressing. Drapery and upholstery.
Props for puppets. Prop and model builder. Member IATSE Locals 1
Stagehands, 52 Motion Pictures and 829 United Scenic Artists. Member ATAC.

CHRIS BOBIN 646-742-0630
347 Fifth Ave., Rm 1102 (34-35th St)   917-683-5239
NY, NY 10016
Hours: by appt.   E-mail: chris@chrisbobin.com
www.chrisbobin.com
Sewn solutions for props, costumes and illustrations. Member ATAC.

Borem Studio 212-750-9066
231 E 50th St. # 2E (2nd & 3rd Aves)   917-334-4335
NY, NY 10022
Hours: by appt.   E-mail: hilda@inch.com
www.inch.com/~hilda
Creating environments, props and sculptures. They specialize in custom
fabrication, design and structural elements in a wide variety of materials for
film, TV, theatre and trade industries. Quick turnaround from a highly
experienced staff. Contact Hilda.

RANDY CARFAGNO PRODUCTIONS .212-947-0302
347 W 39th St. #7E (8-9th Ave)   FAX 212-947-2941
NY, NY 10018
Hours: by appt.   E-mail: randycarfagnoproductions@gmail.com
www.randycarfagnoproductions.com
Puppets, mascots, papier machE and vacuumform masks. All types of
character hats. Oversized puppets and shoes. Member SAG, ATAC.

Cindy Chock 212-246-9662
300 W 55th St. (8th Ave)
NY, NY 10019
Hours: by appt   E-mail: c.chock@att.net
Costumer, seamstress, pattern maker, draper. Bridals, restoration/renovation, leatherwork. Teaches sewing classes in midtown Manhattan.

CINAF DESIGNS 212-501-9090
48 Fairway St.   917-796-4641
Bloomfield, NJ 07003   FAX 973-320-4493
Hours: by appt.   E-mail: cinaf@aol.com
www.cinafdesigns.com
Costume crafts, costume painting and distressing. Drapery and upholstery. Props for puppets. Prop and model builder. Member IATSE Local 1, 829 & Local 52. Member ATAC.

Euro Co. Costumes, Inc. 212-629-9665
254 W 35th St., 15th FL (7-8th Ave)   FAX 212-629-9608
NY, NY 10001
Hours: 9-6 Mon-Fri / or by appt.   E-mail: euroconyc@aol.com
Specializing in custom pieces of hard-to-find fabric effects: textured stretch fabrics, chain-mail, etc.

Geppetto, Inc. 718-398-9792
201 46th St. 2nd FL   FAX 718-622-2991
Brooklyn, NY 11220
Hours: 9-5 Mon-Fri   E-mail: gepstudios@aol.com
www.geppettostudios.com
Soft sculpture animal and body puppet costumes & masks.

DEBORAH GLASSBERG 973-429-2904
53 Spring St.   (cell) 973-930-4878
Bloomfield, NJ 07003
Hours: please call
         E-mail: debglassberg@earthlink.net / deb.glassberg@gmail.com
www.flickr.com/photos/debglassberg
Mask design and construction, face casting, bent reed work, leatherwork. Member ATAC.

Karen Hart 908-931-0998
Hours: by appt.   E-mail: tx2ny@aol.com
Costume design, construction and shopping services.

Martin Izquierdo Studio 212-807-9757
118 W 22nd St., 9th Fl. (6-7th Ave)   FAX 212-366-5249
NY, NY 10011
Hours: 9-7 Mon-Fri   E-mail: izquierdostudio@gmail.com
www.izquierdostudio.com
Full-service costume craft shop.

JERARD STUDIO, INC. 718-852-4128
481 Van Brunt St., Ste. 11D (Beard St)   FAX 718-852-2408
Brooklyn, NY 11231
Hours: 9-6 Mon-Fri   E-mail: mary@jerardstudio.com
www.jerardstudio.com
Structural costumes, masks and mechanics. Member ATAC.

ATAC

JAN KASTENDIECK 212-962-1042
40 Harrison St. Apt 14B   Cell 646-701-3040
NY, NY 10013
Hours: by appt.   E-mail: jgkforce@aol.com
Draper, pattern maker, soft sculpture costumes, foam bodies. Member ATAC.

ARNOLD S. LEVINE, INC. 212-563-5830
555 Eighth Ave., Ste. # 2009 (37-38th St)   FAX 212-563-5838
NY, NY 10018
Hours: 10-5:30 Mon-Fri / or by appt.   E-mail: aslevine@nyc.rr.com
www.asltheatricalmillinery.com
*Custom millinery, masks and costume crafts for all areas of performance.
Member ATAC.*

JENNIE MARINO / MOONBOOTS PRODUCTIONS, INC. 845-359-6262
44 Slocum Ave.   Cell 845-642-0158
Tappan, NY 10983   FAX 845-680-6124
Hours: by appt.   E-mail: jenfx@aol.com
*Special FX make-up, prosthetics, creatures. Prototypes maquettes and prop
fabrication. Masks in foam and cast latex; resin. Mechanical masks, dummies.
Hand, rod, mechanical & full body puppet design and fabrication. Member
ATAC.*

Zoe Morsette 718-784-8894
43-01 21st St., Studio 224A   917-733-1731
Long Island City, NY 11101
Hours: by appt.
*Costume construction in foam, fabric and fake fur. Masks, millinery, costume
accessories.*

MULDER / MARTIN, INC. 610-807-9887
1606 Woodfield Dr.
Bethlehem, PA 18015
Hours: 8-6 Mon-Fri   E-mail: foam@rcn.com
*Speciality costumes for theatre, opera, TV, industrials, sports and promotional
events. The same reasonable and reliable service you have known for over 20
years. No rentals. Member ATAC.*

Carl Paolino Studios 917-957-7305
3801 23rd Ave.   917-282-4756
Astoria, NY 11105   FAX (same)
Hours: by appt. only   E-mail: cpseffects@aol.com
www.paolinostudios.com
Creature costumes & masks, prosthetic makeup.

JODY SCHOFFNER 818-992-6574
24118 Philiprimm St.   cell: 818-421-1736
Woodland Hills, CA 91367
Hours: by appt.   E-mail: sjodye@earthlink.net
Draper and puppet maker. Member ATAC.

Linda C. Schultz 212-222-0477
125 W 96th St. #6J (Columbus-Amsterdam Ave)
NY, NY 10025
Hours: by appt.
Costumer, stylist, wardrobe, draper.

Sean P. McArdle / Hero Props 646-734-2198
18 Bridge St. # 1A
Brooklyn, NY 11201
Hours: by appt.　　　　　　　　　　E-mail: sean@heropropsnyc.com
www.heropropsnyc.com
Prop design and management. Carpentry, welding, turning, casting molding,
upholstery, costume crafts, model making and furniture construction.
Computer graphics design and desktop publishing.

SPS EFFECTS, LLC / SUSAN PITOCCHI 917-519-5805
Hours: by appt.
262 N 6th St., Apt 3
Brooklyn, NY 11211

96 Academy St.　　　　　　　　　　　　　845-292-6942
Liberty, NY 12754　　　　　　　　　　FAX 845-292-6342
www.spseffects.com　　　　　　　　E-mail: spitocchi@earthlink.net
Custom fabrication of props, costumes and sculptures in materials including
foam, fabric, wood, leather, plastics and casting materials.   Member IATSE
Local 52. Member ATAC.

Stone Soup Studios 610-867-4626
301 Broadway
Bethlehem, PA 18015
Hours: 10-4 Tue-Sat　　　　　E-mail: manager@stonesoupbethlehem.com
www.stonesoupbethlehem.com
Working artist studio featuring sophisticated one-of-a kind and limited
edition artist wares. Hand painted silk scarves, ceramics, jewelry, totes and
handbags, baby items fine wood products and more. CREDIT CARDS.

ANNE-MARIE WRIGHT 201-798-7673
280 Third St. Apt # 1　　　　　　　　　　201-424-9114
Jersey City, NJ 07302
Hours: by appt.　　　　　　　E-mail: anne.marie.wright@verizon.net
Costume design and construction for theatre, TV and film. Has sewing
machine, will travel. Member United Scenic Artist #829. Member ATAC.

COSTUME CRAFTSPEOPLE: FABRIC PAINTING & DYEING

Marcella Beckwith 941-586-3282
5119 Lymbar Dr.
Houston, TX 77096
Hours: by appt.　　　　　　　　　　E-mail: hmbeckwith@aol.com
Freelance costume and set designer for film, TV, theatre and print work.
Shopping and costume construction, crafts, millinery, painting and dyeing,
some scenic painting. Member USA Local 829.

EILEEN CONNOR 212-421-4805
300 E 54th St. #25C　　　　　　　　　　917-841-6482
NY, NY 10022
Hours: by appt.
Fabric and costume painting, scenic painting, murals, faux finishes, gilding,
crafts. Member ATAC.

Euro Co. Costumes, Inc. 212-629-9665
    254 W 35th St., 15th FL (7-8th Ave)   FAX 212-629-9608
    NY, NY 10001
    Hours: 9-6 Mon-Fri / or by appt.   E-mail: euroconyc@aol.com
    Specializing in custom pieces of hard-to-find fabric effects: textured stretch
    fabrics, chain-mail, etc.

GENE MIGNOLA, INC. 718-858-8902
    610 Smith Street (3rd Fl)   FAX 718-858-8667
    Brooklyn, NY 11231
    Hours: 9-5 Mon-Fri   E-mail: GM5919@aol.com
    Custom dyeing and silkscreening. Call before stopping by. Member ATAC.

J. MICHELLE HILL 212-924-6986
    280 Ninth Ave. Apt 9B (26th St)
    NY, NY 10001
    Hours: by appt. only   E-mail: moroccomaiden@gmail.com
    Digital fabric painting and output on cloth, natural fibers and nylon, lycra.
    Computer graphic design in Photoshop, Illustrator and Flash Animation.
    Member ATAC.

JONI JOHNS 203-938-9738
    44 Beeholm Rd.   FAX 203-938-9714
    Redding, CT 06896
    Hours: By Appt.   E-mail: johnsj@jonijohns.com
    www.jonijohns.com
    Custom handpainted fabrics and design development for theatre, dance,
    fashion and interiors. Over 20 years experience. Member ATAC.

Kimtex Fabric Service 973-790-6998
    108 N Seventh St.   FAX 973-790-0438
    Paterson, NJ 07522
    Hours: 7-3 Mon-Fri   E-mail: michaelpetto@yahoo.com
    www.kimtexfabricservice.com
    Sample dyeing services and bulk dyeing up to 200 yards depending on
    weight of fabrics.

Linda LaBelle / The Yarn Tree 718-384-3793
    347 Bedford Ave.   718-384-8030
    Brooklyn, NY 11211   FAX (same)
    Hours: 4-8 Mon-Thurs / 12-7 Sat-Sun / or by appt.
    www.theyarntree.com   E-mail: info@theyarntree.com
    Costume design and construction, design and construction of soft props.
    Custom handwoven fabrics, handknits and fabric painting.

COSTUME CRAFTSPEOPLE: KNITTING & WEAVING

ADELE RECKLIES CO. 718-768-9036
    420 Fourth Ave. #1 (7-8th St)   FAX (same)
    Brooklyn, NY 11215
    Hours: by appt.   E-mail: knitter718@earthlink.net
    www.beadcrochetsnakes.com
    Custom knitwear for theater and film; crocheting and beading. Member
    ATAC.

Linda LaBelle / The Yarn Tree 718-384-3793
347 Bedford Ave.   718-384-8030
Brooklyn, NY 11211   FAX (same)
Hours: 4-8 Mon-Thurs / 12-7 Sat-Sun / or by appt.
www.theyarntree.com   E-mail: info@theyarntree.com
Costume design and construction, design and construction of soft props.
Custom handwoven fabrics, handknits and fabric painting.

COSTUME CRAFTSPEOPLE: MAKE-UP ARTISTS

JENNIE MARINO / MOONBOOTS PRODUCTIONS, INC. 845-359-6262
44 Slocum Ave.   Cell 845-642-0158
Tappan, NY 10983   FAX 845-680-6124
Hours: by appt.   E-mail: jenfx@aol.com
Special FX make-up, prosthetics, creatures. Prototypes maquettes and prop
fabrication. Masks in foam and cast latex; resin. Mechanical masks, dummies.
Hand, rod, mechanical & full body puppet design and fabrication. Member
ATAC.

Carl Paolino Studios 917-957-7305
3801 23rd Ave.   917-282-4756
Astoria, NY 11105   FAX (same)
Hours: by appt. only   E-mail: cpseffects@aol.com
www.paolinostudios.com
Creature costumes & masks, prosthetic makeup.

COSTUME CRAFTSPEOPLE: MASKS

ABS Art Effects LLC 315-422-5825
110 Dorset Road
Syracuse, NY 13210
Hours: by appt.   E-mail: andrewbenepe@gmail.com
Custom design and fabrication of all types of masks, animals and monsters a
specialty.

Borem Studio 212-750-9066
231 E 50th St. # 2E (2nd & 3rd Aves)   917-334-4335
NY, NY 10022
Hours: by appt.   E-mail: hilda@inch.com
www.inch.com/~hilda
Creating environments, props and sculptures. They specialize in custom
fabrication, design and structural elements in a wide variety of materials for
film, TV, theatre and trade industries. Quick turnaround from a highly
experienced staff. Contact Hilda.

RANDY CARFAGNO PRODUCTIONS .212-947-0302
347 W 39th St. #7E (8-9th Ave)   FAX 212-947-2941
NY, NY 10018
Hours: by appt.   E-mail: randycarfagnoproductions@gmail.com
www.randycarfagnoproductions.com
Puppets, mascots, papier mache and vacuumform masks. All types of
character hats. Oversized puppets and shoes. Member SAG, ATAC.

Enrapturing Revisions 404-316-9141
3459 Glensford Dr. (Mistyvalle Rd)
Decatur, GA 30032
Hours: 10-7 Mon-Fri by appt.   E-mail: rosemarykimble@gmail.com
www.rosemaryi.com
***Custom Mardi Gras and Carnival masks. Also, bodypainting and henna
tattoos for events. Speak to Rosemary Kimble. See website for online store.***

Global Effects, Inc. 818-503-9273
7115 Laurel Canyon Blvd.   FAX 818-503-9459
N. Hollywood, CA 91605
Hours: by appt.   E-mail: chris@globaleffects.com
www.globaleffects.com
***Higy Quality replicas of NASA Space Suits and fabrication of armour,
vacuumforming, etc. Leather masks, creature suits, ventilated walk-around
costumes. Medieval: armour, weapons, jewelry. Very pleasant to deal with.
RENTALS. CREDIT CARDS.***

RODNEY GORDON, INC. 212-594-6658
519 Eighth Ave., 11th Fl. (35-36th St)   FAX 212-594-6693
NY, NY 10018
Hours: 10-6 Mon-Fri   E-mail: rodneygordoninc@hotmail.com
Custom-made theatrical jewelry, armor, masks and millinery. Member ATAC.

Yvette Helin Studio 718-389-8797
1205 Manhattan Ave., Unit 136 (New Town Creek)   Cell 917-617-5935
Brooklyn, NY 11222
Hours: 9-5 Mon-Fri, or by appt.   E-mail: yvette@yvettehelinstudio.com
www.yvettehelinstudio.com
Entertainment costume designer, maker. Specialty costumes.

MARIAN JEAN 'KILLER' HOSE, LLC 212-594-0990
307 W 38th St., Ste 1110 (8-9th Ave)   917-596-6405
NY, NY 10018   Fax 212-594-0990
Hours: by appt.   E-mail: oxoxkill@nyc.rr.com
www.myspace.com/oxoxkill
***Custom costume crafts; sculptural wire framework, foam work, masks,
millinery, wings, character costumes and soft goods. Member ATAC.***

Ralph Lee 212-929-4777
55 Bethune St. # D405 (Bethune-Washington)
NY, NY 10014
Hours: by appt.   E-mail: info@mettawee.org
www.mettawee.org
Masks, larger-than-life puppets and costumes; wide range of materials.

ARNOLD S. LEVINE, INC. 212-563-5830
555 Eighth Ave., Ste. # 2009 (37-38th St)   FAX 212-563-5838
NY, NY 10018
Hours: 10-5:30 Mon-Fri / or by appt.   E-mail: aslevine@nyc.rr.com
www.asltheatricalmillinery.com
***Custom millinery, masks and costume crafts for all areas of performance.
Member ATAC.***

JENNIE MARINO / MOONBOOTS PRODUCTIONS, INC. 845-359-6262
44 Slocum Ave. Cell 845-642-0158
Tappan, NY 10983 FAX 845-680-6124
Hours: by appt. E-mail: jenfx@aol.com
Special FX make-up, prosthetics, creatures. Prototypes maquettes and prop fabrication. Masks in foam and cast latex; resin. Mechanical masks, dummies. Hand, rod, mechanical & full body puppet design and fabrication. Member ATAC.

MASK ARTS CO. / STANLEY ALLAN SHERMAN 212-243-4039
203 W 14th St. Studio 5F (7th Ave) (Cell) 917-836-6764
NY, NY 10011
Hours: by appt. E-mail: stanley@maskarts.com
www.maskarts.com, www.commediau.com
Handcrafted molded leather and neoprene latex masks for theater, opera, wrestling, dance, Commedia dell'Arte, teaching and more. Specializes in custom masks, custom fitted leather clown noses and neutral masks. Mask repair, odd projects, custom leather projects, teaching mask making and Commedia dell'Arte. RENTALS. Member ATAC.

Stacy Morse 802-257-5660
139 Main St., Ste. #7
Brattleboro, VT 05301
Hours: by appt. E-mail: smorse@comcast.net
Big Heads, realistic, oversized portrait heads and masks. Custom-built logo characters.

Zoe Morsette 718-784-8894
43-01 21st St., Studio 224A 917-733-1731
Long Island City, NY 11101
Hours: by appt.
Costume construction in foam, fabric and fake fur. Masks, millinery, costume accessories.

Carl Paolino Studios 917-957-7305
3801 23rd Ave. 917-282-4756
Astoria, NY 11105 FAX (same)
Hours: by appt. only E-mail: cpseffects@aol.com
www.paolinostudios.com
Prosthetics, lifecasting, creature makeup. Speak to Carl.

Paragon Props 866-859-5059
2342 Wyecroft Rd., Unite G-1 905-469-0061
Oakville, Ontario, Canada L6L 5N2 FAX 905-469-0062
Hours: 8-4:30 Mon-Fri E-mail: sdiamond@paragonprops.com
www.paragonprops.com
Props, masks, puppets, special effects, etc. Visit website for photos.

Julie Prince 212-486-9249
141 E 56th St. #9G (Lex-3rd Ave) 818-353-4525
NY, NY 10022 FAX (same)
Hours: by appt. E-mail: portraicast@aol.com
www.portraicast.com
Life-casting; masks, sculptures and fragments; also props. In California call 818-353-4525.

Roxana Ramseur 917-535-6086
161 Withers St., Apt 3R
Brooklyn, NY 11211
Hours: by appt.　　　　　E-mail: roxana.ramseur@gmail.com
www.roxanaramseur.tumblr.com
Costume designer with fashion background. Theatrical millinary and crafts.

JODY SCHOFFNER 818-992-6574
24118 Philiprimm St.　　　　　　　　　　(cell) 818-421-1736
Woodland Hills, CA 91367
Hours: by appt.　　　　　E-mail: sjodye@earthlink.net
Draper and puppet maker. Member ATAC.

JAMES SEFFENS 212-246-1453
405 W 44th St. (9-10th Ave)
New York, NY 10036
Hours: by appt.　　　　　E-mail: jim@jimseffens.com
www.jimseffens.com
Custom masks and some stock designs. No rentals. CREDIT CARDS.
Member ATAC

Semmerling and Schefer Mask Studio 773-596-5001
2005 W Montrose　　　　　　　　　　　773-697-5012
Chicago, IL 60618
Hours: by appt.　　　　　E-mail: jeff@maskartists.com
www.maskartists.com
Custom masks in comfortable leather and other fine materials. Visit website
to view stock masks for theatre, dance, collectors, masquarade. Contact Jeff
or Sonja.

Manju Shandler Design 917-826-3588
Hours: by appt.　　　　　E-mail: manju@nyc.rr.com
www.manjushandler.com
Specializing in costume design and building of foam sculptured costumes,
puppets, masks and props.

MARI TOBITA 212-254-8614
235 E 10th St., Apt 4D　　　　　　　　(cell) 917-304-5280
NY, NY 10003　　　　　　　　　　　　FAX 212-254-8614
Hours: by appt.　　　　　E-mail: maritobita@aol.com
Theatrical masks, puppets, wooden marionettes, sculpture, props and
costume crafts. Member USA Local 829. Member ATAC.

COSTUME CRAFTSPEOPLE: MILLINERY

ADORNMENTS BY SHARON 404-877-4469
393 Fifth St. #2　　　　　　　　　　　FAX 404-874-8452
Atlanta, GA 30308
Hours: by appt.　　　　　E-mail: sharon@adornmentsbysharon.com
www.adornmentsbysharon.com
Unique handcrafted bridal headpieces, jewelry and accessories. Custom
work created for clients throughout the country. Call or e-mail for a free
consultation. Member ATAC.

Anne Guay, Inc. 917-225-6550
　689 Myrtle Ave. # 5-H (Spencer)　　　　　　FAX 718-852-7589
　Brooklyn, NY 11205
　Hours: By Appt.　　　　　　　　　　　E-mail: info@anneguay.com
　www.anneguay.com
　Custom millinery, fashion accessories, costume crafts, soft goods for display,
　stage, print, TV and film. High-end draperies and fabric treatments. CREDIT
　CARDS.

Marcella Beckwith 941-586-3282
　5119 Lymbar Dr.
　Houston, TX 77096
　Hours: by appt.　　　　　　　　　　E-mail: hmbeckwith@aol.com
　Freelance costume and set designer for film, TV, theatre and print work.
　Shopping and costume construction, crafts, millinery, painting and dyeing,
　some scenic painting. Member USA Local 829.

CORRINNA GRIFFIN 917-544-1287
　1040 Bushwick Ave.
　Brooklyn, NY 11211
　Hours: by appt.　　　　　　　　　　E-mail: corgriffin@gmail.com
　Millinery, costume crafts and event planning. Member ATAC.

Eia Millinery Design 773-975-5959
　1620 W Nelson St.
　Chicago, IL 60657
　Hours: by appt.　　　　　　　　　　E-mail: info@eiahatart.com
　www.eiahatart.com
　Custom millinery and headpieces for fashion, theatre, film and advertising.
　RENTALS. CREDIT CARDS.

RODNEY GORDON, INC. 212-594-6658
　519 Eighth Ave., 11th Fl. (35-36th St)　　　　FAX 212-594-6693
　NY, NY 10018
　Hours: 10-6 Mon-Fri　　　　　E-mail: rodneygordoninc@hotmail.com
　Custom-made theatrical jewelry, armor, masks and millinery. Member ATAC.

MARIAN JEAN 'KILLER' HOSE, LLC 212-594-0990
　307 W 38th St., Ste 1110 (8-9th Ave)　　　　　917-596-6405
　NY, NY 10018　　　　　　　　　　　　　Fax 212-594-0990
　Hours: by appt.　　　　　　　　　　E-mail: oxoxkill@nyc.rr.com
　www.myspace.com/oxoxkill
　Custom costume crafts; sculptural wire framework, foam work, masks,
　millinery, wings, character costumes and soft goods. Member ATAC.

ARNOLD S. LEVINE, INC. 212-563-5830
　555 Eighth Ave., Ste. # 2009 (37-38th St)　　FAX 212-563-5838
　NY, NY 10018
　Hours: 10-5:30 Mon-Fri / or by appt.　　　　E-mail: aslevine@nyc.rr.com
　www.asltheatricalmillinery.com
　Custom millinery, masks and costume crafts for all areas of performance.
　Member ATAC.

Lynne Mackey 212-352-0668
261 W 35th St. # 405 (7-8th Ave)   FAX 212-352-0766
NY, NY 10001
Hours: by appt.
Custom millinery.

Zoe Morsette 718-784-8894
43-01 21st St., Studio 224A   917-733-1731
Long Island City, NY 11101
Hours: by appt.
***Costume construction in foam, fabric and fake fur. Masks, millinery, costume
accessories.***

GARY WHITE / THE CUSTOM HATTER 716-896-3722
1318 Broadway St.   716-474-3071
Buffalo, NY 14212
Hours: 10-5 Mon-Fri   www.custom-hatter.com
***Designing and creating custom-made mens dress, Western felt and fine
Panama straw hats. Period accurate from 1800 to 2006. Hat renovating,
reconstruction and blocking. CREDIT CARDS. Member ATAC.***

COSTUME PATTERNS

Alter Years for the Costumer 626-569-9919
P.O. Box 98   FAX 626-569-9909
Rosemead, CA 91770
Store Hours: 10-5:30 Mon-Fri or by appt.   E-mail: sales@alteryears.com
www.alteryears.com
***Mail order service for historical, ethnic and dance patterns. Costume books.
Corsetry and millinery supplies. 200+ page catalog ($5 or $8 priority mail)
Now offering classes. CREDIT CARDS.***

Amazon Drygoods Ltd. 563-322-6800
411 Brady St.   800-798-7979
Davenport, IA 52801   FAX 563-322-4003
Hours: 9-5 Mon-Fri   E-mail: info@amazondrygoods.com
www.amazondrygoods.com
***A large selection of patterns, shoes, clothing and general items from the
Victorian era. General catalog $4, Shoe catalog $5, Pattern catalog $7,
Window treatments catalog $3. First class mail. CREDIT CARDS.***

Harper House 630-837-0926
2100 Green Bridge Lane
Hanover Park, IL 60133
Hours: 8:30-4:30 Mon-Fri, 24-hr. fax and voice mail.
www.longago.com   E-mail: mjak88@comcast.net
***Costume history books, period and ethnic patterns from 650 AD to 1950.
Chatelaine pins, sewing and needlework accessories, hoop skirts. Catalog $7.***

JAN KASTENDIECK 212-962-1042
40 Harrison St. Apt 14B   Cell 646-701-3040
NY, NY 10013
Hours: by appt.   E-mail: jgkforce@aol.com
Draper, pattern maker, soft sculpture costumes, foam bodies, puppets.
Member ATAC.

Lark Books 828-253-0467
67 Broadway
Asheville, NC 28801
Hours: 9-8:30 Mon-Fri / 24-hour customer service
www.larkbooks.com   E-mail: customerservice@larkbooks.com
Large variety of craft, beading, textiles, needlework fiberarts and books.
Folkwear patterns. Catalog available.

Pattern Works, Intl. 616-458-5987
874 Houseman NE   FAX 616-458-6138
Grand Rapids, MI 49503
Hours: 8-5 Mon-Fri   E-mail: isabelle@patternworks-intl.com
www.patternworks-intl.com
Computerized pattern drafting programs. Offers classes to learn software.
(PC Pattern requires Auto-cad to run, however PW Studio is a stand-alone
program.) Patterns made from your garments, custom patterns from
sketches, photos or research. CREDIT CARDS.

Patterns of History Service 608-264-6428
30 North Carroll St.   FAX 608-264-6575
Madison, WI 53703
Hours: 8-5 Mon-Fri   E-mail: leslie.bellais@wisconsinhistory.org
www.wisconsinhistory.org/patterns
Authentic patterns from 1835-1896, good directions, clear patterns, brochure
available. Patterns sold at State Historical Society of Wisconsin Gift Shop.
CREDIT CARDS.

Richard the Thread / Roy Cooper 310-837-4997
10405 Washington Blvd.   800-473-4997
Culver City, CA 90222   FAX 310-836-4996
Hours: 7-4 Mon-Fri   E-mail: info@richardthethread.com
www.richardthethread.com
Gothic through Edwardian, etc., men's and women's patterns, dress forms;
catalog $3. UPS-COD and CREDIT CARDS.

Seattle Fabrics 206-525-0670
8702 Aurora Ave. N (N 87th St)   866-925-0670
Seattle, WA 98103   FAX 206-525-0779
Hours: 9-6 Mon-Sat   E-mail: seattlefabrics@msn.com
www.seattlefabrics.com
Outdoor and recreational fabric & hardware. Specialty fabrics, webbing,
thread and zippers; neoprene and closed cell foam. Patterns for outdoor and
sports attire; equestrian, tents and backpacks. Fabric samples available.
CREDIT CARDS.

R.L. Shep Publications 707-964-8662
PO Box 2706   FAX 707-964-8662
Fort Bragg, CA 95437
Hours: 9:30-5 Mon-Sat   E-mail: fsbks@mcn.org
www.rlshep.com
Publisher of books from the Regency Period to 1920s tailoring, costume and
patterns. Mail order only. Free brochure on request. Contact Fred Struthers.
CREDIT CARDS.

Stretch & Sew 800-547-7717
2035 S El Camino Dr.
Tempe, AZ 85282
Hours: 7:30-4:30 Mon-Fri MST   E-mail: stretch-and-sew@worldnet.att.net
www.stretch-and-sew.com
Garment patterns for stretch materials. Catalog available. Mail order.
CREDIT CARDS.

James Townsend & Son 800-338-1665
PO Box 415, 133 N First St.   574-594-5852
Pierceton, IN 46562   FAX 574-594-5580
Hours: 9-5 Mon-Fri   E-mail: jastown@jastown.com
www.jastown.com
18th and 19th century costume patterns, clothing and hats; repro colonial
household goods. Catalog. CREDIT CARDS.

Vintage Fashion Library . . . .
400 Thelma Ave.
Xenia, OH 45385
Hours: 24-hr. Web   E-mail: laura@vintagefashionlibrary.com
www.vintagefashionlibrary.com
Large collection of vintage and antique fashion patterns and related materials
including clothing patterns for men, women and children and vintage fashion
magazines and pattern catalogues. PAYPAL, checks and money orders.
Western Union transfers please contact Laura for payment instructions.

Vintage Pattern Lending Library 510-655-3091
869 Aileen St.   FAX 510-654-6442
Oakland, CA 94608
Hours 9-5 Mon-Fri / 24-hr web-site   E-mail: librarian@vpll.org
www.vpll.org
The Vintage Pattern Lending Library preserves, archives, and replicates
historic fashion patterns from 1840 through 1950, vintage sewing
publications, and fashion prints of the past. High quality, user-friendly print
replications of our patterns and copies of our publications are available for
purchase to our guests and purchase or loan to Library members. See web-
site for membership information. CREDIT CARDS.

COSTUME RENTALS

Abracadabra 212-627-5194
19 W 21st St. (5-6th Ave)   FAX 212-627-7435
NY, NY 10001
Hours: 11-7 Mon-Sat / 12-5 Sun
www.abracadabrasuperstore.com
Many kinds of Halloween and theatrical costumes for rent; also masks,
theatrical make-up and costume accessories. Gag, gift and gadget shop.
Magic tricks, special effects and novelties. Catalog available online.
RENTALS. CREDIT CARDS.

Alias Costume Rental 212-564-1530
231 W 29th St. # 608 (6-7th Ave)   FAX 212-564-1534
NY, NY 10001
Hours: 9-6 Mon-Fri / Sat and after hours by Appt.
www.aliascostumesnyc.com   E-mail: info@aliascostumesnyc.com
Alias is open to serve the needs of the film, theatre, commercial and print
community. Large stock of men's and women's vintage clothing, uniforms
(police, firemen, medical, security, hospitality), work wear, theatrical
costumes, accessories and shoes. RENTALS.

Backstage, Inc. 202-544-5744
545 Eighth St. SE   FAX 202-544-7025
Washington, DC 20003
Hours: 11-7 Mon-Sat   E-mail: backstagebooks@aol.com
http://backstagebooks.com
Theatre books and scripts; quarterly newsletter on new releases; mail orders.
Also dancewear, masks, makeup and some costumes for rent. RENTALS
CREDIT CARDS.

Costume Armour, Inc. 845-534-9120
PO Box 85, 2 Mill St.   FAX 845-534-8602
Cornwall, NY 12518
Hours: 8-4 Mon-Fri   E-mail: info@costumearmour.com
www.costumearmour.com
Fabrication of lightweight armour and helmets in a variety of periods and
styles. RENTALS.

The Costume Collection 212-989-5855
601 W 26th St., 3rd Fl. (11-12th Ave)   FAX 212-206-0922
NY, NY 10001
Hours: 9-5:30 Mon-Fri by appt.   E-mail: costume@tdf.org
www.tdf.org
Rental for non-profit organizations only. Will pull costumes for shows
through mail order (outside city limits only); some construction. RENTALS.

Costume Rentals Corp. 800-400-7444
11149 Vanowen St.   818-753-3700
N. Hollywood, CA 91605   FAX 818-753-3737
Hours: 8-6 M-F   E-mail: crcresearch@hughes.net
www.costumerentalscorp.com
All types of uniforms for rent only. Will ship. Only RENTALS. CREDIT CARDS.

Costume World 800 258-0333
950 S Federal Hwy.   954-428-6266
Deerfield Beach, FL 33441   FAX 954-428-4959
Hours: 10-7 Mon-Fri / 10-6 Sat
www.costumeworld.com
Show packages for all major musicals. Will do small rentals. Store locations in Pittsburg, Dallas and headquarters in Deerfield Beach that specialize in Halloween rentals, make-up and wig supplies. 55,000 square feet of costumes. Costume plots available. RENTALS. CREDIT CARDS.

Creative Costume Co. 212-564-5552
242 W 36th St., 8th Fl. (7-8th Ave)   FAX 212-564-5613
NY, NY 10018
Hours: 9:30-4:30 Mon-Fri   E-mail: costume@creativecostume.com
www.creativecostume.com
Large stock of character costumes. RENTALS. CREDIT CARDS.

Early Halloween 212-691-2933
130 W 25th St., 11th Fl. (6-7th Ave)   FAX 212-243-1499
NY, NY 10001
Hours: by appt. only   E-mail: earlyhalloween@aol.com
www.earlyhalloween.com
Vintage clothing, hats, shoes and accessories. Also vintage luggage and memorabilia. RENTAL only.

Francis Hendy NY 212-354-4764
244 W 39th St., 11th Fl. (7-8th Ave)   FAX 212-354-4765
NY, NY 10018
Hours: 10-7 Mon-Sat   E-mail: info@francishendy.com
www.francishendy.com
Costumes for music videos and theater. Fashion design and production. Contact Charmain. RENTALS. CREDIT CARDS.

Frock 212-594-5380
170 Elizabeth St. (Spring-Kenmare)   FAX 212-594-5684
NY, NY 10012
Hours: 12-7 Mon-Sat / 12-5 Sun   E-mail: info@frocknyc.dom
www.frocknyc.com
Sale and rental of vintage women's designer and couture clothing and accessories. Lesser known labels available also. Late 60s to late 90s. Website has photos of many items. RENTALS. CREDIT CARDS.

Goodspeed Musicals Costume Rental 860-322-0836
33 North Main St. Norma Terris Theatre   FAX 860-526-4086
Chester, CT 06412
Hours: 9:15 to 5 Mon-Fri   E-mail: costume-rentals@goodspeed.org
www.goodspeed.org/rentals
Goodspeed Costume Rentals is proud of the wide variety of costumes in our collection. With over 250,000 garments, plus hats and accessories, you will find just about anything you need for your productions. Call to schedule an appointment. RENTALS. CREDIT CARDS.

Halloween Adventure 212-673-4546
    104 Fourth Ave. (11-12th St)   FAX 212-358-0927
    NY, NY 10003
    Hours: 11-8 Mon-Sat / 12-7 Sun
    www.newyorkcostumes.com
    The masters of masquerade with the city's largest selection of costumes, masks, wigs, magic supplies and theatrical make-up, plus custom fangs, f/x kits and much more. CREDIT CARDS.

Hero Wardrobe 212-929-4376
    1 W 21st St., Street Level (5-6th Ave)   FAX 212-929-4333
    NY, NY 1010
    Hours: 9-6 Mon-Fri   E-mail: lani@herowardrobe.com
    www.HEROwardrobe.com
    Uniforms, vintage (men's, women's, & children's), footwear, big & tall, accessories and novelty items. RENTALS. CREDIT CARDS.

Malabar Ltd. 416-598-2581
    14 McCaul St.   FAX 416-598-3296
    Toronto, Ontario, CAN M5T1V6
    Hours: 9:30-6 Mon-Fri / 10-5 Sat   E-mail: b-a-star@malabar.net
    www.malabar.net
    Large costume rental house. Recently adding new costumes and accessories for Halloween. Large selection of opera costumes. Visit website to view some of their stock. CREDIT CARDS.

David Samuel Menkes 212-989-3706
    144 Fifth Ave., 3rd Fl. (19-20th St)
    NY, NY 10011
    Hours: by appt.   E-mail: dsm@davidmenkesleather.com
    www.davidmenkesleather.com
    High quality handcrafted custom leatherwork, theatrical and personal. RENTALS. No credit cards.

Norcostco, Inc. 973-575-3503
    333A Rt. 46 W   800-220-6940
    Fairfield, NJ 07004   FAX 973-575-2563
    Hours: 9:30-6 Mon-Fri / 10-5 Sat (Winter)   E-mail: newjersey@norcostco.com
    www.norcostco.com
    Theatrical supply house, including costumes. Catalog. RENTALS. CREDIT CARDS.

The Sentry Post 610-520-1283
    222 Ashwood Rd. (office)   610-842-2609
    Villanova, PA 19085   FAX 610-520-1284
    Hours: 9:15-5:30 Mon-Fri by appt.
    Authentic historic or military wardrobe, made to order or rental. Very knowledgeable and helpful over the phone; also historic and military props (accoutrements and swords).

COSTUME RENTALS

Spotlight Costumes, LLC 412-381-7733
1503 E Carson St. (S 16th St)   800-256-8645
Pittsburgh, PA 15203   FAX 412-381-0260
Hours: 10-6 Mon-Sat / 12-9 (October)   E-mail: info@spotlightcostumes.com
www.spotlightcostumes.com
*Costume rental and construction. In-house design services available. Also
wigs, masks and make-up. RENTALS. CREDIT CARDS.*

Frankie Steinz Costumes 212-925-1373
580 Broadway Ste 309
New York, NY 10012
Hours: by Appt.   E-mail: info@frankiesteinz.com
www.frankiesteinz.com
*Halloween rentals, rentals for children and custom costumes for music
videos, TV shows and advertising. RENTALS.*

Western Costume 818-760-0900
11041 Vanowen St.   FAX 818-508-2190
N. Hollywood, CA 91605
Hours: 8-5:30 Mon-Sat   E-mail: wccmail@westerncostumes.com
www.westerncostume.com
*One of the largest costume rental houses on the West Coast; film stock.
CREDIT CARDS.*

COSTUME SHOP & WARDROBE SUPPLIES

Allracks Industry, Inc. 212-244-1069
361 W 36th St. (8-9th Ave)   FAX 212-279-3879
NY, NY 10018
Hours: 8:30-4:30 Mon-Fri   E-mail: info@allracks.net
www.allracks.net
*Garment rack sales and rentals. All types of pipes and fittings. CREDIT
CARDS.*

American Hanger and Fixture Corp. 908-282-1982
410 Clermont Terrace   800-221-2790
Union, NJ 07083   FAX 908-282-6874
Hours: 9-5 Mon-Fri   E-mail: help@americanhanger.com
www.americanhanger.com
*Good selection of hangers, fixtures, tags, steamers, clothing racks, signage &
poly bags. Everything for your wardrobe needs. CREDIT CARDS.*

Basic Mfg. Co. 718-871-6106
3611 14th Ave. (36-37th St)   800-964-9973
Brooklyn, NY 11218   FAX 718-871-3616
Hours: 9-5 Mon-Thur / 9-2 Fri   E-mail: ebasicltd@aol.com
www.basicltd.com
Wholesale garment bags. Large orders only. CREDIT CARDS.

Manhattan Wardrobe Supply 212-268-9993
245 W 29th St., 8th Fl. (7-8th Ave)   FAX 212-268-1210
NY, NY 10001
Hours: 9-5:45 Mon-Fri   E-mail: info@wardrobesupplies.com
www.wardrobesupplies.com
Supplier of wardrobe expendables for film, television, theater and schools.
Cleaning supplies, clear garment bags, ageing supplies, etc. Will deliver or
ship. Visit website to find new products to try. Catalog or shop online. Fax
or e-mail orders 24-hrs. Will accept P.O.s or CREDIT CARDS.

Minnesota Chemical 651-646-7521
2285 Hampden Ave.   800-328-5689
St. Paul, MN 55114   FAX 651-649-1101
Hours: 8-4:30 Mon-Fri
www.minnesotachemical.com
Commercial laundry and drycleaning equipment and supplies; parts and
service. CREDIT CARDS.

Pincover Industrial Supply Co., Inc. .212-569-1010
4730 Broadway (near G.W. Bridge)   800-282-5233
NY, NY 10040   FAX 212-942-8486
Hours: 8:30-4:30 Mon-Thurs
Razor blades for industrial use.

Richard the Thread / Roy Cooper 310-837-4997
10405 Washington Blvd.   800-473-4997
Culver City, CA 90222   FAX 310-836-4996
Hours: 7-4 Mon-Fri   E-mail: info@richardthethread.com
www.richardthethread.com
Dressforms, corset supplies, notions, irons and steamers. Catalog $3. UPS-
CODs. CREDIT CARDS.

Ronis Bros. 516-887-5266
39 Harriet Pl.   FAX 516-887-5288
Lynbrook, NY 11563
Hours: 8-4:30 Mon-Fri
www.ronis.com
Manufacturers of Royal forms; dress and accessory forms. Very helpful.
CREDIT CARDS.

Travel Auto Bag Co., Inc. 212-840-0025
264 W 40th St. (7-8th Ave)   (Outside NY) 800-840-0095
NY, NY 10018   FAX: 212-302-8267
Hours: 9-4:30 Mon-Fri   E-mail: info@travelautobag.com
www.travelautobag.com
All types of garment bags, collapsible rolling racks, steamers, hangers,
mannequins and display fixtures. Not a store, they will mail anywhere, free
delivery within garment district or you can pick up order. Shop using the
website. Staff is nice and knowledgeable. CREDIT CARDS.

CURTAINS & DRAPERIES: THEATRICAL

Adirondack Studio 518-638-8000
439 County Rt 45   FAX 518-761-3362
Argyle, NY 12809
Hours: 9-5 Mon-Fri
www.adirondackscenic.com
Theatrical soft goods, backdrops, drapery murals, scenery.

Anne Guay, Inc. 917-225-6550
689 Myrtle Ave. # 5-H (Spencer)   FAX 718-852-7589
Brooklyn, NY 11205
Hours: By Appt.   E-mail: info@anneguay.com
www.anneguay.com
*Custom millinery, fashion accessories, costume crafts, soft goods for display,
stage, print, TV and film. High-end draperies and fabric treatments. CREDIT
CARDS.*

Associated Drapery & Equipment Co. .516-671-5245
40 Sea Cliff Ave.   FAX 516-674-2213
Glen Cove, NY 11542
Hours: 8-4 Mon-Fri
*Custom-made curtains and draperies; also scenic fabrics. Contact Chesky
Weiss.*

B.N. Productions, Inc. 978-352-4730
P.O. Box 353   FAX 978-352-4731
Boxford, MA 01921
Hours: 8:30-5 Mon-Fri   E-mail: sales@bnproductions.com
www.bnproductions.com
Theatrical rigging, drapery and traveler track systems. CREDIT CARDS.

BMI Supply 518-793-6706
571 Queensbury Ave.   800-836-0524
Queensbury, NY 12804   FAX 518-793-6181
Hours: 8-6 Mon-Fri   E-mail: bminy@bmisupply.com
www.bmisupply.com
*A full-line theatrical supply house and on-site contractor. Retail and
wholesale at everyday wholesale prices. Special effects. Sales only. CREDIT
CARDS.*

Brent Porter Fabrications & Interiors Ltd. 212-594-5323
260 W 35th St. #403 (7-8th Ave)   (cell) 917-880-5961
NY, NY 10001   FAX 212-594-5099
Hours: 9-5 Mon-Fri   E-mail: bpfabrications@msn.com
*Experienced theatrical and film upholstery and soft goods. Quick service,
reasonable prices.*

Consolidated Display Co., Inc. 630-851-8666
1210 US Hwy 34   (toll free) 888-851-SNOW
Oswego, IL 60543   FAX 630-851-8756
Hours: 7:30-4 Mon-Fri   E-mail: buzzp@aol.com
www.letitsnow.com
Custom mylar fringe draperies at stock prices. CREDIT CARDS.

Contract Workroom / Janet Girard 718-782-6430
   300 Morgan Ave. (Metropolitan-Grand St)   FAX 718-782-3805
   Brooklyn, NY 11211
   Hours: by appt.
   Custom draperies, window treatments, upholstery, fabric tension structures;
   quilting, soft sculpture, leather sculpture, fabric painting.

Drape Kings 201-770-9950
   3200 Liberty Ave. Unit 2C   888-372-7363
   North Bergen, NJ 07047   FAX 201-770-9956
   Hours: 9-5 Mon-Fri   E-mail: info@drapekings.com
   www.drapekings.com
   Pipe & drape rental systems. Many colors and fabrics to choose from. Drapery
   by the Foot. RENTALS ONLY. CREDIT CARDS.

Gerriets International 609-758-9121
   130 Winterwood Ave   800-369-3695
   Ewing, NJ 08638   FAX 609-758-9596
   Hours: 8:30-5 Mon-Fri   E-mail: mail@gi-info.com
   www.gi-info.com
   Materials in stock and to order; finished draperies and hardware, projection
   screens, wide muslin and drops. Online catalog. Shipping. Big screens for
   RENTAL.

I. Weiss and Sons, Inc. 718-706-8139
   2-07 Borden Ave. (Vernon-Jackson Ave)   888-325-7192
   Long Island City, NY 11101   FAX 718-482-9410
   Hours: 8-5:30 Mon-Fri   E-mail: info@iweiss.com
   www.iweiss.com
   Cycs, scrims, rain curtains and hardware.

Joseph C. Hansen Co., Inc. 201-222-1677
   629 Grove St., Lot # 26 (16-17th St)   866-988-8055
   Jersey City, NJ 07310   FAX 201-222-1699
   Hours: 9-5 Mon-Fri   E-mail: info@jchansen.com
   www.jchansen.com
   Theatrical curtain rental: cycs, scrims, velours, painted drops, star drops,
   curtain track, stands and dance floor. Brochure available. RENTALS. CREDIT
   CARDS.

Limelight Productions, Inc. 413-243-4950
   471 Pleasant St.   800-243-4950
   Lee, MA 01238   FAX 413-243-4993, 800-243-4951
   Hours: 9-5 Mon-Fri
   www.limelightproductions.com
   Custom theatrical curtains. Authorized service for Rosco foggers, ETC
   dimming and control and Strong followspots. Catalog. CREDIT CARDS.

Oasis/Stage Werks 801-363-0364
   249 Rio Grande St.   FAX 801-575-7121
   Salt Lake City, UT 84101
   Hours: 9-6 Mon-Fri
   www.oasis-stage.com
   Custom made grand drapes, scrim, muslin drops, blacks, outdoor draperies,
   display, skirting. Traveler track and bulk fabric sales. Installations. CREDIT
   CARDS.

Production Advantage, Inc. 802-651-6915
P.O. Box 1700   800-424-99914
Williston, VT 05495   FAX 877-424-9991
Hours: 8:30-6 Mon-Fri   E-mail: sales@proadv.com
www.proadv.com
Catalog sales of hardware, lighting, rigging, scenic material, soft goods, sound equipment and expendables to the entertainment industry. All major brands carried. Catalog. CREDIT CARDS.

Reynolds Drapery Service, Inc. 315-845-8632
7440 Main St.   FAX 315-845-8645
Newport, NY 13416
Hours: 8-4 Mon-Fri   E-mail: rynldpry@ntc.net.com
Manufacture, cleaning and repair of theatrical drapery. P.O.s accepted. No credit cards.

Rose Brand 800-223-1624
                                                                 FAX 800-594-7424

4 Emerson Lane(15-16th St)   800-223-1624
Secaucus, NJ 07094   201-809-1730
Hours: 8-5 Mon-Fri   FAX 201-809-1851

10616 Lanark St.   800-360-5056
Sun City, CA 91352   818-505-6290
Hours: 8-5 Mon-Fri   FAX 818-505-6293
www.rosebrand.com   E-mail: sales@rosebrand.com
Custom-sewn stage draperies. Drops, mylar rain curtains, backdrops and fiber optics. Largest selection of theatrical textiles nationwide as well as full range of theatrical supplies. Call or fax for catalog. CREDIT CARDS.

Whaley's / Bradford, Ltd. 011-44-127-457-6718
Harris Ct., Great Horton   011-44-127-452-1309
Bradford, West Yorkshire, England BD7 4EQ
www.whaleys-bradford.ltd.uk   E-mail: info@whaleysltd.co.uk
Located in the UK, Whaley's has curtain fabrics as well as many natural fiber fabrics that are sold prepared for dyeing and printing. Visit their website to order fabrics, drapes or basic fabrics for costumes. They have a separate export department. CREDIT CARDS.

CURTAINS, DRAPERIES, SHADES & BLINDS

Martin Albert Interiors 212-673-8000
9 E 19th St. (B'way-5th Ave)   800-525-4637
NY, NY 10003   FAX 212-673-8006
Hours: 9-5 Mon-Fri   E-mail: mail@martinalbert.com
www.martinalbert.com
Custom window treatments, upholstery and slipcovers. Custom furniture. RENTALS. CREDIT CARDS.

AllState Glass Corp. 212-226-2517
85 Kenmare St. (Lafayette-Mulberry St)   FAX 212-966-7904
NY, NY 10012
Hours: 8-4:30 Mon-Fri
www.allstateglasscorp.com
Good selection shades and blinds. Shades, one-and two-inch blinds, verticals,
pleated shades, woven wooden blinds. Custom and stock shower enclosures
glass and mirrors. Speak to Sydelle Philips. CREDIT CARDS.

BZI Distributors 212-966-6690
314 Grand St. (Basement level of Harry Zarin) (Allen-Grand St.)FAX 212-966-8962
NY, NY 10002
Hours: 9-6 Sun-Fri / 10-6 Sat
www.zarinfabrics.com
Vertical and mini-blinds, many styles of curtain rods and hardware.
Trimmings, upholstery supplies, foam rubber. Contact David or Gerry. $25
minimum on CREDIT CARDS.

Circle Fabrics / Circle Visual, Inc. 212-719-5153
225 W 37th St. 16th FL (7-8th Ave)   FAX 212-704-0918
NY, NY 10018
Hours: 9-5:30 Mon-Fri   E-mail: sales@circlevisual.com
www.circlevisual.com
Custom tablecloths, slipcovers, pillows, banners, printing, embroidery,
fixtures and fabrics. Everything made to order. Quick delivery. Digital
printing for vinyl signs. Visit website to view clientele. CREDIT CARDS.

DFB Sales 718-729-8310
21-07 Borden Ave. (Bordon-21st St)   800-433-4546
Long Island City, NY 11101   FAX 718-706-0526
Hours: 9-5 Mon-Fri   E-mail: dfb@dfbsales.com
www.dfbsales.com
Custom draperies in their workshop. Blinds and shades to order. Many film
credits. Great website. Catalog.

Drapery Exchange 203-655-3844
14 Center St. (Post Rd)   FAX 203-831-8510
Darien, CT 06820
Hours: 10-5 Mon-Fri / 10-1:30 Sat   E-mail: kathy@drapexdarien.com
www.drapexdarien.com
High-end drapery consignment store. CREDIT CARDS.

Eldridge Textile Co. 732-544-4500
22 Meridian Rd. # 3   800-635-4399
Eatontown, NJ 07724   FAX 732-544-4555
Hours: 9:30-6 Mon-Fri   E-mail: custserv@eldridgetextile.com
www.eldridgetextile.com
Sheets, bedding, towels, tablecloths and custom window treatments. $3
refundable charge for catalog. Will ship. Catalog available online. CREDIT
CARDS.

Epstein's Paint Center 212-265-3960
   822 Tenth Ave. (54-55th St)   800-464-3432
   NY, NY 10019   FAX 212-765-8841
   Hours: 8-5:30 Mon-Fri / 8:30-3 Sat   E-mail: sales@epsteinspaint.com
   www.epsteinspaint.com
   Many styles of blinds and shades, custom service within 24-hrs. Also large stock of floor coverings, wallpaper, scenic/household paints, tints and dyes. See Marty. CREDIT CARDS.

Harry Zarin Co. 212-925-6112
   314 Grand St. (Allen-Orchard St)   FAX 212-925-6584
   NY, NY 10002
   Hours: 9-7 Mon-Thurs / 9-6 Fri / 10-6 Sun
   www.zarinfabrics.com
   Large selection of drapery and upholstery fabrics; fair prices. CREDIT CARDS.

Horizon Window Treatments 212-759-4111
   133 W 24th St. (6-7th Ave)   FAX 212-317-0437
   NY, NY 10011
   Hours: 9-7 Mon-Fri / 11-5 Sat-Sun   E-mail: customer@horizonnyc.com

   888 Lexington Ave.(66th St)   212-772-1400
   NY, NY 10021   FAX 212-794-2913
   Hours: 7-7 Mon-Fri / 8-6 Sat / 11-5 Sun
   www.horizonyc.com
   Best showroom in Manhattan for all your window treatment solutions, roller shades, blinds, drapes, cornices, roman and balloon shades. Free measurements. Visit web address for other locations. CREDIT CARDS.

Janovic Plaza 212-772-1400
   888 Lexington Ave.(66th St)   FAX 212-794-2913
   NY, NY 10021
   Hours: 7-7 Mon-Fri / 8-6 Sat / 11-5 Sun

   1555 Third Ave.(87th St)   212-289-6300
   NY, NY 10128   FAX 212-289-6831
   Hours: 7-6:30 Mon-Fri / 9-6 Sat / 11-5 Sun

   159 W 72nd St.(Amsterdam-Columbus Ave)   212-595-2500
   NY, NY 10023   FAX 212-724-7846
   Hours: 7:30-6:30 Mon-Fri / 9-6 Sat / 11-5 Sun

   161 Sixth Ave.(Spring St)   212-627-1100
   NY, NY 10013   FAX 212-924-7641
   Hours: 7:30-6:30 Mon-Fri / 9-6 Sat / 11-5 Sun

   215 Seventh Ave.(22nd-23rd St)   212-645-5454
   NY, NY 10011   FAX 212-691-1504
   Hours: 7:30-6:30 Mon-Fri / 9-6 Sat / 11-5 Sun

   2680 Broadway(102nd St)   212-531-2300
   NY, NY 10025   FAX 212-932-3476
   Hours: 7:30-6:30 Mon-Fri / 9-6 Sat / 11-5 Sun

   292 Third Ave.(22nd-23rd St)   212-777-3030
   NY, NY 10010   FAX 212-253-0985
   Hours: 7:30-6:30 Mon-Fri / 9-6 Sat / 11-5 Sun

Janovic Plaza (cont.) 212-477-6930
　80 Fourth Ave.(10th St)　　　　　　　　　　　　FAX 212-254-4628
　NY, NY 10003
　Hours: 7:30-6:30 Mon-Fri / 9-6 Sat / 11-5 Sun

　30-35 Thompson Ave.(Van Dam & Queens Blvd)　　　　　347-418-3480
　Long Island City, NY 11101　　　　　　　　Orders 718-392-3999
　Hours: 7-6 Mon-Fri / 8-4 Sat　　　　　　　　FAX 718-784-4564
　www.janovic.com
　Window shades and vertical blinds, in stock or custom work. CREDIT
　CARDS.

Marc Tash Interiors 212-385-2253
　2483 65th St. (24th Ave-Dayhill Rd)　　718-336-3326 or 800-MARC TASH
　Brooklyn, NY 11204
　Hours: by appt.　　　　　　　　E-mail: info@marctashinteriors.com
　www.marctashinteriors.com
　Custom drapery and window treatments. Re-upholstery and slipcovers.
　Complete design service and installation. Wood blinds, Roman and balloon
　shades, valances and cornices. Marc will pick up and deliver items for re-
　upholstery. CREDIT CARDS.

Morgik Metal Designs 212-463-0304
　145 Hudson St. (at Hubert St)　　　　　　　　　　　800-354-5252
　NY, NY 10013　　　　　　　　　　　　　FAX 212-463-0329
　Hours: 8-4 Mon-Fri　　　　　　　　　E-mail: sales@morgik.com
　www.morgik.com
　Wrought-iron furniture, drapery rods and other metal products. Contact
　Dorothy, Larry, or Mihail. CREDIT CARDS.

Pintchik Home Hardware and Decorating Center 718-783-3333
　478 Bergen St. (Flatbush Ave)　　　　　　　　FAX 718-857-7932
　Brooklyn, NY 11217
　Hours: 7:30-6:50 Mon-Fri / 8:30-5:50 Sat / 9-5:50 Sun
　Shades and blinds of all types. Paints, hardware and flooring. CREDIT
　CARDS.

Roy Rudin Decorators, Inc. 718-786-7267
　5024 46th St.　　　　　　　　　　　　　　　718-786-8352
　Woodside, NY 11377　　　　　　　　　　FAX 718-786-8408
　Hours: 9-5 Mon-Fri　　　　　　　E-mail: dan46te@earthlink.net
　Experienced theatrical and film upholstery and soft goods.

The Terrence Conran Shop 212-755-9079
　888 Broadway Lower Level (18-19th St)　　　　FAX 212-755-3989
　NY, NY 10003
　Hours: 11-8 Mon-Fri / 10-7 Sat / 12-6 Sun
　　　　　　　　　　E-mail: terenceconranshop@conranusa.com
　www.conranusa.com
　Designer furniture, household, bedding and bath, textiles and hardware. Very
　nice people. Will do rentals to film and television. CREDIT CARDS.

WolfHome 800-220-1893
936 Broadway (22nd St)   646-602-3246
NY, NY 10010   FAX 212-254-7105
Hours: 10-7 Mon-Sat / 11-6:30 Sun
www.wolfhome-ny.com
Beautiful high-end fabrics. Large selection of embroidered silks. Some ready made pillows, drapes and curtains. Interior goods and furniture made to order, shades and window treatments, reupholstery service. They have their own mills and can custom weave and color. Workroom on premises for custom work. Fast deadlines no problem. Very helpful and willing to accommodate entertainment business needs. CREDIT CARDS.

DEPARTMENT & VARIETY STORES

Arrow Wholesale Co. 508-753-5830
28 Water St. (Mercer St)   800-452-6310
Worcester, MA 01604   FAX 508-753-5316
Hours: 9-6 Mon-Fri   E-mail: info@arrowonthenet.com
www.arrowonthenet.com
Rit and Tintex by the dozen. Commercial stationery and school supplies, also seasonal merchandise and props. Wholesale. Supplier of Mom & Popî Five & Dime items.

Bergdorf Goodman 212-753-7300
754 Fifth Ave. (57-58th St)   (studio services) 212-872-8772
NY, NY 10019
Hours: 10-8 Mon-Sat (Sat until 7) / 12-6 Sun
www.bergdorfgoodman.com
High-fashion clothing department store. Contact Betty Halbreich for both men's and women's studio services, by appt. only. CREDIT CARDS.

Bloomingdales 212-705-2000
1000 Third Ave. (59th St)   (Studio Services) 212-705-3673
NY, NY 10022   FAX 212-705-3939
Hours: 10-6 Mon-Fri
www.bloomingdales.com
Designer clothing, housewares, linens, draperies; very stylish. Contact Barbara D-Arsanel. CREDIT CARDS.

Conway Stores 212-967-3460
1345 Broadway(35-36th St)
NY, NY 10018
Hours: 8-8 Mon-Fri / 9:30-8 Sat / 10:30-7 Sun

450 Seventh Ave.(34-35th St)   212-967-1371
NY, NY 10001
Hours: 8-8 Mon-Sun

245 W 34th St.(7-8th Ave)   212-868-0002
NY, NY 10001
Hours: 8-8 Mon-Fri / 9:30-8 Sat / 10:30-7 Sun
Reasonably priced clothing, footwear and accessories and various housewares. Call 212-967-5300 for info on all locations. CREDIT CARDS.

Hammacher-Schlemmer 212-421-9000
147 E 57th St. (Lexington-3rd Ave)   800-421-9002
NY, NY 10022   FAX 212-644-3875
Hours: 10-6 Mon-Sat
www.hammacher.com
Unusual gifts items and gadgets. Catalog. CREDIT CARDS.

IKEA 800-434-IKEA
1000 IKEA Dr.(Exit 13A off NJ Tpke)   908-289-4488
Elizabeth, NJ 07201
Hours: 10-9 Mon-Sat / 10-8 Sun

D-E

IKEA (cont.) 800-434-IKEA
1100 Broadway Mall(LIE Exit 41S or NSP Exit 35S)   516-681-4532
Hicksville, NY 11801
Hours: 10-9 Mon-Sun

1 Beard St.(Columbia-Otsego   718-246-4532
Brooklyn, NY 11231
Hours: 10-9 Mon-Sun
www.ikea.com
International Swedish department store for the home; specializing in
furniture and home furnishings; inexpensive. Visit website for other locations
nationwide. Catalog. CREDIT CARDS.

K-Mart 212-760-1188
250 W 34th St.(7-8th Ave)
NY, NY 10019
Hours: 8-10 Mon-Thurs / 9-10 Fri-Sun

770 Broadway(8th St)   212-673-1540
NY, NY 10003-9535
Hours: 8-10 Daily
www.kmart.com
A/V equipment, sporting goods, camping gear, household goods. P.O.s. See
website for other locations. CREDIT CARDS.

Lord & Taylor 212-391-3344
424 Fifth Ave. (38-39th St)   (studio services) 212-391-3519
NY, NY 10018
Hours: 10-8:30 Mon-Tue, Thur-Fri / 9-8:30 Wed / 10-7 Sat / 11-7 Sun
www.lordandtaylor.com
Stylish women's clothing; good kitchenware department. CREDIT CARDS.

Macy's Department Store 212-695-4400
151 W 34th St. (B'way-7th Ave)
NY, NY 10001
Hours: 10-9:30 Mon-Sat / 11-8 Sun
www.macys.com
The world's largest department store; great kitchenware, housewares and
gifts. Store hours vary by season. CREDIT CARDS.

Saks Fifth Ave. Studio Service . . . .(studio services) 212-940-4560
611 Fifth Ave.(49-50th St)   (store) 212-753-4000
NY, NY 10022
Hours: 10-6 Mon-Fri

9600 Wilshire Blvd.   (store) 310-275-4211
Beverly Hills, CA 90212
Hours: 10-6 Mon-Fri (10-8:30 Thurs) / 10-7 Sat / 12-6 Sun
www.sacksfifthavenue.com
Fashionable clothing and accessories for men, women, children. Great memo
service for stylists and costume designers. Also linens and home furnishings.
CREDIT CARDS.

D-E

DIGITAL DISPLAY

Ace Banner, Flag & Graphics Co. 212-620-9111
107 W 27th St. (6th Ave)   800-675-9112
NY, NY 10011   FAX 212-463-9128
Hours: 7:30-4 Mon-Fri   E-mail: service@acebanner.com
www.acebanner.com / www.acebannershop.com
Foreign and domestic flags; custom banners; screen-printing. CREDIT CARDS.

Baumwell Graphics, Inc. 704-814-4550
8923 Providence Estates Ct.   888-266-7246
Charlotte, NC 28270
Hours: 9-6 Mon-Fri   E-mail: clyde@chromatype.com
www.chromatype.com
Typesetting, desktop publishing services, design, layout, photostats and laser engraving. Contact Clyde Baumwell. Also custom transfers. CREDIT CARDS.

Big Apple Sign Corp. 212-629-3650
247 W 35th St. (7-8th Ave)   877-244-2775
NY, NY 10001   FAX 212-629-4954
Hours: 9-5:30 Mon-Fri   E-mail: amir@bigapplegroup.com
www.bigapplegroup.com
Full-service sign company; 24-hr. service available. CREDIT CARDS.

Circle Fabrics / Circle Visual, Inc. .212-719-5153
225 W 37th St. 16th FL (7-8th Ave)   FAX 212-704-0918
NY, NY 10018
Hours: 9-5:30 Mon-Fri   E-mail: sales@circlevisual.com
www.circlevisual.com

Custom tablecloths, slipcovers, pillows, banners, printing, embroidery, fixtures and fabrics. Everything made to order. Quick delivery. Digital printing for vinyl signs. Visit website to view clientele. CREDIT CARDS.

COMP 24 212-627-4000
127 W 30th St., 4th Fl. (6-7th Ave)   800-848-7716
NY, NY 10001   FAX 212-627-4287
Hours: 8-8 Mon-Fri
www.comp24.com
The largest packaging prototype facility in the world, specializing in color correct comps for advertising. Digital direct proofing and silkscreening; transfers; banners to bus wraps.

DUNHAM STUDIOS 518-494-3930
10 Dunham's Loop   FAX 518-494-3688
Pottersville, NY 12860
Hours: 9-5 Mon-Fri   E-mail: clarke@dunhamstudios.com
www.dunhamstudios.com
All category member USA Local #829. Designer of scenery, lighting & projections for Broadway, International Opera and national television. 2 Tony, 5 Drama Desk Nominations; Maharam Award, Jefferson Award. Custom design and fabrication of exhibits, architectural models and store interiors. Specializing in historically accurate and fantasy model railroads for museums and corporations. Also custom large format printing, murals, props and cut vinyl signs. Member ATAC.

D-E

Manhattan Neon Sign Corp. 212-714-0430
640 W 28th St.   FAX 212-947-3906
NY, NY 10001
Hours: 9-5 Mon-Fri / or by appt.   E-mail: sales@manhattanneon.com
www.manhattanneon.com
Custom-made neon and rentals, 3-D props and displays, large-format full-
color graphics, LED moving message signs and vinyl signs, cut acrylic, wood
metal and foam. Contact Peter.

National Flag & Display Co., Inc. 212-462-4000
22 W 21st St., 7th Fl. (5-6th St)   FAX 212-462-2624
NY, NY 10010
Hours: 9-5:30 Mon-Fri / eves. & weekends by appt.
www.nationalflag.com   E-mail: hsiegel@nationalflag.com
Manufacturers of banners, flags, backdrops and wall murals. Applique,
silkscreen, inkjet, dye-sublimation and electrostatic full-color printing. Rush
orders. RENTALS. CREDIT CARDS.

Revolution Graphics & Design 212-741-7122
Pier 40, Ground floor (West St)   FAX 212-633-6101
NY, NY 10014
Hours: 8:30-5 Mon-Fri   E-mail: bob@revolutiongraphics.com
www.revolutiongraphics.com
Digital signage, graphics, props/design, photo, trade show display, scenery
and exhibits. CREDIT CARDS.

Wang & Frederickson, Inc. 917-251-4702
1 North 12th St., Ste 316/7A   FAX 212-459-0192
Brooklyn, NY 11211
Hours: by appt.   E-mail: info@wangandfrederickson.com
www.wangandfrederickson.com
Wide format printing services.

DISPLAY HOUSES & MATERIALS

Bond Parade Float, Inc. 973-778-3333
111 Clifton Blvd.   FAX 973-778-6950
Clifton, NJ 07011
Hours: 8:30-4:30 Mon-Sat   E-mail: bondfloat@aol.com
www.bondparadefloats.com
Parade floats and float ornaments. RENTALS.

Concept Design Productions 626-932-0082
718 S. Primrose Ave.   800-846-0717
Monrovia, CA 91016   FAX 626-932-0072
Hours: 9-6 Mon-Fri   E-mail: info@conceptdesigninc.com
www.conceptdesigninc.com
Rental house for structural systems, props and scenic elements. Full sets
and support services available. Check out their website for full listings. Also
custom-built items. See James Leverton. RENTALS.

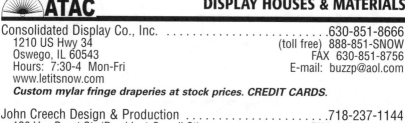

Consolidated Display Co., Inc. 630-851-8666
1210 US Hwy 34 (toll free) 888-851-SNOW
Oswego, IL 60543 FAX 630-851-8756
Hours: 7:30-4 Mon-Fri E-mail: buzzp@aol.com
www.letitsnow.com
Custom mylar fringe draperies at stock prices. CREDIT CARDS.

John Creech Design & Production 718-237-1144
129 Van Brunt St. (President-Carroll St) FAX 718-237-4133
Brooklyn, NY 11231
Hours: 8-6 Mon-Fri E-mail: shop@jcdp.biz
www.webuildeverything.com
Custom scenery, props and special effects for theatre, film, television and display.

DUNHAM STUDIOS 518-494-3930
10 Dunham's Loop FAX 518-494-3688
Pottersville, NY 12860
Hours: 9-5 Mon-Fri E-mail: clarke@dunhamstudios.com
www.dunhamstudios.com
All category member USA Local #829 Designer of scenery, lighting & projections for Broadway, International Opera and national television. 2 Tony, 5 Drama Desk Nominations; Maharam Award, Jefferson Award. Custom design and fabrication of exhibits, architectural models and store interiors. Specializing in historically accurate and fantasy model railroads for museums and corporations. Also custom large format printing, murals, props and cut vinyl signs. Member ATAC.

F.A.S.T. Corp. 608-269-7110
PO Box 258, 14177 County Hwy Q FAX 608-269-7514
Sparta, WI 54656
Hours: 8-5 Mon-Fri E-mail: info@fastkorp.com
www.fastkorp.com
Large scale fiberglass animals and shapes, amusement slides, fountains and trademarks. Online catalog. CREDIT CARDS.

Gabriel Logan 740-380-6809
1689 E Front St. 800-780-0004
Logan, OH 43138 FAX 740-380-6698
Hours: 8-5 Mon-Fri E-mail: info@gabriellogan.com
www.gabriellogan.com
Manufacturer of custom cubes, pedestals, slatwall and geometric display fixtures. Available in many styles and colors in laminate, veneer and faux stone finishes. P.O.s accepted. CREDIT CARDS.

Geppetto, Inc. 718-398-9792
201 46th St. 2nd FL FAX 718-622-2991
Brooklyn, NY 11220
Hours: 9-5 Mon-Fri E-mail: gepstudios@aol.com
www.geppettostudios.com
Custom construction of soft sculpture promotion and display props, character costumes, foam rubber masks, oversized foam props and 3-D illustrations. Contact Scott; brochure available.

Gotham Scenic 201-868-1007
   71 West Side Ave. (W Houston-West St)   212-741-3399
   North Bergen, NY 07047   FAX 201-868-1367
   Hours: 8-5 Mon-Fri
   www.gothamscenic.com
*Full-service union scene shop. Specializes in theatre, TV, displays and
exhibits. High quality and competitive pricing. Talk to John Prisco.*

Kadan Productions, Inc. 212-674-7080
   3200 Liberty Ave., Bldg 3 (Paterson Plank Rd)   FAX 212-674-7244
   North Bergen, NJ 07047
   Hours: 9-6 Mon-Fri
   www.kadaninc.com
*Full-service staging, lighting, audio/video, set construction and design
company. Extensive experience in fashion, corporate conventions and special
events. Can provide video graphics and slide projection. Will design or make
any part of your design happen.*

Blaine Kern Artists, Inc. / Mardi Gras World 504-361-7821
   1380 Port of New Orleans Pl.   800-362-8213
   New Orleans, LA 70130   FAX 504-558-1865
   Hours: 8-5 Mon-Fri   E-mail: sabine@martigrasworld.com
   www.mardigrasworld.com
*Custom and stock. Extensive inventory from 47 years of Mardi Gras Parade
floats; papier mache, fiberglass props, figures, statuary, masks. Brochure
available. Tours of facilities as well as workshops on mask making. P.O.s
accepted. Beautiful website. RENTALS. CREDIT CARDS.*

Lockfast 800-543-7157
   8481 Duke Blvd   FAX 513-701-6936
   Mason, OH 45040
   Hours: 8:30-5 Mon-Fri   E-mail: sales@lockfast.com
   www.lockfast.com
*Providing standard and custom hook-and-loop fastening products, velcro
compatible fabric, plus graphics cases for the display industry. Display loop
fabric available in 34 colors! CREDIT CARDS.*

Main Attractions 732-225-3500
   85 Newfield Ave. (Raritan Ctr Pkwy)   800-394-3500
   Edison, NJ 08837   732-225-2110
   Hours: 9:30-5 Mon-Fri   E-mail: events@mainattractions.com
   www.mainattractions.com
*Special events contractors; specializing in custom tent rentals, restroom
trailers, decor, portable staging, lighting and the production of displays and
signage. Visit website to see the full spectrum of their products. RENTALS.
CREDIT CARDS.*

Mechanical Displays, Inc. 718-258-5588
   4420 Farragut Rd. (E 45th St)   FAX 718-258-6202
   Brooklyn, NY 11203
   Hours: 8-4:30 Mon-Fri   E-mail: info@mechanicaldisplays.com
   www.mechanicaldisplays.com
*Stock and custom animated figures with simple or pneumatic mechanisms;
also turntables. See Lou Nasti for photos and price list. P.O.s accepted. No
credit cards.*

D-E

New York Store Fixture Company 914-591-1100
145 Palisade St. Ste. 249   800-336-8353
Dobbs Ferry, NY 10522   FAX 914-591-1070
Hours: by appt.   E-mail: info@nystorefixture.com
www.nystorefixture.com
Distributor of Metro Shelving and components. Black and chrome in stock, 11 more colors as special order. New and used display cases. Catalog. Some rentals. CREDIT CARDS.

Provost Displays, Inc. 800-555-3772
501 W Washington St., 2nd Fl.   610-279-3970
Norristown, PA 19401   FAX 610-279-3968
Hours: 8-5:30 Mon-Thurs   E-mail: toprovost@verizon.net
www.provostdisplays.com
Vacuumformed architectural & scenic panels. Manufacturers of GIANTFORM; flame and weatherproof vacuumformed plastic decorative panels up to 4' x 12'. Custom molds made to order. Free shipping to NY and NJ areas. Catalog of stock designs available. CREDIT CARDS.

Robelan Displays, Inc. 516-564-8600
395 Westbury Blvd.   FAX 516-564-8077
Hempstead, NY 11550
Hours: 9-5 Mon-Fri   E-mail: main@robelan.net
www.robelan.net
Display props and fabrication, foliage, artificial snow, snow blankets. Phone orders. P.O.s with approved account. CREDIT CARDS.

BILL RYBAK / 3D DESIGN & FABRICATION 917-929-9124
59 South St.
Highland, NY 12528
Hours: by appt.   E-mail: billrybak@yahoo.com
www.billrybak.com
Custom design and fabrication of props, displays, showroom interiors, models and sculpture. Digital props and models imaging.

Spaeth Design 212-489-0770
629 W 54th St., 6th Fl. (10-11th Ave)   FAX 212-265-6261
NY, NY 10019
Hours: 8:30-5 Mon-Fri   E-mail: stephen@spaethdesign.com
www.spaethdesign.com
Custom animated displays, animatronic characters, props and seasonal decor; contact Sandy Spaeth. P.O.s accepted. Freight entrance: 630 W 55th Street.

Superior Specialties, Inc. 800-666-2545
2517 N Casaloma Dr. / P.O. Box 7170   920-560-6262
Appleton, WI 54912   FAX 920-727-3115
Hours: 8-5 Mon-Fri   E-mail: backgrounds@superspec.com
www.superspec.com
To the trade only. Custom decorative items; haybales, display carts, etc. CREDIT CARDS.

DOLLS, DOLL PARTS & DOLLHOUSES

All About Dolls 973-770-3228
72 Lakeside Blvd.   800-645-DOLL
Hopatcong, NJ 07843   FAX 973-398-6338
Hours: 9-4 Mon-Fri   E-mail: sales@allaboutdolls.com
www.allaboutdolls.com
Doll supplies primarily for porcelain dolls. Mail order only. $7 for catalog or check out online catalog. No minimum. CREDIT CARDS.

Creative Toymakers / Toys 2 Wish 4 860-228-3102
93 Mill Plain Rd.(Teacher - Parent Store)   203-794-0577
Danbury, CT 06811   FAX 203-798-9854
Hours: 10-6 Mon-Fri / 10-5 Sat

127 Main St.   860-657-8697
Hebron, CT 06248   FAX 860-228-5272
Hours: 10-6 Mon-Sat / 12-4 Sun   E-mail: info@toys2wish4.com
www.toys2wish4.com
Dolls and doll furniture; also general and educational toys. Two hours from Manhattan.

Manhattan Dollhouse 212-644-9400
767 Fifth Ave. (59th St) FAO Schwartz   888-646-1976
NY, NY 10003
Hours: 10-7 Mon-Thurs / 10-8 Fri / 11-6 Sun
www.manhattandollhouse.com
Doll house kits, furniture, dolls, miniatures. Certified Bespaq dealer. Visit website. RENTALS. CREDIT CARDS.

Tiny Doll House 212-744-3719
314 E. 78th St. (80-81st St)
NY, NY 10075
Hours: 11-5 Mon-Fri / 11-4 Sat
www.tinydollhousenyc.com
Dollhouse mouldings, turnings, decorative castings, lighting systems and parts. CREDIT CARDS.

DOWN, BATTING & FIBERFILL
See also: UPHOLSTERY TOOLS & SUPPLIES

BZI Distributors 212-966-6690
314 Grand St. (Basement level of Harry Zarin) (Allen-Grand St.)FAX 212-966-8962
NY, NY 10002
Hours: 9-6 Sun-Fri / 10-6 Sat
www.zarinfabrics.com
Foam rubber and upholstery supplies. Contact David or Gerry. $25 minimum on CREDIT CARDS.

Canal Rubber Supply Co. 212-226-7339
329 Canal St. (Greene St)   800-444-6483
NY, NY 10013   FAX 212-219-3754
Hours: 9-4:45 Mon-Fri / 9-3:45 Sat
www.canalrubber.com
Fluffy Dacron batting by the yard or roll. Sheet rubber, foam mats, hoses and tubing. CREDIT CARDS.

Economy Foam & Futons 212-475-4800
56 8th St. (5-6th Ave)   FAX 212-475-2727
NY, NY 10011
Hours: 10-7 Mon-Thurs / Fri call for hours / 10:30-6 Sun
                 E-mail: sales@economyfoamandfutons.com
www.economyfoamandfutons.com
Batting by the bag or roll; foam rubber sheets, shapes; pillows; vinyl fabrics; futons. Custom pillow and pad covering. CREDIT CARDS.

Fairfield 800-980-8000
P.O. Box 1157   800-243-0989
Danbury, CT 06813   FAX 203-792-9710
Hours: 8-5 Mon-Fri   E-mail: consumer@poly-fil.com
www.poly-fil.com
Fiber, batting, pillows; polyester, bamboo and cotton. Volume discounts, wholesale only (must have tax number). Minimum order is 2 cartons. Phone orders and P.O.s accepted. CREDIT CARDS.

Mike & Misha Pillow & Quilts, Inc. 212-260-7270
133 W 25th St. # 2W (6-7th Ave)
NY, NY 10001
Hours: By appt. only
Makes pillows and cushions.

DRAPERY HARDWARE AND SUPPLIES

BZI Distributors 212-966-6690
314 Grand St. (Basement level of Harry Zarin) (Allen-Grand St.)FAX 212-966-8962
NY, NY 10002
Hours: 9-6 Sun-Fri / 10-6 Sat
www.zarinfabrics.com
Vertical and mini-blinds, many styles of curtain rods and hardware. Trimmings, upholstery supplies, foam rubber. Contact David or Gerry. $25 minimum on CREDIT CARDS.

Greenberg & Hammer, Inc. 212-246-2835
535 Eighth Ave. 6th Fl. North (36-37th St)   800-955-5135
NY, NY 10018   FAX 212-765-8475
Hours: 9-5 Mon-Fri   E-mail: greenberghammer1@cs.com
www.greenberg-hammer.com
Enormous selection of sewing notions, sewing tools and wardrobe kit supplies; phone and mail orders; see Frank. CREDIT CARDS.

Royal American Wallcraft, Inc. 800-330-9435
501 Central Ave.   386-698-1236
Crescent City, FL 32112   FAX 800-445-2147
Hours: 10-5 Mon-Fri   E-mail: royalm@gmail.com
www.bentleybrothers.com
Drapery hardware, some wall fabrics. Wholesale to the trade. **CREDIT**
CARDS.

Textol Systems, Inc. 201-935-1220
435 Meadow Lane   800-624-8746
Carlstadt, NJ 07072   FAX 201-935-1824
Hours: 8-5 Mon-Fri   E-mail: sales@textol.com
www.textol.com
Drapery supplies and velcro just about anyway you need it. **Super nice**
service. CREDIT CARDS.

DRYCLEANERS

Lincoln Terrace Cleaners 212-874-3066
149 Amsterdam Ave. (66th St)
NY, NY 10023
Hours: 7-7 Mon-Fri / 8-6 Sat
Theatrical drycleaning.

Meurice Garment Care 516-627-6060
249 Plandome Rd. (29-30th St)   24 hr. Hotline 800-240-3377
Manhasset, NY 11030   FAX 516-627-2943
Hours: 9-6 Mon-Sat   E-mail: clothesdr@aol.com
www.garmentcare.com
Fine care for any materials. Garment restoration a specialty. Contact Wayne
Edelman.

Minerva Cleaners 718-729-4566
37-22 34th St. (37-38 Ave)   FAX 718-729-4344
Long Island City, NY 11101
Hours: 7-6 Daily   E-mail: minervacleaners@aol.com
Reasonable prices and fast service; theatrical drycleaning. Contact Mary.
CREDIT CARDS.

Neighborhood Cleaners Association .212-967-3002
252 W 29th St. (7-8th Ave)   800-888-1622
NY, NY 10001
Hours: 9-5 Mon-Fri   E-mail: info@nca-i.com
www.nca-i.com
Theatrical drycleaning; very cooperative; very good. **CREDIT CARDS.**

Ernest Winzer 718-294-2400
1828 Cedar Ave. (179th-Major Deegan)   877-WINZER1
Bronx, NY 10453   FAX 718-294-2729
Hours: 6:30-5 Mon-Fri, Radio Dispatch 24-hrs.   E-mail: borntoclean@yahoo.com
www.ernestwinzer.com
The theatrical dry cleaner. Cleaning, restoration, tailoring, alterations; beads,
pleats, any fabric; multi-cleaning processes; overnight service; water/stain
repellency; fire retardancy; leather/suede/fur.

DYERS

Dye Pro Services, Inc. 403-273-9348
Bay # 14, 4816-35B St. SE   FAX 403-273-9371
Calgary, AB, Canada T2B3N1
Hours: 7-9pm Mon-Fri   E-mail: dylon@dyeproservices.com
www.dyeproservices.com
Custom color textile dyeing, garment dying, antique pleating, marbling, ombre dyeing, silk-screening and discharge dying and printing. Over 16 years experience in the industry. Mail order Dylon and satin shoe dye. Speak to Emily.

D-E

Dye-Namix, Inc. 212-941-6642
151 Grand St. 2nd FL   FAX 212-941-7407
NY, NY 10013
Hours: 9:30-6 Mon-Fri / or by appt.   E-mail: info@dyenamix.com
www.dyenamix.com
Creative dyeing, painting and silkscreening of samples, yardages and garments for the fashion, theatre and film industries. Contact Raylene Marasco for project estimates. No credit cards.

GENE MIGNOLA, INC.. 718-858-8902
610 Smith St., (3rd Fl)   FAX 718-858-8667
Brooklyn, NY 10001
Hours: 9-5 Mon-Fri   E-mail: GM5919@aol.com
Custom dyeing and silkscreening. Call before stopping by. Member ATAC.

Martin Izquierdo Studio 212-807-9757
118 W 22nd St., 9th Fl. (6-7th Ave)   FAX 212-366-5249
NY, NY 10011
Hours: 9-7 Mon-Fri   E-mail: izquierdostudio@gmail.com
www.izquierdostudio.com
Dyeing, silkscreening and fabric painting for theatre, film, commercials, display and video.

Meurice Garment Care 516-627-6060
249 Plandome Rd. (29-30th St)   24 hr. Hotline 800-240-3377
Manhasset, NY 11030   FAX 516-627-2943
Hours: 9-6 Mon-Sat   E-mail: clothesdr@aol.com
www.garmentcare.com
Small quantity dyeing of material and garments for fashion and entertainment industries. Contact Wayne Edelman.

The professional trade association for artists and craftspeople working in theatre, film, television and advertising

ATAC Membership 2010-11

Sharlot Battin
  Montana Leatherworks
Chris Bobin
Sharon Braunstein
Randy Carfagno
Nadine Charlsen
Eileen Connor
Mary Creede
Margaret Cusack
Cindy Anita Fain
  CINAF Designs
James Feng
Keen Gat
Deborah R. Glassberg
Rodney Gordon
Joseph Gourley
Corrinna Griffin
Jung K. Griffin
Denise Grillo
  Offstage Design
Stockton Hall
Karen Hart
Suzanne Hayden

Marian Jean "Killer" Hose
J. Michelle Hill
Louise Hunnicutt
John Jerard
  Jerard Studio
Joni Johns
Jan Kastendieck
Rachel Keebler
  Cobalt Studios
Amanda Klein
Arnold S. Levine
  Arnold S. Levine, Inc.
Janet Linville
Jeanne Marino
  Moonboots Productions
Jerry Marshall
Betsey McKearnan
Gene Mignola
  Gene Mignola, Inc.
Mary Mulder
  Mulder / Martin, Inc.
Susan Pitocchi
Elizabeth Popeil

Adele Recklies
Monona Rossol
  Arts, Crafts, & Theatre
  Safety (A.C.T.S.)
Bill Rybak
Jody Schoffner
James R. Seffens
Lisa Shaftel
  Shaftel S2DO
Stanley Allen Sherman
  Mask Arts Company
Linda Skipper
Michael Smanko
  Prism Prips
Sarah Timberlake
  Timberlake Studios
Mari Tobita
US Institute for Theatre
  Tech. (USITT)
Monique Walker
Anne-Marie Wright
John Yavroyan
  Yavroyan & Nelsen, LTD

For membership information visit our website at
www.ATACBIZ.com
Email: info@ATACBIZ.com
Or drop us a line at:

ATAC Membership Application
Anne-Marie Wright
280 Third St. Apt # 1
Jersey City, NJ 07302-2759

ELECTRICAL & ELECTRONIC SUPPLIES

A. P. W. Co., Inc. 973-627-0643
  5 Astroplace, Ste. B   FAX 973-627-0643
  Rockaway, NJ 07866
  Hours: 8-4 Mon-Fri   E-mail: sales@apwcoinc.com
  www.apwcoinc.com
  A.C. or D.C. electromagnets.

Barbizon 212-586-1620
  456 W 55th St.(9-10th Ave)
  NY, NY 10019   800-582-9941
  Hours: 8-5 Mon-Fri / 9-1 Sat   FAX 212-247-8818

  3 Draper St.   781-935-3920
  Woburn, MA 01801   FAX 781-935-9273
  Hours: 8:15-5:30 Mon-Fri / 9-2 Sat

  6437G General Green Way   703-750-3900
  Alexandria, VA 22312   800-922-2972
  Hours: 9-5 Mon-Fri / 9-12 Sat   FAX 703-750-1448

  11551 Interchange Circle South   954-919-6495
  Miramar, FL 33025   800-535-4083
  Hours: 9-6 Mon-Fri / 9-1 Sat   FAX 954-919-6606

  101 Krog St.   404-681-5124
  Atlanta, GA 30307   FAX 404-681-5315
  Hours: 8:30-5:30 Mon-Fri / 9-1 Sat

  1016 McClelland Ct.   704-372-2122
  Charlotte, NC 28206   FAX 704-372-7422
  Hours: 8:30-5:30 Mon-Fri / 9-12 Sat

  8269 E 23rd Ave., Ste 111   303-394-9875
  Denver, CO 80238   800-290-8643
  Hours: 8:30-5 Mon-Fri   FAX 303-355-5996
  www.barbizon.com
  Theatrical lighting supplier; GE, Sylvania, HMI lamps, etc. Visit web address
  for other locations. CREDIT CARDS.

Blan Electronics 718-746-5222
  157-48 26th Ave   FAX 718-746-5219
  Flushing, NY 11354
  Hours: Call for Appt.   E-mail blannyc@aol.com
  Electronics; special relays, switches, solenoids, etc. Speak to Mike or Bart.

H. L. Dalis, Inc. 800-HLDALIS
  35-35 24th St. (35-36th Ave)   718-361-1100
  Long Island City, NY 11106   FAX 718-392-7654
  Hours: 9-5 Mon-Fri   E-mail: hldalis@aol.com
  www.hldalis.com
  Distributors for industrial and broadcasting electronics. Everything from
  antennas to fuses to wire, cable/accessories.

D-E

D-E

Eighth Avenue Lighting, Inc. 212-279-1323
545 Eighth Ave. (37-38th St)   FAX 212-279-1324
NY, NY 10018
Hours: 9-6 Mon-Sat
Electrical supplies, lighting fixtures, halogen lamps, track lights, novelty lights, paper lanterns, and a full line of light bulbs. CREDIT CARDS.

Home Depot 800-553-3199
550 Hamilton Ave.(16-17th St)   718-832-8553
Brooklyn, NY 11232
Hours: 6-12pm Mon-Sat / 8-9pm Sun

124-04 31st Ave.(College Point Blvd)   718-661-4608
Flushing, NY 11354   FAX 718-670-3437
Hours: 6-11pm Mon-Sat / 7-9pm Sun

40 W 23rd St.(5-6th Ave)   212-929-9571
NY, NY 10010
Hours: 7-9pm Mon-Sat / 8-7 Sun

980 Third Ave.(58-59th St)   212-888-1512
NY, NY 10022
Hours: 7-9pm Mon-Sat / 8-7 Sun

50-10 Northern Blvd.(50th St-Newtown Rd)   718-278-9031
Long Island City, NY 11101
Hours: 6-11pm Mon-Sat / 8-9pm Sun
www.homedepot.com
Hardware, tools, lumber, plumbing supplies, gardening supplies, electrical and lighting supplies. Windows, doors and cabinets. Queens and Brooklyn locations open 24-hrs. for those emergency needs (less crowded then, too.) Check web for additional locations. CREDIT CARDS.

Jensen Tools, Inc. 602-414-4483
7815 S 46th St.   800-426-1194
Phoenix, AZ 85044   FAX 800-366-9662
Hours: 6-5:30 Mon-Fri
www.stanleysupplyservice.com
Electronic test tools, cases, dental tools. CREDIT CARDS.

Perfection Electricks 718-383-1155
1155 Manhattan Ave. (Commercial St)   FAX 718-383-1157
Brooklyn, NY 11222
Hours: 8:30-4:30 Mon-Fri   E-mail: marty@perfectionelectricks.com
www.perfectionelectricks.com
A custom electronics manufacturer specializing in game show equipment, custom control devices and technology support for artists. Talk to Marty. RENTALS.

Radio Shack 800-843-7422
625 8th Ave.(Port Authority Bus Terminal)   212-564-9427
NY, NY 10018
Hours: 7-9 Mon-Fri / 9-8 Sat / 10-7 Sun

Radio Shack (cont.) 212-279-1560
901 Ave. of the Americas(Manhattan Mall)
NY, NY 10001
Hours: 9-9 Mon-Fri / 10-8 Sat / 11-7 Sun

50 E 42nd St.(5th-Mad Ave)   212-953-6050
NY, NY 10017
Hours: 8-8 Mon-Fri / 9-7 Sat / 11-6 Sun
www.radioshack.com
Good supplier of radio, telephone, electronic items and components. Catalog.
See website for other locations nationwide. CREDIT CARDS.

D-E

Switches Unlimited 718-478-5000
34-11 56th St. (B'way-34th Ave)   800-569-6130
Woodside, NY 11377   FAX 718-672-6370
Hours: 8:30-5 Mon-Fri   E-mail: info@switchesunlimited.com
www.switchesunlimited.com
Switches, indicator lights, panel lights. Speak to Doug. CREDIT CARDS.

Techni-Tool 610-941-2400
1547 N Trooper Rd.   800-832-4866
Worchester, PA 19490   FAX 610-828-5623
Hours: 8-8 Mon-Fri   E-mail: sales@techni-tool.com
www.techni-tool.com
Specializes in electronic tools and testing tools; catalog. CREDIT CARDS.

Tudor Electrical Supply Co., Inc. 212-867-7550
222-226 E 46th St. (2nd-3rd Ave)   FAX 212-867-7569
NY, NY 10017
Hours: 8:30-5 Mon-Thurs / 8:30-4:30 Fri
Electrical supplies. Speak to Steve Kramer. CREDIT CARDS.

Union Connector 631-753-9550
40 Dale St.   FAX 631-753-9560
West Babylon, NY 11704
Hours: 9-5 Mon-Fri
www.unionconnector.com
Lighting panels and boxes, patch panels, plugs connectors, adapters, wiring
and power distribution equipment. Speak to Richard Wolpert. RENTALS.

ELECTRICAL DEVICES: ANTIQUE & DUMMY

Harry Poster - Vintage TVs 201-794-9606
1310 Second St.
Fairlawn, NJ 07410
Hours: 24 hours 7 days a week by appt.   E-mail: tvs@harryposter.com
www.harryposter.com
Vintage televisions; props and 24 frame. Signs, radios, tubes, TV-shop items.
Very helpful website. Sales and RENTALS.

ELEVATORS

Century Elevator 718-937-6200
    25-25 49th St. (12-13th Ave)   FAX 718-361-5731
    Long Island City, NY 11103
    Hours: 8:30-5 Mon-Fri   E-mail: andrew @centuryelevator.com
    www.centuryelevator.com
    Installations, repair and maintenance. Brochures. Contact C. Mickey Wolcson.

Certified Elevator & Escalator Products Inc. 718-392-5658
    46-10 Vernon Blvd.   800-221-9553
    Long Island City, NY 11101   FAX 718-392-0817
    Hours: 7-6 Mon-Fri   E-mail: sean@certifiedelevator.com
    www.certifiedelevator.com
    Elevator and escalator parts and fixtures. CREDIT CARDS.

EMBROIDERY, PLEATING & BUTTONHOLES

A-1 Pleating 323-653-5557
    8318 1/4 W Third St. (moved to back of building - go thru. alley)
    Los Angeles, CA 90048   FAX 323-653-5569
    Hours: 9:30-5 Mon-Fri
    ***Custom pleating, fabric covered buttons, belts, buckles. Carries large
    selection of rhinestone and metal buckles. No Credit Cards.***

Lalon Alexander 646-262-7860
    NY, NY   512-376-7000
    Hours: by appt.   E-mail: beads@elephantembellishments.com
    www.elephantembellishments.com
    ***Custom beading and embroidery services; trained at the Lesage School in
    Paris, France.***

Artisan Silkscreen & Embroidery 718-526-0600
    179-10 93rd Ave. (6-7th Ave)   FAX 718-526-5700
    Jamaica, NY 11433
    Hours:9-5 Mon-Thurs / 9-3 Fri   E-mail: info@artisansilkscreen.com
    www.artisansilkscreen.com
    ***Custom silkscreening, t-shirts, jackets, etc., yours or theirs; also posters,
    signs, etc. Catalog available. CREDIT CARDS.***

CHRIS BOBIN 646-742-0630
    347 Fifth Ave., Rm 1102 (34-35th St)   917-683-5239
    NY, NY 10016
    Hours: by appt.   E-mail: chris@chrisbobin.com
    www.chrisbobin.com
    ***Sewn solutions for props, costumes and illustrations. Unique works created
    to your specifications. Beautiful stuff. Call for free color flyer. Member ATAC.***

Bonnaz Embroidery Co. 201-943-8163
    373 Henry St.   FAX 201-943-1215
    Fairview, NJ 07022
    Hours: 9-5 Mon-Fri   E-mail: embroideryusa@msn.com
    ***Custom embroidery at reasonable prices. They do Bonnaz and vermicelli
    embroidery. See Alex.***

D-E

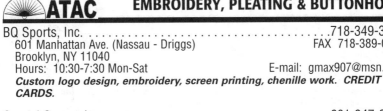

BQ Sports, Inc. 718-349-3528
601 Manhattan Ave. (Nassau - Driggs)   FAX 718-389-0143
Brooklyn, NY 11040
Hours: 10:30-7:30 Mon-Sat   E-mail: gmax907@msn.com
Custom logo design, embroidery, screen printing, chenille work. CREDIT CARDS.

Crystal Crown, Inc. 601-947-8074
183 Webb Davis Rd.   888-278-9531
Lucedale, MS 39452   FAX: 601-947-1860
Hours: 7:30-5 Mon-Thurs   E-mail: crystal@datasync.com
www.crystalcrown.com
USA manufacturer of crowns, tiaras, scepters, jewelry, and embroidered Sashes for beauty pageants and weddings. Very reasonable prices and quick service. CREDIT CARDS.

MARGARET CUSACK 718-237-0145
124 Hoyt St. (Dean St)   718-909-4402
Brooklyn, NY 11217   FAX 718-237-0145
Hours: by appt.   E-mail: cusackart@aol.com
www.margaretcusack.com
Unique stitched artwork, samplers, soft sculpture, quilted hangings, portraits and props that have warmed up the images of clients from AT&T to Aunt Millie's Spaghetti Sauce. Member ATAC.

Fashion Design Concepts 646-366-7627
242 W 38th St., Rm. 200 (7-8th Ave)   FAX: 646-366-7628
NY, NY 10018
Hours: 9-5 Mon-Fri   E-mail: info@fdconcepts.com
www.fdconcepts.com
A versatile embellishment service company in tune with the latest trends. Providing original designs and customized creations in masterful handwork techniques including embroidery, beading and smocking. CREDIT CARDS.

Ideal 718-252-5090
1816 Flatbush Ave.(Avenue K)   FAX 718-692-0492
Brooklyn, NY 11210
Hours: 9-7:30 Mon-Fri / 10-7 Sat / 11-6 Sun

1575 Unionport Rd.   718-239-4010
Bronx, NY 10462
Hours: 10-7 Mon-Sat / 10:30-5:30 Sun
www.idealuniform.com
Custom silkscreening and embroidery on hats, t-shirts, jackets, bags, etc. Our merchandise or yours. CREDIT CARDS.

Kraus & Sons, Inc. 212-620-0408
261 W 35th St. (7-8th Ave)   FAX 212-924-4081
NY, NY 10001
Hours: 9-5 Mon-Fri   E-mail: info@krausbanners.com
www.krausbanners.com
Embroidered, silkscreened or appliqued banners and flags; custom trophies and ribbons; established 1886. No credit cards.

Penn & Fletcher, Inc. 212-239-6868
21-07 41st Ave., 5th Fl.   FAX 212-239-6914
Long Island City, NY 11101
Hours: 9-5 Mon-Fri   E-mail: mail@pennandfletcher.com
www.pennandfletcher.com
Custom embroidery, hand beading specialists; also high quality laces and trims. CREDIT CARDS.

R & C Apparel Corp. 212-239-4155
344 W 38th St. (7-8th Ave)   FAX 212-239-4251
NY, NY 10018
Hours: 9-5 Mon-Fri   E-mail: RCApparel@yahoo.com
Smocking and tucking, multi-head embroidery, pleating, cross cut and bias, cordage and braids. Passamenteries, bonnaze embroidery, fancy stitching. Sample cutting. Will do small or large runs. Talk to Ramdat.

Regal Flags & Poles, Inc. 561-455-8000
1395 NW 17th Ave., Ste. 112B   800-858-8776
Delray Beach, FL 33445   FAX 561-404-4954
Hours: 24-hr. web / 8:30-5 Mon-Fri   E-mail: customerservice@flags.com
www.flags.com
Flags for all occasions. State, country, territoral, international, corporate logos, military, sports, nautical, historical, Nascar and racing, attention flags, pennants and banners. Custom work, as well as embroidery patches and needlepoint products. Patriotic decorations. Hardware and flagpoles. Great website. Very helpful. CREDIT CARDS.

Regal Originals, Inc. 212-921-0270
247 W 37th St. # 3 (7-8th Ave)   FAX 212-575-1893
NY, NY 10018
Hours: 7-6:30 Mon-Fri
Pleating, shirring, smocking, piping, applique, embroidery; good and fast; speak to Roger Cohen.

Stanley Pleating & Stitching Co. 212-868-2920
242 W 36th St., 5th Fl. (7-8th Ave)   FAX 212-868-2939
NY, NY 10018
Hours: (drop off) 12:30-1:15 and 4:30-5:30 Mon-Fri
Many forms of fabric embellishments; pleating, tucking, crochet, hand beading, bonnaz embroidery, applique decorative stitching, nail heads and rhinestoning. Speak to Stuart Meyer.

Vogue Too Pleating, Stitching, Embroidery, Inc. 212-345-8976
265 W 37th St. 14th Fl. (8th Ave)   FAX 212-354-8975
NY, NY 10018
Hours: 8:30-5 Mon-Fri   E-mail: gclark@voguetoo.com
Pleating, stitching, embroidery, computerized embroideries, tucking, hemstitch, saddlestitch, passementry, ruffles, shirring, beading, spaghetti, bias cutting, flowers, covered belts, & covered buttons. Great prices.

D-E

EROTIC GOODS

David Samuel Menkes 212-989-3706
144 Fifth Ave., 3rd Fl. (19-20th St)
NY, NY 10011
Hours: by appt.   E-mail: dsm@davidmenkesleather.com
www.davidmenkesleather.com
High quality handcrafted custom leatherwork, theatrical and personal.
RENTALS. No credit cards.

Pink Pussycat Boutique 718-369-0088
355 5th Ave
Brooklyn, NY 11215
Hours: 12-1am Sun-Thurs / 12:30-3am Fri & Sat
www.pinkpussycat.com   E-mail: internet@pinkpussycat.com
Leather, studs, lingerie, inflatable dolls, handcuffs, sex toys. Mail orders.
Catalog. Manhattan store re-locating in 2010, address not available at
publishing. CREDIT CARDS.

The Pleasure Chest 212-242-2158
156 Seventh Ave. S (Charles-Perry St)   800-753-4536
NY, NY 10014   FAX 212-647-7073
Hours:10-Midnight daily   E-mail: zack@thepleasurechest.com
www.thepleasurechest.com
Erotic postcards, leather goods, lingerie, S & M items, sex toys. Shipping.
CREDIT CARDS.

Toys in Babeland 800-658-9119
94 Rivington St.(Orchard & Ludlow)   212-375-1701
NY, NY 10002   FAX 212-375-1706
Hours: 12-10 Sun-Wed / 12-11 Thurs-Sat

43 Mercer St.(Broome & Grand)   212-966-2120
NY, NY 10013   FAX 212-966-2144
Hours: 11-10 Mon-Sat / 11-7 Sun

707 E Pike St.   206-328-2914
Seattle, WA 98122   FAX 206-328-2994
Hours: 11-10 Mon-Sat / 12-7 Sun

462 Bergen(5th-Flatbush Ave)   718-638-3820
Brooklyn, NY 11217   FAX 718-638-3751
Hours: 12-9 Mon-Sat / 12-7 Sun   E-mail: clair@babeland.com
www.babeland.com
Erotic dildos, leather items and sexual adventure toys. Mail order. Catalog
available. Extra nice employees. CREDIT CARDS.

ETHNIC GOODS: CENTRAL & SOUTH AMERICA

Beads of Paradise 212-620-0642
16 E 17th St. (5th Ave-B'way)   FAX 212-741-3780
NY, NY 10003
Hours: 11-7:30 Sat / 12-6:30 Sun   E-mail: beadsofparadise@hotmail.com
www.beadsofparadisenyc.com
A selection of African jewelry, beads, sculpture and a few fabrics. Richard
Meyer Gallery (African sculpture, pottery and antique fabrics) is in back.
Retail and wholesale (min. for wholesale is $150). Will ship, no swatching.
RENTALS. CREDIT CARDS.

Pan American Phoenix 212-570-0300
857 Lexington Ave. (64-65th St)   FAX 212-535-3383
NY, NY 10065
Hours: 10:30-6:30 Mon-Fri / 11-6 Sat   E-mail: shop@panamphoenix.com
www.panamphoenix.com
Mexican and Latin American imports: clothing, decorative accessories and
fabrics. Speak to Mary Bartos. RENTALS. CREDIT CARDS.

Reign Trading Co. 626-307-7755
3838 Walnut Grove Ave.   Fax: 626-307-7744
Rosemead, CA 91770
Hours: 24-hr. website   E-mail: reigntrading@earthlink.net
www.mexicansugarskull.com / www.mexicancalendargirl.com
One of the best internet sources for Mexican Folk Art, cooking supplies, sugar
skull supplies and information regarding anything historical Mexican. Very
knowledgable staff and extra friendly. RENTALS. CREDIT CARDS.

ETHNIC GOODS: SPANISH

Menkes 212-541-8401
250 W 54th St., 8th Fl. (B'way-8th Ave)   877-227-5460
NY, NY 10019   FAX 212-541-7409
Hours: 11-6 Mon-Sat   E-mail: menkesny@verizon.net
www.menkes.es
Flamenco shoes, clothing and accessories. Spanish combs, bullfighter
apparel. Castanets.

ETHNIC GOODS: AFRICAN & WEST INDIAN

Africa Imports 201-457-1995
240 S Main St. Unit A   800-500-6120
South Hackensack, NJ 07606   FAX 866-457-1910
Hours: 8-7 Mon-Fri / 10-4 Sat   E-mail: africa@africaimports.com
www.africaimports.com
African imported goods. Hats, belts, Africa mudcloth and Kubba cloth,
jewelry, clothing and art. Great website. Catalog. CREDIT CARDS.

Ages Tribal Arts 330-434-1010
194 Myrtle Pl. (Maple)
Acron, OH 44303
Hours: by appt.   E-mail: eric@agestribalarts.com
www.agestribalarts.com
Tribal arts, masks, statues, artifacts, jewelry, fossilized ivory carvings and
pendents, antique prints and etchings. Consolations on tribal art,
specializing in Buddhist, Hindu, Indonesia and African art. RENTALS. CREDIT
CARDS.

D–E

Back to Africa Imports 718-492-5100
140 58th St. Bldg. A, 6th Fl (2nd Ave)   888-282-3563
Brooklyn, NY 11220   FAX 718-492-5150
Hours: 9-7 Mon-Thurs / 9-3 Fri   E-mail: info@back2africa.com
www.back2africa.com
Wonderful selection of African art, statues, textiles, beads, artifacts, masks,
musical instruments and incense burners. CREDIT CARDS.

Bangally African Expo 212-627-6489
30 Greenwich Ave. (6-7th Ave)   FAX 212-627-6936
NY, NY 10011
Hours: 11-9 Sun-Thurs / 11-10 Fri-Sat   E-mail: bangally@bangally.com
www.bangally.com
African imports: clothing, hats, fabric, jewelry, furniture, baskets, masks,
drums and handicrafts. RENTALS. CREDIT CARDS.

Beads of Paradise 212-620-0642
16 E 17th St. (5th Ave-B'way)   FAX 212-741-3780
NY, NY 10003
Hours: 11-7:30 Sat / 12-6:30 Sun   E-mail: beadsofparadise@hotmail.com
www.beadsofparadisenyc.com
A selection of African jewelry, beads, sculpture and a few fabrics. Richard
Meyer Gallery (African sculpture, pottery and antique fabrics) is in back.
Retail and wholesale (min. for wholesale is $150). Will ship, no swatching.
RENTALS. CREDIT CARDS.

JS Imports 212-242-7212
865 Broadway   FAX 212-627-8621
NY, NY 10003
Hours: 9-5:30 Mon-Thurs / 9-4 Fri   E-mail: sdebbah@verizon.net
African art.

Kalustyan's 212-685-3451
123 Lexington Ave. (28-29th St)   800-352-3451
NY, NY 10016   FAX 212-683-8458
Hours: 10-8 Mon-Sat / 11-7 Sun   E-mail: sales@kalustyans.com
www.kalustyans.com
Food items from India, Africa and Cuba. Excellent source for exotic spices.
Most helpful with shopping needs. Also nice selection of cooking utensils,
etc. CREDIT CARDS.

Liberty House 212-932-1950
2878A Broadway (112th St)   FAX 212-932-3467
NY, NY 10025
Hours: 10-6:45 Mon-Wed / 10-7:45 Thurs-Fri / 12-5:45 Sun
www.libertyhousenyc.com   E-mail: info@libertyhousenyc.com
Clothing and jewelry for women. Accessories, Kilim rugs. Objects from
everywhere. CREDIT CARDS.

ETHNIC GOODS: EAST INDIAN

Ages Tribal Arts 330-434-1010
194 Myrtle Pl. (Maple)
Acron, OH 44303
Hours: by appt.   E-mail: eric@agestribalarts.com
www.agestribalarts.com
Tribal arts, masks, statues, artifacts, jewelry, fossilized ivory carvings and
pendents, antique prints and etchings. Consolations on tribal art,
specializing in Buddhist, Hindu, Indonesia and African art. RENTALS. CREDIT
CARDS.

Butala Emporium, Inc. 212-684-4447
108 E 28th St. (Park & Lex Ave)
New York, NY 10016
Hours: 10:30-8 Daily   E-mail: service@indousplaza.com
www.indousplaza.com
Indian household items, dishes, jewelry, rugs, food items and furniture.
RENTALS. CREDIT CARDS.

Deepa Fabrics, Inc. 212-997-8570
270 W 39th St., 3 FL (8th Ave)   212-354-3732
NY, NY 10018   FAX 212-398-6331
Hours: 10-5 Mon-Fri   E-mail: ushafabric@aol.com
Indian silks and saris.

Himalayan Crafts 212-787-8500
2007 Broadway (68-69th St)   FAX 212-787-8548
NY, NY 10023
Hours: 11-7:30 Mon-Fri / 11-7 Sat / 12-6 Sun   E-mail: himacraft@aol.com
www.himalayancraft.com
Objects and textiles, hand crafts, statues, paintings, beads and jewelry.
RENTALS. CREDIT CARDS.

Kalustyan's 212-685-3451
123 Lexington Ave. (28-29th St)   800-352-3451
NY, NY 10016   FAX 212-683-8458
Hours: 10-8 Mon-Sat / 11-7 Sun   E-mail: sales@kalustyans.com
www.kalustyans.com
Food items from India, Africa and Cuba. Excellent source for exotic spices.
Most helpful with shopping needs. Also nice selection of cooking utensils,
etc. CREDIT CARDS.

Phyllis Leibowitz 212-627-1436
   7 E 14th St. #223 (5-6th Ave)   Cell 917-881-3429
   NY, NY 10003
   Hours: by appt.   E-mail: phyllis@inch.com
   www.phyllisleibowitz.com
   Imports furniture, accessories and antique textiles from India. RENTALS.
   CREDIT CARDS.

Paracelso 212-966-4232
   414 West Broadway (Prince-Spring St)
   NY, NY 10012
   Hours: 12:30-7 daily
   Women's clothing. CREDIT CARDS.

Tabwa 212-924-8444
   66 Greenwich Ave. (Perry-7th Ave)   FAX 212-924-8444
   NY, NY 10011
   Hours: 12-8 Mon-Fri / 12-7 Sat   E-mail: tabwa.com@verizon.net
   www.tabwa.com
   Wonderful selection of baskets, as well as small rugs, decorative accessories,
   vintage fabrics, ikats and block print Indian fabrics. Contact Carl. CREDIT
   CARDS.

D-E

ETHNIC GOODS: MIDDLE EASTERN

Aegean Imports 650-593-8300
   Lyell St.   FAX 650-593-8000
   San Carlos, CA 94070
   Hours: 8:30-5 Mon-Fri
   Greek fishermen's hats; quantity mail order only. CREDIT CARDS.

Jacques Carcanagues, Inc. 212-925-8110
   21 Greene St. (Canal-Grand)   FAX 212-925-8112
   NY, NY 10013
   Hours: 11:30-6:30 Tue-Sat   E-mail: carcan@jcarcan.com
   www.jacquescarcanagues.com
   Middle to Far Eastern clothing, jewelry, rugs, textiles, furniture, baskets,
   wicker items. RENTALS. CREDIT CARDS.

Rashid Music Co. 718-852-3295
   155 Court St. (Pacific St)   800-843-9401
   Brooklyn, NY 11201   FAX 718-643-9522
   Hours: 10-7 Mon-Sat   E-mail: webmaster@rashid.com
   www.rashid.com
   Music, DVD's, books, periodicals, castanets, giftware, videos. Phone orders.
   CREDIT CARDS.

Sheherazade Imports, LLC 212-539-1771
   121 Orchard St. (Delancey)   FAX 212-539-1774
   NY, NY 10002
   Hours: 11-7 Mon, Wed-Fri / 23-7 Sat-Sun (closed Tuesdays)
                E-mail: sheherazade@verizon.net
   Authenic handcrafted home furnishings from the Middle East. CREDIT
   CARDS.

ETHNIC GOODS: ORIENTAL

Air Market 212-995-5888
97 Third Ave. (near 12th St)   FAX 212-995-5771
NY, NY 10003
Hours: 12-7 Tue-Sun
A treasure trove of Mr. Friendly paraphernalia. Also clothing, mostly
Japanese. CREDIT CARDS.

Ancient Grounds 206-749-0747
1220 First Ave. (University St)
Seattle, WA 98101
Hours: 7-6 Mon-Fri   E-mail: agrounds@live.com
Tribal and ethographic art from Japan, Borneo and the American Pacific NW
coast. RENTALS. CREDIT CARDS.

Bikini Bar 212-571-6737
148 Duane St. (Church-W B'way)
NY, NY 10013
Hours: 12-7 Tue-Sat   E-mail: surf@bikinibar.com
www.bikinibar.com
Vintage Hawaiian rattan furniture, surfboards, travel posters and collectibles.
Surf Attire. Contact Aileen Oser or Stuart Smith. RENTALS

Handloom Batik 518-828-2205
532 Warren St.
Hudson, NY 12534
Hours: 12-7 Wed-Sat / 1-6 Sun / Call for Appt. before visiting store
www.handloombatik.com   E-mail: usha@handloombatik.com
Asian imports; beautiful batik and handwoven fabrics; reasonably priced.
Paper, soapstone carvings. Accepts personal checks.

Hula Supply Center 808-941-0100
1008 Isenberg St.   800-237-3347
Honolulu, HI 96826   FAX 808-947-6757
Hours: 9-6 Mon-Fri / 9-5 Sat
www.hulasupplycenter.com
Hawaiian, Tahitian, Samoan, Maori costumes and dance instruments.
CREDIT CARDS.

Indonesian Batiks 360-299-3968
14816 Hoxie Ln.
Anacortes, WA 98221
Hours: by appt.   E-mail: info@indobatiks.com
www.indobatiks.com
Batik art panels, many designs and sizes. Retail and wholesale. CREDIT
CARDS.

Kam Man Food Products, Inc. 212-571-0330
200 Canal St. (Mott & Mulberry)   212-571-0331
NY, NY 10013   FAX 212-766-9085
Hours: 9-8:30 Mon-Sun
Tops in Oriental food products, Chinese & Japanese kitchenware and
household items. Two great floors to shop. Very friendly and helpful staff.
CREDIT CARDS.

Leekan Design 212-226-7226
4 Rivington St. (Bowery-Christie St.)   FAX 212-226-3419
NY, NY 10012
Hours:11-6 Mon-Fri / 11-7 Sat / 12-6 Sun   E-mail: info@leekandesigns.com
www.leekandesigns.com
Chinese jewelry and handicrafts; great selection. Folk Art, rugs, textiles,
ceramics, baskets, musical instruments. Architectural elements and furniture.
CREDIT CARDS.

Mitsuawa Market Place 201-941-9113
595 River Rd.
Edgewater, NJ 07020
Hours: 9:30-9 Mon-unt
Shopping plaza with Japanese goods only. Including furnishings, toys,
clothing and food. Has shuttle bus from Port Authority. CREDIT CARDS.

Miya Shoji & Interiors, Inc. 212-243-6774
145 W 26th St. (6-7th Ave)   FAX 212-243-6780
NY, NY 10001
Hours: 10-6 Mon-Fri
Shoji screens, lamps, cabinets. RENTALS. CREDIT CARDS.

The Oriental Dress 212-349-0818
38 Mott St. (Bayard)
NY, NY 10013
Hours: 10-6:30 Mon-Wed, Fri / Closed on Thurs
Chinese brocade. Silk fabric.

Pearl River Chinese Products Emporium 212-431-4770
477 Broadway (Grand-Broome)   800-878-2446
NY, NY 10013   FAX 212-925-6711
Hours: 10-7:20 Daily
www.pearlriver.com
A Chinese department store. Chinese groceries, cookware, dishware,
clothing, fans, paper lanterns, umbrellas, tablecloths; great selection. CREDIT
CARDS.

Vision of Tibet 212-995-9276
167 Thompson St. (Houston-Bleecker St)   FAX   (same)
NY, NY 10012
Hours: 11-7 Daily   E-mail: info@visionoftibet.com
www.visionoftibet.com
Treasures from the Himalayan Kingdom. Jewelry, masks, carpets, furniture.
Phone orders. RENTALS. CREDIT CARDS.

D-E

Yung Kee Trading, Inc. 212-679-3778
838 Sixth Ave. (29-30th St)   FAX 212-532-8651
NY, NY 10001
Hours: 8:30-6 Mon-Fri / 8:30-5 Sat   E-mail: order@ykgroup.com
www.ykgroup.com
Wholesale Oriental goods. No credit cards.

ETHNIC GOODS: RUSSIAN & EASTERN EUROPEAN

A La Vieille Russie, Inc. 212-752-1727
781 Fifth Ave. (59th St)
NY, NY 10022
Hours: 10-5 Mon-Fri / 11-4 Sat (closed Sat; June-Aug)   E-mail: alvr@alvr.com
www.alvr.com
Fine Russian antiques. Online catalog. CREDIT CARDS.

Ernst Licht Imports & Mfg. 610-987-3298
347 Main St. and Friedensburg Rd.   800-776-3298
Oley, PA 19547   FAX 610-987-6007
Hours: 9-5 Mon-Fri / 9-3 Sat   E-mail: ernslicht@ernstlicht.com
www.ernstlicht.com
Bavarian apparel. Folk and festival costumes for men, women and children.
Lederhosen. Mail order and store. CREDIT CARDS.

Singer Clothing Co. 718-384-6200
116 Lee Ave.   FAX (same)
Brooklyn, NY 11211
Hours: 10:30-7:30 Sun-Thurs / 10:30-2 Fri
Large stock; custom-made clothing worn by Russian and Polish nobles; other
period suits. CREDIT CARDS.

Surma The Ukrainian Shop 212-477-0729
11 E 7th St. (2nd-3rd Ave)   FAX 212-473-0439
NY, NY 10003
Hours: 11-6 Mon-Fri / 11-4 Sat   E-mail: surma@brama.com
www.surmastore.com
Slavic general store: Embroidered blouses, scarves, wooden Easter eggs
(hollow ostrich, goose, etc.) Other objets d'art from Russia, Poland and the
Ukraine. RENTALS. CREDIT CARDS.

ETHNIC GOODS: SCOTTISH & IRISH

Scottish Tartans Museum & Gift Shop 828-524-7472
86 E Main St.
Franklin, NC 28734
Hours: 10-5 Mon-Sat   E-mail: tartans@scottishtartans.org
www.scottishtartans.org
The only American extension of the Scottish Tartans Society in Scotland. Will
rent Kilts. Gift shop has a large selection of tartans and other Highland
apparel and Scottish products. CREDIT CARDS.

ETHNIC GOODS: THE AMERICAS & AMERICAN INDIAN

Abracadabra 212-627-5194
19 W 21st St. (5-6th Ave)   FAX 212-627-7435
NY, NY 10001
Hours: 11-7 Mon-Sat / 12-5 Sun
www.abracadabrasuperstore.com
Indian costumes, headdresses, necklaces, spears, peace pipes, bells, etc. Also 6 ft. cigar store Indians. Catalog available online. RENTALS. CREDIT CARDS.

Ancient Grounds 206-749-0747
1220 First Ave. (University St)
Seattle, WA 98101
Hours: 7-6 Mon-Fri   E-mail: agrounds@live.com
Tribal and ethographic art from Japan, Borneo and the American Pacific NW coast. RENTALS. CREDIT CARDS.

Classic Hawaiian Products 808-277-5323
1860 Ala Moana Blvd # 810
Honolulu, HI 96815
Hours: 9-6 (Hawaiian Time) Mon-Fri
        E-mail: customerservice@classichawaiianproducts.com
www.classichawaiianproducts.com
Good selection of Hawaiian clothing; childrens, baby and adult sizes, jewelry, beachwear, fabrics and home decor. Be sure to make time for your orders, they need extra time for quick deliveries.

The Common Ground, Inc. 212-989-4178
55 W 16th St. (5-6th Ave)   FAX 212-620-3122
NY, NY 10014
Hours: 12-7 Tue-Sat   E-mail: thecommonground@att.net
www.thecommonground.8m.net
Antique and contemporary American Indian jewelry, clothing, pottery, furniture. Phone orders. RENTALS. CREDIT CARDS.

Crazy Crow Trading Post 800-786-6210
1801 Airport Rd.   903-786-2287
Pottsboro, TX 75076   FAX 903-786-9059
Hours: 7:30-5:30 Mon-Fri CST   E-mail: orders@crazycrow.com
www.crazycrow.com
Indian craft supply house; mail and phone orders only; catalog $3. CREDIT CARDS.

Crows Nest Trading Co. 800-900-8558
3205 Airport Blvd NW, P.O. Box 3975   FAX 800-900-3136
Wilson, NC 27895
Hours: 9-5 Mon-Fri / 24-hr. website   E-mail: info@crowsnestrading.com
www.crowsnesttrading.com
Leather, western rugged furnishings. Also kitchen, garden and rugs. Western and cowboy themed. Great catalog. CREDIT CARDS.

D-E

Grey Owl Indian Crafts 732-389-4626
15 Meridian Rd.   (orders) 800-487-2376
Eatontown, NJ 07724   FAX 732-389-4629
Hours: 9-5 Mon-Fri   E-mail: sales@greyowlcrafts.com
www.greyowlcrafts.com
Kits for American Indian headdresses and crafts; catalog. **CREDIT CARDS.**

HawwaiianKineStuff.com 800-793-0901
4348 Waialae Ave. # 182
Honolulu, HI 96816
Hours: 10-5 (Hawaiian Time) Mon-Sat
www.hawaiiankinestuff.com   E-mail: customerservice@hawaiiankinestuff.com
Excellent source for EVERYTHING Hawaiian. Aloha wear, food items, tiki items, jewelry, silk leis and Hawaiian art prints. They actually answer the phone Aloha! **CREDIT CARDS.**

La Sirena Mexican Folk Art 212-780-9113
27 E 3rd St. (2nd Ave-Bowery)
NY, NY 10003
Hours: 12-7 Everyday   E-mail: info@lasirenanyc.com
www.lasirenanyc.com
La Sirena is a Mexican Folk Art store in New York City reflecting the beauty and richness of the country of Mexico and the people who live there. The store is filled with arts and crafts from all over Mexico. Much of the work is crafted by families whose traditions have been handed down form generation to generation. **CREDIT CARDS.**

Matoska Trading Company 714-516-9940
611 W Chapman Ave. (N. Parker -N. Pixley)   800-926-6286
Orange, CA 92868   FAX 800-249-9375
Hours: 11-6 Tue-Sat   E-mail: matoska@matoska.com
www.matoska.com
Native American craft supplies, books,feathers, buckskin, leather, beads, music and more. Shop online or visit their store. **CREDIT CARDS.**

R & P Trading 903-613-2012
203 Pack Saddle
Holly Lake Ranch, TX 75765
Hours: 24-hrs. by website   E-mail: sales@rptrading.biz
www.rptrading.biz
Wooden wagons, butter churns, porch swings, Old West and Civil War historic merchandise, hay, barrels and Amish products. Very nice and helpful staff. **CREDIT CARDS.**

Western Canvas, LLC 800-587-6707
86 McNeil Lane   307-587-6707
Cody, WY 82414   FAX 307-587-8186
Hours: 9-12, 1-5 Mon-Fri   E-mail: info@westerncanvas.com
www.westerncanvas.com
Authenic handmade tipis. Various styles. Mail order and online shopping. **CREDIT CARDS.**

Western Crafts & Gifts Co. 407-578-6833
  40 Taylor St.   407-656-0853
  Ocoee, FL 34761
  Hours: 10-6 Mon-Fri / 10-5 Sat   E-mail: westerncrafts@aol.com
  Native American Indian art, pipes, beadwork, kachinas, crafts and craft
  supplies. CREDIT CARDS.

Western Spirit 800-976-9287
  395 Broadway (Walker)   212-343-1476
  NY, NY 10013   FAX 212-343-0257
  Hours: 10:30-7:30 Mon-Fri / 11-8 Sat-Sun   E-mail: iwesternspiritj@yahoo.com
  www.westernspiritny.com
  Largest Western shop in NYC. Native American art, crafts, jewelry, pottery,
  leathercraft and headdresses. Western clothing in men's, women's and
  children's sizes. Toys. CREDIT CARDS.

EVENT PLANNERS
See also: PARTY PLANNERS

Access Event Services 800-823-5515
  322 Seaman St.   FAX 732-246-4456
  New Brunswick, NJ 08901
  Hours: 24-hr operation, call when you need us   E-mail: ed@8008235515.com
  www.redcarpetarrivals.com
  Event industries red carpet arrivals production company. Offering top notch
  equipment, bright 4K searchlights, Street heat for heating your arrivals area,
  security services and crowd control. Un-paralleled customer service and
  attention to every last detail. Last minute can do attitude. CREDIT CARDS.

Artistry in Motion 818-994-7388
  15101 Keswick St.   FAX 818-994-7688
  Van Nuys, CA 91405
  Hours: 9-6 Mon-Fri   E-mail: confetti@artistryinmotion.com
  www.artistryinmotion.com
  Best in the industry for confetti cannons and confetti. Custom designing for
  each event. CREDIT CARDS.

CORRINNA GRIFFIN 917-544-1287
  1040 Bushwick Ave.
  Brooklyn, NY 11211
  Hours: by appt.   E-mail: corgriffin@gmail.com
  Millinery, costume crafts and event planning. Member ATAC.

Cross It Off Your List 212-725-0122
  915 Broadway, 20th Fl.   888-XOFFLIST
  NY, NY 10010   FAX 212-779-4349
  Hours: By Appt.   E-mail: info@crossitoffyourlist.com
  www.crossitoffyourlist.com
  Event planner for all occasions. Corporate accounts welcome. CREDIT
  CARDS.

ATAC

Event Energizers 917-687-5600
689 Fort Washington Ave. (190th St)   FAX 347-591-6800
NY, NY 10040
Hours: 9-5 Mon-Fri   E-mail: john@eventenergizers.com
www.eventenergizers.com
Full service event planning company with in-house lighting, sound, staging,
florals and cloths. Costuming & Talent Management.

Frankies Carnival Time 877-937-2652
3437 E Tremont Ave. (Bruckner Blvd)   718-823-3033
Bronx, NY 10465   FAX 718-824-2979
Hours: 9-6 Mon-Sat / until 7 Fri / 9-3 Sun   E-mail: frankiebe@aol.com
www.frankiescarnival.com
Carnival games, booths, carts, fun house mirrors, inflatable rides, dunk tanks
and bingo supplies. Hot dog carts, cotton candy and popcorn machines.
Tents, chairs, tables, etc. RENTALS. CREDIT CARDS.

Home Management Systems 718-857-7971
209 St. John's Pl. (7-8th Ave)   FAX 718-623-3974
Brooklyn, NY 11217
Hours: By Appt.   E-mail: RLChadsey@gmail.com
Professional event planner, organizer and home management assistance.
Contact Ruth.

In Order, Inc. 973-744-4835
147 Lorraine Ave.   866-INORDER
Upper Montclair, NJ 07043   FAX 973-744-4641
Hours: 8:30-5:30 Mon-Fri   E-mail: deborah@inorder.com
www.inorder.com
Full-service event planner. Any occasion: Weddings, Birthday Parties, etc.

Main Attractions 732-225-3500
85 Newfield Ave. (Raritan Ctr Pkwy)   800-394-3500
Edison, NJ 08837   732-225-2110
Hours: 9:30-5 Mon-Fri   E-mail: events@mainattractions.com
www.mainattractions.com
Special events contractors; specializing in custom tent rentals, restroom
trailers, decor, portable staging, lighting and the production of displays and
signage. Visit website to see the full spectrum of their products. RENTALS.
CREDIT CARDS.

Maximum Events & Designers 330-284-6239
1017 Camden Ave. SW
Canton, OH 44706
Hours: 8-6 Mon-Fri   E-mail: maxevntsdesigns@yahoo.com
Event planner, coordinator, designer, florist and party favors. RENTALS.
CREDIT CARDS.

NAPO-NY 212-439-1088
459 Columbus Ave., PMB 210
NY, NY 10024
www.napo-ny.net   E-mail: napo@napo-ny.net
National Association of Professional Organizers-Greater New York Chapter.
Professional association whose members specialize in business and personal
organizing, including corporate event planning and party planning.

D-E

Paladin Amusements, Inc. 908-464-0826
　9 Maple Ave.   800-699-8552
　Berkeley Heights, NJ 07922   FAX 908-464-3661
　www.paladinamusements.com   E-mail: paladin@paladinamusements.com
　Rental of Carnival games, trailers, tents, rides, speedball, hi-striker and other
　carnival and amusement equipment. Sales of carnival and boardwalk-type
　prizes and merchandise. RENTALS.

PM Amusements 914-937-1188
　36 Bush Ave.   FAX 914-939-8189
　Port Chester, NY 10573
　Hours: 9-5 Mon-Fri / 10-3 Sat
　www.pmamusements.com
　Now your organization has the opportunity to enjoy an enchanting evening
　of Broadway entertainment without the trip to the Great White Way!
　Entertainment ideas include: magic shows, comedy acts, impersonators,
　game shows and much more. RENTALS. CREDIT CARDS.

D-E

Remember our Balloons 973-316-8200
　623 Eagle Rock Ave.   973-296-0872
　West Orange, NJ 07052
　Hours: by appt. 7 days a week   E-mail: robbie@balloonsbyrobbie.com
　www.balloonsbyrobbie.com
　One-stop shopping for all your decorating needs. From the very quirky to
　regular balloon columns, Robbie is the most unique balloon artist. Visit
　website to see all the fun fantastical shapes he has dreamed up for film and
　TV. CREDIT CARDS.

Shackman Associates 212-753-5900
　240 E 56th St. Ste 2E   FAX 212-753-7070
　NY, NY 10022
　Hours: By Appt.   E-mail: dmc@shackmanassociates.com
　www.shackmanassociates.com
　Full-service professional event planner. Offering a variety of themed parties,
　theatre nights as well as customized sightseeing tours, shopping excursions
　and spouse programs for corporate clients.

Taylor Creative, Inc. 646-336-6808
　150 W 28th St., Ste. 1001 (6-7th Aves)   888-245-4044
　NY, NY 10001   FAX 646-336-6810
　Hours: 9:30-5:30 Mon-Fri   E-mail: info@taylorcreativeinc.com
　www.taylorcreativeinc.com
　Prop rental company specializing in modern furniture. Their rentals are ideal
　for green rooms, photo shoots, product launches, press events and traveling
　tours. They also handle event productions from start to finish. RENTALS.
　CREDIT CARDS.

EXPENDABLES

See also: THEATRICAL SUPPLIES

Barbizon 212-586-1620
456 W 55th St.(9-10th Ave)   800-582-9941
NY, NY 10019   FAX 212-247-8818
Hours: 8-5 Mon-Fri / 9-1 Sat

3 Draper St.   781-935-3920
Woburn, MA 01801   FAX 781-935-9273
Hours: 8:15-5:30 Mon-Fri / 9-2 Sat

6437G General Green Way   703-750-3900
Alexandria, VA 22312   800-922-2972
Hours: 9-5 Mon-Fri / 9-12 Sat   FAX 703-750-1448

11551 Interchange Circle South   954-919-6495
Miramar, FL 33025   800-535-4083
Hours: 9-6 Mon-Fri / 9-1 Sat   FAX 954-919-6606

101 Krog St.   404-681-5124
Atlanta, GA 30307   FAX 404-681-5315
Hours: 8:30-5:30 Mon-Fri / 9-1 Sat

1016 McClelland Ct.   704-372-2122
Charlotte, NC 28206   FAX 704-372-7422
Hours: 8:30-5:30 Mon-Fri / 9-12 Sat

8269 E 23rd Ave., Ste 111   303-394-9875
Denver, CO 80238   800-290-8643
Hours: 8:30-5 Mon-Fri   FAX 303-355-5996
www.barbizon.com
Theatrical lighting supplier; GE, Sylvania, HMI lamps, etc. Visit web address for other locations. CREDIT CARDS.

Chicago Canvas & Supply Co. 773-478-5700
3719 W. Lawrence Ave.   FAX 773-588-3139
Chicago, IL 60625
Hours: 8-4 Mon-Fri Closed 12-1 daily   E-mail: email@chicagocanvas.com
www.chicagocanvas.com
Chicago's leading theatrical supply house. Hardware, curtain track, fabrics, expendables; gaffers tape, drop cloths, velcro, scenic supplies, Deca dyes, artist's canvas as well as muslin. CREDIT CARDS.

Hollywood Rentals Production Services 800-233-7830
19731 Nordhoff St.   FAX 818-407-7875
Northridge, CA 91324
Hours: 8-6 Mon-Fri / mobile car for 24-hr. service
www.hollywoodrentals.com
Fuller's earth, glue, tape and other studio supplies. Will deliver. CREDIT CARDS.

Manhattan Wardrobe Supply 212-268-9993
245 W 29th St., 8th Fl. (7-8th Ave)   FAX 212-268-1210
NY, NY 10001
Hours: 9-5:45 Mon-Fri   E-mail: info@wardrobesupplies.com
www.wardrobesupplies.com

Supplier of wardrobe expendables for film, television, theater and schools.
Cleaning supplies, clear garment bags, ageing supplies, etc. Will deliver or
ship. Visit website to find new products to try. Catalog or shop online. Fax
or e-mail orders 24-hrs. Will accept P.O.s or CREDIT CARDS.

Production Advantage, Inc. 802-651-6915
P.O. Box 1700   800-424-99914
Williston, VT 05495   FAX 877-424-9991
Hours: 8:30-6 Mon-Fri   E-mail: sales@proadv.com
www.proadv.com

Catalog sales of hardware, lighting, rigging, scenic material, soft goods,
sound equipment and expendables to the entertainment industry. All major
brands carried. Catalog. CREDIT CARDS.

Rose Brand 800-223-1624
                                                    FAX 800-594-7424

4 Emerson Lane(15-16th St)
Secaucus, NJ 07094   201-809-1730
Hours: 8-5 Mon-Fri   FAX 201-809-1851

10616 Lanark St.   800-360-5056
Sun City, CA 91352   818-505-6290
Hours: 8-5 Mon-Fri   FAX 818-505-6293
www.rosebrand.com   E-mail: sales@rosebrand.com

Complete line of tapes, muslin, fabrics, paint supplies, hardware, kraft papers,
bogus and semi-wax papers. CREDIT CARDS.

The Set Shop 212-255-3500
36 W 20th St. (5-6th Ave)   800-422-7831
NY, NY 10011   FAX 212-229-9600
Hours: 8:30-6 Mon-Fri   E-mail: info@setshop.com
www.setshop.com

Bee Smokers and juice-style machines. Professional and compact garment
steamers. 50 colors of 9'-0" or 12'-0" wide seamless paper; 12 colors muslin;
Foamcore, Gatorboard. Ten types of ice cubes and shards, large selection of
plexi. CREDIT CARDS.

United Staging & Rigging 203-416-5380
250 Fifth St.   203-416-5380
Bridgeport, CT 06607   FAX 203-416-5387
Hours: 8:30-4:30 Mon-Fri

96 Commerce Way   781-376-9180
Canton, MA 01801   FAX 781-376-9185
Hours: 8-5 Mon-Fri
www.unitedstaging.com

Full selection of gaffers tape, glow tapes and other speciality tapes, tie line,
sash cord as well as a variety of rigging and climbing ropes. CREDIT CARDS.

D-E

EXPENDABLES

Wits End Productions 212-242-9400
547 W 49th St.   212-757-4545
NY, NY 10019   FAX 212-242-1797
Hours: 24-hr. service   E-mail: tvgully@aol.com
www.witsendnyc.com

Excellent company to handle all your production needs for film and photography shoots. They have expendible kits you can rent that contain EVERYTHING you could possibly need for any situation. Rent their trucks full of expendables and you even get a truck driver experienced to assist in any and all your needs. If they don't have what you need, they will buy it. Just added to their stock are mole fans, ladders, 600W generators and much much more. Visit their website to view their extensive RENTALS. CREDIT CARDS.

EYEGLASSES

10/10 212-366-1010
50 Madison Ave. (26-27th St)   FAX 212-366-1466
NY, NY 10010
Hours: 10-7 Mon-Thurs / 10-4 Fri / 12-5:30 Sun   E-mail: ruth@1010optics.com
www.1010optics.com

Eyewear from the outrageous to the sublime; specialize in contact lens fittings. Happy to assist stylists in search of great optical props. RENTALS. CREDIT CARDS.

Clairmont-Nichols, Inc. 212-758-2346
1016 First Ave. (56th St)   FAX 212-750-3583
NY, NY 10022
Hours: 9-6 Mon-Fri / (Tue & Thurs until 7) / 9-5 Sat   E-mail: cno56@aol.com
Good quality; repairs, sales and RENTALS. CREDIT CARDS.

Cohen's Fashion Optical 800-EYES-440
117 Orchard St.(Delancey St)   888-777-5273
NY, NY 10002   212-674-1986
Hours: 10-7 Mon-Sat / 12-6 Sun   FAX 212-475-2082

545 Fifth Ave.(44-45th St)   212-697-0915
NY, NY 10017   FAX 212-490-3362
Hours: 9-7 Mon-Fri / 10-6 Sat / 11-5 Sun

767 Lexington Ave.(60th St)   212-751-6652
NY, NY 10021   FAX 212-688-3016
Hours: 9-8 Mon-Fri / 9-7:30 Sat / 11-6 Sun
www.cohensfashionoptical.com
Low-cost frames. See website for other locations. CREDIT CARDS.

Economy Best Vision Co. 212-243-4884
223 W 14th St. (7-8th Ave)   FAX 212-243-3120
NY, NY 10011
Hours: 10-6 Mon-Fri / 10-3 Sat   E-mail: visionandhearing@earthlink.net
Modern and period eyeglass frames. CREDIT CARDS.

M. Eising & Co. 212-744-1270
1135 Madison Ave. (74th St)
NY, NY 10028
Hours: 10-6 Mon-Fri / 10-3 Sat
Good selection period eyeglasses and pince-nez. CREDIT CARDS.

The Eye Shop 212-673-9450
50 W 8th St. (6th-MacDougal St)
NY, NY 10011
Hours: 10-7 Mon-Fri / 10:30-6:30 Sat / 12-6 Sun
Good selection of styles. RENTALS. CREDIT CARDS.

Jeffrey's Manhattan Eyeland 212-787-3232
2391 Broadway (87-88th St)   FAX 212-579-0620
NY, NY 10024
Hours: 10-7 Mon-Fri / 11-5:30 Sat / 12-5 Sun
Designer frames, period frames, some antique selections. Cat-eyes, etc.
Special lenses available for film shoots. RENTALS. CREDIT CARDS.

E.B. Meyrowitz & Dell 212-840-3881
19 W 44th St. (5-6th Ave)   212-575-1686
NY, NY 10036   FAX 212-575-1747
Hours: 9-5:45 Mon-Fri, 10-4:30 Sat.
Modern eyeglasses and lorgnettes. CREDIT CARDS.

Moscot Opticals 866-MOSCOTS
69 West 14th St.(6th Ave)   212-647-1550
NY, NY 10011
Hours: 10:30-7 Mon-Fri / 10:30-5 Sat / 12-5 Sun

118 Orchard St., 2nd Fl.(Delancey St)   212-477-3796
NY, NY 10002
Hours: 10-7 Mon-Fri / 10-6 Sat / 11-5 Sun
www.moscot.com
Large selection; glasses made while you wait; good prices. CREDIT CARDS.

Unique Eyewear 212-947-4977
19 W 34th St. Rm 1218 (5-6th Ave)   FAX 212-563-6752
NY, NY 10001
Hours: 9-4:45 Mon-Fri / 10-1 Sat
Eyeglasses at wholesale prices. No credit cards.

NOTES

FABRICS

See also: ETHNIC GOODS: All Headings
            FABRICS: All Headings

Associated Fabrics Corporation 201-797-0097
  15-01 Pollitt Dr., Unit 7 (Lexington-Park Ave)   800-232-4077
  Fair Lawn, NJ 07410   FAX 866-710-3850
  Hours: 8:30-4:30 Mon-Fri / closed 12-1 daily   E-mail: info@afcfabrics.com
  www.afcfabrics.com
  Full range of theatrical fabrics: metallics, spandex, fluorescents and novelty
  fabrics. CREDIT CARDS.

B & J Fabrics 212-354-8150
  525 Seventh Ave., 2nd Fl. (38th St)   FAX 212-764-3355
  NY, NY 10018
  Hours: 8-5:45 Mon-Fri / 9-4:45 Sat   E-mail: info@bandjfabrics.com
  www.bandjfabrics.com
  Designer fabrics, linings and ultra suede. Samples can be ordered on-line.
  CREDIT CARDS.

Berenstein Textiles 212-354-5213
  270 W 39th St., 20th FL (7-8th Aves)   800-717-2257
  NY, NY 10018   FAX 212-768-2703
  Hours: 9-6 Mon-Fri   E-mail: info@berensteintextiles.com
  www.berensteintextiles.com
  Wholesale importers and converters specializing in bridal, evening and formal
  wear fabrics. they also carry a full inventory of everyday apparel fabric such
  as wools, rayons, silks and polyesters.

Butterfly Fabrics, Inc. 212-768-3940
  237 W 35th St. (7-8th St)   FAX 212-575-6867
  NY, NY 10018
  Hours: 10-5 Mon-Fri / 9-5 Sat   E-mail: cbutterfly@aol.com
  www.butterflyfabrics.us
  Great selection of silks, rayons and spandex fabrics.   CREDIT CARDS.

Circle Fabrics / Circle Visual, Inc. 212-719-5153
  225 W 37th St. 16th FL (7-8th Ave)   FAX 212-704-0918
  NY, NY 10018
  Hours: 9-5:30 Mon-Fri   E-mail: sales@circlevisual.com
  www.circlevisual.com
  Custom tablecloths, slipcovers, pillows, banners, printing, embroidery,
  fixtures and fabrics. Everything made to order. Quick delivery. Digital
  printing for vinyl signs. Visit website to view clientele. CREDIT CARDS.

Classic Hawaiian Products 808-277-5323
  1860 Ala Moana Blvd # 810
  Honolulu, HI 96815
  Hours: 9-6 (Hawaiian Time) Mon-Fri
                     E-mail: customerservice@classichawaiianproducts.com
  www.classichawaiianproducts.com
  Good selection of Hawaiian clothing; childrens, baby and adult sizes, jewelry,
  beachwear, fabrics and home decor. Be sure to make time for your orders,
  they need extra time for quick deliveries.

D & C Textile Corp. 212-564-6200
212 W 35th St., 16th FL (35-36th St)   FAX 212-268-9730
NY, NY 10001
Hours: 9-5 Mon-Fri
Cottons, poplins, jacquards, broadcloth; will order; one week delivery. No
credit cards.

Day to Day Textile 212-575-1577
214 W 39th St., Store # 5 (7-8th Ave)   FAX 212-575-1588
NY, NY 10018
Hours: 9:30-6:30 Mon-Fri / 10-6 Sat / 1-5 Sun   E-mail: daytodaytextile@aol.com
Wholesale and retail upholstery, drapery, lace, leather, suede and fur fabrics.
CREDIT CARDS.

Fabric for Less 212-391-7504
239 W 39th St. (7-8th Ave)   FAX 212-921-4018
NY, NY 10018
Hours: 9:30-6:30 Mon-Fri / 10-6 Sat / 11-5 Sun
Import, export and domestic fabrics. Large linen selection. Designer fabrics
wholesale and retail. CREDIT CARDS.

Fabric House, Inc. 212-944-7016
214A W 39th St. (7-8th Ave)   FAX 212-944-7018
NY, NY 10018
Hours: 9-7 Mon-Fri / 10-6 Sat / 11-5 Sun
Good source for general fabrics and polar fleece. CREDIT CARDS.

Fishman's Fabrics 312-922-7250
1101 S Desplaines St.   FAX 312-922-7402
Chicago, IL 60607
Hours: 9-5 Mon-Fri / 10-4 Sat   E-mail: info@fishmansfabrics.com
www.fishmansfabrics.com
All kinds of fabrics; in store and mail order. Specializing in designer and
bridal fabrics. Custom reupholstery and drapery available. P.O.s and CREDIT
CARDS.

Full Swing Textiles Collections, Inc. 781-934-6781
22 Tinkertown Ln. (Extention St)   FAX 781-846-0228
Duxbury, MA 02332
Hours: 9-5 Mon-Fri by appt.   E-mail: sales@fullswingtextiles.com
www.fullswingtextiles.com
Fabrics based on patterns from 1910-1950s many tropical patterns; Upholstery
and drapery fabrics. Check website for other fabrics. Wholesale only. Online
shopping only. CREDIT CARDS.

Henry Glass & Co. . . . . .212-686-5194 X 213
49 W 37th St., 14th Fl. (6th Ave)   FAX 212-532-3525
NY, NY 10018
Hours: 9-5 Mon-Fri   E-mail: lliyi@jaflex.com
www.henryglassfabrics.com
Quilting cottons and cotton blends, calicos and flannel. Wholesale only -
5 bolt minimum. See website for patterns and retailers. No credit cards.

Habu 212-239-3546
135 W 29th St., Ste. 804 (7-8th Ave) FAX 212-239-4173
NY, NY 10001
Hours: 10-6 Mon-Sat E-mail: habu@habutextiles.com
www.habutextiles.com
Simple Japanese and American handwoven fabrics of natural materials. Yarns are hand dyed with natural dyes. Visit website for catalog information.

Handloom Batik 518-828-2205
532 Warren St.
Hudson, NY 12534
Hours: 12-7 Wed-Sat / 1-6 Sun / Call for Appt. before visiting storeE-mail: usha@handloombatik.com
www.handloombatik.com
Good selection of beautiful batik and handwoven fabrics, reasonably priced; Asian gift items.

Homespun 888-543-2998
P.O. Box 7287 480-699-9676
Chandler, AZ 85246 FAX 309-413-2805
Hours: 9-4 Mon-Fri
www:homespunfabrics.com
Cotton fabrics 10 feet wide. Custom-made drapes, tablecloths, spreads, etc. or do it yourself. CREDIT CARDS.

Jasco New York LLC 914-421-1365
P.O. Box 246 FAX Same
White Plains, NY 10605
Hours: by appt. E-mail: info@jascofabrics.com
www.jascofabrics.com
Manufacturer of knits; wholesale only.

Kabat Textile Corp. 212-398-0011
247 W 37th St. (7-8th Ave) 516-361-3226
NY, NY 10018
Hours: 9-5 Mon-Fri
Light crepe, silk and poly chiffon; wholesale.

L.P. Thur, Inc. / Fabrics and Home 212-243-4913
101 W 23rd St., Ste. 112 (6-7th Ave) 800-582-2624
NY, NY 10011 FAX 631-462-8216
Hours: 9:30-7 Mon-Thurs / 9:30-5:30 Fri E-mail: info@fabricsandhome.com
www.fabricsandhome.com
Velvets, lame, spandex, cotton lycra, rayons, some upholstery fabrics, blackout fabrics. Swatching OK. Dollar a yard fabrics available by the roll. CREDIT CARDS.

La Lame, Inc. 212-921-9770
132 W 36th St., 11th Fl. (5-6th Ave) FAX 212-302-4359
NY, NY 10018
Hours: 9-5 Mon-Fri E-mail: edschneer@lalame.com
www.lalame.com
Great for ecclesiastical costumes; metallic and non-metallic brocades, ecclesiastical and tapestries. Catalog $5. CREDIT CARDS.

Mendel's Far Out Fabrics 415-621-1287
1556 Haight St.
San Francisco, CA 94117
Hours: 10-5:50 Mon-Sat / 11-4:50 Sun   E-mail: sales@mendels.com
www.mendels.com
An art and funky fabric store. Carry fabric dye, buttons, and trims. Also Haight memorabilia.

Mood Designer Fabrics 212-730-5003
225 W 37th St., 3rd Fl.(7-8th Ave)
NY, NY 10018   FAX 212-221-1932
Hours: 9-7 Mon-Fri / 10-4 Sat

6151 W Pico Blvd.   323-653-6663
Los Angeles, CA 90035   FAX 323-653-6660
Hours: 9:30-7 Mon-Fri / 10-5 Sat   E-mail: info@moodfabric.com
www.moodfabric.com
Great prices, lots of everything. Crowded around noon. Retail and wholesale. CREDIT CARDS.

N.Y. Elegant Fabrics 212-302-4984
222 W 40th St. (7-8th Ave)   212-302-4980
NY, NY 10018   FAX 212-302-4996
Hours: 9-6 Mon-Fri / 10-5 Sat   E-mail: nyelegant@aol.com
Large selection of silks, woolen, cottons, velvet and bridal satins. Swatches available upon request. CREDIT CARDS.

Outdoor Wilderness Fabrics 208-402-0110
123 E Simpliot Blvd.   (orders) 800-693-7467
Caldwell, ID 83605   FAX 800-333-6930
Hours: 8-5 Mon-Thurs / 8-4 Fri   E-mail: owfinc@owfinc.com
www.owfinc.com
Trademark fabrics in poly, nylon, fleece, coated and uncoated, webbing, zippers, plastic buckles. Great prices. Catalog. Swatches available. Call before 1pm for same day shipment. CREDIT CARDS.

P & S Textile 212-226-1534
359 Broadway (Franklin-Leonard St)   212-226-1572
NY, NY 10013   FAX 212-343-1838
Hours: 9:30-6:30 Mon-Thurs / 9:30-3 Fri / 11-5:30 Sun
Fabrics, patterns, notions & trimmings and yarn, needles and how-to books. Wide selection and great prices. CREDIT CARDS.

Paron West / Paron Annex 212-768-3266
206 W 40th St. (7-8th Ave)   FAX 212-768-3260
NY, NY 10018
Hours: 8:30-7 Mon-Thurs / 8:30-5:45 Fri / 9-5 Sat / 11-4 Sun
www.paronfabrics.com
Cottons, silks, woolens, velvets, novelties; quality dress goods. CREDIT CARDS.

Pickering International 415-474-2288
888 Post St.   FAX   415-474-1617
San Francisco, CA 94109
Hours: 9-5 Mon-Fri   E-mail: info@picknatural.com
www.picknatural.com
Import and wholesale company specializing in textiles made from natural fibers. They believe that natural resources are good for our environment and are happy to be a green and clean business. You would be surprised at the products available in silks, cottons, soybean, and much more. Swatches available. 10 yard minimums except for remnants. Custom dyeing minimum 500 yards. CREDIT CARDS.

Pierre Deux 212-644-4891
979 Third Ave., Ste 134 (58-59th St)   FAX   212-644-4893
NY, NY 10022
Hours: 9-5 Mon-Fri / Sat by appt.   E-mail: ddny@pierredeux.com
www.pierredeux.com
French country prints. Reproduction furniture. RENTALS. CREDIT CARDS.

Quest Outfitters 800-359-6931
4919 Hubner Cr.   941-923-5006
Sarasota, FL 34241   FAX   941-923-4246
Hours: 8-4 Mon-Fri   E-mail: info@questoutfitters.com
www.questoutfitters.com
Trademark fabrics in poly and nylon, fleece coated fabrics, neoprene and foam meshes. Roll goods insulated fabrics. Zippers, plastic buckles. CREDIT CARDS.

Reprodepot Fabrics 413-527-4047
115 Pleasant St.   FAX   413-527-6407
East Hampton, MA 01027
Hours: Web 24-hrs.   E-mail: help@reprodepotfabrics.com
www.reprodepotfabrics.com
Largest selection of reproduction vintage fabrics on the Internet. Hard-to-find prints and barkcloth. Swatching available. Very friendly. Great website. CREDIT CARDS.

Reproduction Fabrics.com 406-586-1775
205 Haggerty Ln., Ste. 190   800-380-4611
Bozeman, MT 59715   FAX   406-586-8847
Hours: 12-3 Mon-Fri / or by appt.   E-mail: staff@reproductionfabrics.com
www.reproductionfabrics.com
Excellent source for authentic reproduction cotton fabrics from 1775 to 1950; including authentic linens, toiles, and feedsacks. Friendly staff will assist you in your selections. Swatches available upon request. CREDIT CARDS.

Richard Tie Fabrics 516-577-3406
72 Newton Plaza   FAX   516-577-3306
Plainview, NY 11803
Hours: 9-5 Mon-Fri
www.rtfabrics.com / www.rtfacc.com
Custom fabric both woven and printed. They can do your design in a wide range of colors or pick one of their existing patterns. Also has accories on website.

Rosen & Chadick, Inc. 212-869-0142
561 Seventh Ave., 2nd FL (Corner 40th)   800-225-3838
NY, NY 10018   FAX 212-730-5865
Hours: 8:30-5:45 Mon-Fri / 9-4:30 Sat   E-mail: er@rosenandchadickfabrics.com
www.rosenandchadickfabrics.com
Quality fabrics including woolens, silks, cotton and novelties. CREDIT
CARDS.

Roth International 212-840-1945
13 W 38th St. (5-6th Ave)   FAX 212-391-1033
NY, NY 10018
Hours: 9-5 Mon-Fri   E-mail: rothimport@verizon.net
www.rothinternational.net
Sequin and beaded applique, sequins and rhinestones by the yard, metallic
braids and cords, beaded fringe, bridal headpieces; wholesaler, large orders
only.

Royal Fashion Centre, Inc. 212-398-0215
214 W 39th St.   FAX 212-921-0608
NY, NY 10018
Hours: 9-6:30 Mon-Sat / 12-4 Sun   E-mail: mail@royalfabric.com
www.royalfabric.com
Importers, exporters wholesalers and retail of exclusive fabrics, embroideries,
laces and trimming. CREDIT CARDS.

Rupert, Gibbon, & Spider, Inc. 800-442-0455
PO Box 425   707-433-9577
Healdsburg, CA 95448   FAX 707-433-4906
Hours: 8-5 Mon-Fri   E-mail: service@jacquardproducts.com
www.jacquardproducts.com
Fabric paints & dyes, economical full sizes, novelty paints, metallics,
flourescents, sparkles. Catalog. COD. CREDIT CARDS.

Sequins International 718-204-0002
60-01 31st Ave.   FAX 718-204-0999
Woodside, NY 11377
Hours: 8:30-4:30 Mon-Fri
www.sequins.com
Manufacturer of sequin fabrics, stretch and non-stretch, 45", all colors. All
trims. Call for outlets and stores.

Shamash & Sons, Inc. 201-271-0700
57 Hertz Way (5-6th Ave)   FAX 201-271-9718
Secaucus, NJ 07094
Hours: 8:30-5:30 Mon-Fri   E-mail: sales@shamashandsons.com
www.shamashandsons.com
Printed wool challis, silks; interior design section; wholesale and retail.
AMEX.

Stern & Stern Industries, Inc. 212-972-4040
708 Third Ave. (44-45th St)   FAX 212-818-9230
NY, NY 10017
Hours: 9-5 Mon-Fri   E-mail: tom.hogan@steinandstern.com
www.sternandstern.com
Carry teflon fabrics, nylon, polyester, kevlar, aramid and nomex. Swatch
cards available. No credit cards.

Stylecrest Fabrics, Ltd. 212-354-0123
641 59th St. (37-38th St)   800-789-5339
West New York, NJ 07093   FAX 212-354-0279
Hours: 9-6 Mon-Fri / or by appt.   E-mail: stylecrest@aol.com
www.stylecrest.com
Wholesale lames, metals, glitter, sequined velvets, chiffons, satins; better
grade theatrical fabrics. Contact Mary.

Testfabrics, Inc. 570-603-0432
PO Box 26, 415 Delaware Ave.   FAX 570-603-0433
West Pittiston, PA 18643
Hours: 8-5 Mon-Fri   E-mail: testfabric@aol.com
www.testfabrics.com
Lycras, satin, brocade, lame, wools, cotton, rayon, fake fur, velvet. Vintage tie
fabrics, unique weaves and vinyls. 1/2 yard minimum. CREDIT CARDS.

Textile Arts Marketing 914-368-7945
405 Tarrytown Rd., Ste. 1558   888-775-4774
White Plains, NY 10607   FAX 914-428-6557
Hours: 9-5 Mon-Fri / or by appt.   E-mail: info@textileartsmarketing.com
www.textileartsmarketing.com
Imported and customized fabrics, buttons and trimmings. Also custom
weaving, knitting, printing and dyeing. In-stock fabrics include silk, cotton,
synthetics and linen. They do prototypes for the garment industry so custom
work minimums are flexible.

Textile Discount Outlet 773-847-0572
2121 W 21st St. (S. Leavitt-S Hoyne Ave)
Chicago, IL 60608
Hours: call for hours
Great place to find a lot of fun and weird stuff. The prices are awesome,
around $5/yd. Keep an open mind when you go there, you'll never know
what you'll find. Call for hours, they fluctuate. CREDIT CARDS.

Velvets, Inc. 973-379-4272
PO Box 165 / 286 Taylor Rd. S.   FAX 973-379-7460
Short Hills, NJ 07078
Hours: 9-5 Mon-Fri   E-mail: velvetsinc@comcast.net
www.velvets.org
Wholesale by the yard or piece; order from color card; will custom dye large
quantities. CREDIT CARDS.

VITEL Industries 847-299-9750
1026 North Ave.   FAX 847-299-7686
Des Plaines, IL 60016
Hours: 9-5 Mon-Fri   E-mail: vitelindustries@msn.com
Wide selection of fabrics and trims for costume and scenic design.
Specializing in metallic blends, brocades, sheers and holograms. Samples
upon request. Speak to John.

Vogue Fabrics 847-864-9600
718-732 Main St.
Evanston, IL 60202   FAX 847-475-9858
Hours: 9-9 Mon & Thurs / 9-5:30 Tue-Wed, Fri-Sat / 12-5 Sun

Vogue Fabrics (cont.) 312-829-2505
623-627 W Roosevelt Rd.
Chicago, IL 60607   FAX 312-829-8222
Hours: 9:30-6 Mon-Sat / 9:30-8 Thurs / 12-5 Sun

16919 Torrance St.   708-474-4200
Lansing, IL 60438   FAX 708-889-0571
Hours: 11:30-8 Mon & Thurs / 9:30-6 Tue-Wed, Fri & Sat / 12-5 Sun
www.myvoguefabrics.com
Thousands of fabrics: stretch, cotton, knits, sheers, cottons, etc. Swatching
service available thru web address... Some fabrics available wholesale. Call
for warehouse location (847) 864-1270. CREDIT CARDS.

Weavers Fabrics, Inc. 212-840-1492
257-B W 39th St. (7-8th Ave)   FAX 212-840-1575
NY, NY 10018
Hours: 9-6:30 Mon-Fri / 10-6 Sat
Importer of exclusive novelties, silks, woolens, velvets, laces, linens,
embroideries, cottons, sheers, brocades, theatrical and bridal fabrics. Extra
helpful service wholesale and retail. Also quality batting. CREDIT CARDS.

Whaley's / Bradford, Ltd. 011-44-127-457-6718
Harris Ct., Great Horton   011-44-127-452-1309
Bradford, West Yorkshire, England BD7 4EQ
www.whaleys-bradford.ltd.uk   E-mail: info@whaleysltd.co.uk
Located in the UK, Whaley's has curtain fabrics as well as many natural fiber
fabrics that are sold prepared for dyeing and printing. Visit their website to
order fabrics, drapes or basic fabrics for costumes. They have a separate
export department. CREDIT CARDS.

Wimpfheimer Velvets 212-563-3400
226 W 37th St., 12th Fl (34th St)   800-224-7167
NY, NY 10118   FAX 212-629-6431
Hours: 8-4:30 Mon-Fri   E-mail: info@wimpvel.com
www.wimpvel.com
Rayon, velvet, velveteen; 18-20 yd. minimum. CREDIT CARDS.

FABRICS: BURLAP, CANVAS, GAUZE, MUSLIN

Dazian, Inc. . . . . .East Coast 877-232-9426
                                               West Coast 877-432-9426

124 Enterprise Ave. S   201-549-1000
Secaucus, NJ 07096   877-232-9426
Hours: 9-5 Mon-Fri by appt. only   FAX 201-549-1055

27 W 20th St., Ste 903(in the George Dell Showroom)   212-206-3515
NY, NY 10011   FAX 212-206-3516
Hours: 9-5 Mon-Fri / Call Secaucus location for appointments

7120 Case Ave.(Burbank Airport Business Park)   818-287-3800
North Hollywood, CA 91605   FAX 818-287-3810
Hours: 8-5 Mon-Fri   www.dazian.com
Canvas, burlap, gauze, muslin and more; samples on request. Also Foss
shape and Wonderflex. CREDIT CARDS.

Gerriets International 609-758-9121
130 Winterwood Ave
Ewing, NJ 08638
Hours: 8:30-5 Mon-Fri
www.gi-info.com
800-369-3695
FAX 609-758-9596
E-mail: mail@gi-info.com

Canvas, burlap, gauze & seamless muslin up to 41' wide. Sample cards &
catalog available. RENTALS.

Rose Brand 800-223-1624
FAX 800-594-7424

4 Emerson Lane(15-16th St)
Secaucus, NJ 07094
Hours: 8-5 Mon-Fri
800-223-1624
201-809-1730
FAX 201-809-1851

10616 Lanark St.
Sun City, CA 91352
Hours: 8-5 Mon-Fri
www.rosebrand.com
800-360-5056
818-505-6290
FAX 818-505-6293
E-mail: sales@rosebrand.com

Custom sewing. Large stock & selection of F.R. & N.F.R. muslins, extra-wide
seamless muslin, canvas, burlap, cotton scrim and gauze. Call or fax for
catalog. CREDIT CARDS.

Seattle Fabrics 206-525-0670
8702 Aurora Ave. N (N 87th St)
Seattle, WA 98103
Hours: 9-6 Mon-Sat
www.seattlefabrics.com
866-925-0670
FAX 206-525-0779
E-mail: seattlefabrics@msn.com

Outdoor and recreational fabric & hardware. Specialty fabrics, webbing,
thread and zippers; neoprene and closed cell foam. Patterns for outdoor and
sports attire; equestrian, tents and backpacks. Fabric samples available.
CREDIT CARDS.

Trivantage 732-868-8400
16 World's Fair Dr.
Somerset, NJ 08873
Hours: 8-5 Mon-Fri
www.trivantage.com
800-544-3675
FAX 732-563-4400

Acrylic, vinyl, laminates, cotton duck, awning fabrics and hardware and other
specialty fabrics; wholesale only. CREDIT CARDS.

FABRICS: DRAPERY, SLIPCOVER, & UPHOLSTERY

Baranzelli 212-753-6511
938 Third Ave.
NY, NY 10022
Hours: 10-6 Mon-Fri / 12-4 Sun
www.baranzelli.com
FAX 212-759-2558

E-mail: info@baranzelli.com

Outlet for Scalamandre fabrics; trims and casements; good about swatching.
CREDIT CARDS.

The Barn 203-334-3396
50 Hurd Ave. (Grand St)   FAX 203-367-7864
Bridgeport, CT 06604
Hours: 10-5 Mon-Sat
www.thebarn-bridgeport.com
Great upholstery fabrics; also drapery, slipcover and general fabrics. *CREDIT CARDS.*

Beckenstein's Home Fabric & Interiors 212-366-5142
32 W 20th St. (5-6th Ave)   FAX 212-366-4274
NY, NY 10002
Hours: 10-6 Mon-Sat / 12-5 Sun   E-mail: beckfab@aol.com
www.beckinsteinfabrics.com
Good selection of upholstery and drapery fabrics, lace curtain panels; also some trims. Stock and remnants in basement. CREDIT CARDS.

Frank Bella & Co., Inc. 516-932-3838
485-17 Broadway   800-645-7560
Hicksville, NY 11801   FAX 516-932-7347
Hours: 8:30-4:30 Mon-Fri / 8-12 Sat   E-mail: fbellajr@verizon.net
www.frankbellacompany.com
Distributor of U.S. Naugahyde; wholesale and retail, upholstery fabrics. Sample book available.

Calico Corners 914-698-9141
1040 Mamaroneck Ave.   800-213-6366
Mamaroneck, NY 10543   FAX 914-698-6057
Hours: 10-5 Mon-Wed / 10-7 Thurs / 10-5 Fri-Sat / 12-5 Sun
www.calicocorners.com
Large selection of discounted drapery and upholstery fabrics. Visit web address for other locations. CREDIT CARDS.

Clarence House 212-752-2890
979 Third Ave., Ste. 205   800-221-4704
NY, NY 10022   FAX 212-755-3314
Hours: 9-5 Mon- Fri   E-mail: info@clarencehouse.com
www.clarencehouse.com
Showroom to the trade only. Repros of traditional and historical patterns; some trims. Very expensive. CREDIT CARDS.

Design Tex 800-221-1540
200 Varick St., 8th Fl.   212-886-8200
NY, NY 10014   FAX 212-886-8219
Hours: 9-5 Mon-Fri

979 Third Ave., Ste. 232(D&D Bldg. 59th St)   212-752-2535
NY, NY 10022   FAX 212-838-5668
Hour: 9-5 Mon-Fri
www.designtexgroup.com
Vinyl, textile, and acoustical wallcovering, rugs, digital panels, and upholstery fabrics. See website for other showroom locations or call 800-221-1540.

Diana Fabrics 212-302-0006
269 W 39th St. (7-8th Ave)   917-723-5357
NY, NY 10018
Hours: 9:30-7 Mon-Sat / 11-5 Sun   E-mail: dmahrachdesigns@comcast.net
All kinds of exclusive fabrics; denim, silk, velvet, brocade, fur, upholstery.
Shipping available. CREDIT CARDS.

Donghia Textiles 212-935-3713
979 Third Ave. Ste. 613   FAX 212-935-9707
NY, NY 10022
Hours: 9-5 Mon-Fri   E-mail: mail@donghia.com
www.donghia.com
Showroom to the trade. Contemporary and deco-styled patterns of fabrics
and wallcoverings. Some furniture. See website for other locations.

F

Full Swing Textiles Collections, Inc. 781-934-6781
22 Tinkertown Ln. (Extention St)   FAX 781-846-0228
Duxbury, MA 02332
Hours: 9-5 Mon-Fri by appt.   E-mail: sales@fullswingtextiles.com
www.fullswingtextiles.com
Fabrics based on patterns from 1910-1950s many tropical patterns; Upholstery
and drapery fabrics. Check website for other fabrics. Wholesale only. Online
shopping only. CREDIT CARDS.

Harry Zarin Co. 212-925-6112
314 Grand St. (Allen-Orchard St)   FAX 212-925-6584
NY, NY 10002
Hours: 9-7 Mon-Thurs / 9-6 Fri / 10-6 Sun
www.zarinfabrics.com
Large selection of drapery and upholstery fabrics; fair prices. CREDIT CARDS.

Homespun 888-543-2998
P.O. Box 7287   480-699-9676
Chandler, AZ 85246   FAX 309-413-2805
Hours: 9-4 Mon-Fri
www.homespunfabrics.com
Cotton fabrics 10 feet wide. Custom-made drapes, tablecloths, spreads, etc.
or do it yourself. CREDIT CARDS.

Joe's Fabric Warehouse 212-674-7089
102 & 110 Orchard St. (at Delancey St)   FAX 212-674-3651
NY, NY 10002
Hours: 9-6 Sun-Thurs / 9-3 Fri   E-mail: sales@joefabrics.com
www.joefabrics.com
Large and beautiful selection, most current design fabrics. Swatching.
Shipping available. CREDIT CARDS.

Kravet Fabrics 800-645-9068
979 Third Ave., Ste. 324(58-59th St) (D&D Building)   212-421-6363
NY, NY 10022   FAX 212-751-7196
Hours: 9-5 Mon-Fri

200 Lexington Ave., 4th Fl.   212-725-0340
NY, NY 10016   FAX 212-684-7350
Hours: 9-5 Mon-Fri

Kravet Fabrics (cont.) 800-645-9068
225 Central Ave. S   516-293-2000
Bethpage, NY 11714   FAX 516-293-2737
Hours: 10-4 Mon-Fri
www.kravet.com
To the trade (account required); large selection, all kinds of drapery, sheer and upholstery fabrics and trims. Recently added furnitre, carpets and furnishings. Large quantities available. Very helpful; swatching. Reasonably priced.

M & A Decorators 212-226-3910
294 Grand St. (Eldridge & Allen)   FAX 212-334-5273
NY, NY 10002
Hours: 9:30-6 Sun-Thurs / 9:30-4 Fri / Closed Sat
Blinds, fine fabrics, upholstery, bed coverings, window designs, imported tablecloths. CREDIT CARDS.

Marimekko Store 212-628-8400
1262 Third Ave. (72nd-73rd St)   800-527-0624
NY, NY 10021   FAX 212-628-2814
Hours: 10-7 Mon-Sat / 12-5 Sun   E-mail: info@kiitosmariemekko.com
www.kiitosmarimekko.com
Stylish contemporary fabrics, Wallpaper and large scale prints. Pricey. CREDIT CARDS.

Rose Brand 800-223-1624
                                  FAX 800-594-7424

4 Emerson Lane(15-16th St)   800-223-1624
Secaucus, NJ 07094   201-809-1730
Hours: 8-5 Mon-Fri   FAX 201-809-1851

10616 Lanark St.   800-360-5056
Sun City, CA 91352   818-505-6290
Hours: 8-5 Mon-Fri   FAX 818-505-6293
www.rosebrand.com   E-mail: sales@rosebrand.com
Custom-sewn draperies. Individual attention by experienced sales staff. Call for custom sewn goods quote. Fast service. Velour, silks, satin, bengaline, muslin. Call or fax for catalog. CREDIT CARDS.

Arthur Sanderson & Sons 212-319-7220
979 Third Ave. (58-59th St)   FAX 212-593-6184
NY, NY 10022
Hours: 9-5 Mon-Fri   E-mail: sales@zoffany.com
www.sanderson-uk.com
To the trade. William Morris, arts and crafts wall covering and decorator fabrics. Expensive.

Scalamandre 212-376-2900
222 E 59th St. (2nd-3rd Ave)   800-932-4361
NY, NY 10022   FAX 212-688-7531
Hours: 9-6 Mon-Fri   E-mail: info@scalamandre.com
www.scalamandre.com
Showroom to the trade (account required). Wide selection of drapery, upholstery, decorator fabrics and trimmings; very expensive. Warehouse location in Hauppauge, NY. CREDIT CARDS.

F. Schumacher & Co (showroom) 212-415-3900
979 Third Ave., Ste. 832 (59th St)　　　　　　　　　　　800-523-1200
NY, NY 10022　　　　　　　　　　　　　　　　　FAX 212-415-3907
Hours: 9-5 Mon-Fri
www.fsco.com
Showroom to the trade (account required); collection of historic reproduction
wallpaper and matching fabrics. Will occasionally place fabrics in high-profile
movies and theaters.

Sheila's Decorating 212-777-3767
68 Orchard St. (Grand St)　　　　　　　　　　　FAX 212-777-7076
NY, NY 10002
Hours: 10-6 Sun-Fri　　　　　　　　　E-mail: info@sheilasdecorating.com
www.sheilasdecorating.com
Well-displayed and reasonably priced fabrics, furnishings and accessories.
CREDIT CARDS.

The Silk Trading Co. 323-954-9280
360 South La Brea Ave.　　　　　　　　　　　　　　888-SILK-302
Los Angeles, CA 90036　　　　　　　　　　　　FAX 323-954-8024
Hours: 9-6 Mon-Fri / 9-5 Sat
www.silktrading.com
Decorate without modesty. Wonderful selection of drapery and upholstery
fabrics. Custom drapes, upholstery and decorator's paints. Some trims and
tassels. CREDIT CARDS.

Sommer's Plastic Products Co., Inc. 973-777-7888
31 Styertowne Rd.　　　　　　　　　　　　　　　　800-225-7677
Clifton, NJ 07012　　　　　　　　　　　　　　　FAX 973-777-7890
Hours: 9-5 Mon-Fri　　　　　　　　　　E-mail: sales @sommers.com
www.sommers.com
Plastic fabrics, synthetic leathers and furs for apparel, footwear, luggage and
leather goods, home furnishing, wallcovering and upholstery.

Stroheim & Romann, Inc. 212-486-1500
979 Third Ave., Ste. 102 (58-59th St)　　　　　　FAX 212-980-1782
NY, NY 10022
Hours: 9-5 Mon-Fri　　　　　　　　　　　　E-mail: info@stroheim.com
www.stroheim.com
Showroom to the trade only; upholstery and drapery fabrics; order 24-hrs.
before pick-up. CREDIT CARDS.

Textile Discount Outlet 773-847-0572
2121 W 21st St. (S. Leavitt-S Hoyne Ave)
Chicago, IL 60608
Hours: call for hours
Great place to find a lot of fun and weird stuff. The prices are awesome,
around $5/yd. Keep an open mind when you go there, you'll never know
what you'll find. Call for hours, they fluctuate. CREDIT CARDS.

Whaley's / Bradford, Ltd. 011-44-127-457-6718
Harris Ct., Great Horton   011-44-127-452-1309
Bradford, West Yorkshire, England BD7 4EQ
www.whaleys-bradford.ltd.uk   E-mail: info@whaleysltd.co.uk
*Located in the UK, Whaley's has curtain fabrics as well as many natural fiber
fabrics that are sold prepared for dyeing and printing. Visit their website to
order fabrics, drapes or basic fabrics for costumes. They have a separate
export department. CREDIT CARDS.*

WolfHome 800-220-1893
936 Broadway (22nd St)   646-602-3246
NY, NY 10010   FAX 212-254-7105
Hours: 10-7 Mon-Sat / 11-6:30 Sun
www.wolfhome-ny.com
*Beautiful high-end fabrics. Large selection of embroidered silks. Some ready
made pillows, drapes and curtains. Interior goods and furniture made to
order, shades and window treatments, reupholstery service. They have their
own mills and can custom weave and color. Workroom on premises for
custom work. Fast deadlines no problem. Very helpful and willing to
accommodate entertainment business needs. CREDIT CARDS.*

FABRICS: FELT, VINYL, HOOK & LOOP, LAMINATES

Aetna Felt Corp. 610-791-0900
2401 W Emaus Ave.   800-526-4451
Allentown, PA 18103   FAX 610-791-5791
Hours: 8:30-4:30 Mon-Fri   E-mail: info@aetnafelt.com
www.aetnafelt.com
Industrial, light and novelty felt; swatch catalog. CREDIT CARDS.

American Felt & Filter Co. 845-561-3560
361 Walsh Ave.   FAX 845-561-0963
New Windsor, NY 12553
Hours: 8-5 Mon-Fri   E-mail: affco@affco.com
www.affco.com
Industrial, hat and lightweight felt; color cards; call for information.

Apex Plastic Industries, Inc. 800-APEX-INC
1400 Greenleaf Ave.
Elk Grove Village, IL 60007
Hours: 8-5 Mon-Fri   E-mail: info@apexplasticinc.com
www.apexplasticinc.com
*Large selection of plastics and vinyls, many felt-backed for upholstery.
Interesting textures, patterns and colors. CREDIT CARDS.*

Frank Bella & Co., Inc. 516-932-3838
485-17 Broadway   800-645-7560
Hicksville, NY 11801   FAX 516-932-7347
Hours: 8:30-4:30 Mon-Fri / 8-12 Sat   E-mail: fbellajr@verizon.net
www.frankbellacompany.com
*Distributor of U.S. Naugahyde; wholesale and retail, upholstery fabrics.
Sample book available.*

BZI Distributors 212-966-6690
314 Grand St. (Basement level of Harry Zarin) (Allen-Grand St.)
NY, NY 10002   FAX 212-966-8962
Hours: 9-6 Sun-Fri / 10-6 Sat
www.zarinfabrics.com
Vertical and mini-blinds, many styles of curtain rods and hardware.
Trimmings, upholstery supplies, foam rubber. Contact David or Gerry. $25
minimum on CREDIT CARDS.

Central Shippee 973-838-1100
46 Star Lake Rd.   800-631-8968
Bloomingdale, NJ 07403   FAX 973-838-8273
Hours: 9-11 Tue-Thrus   E-mail: felt@webspan.net
www.thefeltpeople.com
Felt for every purpose. Catalog; industrial and decorator felt, quick and
helpful service. Swatch cards available. CREDIT CARDS.

Design Craft Fabric Corp. 847-904-7000
2230 Ridge Dr.   800-755-1010
Glenview, IL 60025   FAX 847-904-7102
Hours: 8:30-5 Mon-Fri   E-mail: dcinfo@design-craft.com
www.design-craft.com
Wholesaler of foam-backed fabric, 60" wide loop weave fabric for hook and
loop applications; attaches like magic.î

Economy Foam & Futons 212-475-4800
56 8th St. (5-6th Ave)   FAX 212-475-2727
NY, NY 10011
Hours: 10-7 Mon-Thurs / Fri call for hours / 10:30-6 Sun
                         E-mail: sales@economyfoamandfutons.com
www.economyfoamandfutons.com
Vinyl fabrics, foam rubber sheets, shapes, batting. CREDIT CARDS.

The Felters Co. 864-576-7900
5965 Hwy 221   800-845-7596
Roebuck, SC 29376   FAX 864-574-5235
Hours: 8-5 Mon-Fri   E-mail: billA@felters.com
www.felters.com
Wholesale manufacturer of industrial and decorator non-woven felt; swatch
card available.

Lockfast 800-543-7157
8481 Duke Blvd   FAX 513-701-6936
Mason, OH 45040
Hours: 8:30-5 Mon-Fri   E-mail: sales@lockfast.com
www.lockfast.com
Providing standard and custom hook-and-loop fastening products, velcro
compatible fabric, plus graphics cases for the display industry. Display loop
fabric available in 34 colors! CREDIT CARDS.

Mendel's Far Out Fabrics 415-621-1287
1556 Haight St.
San Francisco, CA 94117
Hours: 10-5:50 Mon-Sat / 11-4:50 Sun   E-mail: sales@mendels.com
www.mendels.com
An art and funky fabric store. Carry fabric dye, buttons, and trims. Also Haight memorabilia.

National Nonwovens 413-527-3445
PO Box 150, 180 Pleasant St.   800-333-3469
Easthampton, MA 01027   FAX 413-527-9570
Hours: 8-5 Mon-Fri   E-mail: sales@nationalnonwovens.com
www.nationalnonwovens.com
Manufacturer and die cutter of wool and synthetic felts and non-woven fabrics.

Sammons Preston 800-323-5547
1000 Remington Blvd., Ste. 210   630-378-6000
Bolingbrook, IL 60440   FAX 630-378-6010
Hours: WEB 24-hrs.   E-mail: sp@patterson-medical.com
www.sammonspreston.com
Thermoplastic (Roylan), Velcro and miscellaneous post-op therapy items.

Seattle Fabrics 206-525-0670
8702 Aurora Ave. N (N 87th St)   866-925-0670
Seattle, WA 98103   FAX 206-525-0779
Hours: 9-6 Mon-Sat   E-mail: seattlefabrics@msn.com
www.seattlefabrics.com
Outdoor and recreational fabric & hardware. Specialty fabrics, webbing, thread and zippers; neoprene and closed cell foam. Patterns for outdoor and sports attire; equestrian, tents and backpacks. Fabric samples available. CREDIT CARDS.

Supreme Felt & Abrasives Co. 708-344-0134
4425 James Pl.   FAX 708-344-0285
Melrose Park, IL 60160
Hours: 8-4:30 Mon-Fri   E-mail: supremefelt@aol.com
www.supremefelt.com
Industrial felt.

FABRICS: FUR AND PILE

Big 4 Fabrics 973-777-4143
1000 Main Ave.   800-USA-PILE
Clifton, NJ 07011   FAX 973-777-5014
Hours: 9-3 Mon-Thurs / 9-2 Fri
www.big4fabrics.com
One of the largest sources for faux fur fabrics. They also carry a large inventory of nylon lycra, spandex, cotton lycra and stretch velvet. CREDIT CARDS.

Diana Fabrics 212-302-0006
   269 W 39th St. (7-8th Ave)   917-723-5357
   NY, NY 10018
   Hours: 9:30-7 Mon-Sat / 11-5 Sun   E-mail: dmahrachdesigns@comcast.net
   All kinds of exclusive fabrics; denim, silk, velvet, brocade, fur, upholstery.
   Shipping available. CREDIT CARDS.

Fabulous-Furs 800-848-4650
   20 W Eleventh St.   859-291-3300
   Covington, KY 41011   FAX 859-291-9687
   Hours: 9-5 Mon-Fri / 10-3 Sat / 24-7 Catalog
   www.fabulousfurs.com   E-mail: custserv@fabulousfurs.com
   Full line of fur fabrics, patterns, fur coat kits, sewing notions; also
   instructional books and patterns. Phone orders. CREDIT CARDS.

National Fiber Technologies 978-686-2964
   300 Canal St.   800-842-2751
   Lawrence, MA 01840   FAX 978-686-1497
   Hours: 8:30-5 Mon-Fri   E-mail: info@nftech.com
   www.nftech.com
   Manufacturer of long-and short-hair fur fabrics in any color, density or
   length. Available with tinsel or iridescent fibers on standard or 4-way stretch
   backing. Production of custom-made fabrics is 2-3 weeks, less for a rush
   order.

FABRICS: LINING, INTERFACING, FUSIBLE

Acker & Jablow Fabrics 212 216-1300
   519 Eighth Ave., 5th Fl. (35-36th St)   FAX 212-216-1400
   NY, NY 10018
   Hours: 9-5 Mon-Fri
   Distributors of lining, underlining, rayon, siri; swatch cards available.
   Wholesale.

Fabric Czar USA, Inc. 212-475-6666
   257 W 39th St. (7-8th Ave)   800-221-2727
   NY, NY 10018   FAX 212-473-1710
   Hours: 9-5 Mon-Fri
   www.fabricczar.com
   Complete line of lining fabrics, canvas interfacing; also good selection of
   quality woolens. CREDIT CARDS.

FABRICS: SCENIC

Associated Drapery & Equipment Co. 516-671-5245
   40 Sea Cliff Ave.   FAX 516-674-2213
   Glen Cove, NY 11542
   Hours: 8-4 Mon-Fri
   Custom-made curtains and draperies; also scenic fabrics. Contact Chesky
   Weiss.

Chicago Canvas & Supply Co. 773-478-5700
3719 W. Lawrence Ave.   FAX 773-588-3139
Chicago, IL 60625
Hours: 8-4 Mon-Fri Closed 12-1 daily   E-mail: email@chicagocanvas.com
www.chicagocanvas.com
Chicago's leading theatrical supply house. Hardware, curtain track, fabrics,
expendables; gaffers tape, drop cloths, velcro, scenic supplies, Deca dyes,
artist's canvas as well as muslin. CREDIT CARDS.

Dazian, Inc. . . . . .East Coast 877-232-9426
                                              West Coast 877-432-9426

124 Enterprise Ave. S   201-549-1000
Secaucus, NJ 07096   877-232-9426
Hours: 9-5 Mon-Fri by appt. only   FAX 201-549-1055

27 W 20th St., Ste 903(in the George Dell Showroom)   212-206-3515
NY, NY 10011   FAX 212-206-3516
Hours: 9-5 Mon-Fri / Call Secaucus location for appointments

7120 Case Ave.(Burbank Airport Business Park)   818-287-3800
North Hollywood, CA 91605   FAX 818-287-3810
Hours: 8-5 Mon-Fri
www.dazian.com
Scrim, muslin, velour, etc.; catalog and/or color cards on request. CREDIT
CARDS.

Gerriets International 609-758-9121
130 Winterwood Ave   800-369-3695
Ewing, NJ 08638   FAX 609-758-9596
Hours: 8:30-5 Mon-Fri   E-mail: mail@gi-info.com
www.gi-info.com
Complete line of scenic fabrics. Call for samples. RENTALS.

Production Advantage, Inc. 802-651-6915
P.O. Box 1700   800-424-99914
Williston, VT 05495   FAX 877-424-9991
Hours: 8:30-6 Mon-Fri   E-mail: sales@proadv.com
www.proadv.com
Catalog sales of hardware, lighting, rigging, scenic material, soft goods,
sound equipment and expendables to the entertainment industry. All major
brands carried. Catalog. CREDIT CARDS.

Rose Brand 800-223-1624
                                                    FAX 800-594-7424
4 Emerson Lane(15-16th St)
Secaucus, NJ 07094   201-809-1730
Hours: 8-5 Mon-Fri   FAX 201-809-1851

10616 Lanark St.   800-360-5056
Sun City, CA 91352   818-505-6290
Hours: 8-5 Mon-Fri   FAX 818-505-6293
www.rosebrand.com   E-mail: sales@rosebrand.com
Custom sewing. Large stock and selection of F.R. & N.F.R. muslins, extra-
wide seamless muslin, canvas, cyc, scrim, leno, scenery netting, burlap, felt,
metallics. Call or fax for catalog. CREDIT CARDS.

The Set Shop 212-255-3500
36 W 20th St. (5-6th Ave)   800-422-7831
NY, NY 10011   FAX 212-229-9600
Hours: 8:30-6 Mon-Fri   E-mail: info@setshop.com
www.setshop.com
Bee Smokers and juice-style machines. Professional and compact garment steamers. 50 colors of 9'-0" or 12'-0" wide seamless paper; 12 colors muslin; Foamcore, Gatorboard. Ten types of ice cubes and shards, large selection of plexi. CREDIT CARDS.

Valley Forge Fabrics, Inc. 800-223-7979
2981 Gateway Dr.   954-971-1776
Pompano Beach, FL 33069   FAX 954-968-1775
Hours: 8:30-5:30 Mon-Fri   E-mail: info@valleyforge.com
www.valleyforge.com
Velours, muslin, scrim, cyc and acoustical fabrics; manufacturer of flame-retardant fabrics; samples available. Speak to Bernie. CREDIT CARDS.

FABRICS: SHEERS, NETS & LACES

Apex Mills 516-239-4400
168 Doughty Blvd.   800-989-2739
Inwood, NY 11096   FAX 516-239-4951
Hours: 9-5 Mon-Fri   E-mail: info@apexmills.com
www.apexmills.com
Polyester mesh fabrics.

Beckenstein's Home Fabric & Interiors 212-366-5142
32 W 20th St. (5-6th Ave)   FAX 212-366-4274
NY, NY 10002
Hours: 10-6 Mon-Sat / 12-5 Sun   E-mail: beckfab@aol.com
www.beckinsteinfabrics.com
Good selection of upholstery and drapery fabrics, lace curtain panels; also some trims. Stock and remnants in basement. CREDIT CARDS.

Berenstein Textiles 212-354-5213
270 W 39th St., 20th FL (7-8th Aves)   800-717-2257
NY, NY 10018   FAX 212-768-2703
Hours: 9-6 Mon-Fri   E-mail: info@berensteintextiles.com
www.berensteintextiles.com
Wholesale importers and converters specializing in bridal, evening and formal wear fabrics. they also carry a full inventory of everyday apparel fabric such as wools, rayons, silks and polyesters.

Novik Sales 516-599-8678
84 Atlantic Ave.   FAX 516-599-8696
Lynbrook, NY 11563
Hours: 10-5 Mon-Fri / Call first
Lace motifs and yardage; net, tulle, maline, marquisette; wholesale only, must order from sample books.

ATAC

Owl Mills 732-942-8025
500 James St. Unit 11   FAX 732-907-2621
Lakewood, NJ 08701
Hours: 9-5 Mon-Fri   E-mail: owlmills@gmail.com
www.owlmills.com
Silk organza, sheers, nets, linens. Popular plain and metallic braids, ribbons and cord trims imported from Europe. Swatching. No credit cards.

Seattle Fabrics 206-525-0670
8702 Aurora Ave. N (N 87th St)   866-925-0670
Seattle, WA 98103   FAX 206-525-0779
Hours: 9-6 Mon-Sat   E-mail: seattlefabrics@msn.com
www.seattlefabrics.com
Outdoor and recreational fabric & hardware. Specialty fabrics, webbing, thread and zippers; neoprene and closed cell foam. Patterns for outdoor and sports attire; equestrian, tents and backpacks. Fabric samples available. CREDIT CARDS.

Sterling Net 973-783-9800
18 Label St.   800-342-0316
Montclair, NJ 07042   FAX 973-783-9808
Hours: 9-5 Mon-Fri   E-mail: info@sterlingnets.com
www.sterlingnets.com
Theatrical, decorative, agricultural, fishing, cargo nets; bulk and custom.

Tinsel Trading 212-730-1030
1 W 37th St. (5-6th Ave)   FAX 212-768-8823
NY, NY 10018
Hours: 9:45-5:30 Mon-Fri / 11-5 some Sat (call first)
www.tinseltrading.com   E-mail: sales@tinseltrading.com
Gold mesh fabrics, metallic and antique trims, vintage flowers, fruit stamens, buttons, fringes, cords, tassels, horsehair, ribbons, etc. Also upholstery gimps and trims. $75 minimum order for shipping. CREDIT CARDS.

Weavers Fabrics, Inc. 212-840-1492
257-B W 39th St. (7-8th Ave)   FAX 212-840-1575
NY, NY 10018
Hours: 9-6:30 Mon-Fri / 10-6 Sat
Importer of exclusive novelties, silks, woolens, velvets, laces, linens, embroideries, cottons, sheers, brocades, theatrical and bridal fabrics. Extra helpful service wholesale and retail. Also quality batting. CREDIT CARDS.

FABRICS: SILK

Bach International LLC 201-964-1900
425 Paterson Ave   FAX 201-964-9844
East Rutherford, NJ 07073
Hours: 10-5 Mon-Fri / by appt.
www.bachinternational.com
Wholesale only; beautiful Indian raw silks by the bolt.

Baranzelli 212-753-6511
   938 Third Ave.   FAX 212-759-2558
   NY, NY 10022
   Hours: 10-6 Mon-Fri / 12-4 Sun   E-mail: info@baranzelli.com
   www.baranzelli.com
   Outlet for Scalamandre fabrics; trims and casements; good about swatching.
   CREDIT CARDS.

C & J Textiles 212-354-0040
   230 W 38th St., 7th FL (7-8th Ave)   FAX 212-704-9771
   NY, NY 10018
   Hours: 9-5 Mon-Fri   E-mail: sales@cjtextile.com
   Specializing in fine silk fabrics. No minimum.

Calamo Silk 212-840-1570
   55 W 39th St., 14th Fl.(5-6th Ave)   212-840-1570
   NY, NY 10018   FAX 212-704-2086
   Hours: 9-5 Mon-Fri Call for appt.

   110 E 9th St. Ste. B1271   213-622-3800
   Los Angeles, CA 90079   FAX 213-622-6900
   Hours: 9-5 Mon-Fri   E-mail: info@calamosilk.com
   www.calamosilk.com
   Silks at good prices.

Exotic Silks 800-845-7455
   1959 Leghorn   650-965-7760
   Mountain View, CA 94043   FAX 650-965-0712
   Hours: 8:30-5:30 Mon-Fri   E-mail: silks@exoticsilks.com
   www.exoticsilks.com
   Just about everything you can imagine in silk is at this location, over 1400
   silks in every color. Business accounts must be set up before ordering.
   Reasonable priced. Minimum quantity is 15-17 yards per piece, 28 yards for
   velvets, and 1/2 dozen of all other items. The minimum sale is $100. CREDIT
   CARDS.

N.Y. Elegant Fabrics 212-302-4984
   222 W 40th St. (7-8th Ave)   212-302-4980
   NY, NY 10018   FAX 212-302-4996
   Hours: 9-6 Mon-Fri / 10-5 Sat   E-mail: nyelegant@aol.com
   Large selection of silks, woolen, cottons, velvet and bridal satins. Swatches
   available upon request. CREDIT CARDS.

Oriental Silk, Co. 323-651-2323
   8377 Beverly Blvd.   FAX (same)
   Los Angeles, CA 90048
   Hours: 9-5 Mon-Fri
   www.orientalsilk.com
   Direct importer of silks. Mail order. Swatching available. CREDIT CARDS.

Owl Mills 732-942-8025
500 James St. Unit 11   FAX 732-907-2621
Lakewood, NJ 08701
Hours: 9-5 Mon-Fri   E-mail: owlmills@gmail.com
www.owlmills.com
Silk organza, sheers, nets, linens. Popular plain and metallic braids, ribbons and cord trims imported from Europe. Swatching. No credit cards.

Pickering International 415-474-2288
888 Post St.   FAX 415-474-1617
San Francisco, CA 94109
Hours: 9-5 Mon-Fri   E-mail: info@picknatural.com
www.picknatural.com
Import and wholesale company specializing in textiles made from natural fibers. They believe that natural resources are good for our environment and are happy to be a green and clean business. You would be surprised at the products available in silks, cottons, soybean, and much more. Swatches available. 10 yard minimums except for remnants. Custom dyeing minimum 500 yards. CREDIT CARDS.

The Silk Trading Co. 323-954-9280
360 South La Brea Ave.   888-SILK-302
Los Angeles, CA 90036   FAX 323-954-8024
Hours: 9-6 Mon-Fri / 9-5 Sat
www.silktrading.com
Decorate without modesty. Wonderful selection of drapery and upholstery fabrics. Custom drapes, upholstery and decorator's paints. Some trims and tassels. CREDIT CARDS.

Super Textile Co., Inc. 212-643-8700
134 W 37th St., 4th Fl. (B'way-7th Ave)   800-548-1722
NY, NY 10018   FAX 212-594-5002
Hours: 9-4:30 Mon-Thurs / 9-3 Fri
Gorgeous silks at reasonable prices; retail or wholesale.

Thai Silks 650-948-8611
252 State St.   800-722-SILK (7455)
Los Altos, CA 94022   FAX 650-948-3426
Hours: 9-5:30 Mon-Sat   E-mail: silks@thaisilks.com
www.thaisilks.com
Mail order, swatch club, brochure. All kinds of silks. CREDIT CARDS.

WolfHome 800-220-1893
936 Broadway (22nd St)   646-602-3246
NY, NY 10010   FAX 212-254-7105
Hours: 10-7 Mon-Sat / 11-6:30 Sun
www.wolfhome-ny.com
Beautiful high-end fabrics. Large selection of embroidered silks. Some ready made pillows, drapes and curtains. Interior goods and furniture made to order, shades and window treatments, reupholstery service. They have their own mills and can custom weave and color. Workroom on premises for custom work. Fast deadlines no problem. Very helpful and willing to accommodate entertainment business needs. CREDIT CARDS.

FABRICS: STRETCH, CORSET & SPANDEX

Big 4 Fabrics 973-777-4143
1000 Main Ave.   800-USA-PILE
Clifton, NJ 07011   FAX 973-777-5014
Hours: 9-3 Mon-Thurs / 9-2 Fri
www.big4fabrics.com
One of the largest sources for faux fur fabrics. They also carry a large inventory of nylon lycra, spandex, cotton lycra and stretch velvet. CREDIT CARDS.

Farthingales 519-275-2374
286 Monteith Ave.
Stratford, Ontario, CANADA N5A2P8   FAX 519-275-2376
Hours: call for appt.   E-mail: 1sparks@farthingales.on.ca
www.farthingales.on.ca

3306 Pico Blvd(West of Santa Monica Freeway)   310-392-1787
Santa Monica, CA 90404
Hours: by appt. only   E-mail: sales@farthingalesla.com
www.farthingalesla.com
North America's largest source for costume corset fabrics, bones, zigzag wire, wiggle bones and busks. Hoopsteel, crinoline, tutu net and stiff period shirt interfacing. Grommets, hooks and eyes, buckles, garters and historic sewing patterns. Dyable silks and cottons. View website for new products and ordering, no telephone orders. Los Angeles location only carries corsets. CREDIT CARDS.

La Lame, Inc. 212-921-9770
132 W 36th St., 11th Fl. (5-6th Ave)   FAX 212-302-4359
NY, NY 10018
Hours: 9-5 Mon-Fri   E-mail: edschneer@lalame.com
www.lalame.com
Metallic prints, velvets, tricots, flocked and embroideries, patent coatings, laces, sequins, novelties. CREDIT CARDS.

Milliken & Co. 917-542-3740
350 Madison Ave. (44-45th St)
NY, NY 10017
Hours: 9-5 Mon-Fri
www.milliken.com
Milliskin, nylon, Lycra, activewear; wholesale only.

New York Theatrical Supplies, Inc. .212-840-3120
263 W 38th St. (7-8th Ave)   FAX 212-354-7432
NY, NY 10018
Hours: 9-6 Mon-Fri / 10-5 Sat
Spandex, stretch fabrics, glitz and feathers. CREDIT CARDS.

Rose Brand 800-223-1624
                FAX 800-594-7424
4 Emerson Lane(15-16th St)
Secaucus, NJ 07094   201-809-1730
Hours: 8-5 Mon-Fri   FAX 201-809-1851

Rose Brand (cont.) 800-223-1624
    10616 Lanark St.   800-360-5056
    Sun City, CA 91352   818-505-6290
    Hours: 8-5 Mon-Fri   FAX 818-505-6293
    www.rosebrand.com   E-mail: sales@rosebrand.com
    120" Spandex, 120" F.R. poly stretch, colored spandex, metallic stretch fabrics, 60" power stretch, 46" super stretch. Also costume fabrics and ballet nets. Call or fax for catalog. CREDIT CARDS.

Spandex House, Inc. 212-354-6711
    263 W 38th St., 2nd Fl. (7-8th Ave)   FAX 212-354-7432
    NY, NY 10018
    Hours: 9-6 Mon-Fri / 10-5 Sat   E-mail: sales@spandexhouse.com
    www.spandexhouse.com
    Specializing in spandex and Lycra. Also theatrical, costume and display fabrics. CREDIT CARDS.

Stretch World, Inc. 212-398-3004
    252 W 38th St. (7-8th Ave)   FAX 212-398-3003
    NY, NY 10018
    Hours: 9-7 Mon-Sat / 11-7 Sun   E-mail: buy@stretchworld.com
    www.stretchworld.com
    All kinds of stretch fabrics.

FABRICS: WOOLENS & UNIFORM

M. J. Cahn Co., Inc. 212-563-7292
    510 W 27th St. (10-11th Ave)   FAX 212-563-7299
    NY, NY 10001
    Hours: 8:30-4 Mon-Fri   E-mail: woolens@gmail.com
    www.wovenfabrics.com
    Woolens for uniforms and menswear; period fabrics. Also carries cotton and synthetics.

Fabric Czar USA, Inc. 212-475-6666
    257 W 39th St. (7-8th Ave)   800-221-2727
    NY, NY 10018   FAX 212-473-1710
    Hours: 9-5 Mon-Fri
    www.fabricczar.com
    Fine suit woolens to uniform weight wool, shirt fabrics; good selection. CREDIT CARDS.

M. Grabie Woolen Co., Inc. 718-268-7444
    107-40 Queens Blvd., Rm. 208   FAX 718-268-0074
    Forest Hills, NY 11375
    Hours: 9-5:30 Mon-Fri   E-mail: grabiewoolen@aol.com
    www.grabiewoolen.com
    Manufacturers of Australian Merino woolens and wool blends. Also a fine line of gabardines, twill crepe, pique and flannels. Many colors to choose from, no minimums. Swatch book, phone and fax orders. No credit cards.

F

N.Y. Elegant Fabrics 212-302-4984
    222 W 40th St. (7-8th Ave)   212-302-4980
    NY, NY 10018   FAX 212-302-4996
    Hours: 9-6 Mon-Fri / 10-5 Sat   E-mail: nyelegant@aol.com
    Large selection of silks, woolen, cottons, velvet and bridal satins. Swatches
    available upon request. CREDIT CARDS.

York Fabrics 914-481-5549
    33 New Brodd St., Unit LL3 (35-34th St)   800-303-0409
    Port Chester, NY 10573   Fax 914-481-5549
    Hours: 9:30-5 Mon-Fri   E-mail: sales@yorkfabrics.com
    www.yorkfabrics.com
    York Fabrics specializes in in-stock worsted and wool fabrics in various
    textures, colors and patterns. There is a huge selection of fine suiting fabrics
    in super 100's, 110's and 100% woolens. Period pieces and authentic looking
    woolens. Wholesale and retail. CREDIT CARDS.

FEATHERS

AA Feather Company / Gettinger Feathers 212-695-9470
    16 W 36th St., FL 8 (5-6th Ave)   FAX 212-695-9471
    NY, NY 10018
    Hours: 9-5 Mon, Wed-Thurs / 9-1 Fri   E-mail: gettfeath@aol.com
    www.gettingerfeather.com
    Colorful feathers and boas, silk flowers, etc.

American Plume & Fancy Feather Co., Inc. 800-521-1132
    P.O. Box 566 / 4 Skyline Dr. (7-8th Ave)   (outside NY) 800-962-8544
    Clarks Summit, PA 18411   FAX 570-586-3008
    Hours: 9-4 Mon- Fri   E-mail: apff@epix.net
    www.americanplume.com
    Natural and dyed feathers, boas, ostrich, marabou, chandelle, turkey, etc;
    referrals for smaller orders available. Nice people. CREDIT CARDS.

Associated Fabrics Corporation 201-797-0097
    15-01 Pollitt Dr., Unit 7 (Lexington-Park Ave)   800-232-4077
    Fair Lawn, NJ 07410   FAX 866-710-3850
    Hours: 8:30-4:30 Mon-Fri / closed 12-1 daily   E-mail: info@afcfabrics.com
    www.afcfabrics.com
    Nice ostrich plumes over 18î, ask for Bruce. CREDIT CARDS.

Cinderella Flower & Feather Corporation 212-564-2929
    48 W 37th St. (5-6th Ave)   FAX 212-594-0071
    NY, NY 10018
    Hours: 9-6 Mon-Fri / 10-4 Sat   E-mail: cinderella@margola.com
    Fancy feathers, boas, flowers, fruit. Merged with Margola Corporation.
    CREDIT CARDS.

Dersh Feather & Trading Corp. 212-714-2806
    25 W 38th St. (5-6th Ave)   FAX 212-239-1407
    NY, NY 10018
    Hours: 9-5 Mon-Fri   E-mail: dershfeather@aol.com
    www.dershfeather.com
    Good selection of feathers; recommended. Catalog.

Eskay Novelty 212-391-4110
34 W 38th St., FL 3 (5-6th Ave)   800-237-2202
NY, NY 10018   FAX 212-921-7926
Hours: 8-4 Mon-Thurs / 8-12 Fri   E-mail: sales@eskaynovelty.com
www.eskaynovelty.com
Excellent selection of all types of feathers. Phone orders accepted until 8pm
Mon-Thurs. Will make custom boas. CREDIT CARDS.

The Feather Place 212-719-0345
40 W 38th St., 3rd Fl. (5-6th Ave)
NY, NY 10018
Hours: 9 - 5 Mon - Fri   E-mail: websales@featherplace.com
www.featherplace.com
Feathers of all kinds, small to large quantities. Catalog available online. See
website for other locations and product availability.

Grey Owl Indian Crafts 732-389-4626
15 Meridian Rd.   (orders) 800-487-2376
Eatontown, NJ 07724   FAX 732-389-4629
Hours: 9-5 Mon-Fri   E-mail: sales@greyowlcrafts.com
www.greyowlcrafts.com
Feathers for American Indian headdresses; also beads, kits. CREDIT CARDS.

Hai's Trimming Co. 212-764-2166
242 W 38th St. (7-8th Ave)   FAX (same)
NY, NY 10018
Hours: 10-6 Mon-Fri / 10-5 Sat
All kinds of trims; bridal accessories. Good stock of heat fix and glue on
rhinestones, ribbons, buttons, etc. Beaded trims and feathers. Vinyl repair
glues and adhesives that stick vinyl to vinyl. CREDIT CARDS.

M & J Trimmings . . . . .1-800-9MJ TRIM
1008 Sixth Ave. (37-38th St)   212-204-9595
NY, NY 10018   FAX 212-704-8090
Hours: 9-8 Mon-Fri / 10-6 Sat / 12-6 Sun   E-mail: info@mjtrim.com
www.mjtrim.com
Pricey; ribbons, buttons, buckles, frogs, beads, rhinestones, handbag handles
and Swarovski heatsets. CREDIT CARDS.

Manny's Millinery Supply Co. 212-840-2235
26 W 38th St. (5-6th Ave)   FAX 212-944-0178
NY, NY 10018
Hours: 11-6 Tue-Thurs / 11-4:30 Fri   E-mail: info@mannys-millinery.com
www.mannys-millinery.com
Manny's will be staying open, however they are streamlining their inventory.
Limited quantities of straw and felt bodies. Visit website or call for updated
information. Large selection of flowers, tubular horsehair braid, veiling, and
feathers. Shop online. Be sure to call before dropping by store. CREDIT
CARDS.

Matoska Trading Company 714-516-9940
    611 W Chapman Ave. (N. Parker -N. Pixley)   800-926-6286
    Orange, CA 92868   FAX 800-249-9375
    Hours: 11-6 Tue-Sat   E-mail: matoska@matoska.com
    www.matoska.com
    Native American craft supplies, books,feathers, buckskin, leather, beads,
    music and more. Shop online or visit their store. CREDIT CARDS.

New York Theatrical Supplies, Inc. 212-840-3120
    263 W 38th St. (7-8th Ave)   FAX 212-354-7432
    NY, NY 10018
    Hours: 9-6 Mon-Fri / 10-5 Sat
    Spandex, stretch fabrics, glitz and feathers. CREDIT CARDS.

Roth International 212-840-1945
    13 W 38th St. (5-6th Ave)   FAX 212-391-1033
    NY, NY 10018
    Hours: 9-5 Mon-Fri   E-mail: rothimport@verizon.net
    www.rothinternational.net
    Pure silk flowers, feathers and good selection of trimmings; wholesaler, large
    orders only.

S.A. Feathers 800-226-8698
    5852 Enterprise Pkwy.   FAX 239-693-6912
    Ft. Myers, FL 33905
    Hours: 8-3:30 Mon-Fri   E-mail: info@safeathercompany.com
    www.safeathercompany.com
    Natural and custom-dyed feathers by the pound, boas and band plumes.
    CREDIT CARDS.

M. Schwartz & Sons, Inc. 631-234-7722
    45 Hoffman Ave.   FAX 631-234-7817
    Hauppauge, NY 11788
    Hours: 8:30-5 Mon-Fri
    www.mschwartzfeather.com
    Wholesale feathers.

FIREARMS & WEAPONRY

See also: ARMOR
         POLICE EQUIPMENT

Ace Video & Props 718-392-1100
    37-24 24th St., Ste. 106 (Houston & West St)   212-206-1475
    Long Island City, NY 11101   FAX 718-392-1155
    Hours: 10-6 Mon-Fri / 10-2 Sat by appt.
             E-mail: acevideorentals@gmail.com / acepropsnyc@gmail.com
    www.aceprops.com
    Working and non-working replicas of firearms; Uzzis, .357 Magnums, etc.
    RENTALS. CREDIT CARDS.

Altered Anatomy FX / BNT Studios .951-653-3658
20841 Bakal Dr.   FAX 909-653-9468
Riverside, CA 92508
Hours: 9-7 Mon-Fri   E-mail: bill@bntstudios.com
www.bntstudios.com
Armor, creatures, puppets, helmets, bodysuits. Rapid prototyping, CNC prototyping.

American Fencers Supply/ The Armoury 415-863-7911
1027 Terra Nova Blvd.   650-359-7911
Pacifica, CA 94044   FAX 415-431-7931
Hours: 9-5 Mon-Fri / 10-4 Sat E-mail: amfence@amfence.com
www.amfence.com
Period swords, rapiers, daggers, etc; chain mail. Catalog available. CREDIT CARDS.

Blade Fencing 212-244-3090
245 W 29th St. (7-8th Ave)   800-828-5661
NY, NY 10001   FAX 212-244-3090
Hours: 10-6 Mon-Fri / 11-3 Sat-Sun E-mail: bladefencing@gmail.com
www.blade-fencing.com
Fencing and stage equipment and clothing; catalog. CREDIT CARDS.

Centre Firearms Co., Inc. 212-244-4040
10 W 37th St., 7th FL (5-6th Ave)   FAX 212-947-1233
NY, NY 10018
Hours: 9-3:30 Mon-Fri   E-mail: centrefire@aol.com
www.centrefirearms.com
Complete NYC-approved weapons, blanks, props; gunsmithing. Call to verify specific need for permits. Seminars offered on firearm handling, pertinent laws and safety. Needless to say, a knowledgeable staff. RENTALS. CREDIT CARDS.

Collector's Armoury 703-493-9120
PO Box 1050   800-336-4572
Lorton, VA 22199   FAX 703-493-9424
Hours: 8:30-5 Mon-Fri EST E-mail: sales@collectorsarmoury.com
www.collectorsarmoury.com
Great prop and costume prop weapons. Color catalog available. Contact theatrical department. CREDIT CARDS.

Costume Armour, Inc. 845-534-9120
PO Box 85, 2 Mill St.   FAX 845-534-8602
Cornwall, NY 12518
Hours: 8-4 Mon-Fri   E-mail: info@costumearmour.com
www.costumearmour.com
Replica weapons, arms, armor. Also custom work. Catalog. RENTALS.

Frank's Sport Shop . . . .(Store) 718-299-9628
430 E Tremont Ave. (Park Ave)   (Office) 212-945-0020
Bronx, NY 10457   FAX 718-583-1652
Hours: 9-8 Mon-Fri / 9-6 Sat E-mail: info@frankssports.com
www.frankssports.com
Complete line of hunting and archery equipment and clothing. Also sporting goods and career apparel. Catalog available online. RENTALS. CREDIT CARDS.

Historic Arms & Armor 760-789-2299
17228 Voorhes Ln.   FAX 760-789-6644
Ramona, CA 92065
Hours: 9-6 Mon-Fri, by appt.   E-mail: info@historicenterprises.com
www.historicenterprises.com
Ancient Greek to vacuumform sci-fi armor. Specializes in medieval and
renaissance. RENTALS.

J&M Special Effects 718-875-0140
524 Sackett St.   FAX 718-596-8329
Brooklyn, NY 11217
Hours: 9-4 Mon-Fri by appt.   E-mail: info@jmfx.net
www.jmfx.net
Full-service special effects shop; design, construction, rental, sales of
equipment and supplies. Custom and stock, real or replicas. RENTALS.

Movie Gun Services Company 866-888-2025
PO Box 268
Babylon, NY 11702
Hours: by appt.   E-mail: mgs@moviegunservices.com
www.moviegunservices.com
Exotic weapon props for TV, film and print. Theatrical explosives supplies.
RENTALS. CREDIT CARDS.

Museum Replicas Ltd. 800-883-8838
P.O. Box 840 / 2147 Gee Mills Rd.   FAX 770-388-0246
Conyers, GA 30013
Hours: 9-6 Mon-Fri / 10-4 Sat   E-mail: custserv@museumreplicas.com
www.museumreplicas.com
Replica swords, daggers, rapiers, battle and pole axes, helmets, etc.; catalog.
CREDIT CARDS.

New Hope Martial Arts Supplies 212-643-8216
823 Sixth Ave., 2nd Fl. (28-29th St)   FAX 212-643-8273
NY, NY 10001
Hours: 10-7 Mon-Sat
www.newhopemartialarts.com
Martial arts supplies, oriental gifts, cutlery and posters. Some videos of
martial arts. CREDIT CARDS.

The Noble Collection 800-866-2538
PO Box 1476
Sterling, VA 20167
Hours: 9-5 Mon-Fri (customer service)
                         E-mail: customerservice@noblecollection.com
www.noblecollection.com
Historic and fantasy reproduction armor and sword. Life-size reproductions of
15th century armor and Samurai armor. Mail order only, call for catalog.
Layaway plan available. CREDIT CARDS.

Prop Masters, Inc. 818-846-3915
272 Empire Ave   FAX 818-846-1278
Burbank, CA 91504
Hours: 9-5 Mon-Fri
www.propmastersinc.com
Armor, robots and vacuumforming. Contact Henry.

SFX Design, Inc. 817-599-0800
2500 I-20 E
FAX 817-599-0496
Weatherford, TX 76087
Hours: 8-4 Mon-Fri
E-mail: info@sfxdesigninc.com
www.sfxdesigninc.com
Stock and custom gobos. Decorative and fighting swords, handguns, rifles, machine guns; any period, able to fire blanks. Breakaway resin to mold your own bottles, glass, panes, etc. Fog-Master machines and Aquafog component; also cobweb system. Pyrotechnics and miniature pneumatics, blood effects, atmospherics; custom projects. Great website. Catalog. No credit cards.

Starfire Swords, Ltd. 607-589-7978
74 Railroad Ave.
FAX 607-589-6630
Spencer, NY 14883
Hours: 10-2 Mon-Fri
E-mail: orders@starfireswords.com
www.starfireswords.com
Makes swords, daggers and metal weaponry for costume, decoration and stage combat. Also carries leather scabbards and accoutrements, for their own blades. Good selection. RENTALS. CREDIT CARDS.

Sword in the Stone Crafts 905-299-5550
152 Commercial St.
Milton, Ontario, Canada L9T 2J2
Hours: 9-5 Mon-Fri
E-mail: spike@ica.net
www.swordinthestone.ca
Skilled artisans working primarily in leather, specializing in custom-made gunleather and holsters, armour, belts, bags, pouches and cases, scabbards and sheaths, custom leather carving and more. RENTALS. CREDIT CARDS.

U.S. Cavalry 270-351-7000
2855 Centennial Ave.
800-777-7172
Radcliff, KY 40160
FAX 270-352-0266
Hours: 10-6:30 Mon-Fri / 9-5 Sat / 11-5 Sun
www.uscav.com
Military sabers, arms. Catalog. CREDIT CARDS.

Weapons Specialists 212-941-7696
33 Greene St. Loft #1W (Grand St)
Rick Washburn 917-626-6873
NY, NY 10013
FAX 212-941-7654
Hours: 9-6 Mon-Fri / other times by appt.
E-mail: rick@weaponspecialists.com
www.weaponspecialists.com
Weapons rentals from prehistoric to futuristic. NYC-approved firearms; medieval, colonial, western and most period weapons. Consultation, training and safety supervision. 24-hr. service available. RENTALS. CREDIT CARDS.

FIREPLACES & EQUIPMENT

A & R Asta Ltd. 212-750-3364
1152 Second Ave. (60-61st St)   FAX 212-751-5418
NY, NY 10021
Hours: 9:30-5 Mon-Fri / Weekends by appt. only   E-mail: asta1152@aol.com
*Custom marble cutting for tables, sinks, fireplaces, antique fireplace
accessories and marble statuary. Fireplace installation. Contact Vincent.
RENTALS.*

Danny Alessandro Ltd. 212-421-1928
308 E 59th St. (2nd-3rd Ave)   212-759-8210
NY, NY 10022   FAX 212-759-3819
Hours: 9-5 Mon-Fri / or by appt.
*Period reproduction mantels and fireplace accessories. Phone orders and
delivery. RENTALS. CREDIT CARDS.*

Demolition Depot / Irreplaceable Artifacts 212-860-1138
216 E 125th St.(2nd-3rd Ave)
NY, NY 10035   FAX 212-860-1560
Hours: 10-6 Mon-Sat / 12-5 Sun

428 Main St.   860-344-8576
Middletown, CT 06457   FAX 860-638-0834
Hours: by appt. only call 212-860-1138   E-mail: info@demolitiondepot.com
www.demolitiondepot.com
*Architectural ornamentation from demolished buildings; antique fireplaces.
100,000 sq. ft. warehouse by appt. RENTALS.*

Elizabeth Street Gallery, Inc. 212-941-4800
209 Elizabeth St. (Spring-Prince St.)   FAX 212-274-0057
NY, NY 10012
Hours: 10-5 Mon-Fri call for appt.   E-mail: info@elizabethstreetgallery.com
www.elizabethstreetgallery.com
*French, English and American stone and marble fireplaces. 17th-19th century
garden statuary and furniture; columns, pilasters and keystones. Also studio
collection of reproductions based on historical designs. RENTALS. CREDIT
CARDS.*

J&M Special Effects 718-875-0140
524 Sackett St.   FAX 718-596-8329
Brooklyn, NY 11217
Hours: 9-4 Mon-Fri by appt.   E-mail: info@jmfx.net
www.jmfx.net
Special effects company. Rentals of gas fueled fireplace rigs.

William H. Jackson Co. 212-753-9400
18 E 17th St. (2nd-3rd Ave)   FAX 212-753-7872
NY, NY 10003
Hours: 9:30-5 Mon-Thurs / 9:30-4 Fri
www.wmhj.com
*Antique reproduction mantels and fireplace accessories. Phone orders and
delivery available. Contact Donald Nelson. CREDIT CARDS.*

Lehman's 330-857-5757
One Leham Cr. / P.O. Box 270   888-438-5346
Kidron, OH 44636   FAX 888-780-4975
Hours: 8-5:30 Mon-Sat / Thurs til 8   E-mail: GetLehmans@aol.com
www.lehmans.com
Housewares, oil lamps, cast-iron cookery, wood cook stoves, homestead tools. Rustic old-fashioned stuff. Non-electric Amish products. Plus, all those old-fashioned health and beauty products, canning supplies, food and laundry supplies. Great catalog ($10 including shipping) or shop online. CREDIT CARDS.

Leo Design 212-929-8466
413 Bleeker St. (Bank-W 11th St)
NY, NY 10014
Hours: 12-8 Mon-Sat / 12-6 Sun
Wrought-iron and cast Arts and Crafts andirons, pottery and other gift items. Checks preferred on deposit. RENTALS. CREDIT CARDS.

FIRERETARDING SERVICES & SUPPLIES
See also: FABRICS: Scenic

Associated Drapery & Equipment Co....................516-671-5245
40 Sea Cliff Ave.   FAX 516-674-2213
Glen Cove, NY 11542
Hours: 8-4 Mon-Fri
Flameproofing service and compounds; also custom-made curtains and drapes; contact Chesky Weiss. Catalog.

BMI Supply 518-793-6706
571 Queensbury Ave.   800-836-0524
Queensbury, NY 12804   FAX 518-793-6181
Hours: 8-6 Mon-Fri   E-mail: bminy@bmisupply.com
www.bmisupply.com
Carries a full range of products for flameproofing, including Fire Retardant 279-7, an excellent product for synthetics. Catalog. CREDIT CARDS.

Tom Carroll Scenery, Inc. 201-432-9047
25 Pollock Ave.   FAX 201-434-1146
Jersey City, NJ 07305
Hours: 8-4 Mon-Fri   E-mail: tcarrollscenery@comcast.net
www.tomcarrollscenery.com
Custom scenery and props for theater, TV, film and industrials. Licensed to issue flameproof certificates.

H.J. Murray Co. 212-227-7050
66 Reade St. (Church-B'way)   FAX 212-962-6263
NY, NY 10007
Hours: 7:30-4:30 Mon-Fri   E-mail: hjmurrayco@aol.com
Sell fire protection equipment wholesale; valves, new extinguishers, etc. CREDIT CARDS.

I. Weiss and Sons, Inc. 718-706-8139
2-07 Borden Ave. (Vernon-Jackson Ave)   888-325-7192
Long Island City, NY 11101   FAX 718-482-9410
Hours: 8-5:30 Mon-Fri   E-mail: info@iweiss.com
www.iweiss.com
Flameproofing service. Also carry flame-retardant scenic fabrics.

Plastic Coatings Corporation 304-755-9151
4904 Teays Valley Rd.   800-279-9151
Scott Depot, WV 25560   FAX 304-755-0229
Hours: 8-4:30 Mon-Fri   E-mail: jaxsan@verizon.net
www.jaxsancoatings.com
Manufacturers of Jaxsan 600, a fibrous acrylic latex coating that is weather resistant and fire retardant. Friendly technical assistance over the phone. CREDIT CARDS.

Reynolds Drapery Service, Inc. 315-845-8632
7440 Main St.   FAX 315-845-8645
Newport, NY 13416
Hours: 8-4 Mon-Fri   E-mail: rynldpry@ntc.net.com
Flameproofing service for theatrical draperies as well as ìdo it yourselfî kits. No credit cards.

Rose Brand 800-223-1624
         FAX 800-594-7424

4 Emerson Lane(15-16th St)   800-223-1624
Secaucus, NJ 07094   201-809-1730
Hours: 8-5 Mon-Fri   FAX 201-809-1851

10616 Lanark St.   800-360-5056
Sun City, CA 91352   818-505-6290
Hours: 8-5 Mon-Fri   FAX 818-505-6293
www.rosebrand.com   E-mail: sales@rosebrand.com
Full line of flame retardant additives and solutions. Also pretreated certificated flame retardant fabrics in many weights and sizes. Custom flame treatment services for non-flame retardant fabrics. Call or fax for catalog. CREDIT CARDS.

Spartan Flame Retardants 800-435-5700
345 E Terra Cotta Ave.   815-459-8500
Crystal Lake, IL 60014   FAX 815-459-8560
Hours: 9-5 Mon-Fri   E-mail: spartan@mc.net
www.spartancompany.com
Formerly Flameproof Chemical Co. Distributors of DuPont fire retardants. P.O.s. No credit cards.

Turning Star, Inc. 212-696-2410
229 Bond St.   718-254-0534
Brooklyn, NY 11217   FAX 718-254-0538
Hours: 8-5 Mon-Fri   E-mail: info@turningstar.com
www.turningstar.com
Quality-assured flame proofing and fire retardant protection that is recognized by fire departments across the country. Also sells flame retardant products. CREDIT CARDS.

Zeller International, Ltd. 607-363-7792
15261 Highway 30   FAX 607-363-2071
Downsville, NY 13755
Hours: 9-5 Mon-Fri   E-mail: contact@zeller-int.com
www.zeller-int.com
Products for flameproofing of costumes, scenery, paint and objects. Also
waterproofing for fabric. Some minimums apply. Contact Carla Zelaschi.
Catalog. CREDIT CARDS.

FISHING TACKLE

Capitol Fishing Tackle 212-929-6132
132 West 36th St. (7 Ave-Bway)   FAX 212-929-0039
NY, NY 10018
Hours: 10-7 Mon-Fri / 10-5 Sat   E-mail: tom@capitolfishing.com
www.capitolfishing.com
A good selection of fly and line equipment. Tackle, lead weights,
monofilament, black nylon fishline, and high-test squid line. Waders, big
game fishing reels and poles. Small and large orders. CREDIT CARDS.

Gudebrod Industries, Inc. 610-327-4050
274 Shoemaker Rd.   877-249-2211
Pottstown, PA 19464   FAX 610-327-4588
Hours: 8:30-4:30 Mon-Fri   E-mail: sales@gudebrod.com
www.gudebrod.com
Braided fishline, variety of tests on spools. $150 minimum.

The Orvis Company 212-827-0698
522 Fifth Ave. (44-45th St)   FAX 212-827-0602
NY, NY 10036
Hours: 9-6 Mon-Wed, Fri / 9-7 Thurs / 10-5 Sat / 12-5 Sun
www.orvis.com
Fly fishing supplies. Gentlemen's hunting and fishing equipment and
clothing. Catalog available. CREDIT CARDS.

FLAGS & BANNERS

AAA American Flag Decorating Co., Inc. 212-279-4644
36 W 37th St., 9th Fl. (5-6th Ave)   FAX 212-695-8392
NY, NY 10018
Hours: 8:30-4 Mon-Thurs / 8:30-3:30 Fri   E-mail: aaaamericanflag@verizon.net
Stock and custom banners, flags and bunting. Screen and applique work.
Contact Ian. RENTALS. CREDIT CARDS.

Ace Banner, Flag & Graphics Co. .212-620-9111
107 W 27th St. (6th Ave)   800-675-9112
NY, NY 10011   FAX 212-463-9128
Hours: 7:30-4 Mon-Fri   E-mail: service@acebanner.com
www.acebanner.com / www.acebannershop.com
Foreign and domestic flags; custom banners; screen-printing. CREDIT
CARDS.

All Suffolk Flag Rental Service 631-589-2295
812 Sayville Ave. (13th St)　　　　　　　　　　　　　　　800-734-4144
Bohemia, NY 11716　　　　　　　　　　　　　　FAX 631-589-8141
Hours: 9-6 Mon-Fri / 9-2 Sat-Sun (call first)
Flags, bunting, pennants and windsocks; will ship same day; contact Joan
Dougherty. P.O.s accepted. RENTALS. CREDIT CARDS.

Arista Flag Corp. 845-246-7700
157 W Saugerties Rd.　　　　　　　　　　　　　FAX 845-246-7786
Saugerties, NY 12477
Hours: 8:30-5 Mon-Fri　　　　　　　　　E-mail: sales@aristaflag.com
www.aristaflag.com
Manufacturer of vinyl flags and banners; custom orders. Screen and applique
work. $25 minimum. P.O.s accepted. CREDIT CARDS.

Art Flag Co., Inc. 212-334-1890
8 Jay St. (Greenwich-Hudson St)　　　　　　　　　　　800-ART-FLAG
NY, NY 10013　　　　　　　　　　　　　　FAX 212-941-9631
Hours: 8-5:30 Mon-Fri　　　　　　　　　E-mail: info@artflag.com
www.artflag.com
Custom and stock, flags and banners. P.O.s and CREDIT CARDS.

Big Apple Sign Corp. 212-629-3650
247 W 35th St. (7-8th Ave)　　　　　　　　　　　　　877-244-2775
NY, NY 10001　　　　　　　　　　　　　　FAX 212-629-4954
Hours: 9-5:30 Mon-Fri　　　　　　E-mail: amir@bigapplegroup.com
www.bigapplegroup.com
Full-service sign company; 24-hr. service available. CREDIT CARDS.

Broadway Banner & Flag Company .518-792-1776
1940 Route 32 N (Rt 50)　　　　　　　　　　　FAX 518-792-4693
Gansevoort, NY 12831
Hours: 10-6 Tue-Fri / 12/4 Sat　　　E-mail: info@broadwaybanner.com
www.broadwaybanner.com
Flags and banners. All State, territories, Scout's and veteran's flags.
Hardware, poles and flag kits. Great website. CREDIT CARDS.

CRW Flags, Inc. 410-766-6106
7306 E. Furnace Branch Rd.　　　　　　　　　　　800-662-6106
Glen Burnie, MD 21060
Hours: 9-6 Mon-Sat　　　　　　　　　E-mail: gw@crwflags.com
www.crwflags.com
Offering flags of all nations in various sizes, as well as flagpoles and flag
related hardware and accessories. Also custom, novelty, boating, racing and
military flags. Web-site full of information as well as flag etiquette. CREDIT
CARDS.

Flag One 866-666-3524
P.O. Box 191053　　　　　　　　　　　　　FAX 866-233-3524
St. Louis, MO 63118
Hours: Web 24-hrs.　　　　　　　　　E-mail: contact@flagone.com
www.flagone.com
Flags and banners from around the world. USA city flags, religious, regional
& territory, civilian, military, rainbow pride flags as well as custom banners.
Various materials available. Great website. CREDIT CARDS.

F

Flagman of America 860-678-0275
22 Old Avon Village / P.O. Box 440   800-835-2462
Avon, CT 06001   FAX 860-678-8812
Hours: 24-hr website   E-mail: info@flagman.com
www.flagman.com
US Flags, custom, military, racing, marine, religious flags, and historical
flags. Flag poles, hardware and various outdoor signs for home and garden.
Speedy and courteous service. CREDIT CARDS.

Kraus & Sons, Inc. 212-620-0408
261 W 35th St. (7-8th Ave)   FAX 212-924-4081
NY, NY 10001
Hours: 9-5 Mon-Fri   E-mail: info@krausbanners.com
www.krausbanners.com
Embroidered, silkscreened or appliqued banners and flags; custom trophies
and ribbons; established 1886. No credit cards.

Main Attractions 732-225-3500
85 Newfield Ave. (Raritan Ctr Pkwy)   800-394-3500
Edison, NJ 08837   732-225-2110
Hours: 9:30-5 Mon-Fri   E-mail: events@mainattractions.com
www.mainattractions.com
Special events contractors; specializing in custom tent rentals, restroom
trailers, decor, portable staging, lighting and the production of displays and
signage. Visit website to see the full spectrum of their products. RENTALS.
CREDIT CARDS.

Manhattan Neon Sign Corp. 212-714-0430
640 W 28th St.   FAX 212-947-3906
NY, NY 10001
Hours: 9-5 Mon-Fri / or by appt.   E-mail: sales@manhattanneon.com
www.manhattanneon.com
Custom-made neon and rentals, 3-D props and displays, large-format full-
color graphics, LED moving message signs and vinyl signs, cut acrylic, wood
metal and foam. Contact Peter.

National Flag & Display Co., Inc. 212-462-4000
22 W 21st St., 7th Fl. (5-6th St)   FAX 212-462-2624
NY, NY 10010
Hours: 9-5:30 Mon-Fri / eves. & weekends by appt.
                                     E-mail: hsiegel@nationalflag.com
www.nationalflag.com
Manufacturers of banners, flags, backdrops and wall murals. Applique,
silkscreen, inkjet, dye-sublimation and electrostatic full-color printing. Rush
orders. RENTALS. CREDIT CARDS.

Quinn Flags 800-353-2468
316 Broadway
Hanover, PA 17331
Hours: 9-5 Mon-Fri   E-mail: info@quinnflags.com
www.quinnflags.com
American flags, bunting, state, territory and world flags and weathervanes.
Website has many more items as well as info on proper flag etiquette. Very
nice staff. CREDIT CARDS.

Regal Flags & Poles, Inc. 561-455-8000
1395 NW 17th Ave., Ste. 112B   800-858-8776
Delray Beach, FL 33445   FAX 561-404-4954
Hours: 24-hr. web / 8:30-5 Mon-Fri   E-mail: customerservice@flags.com
www.flags.com
Flags for all occasions. State, country, territoral, international, corporate logos, military, sports, nautical, historical, Nascar and racing, attention flags, pennants and banners. Custom work, as well as embroidery patches and needlepoint products. Patriotic decorations. Hardware and flagpoles. Great website. Very helpful. CREDIT CARDS.

SaratogaFlag.com 518-792-1776
1940 Route 32 N (Route 50)   FAX 518-792-4693
Ganesvoort, NY 12831
Hours: 11-5 Tue-Fri / 12-4 Sat / 24-hr Web   E-mail: info@sarasotaflag.com
www.saratogaflag.com
Custom flags, banners & theatrical backdrops. USA, historical, world and military flags, flagpoles and accessories. Truck and car lettering. CREDIT CARDS.

Sign Design of New York 718-392-0779
33-26 Northern Blvd.   FAX 718-937-6935
Long Island City, NY 11101
Hours: 9-6 Mon-Fri   E-mail: info@sdgny.com
www.sdgny.com
Manufacturer of all types of custom signage and visual display materials. Services from design to installations. CREDIT CARDS.

Sign Expo 212-925-8585
102 Franklin St.   FAX 212-680-0195
NY, NY 10013
Hours: 9-5:30 Mon-Fri   E-mail: signs@signexpo.com
www.signexpo.com
Banners, awnings, signs, letters, neon.

Specialty Sign Co., Inc. 212-243-8521
54 W 21st St., 2nd Fl. (5-6th Ave.)   800-394-3433
NY, NY 10010   FAX 212-243-6457
Hours: 9-5 Mon-Fri   E-mail: sales@specialtysigns.com
www.specialtysigns.com
Computer cut pre-spaced vinyl graphics. Indoor and outdoor use. Any size up to 48" high. Specialize in rush jobs. Helpful with questions. CREDIT CARDS.

The Flag Shop, Inc. 410-625-2212
301 Light St.   877-883-5247
Baltimore, MD 21202
Hours: 10-9 Mon-Sat / 11-7 Sun
www.flagshopinc.com
Flags of all Nations and States. Also wonderful assortment of flag-related items; t-shirts, balls, hats, posters, pins, etc. Embroidered patches with countries and various police emblems. Very nice people. Will ship. Catalog. CREDIT CARDS.

FLOCKING SERVICES & SUPPLIES

American Flock Association 617-303-6288
6 Beacon St., Ste. 1125   FAX 617-542-2199
Boston, MA 02108
Hours: 9-5 Mon-Fri   E-mail: info@flocking.org
www.flocking.org
Free directory guide to the flocking industry.

DonJer Products Co. 815-247-8775
13142 Murphy Rd.   800-336-6537
Winnebago, IL 61088   FAX 815-247-8644
Hours: by appt.   E-mail: info@donjer.com
www.donjer.com
Spray-on suede flock fibers, adhesive and equipment. Mail order. CREDIT CARDS.

FLOOR COVERINGS
See also: ANTIQUES: All Headings
             DANCE & STAGE FLOORING
             TILE, BRICKS & COBBLESTONES

ABC Carpet & Home Co., Inc. 212-473-3000
888 Broadway(19th St)
NY, NY 10003   FAX 212-777-3713
Hours: 10-8 Mon - Fri / 10-7 Sat / 11-6:30 Sun

1055 Bronx River Ave.(Bruckner Blvd) Outlet   718-842-8772
NY, NY 10472   FAX 718-812-6905
Hours: 10-7 Mon - Fri / 10-7 Sat / 11-6 Sun
www.abccarpet.com
Rugs, carpets, carpet remnants and runners. Also linens, furniture, antiques and decorative items. CREDIT CARDS.

Aronson's Floorcovering 212-243-4993
135 W 17th St. (6-7th Ave)   FAX 212-675-5939
NY, NY 10011
Hours: 9-6 Mon-Fri / 11-4 Sat
www.aronsonsfloors.com
Large selection of linoleum & vinyl, carpets and wood flooring in stock. Friendly service, speak to Soni or Laura. Samples available. CREDIT CARDS.

Gillian Bradshaw-Smith 214-948-8472
311 N Winnetka Ave.
Dallas, TX 75208
Hours: by appt.   E-mail: gillbs@swbell.net
www.gillianbradshaw-smith.net
Set Design and scenic painting. Custom murals, floorcloths and drops. Speak to Gillian Bradshaw-Smith.

Carpet Factory Outlet 212-988-5326
  1492 First Ave. (78th St)   FAX 212-288-6029
  NY, NY 10021
  Hours: 8-6 Mon-Fri / 10-5 Sat   E-mail: info@carpetfactoryoutlet.com
  www.carpetfactoryoutlet.com
  Carpet, linoleum, area rugs, remnants. Area rugs bound same day binding,
  over 1000 remnants. Contact Vincent. CREDIT CARDS.

Carpet Fashions 212-683-1888
  501 Fifth Ave. (42nd St)   FAX 212-683-4074
  NY, NY 10016
  Hours: by appt.   E-mail: info@carpetfashions.net
  www.carpetfashions.net
  Custom-made carpets and rugs to the trade.

Chelsea Floor Covering Acquisition Corp. 212-243-0375
  139-41 W 19th St. (6-7th Ave)   FAX 212-727-7958
  NY, NY 10011
  Hours: 8-4:30 Mon-Fri   E-mail: kbosco@chelseafloors.com
  www.chelseafloors.com
  Carpet, all kinds of tile, wood floors; carpet and tile adhesives; will contract
  installation. Speak to Ron. CREDIT CARDS.

Crows Nest Trading Co. 800-900-8558
  3205 Airport Blvd NW, P.O. Box 3975   FAX 800-900-3136
  Wilson, NC 27895
  Hours: 9-5 Mon-Fri / 24-hr. website   E-mail: info@crowsnestrading.com
  www.crowsnesttrading.com
  Leather, western rugged furnishings. Also kitchen, garden and rugs. Western
  and cowboy themed. Great catalog. CREDIT CARDS.

Design Tex 800-221-1540
  200 Varick St., 8th Fl.   212-886-8200
  NY, NY 10014   FAX 212-886-8219
  Hours: 9-5 Mon-Fri

  979 Third Ave., Ste. 232(D&D Bldg. 59th St)   212-752-2535
  NY, NY 10022   FAX 212-838-5668
  Hour: 9-5 Mon-Fri
  www.designtexgroup.com
  Vinyl, textile, and acoustical wallcovering, rugs, digital panels, and upholstery
  fabrics. See website for other showroom locations or call 800-221-1540.

Eliko Antique Carpets 212-725-1600
  102 Madison Ave., 4th Fl. (29-30th St)   FAX 212-725-1885
  NY, NY 10016
  Hours: 9-5 Mon-Fri   E-mail: elikorugs@aol.com
  www.elikorugs.com
  Antique and semi-antique carpets. 5500 rugs in inventory.

Epstein's Paint Center 212-265-3960
   822 Tenth Ave. (54-55th St)   800-464-3432
   NY, NY 10019   FAX 212-765-8841
   Hours: 8-5:30 Mon-Fri / 8:30-3 Sat   E-mail: sales@epsteinspaint.com
   www.epsteinspaint.com
   ***Many styles of blinds and shades, custom service within 24-hrs. Also large
   stock of floor coverings, wallpaper, scenic/household paints, tints and dyes.
   See Marty. CREDIT CARDS.***

Essee's Dial-A-Floor 212-281-9083
   3531 Broadway (145th St)   800-845-3722
   NY, NY 10031   FAX 212-281-1289
   Hours: 8-6 Mon-Fri / 9-5 Sat   E-mail: brucegen@aol.com
   www.dialafloor.com
   ***Cheap linoleum, vinyl floor tile, sustainable options, carpet and rugs. Large
   selection. CREDIT CARDS.***

Harooni Originals, Inc. 212-532-4133
   135 Madison Ave. (31st St)   516-330-1997
   NY, NY 10016   FAX 212-779-3097
   Hours: 10-6 Mon-Fri   E-mail: harooniny@aol.com
   www.harooni.com
   ***Wonderful selection of palace-sized rugs and many other sizes. Works well
   with Film and TV shows for RENTALS. CREDIT CARDS.***

Victor Henschel 212-688-1732
   215 E 59th St. (2nd-3rd Ave)   FAX 212-755-0578
   NY, NY 10022
   Hours: 10-5 Mon-Fri
   Carpet; good source for linoleum, will order. RENTALS. AMEX.

Kravet Fabrics 800-645-9068
   979 Third Ave., Ste. 324(58-59th St) (D&D Building)   212-421-6363
   NY, NY 10022   FAX 212-751-7196
   Hours: 9-5 Mon-Fri

   200 Lexington Ave., 4th Fl.   212-725-0340
   NY, NY 10016   FAX 212-684-7350
   Hours: 9-5 Mon-Fri

   225 Central Ave. S   516-293-2000
   Bethpage, NY 11714   FAX 516-293-2737
   Hours: 10-4 Mon-Fri
   www.kravet.com
   ***To the trade (account required); large selection, all kinds of drapery, sheer and
   upholstery fabrics and trims. Recently added furnitre, carpets and
   furnishings. Large quantities available. Very helpful; swatching. Reasonably
   priced.***

Nemati Collection 212-486-6900
   1059 Third Ave., 3rd Fl.   877-7NEMATI
   NY, NY 10021   FAX 212-755-8428
   Hours: 9-6 Mon-Thurs / 9-5 Fri   E-mail: info@nematicollection.com
   www.nematicollection.com
   ***Rare and antique Oriental and European carpets and tapestries. All weaving
   and cleaning done by hand. RENTALS. CREDIT CARDS.***

Rug Warehouse 212-779-7373
1 E 28th St. # 5 (Madison-5th Ave)   FAX 212-779-8140
NY, NY 10016
Hours: by appt. only
Good selection of Oriental and contemporary area rugs. RENTALS. CREDIT
CARDS.

FLOOR: DANCE & STAGE

American Harlequin Corp. 800-642-6440
1531 Glen Ave.   856-234-5505
Moorestown, NJ 08057   FAX 856-231-4403
Hours: 9-8 Mon-Fri   E-mail: dance@harlequinfloors.com
www.harlequinfloors.com
Inventory on East and West Coasts to service entire country; dance, stage
and exhibit flooring.

Gerriets International 609-758-9121
130 Winterwood Ave   800-369-3695
Ewing, NJ 08638   FAX 609-758-9596
Hours: 8:30-5 Mon-Fri   E-mail: mail@gi-info.com
www.gi-info.com
Vario portable dance floor, 63" wide in 8 colors. Also stocks scenic fabrics and
materials. RENTALS.

Joseph C. Hansen Co., Inc. 201-222-1677
629 Grove St., Lot # 26 (16-17th St)   866-988-8055
Jersey City, NJ 07310   FAX 201-222-1699
Hours: 9-5 Mon-Fri   E-mail: info@jchansen.com
www.jchansen.com
Theatrical curtain rental: cycs, scrims, velours, painted drops, star drops,
curtain track, stands and dance floor. Brochure available. RENTALS. CREDIT
CARDS.

Main Attractions 732-225-3500
85 Newfield Ave. (Raritan Ctr Pkwy)   800-394-3500
Edison, NJ 08837   732-225-2110
Hours: 9:30-5 Mon-Fri   E-mail: events@mainattractions.com
www.mainattractions.com
Special events contractors; specializing in custom tent rentals, restroom
trailers, decor, portable staging, lighting and the production of displays and
signage. Visit website to see the full spectrum of their products. RENTALS.
CREDIT CARDS.

Oasis/Stage Werks 801-363-0364
249 Rio Grande St.   FAX 801-575-7121
Salt Lake City, UT 84101
Hours: 9-6 Mon-Fri
www.oasis-stage.com
D'anser floor, resilient sub-floor, 30'x40' rentable dance floor. P.O.s. RENTALS.
CREDIT CARDS.

Production Advantage, Inc. 802-651-6915
P.O. Box 1700   800-424-99914
Williston, VT 05495   FAX 877-424-9991
Hours: 8:30-6 Mon-Fri   E-mail: sales@proadv.com
www.proadv.com
Catalog sales of hardware, lighting, rigging, scenic material, soft goods,
sound equipment and expendables to the entertainment industry. All major
brands carried. Catalog. CREDIT CARDS.

Rose Brand 800-223-1624
                                                                FAX 800-594-7424

4 Emerson Lane(15-16th St)   800-223-1624
Secaucus, NJ 07094   201-809-1730
Hours: 8-5 Mon-Fri   FAX 201-809-1851

10616 Lanark St.   800-360-5056
Sun City, CA 91352   818-505-6290
Hours: 8-5 Mon-Fri   FAX 818-505-6293
www.rosebrand.com   E-mail: sales@rosebrand.com
Complete line of stage flooring available for sale or rent. Studio show floor
and Roscotiles, cleaners and tape. Call or fax for catalog. CREDIT CARDS.

StageStep, Inc. 215-636-9000
4701 Bath St. # 46B   800-523-0960
Philadelphia, PA 19137   FAX 267-672-2912
Hours: 9-5 Mon-Fri   E-mail: stagestep@stagestep.com
www.stagestep.com
Full line of dance floors. Also Mirrorlite™, books, records, CDs, videos.
Catalog and samples. CREDIT CARDS.

Steel Deck NY, Inc. 718-599-3700
143-145 Banker St.   877-60-STAGE
Brooklyn, NY 11222   FAX 718-599-3800
Hours: 9-5 Mon-Fri   E-mail: info@steeldeckny.com
www.steeldeckny.com
Open steel deck stage floor and platforming. Easy to assemble. Standard
and custom sizes. Very helpful, friendly staff. Speak to Rob. CREDIT CARDS.

United Staging & Rigging 203-416-5380
250 Fifth St.
Bridgeport, CT 06607   FAX 203-416-5387
Hours: 8:30-4:30 Mon-Fri

96 Commerce Way   781-376-9180
Canton, MA 01801   FAX 781-376-9185
Hours: 8-5 Mon-Fri
www.unitedstaging.com
CM Motors, Stageright staging, roofs, Genie lifts, soft goods, truss, rugging.
Large RENTALS inventory. Contact Doug Frawley (CT) or Jon Sharpe (MA).

FLORAL SUPPLIES
See also: ARTIFICIAL FLOWERS, PLANTS & FOOD
For containers: BASKETS & WICKER ITEMS
                POTTERY & GREENWARE

A.C. Moore 201-902-0377
400 Mill Creek Dr. (Mill Creek Mall Area)
Secaucus, NJ 07094
Hours: 99 Mon-Fri / 9-8 Sat-Sun
www.acmoore.com
Chain based craft supply store. General crafts, art materials & framing, yarn and needlecrafts, wedding supplies and more. Visit website for other 95 locations across the USA. CREDIT CARDS.

B & J Florist's Supply 212-564-6086/7
103 W 28th St.   212-564-6088
NY, NY 10001
Hours: 7-5 Mon-Sat
Wholesale florist supplies, baskets and glassware. Wonderful selection of ribbons; wired and unwired, sheers, tulle. Seasonal items, Christmas ornaments, fruits & vegetables. CREDIT CARDS.

Bill's Flower Market, Inc. 212-889-8154
816 Sixth Ave. (28th St)   FAX 212-889-2352
NY, NY 10001
Hours: 8-6 Mon-Fri / 9-5 Sat   E-mail: bfm816@aol.com
www.billsflowermarket.com
Live flowers, baskets, floral supplies and large selection of feathers, artificial birds. CREDIT CARDS.

Dry Nature Designs 212-695-8911
245 W 29th St. (7-8th Ave)   FAX 212-695-4104
NY, NY 10001
Hours: 8:30-5 Mon-Fri / 9:30-5:30 Sat   E-mail: drynaturedesigns@aol.com
www.drynature.com
Great selection of natural earth & nature products. Branches, corals, porcupine quills, ostrich & emu eggs, dry fruits & flowers, gourds, grasses, grains & fall leaves, driftwood and more. Designer arrangements. A must see located in the Floral District of NYC. Visit website for really cool photos of shop. CREDIT CARDS.

Hionis Greenhouses, Inc. 908-534-7710
4 Coddington Rd.   FAX 908-534-7720
Whitehouse Station, NJ 08889
Hours: 9-6 Mon-Fri / 9-4 Sat   E-mail: hionisplants@yahoo.com
www.hionisgreenhouses.com
Flowering plants indoor and outdoor trees, florist supplies, orchids, pottery and holiday supplies. CREDIT CARDS. RENTALS.

Jamali Garden & Hardware Supplies, Inc. 212-244-4025
149 W 28th St. (6-7th Ave)   212-594-5265
NY, NY 10001   FAX 212-967-8196
Hours: 6:30-5 Mon-Sat
www.jamaligarden.com
Hardware, garden supplies and floral supplies. Complete line of potting soil and fertilizers. Great selection of pottery from around the world and unique containers. CREDIT CARDS.

Charles Lubin Co. 914-968-5700
145 Saw Mill River Rd.   FAX 914-968-5723
Yonkers, NY 10701
Hours: 7:30-4:30 Mon-Fri
www.lubinflowers.com
Silk flowers for decoration, home and store display, fashion and packaging.

Paramount Wire Co., Inc. 973-672-0500
2-8 Central Ave.   FAX 973-674-0727
East Orange, NJ 07018
Hours: 9-5 Mon-Fri
www.parawire.com
Millinery, piano, ribbon wire, cotton and rayon covered wire, paper stakes. $100 minimum.

FLOWERS & PLANTS: LIVE
See also: BASKETS & WICKER ITEMS
            POTTERY & GREENWARE

American Foliage & Design Group 212-741-5555
122 W 22nd St. (6-7th Ave)   FAX 212-741-9499
NY, NY 10011
Hours: 8-5 Mon-Fri   E-mail: afdesigngr@aol.com
www.americanfoliagedesign.com
Silk and live flowers for TV, commercials, special events. RENTALS.

Bill's Flower Market, Inc. 212-889-8154
816 Sixth Ave. (28th St)   FAX 212-889-2352
NY, NY 10001
Hours: 8-6 Mon-Fri / 9-5 Sat   E-mail: bfm816@aol.com
www.billsflowermarket.com
Live flowers, baskets, floral supplies and large selection of feathers, artificial birds. CREDIT CARDS.

Castle & Pierpont Event Design Ltd. 212-244-8668
29 Prince St. (Elizabeth-Mott)   FAX 212-244-7935
NY, NY 10012
Hours: 12-8 Mon-Sun
www.castlepierpont.com
Fresh flower arrangements; complete special events design and supplies. RENTALS. CREDIT CARDS.

Chelsea Garden Center 877-846-0565
   580 Eleventh Ave.(44th St)   212-727-7100
   NY, NY 10036   212-727-3434
   Hours: 9-7 Everyday (Winter hours: 10-5 Wed-Sun)   FAX 212-727-3637

   444 Van Brunt St.(Fairway)   718-875-2100
   Brooklyn, NY 11231   E-mail: info@chelseagardencenter.com
   www.chelseagardencenter.com
   Plants, trees, shrubs, flowers, large and small planters, landscape supplies
   and landscaping. Fountains, furniture and pottery available for RENTALS.
   CREDIT CARDS.

Flowers by Reuven 212-564-4740
   255 W 36th St., MR 203 (7-8th Ave)   FAX 212-564-4154
   NY, NY 10023
   Hours: b appt.   E-mail: laura.reuvens@yahoo.com
   www.flowersbyreuven.com
   Provides live plants and floral arrangements to many of NYC's daytime
   dramas. Knowledgeable and reliable. Only events and special orders.
   CREDIT CARDS.

G. Page Flowers 212-741-8928
   120 W 28th St. (6-7th Ave)   FAX 212-741-8968
   NY, NY 10001
   Hours: 6-2:30 Mon-Sat   E-mail: info@gpage.com
   www.gpage.com
   Fresh flowers, wholesale and retail. CREDIT CARDS.

Wendy Goidell 212-362-6168
   140 Riverside Dr.   917-797-6604
   NY, NY 10024
   Hours: by appt.
   Flower and plant design for film, commericals, print work and special events.

Hillcrest Gardens 201-599-3030
   95 W Century Rd.   FAX 201-599-3064
   Paramus, NJ 07652
   Hours: 6-5 Mon-Fri / 6-12 Sat / 8-11 Sun
   Complete line of silk flowers and greenery, also fruit. Helpful and friendly
   service. Contact Tom x234.

Hionis Greenhouses, Inc. 908-534-7710
   4 Coddington Rd.   FAX 908-534-7720
   Whitehouse Station, NJ 08889
   Hours: 9-6 Mon-Fri / 9-4 Sat   E-mail: hionisplants@yahoo.com
   www.hionisgreenhouses.com
   Flowering plants indoor and outdoor trees, florist supplies, orchids, pottery
   and holiday supplies. CREDIT CARDS. RENTALS.

L. DeLea & Sons, Inc. 631-368-8022
444 Elwood Rd. (Jericho Tpke-Clay Rd)   800-244-7637
E. Northport, NY 11731   FAX 631-368-9382
Hours: 6-5 Mon-Fri
www.deleasodfarms.com
A large sod farm and landscape supply company filling large or small orders. Delivery service available on purchases of 600 sq. ft. or more. Contact Joel or Vinnie. CREDIT CARDS.

Midtown Greenhouse Garden Center 718-636-0020
115 Flatbush Ave. (4th Ave)   FAX 718-858-0641
Brooklyn, NY 11217
Hours: 9-6 Mon-Sat / 9-5 Sun
Gardening supplies, flowers, plants, sod, pots; will deliver. CREDIT CARDS.

Seaport Flowers 718-858-6443
214 Hicks St. (Montague-Remsen)   718-222-8650
Brooklyn, NY 11201
Hours: 11-7 Tue-Fri / 11-6 Sat / 12-5 Sun   E-mail: amy@seaportflower.com
www.seaportflowers.com
Fresh flower arrangements with imaginative selection of containers for corporate, residential and special events. Friendly, personal service. CREDIT CARDS.

Stone Kelly 212-245-6611
736 11th Ave. (52nd St)   FAX 212-245-6020
NY, NY 10019
Hours: 9:30-5 Mon-Fri / 10-5 Sat   E-mail: info@stonekelly.com
www.stonekelly.com
Fresh flower arrangements for commercials, events, residential. Great style. Contact Jen Stone.

Surroundings 212-580-8982
1351 Amsterdam Ave. (MLKJr Blvd - 126th St)   800-567-7007
NY, NY 10027   FAX (orders only) 212-579-7453
Hours: 9-6 Mon-Fri / 10-6 Sat-Sun
www.surroundingsflowers.com
Designs special events: flowers and themed gift baskets only. CREDIT CARDS.

Wilkens Fruit & Fir Farm 914-245-5111
1335 White Hill Rd.   FAX 914-245-4099
Yorktown Heights, NY 10598
Hours: by appt.
www.wilkensfarm.com
Christmas trees; available year round, all sizes; 45 min. from Manhattan.

F

FLYING EFFECTS

Flying by Foy 702-454-3300
   3275 E Patrick Ln.   702-454-3500
   Las Vegas, NV 89120   FAX 702-454-7369
   Hours: 8:30-5:30 Mon-Fri   E-mail: foymail@flybyfoy.com
   www.flybyfoy.com
   Custom flying and spectacle effects by contract.

ZFX Flying Illusions 502-637-2500
   611 Industry Road   FAX 502-637-7878
   Louisville, KY 40208
   Hours: 9-5 Mon-Fri   E-mail: zfx@zfxflying.com
   www.zfxflying.com
   Flying effects for film, television and theatre. Visit website for other
   locations. Contact Katie Rubin.

FOAM SHEETING & SHAPES
See also: UPHOLSTERY TOOLS & SUPPLIES

Canal Rubber Supply Co. 212-226-7339
   329 Canal St. (Greene St)   800-444-6483
   NY, NY 10013   FAX 212-219-3754
   Hours: 9-4:45 Mon-Fri / 9-3:45 Sat
   www.canalrubber.com
   Good stock of foam rubber, variety of types, sizes, thicknesses and densities;
   also latex and rubber tubing. CREDIT CARDS.

Cellofoam, Inc. 800-288-7663
   16 Baron Park Rd.   800-332-3626
   Fredericksburg, VA 22405   FAX   540-899-5429
   Hours: 8-5 Mon-Fri   E-mail: info@cellofoam.com
   www.cellofoam.com
   Ethafoam plank and roll, foam rubber, polystyrene; excelsior. Catalog. $35
   minimum on phone orders. CREDIT CARDS.

Dixie Foam Co. 212-645-8999
   113 W 25th St. (6-7th Ave)   800-BED-6060
   NY, NY 10001   FAX 212-645-4055
   Hours: 10-5:30 Mon-Sat   www.dixiefoam.com
   www.dixiefoam@yahoo.com
   Foam rubber, mattress sizes; pricey. Brochures. CREDIT CARDS.

Dura-Foam Products, Inc. 718-894-2488
   63-02 59th Ave.   FAX 718-894-2493
   Maspeth, NY 11378
   Hours: 8-4:30 Mon-Fri   E-mail: durafoaminc@yahoo.com
   Flexible foams in a variety of densities; black and white only. Has different
   size dies for cutting foam rods. No minimum, no catalog.

FOAM SHEETING & SHAPES

DuraLast Products Corp. 901-323-8448
580 Tillman, Ste. 5   888-323-8448
Memphis, TN 38112   FAX 901-323-8442
Hours: 8-4:30 Mon-Fri   E-mail: nathan@duralast.com
www.duralast.com
*Rubberized hog hair media, a natural fiber used to create various special
effects; sound effects construction, sound dampening, rain making, etc.
Available in various sizes and thicknesses. Also air conditioner filters.
CREDIT CARDS.*

Economy Foam & Futons 212-475-4800
56 8th St. (5-6th Ave)   FAX 212-475-2727
NY, NY 10011
Hours: 10-7 Mon-Thurs / Fri call for hours / 10:30-6 Sun
                            E-mail: sales@economyfoamandfutons.com
www.economyfoamandfutons.com
*Foam rubber sheets, shapes, batting by the bag or roll, pillow shapes, vinyl
fabrics, futons. CREDIT CARDS.*

IR Specialty Foams 888-804-8242
3900 B 20th St. E   800-426-7944
Fife, WA 98424   FAX 888-922-5339
Hours: 8:30-4:30 Mon-Fri / 24-hr. website   E-mail: csfife@irfoam.com
www.irfoam.com
*Extensive variety of foams, including aerated and many closed cell types.
Service is excellent. They carry excellent quality flexible foams cut to
whatever thickness you desire and will ship as little as one sheet. Visit
website to request their tri-fold catalog.*

Kamco Supply 718-768-1234
80 21st St.(3rd Ave)
Brooklyn, NY 11232   FAX 718-788-8607
Hours: 7-5 Mon-Fri

153 Tenth Ave.(19th St)   212-736-7350
NY, NY 10011   FAX 212-564-6436
Hours: 6-5 Mon-Fri / 7-12 Sat
www.kamco.com
*Brochure available. Sheet plastic foam, Insta-foam, other foams; good stock,
reasonable prices. No minimum. CREDIT CARDS.*

Quality Foam Designs 574-293-5547
2600 S Nappanee St.   FAX 574-294-6283
Elkhart, IN 46517
Hours: 8-5 M-F   E-mail: info@centuryfoam.com
www.qualityfoamdesigns.com
*This helpful friendly company sells stock and custom novelty foam products.
Made from safe toy spec foam. Imprinting available as well as color
matching foam for large quantity jobs. Speak to Sandy. CREDIT CARDS.*

Rempac Foam Corp. 973-881-8880
370 W. Passaic St.   800-394-7885
Rochelle Park, NJ 07602   FAX 973-881-9368
Hours: 8:30-5 Mon-Fri
www.rempac.com
Ethafoam rod and sheet, beadboard; will die cut foam. $1500 minimum order.
Brochure.

Rogers Foam Corp. 617-623-3010
20 Vernon St.   FAX 617-629-2585
Somerville, MA 02145
Hours: 8-5 Mon-Fri   E-mail: info@rogersfoam.com
www.rogersfoamcorp.com
Scottfoam and other foams. $300 minimum. No catalog.

Seattle Fabrics 206-525-0670
8702 Aurora Ave. N (N 87th St)   866-925-0670
Seattle, WA 98103   FAX 206-525-0779
Hours: 9-6 Mon-Sat   E-mail: seattlefabrics@msn.com
www.seattlefabrics.com
Outdoor and recreational fabric & hardware. Specialty fabrics, webbing,
thread and zippers; neoprene and closed cell foam. Patterns for outdoor and
sports attire; equestrian, tents and backpacks. Fabric samples available.
CREDIT CARDS.

Snow Craft Co., Inc. 516-739-1399
200 Fulton Ave.   FAX 516-739-1637
Garden City Park, NY 11040
Hours: 9-5 Mon-Fri
Foam, will cut to size; other foams and packing materials; delivery is extra.
$150 minimum. CREDIT CARDS.

Strux Corp. 516-768-3969
P.O. Box 536   FAX 631-422-5740
Lindenhurst, NY 11757
Hours: 8-4:30 Mon-Fri   E-mail: bob@strux.com
www.strux.com
Complete line of urethane foams in assorted densities and thicknesses.
Sample kit available. CREDIT CARDS.

Urethane Products Co., Inc. / Lorraine Textile Specialties 516-488-3600
PO Box 308, 1750 Plaza Ave.
New Hyde Park, NY 11040
Hours: 7-5 Mon-Fri
Great source for polyurethane foam sheeting for animal costumes, kapok
stuffing; excellent selection and prices, $80 minimum.   Contact Gary Hall.

FOG MACHINES & FOG JUICE
See also: SPECIAL EFFECTS SERVICES

Abracadabra 212-627-5194
19 W 21st St. (5-6th Ave)   FAX 212-627-7435
NY, NY 10001
Hours: 11-7 Mon-Sat / 12-5 Sun
www.abracadabrasuperstore.com
Fog machines, bubble machines and smoke effects. Catalog available online.
RENTALS. CREDIT CARDS.

City Theatrical, Inc. 201-549-1160
475 Barell Ave.   800-230-9497
Carlstadt, NJ 07072   FAX 201-549-1161
Hours: 7-6 Mon-Fri   E-mail: info@citytheatrical.com
www.citytheatrical.com
Manufacturer of Aquafog 3300, a dry ice fog machine and other unique
lighting accessories.

EFEX Rentals 718-505-9465
5805 52nd Ave. (43rd Ave)   FAX 718-505-9631
Woodside, NY 11377
Hours: 8:30-5:30 Mon-Fri   E-mail: efexrentals@verizon.net
www.efexrentals.com
Distributors of many types of fog machines and fog juice; also special effects
materials; snow, breakaways, turntables and rigging. Catalog available. P.O.s
accepted. RENTALS.

Group One Ltd. 516-249-1399
70 Sea Ln.   FAX 516-249-8870
Farmingdale, NY 11735
Hours: 9-5:30 Mon-Fri   E-mail: sales@g1limited.com
www.g1limited.com
Exclusive US distributor for lighting and audio products including: Digico,
Belestion, Blue Sky, Elektralite, Pulsar. No credit cards.

J&M Special Effects 718-875-0140
524 Sackett St.   FAX 718-596-8329
Brooklyn, NY 11217
Hours: 9-4 Mon-Fri by appt.   E-mail: info@jmfx.net
www.jmfx.net
All types of fog/smoke systems and supplies; design services. RENTALS.

Mutual Hardware Corp. 718-361-2480
36-27 Vernon Blvd.   866-361-2480
Long Island City, NY 11106   FAX 718-786-9591
Hours: 8:30-4:30 Mon-Fri
www.mutualhardware.com
Fog machines, fog juice in stock; theatrical hardware. Contact John or Sal.

Rosco Laboratories, Inc. 203-708-8900
52 Harbor View Ave.   800-ROSCONY
Stamford, CT 06902   FAX 203-708-8919
Hours: 9-5 Mon-Fri   E-mail: info@rosco.com
www.rosco.com
Fog machines and chemicals for specilized applications. Shipping available.

 **ATAC**

The Set Shop 212-255-3500
36 W 20th St. (5-6th Ave) 800-422-7831
NY, NY 10011 FAX 212-229-9600
Hours: 8:30-6 Mon-Fri E-mail: info@setshop.com
www.setshop.com
Bee Smokers and juice-style machines. Professional and compact garment steamers. 50 colors of 9'-0" or 12'-0" wide seamless paper; 12 colors muslin; Foamcore, Gatorboard. Ten types of ice cubes and shards, large selection of plexi. CREDIT CARDS.

SFX Design, Inc. 817-599-0800
2500 I-20 E FAX 817-599-0496
Weatherford, TX 76087
Hours: 8-4 Mon-Fri E-mail: info@sfxdesigninc.com
www.sfxdesigninc.com
Stock and custom gobos. Decorative and fighting swords, handguns, rifles, machine guns; any period, able to fire blanks. Breakaway resin to mold your own bottles, glass, panes, etc. Fog-Master machines and Aquafog component; also cobweb system. Pyrotechnics and miniature pneumatics, blood effects, atmospherics; custom projects. Great website. Catalog. No credit cards.

SLD Lighting 212-245-4155
318 W 47th St. (8-9th Ave) 800-245-6630
NY, NY 10036 FAX 212-956-6537
Hours: 9-5:30 Mon-Wed, Fri / 9-6:30 Thurs E-mail: sales@sldlighting.com
www.sldlighting.com
Stocking distributor of major lighting/sound manufacturers and specialty items. Retail store and mail order department. Full-line catalog available. Shipping worldwide. RENTALS. CREDIT CARDS.

Zeller International, Ltd. 607-363-7792
15261 Highway 30 FAX 607-363-2071
Downsville, NY 13755
Hours: 9-5 Mon-Fri E-mail: contact@zeller-int.com
www.zeller-int.com
Smoke, fog and steam products and effects. Wholesale and retail. Some minimums apply. Contact Carla Zelaschi. Catalog. CREDIT CARDS.

FRAMES & FRAMING

APF Holdings, Inc. 212-308-6152
219 E 60th St. (2nd-3rd Ave) FAX 212-421-2187
NY, NY 10021
Hours: 9:30-5:30 Mon-Fri / 11-4 Sat (June-Aug) E-mail: info@apfgroup.com
www.apfgroup.com
Custom framing and restoration. Catalog. CREDIT CARDS.

Arthur Brown International Pen Shop 212-575-5555
2 W 45th St. (5-6th Ave) 800-772-PENS
NY, NY 10036 FAX 212-575-5825
Hours: 9-6:15 Mon-Fri / 10-6 Sat E-mail: penshop@artbrown.com
www.artbrown.com
Stationery, Ink and refills, desk sets and ink pens. CREDIT CARDS.

Bark Frameworks, LLC 212-431-9080
   21-24 44th Ave.   718-752-1919
   Long Island City, NY 11101   FAX 718-392-5546
   Hours: 9-6 Mon-Fri or by appt.   E-mail: inquiries@barkframeworks.com
   www.barkframeworks.com
   Museum-quality framing; expensive but worth it. CREDIT CARDS.

Chelsea Frames 212-807-8957
   197 Ninth Ave. (21st-22nd St)   FAX 212-924-3208
   NY, NY 10011
   Hours: 10-7:30 Mon-Thurs / 10-6 Fri-Sat / 11-5 Sun   E-mail: cfby@aol.com
   www.chelseaframes.com
   *Custom and archival framing. Art restoration and antique prints. Custom
   mirrors. Delivery and rush services available. CREDIT CARDS.*

G. Elter - Framed on Madison, Inc. .212-734-4680
   976 Lexington Ave. (71-72nd St)   FAX 212-219-9573
   NY, NY 10021
   Hours: 10-6 Mon-Sat / Thurs until 7   E-mail: contact@framedonmadison.com
   www.framedonmadison.com
   *Victorian and other antique and modern picture frames in a choice of
   materials. CREDIT CARDS.*

Frames For You, Inc. 212-874-2337
   136 W 72nd St. (Columbus-B'way)   FAX 212-874-2529
   NY, NY 10023
   Hours: 10-7:30 Mon-Thurs / 10-6:30 Fri / 10-6 Sat / 12-5 Sun
   www.framesforyounyc.com
   Custom frames, quick turnaround; see owner, Bernard. CREDIT CARDS.

Heritage Frame & Picture Co. 914-332-5200
   8 Main St. (Bway)   Pick Up's 212-233-3205
   Tarrytown, NY 10591   FAX 914-332-4364
   Hours: 10-4 Wed-Fri / 10-5 Sat   E-mail: heritageframe@hotmail.com
   www.heritageframe.com
   *Framing, lamination; mats cut and glass replaced while you wait. Free Pick-
   ups in NYC on Mondays. Catalog. RENTALS. CREDIT CARDS.*

Julius Lowy Frame & Restoring Co., Inc. 212-861-8585
   223 E 80th St. (2nd-3rd Ave)   FAX 212-988-0443
   NY, NY 10021
   Hours: 9-5:30 Mon-Fri
   www.lowyonline.com
   *Good selection of ornate antique frames; also restoration and reproduction of
   frames and furniture. Will ship. CREDIT CARDS.*

Lee's Art Shop & Studio 212-247-0110
   220 W 57th St. (B'way-7th Ave)   FAX 212-581-7023
   NY, NY 10019
   Hours: 9-7:30 Mon-Fri / 10-7 Sat / 11-6 Sun   E-mail: info@leesartshop.com
   www.leesartshop.com
   Framing supplies, custom framing; art supplies. CREDIT CARDS.

Manhattan Frame & Art 212-268-5643
350 Seventh Ave. #903 (29-30th St)   FAX 212-268-5644
NY, NY 10001
Hours: 9:30-5 Mon-Fri   E-mail: manhattanframe@manhattanframe.com
www.manhattanframe.com
Very helpful. Picture framing at better prices; professional custom picture framing. Mention THE ENTERTAINMENT SOURCEBOOK and receive a 15% discount. All work done on site. Will ship. CREDIT CARDS.

New York Central II - Framing & Furniture Annex 212-420-6060
102 Third Ave. (12-13th St)   FAX 212-674-8144
NY, NY 10003
Hours: 9:30-6:15 Mon-Sat
www.nycentralart.com
Large selection of ready-made frames; custom framing, glass and mat cutting, dry mounting, shrink wrapping; also studio furniture and easels. RENTALS. CREDIT CARDS.

One Hour Framing Shop 212-869-5263
15 E 40th St.(Madison-5th Ave)
NY, NY 10016   800-427-7058
Hours: 9-6:30 Mon-Fri   FAX 212-391-4631

575 Lexington Ave. (in Cameraland)(51st-52nd St)   212-888-9130
NY, NY 10022
Hours: 9-6:30 Mon-Fri   E-mail: Waseem@onehourframing.com
www.onehourframing.com
Metal, wood frames, custom framing, dry mounting. Offers some discount prices; will cut glass and mats while you wait. Will ship. CREDIT CARDS.

Paris Fine Custom Framing 212-873-5602
323 Amsterdam Ave. (75-76th St)   FAX 212-877-4122
NY, NY 10023
Hours: 11-7 Mon-Sat / 12-6 Sun
www.parisframemakers.com
Custom framing, lithographs, serigraphs and photographs. CREDIT CARDS.

Pearl Paint / World's Largest Creative Resource 800-451-7327
308 Canal St.(B'way-Church St)   212-431-7932
NY, NY 10013   (mail order) 800-221-6845
Hours: 9-7 Mon-Fri / 10-7 Sat / 10-6 Sun   FAX 212-431-6798

42 Lispenard St. (Craft & Home Center)(B'way-Church St)   212-226-3717
NY, NY 10013   800-221-6845
Hours: 9-7 Mon-Fri / 10-7 Sat / 10-6 Sun

776 Rt. 17 N   201-447-0300
Paramus, NJ 07652   FAX 201-447-4012
Hours: 10-9 Mon-Sat

1033 E Oakland Park Blvd.(Corp. Office)   954-567-9678
Ft. Lauderdale, FL 33334
www.pearlpaint.com
Large selection of section frames and stock sizes at very good prices; art supplies; catalog. Online shopping available. CREDIT CARDS.

J. Pocker & Son, Inc. 800-838-4588
135 E 63rd St. (Lexington-Park Ave)   212-838-5488
NY, NY 10065   FAX 212-750-2053
Hours: 9-5:30 Mon-Fri / 10-5:30 Sat   E-mail: info@jpocker.com
www.jpocker.com
Frames, custom framing, dry mounting; posters and prints. Will ship. CREDIT CARDS.

Yale Picture Frame Corp. 718-788-6200
770 Fifth Ave. (27-28th St)   (outside NY) 800-331-YALE
Brooklyn, NY 11232   FAX 718-788-5852
Hours: 8-5 Mon-Thur / 8-3 Fri / 11-3 Sun
www.yalepf.com
Custom and ready-made frames; also glass, matting, etc. Excellent work. Can handle rush. Catalog of available frame mouldings. Will ship. CREDIT CARDS.

F

FURNITURE: CHILDREN'S

Schneider's Juvenile Furniture 212-228-3540
41 W 25th St. (B'way - 6th Ave)
NY, NY 10010
Hours: 10-6 Mon-Sat / 10-8 Tue
www.schneidersbaby.com
Children's furniture, carriages, car seats and accessories. See Allen. RENTALS. CREDIT CARDS.

FURNITURE: CONTEMPORARY

Aero Studios, Ltd. Thomas O'Brien .212-966-1500
419 Broome St.   212-966-4700
NY, NY 10013   FAX 212-966-4701
Hours: 11-6 Mon-Sat   E-mail: aeroltd@aol.com
www.aerostudios.com
Contemporary and "contemporary antique" furniture retail store and design studio. RENTALS. CREDIT CARDS.

B&B Italia USA, Inc. 800-872-1697
150 E 58th St.   212-758-4046
NY, NY 10155   FAX 212-758-9155
Hours: 9:30-6 Mon-Fri / 12-6 Sat-Sun   E-mail: info@bebitalia.com
www.bebitalia.com
Contemporary Italian furniture and accessories. Soho store: 138 Greene St. NYC. CREDIT CARDS.

Cassina USA, Inc. 800-770-3568
155 E 56th St.   212-245-2121
NY, NY 10022   FAX 212-245-1340
Hours: 9-6 Mon-Fri / 12-5 Sat

151 Wooster St.   212-228-8186
NY, NY 10012   FAX 212-228-6181
Hours: 10-7 Mon-Fri / 12-6 Sat-Sun   E-mail: info2@cassinausa.com
www.cassinausa.com
Classic Italian design. Limited RENTALS for print or film. CREDIT CARDS.

Dakota Jackson, Inc 212-838-9444
    979 Third Ave., Ste 407 (58-59th St)   FAX 212-758-6413
    NY, NY 10022
    Hours: 9-5:30 Mon-Thurs / 9-5 Fri   www.dakotajackson.com
    Contemporary designer furniture; seating, cabinets, desks, tables. Sales only.
    No credit cards.

Dennis Miller Assoc.,Inc. 212-684-0070
    200 Lexington Ave # 1510 (32nd-33rd St)   FAX 212-684-0776
    NY, NY 10016
    Hours: 9-5 Mon-Fri or by appt.   www.dennismiller.com
    Contemporary furniture.

Glendale Custom Furniture, Inc. 718-326-2700
    71-08 80th St.   FAX 718-894-2528
    Glendale, NY 11385
    Hours: 9-5 Mon-Fri   E-mail: gpc@nyc.rr.com
    www.thepacecollection.com
    Modern and high-tech furniture and custom work; expensive. Catalog $35.
    No Credit Cards.

Jennifer Convertibles 212-677-6862
    902 Broadway (19-20th St)   Office 718-358-5783
    NY, NY 10010
    Hours: 10-9 Mon-Fri / 10-6 Sat / 11-6 Sun
    www.jenniferfurniture.com
    Large selection of sofas and loveseats in both sleeper and regular styles;
    many items in stock for immediate delivery; good prices. Call 1-800-
    JENNIFER or check website for other locations. CREDIT CARDS.

Knoll 212-343-4000
    76 Ninth Ave., 11th FL (15-16th St)   800-343-5665
    NY, NY 10011   FAX 212-343-4180
    Hours: 10-5 Mon-Fri   E-mail: nyc@knoll.com
    www.knoll.com
    Modern classic and high-tech furniture; expensive. See website for other USA
    locations. Catalog.

Lillian August Designs, Inc. 203-847-3314
    32 Knight St. (North Ave-Park St)   FAX 203-852-0524
    Norwalk, CT 06851
    Hours: 10-7 Mon-Sat / 11-6 Sun   E-mail: kcavalier@lillianaugust.com
    www.lillianaugust.com
    100,000 sf of contemporary, antique and imported furnishings and
    accessories. Home and garden. Contact Kim at X 3019. RENTALS. CREDIT
    CARDS.

modprop 212-628-7582
    1044 Madison Ave. (79-80th St)
    NY, NY 10021
    Hours: 9-5 Mon-Fri   E-mail: info@modprop.com
    www.modprop.com
    Modern funiture prop rental house. Specializing in contemporary furniture,
    they rent anything from vintage automobiles, shooting locations to plates
    and glasses. Wide selections in superior condition. Speak to Stephen.
    RENTALS. CREDIT CARDS.

Poltrona Frau 212-777-7592
145 Wooster St.   FAX 212-777-8481
NY, NY 10012
Hours: 10-7 Mon-Fri / 12/6 Sat-Sun
www.frauusa.com
High-end contemporary leather furniture. RENTALS. CREDIT CARDS.

The Terrence Conran Shop 212-755-9079
888 Broadway Lower Level (18-19th St)   FAX 212-755-3989
NY, NY 10003
Hours: 11-8 Mon-Fri / 10-7 Sat / 12-6 Sun
www.conranusa.com   E-mail: terenceconranshop@conranusa.com
Designer furniture, household, bedding and bath, textiles and hardware. Very nice people. Will do rentals to film and television. CREDIT CARDS.

Two Jakes 718-782-7780
320 Wythe Ave. (Grand & S. 1st St)   888-2jakes2
Brooklyn, NY 11211   FAX 718-782-7259
Hours: 11-7 Tue-Sun   E-mail: info@twojakes.com
www.twojakes.com
Retail furniture specializing in classic 20th century modern office furniture; Steelcase, Knoll, Henry Miller, etc. If it is well-made, they probably carry it. Check website for their ever-changing inventory. CREDIT CARDS.

FURNITURE: CUSTOM & UNFINISHED

Furniture Design by Knossos 212-242-0966
538 Sixth Ave. (14-15th St)   FAX 212-727-9316
NY, NY 10011
Hours: 10-7 Mon-Fri / 10-6 Sat /11-5 Sun
Custom and ready-made unfinished French country furniture. CREDIT CARDS.

Gothic Cabinet Craft 888-801-3100
1601 Second Ave.(83rd St)   212-288-2999
NY, NY 10028   FAX 212-427-3618
Hours: 10-8 Mon-Wed/ 10-7 Tues, Thurs, Sat / 11-6 Sun

2652 Broadway(100th-101st St)   212-678-4368
NY, NY 10025
Hours: 10-7 Mon-Fri / 10-6 Sat / 11-5 Sun

360 Sixth Ave.(Washington-Waverly St)   212-982-8539
NY, NY 10014   FAX 212-982-8543
Hours: 10-8 Mon-Wed / 10-9 Thurs / 10-7 Sat / 11-6 Sun

104 Third Ave.(13th St)   212-420-9556
NY, NY 10010   FAX 212-477-7597
Hours: 10-8 Mon, Thurs / 10-7 Tues, Wed, Fri / 11-7 Sat / 12-6 Sun

Gothic Cabinet Craft (cont.) 212-420-9556
   58-77 57th St.(Grand Ave Clearance Ctr)   347-881-1458
   Maspeth, NY
   Hours: 10-6 Mon-Sat / 11-5 Sun   E-mail: info@gothiccabinetcraft.com
   www.gothiccabinetcraft.com
   Custom and ready-made unfinished furniture; formica work; cheap. See
   website for additional locations. CREDIT CARDS.

Green Life LLC 800-982-3880
   21 Whitney Dr.   FAX 888-316-5461
   Milford, OH 45150
   Hours: 9-5 Mon-Fri / 9-5:30 Sat / WEB 24-hrs.
   www.arthurlauer.com   E-mail: customerservice@arthurlauer.com
   Outdoor furniture in classic designs. Some pieces fully assembled, others
   flat packed. If you live in the Northeast, they offer "White Glove Delivery."
   CREDIT CARDS.

Pierre Deux 212-644-4891
   979 Third Ave., Ste 134 (58-59th St)   FAX 212-644-4893
   NY, NY 10022
   Hours: 9-5 Mon-Fri / Sat by appt.   E-mail: ddny@pierredeux.com
   www.pierredeux.com
   French country prints. Reproduction furniture. RENTALS. CREDIT CARDS.

Smith & Watson, Inc. 212-686-6444
   200 Lexington Ave., Ste 801 (32nd-33rd St)   FAX 212-686-6606
   NY, NY 10016
   Hours: 9-5 Mon-Fri   E-mail: inquiries@smithwatson.com
   www.smith-watson.com
   English and American reproductions; catalog available. Also custom furniture.
   RENTALS. No credit cards.

FURNITURE: FRAMES

Artistic Frame Co. 212-289-2100
   985 Third Ave.   FAX 212-289-2101
   NY, NY 10022
   Hours: 10-5 Mon-Thurs / 10-1 Fri   E-mail: sales@artisticframe.com
   www.artisticframe.com
   Period reproduction furniture frames, raw, ready for finishing; to the trade.
   Catalog; reasonable. They will also finish and upholster their frames.

Devon Shops 212-686-1760
   111 E 27th St. (Lex-Park Ave S)   FAX 212-686-2970
   NY, NY 10016
   Hours: 10-6 Mon-Fri / Sat-Sun by Appt.   E-mail: winston@devonshop.com
   www.devonshop.com
   Period reproduction furniture; raw frame or finished with muslin. Expensive,
   good quality. RENTALS.

FURNITURE: FRAMES

Ressler Importers, Inc. 212-674-4477
  63 Flushing Ave., Unit 250 (Thompson-Sullivan St)   212-533-5750
  Brooklyn, NY 11205   FAX 212-353-9446
  Hours: 8-5 Mon-Fri / or by appt.   E-mail: resslerimp@aol.com
  www.resslerimporters.com
  Period and contemporary reproductions, raw furniture frames or finished
  with upholstery; reasonable prices; catalog.

FURNITURE: GARDEN

Architectural Artifacts, Inc. 773-348-0622
  4325 N. Ravenswood   FAX 773-348-6118
  Chicago, IL 60613
  Hours: 10-5 Mon-Sun   E-mail: sales@architecturalartifacts.com
  www.architecturalartifacts.com
  80,000 sq. feet of architectural elements. One of the best finds in Chicago.
  Stained glass, fireplace mantels, period lighting, garden furnishings,
  decorative, cast & wrought iron. Must see to believe the stock. Some
  RENTALS.

Chelsea Garden Center 877-846-0565
  580 Eleventh Ave.(44th St)   212-727-7100
  NY, NY 10036   212-727-3434
  Hours: 9-7 Daily (Winter hours: 10-5 Wed-Sun)   FAX 212-727-3637

  444 Van Brunt St.(Fairway)   718-875-2100
  Brooklyn, NY 11231   E-mail: info@chelseagardencenter.com
  www.chelseagardencenter.com
  Plants, trees, shrubs, flowers, large and small planters, landscape supplies
  and landscaping. Fountains, furniture and pottery available for RENTALS.
  CREDIT CARDS.

Crows Nest Trading Co. 800-900-8558
  3205 Airport Blvd NW, P.O. Box 3975   FAX 800-900-3136
  Wilson, NC 27895
  Hours: 9-5 Mon-Fri / 24-hr. website   E-mail: info@crowsnestrading.com
  www.crowsnesttrading.com
  Leather, western rugged furnishings. Also kitchen, garden and rugs. Western
  and cowboy themed. Great catalog. CREDIT CARDS.

Demolition Depot / Irreplaceable Artifacts 212-860-1138
  216 E 125th St.(2nd-3rd Ave)
  NY, NY 10035   FAX 212-860-1560
  Hours: 10-6 Mon-Sat / 12-5 Sun

  428 Main St.   860-344-8576
  Middletown, CT 06457   FAX 860-638-0834
  Hours: by appt. only call 212-860-1138   E-mail: info@demolitiondepot.com
  www.demolitiondepot.com
  Architectural ornamentation from demolished buildings. Cast iron outdoor
  furniture and interesting pieces for the garden. RENTALS.

Eclectic / Encore Properties, Inc. 212-645-8880
620 W 26th St., 4th Fl. (11-12th Ave)   FAX 212-243-6508
NY, NY 10001
Hours: 9-5 Mon-Fri / or by appt.   E-mail: props@eclecticprops.com
www.eclecticprops.com
*Wicker, Adirondack, wrought iron, willow, cast iron, redwood, twig,
architectural ornamentation, poolside, park, outdoor cafe, etc. Can request
rental items thru online catalog. RENTALS. CREDIT CARDS.*

Elizabeth Street Gallery, Inc. 212-941-4800
209 Elizabeth St. (Spring-Prince St.)   FAX 212-274-0057
NY, NY 10012
Hours: 10-5 Mon-Fri call for appt.   E-mail: info@elizabethstreetgallery.com
www.elizabethstreetgallery.com
*Benches, tables, chairs, fountains, birdbaths, gazebos, gates, fences and more
in iron, wood, marble, bronze. Also fireplaces, statuary and architectural
elements. RENTALS. CREDIT CARDS.*

Florentine Craftsmen, Inc. 718-937-7632
46-24 28th St. (Skillman-47th Ave)   800-971-7600
Long Island City, NY 11101   FAX 718-937-9858
Hours: 8-4:30 Mon-Fri   E-mail: info@florentinecraftsmen.com
www.florentinecraftsmen.com
*Cast iron fountains, statues, columns, tables, chairs, benches for outdoor use;
expensive. Download catalog from website. Contact Bill Reany. RENTALS.
CREDIT CARDS.*

Fortunoff Backyard Store 201-262-1700
141 New Jersey Rte. 17)
Paramus, NJ 07652
Hours: 10-9 Mon-Sat
www.fortunoff.com
*Outdoor furniture and accessories. See website for other locations. CREDIT
CARDS.*

Fran's Wicker & Rattan Furniture 800-372-6799
295 Rt. 10 East   FAX 973-584-7446
Succasunna, NJ 07876
Hours: 9-5:30 Mon-Fri (Wed & Thurs until 8:30) / 9:30-6 Sat / 12-5 Sun
www.franswicker.com   E-mail: inquiry@franswicker.com
*Large selection wicker baskets, outdoor rugs, rattan, wicker, teak and cast
aluminum furniture 1 hour from NYC. Ask for Fran Gruber. CREDIT CARDS.*

Green Life LLC 800-982-3880
21 Whitney Dr.   FAX 888-316-5461
Milford, OH 45150
Hours: 9-5 Mon-Fri / 9-5:30 Sat / WEB 24-hrs.
www.arthurlauer.com   E-mail: customerservice@arthurlauer.com
*Outdoor furniture in classic designs. Some pieces fully assembled, others
flat packed. If you live in the Northeast, they offer "White Glove Delivery."
CREDIT CARDS.*

Jensen-Lewis Co., Inc. 212-929-4880
    89 Seventh Ave. (15th St)   FAX 212-727-0845
    NY, NY 10011
    Hours: 10-7 Mon-Sat (Thurs until 8) / 12-5:30 Sun
    www.jensen-lewis.com   E-mail: jlsalesinf@jensen-lewis.com
    Casual residential furnishings for the urban garden. CREDIT CARDS.

Lexington Gardens 212-861-4390
    1011 Lexington Ave. (72nd-73rd St)   FAX 212-988-0943
    NY, NY 10021
    Hours: 10- 6 Mon-Fri / 11-5 Sat   E-mail: inquiry@lexingtongardensnyc.com
    www.lexingtongardensnyc.com
    Wonderful antique iron furniture. Also has oversized garden pots from China
    and Vietnam in various glazes. Selected rentals on the antiques. CREDIT
    CARDS.

Lillian August Designs, Inc. 203-847-3314
    32 Knight St. (North Ave-Park St)   FAX 203-852-0524
    Norwalk, CT 06851
    Hours: 10-7 Mon-Sat / 11-6 Sun   E-mail: kcavalier@lillianaugust.com
    www.lillianaugust.com
    100,000 sf of contemporary, antique and imported furnishings and
    accessories. Home and garden. Contact Kim at X 3019. RENTALS. CREDIT
    CARDS.

Morgik Metal Designs 212-463-0304
    145 Hudson St. (at Hubert St)   800-354-5252
    NY, NY 10013   FAX 212-463-0329
    Hours: 8-4 Mon-Fri   E-mail: sales@morgik.com
    www.morgik.com
    Wrought-iron furniture, drapery rods and other metal products. Contact
    Dorothy, Larry, or Mihail. CREDIT CARDS.

FURNITURE: GENERAL
See also: ANTIQUES
            DEPARTMENT STORES
            PROP RENTAL HOUSES
            THRIFT SHOPS

Allen Office Furniture 212-929-8228
    149 W 21st St. (6-7th Ave)
    NY, NY 10011
    Hours: 9-5 Mon-Sat   E-mail: allenop@aol.com
    Office furniture, new and used. Prop furniture rentals. Steel shelving.
    Contact Jim Howley. RENTALS.

Anything But Costumes 908-788-1727
    111 Mine St.   FAX 908-237-1158
    Flemington, NJ 08822
    Hours: daily by appt.   E-mail: anythingbutcostumes@earthlink.net
    www.anythingbutcostumes.com
    An eclectic collection of furniture and other props and dressing. Very helpful
    over the phone. Will fax or e-mail photos. Deliveries available. RENTALS.

Arenson Office Furnishings, Inc. 212-633-2400
   1115 Broadway, 6th Fl. (24-25th St)   FAX 212-633-2777
   NY, NY 10010
   Hours: 8:30-5:30 Mon-Fri / or by appt.
   www.aof.com
   Good prices, excellent service. Same day delivery. RENTALS.

Art & Industrial Design 212-477-0116
   50 Great Jones St. (4th Ave)   FAX 212-477-1420
   NY, NY 10012
   Hours: 10-5 Mon-Fri / 10-1 Sat   E-mail: info@aid20c.com
   www.aid20c.com
   20th-century and Art Deco furniture, furnishings, art and objects. Also
   collectibles, clocks and lighting fixtures. RENTALS. CREDIT CARDS.

E. J. Audi 212-337-0700
   207 W 25th St. (7-8th Ave)   FAX 212-229-2189
   NY, NY 10010
   Hours: 10-6 Mon-Sat / Thurs until 8 / 12-5 Sun
   www.stickley.com
   Reproduction Mission oak and 18th century furniture in mahogany and
   cherry. Lighting fixtures. Catalog. CREDIT CARDS.

The Chair Factory 212-941-8700
   214 Bowery (Prince & Spring St)   877-7-CHAIRS
   NY, NY 10012   FAX 212-941-0033
   Hours: 9-6 Mon-Thurs / 9-4 Fri / by Appt.   E-mail: sales@thechairfactory.com
   www.thechairfactory.com
   Manufacturers of wood and metal chairs, barstools and tables. Hundreds of
   styles to choose from. CREDIT CARDS.

Cort 212-867-2800
   711 Third Ave. (51st St)   800-962-CORT
   NY, NY 10017   FAX 212-573-6869
   Hours: 9-6 Mon-Fri / Sat by Appt.   E-mail: newyorkdhg-loc@rent-ifr.com
   www.rent-ifr.com
   Modern wooden furniture (hotel like, very generic); some office. Lighting
   fixtures. Good for multiples. Contact Toby in NYC. See website for other
   locations. RENTALS. CREDIT CARDS.

Decorative Crafts, Inc. 203-531-1500
   50 Chestnut St.   800-431-4455
   Greenwich, CT 06830   FAX 203-531-1590
   Hours: 9-4:30 Mon-Fri   E-mail: info@decorativecrafts.com
   www.decorativecrafts.com
   To trade only. Imported brassware, Oriental screens and furniture; catalog.
   CREDIT CARDS.

The Door Store 877 366-7786
   100 Enterprise Ave. S(Clearance Center & Warehouse)   201-864-8844
   Secaucus, NJ 07094   FAX 201-864-7989
   Hours: 10-6 Mon-Sat / 10-8 Thurs / 11-6 Sun

The Door Store (cont.) 212-627-1515
123 W 17th St.(6-7th Ave)
NY, NY 10011
Hours: 10-9 Mon-Sat / 11-7 Sun

1 Park Ave.(33th St)   212-679-9700
NY, NY 10016
Hours: 10-7 Mon-Sat / 11-6 Sun

969 Third Ave.(58th St)
NY, NY 10022
Hours: 10-8 Mon-Sat / 11-6 Sun

1457 Northern Blvd.   516-627+2420
Manhasset, NY 11030
Hours: 10-7 Mon-Sat / 11-6 Sun
www.doorstorefurniture.com
Contemporary furniture; showroom, clearance center and warehouse in
Secaucus. See web address for other locations. CREDIT CARDS.

Eclectic / Encore Properties, Inc. 212-645-8880
620 W 26th St., 4th Fl. (11-12th Ave)   FAX 212-243-6508
NY, NY 10001
Hours: 9-5 Mon-Fri / or by appt.   E-mail: props@eclecticprops.com
www.eclecticprops.com
History for rent. Great selection of older styles and the unusual. Can request
rental items thru online catalog. RENTALS. CREDIT CARDS.

The End of History 212-647-7598
548 1/2 Hudson St. (Perry-Charles St)
NY, NY 10014
Hours: 12-7 Mon-Fri / 1-6 Sat-sun
Collection of vintage glassware, ceramics and lighting. Mostly 50s-60s from
Italy, Scandinavia and America. Has furniture from the same period.
RENTALS. CREDIT CARDS.

Ethan Allen Galleries 212-888-2384
1010 Third Ave. (60-61st St)   FAX 212-888-2730
NY, NY 10065
Hours: 10-8 Mon-Tue, Thurs / 10-6 Wed, Fri-Sat / 12-5 Sun
www.ethanallen.com
American traditional, French country and several contemporary lines of
furniture. RENTALS from 4 floors of display. Check website for other
locations. Catalog. CREDIT CARDS.

Everything Goes 718-273-0568
17 Brook St.   FAX 718-448-6842
Staten Island, NY 10301
Hours: 10:30-6:30 Tue-Sat   E-mail: ganas@well.com
www.etgstores.com
Convenient to the ferry; 4 locations with a constantly changing stock of
estate sale furniture, furnishings and some antiques. Contact Ellen
Oppenheim. See web address for other locations. RENTALS. CREDIT
CARDS.

FURNITURE: GENERAL

Gallery 532 203-858-1432
   50 John St. (John Street Antiques) (Manhattan-Market)   203-324-4677
   Stamford, CT 06902
   Hours: 10:30-5:30 Daily   E-mail: gallery532@aol.com
   Early 20th century (1900-1920) furniture, lighting fixtures and other decorative
   arts. Currently selling at John St. Antiques. Very helpful. RENTALS. CREDIT
   CARDS.

IKEA 800-434-IKEA
   1000 IKEA Dr.(Exit 13A off NJ Tpke)   908-289-4488
   Elizabeth, NJ 07201
   Hours: 10-9 Mon-Sat / 10-8 Sun

   1100 Broadway Mall(LIE Exit 41S or NSP Exit 35S)   516-681-4532
   Hicksville, NY 11801
   Hours: 10-9 Mon-Sun

   1 Beard St.(Columbia-Otsego)   718-246-4532
   Brooklyn, NY 11231
   Hours: 10-9 Mon-Sun
   www.ikea.com
   International Swedish department store for the home; specializing in
   furniture and home furnishings; inexpensive. Visit website for other locations
   nationwide. Catalog. CREDIT CARDS.

Invincible Furniture 973-333-6090
   11-13 Maryland Ave.   888-289-4489
   Paterson, NJ 07503   FAX 973-333-6086
   Hours: 9-5 Mon-Fri
   www.invincibleipf.com
   Period reproduction of furniture; catalog and finish samples available.
   Expensive, high quality. CREDIT CARDS.

Kravet Fabrics 800-645-9068
   979 Third Ave., Ste. 324(58-59th St) (D&D Building)   212-421-6363
   NY, NY 10022   FAX 212-751-7196
   Hours: 9-5 Mon-Fri

   200 Lexington Ave., 4th Fl.   212-725-0340
   NY, NY 10016   FAX 212-684-7350
   Hours: 9-5 Mon-Fri

   225 Central Ave. S   516-293-2000
   Bethpage, NY 11714   FAX 516-293-2737
   Hours: 10-4 Mon-Fri
   www.kravet.com
   To the trade (account required); large selection, all kinds of drapery, sheer and
   upholstery fabrics and trims. Recently added furnitre, carpets and
   furnishings. Large quantities available. Very helpful; swatching. Reasonably
   priced.

F

Lee's Art Shop & Studio 212-247-0110
220 W 57th St. (B'way-7th Ave)   FAX 212-581-7023
NY, NY 10019
Hours: 9-7:30 Mon-Fri / 10-7 Sat / 11-6 Sun   E-mail: info@leesartshop.com
www.leesartshop.com
This West Side showroom has a large selection of modern European
furniture, lighting fixtures and fans; expensive. RENTALS. CREDIT CARDS.

Lillian August Designs, Inc. 203-847-3314
32 Knight St. (North Ave-Park St)   FAX 203-852-0524
Norwalk, CT 06851
Hours: 10-7 Mon-Sat / 11-6 Sun   E-mail: kcavalier@lillianaugust.com
www.lillianaugust.com
100,000 sf of contemporary, antique and imported furnishings and
accessories. Home and garden. Contact Kim at X 3019. RENTALS. CREDIT
CARDS.

Miya Shoji & Interiors, Inc. 212-243-6774
145 W 26th St. (6-7th Ave)   FAX 212-243-6780
NY, NY 10001
Hours: 10-6 Mon-Fri
Shoji screens, lamps, cabinets. RENTALS. CREDIT CARDS.

Mosaic House 212-414-2525
32 W 22nd St. (B'way-6th Ave)   FAX 212-414-2526
NY, NY 10010
Hours: 10-6 Mon-Sat   E-mail: contactus@mosaichse.com
www.mosaichse.com
Moroccan house of tiles and furnishings. Beautiful mosaic tables. Will do
custom work. CREDIT CARDS.

Palumbo 212-734-7630
972 Lexington Ave. (70-71st St)   FAX 212-734-6590
NY, NY 10021
Hours: 11-6 Mon-Fri   E-mail: mail@palumbogallery.com
www.palumbogallery.com
Mid-20th-century furniture. Custom post-war designers like Tommi Parzinger,
Edward Wormley & William Paklmann. Contact Pat Palumbo or Don Silvey.
RENTALS.

Pier 1 Imports 800-245-4595
1550 Third Ave.(87th St)   212-987-1746
NY, NY 10128
Hours: 10-9 Mon-Sat / 11-7 Sun

71 Fifth Ave.(14-15th St)   212-206-1911
NY, NY 10003
Hours: 10-9 Mon-Sat / 11-7 Sun
www.pier1.com
Popular chain of stores carries baskets; wicker furniture and decorative items
for the home. Some lighting, clothing, frames. See website for over 800
locations nationally. Some RENTALS. CREDIT CARDS.

F

The Prop Company / Kaplan and Associates 212-691-7767
111 W 19th St., 8th Fl. (6-7th Ave)   FAX 212-727-3055
NY, NY 10011
Hours: 9-5 Mon-Fri   E-mail: propcompany@yahoo.com
Unique collection of contemporary and antique tables, chairs and much
surface decoration. Contact Maxine Kaplan. CREDIT CARDS.

Props for Today 212-244-9600
330 W 34th St. (8-9th Ave)   FAX 212-244-1053
NY, NY 10001
Hours: 8:30-5 Mon-Fri   E-mail: info@propsfortoday.com
www.propsfortoday.com
Full-service prop house offering sales and rentals on antique to ultra-modern
furniture. Long term rental packages and custom orders available. RENTALS.
CREDIT CARDS.

Regeneration Modern Furniture 212-741-2102
38 Renwick St. (Spring-Canal St)   FAX 212-741-2342
NY, NY 10013
Hours: 12-5 Mon / 12-6 Tue-Sat   E-mail: contact@regenerationfurniture.com
www.regenerationfurniture.com
Specializing in communal seating from mid-20th century. Knoll, Jacobsen,
Wormley, etc. Smaller location in ABC Carpet & Home on Broadway (2nd FL.)
Prices are surprisingly reasonable. RENTALS. CREDIT CARDS.

Sheila's Decorating 212-777-3767
68 Orchard St. (Grand St)   FAX 212-777-7076
NY, NY 10002
Hours: 10-6 Sun-Fri   E-mail: info@sheilasdecorating.com
www.sheilasdecorating.com
Well-displayed and reasonably priced fabrics, furnishings and accessories.
CREDIT CARDS.

Smith & Watson, Inc. 212-686-6444
200 Lexington Ave., Ste 801 (32nd-33rd St)   FAX 212-686-6606
NY, NY 10016
Hours: 9-5 Mon-Fri   E-mail: inquiries@smithwatson.com
www.smith-watson.com
English and American reproductions; catalog available. Also custom furniture.
RENTALS. No credit cards.

Spatial Environmental Elements Ltd. 212-228-3600
89 Fifth Ave., Ste. 904   FAX 212-228-3600
NY, NY 10003
Hours: 10-7 Mon-Sat / 12-6 Sun   E-mail: seeltd@aol.com
www.seeltd.com
Large showroom of modern design furniture; also some lighting, accessories
and objects. RENTALS. CREDIT CARDS.

Victorian Trading Company 800-700-2035
15600 W 99th St.   913-438-3995
Lenexa, KS 66219   FAX 913-438-5225
Hours: 24 on website   www.victoriantradingco.com
Mail order company with an extensive selection of merchandise, including
reproduction Victorian furniture, desk accessories, knick-knacks and garden
items. CREDIT CARDS.

Weissman Furniture Wholesalers 212-213-0088
102 E 31st St. (Park & Lex)   FAX 212-213-0880
NY, NY 10016
Hours: by appt. only   E-mail: larryfurniture@aol.com
Contemporary and some traditional styles of furniture for home, hotel,
healthcare and office. Sofabeds. RENTALS. CREDIT CARDS.

FURNITURE: OFFICE

Allen Office Furniture 212-929-8228
149 W 21st St. (6-7th Ave)
NY, NY 10011
Hours: 9-5 Mon-Sat   E-mail: allenop@aol.com
Office furniture, new and used. Prop furniture rentals. Steel shelving.
Contact Jim Howley. RENTALS.

Arenson Office Furnishings, Inc. 212-633-2400
1115 Broadway, 6th Fl. (24-25th St)   FAX 212-633-2777
NY, NY 10010
Hours: 8:30-5:30 Mon-Fri / or by appt.
www.aof.com
Good prices, excellent service. Same day delivery. RENTALS.

Bergen Office Furniture 212-366-6677
127 W 26th St. (6-7th Ave)   FAX 212-366-5779
NY, NY 10001
Hours: 9-5 Mon-Fri   E-mail: bergenup@aol.com
www.bergenofficefurniture.com
Specialize in vintage office furniture from 1920s-60s and contemporary office
furniture. Also has a furniture refinishing, upholstering and paint shop. Ask
for Ira. RENTALS.

Cort 212-867-2800
711 Third Ave. (51st St)   800-962-CORT
NY, NY 10017   FAX 212-573-6869
Hours: 9-6 Mon-Fri / Sat by Appt.   E-mail: newyorkdhg-loc@rent-ifr.com
www.rent-ifr.com
Modern wooden furniture (hotel like, very generic); some office. Lighting
fixtures. Good for multiples. Contact Toby in NYC. See website for other
locations. RENTALS. CREDIT CARDS.

Dallek 212-684-4848
888 Longfellow Ave. (39-40th St)   800-876-8786
Bronx, NY 10474   FAX 212-576-1036
Hours: 8:45-5:45 Mon-Thurs / 8:45-5 Fri   E-mail: info@dallek.com
www.dallek.com
Office furniture; expensive. Catalog. CREDIT CARDS.

Furniture Rental Associates 212-868-0300
  148 Madison Ave.   800-633-3748
  NY, NY 10016   FAX 212-594-5415
  Hours: 9-6 Mon-Fri or by appt.   E-mail: frarents@aol.com
  www.frarents.com
  Full-service office furniture rentals: traditional, contemporary, modern and
  computer office furniture. Same day service. Reupholstery and refinishing.
  Contact Randie Greenberg. RENTALS. CREDIT CARDS.

Office Furniture Place 212-921-2888
  247 W 37th St., 15th Fl. (7-8th Ave)   FAX 646-395-9110
  NY, NY 10001
  Hours: 9-5:30 Mon-Fri   E-mail: paul@officefurnitureplace.com
  www.officefurnitureplace.com
  Good selection of used office furniture. CREDIT CARDS.

F

Pearl Paint / World's Largest Creative Resource 800-451-7327
  308 Canal St.(B'way-Church St)   212-431-7932
  NY, NY 10013   (mail order) 800-221-6845
  Hours: 9-7 Mon-Fri / 10-7 Sat / 10-6 Sun FAX 212-431-6798

  42 Lispenard St. (Craft & Home Center)(B'way-Church St)   212-226-3717
  NY, NY 10013   800-221-6845
  Hours: 9-7 Mon-Fri / 10-7 Sat / 10-6 Sun

  776 Rt. 17 N   201-447-0300
  Paramus, NJ 07652   FAX 201-447-4012
  Hours: 10-9 Mon-Sat

  1033 E Oakland Park Blvd.(Corp. Office)   954-567-9678
  Ft. Lauderdale, FL 33334
  www.pearlpaint.com
  Easels, drafting machines, flat files, airbrushes, light boxes, office furniture at
  this location. Online shopping available. CREDIT CARDS.

Props for Today 212-244-9600
  330 W 34th St. (8-9th Ave)   FAX 212-244-1053
  NY, NY 10001
  Hours: 8:30-5 Mon-Fri   E-mail: info@propsfortoday.com
  www.propsfortoday.com
  Full-service prop rental house with new and antique office furniture,
  accessories and general dressing. Bulk mail and file paper. RENTALS. CREDIT
  CARDS.

Rehab Vintage 323-935-8438
  7609 Beverly Blvd.   800-668-1020
  Los Angeles, CA 90036   FAX 323-935-7338
  Hours: 10-6 Mon-Fri / 12-5 Sat E-mail: inforehabvintage.net
  www.rehabvintage.net
  Vintage American steel furniture. Old steel locks, lockers, tables, cabinets,
  shelving, etc. Great selection of office furnishings. Expensive. CREDIT
  CARDS.

FURNITURE: OFFICE

Two Jakes 718-782-7780
320 Wythe Ave. (Grand & S. 1st St)   888-2jakes2
Brooklyn, NY 11211   FAX 718-782-7259
Hours: 11-7 Tue-Sun   E-mail: info@twojakes.com
www.twojakes.com
Retail furniture specializing in classic 20th century modern office furniture;
Steelcase, Knoll, Henry Miller, etc. If it is well-made, they probably carry it.
Check website for their ever-changing inventory. CREDIT CARDS.

FURNITURE: PARTS

American Wood Column Corp.   718-782-3163
913 Grand St. (Bushwick-Morgan Ave)   FAX 718-387-9099
Brooklyn, NY 11211
Hours: 8-4:30 Mon-Fri
www.americanwoodcolumn.com
Columns, pedestals and moldings. All types of wood turnings. Will ship
worldwide. Speak to Tom Lupo. Brochure.

H. Arnold Wood Turning, Inc. 914-381-0801
875 Mamaroneck Ave.   866-404-0893
Mamaroneck, NY 10543   FAX 914-381-0804
Hours: 9-5 Mon-Fri   E-mail: info@arnoldwood.com
www.arnoldwood.com
Wholesale only. Custom wood turnings of all types, finials, legs and columns.

FURNITURE: REPAIR & REFINISHING

New York Chair Caning & Repair 212-724-4408
3051 Fulton St. (Shepherd-Highland Pl)
Brooklyn, NY 11208
Hours: 9-5 Mon-Fri / 9-1 Sat or by appt.
Furniture repair, hand and machine caning, rush, splint and wicker repair.
Unclaimed pieces for sale or rent. Contact Jeffrey Weiss.

Poor Richard's Restoration Studio .973-783-5333
101 Walnut St. (N Willow-Walnut Conor)
Montclair, NJ 07042
Hours: by appt.   E-mail: rickford99@yahoo.com
www.rickford.com
All aspects of furniture repair and conservation, from stripping of wood and
reupholstery to reweaving of cane, wicker and rush. Gesso work and painted
finishes. Also antique doll and jewelry repairs, old books and photos. CREDIT
CARDS.

Professional Furniture Finishing, Co. 212-532-0606
200 Lexington Ave. (32nd-33rd St)   FAX 212-689-7068
NY, NY 10016
Hours: 8-4 Mon-Fri   E-mail: profurn@aol.com
Furniture refinishing.

Veteran's Caning Shop 212-564-4560
442 Tenth Ave. (35th St)   866-484-7707
NY, NY 10001
Hours: 7:30- 4:30 Mon-Thur/ 7:30-4 Fri / 8-1 Sat
www.veteranscaning.com   E-mail: veteranscaning@worldnet.att.com
Hand and machine caning, rush and splint seating, also wicker repairs. Pick-up and delivery available. Very nice and helpful people.

Yorkville Caning, Inc. 212-432-6464
3104 60th St. (31st-32nd Ave)   718-274-6464
Woodside, NY 11377   FAX 718-274-8525
Hours: 7:30-4 Mon-Fri   E-mail: yorkvillecaning@aol.com
www.yorkvillecaning.com
Repair of cane, wicker, rush, rattan, splint and wood furniture. Also re-glueing and basic upholstery. No stripping. NJ drop off available.

FURNITURE: RESTAURANT

A Beautiful Bar 212-431-0600
49 E Houston St.   (warehouse) 718-730-5427
NY, NY FAX 212-625-0980
Hours: by appt.   E-mail: info@abeautifulbar.com
www.abeautifulbar.com
Always changing selection of bars and backbars; 8-30 ft. long; Victorian and Deco. Nice on-line catalog. Speak to Steve. RENTALS.

Arenson Office Furnishings, Inc. 212-633-2400
1115 Broadway, 6th Fl. (24-25th St)   FAX 212-633-2777
NY, NY 10010
Hours: 8:30-5:30 Mon-Fri / or by appt.
www.aof.com
Pedestal tables, folding and stacking chairs. RENTALS.

Gargoyles LTD 215-629-1700
120 N Third St.   FAX 215-592-8441
Philadelphia, PA 19106
Hours: 9-5:30 Tue-Fri / 11-6 Sat   E-mail: gargoylesltd@yahoo.com
www.gargoylesltd.com
Theme decor for restaurants. Country and period advertising memorabilia, period advertising mirrors, English and American antiques, Sports memorabilia and scale models. RENTALS. CREDIT CARDS.

Prince Seating 718-363-2300
1355 Atlantic Ave. (Brooklyn-York Ave)   FAX 718-363-9880
Brooklyn, NY 11216
Hours: 9-5 Mon-Fri   E-mail: info@princeseating.com
www.princeseating.com
Manufacturers of wood and metal chairs, barstools and tables. Hundreds of styles to choose from. RENTALS. CREDIT CARDS.

Rite Supermarket Equipment, Inc. 718-292-1800
   3362 Park Ave. (165th St)   FAX 718-665-8340
   Bronx, NY 10456
   Hours: 7:30-4:30 Mon-Fri   E-mail: ritesup@aol.com
   www.ritesupermarketequipment.com
   New and used supermarket and restaurant equipment, refrigerated cases and
   new and used diner booths. Signage and decorations. RENTALS.

Rollhause Seating Products, Inc. 212-334-1111
   134 Grand St. (Crosby-Lafayette St)   800-82-BOOTH
   NY, NY 10013   FAX 212-941-8193
   Hours: 8-4 Mon-Thurs   E-mail: info@seatingproducts.com
   www.seatingproducts.com
   Booths, chairs, tables; stock and custom furniture available. Very nice service.
   Reupholstery service available. RENTALS. CREDIT CARDS.

The Warehouse Store Fixture Co. 203-575-0111
   84 Progress Ln.   FAX 203-575-9140
   Waterbury, CT 06705
   Hours: 8-5 Mon-Fri / 9-2 Sat   E-mail: wsfc@restaurantsupplystore.com
   www.restaurantsupplystore.com
   New and used restaurant tables, chairs, booths, etc.; store and kitchen
   fixtures. CREDIT CARDS.

Yasakart Chair Table Booth Outlet /
   SINO America International Corp. 212-995-1395
   280 Bowery   FAX 212-219-9081
   NY, NY 10012
   Hours: 9:30-6 Mon-Sat
   www.chairny.com
   Chairs, tables, booths, benches, bar and counter stools. Sushi bar signs,
   lighting and Decorative Materials. A real Chinatown experience!

GLASS & MIRRORS

AllState Glass Corp. 212-226-2517
  85 Kenmare St. (Lafayette-Mulberry St)   FAX 212-966-7904
  NY, NY 10012
  Hours: 8-4:30 Mon-Fri
  www.allstateglasscorp.com
  Good selection shades and blinds. Shades, one-and two-inch blinds, verticals,
  pleated shades, woven wooden blinds. Custom and stock shower enclosures
  glass and mirrors. Speak to Sydelle Philips. CREDIT CARDS.

S.A. Bendheim Co., Inc. 212-226-6370
  122 Hudson St. (N Moore St)   800-606-7621
  NY, NY 10013   FAX 212-431-3589
  Hours: 9:30-5 Mon-Fri by appt. only
  www.bendheim.com
  All types of stained and textured glasses, tools and supplies; carries
  replacement different "distortion" degrees of Colonial mouth-blown window
  glass. Also teaches glass leading. CREDIT CARDS.

Capitol Glass & Sash Co., Inc. 212-243-4528
  50-45 Barnett Ave. (Laight)   718-651-8400
  Long Island City, NY 11104   FAX 718-651-8401
  Hours: 7-5 Mon-Fri   E-mail: capitolglass@aol.com
  www.capitolglassnyc.com
  Glazing contractors, complete line of glass and mirrors; also full line of
  millwork and windows. CREDIT CARDS.

Glass Restorations 212-517-3287
  1597 York Ave. (84-85th St)   FAX (same)
  NY, NY 10028
  Hours: 10:30-6 Mon-Fri
  Cuts, grinds and repairs chipped or scratched glass; also repairs broken glass;
  polishes. Speak to Gus. No credit cards.

Morris Glasser & Son, Inc. 212-831-8750
  305 Third Ave.   FAX 212-369-2526
  Brooklyn, NY 11215
  Hours: 8-5 Mon-Fri / 8-1 Sat
  Glass, mirror; very fast and helpful; worth the trip. No credit cards.

James Glass Studio 718-596-6463
  20 Jay St., Ste. 734 (Plymouth St)   FAX Same
  Brooklyn, NY 11201
  Hours: by appt.   E-mail: jamesglassstudio@earthlink.net
  www.jamesglassstudio.com
  Custom sculpting studio, casting in 3D glass, stone and metal. Established
  glass studio for 20 years.

Knickerbocker Plate Glass Corp. 212-247-8500
  439 W 54th St., Ground FL (9-10th Ave)   800-439-8500
  NY, NY 10019   FAX 212-489-1449
  Hours: 8:30-4:30 Mon-Fri
  www.knickerbockerplateglass.com
  24-hr. emergency boarding service. CREDIT CARDS.

G-H

Light Curves / Joan Nicole 845-434-5081
10 Rockview Lane   845-978-7653
Loch Sheldrake, NY 12759   FAX 845-434-5081
Hours: By appt., 24-hr. answering mach.   E-mail: lightcurves@gmail.com
Exquisite custom stained glass, tiffany style, leaded, painted glass, fused glass and mosaic. Also lighting fixtures, glass sculpture and jewelry, folding screens, windows, etc.

Manhattan Shade & Glass Co. 212-288-5616
1299 Third Ave. (Showroom) (74-75th St)   FAX 212-288-7241
NY, NY 10021
Hours: 8:30-5:30 Mon-Fri / 10-5 Sat   E-mail: sales@manhattanshade.com
www.manhattanshadeandglass.com
Wide range of glass, mirror and window treatment products. They sell, fabricate and install. Also extensive upholstery and curtain services. Specialize in motorizing control systems for all types of window coverings. Workroom in on Long Island. CREDIT CARDS.

Nisa Glass Systems, Inc. 212-265-0882
667 Tenth Ave. (47th St)   FAX   212-445-0727
NY, NY 10036
Hours: 8:30-5:30 Mon-Fri
Glass and mirror, plastic and aluminum. No credit cards.

Penn Glass Enterprise 718-641-7979
84-06 Liberty Ave.   800-222-6299
Ozone Park, NY 11417   FAX 718-641-5967
Hours: 7:30-4:30 Mon-Fri   E-mail: pennglass@yahoo.com
www.pennglass.com
Full line of products and services for all glass applications, storefronts. Very friendly. Services the film industry. P.O.s and CREDIT CARDS.

Rosen-Paramount Glass 212-532-0820
45 E 20th St. # 1 (Park Ave S-B'way)   FAX 212-473-7220
NY, NY 10003
Hours: 8-5 Mon-Fri
Glass and mirror. CREDIT CARDS for over $50.

Saraco Glass Corp. 718-871-6500
1267 38th St. (13th Ave)   FAX 718-851-0890
Brooklyn, NY 11218
Hours: 9-5 Mon-Fri / Weekends by appt.
All types of glass and mirrors. No credit cards.

Scanlan Glass 718-369-3645
103 14th St. (2nd-3rd Ave)
Brooklyn, NY 11215
Hours: by appt.   E-mail: kevin@scanlanglass.com
www.scanlanglass.com
Hand blown glass made to order. A complete glass fabrication facility. Hot and cold working equipment available. Classes taught, see web-site for dates. RENTALS.

G-H

GLOVES

Finale, Inc. 602-218-5976
　　4635 N Black Canyon Hwy # 201　　　　　　　877-775-4920
　　Phoenix, AZ 85015　　　　　　　　　　FAX　602-218-5975
　　Hours: 7:30-3:30 Mon-Fri
　　www.finalegloves.com
　　Vinyl and leather men's gloves; ladies' gloves, including long lace, satin,
　　velvet, sheer. Also children's gloves. Online shopping available.

Gaspar Gloves 323-441-1986
　　　　　　　　FAX　323-227-6993Los Angeles, CA 90065
　　Hours:　24-hr web / by appt.　　　　E-mail: glovesbyd@aol.com
　　www.gaspargloves.com
　　Web based glove company.　Custom and stock gloves.　Large selection.
　　Interesting link on website regarding glove etiquette. CREDIT CARDS.

Isotoner Gloves 212-944-1129
　　420 Fifth Ave. (37-38th St)　　　　　　FAX　212-944-6875
　　NY, NY 10016
　　Hours: 8:30-5 Mon-Thurs / 9-1 Fri
　　www.totes.com
　　Manufacturer; will help obtain out-of-season men's and women's gloves in
　　quantity.

La Crasia Gloves 212-803-1600
　　15 W 28th St. # 401 (5-B-way)　　　　　FAX　212-686-5250
　　NY, NY 10001
　　Hours:　By appt. only　　　　　　　E-mail: sales@lacrasia.com
　　www.lacrasia.com
　　Large stock of men's and women's gloves, also does custom work large or
　　small quantities in fabric and leather.　Contact Jay Ruckel for custom work.

Norman Librett, Inc. 914-636-1500
　　64 Main St. (Boston Post Rd)　　　　　FAX　914-636-2783
　　New Rochelle, NY 10801
　　Hours: 8-5 Mon-Fri　　　　　　　E-mail: Librettcord@aol.com
　　Manufacturer of dress and work gloves

GRAPHICS & TYPESETTING

Baumwell Graphics, Inc. 704-814-4550
　　8923 Providence Estates Ct.　　　　　　888-266-7246
　　Charlotte, NC 28270
　　Hours: 9-6 Mon-Fri　　　　　　E-mail: clyde@chromatype.com
　　www.chromatype.com
　　Typesetting, desktop publishing services, design, layout, photostats and laser
　　engraving. Contact Clyde Baumwell. Also makes custom transfers. CREDIT
　　CARDS.

G-H

Beyond Image Graphics 818-547-0899
1853 Dana St.   FAX 818-547-1470
Glendale, CA 91201
Hours: 9-5 Mon-Fri   E-mail: rafi@beyondimagegraphics.com
www.beyondimagegraphics.com
Signs, digital printing, banners, decals, vinyl graphics, vehicle graphics, custom life size cutouts, and much much more. One of the largest graphics houses in Southern California. CREDIT CARDS.

Coloredge Visual 212-594-4800
127 W 30th St.   800-321-8864
NY, NY 10011   FAX 212-594-4488
Hours: 24-hrs.   E-mail: sales@coloredgevisual.com
www.coloredgevisual.com
Transfers, bubble, duplicating chromes, photo CDs and Mac and PC output.

COMP 24 212-627-4000
127 W 30th St., 4th Fl. (6-7th Ave)   800-848-7716
NY, NY 10001   FAX 212-627-4287
Hours: 8-8 Mon-Fri
www.comp24.com
The largest packaging prototype facility in the world, specializing in color correct comps for advertising. Digital direct proofing and silkscreening; transfers; banners to bus wraps.

G.F.I. (Graphics For Industry) 212-889-6202
307 W 36th St. (7-8th Aves)   FAX 212-545-1276
NY, NY 10018
Hours: 9-5:30 Mon-Fri   E-mail: mpahmer@gfiusa.net
www.gfiusa.net
Color correct and replicate product and packaging for TV and film; some modelmaking; transfers; high quality full graphic service.

The Hand Prop Room LP 323-931-1534
5700 Venice Blvd. (Venice & Curson)   FAX 323-931-2145
Los Angeles, CA 90019
Hours: 7-7 Mon-Fri   E-mail: info@hpr.com
www.hpr.com
Full printing and graphics service; newspapers, license plates, IDs, "Greeked" product labels. CREDIT CARDS.

Quad Right 212-222-1220
147 W 95th St. # 1A (Amst-Col Ave)   FAX 212-222-2084
NY, NY 10025
Hours: 9-5:30 Mon-Fri   E-mail: quadright@pipeline.com
www.quadright.com
Graphic design, printing and digital services. CREDIT CARDS.

Sweetbryar Calligraphics 845-679-7335
31 Overlook Dr.
Woodstock, NY 12498
Hours: 10-6 Mon-Sat / by appt. only   E-mail: bryarcalli@aol.com
www.sweetbryar.com
Calligraphy and sign painting, air brushing, hand lettering, logos, banners, posters (all custom), menus. On location if necessary.

G-H

Scott Wilson Graphics 917-846-3106
   201 W 54th St. Apt 3C   212-247-4006
   NY, NY 10019   FAX 212-399-1164
   Hours: 9-6 Mon-Fri
   Small graphics company, transfers, airbrush, some modelmaking. Very
   helpful.

Joan Winters 212-475-6605
   236 E 5th St. #D3 (2nd-3rd Ave)
   NY, NY 10003
   Hours: by appt.   E-mail: joanwinters@earthlink.net
   Graphic design and production services for specialty props including
   magazines, books, newspapers, badges and letterheads. Logos, posters,
   computer typesetting. Major film credits.

G-H

NOTES

HAIR AND WIG DESIGN

Dave Bova 386-366-4649
NY, NY
Hours: by appt.　　　　　　　　　　E-mail: bovaii@hotmail.com
Wig design and special effects make-up. RENTALS. CREDIT CARDS.

The Broadway Wig Company 212-244-5885
217 E 60th St. Ste 201 (3rd Ave)
NY, NY 10022
Hours: by appt.　　　　　　　E-mail: broadwaywigs@earthlink.net
www.broadwaywigs.com
Custom theatrical wigs of distinction. Speak to Robert Charles. CREDIT CARDS.

D.R. Wigs 416-429-1402
48 Coleridge Ave.　　　　　　　　　　　　　　416-816-2564
Toronto, Ontario, Canada M4C 4H5　　　　FAX 416-429-1402
Hours: by Appt.　　　　　　　E-mail: drwigs@sympatico.ca
www.dawnbrides.com
Licensed hairstylist, make-up artist and custom wig builder for film and theatre. Owns over 800 stock wigs for rentals. Can provide crew for make-up and hairstylists for large or small productions. RENTALS. PayPal.

Elsen Associates 412-321-1380
832 Western Ave. (155th St)　　　　　　　FAX 412-487-3182
Pittsburgh, PA 15233
Hours: by appt.　　　　　　　E-mail: info@elsenassociates.com
www.elsenassociates.com
Rental and custom-built wigs for all media; staffed with a network of qualified wig and make-up designers on-site. RENTALS.

Rob Greene 646-296-8686
NY, NY
Hours: by appt.　　　　　　　　　　E-mail: rawbg@aol.com
www.backstageartistry.com
Wig Design. RENTALS. CREDIT CARDS.

Hudson Brown Wigs, LLC 212-727-9447
1133 Broadway, Ste. 1305　　　　　　　　FAX 212-727-9446
NY, NY 10010
Hours: 10-6 Mon-Fri　　　E-mail: contact@hudsonbrownwigs.com
www.hudsonbrownwigs.com
Broadway hair designer, Shrek, Little Mermaid, Legally Blonde among others.

Paul Huntley Ltd. 212-787-5200
312 W 82nd St. (Riverside-West End Ave)　　　　　　FAX (same)
NY, NY 10010
Hours: by appt.
Custom-made, excellent quality wigs; expensive. One of the best.

G-H

Jared Janas 201-349-4444
NY, NY
Hours: by appt. E-mail: jjjanas@hotmail.com
www.backstageartistry.com
Hair and wig design for theater and movies. Also special effects make-up.
Some RENTALS. CREDIT CARDS.

Cookie Jordan 505-577-3516
322 W 55th St. (8-9th Ave)
NY, NY 10019
Hours: by appt. E-mail: jordantrp@mac.com
Fela on Broadway, 25 years hair and make-up design. Wigs for Disney's High
School Musical; National and UK tours. Make-up for South Pacific, The
Bridge Project. RENTALS.

Charles Lapointe 212-868-4070
34 W 35th St. (5-6th Ave)
NY, NY 10001
Hours: by appt. E-mail: ccglspointe@msn.com
Broadway credits include Memphis, Xanadu and The Color Purple. RENTALS.

Leah Loukas 513-265-2891
NY, NY
Hours: by appt. E-mail: loukaslj@hotmail.com
Broadway credits include American Idiot. RENTALS.

Josh Marquette 917-754-3530
Hours: by appt. E-mail: jkmarquette@hotmail.com
Wig designer for Drowsy Chaperone on Broadway. Dept head for 30-Rock.
Some RENTALS.

Mark Adam Rampmeyer 917-548-1989
NY, NY
Hours: by appt. www.wigmanmark@aol.com
Designs and has rentals for all forms of theatrical adventures. RENTALS.

Ashley Ryan 469-387-6733
NY, NY
Hours: by appt. E-mail: ashleylr38@yahoo.com
Broadway and off-Broadway credits for hair and wig design. RENTALS.

Wig Designs 865-455-7017
Hours: by appt. E-mail: cpostiche@comcast.net
Wig design, styling and customizing, specializing in opera. Able to travel.
Brochure available. Contact Sandra Herrara. Sales and RENTALS.

Wigmaster Associates 212-463-0966
174 Fifth Ave. 212-866-2059
NY, NY 10010
Hours: by appt only
www.wigmasterassociates.com
Custom wigs. Online shopping.

G-H

HAIR SUPPLIES & WIGS
See also: BEAUTY SALON EQUIPMENT

Abracadabra 212-627-5194
19 W 21st St. (5-6th Ave)   FAX 212-627-7435
NY, NY 10001
Hours: 11-7 Mon-Sat / 12-5 Sun
www.abracadabrasuperstore.com
Wigs, mustaches and beards. Crepe and human hair. Catalog available online. RENTALS. CREDIT CARDS.

Costume World 800 258-0333
950 S Federal Hwy.   954-428-6266
Deerfield Beach, FL 33441   FAX 954-428-4959
Hours: 10-7 Mon-Fri / 10-6 Sat
www.costumeworld.com
Show packages for all major musicals. Will do small rentals. Store locations in Pittsburg, Dallas and headquarters in Deerfield Beach that specialize in Halloween rentals, make-up and wig supplies. 55,000 square feet of costumes. Costume plots available. RENTALS. CREDIT CARDS.

DeMeo Brothers, Inc. 212-268-1400
2 Brighton Ave. (6-7th Ave)
Passaic, NJ 07055
Hours: Mon-Fri by appt.
Theatrical laces, yak hair, fine European hair, wig-making and hairpiece-making supplies; hair sample matching; order by mail. Price list available. No minimum. CREDIT CARDS.

Frederickís of Hollywood 800-323-9525
6608 Hollywood Blvd.   FAX 602-760-2181
Hollywood, CA 90028
Hours: 8:30-8 Mon-Fri
www.fredericks.com
Sexy lingerie for women and men; bathing suits, hooker shoes and wigs. Catalog and shopping online. Over 200 stores, check the website for a store near you. CREDIT CARDS.

Goldsmith Mannequins 212-366-9040
601 W 26th St. Ste 350 (10-11th Ave)   FAX 212-366-9048
NY, NY 10001
Hours: 9-4 Mon-Fri / Showroom by Appt.   E-mail: info@goldsmith-inc.com
www.goldsmith-inc.com
Manufacturer of mannequins, forms, accessories fixtures and furniture. Visual merchandising. Wig heads. Free catalog. Will ship. RENTALS.

Hair Motion International Corp. 212-689-9738
40 W 27th St. (6th-B'way)   877-240-4004
NY, NY 10001   FAX 212-684-0585
Hours: 7-5:30 Mon-Fri / 7-4:30 Sat / 8-3:30 Sun   E-mail: info@hairmotion.com
www.hairmotion.com
Asian import, human and artifical hair and wigs, also "fun" colored hair and wigs; beauty and nail supplies. Trimming machins, blades, flat and curling irons. CREDIT CARDS.

G-H

Lacey Costume Wig 212-695-1996
318 W 39th St., 10th Fl. (8-9th Ave)   800-562-9911
NY, NY 10018   FAX 212-695-3860
Hours: 10-6 Mon-Fri
Free catalog available. Reasonably priced novelty and period wigs. No
minimum. Contact Elliot, Billy or Mason Kaplan.

Michael Salem Boutique 212-697-0644
300 E 46th St., 2nd Fl. (2nd Ave)   917-412-9739
NY, NY 10017
Hours: by appt only 24/7   E-mail: msaleminc@msn.com
www.michaelsalem.com
Complete line of ladies' clothing for men, including shoes and wigs. CREDIT
CARDS.

National Fiber Technologies 978-686-2964
300 Canal St.   800-842-2751
Lawrence, MA 01840   FAX 978-686-1497
Hours: 8:30-5 Mon-Fri   E-mail: info@nftech.com
www.nftech.com
Custom-made wigs, made with flamesafe Modacrylic fibers, styled as you
specify. Production time 3-4 weeks. Made in USA.

Ray Beauty Supply Co., Inc. 212-757-0175
721 Eighth Ave. (45-46th St)   800-253-0993
NY, NY 10036   FAX 212-459-8918
Hours: 8:30-6 Mon-Wed / 8:30-7 Thurs-Fri / 9-5:15 SatE-mail:
ray.beauty@verizon.net
www.raybeauty.com
Wide variety hair supplies and make-up; beauty salon equipment rental; see
Bobby. Phone orders and shipping available. CREDIT CARDS.

Ricky's 212-769-3678
112 W 72nd St. (Amst-Col)
NY, NY 10024   FAX 212-769-0320
Hours: 9-10 Mon-Fri / 10-9 Sat / 10-8 Sun

1189 First Ave.(Corner of 64th & 1st Ave)   212-879-8361
NY, NY 10021   FAX 212-879-8359
Hours: 10-9 Mon-Sun

332 W 57th St.(8-9th Aves)   212-247-8010
NY, NY 10019   FAX 212-247-8011
Hours: 9-9 Mon-Fri / 10-9 Sat / 9-8 Sun

44 E 8th St.(Corner of Greene St)   212-254-5247
NY, NY 10003   FAX 212-254-6523
Hours: 10-9 Mon-Sun

466 Sixth Ave.(11-12th St)   212-924-3401
NY, NY 10011   FAX 212-924-3404
Hours: 9-10 Mon-Sat / 10-10 Sun

590 Broadway(Prince-Houston St)   212-226-5552
NY, NY 10012   FAX 212-226-5595
Hours: 9-10 Mon-Sat / 10-8 Sun

G-H

Ricky's (cont.) 212-206-0234
267 W 23rd St.(7-8th Ave)
New York, NY 10011   FAX 212-206-0379
Hours: 9-11 Mon-Sat / 10-10 Sun   E-mail: info@rickysnyc.com
www.rickysnyc.com
Way beyond your average drug / cosmetic store. Ricky's is truely an
experience specializing in haircare products, wigs, make-up and some stores
have salons in them. During Halloween all stores carry costume supplies.
Several locations carry costume supplies year round. Check the website for
salon locations. Ricky's is adding additional stores, keep checking website
for their locations. CREDIT CARDS.

United Beauty Products 973-433-0080
216 Little Falls Rd., Unit 7   FAX 973-433-0079
Cedar Grove, NJ 07009
Hours: 9-5 Mon-Fri   E-mail: support@unitedbeauty.com
www.unitedbeauty.com
Beauty salon supplies. Will sell small quantities. Phone orders. Will ship.
RENTALS. CREDIT CARDS.

Wig City 212-421-1618
217 E 60th St. (2nd-3rd Ave)
NY, NY 10022
Hours: 10-5 Mon-Sat
Inexpensive wigs. CREDIT CARDS.

Wigboys Theatrical Wigs 707-763-1978
170 Rainsville Rd.   FAX (Same)
Petaluma, CA 94952
Hours: 9-5 Mon-Fri   E-mail: information@wigboys.com
www.wigboys.com
Wonderful selection of theatrical wigs. Wigs are styled according to your
research. Visit their website to view their stock. Nice folks to deal with.
RENTALS.

HAMPERS

BMI Supply 518-793-6706
571 Queensbury Ave.   800-836-0524
Queensbury, NY 12804   FAX 518-793-6181
Hours: 8-6 Mon-Fri   E-mail: bminy@bmisupply.com
www.bmisupply.com
A full-line theatrical supply house and on-site contractor. Retail and
wholesale at everyday wholesale prices. Special effects. Sales only. CREDIT
CARDS.

I. Weiss and Sons, Inc. 718-706-8139
2-07 Borden Ave. (Vernon-Jackson Ave)   888-325-7192
Long Island City, NY 11101   FAX 718-482-9410
Hours: 8-5:30 Mon-Fri   E-mail: info@iweiss.com
www.iweiss.com
Canvas storage hampers, standard and custom sizes. Plywood tops, swivel
castors.

HAMPERS

Movers Supply House, Inc. 718-671-1200
1476 E 222nd St. (Baychester Ave)   800-432-1MSH
Bronx,, NY 10469   FAX 718-379-4403
Hours: 8-5 Mon-Fri
www.moversupply.com
Packing blankets, loading straps, hampers, j-bars; good prices; will ship COD.
CREDIT CARDS.

Mutual Hardware Corp. 718-361-2480
36-27 Vernon Blvd. (Vernon Blvd)   866-361-2480
Long Island City, NY 11106   FAX 718-786-9591
Hours: 8:30-4:30 Mon-Fri
www.mutualhardware.com
Canvas storage hampers; theatrical hardware. Contact John or Sal.

HANDICRAFTS

Hand-Made by Mary Pat 718-768-3571
25 Jackson Pl. (6-7th Ave)
Brooklyn, NY 11215
Hours: 10-7 Mon-Sat   E-mail: firesun1@hotmail.com
Knitted and crocheted items of all kinds: sweaters, socks, hats, blankets,
dresses, jackets, pants, etc.

The Rocking Horse Shop . . . .+44 (0)1759-368737
Fangfoss   FAX +44 (0)1759-368-194
York, England, YO41 5JH
Hours: 9-4 Mon-Sat (Great Britain)   E-mail: info@rockinghorse.co.uk
www.rockinghorse.co.uk
Everything you need to carve a rocking horse. Bridles, saddles, glass eyes,
real horsehair and artificial manes and tails, rocking hardware, plans, full kits.
Also ¡The Rocking Horse Maker,¡ a wonderful book on the art of carving. Full
color catalog. CREDIT CARDS.

Stone Soup Studios 610-867-4626
301 Broadway
Bethlehem, PA 18015
Hours: 10-4 Tue-Sat   E-mail: manager@stonesoupbethlehem.com
www.stonesoupbethlehem.com
Working artist studio featuring sophisticated one-of-a kind and limited
edition artist wares. Hand painted silk scarves, ceramics, jewelry, totes and
handbags, baby items fine wood products and more. CREDIT CARDS.

Tribeca Potters 212-431-7631
313 W 37th St., 4th Fl. (8-9th Aves)   877-687-0124
NY, NY 10018   FAX 212-431-8938
Hours: 10-5 Mon-Sat / or by appt.   E-mail: tribeccapotters@tribecapotters.com
www.tribecapotters.com
African masks, ceramics, terra-cotta goods. Call on Saturdays during summer.

HARDWARE: DECORATIVE

18th Century Hardware 724-694-2708
131 E 3rd St.   FAX 724-694-9587
Derry, PA 15627
Hours: 8:30-4:30 Tue-Fri
Will reproduce period hardware via sand casting. Does lovely finishing. No Credit Cards.

A.F. Supply 212-243-5400
22 W 21st St., 5th Fl. (5-6th Ave)   800-366-2284
NY, NY 10010   FAX 212-243-2403
Hours: 9-5 Mon-Fri Appointment recommended.   E-mail: info@afnewyork.com
www.afsupply.com / www.afnewyork.com
A treasure trove of thousands of doorknobs. Can adapt old knobs to new mechanisms and vice versa. RENTALS. CREDIT CARDS.

Acorn Manufacturing Company, Inc. 800-835-0121
PO Box 31   508-339-4500
Mansfield, MA 02048   FAX 508-339-0104
Hours: 8-4 Mon-Thurs / 8-1 Fri   E-mail: acorninfo@acornmfg.com
www.acornmfg.com
Forged iron hardware in rough, smooth iron and hand-forged stainless steel. Catalog. Website lists many local distributors. CREDIT CARDS.

Architectural Grille 718-832-1200
42 Second Ave.   (outside of NY only) 800-387-6267
Brooklyn, NY 11215   FAX 718-832-1390
Hours: 8-5 Mon-Thurs / 8-4:30 Fri   E-mail: info@archgrille.com
www.archgrille.com
Bar grilles and perforated grilles in stock. Catalog available.

The Brass Center 212-421-0090
248 E 58th St. (2nd-3rd Ave)   FAX 212-371-7088
NY, NY 10022
Hours: 8:30-5 Mon-Fri   E-mail: info@thebrasscenter.com
www.thebrasscenter.com
Carries the complete line of Baldwin products as well as other major lines. Also bath accessories. Wholesale and retail. CREDIT CARDS.

Decoware, Inc. 718-871-1212
944 McDonald Ave. (Ave F-18th Ave)   877-871-1212
Brooklyn, NY 11218   FAX 718-972-3277
Hours: 9:30-5:30 Mon-Wed / 9:30-6:30 Thurs / 9:30-11:30 Fri / 10-4:30 Sun
www.decow.com   E-mail: sales@decow.com
Large selection of decorative hardware and plumbing fixtures. Delivery service available. CREDIT CARDS.

Gracious Home 212-988-8990
1220, 1217, 1201 Third Ave.(70th-71st St)   212-517-6300
NY, NY 10021   FAX 212-249-1534
Hours: 8-7 Mon-Fri / 9-7 Sat / 10-6 Sun

G-H

Gracious Home (cont.) 212-231-7800
1992 Broadway(67th St)   800-237-3404
NY, NY 10023   FAX 212-875-9976
Hours: 9-9 Mon-Sat / 10-7 Sun   E-mail: info@gracioushome.com
www.gracioushome.com
Decorative hardware, faucets, lighting fixtures and bulbs, towel bars,
hampers, bath accessories; also bed linens, picture frames and decorative
items. CREDIT CARDS.

P.E. Guerin 212-243-5270
23 Jane St. (Greenwich-8th Ave)   FAX 212-727-2290
NY, NY 10014
Hours: 10-4 Mon-Fri by appt   E-mail: peguerin@aol.com
www.peguerin.com
Primarily custom, 4-8 week delivery. Excellent selection of all types of
hardware for your home or palace; catalog; very expensive. CREDIT CARDS.

H.T. Sales 212-265-0747
718 Tenth Ave. (49-50th St.)   877-HARDWARE
NY, NY 10019   FAX 212-262-0150
Hours: 7:30-4:30 Mon-Fri   E-mail: henry@htsalescompany.com
www.htsalescompany.com
Decorative and bath hardware division located at 726 10th Ave. CREDIT
CARDS.

Joseph Biunno Ltd. / Finials Unlimited 718-729-5630
21-07 Borden Ave., 3rd FL   FAX 718-729-5628
Long Island City, NY 11101
Hours: 9-5 Mon-Fri / or by appt.   E-mail: finunlim@aol.com
www.antiquefurnitureusa.com
In stock and custom finials, tiebacks, rosettes, drapery rings, poles.
Wonderful finials in larger (9" x4") sizes. CREDIT CARDS.

Kraft Hardware, Inc. 212-838-2214
315 E 62nd St. (1st-2nd Ave)   FAX 212-644-9254
NY, NY 10065
Hours: 9-5 Mon-Fri
www.kraft-hardware.com
Door, cabinet and bathroom hardware. CREDIT CARDS.

Lumberland Hardware 212-696-0022
368 Third Ave. (29th St)   FAX 212-481-9223
NY, NY 10016
Hours: 9-7 Mon-Sat
Wooden spindles, hardwood, some decorative hardware, mouldings and
power tools; same day delivery for orders received by 1 pm. CREDIT CARDS.

Nanz Custom Hardware 212-367-7000
20 Vandam St. (Varick St)   FAX 212-367-7375
NY, NY 10013
Hours: by appt.   E-mail: info@nanz.com
www.nanz.com
Repro doorknobs and escutcheons. (Individually made glass spheres with
air-bubble "seeds" that resemble antique paperweights.)

Selby Furniture Hardware Co. 718-993-3700
321 Rider Ave. (140th St)   800-224-0059
Bronx, NY 10451   FAX 718-993-3143
Hours: 8:30-4:30 Mon-Fri   E-mail: selbern@aol.com
www.selbyhardware.com
Furniture hardware wholesalers; catalog. $25 walk-in minimum. Shipping charge for orders under $100. CREDIT CARDS.

Simonís Hardware 212-532-9220
421 Third Ave. (29-30th St)   888-274-6667
NY, NY 10016   FAX 212-725-3609
Hours: 8-5:30 Mon-Fri / 8-7 Thurs / 10-6 Sat
                          E-mail: sercice@simons-hardware.com
www.simons-hardware.com
Enormous selection decorative bath, kitchen and functional hardware; go early in the day. Catalog. CREDIT CARDS.

The Terrence Conran Shop 212-755-9079
888 Broadway Lower Level (18-19th St)   FAX 212-755-3989
NY, NY 10003
Hours: 11-8 Mon-Fri / 10-7 Sat / 12-6 Sun
                  E-mail: terenceconranshop@conranusa.com
www.conranusa.com
Designer furniture, household, bedding and bath, textiles and hardware. Very nice people. Will do rentals to film and television. CREDIT CARDS.

Tremont Nail Co. 508-339-4500
PO Box 31   800-835-0121
Mansfield, MA 02048   FAX 508-339-0104
Hours: 8-5 Mon-Thurs / 8-4 Fri
www.tremontnail.com
20 varieties of old-fashioned and special patterned cut nails; catalog. $25 minimum. CREDIT CARDS.

HARDWARE: GENERAL

American Home Hardware 212-765-7356
590 Ninth Ave. (42-43rd St)   FAX 212-757-7045
NY, NY 10036
Hours: 8-7 Mon-Fri / 8:30-6 Sat / 8:30-4 Sun
General neighborhood hardware and housewares store. They carry Benjamin Moore paints, moving supplies and wardrobe boxes. Very nice to deal with. CREDIT CARDS.

B & N Hardware 212-242-1136
12 W 19th St. (5-6th Ave)   FAX 212-255-3973
NY, NY 10011
Hours: 8-5 Mon-Fri / 9-2 Sat
Good selection of hardware, tools, paint. Ask for Dave. CREDIT CARDS.

G-H

Barry Supply Co. 212-242-5200
36 W 17th St. (5-6th Ave)   FAX 212-675-7094
NY, NY 10011
Hours: 10-4 Mon-Fri   E-mail: barsup@hotmail.com
New and obsolete replacement parts for windows and patio doors. Sash weights, tilt latches, etc. No minimum. Any item you can't find, ask. They'll get it for you. No credit cards.

Best Hardware & Mill Supply, Inc. 516 354-0529
406 Jericho Tpke. (Sycamore-Lewis Ave)   FAX 516-354-1908
Floral Park, NY 11010
Hours: 7:30-5:30 Mon-Thurs / 7:30-7 Fri / 8-5 Sat / 10-2:30 Sun
Cobalt drill bits, milling supplies, tools, case-hardened bolts, hardware.
CREDIT CARDS.

Garden Hardware & Supply Co. 212-247-2888
701 Tenth Ave. (47-48th St)   FAX 212-247-2859
NY, NY 10036
Hours: 8:30-5 Mon-Fri / 8:30-2 Sat
Known as "Broadway's Hardware Store," this icon carries a large selection of "to the trade" hardware and supplies. Don't be surprised with the disorganization of the store, Bobby can help you find just about anything.
CREDIT CARDS.

H.T. Sales 212-265-0747
718 Tenth Ave. (49-50th St.)   877-HARDWARE
NY, NY 10019   FAX 212-262-0150
Hours: 7:30-4:30 Mon-Fri   E-mail: henry@htsalescompany.com
www.htsalescompany.com
Decorative and bath hardware division located at 726 10th Ave, tools division located at 718 10th Ave. CREDIT CARDS.

Home Depot 800-553-3199
550 Hamilton Ave.(16-17th St)   718-832-8553
Brooklyn, NY 11232
Hours: 6-12pm Mon-Sat / 8-9pm Sun

124-04 31st Ave.(College Point Blvd)   718-661-4608
Flushing, NY 11354   FAX 718-670-3437
Hours: 6-11pm Mon-Sat / 7-9pm Sun

40 W 23rd St.(5-6th Ave)   212-929-9571
NY, NY 10010
Hours: 7-9pm Mon-Sat / 8-7 Sun

980 Third Ave.(58-59th St)   212-888-1512
NY, NY 10022
Hours: 7-9pm Mon-Sat / 8-7 Sun

50-10 Northern Blvd.(50th St-Newtown Rd)   718-278-9031
Long Island City, NY 11101
Hours: 6-11pm Mon-Sat / 8-9pm Sun
www.homedepot.com
Hardware, tools, lumber, plumbing supplies, gardening supplies, electrical and lighting supplies. Windows, doors and cabinets. Queens and Brooklyn locations open 24-hrs. for those emergency needs (less crowded then, too.) Check web for additional locations. CREDIT CARDS.

G-H

HomeFront Hardware 212-545-1447
202 E 29th St. (2nd-3rd Aves) FAX 212-545-0092
NY, NY 10016
Hours: 24-hr Daily
www.homefronthardware.com
Hardware, housewares and tool rentals. CREDIT CARDS.

Jamali Garden & Hardware Supplies, Inc. 212-244-4025
149 W 28th St. (6-7th Ave) 212-594-5265
NY, NY 10001 FAX 212-967-8196
Hours: 6:30-5 Mon-Sat
www.jamaligarden.com
Hardware, garden supplies and floral supplies. Complete line of potting soil and fertilizers. Great selection of pottery from around the world and unique containers. CREDIT CARDS.

McMaster-Carr Supply Co. 609-259-8900
200 New Canton Way FAX 609-259-3575
Robbinsville, NJ 08691
Hours: 24-hrs. / 7 days E-mail: nj.sales@mcmaster.com
www.mcmaster.com
Top quality items, esp. hardware. A vast selection of even the hard-to-find stuff. Most items available for next day delivery to NYC via UPS. Great catalog. CREDIT CARDS.

Midtown Hardware 212-682-7858
155 E 45th St. (3rd-Lex Ave) FAX 212-986-4674
NY, NY 10017
Hours: 9-6 Mon-Fri / 9-5 Sat
Good selection of hardware, paint and houseware items. CREDIT CARDS.

MSC Industrial Supply Co. 717-865-5888
100 MSC Dr. 800-645-7270
Jonestown, PA 17038 FAX 717-861-5810
Hours: 7-5 Mon-Fri E-mail: branchhbu@mscdirect.com
www.mscdirect.com
Mail order machine tools; drills, reamers, cutters, etc.; great catalog, $25 minimum. Extensive hardware selection. Good one stop shop for large machines and tools. Competitive prices. Also good source for transmission parts. Order by 4 pm and get items delivered next day. Several depots across US. CREDIT CARDS.

Rockler Woodworking and Hardware 800-279-4441
4365 Willow Dr. 763-478-8201
Hamel, MN 55340 FAX 763-478-8395
Hours: Varies with locations E-mail: info@rockler.com
www.rockler.com
Especially good selection of hardware, some for knockdowns, tools, caning supplies, veneers and veneering. Wooden parts, catalog. 30 retail stores. CREDIT CARDS.

G-H

Seattle Fabrics 206-525-0670
8702 Aurora Ave. N (N 87th St)   866-925-0670
Seattle, WA 98103   FAX 206-525-0779
Hours: 9-6 Mon-Sat   E-mail: seattlefabrics@msn.com
www.seattlefabrics.com
*Outdoor and recreational fabric & hardware. Specialty fabrics, webbing,
thread and zippers; neoprene and closed cell foam. Patterns for outdoor and
sports attire; equestrian, tents and backpacks. Fabric samples available.
CREDIT CARDS.*

Sidís Hardware 718-875-2259
345 Jay St. (Myrtle-Willoughby St)   FAX 718-852-3369
Brooklyn, NY 11201
Hours: 8-6:15 Mon-Fri / 8-5:45 Sat / 10-4:45 Sun
www.sidshardware.com   E-mail: info@sidshardware.com
*Large selection of general and household hardware, power tools and
household supplies. CREDIT CARDS.*

Vercesi Hardware 212-475-1883
152 E 23rd St. (3rd-Lex Ave)   FAX 212-979-8482
NY, NY 10010
Hours: 8-7 Mon-Fri / 9-7 Sat / 12-5 Sun   E-mail: acehardwarestore@gmail.com
www.vercesihardware.com
*A wonderfully stocked general hardware store. Electrical and plumbing parts.
Housewares, paints, appliances and window blinds. Accounts welcome. Note
the late hours. CREDIT CARDS.*

Harold C. Wolff, Inc. Hardware 212-227-2128
76 Maiden Ln., Ste 508   FAX 212-385-0794
NY, NY 10038
Hours: 8-4 Mon-Fri
General hardware. CREDIT CARDS.

HARDWOODS & VENEERS

Center Lumber Company 973-742-8300
85 Fulton St.   FAX 973-742-8303
Paterson, NJ 07509
Hours: 7:30-5 Mon-Fri   E-mail: astrid.frank@centerlumber.com
*Great selection of custom mouldings, with many profiles not seen in the
regular catalogs. Youíll need some lead time, but definitely worth it.*

M.L. Condon Co., Inc..............................914-946-4111
250 Ferris Ave.   FAX 914-946-3779
White Plains, NY 10603
Hours: 8-4:30 Mon-Fri
*Hardwood lumber, hardwood and marine plywood and mouldings; planing
and ripping facilities; deliveries. Good prices, no minimum. Good quality.
Catalog. No credit cards.*

G-H

Constantines Wood Center of Florida, Inc. 954-561-1716
   1040 E Oakland Park Blvd.   800-443-9667
   Ft. Lauderdale, FL 33334   FAX 954-565-8149
   Hours: 8:-5:30 Mon-Fri / 9-3 Sat
   www.constantines.com
   *Hardwoods, veneers, exotic woods, moulding, hardware and woodworking
   tools. Good products, good service. Online catalog. Orders shipped. CREDIT
   CARDS.*

Rosenzweig Lumber Corp. 718-585-8050
   801 E 135th St. (near Bruckner Blvd)   800-228-7674
   Bronx, NY 10454   FAX 718-292-8611
   Hours: 7-4 Mon-Fri / 9:30-4 pick-ups   E-mail: admin@rosenzweiglumber.com
   www.rosenzweiglumber.com
   *Good selection hardwoods, veneers, plywood, lumber and mouldings; good
   prices, prompt next day delivery. Catalog. CREDIT CARDS.*

HATS

G-H

Aegean Imports 650-593-8300
   Lyell St.   FAX 650-593-8000
   San Carlos, CA 94070
   Hours: 8:30-5 Mon-Fri
   Greek fishermen's hats; quantity mail order only. CREDIT CARDS.

Bollman Hats Co. 212-981-9945
   411 Fifth Ave., 2nd Fl. (34th St)   FAX 212-981-9848
   NY, NY 10016
   Hours: 8:30-5 Mon-Thurs / 8:30-4:30 Fri
   www.bollmanhats.com
   Manufacturer of period hats. CREDIT CARDS.

Fibre-Metal Products Co. 610-459-5300
   PO Box 248, Baltimore Pike (Rt. 1)   800-523-7048
   Concordville, PA 19331   FAX 800-852-3261
   Hours: 8-4:30 Mon-Fri   E-mail: sales@fibre-metal.com
   www.fibre-metal.com
   Hard hats manufacturer, welding safety. Catalog.

Grey Owl Indian Crafts 732-389-4626
   15 Meridian Rd.   (orders) 800-487-2376
   Eatontown, NJ 07724   FAX 732-389-4629
   Hours: 9-5 Mon-Fri   E-mail: sales@greyowlcrafts.com
   www.greyowlcrafts.com
   Kits for American Indian headdresses and crafts; catalog. CREDIT CARDS.

Halloween Adventure 212-673-4546
   104 Fourth Ave. (11-12th St)   FAX 212-358-0927
   NY, NY 10003
   Hours: 11-8 Mon-Sat / 12-7 Sun
   www.newyorkcostumes.com
   *The masters of masquerade with the city's largest selection of costumes,
   masks, wigs, magic supplies and theatrical make-up, plus custom fangs, f/x
   kits and much more. CREDIT CARDS.*

Hat/Cap Exchange 302-478-9338
PO Box 7507   FAX: 866-270-7668
Wilmington, DE 19803
Hours: 10-4 Mon-Fri   E-mail: John.hatcap@gmail.com
www.hatcapexchange.com
Wholesale hats, good prices; extra charge for split cartons. CREDIT CARDS.

Hatcrafters, Inc. 610-623-2620
20 N Springfield Rd.   866-651-4021
Clifton Heights, PA 19018   FAX 610-284-2620
Hours: 8-5 Mon-Fri   E-mail: info@hatcrafters.com
www.hatcrafters.com
Theatrical hats, stock and custom; military reproductions; catalog. CREDIT CARDS.

J. J. Hat Center 212-239-4368
310 Fifth Ave. (31st-32nd St)   800-622-1911
NY, NY 10001   FAX 212-971-0406
Hours: 9-6 Mon-Fri / 9:30-5:30 Sat   E-mail: www.jjhatctr@aol.com
www.jjhatcenter.com
All types of hats including Stetsons. CREDIT CARDS.

Jacobson Hat Co., Inc. 570-342-7887
1301Ridge Row   800-233-4690
Scranton, PA 18510   FAX 800-882-5428
Hours: 8:30-5:30 Mon-Fri   E-mail: info@jhats.com
www.jhats.com
Theatrical hats and hat frames, novelty and party hats, custom-made; large orders; catalog. CREDIT CARDS.

Keystone Uniform Cap 215-922-5493
801 N Front St.   FAX 215-922-5161
Philadelphia, PA 19123
Hours: 7:30-4 Mon-Fri   E-mail: david@keystoneuniformcap.com
www.keystoneuniformcap.com
Uniform hats. Catalog available. CREDIT CARDS.

Leon Fuks, Inc. 718-567-2257
170 53rd St. (6th Ave)   FAX 718-567-2259
Brooklyn, NY 11232
Hours: 7:30-5:30 Mon-Fri
Straw hats and braids. Mail order. Call before stopping in.

Meyer the Hatter 504-525-1048
120 St. Charles Ave.   800-882-2506
New Orleans, LA 70130   FAX 504-525-0259
Hours: 10-5:45 Mon-Sat   E-mail: info@meyerthehatter.com
www.meyerthehatter.com
The South's largest hat store offering a wide selection of quality hats and caps from the world's leading headwear manufacturers. Visit website for wonderful selection. Celebrating its 64th Anniversary. CREDIT CARDS.

O.K. Uniforms Co. 212-791-9789
253 Church St. (Franklin-Leonard)   FAX 212-791-9795
NY, NY 10013
Hours: 9:45-5:45 Mon-Thurs / 9:45-2 Fri / 12-4 Sun
www.okuniform.com   E-mail: okuniform@gmail.com
Complete selection of uniforms and accessories for all service industries.
Name and logo emblems available. Sales only. CREDIT CARDS.

Peacock's Marching World 928-692-2263
4755 Olympic Dr.   800-733-2263
Kingman, AZ 86401   FAX 928-692-2270
Hours: 9-5:30 Mon-Fri / Call on Saturdays   E-mail: sales@marchingworld.com
www.marchingworld.com
Marching props and accessories for bands and colorguards including hats,
gloves, marching shoes and prop rifles. CREDIT CARDS.

Sacred Feather 608-255-2071
417 State St.   800-208-0699
Madison, WI 53703   FAX 608-255-1626
Hours: 10-6 Mon-Sat / 11-5 Sun   E-mail: badame@sacredfeather.com
www.sacredfeather.com
Derbies, toppers, Western, fedoras, some theatrical, etc.; no catalog. Phone
and mail orders. CREDIT CARDS.

Stetson Hats 816-233-8031
3601 S Leonard Rd.   (factory) 972-494-0511
St. Joseph, MO 64503   FAX 816-233-8032
Hours: 8:30-4:30 Mon-Fri / 8-4 Sat
www.stetsonhat.com
Derbies, toppers, Western hats; wholesale only. Customer service 800-325-
2662. CREDIT CARDS.

Tracey Tooker 212-966-6695
18 Mercer St., 4th FL (Grand/Canal)   561-628-3494
NY, NY 10013   FAX 212-219-1750
Hours: Call for appt.
Custom fashion hats, some stock. CREDIT CARDS.

Top Hats of America 516-599-3188
16 Broadway   FAX 516-599-0408
Malverne, NY 11565
Hours: 8 - 4:30 Mon-Fri   E-mail: dave@tophats.com
Satin top hats, collapsible top hats, custom work, affordable. Catalog.

GARY WHITE / THE CUSTOM HATTER 716-896-3722
1318 Broadway St.   716-474-3071
Buffalo, NY 14212
Hours: 10-5 Mon-Fri
www.custom-hatter.com
Designing and creating custom-made mens dress, Western felt and fine
Panama straw hats. Period accurate from 1800 to 2006. Hat renovating,
reconstruction and blocking. CREDIT CARDS. Member ATAC.

G-H

Worth & Worth 212-265-2887
45 W 57th St. # 602   800-428-7467
NY, NY 10019   FAX 212-265-2998
Hours: 10-6 Mon-Tue / 10-7 Wed-Sat   E-mail: info@hatshop.com
www.hatshop.com
A haberdashery with in-house manufacturing of hats and accessories for over
60 years. CREDIT CARDS.

HOBBY SHOPS & SUPPLIES
See also: ART SUPPLIES
    CASTING AND MODELING SUPPLIES
    DOLLS, DOLL PARTS & DOLLHOUSES

Americaís Hobby Center 800-242-1931
8300 Tonnelle Ave.   201-662-0777
North Bergen, NJ 07047
Hours: 9-5:30 Mon-Fri / 9-4 Sat   E-mail: sales@ahc1931.com
www.ahc1931.com
Train and airplane kits, good for model hardware; slow service; catalogs.
CREDIT CARDS.

Engineering Model Associates 626-912-7016
1020 S Wallace Pl.   800-666-7015
City of Industry, CA 91748   FAX 626-965-2036
Hours: 7:30-4 Mon-Fri   E-mail: plastruct@plastruct.com
www.plastruct.com
Wide selection of plastic scale model parts for architectural and engineering
models. Wholesale and retail. On-line catalog and purchase. Minimum $20.
CREDIT CARDS.

Lifoam Products, Inc. 410-889-1023
235 Schilling Cr., Ste. 111   800-638-1471
Hunt Valley, MD 21031   FAX 800-937-3626
Hours: 8-5 Mon-Fri
www.lifoam.com
Wholesale and retail lichen, surface texturing materials, trees; various local
distributors; catalog. $25 minimum.

M. H. Industries / The Station 717-774-7096
213 9th St. (Bridge St)   FAX 717-774-8862
New Cumberland, PA 17070
Hours: 10-5 Tue-Fri / 10-4 Sat
Basswood stripwood, mouldings, dollhouse lumber, model trains and
accessories, all gauges. Catalog. CREDIT CARDS.

Microform Models, Inc. 508-485-9333
158 Winter St.   877-489-3011
Marlborough, MA 01752
Hours: 8-4:30 Mon-Fri   E-mail: greatservice@microformmodels.com
www.microformmodels.com
Cast metal furniture, props, trees, etc.; great selection in 1/4î, some 1/2î
chairs, inexpensive. Phone orders. Shipping. Catalog with actual size photos.
CREDIT CARDS.

G-H

Plastruct 626-912-7016
1040 S Wallace Pl.   800-666-7015
City of Industry, CA 91748   FAX 626-965-2036
Hours: 7:30-4 Mon-Fri   E-mail: plastruct@plastruct.com
www.plastruct.com
Good selection of model pieces and supplies, 1/2î and 1/4î scale. Catalog $5. CREDIT CARDS.

Polyform Products 847-427-0020
1901 Estes St.   FAX 847-427-0426
Elk Grove Village, IL 60007
Hours: 8-4:30 Mon-Thurs / 7-3:30 Fri   E-mail: info@polyformproducts.com
www.sculpey.com
Sculpey manufacturer. Wholesale and retail. Catalog. CREDIT CARDS.

Railroad Warehouse 732-295-2202
3245 Rte. 88   FAX 732-295-2434
Pt Pleasant, NJ 08742
Hours: 12-5 Mon / 11-6 Tue-Wed / 11-7 Thurs-Fri / 11-5:30 Sat / 11-5 SunE-mail:
rrwhouse@verizon.net
www.railroadwarehouse.net
Custom train maker; hobby and craft supplies. Brand name trains, models.

The Red Caboose 212-575-0155
23 W 45th St. Downstairs (5-6th Ave)   FAX 212-575-0272
NY, NY 10036
Hours: 11:30-7 Mon-Fri / 11:30-5 Sat
www.theredcaboose.com
Brass, simulated surfaces, choppers; train and ship models and accessories. Die-cast airplanes and full range of architectural supplies for model building. Paints, glues and tools. CREDIT CARDS.

Rudy's Hobby & Art 718-545-8280
3516 30th Ave. (35-36th St)
Astoria, NY 11103
Hours: 11-6:30 Wed-Sat
Great hobby shop. Also carries art supplies. No credit cards.

Special Shapes Co., Inc. 773-229-0740
6911 W 59th St.   800 51SHAPE
Chicago, IL 60638   FAX 773-229-0746
Hours: 9-4 Mon-Fri
www.specialshapes.com
Brass rod and structural shapes in 3' lengths, brass strips, sheets and miniature screws; 2-3 week delivery; flier. CREDIT CARDS.

Train World 718-436-7072
751 McDonald Ave. (Ditmas-Cortelyou Rd)   800-541-7010
Brooklyn, NY 11218   FAX 718-972-8514
Hours: 10-6 Mon-Sat   E-mail: orders@trainworld.com
www.trainworld.com
Large stock of trains and accessories. CREDIT CARDS.

G-H

Trainland 516-599-7080
293 Sunrise Hwy
Lynbrook, NY 11563
Hours: 10-6 Mon-Sat   E-mail: orders@trainworld.com
www.trainworld.com
Large stock of trains and accessories. CREDIT CARDS.

HOLIDAY DECORATIONS

Kurt S. Adler 212-924-0900
7 W 34th St. (5th Ave)   FAX 212-807-0575
NY, NY 10010
Hours: 9-5:30 Mon-Fri   www.info@kurtadler.com
www.kurtadler.com
Christmas: lights, decorations, ornaments, nativity scenes. Wholesale, $500
minimum. Catalog.

American Christmas Decorations, Inc. 718-402-9700
1135 Bronx River Ave. (Bruckner Blvd-Westchester Ave)   FAX 718-402-9704
Bronx, NY 10472
Hours: 9-5 Mon-Fri   E-mail: magic@americanxmas.com
www.americanxmas.com
Custom design, installation, removal, storage and refurbishing of holiday
decorations. 2' to 50' Christmas trees; 2' to 20' wreaths, garlands, menorahs,
etc. Also has animated figures. RENTALS.

American Foliage & Design Group .212-741-5555
122 W 22nd St. (6-7th Ave)   FAX 212-741-9499
NY, NY 10011
Hours: 8-5 Mon-Fri   E-mail: afdesigngr@aol.com
www.americanfoliagedesign.com
Silk and live flowers. Christmas creations for TV, print work, special events.
RENTALS.

Authentiques 212-675-2179
255 W 18th St. (7-8th Ave)
NY, NY 10011
Hours: 12-6 Wed-Sat / 1-6 Sun or by appt.   E-mail: fab.stuff@verizon.net
www.fab-stuff.com
Authentic 1950s Christmas decorations. Wonderful selection. Speak to
Robert. Will help in research.

Christmas Cottage 212-333-7380
871 Seventh Ave. (55-56th St)
NY, NY 10019
Hours: 9-7 Mon-Sat / 9-6 Sun
www.thechristmascottage.com
General Christmas decorations; lights, ornaments, nativity scenes. Nice
collectable ornaments and figurines. Also another location in Mystic, CT.
CREDIT CARDS.

G-H

 **ATAC**

HYDRAULICS & PNEUMATICS

The Feather Tree Co. 608-837-7669
PO Box 281   FAX 608-834-9223
Sun Prarie, WI 53590
Hours: 10-5 Mon-Fri / 24-hrs. on website
www.feathertrees.com   E-mail: websitemail@feathertrees.com
The Feather Tree Co. is renewing the art-form of the Goosefeather Christmas Tree. All of their trees are handmade in Wisconsin and use real goose feathers. Trees come in various sizes and 10 different colors. Visit website. CREDIT CARDS.

Hionis Greenhouses, Inc. 908-534-7710
4 Coddington Rd.   FAX 908-534-7720
Whitehouse Station, NJ 08889
Hours: 9-6 Mon-Fri / 9-4 Sat   E-mail: hionisplants@yahoo.com
www.hionisgreenhouses.com
Flowering plants indoor and outdoor trees, florist supplies, orchids, pottery and holiday supplies. CREDIT CARDS. RENTALS.

Superior Studio Specilities 800-354-3049
401 N Western Ave.   312-850-9016
Chicago, IL 60612   FAX 312-850-9026
Hours: 8:30-5 Mon-Fri   Email: chicago@superiorstudio.com

2239 S Yates Ave   323-278-0100
Commerce, CA 90040   FAX 323-278-0111
Hours: 8:30-5 Mon-Fri   Email: la@superiorstudio.com
www.superiorstudio.com
Seamless papers, fake food, wire mannequin frames, foam boards and cutting supplies. CREDIT CARDS.

HYDRAULICS & PNEUMATICS
See also: SCENIC SHOPS
             SPECIAL EFFECTS SERVICES
             THEATRICAL HARDWARE & RIGGING EQUIPMENT

Northern Tool and Equipment 952-894-9510
2800 Southcross Dr. W   FAX 952-894-1020
Burnsville, MN 55306
Hours: 24 hours daily (catalog sales)
www.northerntool.com
Pumps, valves, accessories; catalog available. CREDIT CARDS.

W. B. Equipment Service Co. 914-522-5464
127 Oak St.   866-252-1903
Wood Ridge, NJ 07075   FAX 201-438-7830
Hours: 8-5 Mon-Fri   E-mail: stephen.cireco@verizon.net
www.wbequipment.com
Jacking and specialized equipment. Contact Jack Cireco. RENTALS.

G-H

NOTES

G-H

ICE, DRY ICE & FIREWOOD

Cole Mountain Ice Co. 212-397-1500
FAX 631-929-8111NY
Hours: 8-6 Mon-Sat   E-mail: colemountainice@yahoo.com
Ice, dry ice. Only phone orders or email.

Diamond Ice Cube 212-355-3734
556 River Ave. (149th St)   212-675-4115
Bronx, NY 10451   FAX 718-292-0781
Hours: 7-7 Mon-Sat / 8-12 Sun / (8-5 Sun in Summer)
Ice; block, cube; call day before for dry ice; firewood.

Humphrey's Farm, Inc. / Display Fake Foods 786-955-6584
PO Box 5800 (Mail Order)   FAX 305-749-8099
Miami Lakes, FL 33014
Hours: 9:30-5:30 Mon-Fri   E-mail: sales@displayfackfoods.com
www.displayfake foods.com
Artificial ice chips, shards and cubes. CREDIT CARDS.

Ice Fantasies, Inc. 800-NICE-ICE
220 Plymouth St., Ste. 5A   718-852-4895
Brooklyn, NY 11201   FAX 718-852-0434
Hours: 10-6 Tue-Sat   E-mail: fishman5@mac.com
www.icefantasies.com
*Custom ice props, ice sculpture, snow making. Sound stage and set
experience, live TV and photography. CREDIT CARDS.*

United City Ice Cube Co. 212-563-0819
503 W 45th St. (10-11th Ave)   FAX 212-397-0805
NY, NY 10036
Hours: 6am-9pm daily / call first
www.unitedcityicecube.com
Block, cube, dry ice.

IRONS & STEAMERS

Atlanta Thread & Supply Co. 770-389-9115
695 Red Oak Rd.   800-847-1001
Stockbridge, GA 30281   FAX 800-298-0403
Hours: 8:15-5:30 Mon-Fri   E-mail: awootton@atlantathread.com
www.atlantathread.com
*Wide selection of notions and sewing supplies from industrial machines to
home irons to needles and pins. Very helpful staff. Shipping and phone orders
available. Online catalog. CREDIT CARDS.*

Bernstein Display 212-683-2406
151 W 25th St.   718-237-2215
NY, NY 10001   FAX 718-237-5922
Hours: 9-5 Mon-Fri   E-mail: solutions@bernsteindisplay.com
www.bernsteindisplay.com
*Jiffy steamers, hangers, garment bags, rolling racks and display fixtures. Free
catalog. Shipping. RENTALS. CREDIT CARDS.*

I-K

European Finishing Equipment 201-460-9333
610 Washington Ave.   888-460-9292
Carlstadt, NJ 07072   FAX 201-964-1404
Hours: 9-5 Mon-Fri   E-mail: histeam@prodigy.net
www.histeam.com
Distributor for Namoto gravity-feed steam irons; full line of pressing equipment. On-line shopping available. CREDIT CARDS.

Jiffy Steamer Co. 800-525-4339
PO Box 869, 4462 Ken-Tenn Hwy.   731-885-6690
Union City, TN 38261   FAX 731-885-6692
Hours: 8-4 Mon-Fri
www.jiffysteamer.com
Manufacturers of garment, hat and wig steamers. CREDIT CARDS.

S & G Limited 570-344-4000
1321 E Drinker   FAX 570-343-0618
Dunmore, PA 18512
Hours: 8-4:30 Mon-Fri   E-mail: acpsr@epix.net
www.acpsr.com
Sussman products, new and used, some repairs done. CREDIT CARDS.

The Set Shop 212-255-3500
36 W 20th St. (5-6th Ave)   800-422-7831
NY, NY 10011   FAX 212-229-9600
Hours: 8:30-6 Mon-Fri   E-mail: info@setshop.com
www.setshop.com
Professional and compact garment steamers. RENTALS. CREDIT CARDS.

Sussman Automatic Corp. 718-937-4500
43-20 34th St. (Queens Blvd-43rd Ave)   800-76-STEAM
Long Island City, NY 11101   FAX 718-472-3256
Hours: 8-4 Mon-Fri   E-mail: slg@sussmancorp.com
www.sussmancorp.com
Manufacturer of Sussman irons and steamers; pressing tables. 24-hr, delivery service. Check website for West Coast office.

I-K

JEWELERS' TOOLS & SUPPLIES
See also: METALS & FOILS
            TRIMMINGS

Albest Metal Stamping Corp. 718-388-6000
1 Kent Ave. (N 13-N 14th St)   FAX 718-388-0404
Brooklyn, NY 11211
Hours: 8-5 Mon-Thurs / 8-1 Fri   E-mail: info@albest.com
www.albest.com
Leading manufacturer of metal and plastic hardware. Carries full line of Eisen products. Buckles, clips, military spec. hardware, rings, snap hooks, studs, nailheads, settings. CREDIT CARDS.

Allcraft Jewelry Supply Company 212-279-7077
135 W 29th St., Ste. 205 (6-7th Ave)   800-645-7124
NY, NY 10001   FAX 800-645-7125
Hours: 9-5 Mon-Fri   E-mail: allcrafttools@yahoo.com
www.allcraftdirect.com
Complete jewelers' supply: tools, metals, wire, wax, findings, buffing supplies, flexible shafts; scales, chemicals and soldering supplies. Very helpful. Online catalog.

The Compleat Sculptor, Inc. 212-243-6074
90 Vandam St. (Hudson-Greenwich)   800-9-SCULPT
NY, NY 10013   FAX 212-243-6374
Hours: 9-6 Mon, Thurs-Sat / 9-8 Tue-Wed   E-mail: tcs@sculpt.com
www.sculpt.com
Carries complete line of sculpture materials including; clay, wood, wax, sculpting tools, alabaster, marble, mold-making and casting materials, books, videos, pedestals and bases. Friendly and knowledgeable help. Catalog. Technical support line (212) 367-7561. CREDIT CARDS.

Eastern Findings Corp. 516-747-6640
116 County Courthouse Rd.   800-EFC-6640
Garden City Park, NY 11040   FAX 516-747-6650
Hours: 9-4:30 Mon-Fri   E-mail: sales@easternfindings.com
www.easternfindings.com
Extensive selection of jewelry findings, filigree shapes, chans and also beading supplies. CREDIT CARDS.

Fire Mountain Gems . . . .(orders) 800-355-2137
One Fire Mountain Way   800-423-2319
Grants Pass, OR 97526   FAX 800-292-3473
Hours: 6-6 Mon,Tue,Thurs,Fri / 9-6 Wed / 7-3 Sat
www.firemountaingems.com   E-mail: questions@firemtn.com
Mail order supplies for jewelry making. Their stock includes beads, cabochons, crystal, wire and findings. Fast, friendly service. Online catalog and shopping available. CREDIT CARDS.

C. R. Hill Co. 248-543-1555
2734 W 11 Mile Rd.
Berkley, MI 48072
Hours: 9-6 Mon / 9-4 Tue, Thurs, Fri / 9-12 Sat / Closed Wed & SunE-mail: info@crhill.com
www.crhill.com   E-mail: info@crhill.com
Jewelers' tools, casting supplies, metal sheet and tubing; catalog.

Jewelry Display of New York 212-768-3623
21 W 47th St., 2nd Fl. (5-6th Ave)   1-800-551-9906
NY, NY 10036   FAX 212-575-1198
Hours: 9-5:30 Mon-Fri   E-mail: info@jewelrydisplay.com
www.jewelrydisplay.com
Jewelry display trays,velvet, etc. Free catalog, online shopping.

New York Beads, Inc. 212-382-2994
1026 Sixth Ave. (38-39th St)   212-382-2986
NY, NY 10018   FAX 212-382-1060
Hours: 9-6:30 Mon-Fri / 10-5:30 Sat-Sun
Fine selection of beads, chains, findings and jewelery supplies. Wholesale and retail. CREDIT CARDS.

Ornamental Beads 303-567-2222
5712 W. 38th Ave.   800-876-6762
Wheat Ridge, CO 80212   FAX 303-567-4245
Hours: 10-6 Mon-Sat / 12/4 Sun   E-mail: orna@ornabead.com
www.ornabead.com
Jewelry findings and supplies, new and antique stones and beads, glass stones and clip on earrings. Costume jewelry. 40 years in business. Used by many Broadway shows.

C.S. Osborne Tools 973-483-3232
125 Jersey St.   FAX 973-484-3621
Harrison, NJ 07029
Hours: 8-4:30 Mon-Fri   E-mail: cso@csosborne.com
www.csosborne.com
Tools for metalwork; catalog.

T.W. Smith Welding Supply 718-388-7417
885 Meeker Ave. (Bridgewater-Varick St)   FAX 718-388-8943
Brooklyn, NY 11222
Hours: 7:30-4:30 Mon-Fri   E-mail: info@twsmith.com
www.twsmith.com
Soldering and welding supplies, propane.

JEWELRY

See also: CLOTHING: Antique & Vintage
            COSTUME CRAFTSPEOPLE: Costume Accessories
            ETHINIC GOODS: All Headings

Accessories Palace 212-594-8180
1250 Broadway, Unit D (32nd-33rd St)   FAX 212-594-8179
NY, NY 10001
Hours: 10-6 Mon-Fri / 10-5 Sat   E-mail: info@acc-palace.com
www.acc-palace.com
Wholesale fashion jewelry and accessories. Great selection of rhinestone and beaded jewelry. CREDIT CARDS.

I-K

Archangel Antiques 212-260-9313
334 E 9th St. (1st-2nd Ave)
NY, NY 10003
Hours: 1-7 Tue-Sun or by appt.
www.archangelantiquesnyc.com
Unbelievable selection of vintage buttons, cufflinks and eyeglasses; jewelry,
vintage clothing, collectibles, small furnishings, cigarette cases, etc.
Reasonably priced, very helpful. RENTALS.

Art & Industrial Design 212-477-0116
50 Great Jones St. (4th Ave)   FAX 212-477-1420
NY, NY 10012
Hours: 10-5 Mon-Fri / 10-1 Sat   E-mail: info@aid20c.com
www.aid20c.com
Collectors' jewelry, many pieces by 20th-century artists; 20th-century and Art
Deco furniture and furnishings; decorative accessories. RENTALS. CREDIT
CARDS.

S. Axelrod Co., Inc. 212-594-3022
7 W 30th St., 2nd Fl. (5th-B'way)   FAX 212-947-3787
NY, NY 10001
Hours: 9-5 Mon-Fri   E-mail: sales@axelrodco.com
www.axelrodco.com
Wholesaler of google eyes, decorative trims, rhinestones, metal findings.
Contact Harvey Axelrod. CREDIT CARDS.

Beads of Paradise 212-620-0642
16 E 17th St. (5th Ave-B'way)   FAX 212-741-3780
NY, NY 10003
Hours: 11-7:30 Sat / 12-6:30 Sun   E-mail: beadsofparadise@hotmail.com
www.beadsofparadisenyc.com
A selection of African jewelry, beads, sculpture and a few fabrics. Richard
Meyer Gallery (African sculpture, pottery and antique fabrics) is in back.
Retail and wholesale (min. for wholesale is $150). Will ship, no swatching.
RENTALS. CREDIT CARDS.

C'est Magnifique 212-475-1613
120 MacDougal St. (3rd-Bleecker St)   FAX 212-937-8070
NY, NY 10012
Hours: 12-8 Mon-Fri / 12-9 Sat
www.cest-magnifique.com
Gold and diamond jewelry from all over the world; see Alfred. CREDIT
CARDS.

The Clay Pot 718-788-6564
162 Seventh Ave. (Garfield-1st St)   (catalog) 800-989-3579
Brooklyn, NY 11215   FAX 718-965-1138
Hours: 11-7:30 Mon-Fri / 10:30-7 Sat / 12-6 Sun   E-mail: info@clay-pot.com
www.clay-pot.com
A "pottery gallery" featuring a number of quality potters; glass, jewelry and
wooden crafts. RENTALS. CREDIT CARDS.

I-K

Crystal Crown, Inc. 601-947-8074
183 Webb Davis Rd.   888-278-9531
Lucedale, MS 39452   FAX: 601-947-1860
Hours: 7:30-5 Mon-Thurs   E-mail: crystal@datasync.com
www.crystalcrown.com
USA manufacturer of crowns, tiaras, scepters, jewelry, and embroidered sashes for beauty pageants and weddings. Very reasonable prices and quick service. CREDIT CARDS.

Earrings Plaza 212-685-5666
1263 Broadway (31-32nd St)   800-477-6616
NY, NY 10001   FAX 212-685-5677
Hours: 8-7 Mon-Fri / 8-6 Sat / 9-5 Sun
$10 minimum purchase. Huge and inexpensive selection of costume jewelry. Fills the void of the old Woolworth's jewelry counter. CREDIT CARDS.

Michael C. Fina Co. 212-557-2500
545 Fifth Ave. (45th St)   800-289-3462
NY, NY 10017   FAX 212-557-3862
Hours: 11-8 Mon-Thurs / 10-7 Fri / 10-6 Sat / 11-6 Sun
www.michaelcfina.com
Silver, silverware, china, crystal and jewelry. Good prices. Catalog and online shopping available. CREDIT CARDS.

Full Line Accessories 212-967-5327
67 W 36th St. (6th Ave)   212-216-9253
NY, NY 10018   FAX 212-967-5176
Hours: 9-7 Mon-Sat / 10-6:30 Sun
Inexpensive costume jewelry with an extensive selection of fancy rhinestone pieces. CREDIT CARDS.

The Hammer / Robin David Ludwig .845-679-7335
PO Box 115 (mailing address)   845-532-5724
Bearsville, NY 12409
Hours: by appt.   E-mail: rth@fivepointsband.com
www.sweetbryar.com/hammer/
Custom jewelry and prop pieces; specializes in historically based art; works with gold, silver and brass; also miniature to full scale armor. Portfolio available on request. CREDIT CARDS thru PayPal only.

HawaiianKineStuff.com 800-793-0901
4348 Waialae Ave. # 182
Honolulu, HI 96816
Hours: 10-5 (Hawaiian Time) Mon-Sat
www.hawaiiankinestuff.com   E-mail: customerservice@hawaiiankinestuff.com
Excellent source for EVERYTHING Hawaiian. Aloha wear, food items, tiki items, jewelry, silk leis and Hawaiian art prints. They actually answer the phone Aloha! CREDIT CARDS.

I-K

Georg Jensen Silversmiths 212-759-6457
  687 Madison Ave. (61-62nd St)   FAX 212-355-1529
  NY, NY 10065
  Hours: 10-6 Mon-Sat / 12-5 Sun
  www.georgjensen.com
  Modern design sterling silver, stainless flatware, barware and gifts. Sterling
  silver and 18 carat jewelry and watches. Catalog. Contact Martha Palhno.
  RENTALS. CREDIT CARDS.

Jules J. Karp Coins & Bullion, Inc. 212-943-5770
  125 Maiden Ln.   FAX 212-785-4675
  NY, NY 10038
  Hours: 9-5 Mon-Fri   E-mail: juleskarp2@aol.com
  www.juelskarpcoinsandbullioninc.com
  Rare coins and bullion, currency and jewelry. Buy backs possible. RENTALS.

Kenjo Jewelers 212-333-7220
  40 W 57th St. (5-6th Ave)
  NY, NY 10019
  Hours: 10-6 Mon-Fri /10:30-5:30 Sat
  Jewelry, wedding bands, contemporary watches; pricey; not costume jewelry.
  RENTALS. CREDIT CARDS.

Light Curves / Joan Nicole 845-434-5081
  10 Rockview Lane   845-978-7653
  Loch Sheldrake, NY 12759   FAX 845-434-5081
  Hours: By appt., 24-hr. answering mach.   E-mail: lightcurves@gmail.com
  Exquisite custom stained glass, tiffany style, leaded, painted glass, fused
  glass and mosaic. Also lighting fixtures, glass sculpture and jewelry, folding
  screens, windows, etc.

Lup / Reel Jewelry 212-924-5588
  1133 Broadway, Ste. 1314 (25-26th St)   FAX 212-924-2002
  NY, NY 10010
  Hours: By Appt.   E-mail: jessica@luprocks.com
  www.luprocks.com
  Fashion jewelry and watches from over 100 top designers. Jewelry cleared
  with designers for use in TV, film and print product placement. Diamonds,
  pearls, colored gemstones, platinum and gold available for use. Watches,
  handbags, shoes & sunglasses. No CREDIT CARDS.

Off-Broadway Boutique 212-724-6713
  139 W 72nd St. (B'way-Columbus)   FAX 212-873-3825
  NY, NY 10023
  Hours: 10:30-8 Mon-Fri / 10:30-7 Sat / 1-7 Sun   E-mail: alixcohen@aol.com
  www.boutiqueoffbroadway.com
  Women's tuxedos, gowns, jewelry and accessories. Gently worn star's
  clothes available. Phone orders. Will ship. CREDIT CARDS.

I-K

Parrish Relics 781-438-1497
  P O Box 80039
  Stoneham, MA 02180
  Hours: by appt.   E-mail: jen@parrishrelics.com
  www.parrishrelics.com
  Historical replicas, accessories and jewelry props. Lightweight museum
  quality crown; medieval to Victorian. Design specialists. Visit website to
  order. CREDIT CARDS.

Platinum Guild International USA 949-760-8279
  620 Newport Center Dr.   FAX 949-760-8780
  Newport Beach, CA 92660
  Hours: 8:30-5 Mon-Fri
  www.preciousplatinum.com
  Will loan platinum jewelry for film, photo shoots, television and theatre. Can
  make referrals to NYC jewelry retailers for product placement.

Poor Richard's Restoration Studio 973-783-5333
  101 Walnut St. (N Willow-Walnut Conor)
  Montclair, NJ 07042
  Hours: by appt.   E-mail: rickford99@yahoo.com
  www.rickford.com
  All aspects of furniture repair and conservation, from stripping of wood and
  reupholstery to reweaving of cane, wicker and rush. Gesso work and painted
  finishes. Also antique doll and jewelry repairs, old books and photos. CREDIT
  CARDS.

Sentimento Antiques 212-750-3111
  306 E 61st St., 6rd Fl. (1st-2nd Ave)   FAX 212-750-3839
  NY, NY 10021
  Hours: 10-6 Mon-Fri   E-mail: info@sentimentoantiques.com
  www.sentimentoantiques.com
  Desk accessories, luggage and various small decorative items and jewelry;
  some antique and vintage. No credit cards. RENTALS.

Showroom Seven 212-643-4810
  263 Eleventh Ave.   FAX 212-971-6066
  NY, NY 10018
  Hours: 9-6 Mon-Fri
  Extensive selection of designer fashions; shoes, handbags, hats, gloves, belts
  and scarves. List of designers they carry available upon request. CREDIT
  CARDS.

Victorian Trading Company 800-700-2035
  15600 W 99th St.   913-438-3995
  Lenexa, KS 66219   FAX 913-438-5225
  Hours: 24 on website
  www.victoriantradingco.com
  Mail order company with a wide selection of reproduction Victorian jewelry,
  fans, hat pins, personal grooming items and perfume atomizers. Great
  website. CREDIT CARDS.

I-K

World Gold Council 212-317-3800
    444 Madison Ave. (49-50th St)   FAX 212-688-0410
    NY, NY 10022
    Hours: 9-5 Mon-Fri   E-mail: info@gold.org
    www.gold.org
    Will promote real gold items for film, commercials and still photography.

Yellow Shed Antiques 845-628-0362
    PO Box 706, 571 Rt 6   FAX 845-628-2777
    Mahopac, NY 10541
    Hours: 10-5 Wed-Sun
China, crystal, silver items, memorabilia, quilts, jewelry, posters and prints. 1 hr. from Manhattan. 8,000 sq. ft. of decorative accessories. Contact Mark or Patty. RENTALS. CREDIT CARDS.

I-K

The professional trade association for artists and craftspeople working in theatre, film, television and advertising

ATAC Membership 2010-11

I-K

Sharlot Battin
  Montana Leatherworks
Chris Bobin
Sharon Braunstein
Randy Carfagno
Nadine Charlsen
Eileen Connor
Mary Creede
Margaret Cusack
Cindy Anita Fain
  CINAF Designs
James Feng
Keen Gat
Deborah R. Glassberg
Rodney Gordon
Joseph Gourley
Corrinna Griffin
Jung K. Griffin
Denise Grillo
  Offstage Design
Stockton Hall
Karen Hart
Suzanne Hayden

Marian Jean "Killer" Hose
J. Michelle Hill
Louise Hunnicutt
John Jerard
  Jerard Studio
Joni Johns
Jan Kastendieck
Rachel Keebler
  Cobalt Studios
Amanda Klein
Arnold S. Levine
  Arnold S. Levine, Inc.
Janet Linville
Jeanne Marino
  Moonboots Productions
Jerry Marshall
Betsey McKearnan
Gene Mignola
  Gene Mignola, Inc.
Mary Mulder
  Mulder / Martin, Inc.
Susan Pitocchi
Elizabeth Popeil

Adele Recklies
Monona Rossol
  Arts, Crafts, & Theatre
  Safety (A.C.T.S.)
Bill Rybak
Jody Schoffner
James R. Seffens
Lisa Shaftel
  Shaftel S2DO
Stanley Allen Sherman
  Mask Arts Company
Linda Skipper
Michael Smanko
  Prism Prips
Sarah Timberlake
  Timberlake Studios
Mari Tobita
US Institute for Theatre
  Tech. (USITT)
Monique Walker
Anne-Marie Wright
John Yavroyan
  Yavroyan & Nelsen, LTD

For membership information visit our website at
www.ATACBIZ.com
Email: info@ATACBIZ.com
Or drop us a line at:

ATAC Membership Application
Anne-Marie Wright
280 Third St. Apt # 1
Jersey City, NJ 07302-2759

KEYS & LOCKSMITHS

AAA Locksmiths 212-840-3939
   44 W 46th St. (5-6th Ave)   FAX 212-921-5086
   NY, NY 10036
   Hours: 8-5:30 Mon-Thurs / 8-5 Fri
   Licensed master locksmiths. Safe work and door check service. Member
   ALOA.

Charles Locksmith, Inc. 212-879-2740
   185 E 80th St. (Lex-3rd Ave)   866-OLD-KEYS
   NY, NY 10021   FAX 212-879-4710
   Hours: 8-6 Mon-Sat / 24-hr. emergency service
   www.charleslocksmith.com   E-mail: mike@charleslocksmith.com
   Large selection of antique keys and locks. Hard-to-find keys and locks for
   antique furniture. RENTALS. CREDIT CARDS.

KITCHEN EQUIPMENT: HOUSEHOLD

Bed, Bath and Beyond . . . . .1-800-Go Beyond
   620 Sixth Ave.(18th St)   212-255-3550
   NY, NY 10011   FAX 212-229-1040
   Hours: 8-9 Daily

   410 E 61st St.(1st Ave)   646-215-4702
   NY, NY 10010   FAX 646-215-4713
   Hours: 9-9 Daily

   1932 Broadway(64-65th St)   917-441-9391
   NY, NY 10023
   Hours: 9-10 Daily
   www.bedbathandbeyond.com
   A department store for bedroom, bathroom and kitchen: as well as seasonal.
   Visit the website for other locations across the USA. CREDIT CARDS.

Bowery Kitchen Supplies, Inc. 212-376-4982
   460 W 16th St. in Chelsea Market (9-10th Ave)   FAX 212-242-7360
   NY, NY 10011
   Hours: 9-9 Mon-Fri / 108 Sat / 11-6 Sun   E-mail: bowerykitchen@yahoo.com
   www.bowerykitchens.com
   Wonderful selection of various kitchen supplies both for home or industrial
   use. Located inside the Chelsea Market. CREDIT CARDS.

Bridge Kitchenware 973-287-6163
   563 Eagle Rock Ave.
   Roseland, NJ 07068
   Hours: 9-4 Mon-Fri /10-1 Sat   E-mail: info@bridgekitchenware.com
   www.bridgekitchenware.com
   Large selection of professional cookware, bakeware, cutlery and utensils.
   Great website. CREDIT CARDS.

I-K

Broadway Panhandler 212-966-3434
  65 E 8th St. (B'way-University)   866-266-5927
  NY, NY 10013   FAX 212-966-9017
  Hours: 11-7 Mon-Sat / 11-6 Sun   E-mail: bpisales@broadwaypanhandler.com
  www.broadwaypanhandler.com
  Kitchen equipment and utensils, cake decorating supplies, mugs, etc. No
  rentals. CREDIT CARDS.

The Container Store 800-266-8246
  629 Sixth Ave.(18-19th St)   212-366-4200
  NY, NY 10011
  Hours: 9-9 Mon-Sat / 10-8 Sun

  725 Lexington Ave.(58-59th St)   212-366-4200
  NY, NY 10022
  Hours: 9-9 Mon-Sat / 10-8 Sun
  www.containerstore.com
  For all your organizational needs; bins, files, boxes, metro shelving and closet
  organizers. The Container Store has everything. Contact the website or toll-
  free number for other locations. CREDIT CARDS.

Crows Nest Trading Co. 800-900-8558
  3205 Airport Blvd NW, P.O. Box 3975   FAX 800-900-3136
  Wilson, NC 27895
  Hours: 9-5 Mon-Fri / 24-hr. website   E-mail: info@crowsnestrading.com
  www.crowsnesttrading.com
  Leather, western rugged furnishings. Also kitchen, garden and rugs. Western
  and cowboy themed. Great catalog. CREDIT CARDS.

Dean & Deluca 212-226-6800
  560 Broadway (Spring-Prince St)   800-221-7714
  NY, NY 10012   FAX 212-226-2003
  Hours: 9-8 Mon-Sat / 10-7 Sun
  www.deandeluca.com
  Gourmet supermarket with a large kitchenware department; unique selection
  of tabletop and cooking items. Check web for many more locations. CREDIT
  CARDS.

Forzano Italian Imports, Inc. 914-664-2227
  514 South 5th Ave.   FAX 914-664-8291
  Mt. Vernon, NY 10550
  Hours: 10-10 daily   E-mail: sales@forzanoitalianimports.com
  www.forzanoitalianimports.com
  Everything for the kitchen with an Italian flavor. Online shopping. RENTALS.
  CREDIT CARDS.

Gracious Home 212-988-8990
  1220, 1217, 1201 Third Ave.(70th-71st St)
  NY, NY 10021   212-517-6300
  Hours: 8-7 Mon-Fri / 9-7 Sat / 10-6 Sun   FAX 212-249-1534

  1992 Broadway(67th St)   212-231-7800
  NY, NY 10023   800-237-3404
  Hours: 9-9 Mon-Sat / 10-7 Sun   FAX 212-875-9976
  www.gracioushome.com   E-mail: info@gracioushome.com
  Large selection of housewares, hardware and small appliances. CREDIT
  CARDS.

Home Outlet 718-531-7777
890 E 59th St. (Flatlands)   FAX 718-531-7914
Brooklyn, NY 11234
Hours: 10-6 Mon-Sat
Wide selection of kitchen cabinets for RENTALS. Contact Don. CREDIT CARDS.

The Jar Store 860-826-1881
221 South Street, Bldg F-5   FAX 860-826-1880
New Britain, CT 06051
Hours: 9-5:30 Mon-Fri
www.jarstore.com
Wholesale jar company and candle supply company. Apothecary, storage and many other styles. Excellent selection on website. CREDIT CARDS.

K-Mart 212-760-1188
250 W 34th St.(7-8th Ave)
NY, NY 10019
Hours: 8-10 Mon-Thurs / 9-10 Fri-Sun

770 Broadway(8th St)   212-673-1540
NY, NY 10003-9535
Hours: 8-10 Daily
www.kmart.com
Household goods. Purchase orders accepted. CREDIT CARDS.

Lehman's 330-857-5757
One Leham Cr. / P.O. Box 270   888-438-5346
Kidron, OH 44636   FAX 888-780-4975
Hours; 8-5:30 Mon-Sat / Thurs til 8   E-mail: GetLehmans@aol.com
www.lehmans.com
Housewares, oil lamps, cast-iron cookery, wood cook stoves, homestead tools. Rustic old-fashioned stuff. Non-electric Amish products. Plus, all those old-fashioned health and beauty products, canning supplies, food and laundry supplies. Great catalog ($10 including shipping) or shop online. CREDIT CARDS.

Lowe's 718-249-1151
118 Second Ave. (9th-12th St)   800-445-6337
Brooklyn, NY 11215   FAX 718-249-1154
Hours: 5-12 Mon-Sun
www.lowes.com
Big-box home improvement store that carries gardening supplies, kitchen cabinets, lighting fixtures, tools, lumber and much more. Check website for other locations. CREDIT CARDS.

Pier 1 Imports 800-245-4595
1550 Third Ave.(87th St)   212-987-1746
NY, NY 10128
Hours: 10-9 Mon-Sat / 11-7 Sun

71 Fifth Ave.(14-15th St)   212-206-1911
NY, NY 10003
Hours: 10-9 Mon-Sat / 11-7 Sun   www.pier1.com
Popular chain of stores carries baskets; wicker furniture and decorative items for the home. Some lighting, clothing, frames. See website for over 800 locations nationally. Some rentals. CREDIT CARDS.

I-K

Pottery Barn 888-779-5176
FAX 702-363-2541

1965 Broadway(66-67th St)   212-579-8477
NY, NY 10023
Hours: 10-9 Mon-Sat / 11-7 Sun

127 E 59th St.(Lexington)   917-369-0050
NY, NY 10022
Hours: 10-9 Mon-Sat / 11-7 Sun
www.potterybarn.com
China, glassware, cookware, utensils, etc. Catalog. RENTALS (M-W 10-12,
with credit card deposit). Over 160 stores in USA and Canada. CREDIT
CARDS.

The Prop Company / Kaplan and Associates 212-691-7767
111 W 19th St., 8th Fl. (6-7th Ave)   FAX 212-727-3055
NY, NY 10011
Hours: 9-5 Mon-Fri   E-mail: propcompany@yahoo.com
Contemporary tabletop, decorative accessories, antiques, ephemera and
furniture. A nice collection of linens. RENTALS.

Props for Today 212-244-9600
330 W 34th St. (8-9th Ave)   FAX 212-244-1053
NY, NY 10001
Hours: 8:30-5 Mon-Fri   E-mail: info@propsfortoday.com
www.propsfortoday.com
Large selection of plate and glassware, small appliances and cookware.
Everything for the contemporary or vintage kitchen and dining room.
RENTALS. CREDIT CARDS.

Toaster Central 212-744-3773
1427 York Ave. (76th St)
NY, NY 10021
Hours: by appt.   E-mail: pop@toastercentral.com
www.toastercentral.com
Working vintage toasters, small appliances, coffee pots, etc. from 1920 to
present day. Great website, very helpful. Speak to Michael Sheafe.
RENTALS. AMEX.

Williams-Sonoma 877-812-6235
110 Seventh Ave.(at 17th St)   212-633-2203
NY, NY 10011   FAX 212-206-0826
Hours: 10-8 Mon-Fri / 10-7 Sat / 12-6 Sun

1175 Madison Ave.(86th St)   212-289-6832
NY, NY 10028
Hours: 10-7 Mon-Fri / 10-6 Sat / 12-6 Sun

121 E 59th St.(Park & Lex)   917-369-1131
NY, NY 10022
Hours: 10-8 Mon-Sat / 11/7 Sun

I-K

Williams-Sonoma (cont.) 212-823-9750
10 Columbus Circle Time Warner Building(Columbus Circle)
NY, NY 10022
Hours: 10-7 Mon-Fri / 10-6 Sat / 10-6 Sun
www.williams-sonoma.com
Kitchenware store; china, glassware, cookware, utensils, etc. Catalog. Studio
services available thru corporate offices 415-421-7900. See website for other
locations. CREDIT CARDS.

Zabar's Mezzanine 212-787-2000
2245 Broadway (80th St)   800-697-6301
NY, NY 10024   FAX 212-580-4477
Hours: 8-7:30 Mon-Fri / 8-8 Sat / 9-6 Sun   E-mail: zabarscatalog@zabars.com
www.zabars.com
Extensive selection kitchen equipment, pots, pans, utensils, small electrical
appliances, etc.; very reasonable. Outfitters for the home chef. American and
European items. CREDIT CARDS.

KITCHEN EQUIPMENT: INDUSTRIAL
See also: APPLIANCES
            FURNITURE: Restaurant

All Care Business Machine, Inc. 212-431-3200
184 Bowery (Spring-Delancy St)   866-431-3200
NY, NY 10012   FAX 212-219-1744
Hours: 8-5 Mon-Fri / 9-4 Sat   E-mail: info@acbm-inc.com
www.acbm-inc.com
New and used cash registers, restaurant equipment and safes. RENTAL.
CREDIT CARDS.

Balter Sales 212-674-2960
209 Bowery (Rivington St)   FAX 212-460-5269
NY, NY 10002
Hours: 8-4:15 Mon-Fri   E-mail: lorib@baltersales.com
www.baltersales.com
Wholesaler (to trade only) of restaurant china and glassware servicing film
and TV. CREDIT CARDS.

Bari Restaurant Equipment 212-925-3786
240 Bowery (Houston-Prince St)   212-925-3845
NY, NY 10012   FAX 212-941-7054
Hours: 8-5 Mon-Fri / 9-3 Sat
www.bariequipment.com
Big selection used and new appliances, furnishings. CREDIT CARDS.

Bowery Kitchen Supplies, Inc. 212-376-4982
460 W 16th St. in Chelsea Market (9-10th Ave)   FAX 212-242-7360
NY, NY 10011
Hours: 9-9 Mon-Fri / 108 Sat / 11-6 Sun   E-mail: bowerykitchen@yahoo.com
www.bowerykitchens.com
Wonderful selection of various kitchen supplies both for home or industrial
use. Located inside the Chelsea Market. CREDIT CARDS.

I-K

Bridge Kitchenware 973-287-6163
563 Eagle Rock Ave.
Roseland, NJ 07068
Hours: 9-4 Mon-Fri /10-1 Sat   E-mail: info@bridgekitchenware.com
www.bridgekitchenware.com
Large selection of professional cookware, bakeware, cutlery and utensils.
Great website. CREDIT CARDS.

Chair Up, Inc. 212-353-0056
219 Bowery (Rivington)   FAX 212-353-0202
NY, NY 10012
Hours: 8:30-4:30 Mon-Fri, 8:30-2 Sat
www.chairupny.com
Good selection of restaurant tables, chairs and stools. Talk to Dave. CREDIT
CARDS.

Chef Restaurant Supplies 212-254-6644
294-296 Bowery (Houston St)   800-228-6141
NY, NY 10012   FAX 212-353-0841
Hours: 9-5:30 Mon-Sat / 11-4:30 Sun
www.chefrestaurantsupplies.com
Restaurant supplies, glassware, dishes and woks. CREDIT CARDS.

Daroma Restaurant Equipment Corp. 212-260-2463
231 Bowery (Spring St)   FAX 212-979-1335
NY, NY 10002
Hours: 8:30-5 Mon-Fri / 8:30-3 Sat
Large and small appliances and restaurant supplies including Metro shelving.
RENTALS (certified check required). CREDIT CARDS (for smaller items).

Detecto & Precision Scales 201-944-3888
240 Grand Ave.   800-972-2537
Leonia, NJ 07605   FAX 201-944-3808
Hours: 8:30-4:30 Mon-Fri   E-mail: precisinscales@verizon.net
Scales for every weighing need. RENTALS. CREDIT CARDS.

Eastern Tabletop Manufacturing Company, Inc. 718-522-4142
1943 Pitkin Ave.   888-422-4142
Brooklyn, NY 11207   FAX 718-522-4155
Hours: 9-5 Mon-Thurs / 9-1 Fri / 24-hr website
www.easterntabletop.com   E-mail: sales@easterntabletop.com
Since 1950, Eastern Tabletop Manufacturing Co., Inc. has been dedicated to
manufacturing and designing Silver Plated Holloware and Chafing Dishes for
the food service industry. Trays, beverage servers and cover-ups. Now good
selection of bars, high end carts and pidiums. Visit website for collection.

Kerekes Bakery & Restaurant Equipment Inc. 718-232-7044
6103 15th Ave. (61st-62nd St)   800-525-5556
Brooklyn, NY 11219   FAX 718-232-4416
Hours: 9-5:30 Mon-Thurs / 9-1 Fri / 11-4 Sun   E-mail: sales@bakedeco.com
www.bakedeco.com
They sell everything from a spoon to an oven. Mixers, refrigeration, ovens,
sinks, tables,tabletop machines and racks. Cake decorating, chocolate making
for the professional or the gourmet chef at home. They can furnish your
entire commercial kitchen. CREDIT CARDS.

I-K

The Lighting Showroom, Inc. 212-219-2059
137 Bowery (Broome-Grand St)
NY, NY 10002
Hours: 9:30-5:30 / 7 days a week
Decorative lighting and accessories. Custom design capabilities. Lamps,
chandeliers, sconces, picture lights. CREDIT CARDS.

Regency Service Carts, Inc. 718-855-8304
337-361 Carroll St. (Hoyt-Bond St)   FAX 718-834-8507
Brooklyn, NY 11231
Hours: 8-5 Mon-Fri   E-mail: regeastny@aol.com
www.regencynylv.com
Silver-plated tabletop items, chaffing dishes, domes and dessert carts, room
service carts, holloware; catalog. Wonderful website. RENTALS.

Rite Supermarket Equipment, Inc. .718-292-1800
3362 Park Ave. (165th St)   FAX 718-665-8340
Bronx, NY 10456
Hours: 7:30-4:30 Mon-Fri   E-mail: ritesup@aol.com
www.ritesupermarketequipment.com
New and used supermarket and restaurant equipment, refrigerated cases and
new and used diner booths. Signage and decorations. RENTALS.

Sang Kung Co., Inc. 800-221-2994
110 Bowery (Grand-Hester St)   212-226-4527
NY, NY 10013   FAX 212-219-3615
Hours: 9-5:30 Mon-Sat   E-mail: info@sangkung.com
www.sangkung.com
Reasonably priced Chinese restaurant supplies and cookware, knives and
food preparation bowls. And a baking section to die for... HUGE muffin tins
for when you're baking for a party of 30. CREDIT CARDS.

Samuel Underberg, Inc. 718-363-0787
1784 Atlantic Ave. (Utica)   FAX 718-363-0786
Brooklyn, NY 11213
Hours: 8-4 Mon-Fri
Complete supplies for food stores and butcher shops. Shopping carts, scales,
baskets, platters, utensils and knives, pans and trays, price markers, paper
cutters, plastic dividers for deli cases, blackboards and numbered ticket
dispensers. RENTALS.

The Warehouse Store Fixture Co. 203-575-0111
84 Progress Ln.   FAX 203-575-9140
Waterbury, CT 06705
Hours: 8-5 Mon-Fri / 9-2 Sat   E-mail: wsfc@restaurantsupplystore.com
www.restaurantsupplystore.com
Immense stock, new and used, of store and kitchen fixtures. CREDIT CARDS.

I-K

NOTES

I-K

LABELS: WOVEN & PRINTED

All City Label & Tag Co. 212-244-9293
    261 W 35th St. (6-7th Ave)   800-LABEL-11
    NY, NY 10001   FAX 212-244-9295
    Hours: 9-4 Mon-Fri
    www.allcitylabel.com
    Printed and woven labels. CREDIT CARDS.

Harvard Label & Tag Co. 212-736-8434
    225 W 35th St., 11th Fl. (7-8th Ave)   800-266-9161
    NY, NY 10001   FAX 212-629-4198
    Hours: 9-5 Mon-Fri
    www.auburnlabel.com
    Formerly Auburn Label & Tag Co. Woven and printed labels, tags, stickers and patches. 5000 label minimum.

Ideal 718-252-5090
    1816 Flatbush Ave.(Avenue K)
    Brooklyn, NY 11210   FAX 718-692-0492
    Hours: 9-7:30 Mon-Fri / 10-7 Sat / 11-6 Sun

    1575 Unionport Rd.   718-239-4010
    Bronx, NY 10462
    Hours: 10-7 Mon-Sat / 10:30-5:30 Sun
    www.idealuniform.com
    Custom labels for your labeling needs, woven and printed. All sizes and colors available. CREDIT CARDS.

Treo Label & Tag Co., Inc. 718-384-3300
    36 Broadway (Wythe-Kent)   FAX 718-388-7308
    Brooklyn, NY 11211
    Hours: by appt.
    Woven labels and tags and printed ribbon.

LADDERS, LIFTS & SCAFFOLDING

Manhattan Ladder Co., Inc. 800-229-3352
    122 Woodworth Ave. (31st Rd)   800-229-2960
    Yonkers, NY 10702
    Hours: 7-4 Mon-Fri   E-mail: nyladder@aol.com
    www.newyorkladder.com
    Wood and aluminum ladders, scaffolding; delivery. Affiliate of CT Ladder & Scafold Co. RENTALS. CREDIT CARDS.

Putnam Rolling Ladder Co., Inc. 212-226-5147
    32 Howard St. (B'way-Lafayette St)   FAX 212-941-1836
    NY, NY 10013
    Hours: 8:30-4 Mon-Fri   E-mail: putnam1905@aol.com
    www.putnamrollingladder.com
    All types of ladders: amazing selection in catalog; custom work. Delivery. Great online catalog. CREDIT CARDS.

J. Racenstein Co. 201-809-1680
74 Henry St.   800-221-3748
Secaucus, NJ 07094   FAX 201-348-1385
Hours: 8:30-4:30 Mon-Fri   E-mail: helpdesk@jracenstein.com
www.jracenstein.com
Natural Mediterranean sponges and synthetics. Window cleaning and janitorial supplies. Ladders, harnesses, and safety equipment. Extra cool website. CREDIT CARDS.

Safway Services, Inc. 718-383-8400
31-31 123rd St.   800-640-8778
Flushing, NY 11354   FAX 718-321-8106
Hours: 6:30-3 Mon-Fri   E-mail: jamie.kelly@safway.com
www.safway.com
Bleachers, ladders, lifts and scaffolding; delivery available. Catalog. RENTALS. CREDIT CARDS.

York Ladder, Inc. 718-784-6666
37-20 12th St. (38th Ave)   800-640-YORK
Long Island City, NY 11101   FAX 718-482-9016
Hours: 7-3 Mon-Fri   E-mail: info@yorksscaffold.com
www.yorkscaffold.com
All types of ladders, scaffolding, suspended systems. Catalog. RENTALS. CREDIT CARDS.

LAMINATES
See also: LUMBER

L.I. Laminates 631-234-6969
35 Engineers Rd., Ste 100   (outside NY) 800-221-5454
Hauppauge, NY 11788   FAX 631-234-5590
Hours: 7:30-6 Mon-Thurs / 7:30-4 Fri / 7:30-1 Sat
Water-based, non-toxic finishing products. Pre-curved plywood. CREDIT CARDS.

LeNobel Lumber Co., Inc. 212-246-0150
38-20 Review Ave.   718-784-5230
Long Island City, NY 11101   FAX 718-784-1422
Hours: 8-5 Mon-Fri / (closed for lunch 12-1) Pick-up until 3:30
www.lenoblelumber.com   E-mail: website.lenoble@att.net
Doors, plywood, laminates, mouldings, masonite, millwork, windows, Sonotube. Cutting 1-3:30 pm. Delivery. Cash, certified check or accounts only.

Manhattan Laminates Ltd. 212-255-2522
624 W 52nd St. (11-12th Ave)   FAX 212-255-4670
NY, NY 10011
Hours: 7:30-5 Mon-Fri
www.manhattanlaminates.com
Large selection. Metal laminate, Formica, MDF, foamcore, plywood, tools, glue, hardware, hindges and slides. Delivery. CREDIT CARDS.

Midtown Lumber 212-675-2230
276 W 25th St. (7-8th Ave)   FAX 212-675-2642
NY, NY 10001
Hours: 7-4:30 Mon-Fri
Good selection of Formica and other laminates; moldings, hardwood flooring,
tileboard, glass block, hardware and lumber cut to size. Contact Mike.
CREDIT CARDS.

Plastic-Craft Product Corp. 845-358-3010
744 W Nyack Rd.   800-627-3010
West Nyack, NY 10994   FAX 845-358-3007
Hours: 8-5 Mon-Fri   E-mail: info@plastic-craft.com
www.plastic-craft.com
Plastic sheets, rods and tubes; laminates, adhesives. For custom designs,
contact Mark. CREDIT CARDS.

Tulnoy Lumber 718-901-1700
1620 Webster Ave. (173rd St)   800-899-5833
Bronx, NY 10457   FAX 718-229-8920
Hours: 7-5 Mon-Fri   E-mail: sales@tulnoylumber.com
www.tulnoylumber.com
Stocks Formica, Wilsonart, Pionite ARPA. Also mouldings, Gatorboard, etc.
Contact Peter Tulchin.

Wilson Art 866-455-8297
250 Karin (19th Ave)   516-935-6980
Hicksville, NY 11801   FAX 516-935-6875
Hours: 8-4:30 Mon-Fri
www.wilsonart.com
Stocks Wilsonart brand decorative laminate and tambours; warehouse and
executive office here. Delivery ($50 minimum). CREDIT CARDS.

LAMINATING SERVICES

Idesco Corp. 212-889-2530
37 W 26th St. (B'way-6th Ave)   800-336-1383
NY, NY 10010   FAX 212-889-7033
Hours: 9-4:45 Mon-Fri   E-mail: info@idesco.com
www.idesco.com
All kinds of laminating, fast service. $75 min. on shipped items. CREDIT
CARDS.

LAMPSHADES & PARTS

Action Lighting, Inc. 406-586-5105
310 Ice Pond Rd.   800-248-0076
Bozeman, MT 59715   FAX 406-585-3078
Hours: 8-5 Mon-Fri closed 11:30-12:30 daily E-mail: catalog@actionlighting.com
www.actionlighting.com
Bulbs of all kinds. Great catalog and website. Staff very helpful. Orders
under $25 will be charged a small order fee of $7.50. CREDIT CARDS.

ATAC

The Alpha Workshops 212-594-7320
245 W 29th St., Ste. 14th FL (7-8th Ave)   FAX 212-594-4832
NY, NY 10001
Hours: by appt only.   E-mail: info@alphaworkshops.org
www.alphaworkshops.org
Custom hand-painted lampshades on paper or fabric in any style. CREDIT CARDS.

Broome Lampshade, Inc. 212-431-9666
325 Broome St. (Bowery-Chrystie St)   FAX 212-431-9866
NY, NY 10002
Hours: 9:30-6 Mon-Fri / 10-4 Sat-Sun   E-mail: goshades@aol.com
www.lampshadesny.com
Large stock of fabric and parchment shades. Custom work, recovering available. Also does lamp repair, rewiring and restoration. Contact Rony.

City Knickerbocker, Inc. 212-586-3939
665 Eleventh Ave, 2nd Fl. (corner 48th)   FAX 212-262-2889
NY, NY 10019
Hours: 8:30-5 Mon-Fri   E-mail: info@cityknickerbocker.com
www.cityknickerbocker.com
Convenient midtown location. The best stop for rental of antique and some contemporary lighting fixtures and shades. Lighting repair and rewiring. Some halogen repairs. Nice people; see Ken or Scott. RENTALS. CREDIT CARDS.

Grand Brass Lamp Parts, Inc. 212-226-2567
51 Railroad Ave.   FAX 212-226-2573
West Haven, CT 06516
Hours: 9-4 Mon-Fri   E-mail: sales@grandbrass.com
www.grandbrass.com
Lamp bases, globes, chimneys, metal shades and lamp hardware. Many odd parts. Cloth covered electrical wire. Mogul bases. Lighting repair, including halogen. Very informative website. CREDIT CARDS.

Igmor Crystal Lite Corp 212-243-2400
45 W 25th St. (5th Ave)   FAX 212-627-9591
NY, NY 10010
Hours: 9-4:30 Mon-Fri / closed 12-1
www.igmorcrystal.com
Crystals, crystal chandelier components. CREDIT CARDS.

Just Bulbs 212-228-7820
220 E 60th St. (2nd-3rd Ave)   FAX 212-888-5704
NY, NY 10022
Hours: 10-7 Mon-Sat / 12-6 Sun   E-mail: sales@justbulbsnyc.com
www.justbulbs.com
Everything in light bulbs, including novelty string lights; pricey. CREDIT CARDS.

Just Shades 212-966-2757
   21 Spring St. (Elizabeth-Mott St)   FAX 212-334-6129
   NY, NY 10012
   Hours: 9:30-6 Tue-Fri / 9:30-5 Sat / Thur till 8   E-mail: info@justshadesny.com
   www.justshadesny.com
   Extensive selection of lampshades in silk, paper and parchment. Stock and
   custom. Knowledgeable and friendly staff. CREDIT CARDS.

Light Curves / Joan Nicole 845-434-5081
   10 Rockview Lane   845-978-7653
   Loch Sheldrake, NY 12759   FAX 845-434-5081
   Hours: By appt., 24-hr. answering mach.   E-mail: lightcurves@gmail.com
   Exquisite custom stained glass, tiffany style, leaded, painted glass, fused
   glass and mosaic. Also lighting fixtures, glass sculpture and jewelry, folding
   screens, windows, etc.

Nowell's Lighting 415-332-4933
   615 Irwin St. (Lincoln-Anderson Dr)   FAX 415-332-4936
   San Raphael, CA 94961
   Hours: 9:30-5 Tue-Sat   E-mail: sales@nowellslighting.com
   www.nowellslighting.com
   Reproduction and antique Victorian and Edwardian fixtures and shades;
   custom work. Rewiring and repairs, including halogens.

Oriental Lamp Shade Co., Inc. 212-873-0812
   223 W 79th St.(B'way-Amsterdam)
   NY, NY 10024   FAX 212-873-0898
   Hours: 10-6 Mon-Sat

   816 Lexington Ave.(62nd-63rd St)   212-832-8190
   NY, NY 10021   FAX 212-758-5367
   Hours: 10-5:30 Mon-Sat   E-mail: olsc@att.net
   www.orientallampshade.com
   Good selection of stock shades; custom work available. Rewiring, repairs and
   restoration. Contact Ron.

Owl Mills 732-942-8025
   500 James St. Unit 11   FAX 732-907-2621
   Lakewood, NJ 08701
   Hours: 9-5 Mon-Fri   E-mail: owlmills@gmail.com
   www.owlmills.com
   Silk organza, sheers, nets, linens. Popular plain and metallic braids, ribbons
   and cord trims imported from Europe. Swatching. No credit cards.

Sundial Vintage Electric 413-582-6909
   PO Box 803   FAX 413-582-6908
   Northampton, MA 01061
   Hours: by appt.   E-mail: customerserv@sundialwire.com
   www.sundialwire.com
   Sundial Vintage Electric is a supplier of new, cloth covered, braided electrical
   wire, which is custom-manufactured to replicate vintage electrical wire.
   Great website. Go visit.

Weiss & Biheller 212-979-6990
    116 E 16th St., 9th Fl. (Park-Irving Pl)   888-296-8919
    NY, NY 10003   FAX 212-979-8283
    Hours: 9-4:45 Mon-Fri
    www.weissandbiheller.com
    Large stock of chandeliers, sconces, lamp parts, also crystal trimmings.
    Wholesale only. $50 min.

LEATHER & FUR
For fake fur, see FABRICS: Fur & Pile

Aadar Leather 212-647-9334
    154 W 27th St. (6-7th Ave)   212-647-9340
    NY, NY 10001   FAX 212-647-9342
    Hours: 10-5 Mon-Thur / 11-2 Sun
    Full skins and leather remnants. Upholstery and garment leathers, suede,
    hair on cowhides, printed, solids, snakeskins and more. CREDIT CARDS.

Alliance Leather Imports, Ltd. 212-736-7044
    555 Eighth Ave., Ste 1601 (37-38th St)   917-587-7434
    NY, NY 10018   FAX 212-736-7045
    Hours: 10-5 Mon-Thurs / 10-2 Fri   E-mail: hideimpex@aol.com
    Supplier of leather and fur skins in smooth, embossed and fancy leathers as
    well as hair-on sking. CREDIT CARDS.

Behrle NYC 212-279-5626
    440 W 34th St # 4B (9-10th Aves)
    NY, NY 10001
    Hours: by appt. only   E-mail: behryenyc@gmail.com
    www.behrlenyc.com
    Custom leather clothing ranging from corsetry, cordovan lacing, applique etc.
    Original designs for the home including curtains, upholstery and pillows.
    Member IATSE USA Local 829. RENTALS. CREDIT CARDS.

Dualoy, Inc. 212-736-3360
    149 W 36th St., 4th FL (6th-7th Ave)   FAX 212-594-8327
    NY, NY 10018
    Hours: 9-5 Mon-Fri   E-mail: peter@dualoy.com
    www.dualoy.com
    Large selection of European aniline dyed hides for upholstery and interiors.
    Also carry lamb parchment, leather floor tiles, shagreen and woven leather.
    Very helpful. Speak to Peter.

Fabulous-Furs 800-848-4650
    20 W Eleventh St.   859-291-3300
    Covington, KY 41011   FAX 859-291-9687
    Hours: 9-5 Mon-Fri / 10-3 Sat / 24-7 Catalog
    www.fabulousfurs.com   E-mail: custserv@fabulousfurs.com
    Full line of fur fabrics, patterns, fur coat kits, sewing notions; also
    instructional books and patterns. Phone orders. CREDIT CARDS.

The Leather Factory 800-433-3201
    1818 N Cameron St.   717-236-8142
    Harrisburg, PA 17103   FAX 717-236-0752
    Hours: 8-6 Mon-Fri / 9-4 Sat   E-mail: harrisburg@leatherfactory.com

    4726 S. Salina St.   315-492-2225
    Syracuse, NY 13205   FAX 315-492-6312
    Hours: 8-6 Mon-Fri / 9-4 Sat   E-mail: syracuse@leatherfactory.com
    www.tandyleatherfactory.com
    Leather and leather tooling supplies. Visit their website for other locations.
    CREDIT CARDS.

Leather Impact 212-302-2332
    256 W 38th St. (7-8th Ave)   FAX 212-730-2486
    NY, NY 10018
    Hours: 9:30-5 Mon-Fri
    Garment leathers, skins, suedes, printed suedes and embossed leathers.
    Limited swatching. Wholesale only, no min. Will ship. No credit cards.

Mokuba 212-869-8900
    55 W 39th St. (5-6th Ave)
    NY, NY 10018
    Hours: 9-5 Mon-Fri
    Over 3,500 square feet of decorative ribbons and trims. Every fabric, shape,
    size and color imaginable; stretchable faux fur trims, braided leathers and
    washable fake suedes. Bugle-beaded tassle ribbons. Company based in
    Japan and has more than 43,000 items. CREDIT CARDS.

Rawhides Custom Leatherware 201-333-2571
    P.O. Box 2146
    Secaucus, NJ 07096
    Hours: by appt.   E-mail: hidemaster@rawhides.com
    www.rawhides.com
    Custom leather clothing, theatrical costumes, garments or accessories. Visit
    website for ordering information. CREDIT CARDS.

Renar Leather Co. 212-349-2075
    4645 Mill Ave. (6th Ave)   212-349-2076
    Brooklyn, NY 11234   FAX (call first)
    Hours: 9-3 Mon-Fri by appt. only
    Chamois, shoe, garment, novelty leathers.

Sommer's Plastic Products Co., Inc. 973-777-7888
    31 Styertowne Rd.   800-225-7677
    Clifton, NJ 07012   FAX 973-777-7890
    Hours: 9-5 Mon-Fri   E-mail: sales @sommers.com
    www.sommers.com
    Plastic fabrics, synthetic leathers and furs for apparel, footwear, luggage and
    leather goods, home furnishing, wallcovering and upholstery.

LEATHER & FURRIERS TOOLS & SUPPLIES

Albest Metal Stamping Corp. 718-388-6000
1 Kent Ave. (N 13-N 14th St)   FAX 718-388-0404
Brooklyn, NY 11211
Hours: 8-5 Mon-Thurs / 8-1 Fri   E-mail: info@albest.com
www.albest.com
Leading manufacturer of metal and plastic hardware. Carries full line of Eisen products. Buckles, clips, military spec. hardware, rings, snap hooks, studs, nailheads, settings. CREDIT CARDS.

Samuel Bauer & Sons, Inc. 212-868-4190
244 W 30th St. (7-8th Ave)   FAX 212-967-7076
NY, NY 10001
Hours: 9-5 Mon-Thur / 9-2:30 Fri   E-mail: info@samuelbauer.com
www.samuelbauer.com
Furriers supplies; dyes markers and sprays for fur. CREDIT CARDS.

Fiebing Company, Inc. 414-271-5011
PO Box 694   800-558-1033
Milwaukee, WI 53201   FAX 414-271-3769
Hours: 6:30-3:30 Mon-Fri   E-mail: custserv@fiebing.com
www.fiebing.com
Manufacturer of the popular leather dyes; chart of products available. Website will direct you to retail locations by state.

Kaufman Shoe Repair Supplies, Inc. 212-777-1700
346 Lafayette St. (Bond-Bleecker St)   FAX 212-777-1747
NY, NY 10012
Hours: 6:30-2 Sun-Fri
Barge, Magix, dyes, skins, shoe rubber, lacing and some small quantities of leather. Mostly wholesale; will not sell in small quantities. CREDIT CARDS.

The Leather Factory 800-433-3201
1818 N Cameron St.   717-236-8142
Harrisburg, PA 17103   FAX 717-236-0752
Hours: 8-6 Mon-Fri / 9-4 Sat   E-mail: harrisburg@leatherfactory.com

4726 S. Salina St.   315-492-2225
Syracuse, NY 13205   FAX 315-492-6312
Hours: 8-6 Mon-Fri / 9-4 Sat   E-mail: syracuse@leatherfactory.com
www.tandyleatherfactory.com
Leather and leather tooling supplies. Visit their website for other locations. CREDIT CARDS.

Louis Birns & Sons, Ltd. 518-690-7141
6 Charles Blvd.   800-533-3023
Guilderland, NY 12084   FAX 518-690-7142
Hours: 8-5 Mon-Fri   E-mail: lbssons@vuno.com
Wholesale to the shoe and leather repair trades. Pre-cut leather soles, half soles and heels. Lacings, leather dyes and glues, shoemaker supplies. CREDIT CARDS.

National Leather & Shoe Findings Co. 718-797-3434
   617 Sackett St. (3rd-4th Ave)   800-797-3884
   Brooklyn, NY 11271   FAX 718-797-3484
   Hours: 7:30-4 Mon-Fri
   Good stock Magix, leather dyes, shoe rubber and lacing; phone in orders and
   pick-up.

Ohio Travel Bag 440-498-1955
   6481 Davis Industrial Pkwy.   800-800-1941
   Solon, OH 44139   FAX 440-498-9811
   Hours: 8-5 Mon-Fri   E-mail: info@ohiotravelbag.com
   www.ohiotravelbag.com
   Wholesale buckles and hardware for leatherwork; catalog.

C.S. Osborne Tools 973-483-3232
   125 Jersey St.   FAX 973-484-3621
   Harrison, NJ 07029
   Hours: 8-4:30 Mon-Fri   E-mail: cso@csosborne.com
   www.csosborne.com
   Leather dyes, leather needles, etc. Catalog.

Veteran Leather Co. 718-786-9000
   36-14 35th St. (4th Ave)   FAX 718-786-0701
   Long Island City, NY 11106
   Hours: 8:30-4:30 Mon-Fri   E-mail: sales@veteranleather.com
   www.veteranleather.com
   Skins, leather dyes and needles. Catalog available. CREDIT CARDS.

Western Crafts & Gifts Co. 407-578-6833
   40 Taylor St.   407-656-0853
   Ocoee, FL 34761
   Hours: 10-6 Mon-Fri / 10-5 Sat   E-mail: westerncrafts@aol.com
   Leather working tools and supplies. Crafting supplies and hides. CREDIT
   CARDS.

LIGHTING & PROJECTION EQUIPMENT

Ace Video & Props 718-392-1100
   37-24 24th St., Ste. 106 (Houston & West St)   212-206-1475
   Long Island City, NY 11101   FAX 718-392-1155
   Hours: 10-6 Mon-Fri / 10-2 Sat by appt.
           E-mail: acevideorentals@gmail.com / acepropsnyc@gmail.com
   www.aceprops.com
   All types of film and TV lighting equipment; film, slide and video projection
   equipment. RENTALS. CREDIT CARDS.

Cinemills Corp. 877-262-4647
   2021 Lincoln St.   818-843-4560
   Burbank, CA 91504   FAX 818-843-7834
   Hours: 8-5 Mon-Fri   E-mail: sales@cinemills.com
   www.cinemills.com
   Mfgrs. Blackout Foil, a heat resistant, black-matte aluminum foil for masking
   light leaks. California: 800-692-6700. RENTALS. CREDIT CARDS.

GAM Products, Inc. 323-935-4975
4975 W Pico Blvd.   FAX 323-935-2002
Los Angeles, CA 90019
Hours: 8-5:30 Mon-Fri   E-mail: sales@gamonline.com
www.gamonline.com
Sells steel projection templates (gobos), scenic projectors, color filters;
special effects, lighting and controls. Catalog. P.O.s accepted. CREDIT CARDS

The Light Source 704-504-8399
3935 Westinghouse Blvd.   FAX 704-588-4637
Charlotte, NC 28273
Hours: 8-5 Mon-Fri   E-mail: mail@thelightsource.com
www.thelightsource.com
Theatrical and TV lighting equipment. Makes extruded aluminum lighting
clamps: Mega-Clamps, Mega-Bergers and Mega-Handles. Also Mega-Lite,
large variable focus floodlights.

Musson Theatrical 800-THEATER
890 Walsh Ave.   408-986-0210
Santa Clara, CA 95050   FAX 408-986-9552
Hours: 8:30-5:30 Mon-Fri / 10-2 Sat   E-mail: info@musson.com
www.musson.com
Great West Coast full-service supply for lighting and sound. Very
knowledgable and helpful. Contact Bob Smay. RENTALS.

O'Ryan Industries 360-892-0447
PO Box 1736 (for mail request)   800-426-4311
Vancouver, WA 98668   FAX 360-892-6742
Hours: 7:30-5 Mon-Thurs
www.oryanindustries.com
Laser light systems, audio driven or manual. Low voltage lights and fiber
optics for water conditions (pool and spa). Fiber optics for microscopes.
Catalog. CREDIT CARDS.

LIGHTING & PROJECTION EQUIPMENT: MANUFACTURERS

Altman Stage Lighting Co., Inc. 914-476-7987
57 Alexander St.   800-4ALTMAN
Yonkers, NY 10701   FAX 914-966-1980
Hours: 9:30-5 Mon-Fri   E-mail: info@altmanlighting.com
www.altmanlighting.com
Manufacturer of theatre, film and TV luminaries. Catalog. RENTALS. No credit
cards.

Arri 818-841-7070
600 N Victory Blvd.
Burbank, CA 91502   FAX 818-848-4028
Hours: 8:15-5 Mon-Fri

617 Rt. 303   845-353-1400
Blauvelt, NY 10913   FAX 845-425-1250
Hours: 9-5:30 Mon-Fri   E-mail: arriflex@arri.com
www.arri.com
Specializing in HMI lighting instruments and projectors. CREDIT CARDS.

City Theatrical, Inc. 201-549-1160
475 Barell Ave.   800-230-9497
Carlstadt, NJ 07072   FAX 201-549-1161
Hours: 7-6 Mon-Fri   E-mail: info@citytheatrical.com
www.citytheatrical.com
Manufacturer of unique lighting accessories, including Blacktak Light Mask
Foil, AquaFog dry ice foggers, CandleLite flicker candles. Distributor of
Lightwright lighting software.

Cooper Controls / North America 800-553-3879
203 Cooper Circle
Peachtree City, GA 30269
Hours: 8-5 Mon-Fri   E-mail: controlsales@cooperindustries.com
www.cooperindustries.com
Dimming systems and lighting controls, including installation systems and
portable gear for live performance, theme park and convention centers.

Creative Stage Lighting 518-251-3302
PO Box 567, 149 Route 28N   FAX 518-251-2908
North Creek, NY 12853
Hours: 8:30-5 Mon-Fri   E-mail: Info@creativestagelighting.com
www.creativestagelighting.com
Wholesale distributor of lighting and rigging supplies. Custom fabrication of
electrical systems. RENTALS. CREDIT CARDS.

DeSisti Lighting 908-317-0020
1011 Route 22 E, Unit D   FAX 908-317-0021
Mountaininside, NJ 07092
Hours: 9-4 Mon-Fri   E-mail: frank_kosuda@desistiusa.com
www.desistilighting.com
Design and manufacturer of complete motorized and robotic lighting and
rigging systems for film, television, photographic and location lighting.

Electronic Theatre Controls, Inc. (ETC) 800-688-4116
630 Ninth Ave., Ste 1001(45th St)   212-397-8080
NY, NY 10036   FAX 212-397-4340
Hours: 9-5 Mon-Fri

6640 Sunset Blvd., Ste 200   323-461-0216
Los Angeles, CA 90028   FAX 323-461-7830
Hours: 9-5 Mon-Fri

3031 Plesant View   608-831-4116
Middleton, WI 53562   FAX 608-836-1736
Hours: 8-5 Mon-Fri

3031 Pleasant View Rd.   608-831-4116
Middleton, WI 53562   FAX 608-836-1736
Hours: 8-5 Mon-Fri
www.etcconnect.com
Manufactures a complete line of sophisticated entertainment lighting
equipment, including control consoles, dimming equipment, interface
products and architectural lighting systems.

Goddard Design Co. 718-599-0170
51 Nassau Ave.   FAX 718-599-0172
Brooklyn, NY 11222
Hours: 10-6 Mon-Fri   E-mail: sales@goddarddesign.com
www.goddarddesign.com

Designers and manufacturers. of theatrical electronics. DMX test equipment 512 and distribution, intercom systems, scenery mechanization controllers. DMX or RDM Consulting.

Group One Ltd. 516-249-1399
70 Sea Ln.   FAX 516-249-8870
Farmingdale, NY 11735
Hours: 9-5:30 Mon-Fri   E-mail: sales@g1limited.com
www.g1limited.com

Exclusive US distributor for lighting and audio products including: Digico, Belestion, Blue Sky, Elektralite, Pulsar. No credit cards.

Lex Products Corp. 203-363-3738
401 Shippan Ave.   800-643-4460
Stamford, CT 06902   FAX 203-363-3742
Hours: 8:30-5:30 Mon-Fri   E-mail: info@lexproducts.com
www.lexproducts.com

Manufacturer of electrical cable assemblies and distribution boxes for the entertainment industry. Master distributor of bulk cable and connectors like ECT cam connectors, Leviton, American Insulated.

Lighting & Electronics 845-297-1244
Market St., Industrial Park   800-553-1244
Wappingers Falls, NY 12590   FAX 845-297-9270
Hours: 8:30-5 Mon-Fri   E-mail: info@le-us.com
www.le-us.com

Manufacturer of lighting fixtures for professional, educational, community stage and studio. Products include the Mini-Strip, Broad Cyc and Micro-Fill, along with full lines of ellipsoidals, fresnels, etc. Specializing in dimming fluorescents.

Motion Laboratories 914-788-8877
520 Furnace Dock Rd.   800-227-6784
Cortlandt Manor, NY 10567   FAX 914-788-8866
Hours: 9-6 Mon-Fri   E-mail: info@motionlabs.com
www.motionlabs.com

Manufacturer of electrical distribution and motor control products. Good technical support.

Rosco Laboratories, Inc. 203-708-8900
52 Harbor View Ave.   800-ROSCONY
Stamford, CT 06902   FAX 203-708-8919
Hours: 9-5 Mon-Fri   E-mail: info@rosco.com
www.rosco.com

Stainless steel, glass and dichroic gobos; also complete line of projection screens and color media. Shipping available.

Strand Lighting 800-733-0564
6603 Darin Way   714-230-8200
Cypress, CA 90630   FAX 714-899-0042
Hours: 8-5 Mon-Fri   E-mail: sales@strandlight.com
www.strandlight.com
Lighting equipment, controls and fixtures for all entertainment mediums.
RENTALS. CREDIT CARDS.

T.P.R. Enterprises Ltd. 914-698-1141
644 Fayette Ave.   FAX 914-698-9419
Mamaroneck, NY 10543
Hours: 9:30-5:30 Mon-Fri   E-mail: info@tprilites.com
www.tprlites.com
Mfgr. and importer of special effects lighting equipment. Offers a complete
and versatile line of fiber optics.

Theatre Effects 800-791-7646
11707 Chesterdale Rd.   513-772-7646
Cincinnati, OH 45246   FAX 513-772-3579
Hours: 9-5 Mon-Fri   E-mail: service@theatrefx.com
www.theatrefx.com
Manufacturer and distributor of special effects with fire and smoke. Confetti
and streamer cannons, fog machines, bubble machines, snow machines. Free
catalog available. RENTALS. CREDIT CARDS.

Tomcat USA, Inc. 432-694-7070
2160 Commerce   FAX 432-689-3805
Midland, TX 79703
Hours: 8-5 Mon-Fri   E-mail: info@tomcatusa.com
www.tomcatglobal.com
Engineering and manufacturing of custom and standard trussing, lighting
support and roof systems. Has full line of rigging accessories, custom cable
assemblies, chain hoists, motions controls. CREDIT CARDS.

LIGHTING & PROJECTION EQUIPMENT: RENTALS, SALES & SERVICES

14th St. Stage Lighting, Inc. 212-645-5491
430 W 14th St. Basement (9-10th Ave)   FAX 212-645-5491 at prompt *14
NY, NY 10014
Hours: 10-4 Mon-Fri / 10-1 Sat   E-mail: info@14thstreetstagelighting.com
www.14thstreetlstagelighting.com
Full sales and rental of equipment and perishables. Reasonable rates.
RENTALS. CREDIT CARDS.

4Wall Entertainment 866-492-5540
2 Empire Blvd.   201-329-9878
Moonachie, NJ 07074   FAX 201-329-9890
Hours: 9-5 Mon-Fri

3325 W. Sunset Rd., Ste. F   702-263-3858
Las Vegas, NV 89118   FAX 702-263-3863
Hours: 9-5 Mon-Fri

4Wall Entertainment (cont.) 866-492-5540
2850 S. Roosevelt St., Ste. 101   480-212-0140
Tempe, AZ 85282   FAX 480-212-0141
Hours: 9-5 Mon-Fri

10 Azar Ct.   410-242-3322
Halethorpe, MD 21227
Hours: 9-5 Mon-Fri
www.4wallentertainment.com
Full-service lighting rental, sales and service. Visit web for additional locations. RENTALS.

Advanced Lighting & Sound Solutions 860-643-8401
PO Box 837 / 163 Slater St. Unit # 4   800-622-8872
Manchester, CT 06045   FAX 860-643-9032
Hours: 9-6 Mon, Fri / 9-5 Tue-Thur   E-mail: sales@alss1.com
www.alss1.com
Sales, service and installation of lighting and sound equipment and supplies. RENTALS. CREDIT CARDS.

All Bulbs & Expendables 516-766-2266
Mottingham Rd.   FAX 516-766-2299
Rockville Centre, NY 11570
Hours: 9-6 Mon-Fri   E-mail: sales@allbulbs.com
www.allbulbs.com
Major brands and types of bulbs, fixtures, gel, sockets, tape products, etc. Mention you saw us in The Entertainment Sourcebook and receive a 5% discount. CREDIT CARDS.

Altman Stage Lighting Co., Inc. 914-476-7987
57 Alexander St.   800-4ALTMAN
Yonkers, NY 10701   FAX 914-966-1980
Hours: 9:30-5 Mon-Fri   E-mail: info@altmanlighting.com
www.altmanlighting.com
Manufacturer of theatre, film and TV luminaries. Catalog. RENTALS. No credit cards.

Barbizon 212-586-1620
456 W 55th St.(9-10th Ave)
NY, NY 10019   800-582-9941
Hours: 8-5 Mon-Fri / 9-1 Sat   FAX 212-247-8818

3 Draper St.   781-935-3920
Woburn, MA 01801   FAX 781-935-9273
Hours: 8:15-5:30 Mon-Fri / 9-2 Sat

6437G General Green Way   703-750-3900
Alexandria, VA 22312   800-922-2972
Hours: 9-5 Mon-Fri / 9-12 Sat   FAX 703-750-1448

11551 Interchange Circle South   954-919-6495
Miramar, FL 33025   800-535-4083
Hours: 9-6 Mon-Fri / 9-1 Sat   FAX 954-919-6606

101 Krog St.   404-681-5124
Atlanta, GA 30307   FAX 404-681-5315
Hours: 8:30-5:30 Mon-Fri / 9-1 Sat

Barbizon (cont.) 704-372-2122
1016 McClelland Ct.
Charlotte, NC 28206   FAX 704-372-7422
Hours: 8:30-5:30 Mon-Fri / 9-12 Sat

8269 E 23rd Ave., Ste 111   303-394-9875
Denver, CO 80238   800-290-8643
Hours: 8:30-5 Mon-Fri   FAX 303-355-5996
www.barbizon.com
Theatrical lighting supplier; GE, Sylvania, HMI lamps, etc. Visit web address
for other locations. CREDIT CARDS.

Bentley Meeker Lighting & Staging, Inc. 212-722-3349
465 10th Ave. 2nd FL   FAX: 212-722-8803
NY, NY 10018
Hours: 10-6 Mon - Fri   E-mail: mail@bentleymeeker.com
www.bentleymeeker.com
Full-service lighting, staging and audio firm specializing in live events,
parties, fashion shows, etc.

Bestek Lighting & Staging 631-643-0707
98 Mahan St.   631-643-0760
West Babylon, NY 11704   FAX 631-643-0764
Hours: 9-5 Mon-Fri   E-mail: production@bestek.com
www.bestek.com
Full production services including lighting, AV, stages, sets, platforms, rentals
and installation for special events, corporate meetings, live shows.
RENTALS. CREDIT CARDS.

BMI Supply 518-793-6706
571 Queensbury Ave.   800-836-0524
Queensbury, NY 12804   FAX 518-793-6181
Hours: 8-6 Mon-Fri   E-mail: bminy@bmisupply.com
www.bmisupply.com
A full-line theatrical supply house and on-site contractor. Retail and
wholesale at everyday wholesale prices. Special effects. Sales only. CREDIT
CARDS.

BML / Blackbird Theatrical Services 201-617-8900
1 Aquarium Dr.   FAX 201-617-8908
Secaucus, NJ 07094
Hours: 9-6 Mon-Fri   E-mail: mail@bmlblackbird.com
www.bmlblackbird.com
Full-service production house. Lighting packages for rock and roll, theatre,
special events, etc. Over 25 years in the business. RENTALS. CREDIT
CARDS.

BTL Productions 201-943-4190
815 Fairview Ave., Unit 11 (Tracey Ave)   FAX 201-943-4191
Fairview, NJ 07022
Hours: 9-5 Mon-Fri
www.bltprod.com
Full service production company providing project management, design (scenic, lighting and sound.) Fabrication and installation. Extensive experience in fashion shows and special / corporate events as well as theatre and television. the will help you design or realize your design. Custom logos and backdrops. RENTALS.

Bulbtronics, Inc. 800-588-BULB
720 Ninth Ave.(49th & 50th St)   212-765-6190
NY, NY 10019   FAX 212-765-6195
Hours: 9-5 Mon-Fri

1054 N Cahuenga Blvd.   323-461-6262
Hollywood, CA 90038   FAX 213-461-7307
Hours: 9-5 Mon-Fri

45 Banfi Plaza(Headquarters)   631-249-2272
Farmingdale, NY 11735   800-654-8542
Hours: 9-5 Mon-Fri   FAX 631-249-6066
                                  E-mail: sttv@bulbtronics.com

9460 Delegates Dr Suite 119   407-857-1777
Orlando, FL 32837   866-675-2852
Hours: 9-5 Mon-Fri   FAX 407-857-1115
www.bulbtronics.com   E-mail: custserv@bulbtronics.com
Full-service lamp and bulb distributor. Also supplies; gaffer tape, blackwrap, color media, patterns, sockets and fixtures; ask for stage and studio dept. Brochure and price list available. Check website for other locations. CREDIT CARDS.

Christie Lites Ltd. 416-644-1010
100 Carson St. Unit A   FAX 416-644-0404
Toronto, ON, Canada M8W 3R9
Hours: 8-5 Mon-Fri

7662 Currency Dr.   407-856-0016
Orlando, FL 32809   FAX 407-856-0765
Hours: 8-5 Mon-Fri

4801 Sharp St.   214-637-3535
Dallas, TX 75247   FAX 214-637-4343
Hours: 8-5 Mon-Fri

231 Third Ave. NE   212-685-0016
Yonkers, NY 10705   FAX 914-969-1073
Hours: 8-5 Mon-Fri

3686 Bainbridge Ave.(Vancouver Area)   604-255-9943
Burnaby, BC, Canada V5A 2T4   FAX 604-255-9194
Hours: 8-5 Mon-Fri

Christie Lites Ltd. (cont.) 877-668-2207
4340 N. Lamb Blvd.
Las Vegas, NV 89115
Hours: 8-5 Mon-Fri
www.christielites.net
*A full-service theatrical and rock & roll lighting company providing sales,
rentals and production services. Specialists in the packaging of complete
systems for both touring and installation. Manufacturer of ColoRocket
colorchanger systems. Large inventory of various intelligent lights.
RENTALS.*

Cine 60 347-527-1175
630 Ninth Ave., 2nd FL (44-45th St)   917-239-8119
NY, NY 10036   FAX 347-730-4496
Hours: 8:30-5 Mon-Fri   E-mail: sales@cine60newyork.com
www.cine60newyork.com
*Film and video equipment; source for battery belts and packs. RENTALS.
CREDIT CARDS.*

Circuit Lighting, Inc. 732-968-9533
299 Route 22 E., Ste 12(Colonial Square Mall)   FAX 732-968-9231
Greenbrook, NJ 08812
Hours 9-5 Mon-Fri   E-mail: info@circuitlighting.com
www.circuitlighting.com
*Specializes in video/television, corporate and concert production.
Multilingual staff. Sales and repair of equipment. RENTALS. CREDIT
CARDS.*

Dimmer Performance Electronics, Inc. 201-262-7299
326 Sherwood Dr.   FAX 201-262-0444
Paramus, NJ 07652
Hours: 8:30-6 Mon-Fri
*A field service company. Authorized service for Macro Electronics, Electronics
Diversified and Microlite Corp. Specialist in Kliegl products, with large
inventory of spare parts.*

Duplication Depot 631-752-0608
215-B Central Ave.   800-950-0608
Farmingdale, NY 11735   FAX 631-752-3607
Hours: 9-5 Mon-Fri   E-mail: copymydist@gmail.com
www.duplicationdepot.com
*Audio-visual services; duplicating, editing and staging. Also projection
equipment; reasonable prices. RENTALS. CREDIT CARDS.*

Gerriets International 609-758-9121
130 Winterwood Ave   800-369-3695
Ewing, NJ 08638   FAX 609-758-9596
Hours: 8:30-5 Mon-Fri   E-mail: mail@gi-info.com
www.gi-info.com
*Manufacturer of projection cycloramas and screens made of six different,
inherently flame-retardant, front/rear projection materials; ultrasonically
welded to sizes up to 100' high. RENTALS.*

High Output, Inc. 781-364-1800
495 Turnpike St.
Canton, MA 02021   781-364-1900
Hours: 8:30-5:30 Mon-Fri

4 Warren Ave. # 6   207-854-4737
Westbrook, ME 04092   FAX 207-854-4746
Hours: 9-5 Mon-Fri

301 Iron Horse Way, Bldg. 62   401-521-0676
Providence, RI 02908   FAX 401-521-0776
Hours: 8:30-5:30 Mon-Fri

62 Brigade St.   888-744-1400
Charleston, SC 29403   843-722-3600
Hours: 8:30-5 Mon-Fri   FAX 843-722-3607

300 State St., Ste. 318   860-437-3600
New London, CT 06320

                                                       FAX 860-437-0404
www.highoutput.com   E-mail: sales@highoutput.com
Lighting equipment for theatre. Maintains a complete stock of color, lamps
and supplies at all locations. Can provide installation of lighting, control,
dimming, curtains and rigging. Also New England's largest provider of film
and television lighting. Shop online. RENTALS. CREDIT CARDS.

Hudson Scenic Studio 914-375-0900
130 Fernbrook St.   FAX 914-378-9134
Yonkers, NY 10705
Hours: 8:00-5:30 Mon-Fri   E-mail: info@hudsonscenic.com
www.hudsonscenic.com
Union lighting shop. Speak to Neil Mazzella. RENTALS.

Kadan Productions, Inc. 212-674-7080
3200 Liberty Ave., Bldg 3 (Paterson Plank Rd)   FAX 212-674-7244
North Bergen, NJ 07047
Hours: 9-6 Mon-Fri
www.kadaninc.com
Full-service staging, lighting, audio/video, set construction and design
company. Extensive experience in fashion, corporate conventions and special
events. Can provide video graphics and slide projection. Will design or make
any part of your design happen.

Ken Logert Productions 718-292-1257
2680 Park Ave. (141st St)   FAX 718-742-2461
Bronx, NY 10451
Hours: 9-5 Mon-Fri / call for appt.   E-mail: info@klprods.com
www.klprods.com
One-stop, full-service equipment provider of lighting, audio/video and
projection equipment for concerts, special events, promotions and
environmental production services. RENTALS. CREDIT CARDS.

Lee Filters 818-238-1220
2237 N Hollywood Way   800-576-5055
Burbank, CA 91505   FAX 818-238-1228
Hours: 8-5 Mon-Fri   E-mail: mail@leefiltersusa.com
www.leefilters.com / www.leefiltersusa.com
Has Blackfoil 280, a heat resistant, flexible foil. Color media and lighting patterns. One of the world's largest manufacturers of color filters. See website for list of dealers.

Lighting & Electronics 845-297-1244
Market St., Industrial Park   800-553-1244
Wappingers Falls, NY 12590   FAX 845-297-9270
Hours: 8:30-5 Mon-Fri   E-mail: info@le-us.com
www.le-us.com
Manufacturer of lighting fixtures for professional, educational, community stage and studio. Products include the Mini-Strip, Broad Cyc and Micro-Fill, along with full lines of ellipsoidals, fresnels, etc. Specializing in dimming fluorescents.

Lights Up and Cue Sound 516-505-3900
25 Hempstead Gardens Dr.   FAX 516-505-3939
West Hempstead, NY 11552
Hours: 8:30-5 Mon-Fri   E-mail: frankb@lighsupandcuesound.com
www.lightsupandcuesound.com
Full production light and sound company. Installation services. Complete special events lighting and contracting services for indoor/outdoor venues and touring shows.

Lite-Trol Services 516-681-5288
485 W John St.   800-548-3876
Hicksville, NY 11801   FAX 516-681-7288
Hours: 9-5 Mon-Fri   E-mail: litetrol@aol.com
www.litetrol.com
Repair and maintenance of theatrical and architectural lighting systems. Contact Steve Short.

Main Attractions 732-225-3500
85 Newfield Ave. (Raritan Ctr Pkwy)   800-394-3500
Edison, NJ 08837   732-225-2110
Hours: 9:30-5 Mon-Fri   E-mail: events@mainattractions.com
www.mainattractions.com
Special events contractors; specializing in custom tent rentals, restroom trailers, decor, portable staging, lighting and the production of displays and signage. Visit website to see the full spectrum of their products. RENTALS. CREDIT CARDS.

Oasis/Stage Werks 801-363-0364
249 Rio Grande St.   FAX 801-575-7121
Salt Lake City, UT 84101
Hours: 9-6 Mon-Fri
www.oasis-stage.com
Rental, sales and service. Vari Lite 300 Series dealer, ETC Source tours in stock, Optikinetics dealer and repair. RENTALS. CREDIT CARDS.

PLS Staging 973-857-7242
   371 Little Falls Road   800-783-4757
   Cedar Grove, NJ 07009   FAX 973-857-8867
   Hours: 9-5 Mon-Fri / 24-hr. paging service
   www.plsstaging.com
   Full-service audio-visual company. Rentals speak to Scott. RENTALS.
   CREDIT CARDS.

PRG 201-758-4000
   539 Temple Hill Rd.   845-567-5700
   New Windsor, NY 12553   FAX 845-567-5800
   Hours: 8-6 Mon-Fri

   7777 West Side Ave.   201-758-4000
   North Bergen, NJ 07047   FAX 201-758-4312
   Hours: 8-6 Mon-Fri

   250 E Sandford Blvd.   914-662-3540
   Mt. Vernon, NY 10550   FAX 914-668-6844
   Hours: 8-6 Mon-Fri

   9111 Sunland Blvd.   818-252-2600
   Sun Valley, CA 91352   818-262-3983
   Hours: 8-6 Mon- Fri   FAX 818-252-2620

   6050 S Valley View Blvd.   702-942-4774
   Las Vegas, NV 89118   702-942-4774
   Hours: 8-6 Mon-Fri   FAX 702-942-4772

   2480 Tedlo St.   905-270-9050
   Mississauga, ON L5A 3V3   FAX 905-270-2590
   Hours: 8-6 Mon-Fri

   1902 Cypress Lake Dr., Ste 100   407-855-8060
   Orlando, FL 32837   FAX 407-855-8059
   Hours: 8-6 Mon-Fri

   8351 Eastgate Blvd.   615-834-3190
   Mount Juliette, TN 37122   FAX 615-834-3192
   Hours: 8-6 Mon-Fri

   8617 Ambassador Row Ste. 120   214-630-1963
   Dallas, TX 75247   FAX 214-630-5867
   Hours: 8-6 Mon-Fri

   11801 E. 33rd Ave., Ste. D   303-341-4848
   Aurora, CO 80010   FAX 702-942-4623
   Hours: 8-6 Mon-Fri   E-mail: prg.com
   www.prg.com
   **_Full-service lighting rental, sales and service, serving theatre, corporate
theatre, television and special event markets. Systems group specializes in
turn-key permanent installations. Image Systems group provides expertise in
large format projection systems. RENTALS_**

Production Advantage, Inc. 802-651-6915
P.O. Box 1700   800-424-99914
Williston, VT 05495   FAX 877-424-9991
Hours: 8:30-6 Mon-Fri   E-mail: sales@proadv.com
www.proadv.com
Complete line of lamps, filters, patterns, connectors, cable, instruments and
accessories. Catalog available and approved P.O.s accepted. Catalog.
CREDIT CARDS.

Raven Screen Corp. 845-782-1844
112 Spring St.   800-847-6906
Monroe, NY 10950   FAX 845-782-1840
Hours: 8:30-5 Mon-Fri   E-mail: info@ravenscreen.com
www.ravenscreen.com
Carries all scope of projection screening, glass, fabrics, etc. Chalk and tack
boards, lecture units and other AV furniture.

RKL Lighting Co., Inc. 201-261-3383
380 N Fairview Ave.   FAX 201-261-3066
Paramas, NJ 07652
Hours: 9-6 Mon-Fri   E-mail: rkliegl@rkllighting.com
www.rkllighting.com
A dealer for theatrical, film and television lighting markets. Specializing in
Altman, Electronics Diversified, Rosco and Strong. Contact John or Karen
Kleigl.

Scharff Weisberg, Inc. 212-582-2345
36-36 33rd St.   800-477-SHOW
Long Island City, NY 11106   FAX 718-610-1750
Hours: 9-5:30 Mon-Fri / 24 hr Tech Support
www.swinyc.com   E-mail: scharffweisberg@swinyc.com
Rents, sells, stages and installs a full line of audio, video and multimedia
equipment. Specializes in video projection, image magnification, computer
data display, sound and video walls. Developing a full-service lighting
division. RENTALS.

Science Faction 212-586-1911
333 W 52nd St., FL 9 (Park-3rd Ave)
NY, NY 10019
Hours: 9:30-6 Mon-Fri   E-mail: info@sciencefaction.com
www.sciencefaction.com
Laser special effects, including ability to digitize and animate from flat line
art.

See Factor Industry, Inc. 718-784-4200
37-11 30th St. (37th Ave)   FAX 718-784-0617
Long Island City, NY 11101
Hours: 9-5 Mon-Fri
www.seefactor.com
Supplying equipment and services to local, national and international shows,
concert tours and industrials.

SFX Design, Inc. 817-599-0800
2500 I-20 E   FAX 817-599-0496
Weatherford, TX 76087
Hours: 8-4 Mon-Fri   E-mail: info@sfxdesigninc.com
www.sfxdesigninc.com
Stock and custom gobos. Decorative and fighting swords, handguns, rifles,
machine guns; any period, able to fire blanks. Breakaway resin to mold your
own bottles, glass, panes, etc. Fog-Master machines and Aquafog
component; also cobweb system. Pyrotechnics and miniature pneumatics,
blood effects, atmospherics; custom projects. Great website. Catalog. No
credit cards.

SLD Lighting 212-245-4155
318 W 47th St. (8-9th Ave)   800-245-6630
NY, NY 10036   FAX 212-956-6537
Hours: 9-5:30 Mon-Wed, Fri / 9-6:30 Thurs   E-mail: sales@sldlighting.com
www.sldlighting.com
Stocking distributor of major lighting/sound manufacturers and specialty
items. Retail store and mail order department. Full-line catalog available.
Shipping worldwide. RENTALS. CREDIT CARDS.

Staging Techniques 212-736-5727
210 W Lincoln Ave. (8-9th Ave)   FAX 914-664-3919
Mt. Vernon, NY 10050
Hours: 9-5 Mon-Fri   E-mail: info@stagingtechniques.com
www.stagingtechniques.com
Audio-visual house; programming facilities, screening room. RENTALS.
AMEX.

Times Square Lighting 845-947-3034
5 Holt Dr.   FAX 845-947-3047
Stony Point, NY 10980
Hours: 8:30-5 Mon-Fri

214 W 29th St.(7th-8th Ave)   212-391-5865
NY, NY 10001   FAX 917-591-0815
Hours: 8:30-5 Mon-Fri
www.tslight.com   E-mail: info@tslight.com
Manufacturer of lighting instruments and fog machines. CREDIT CARDS.

U.S. Balloon Mfg. Co. 718-492-9700
140 58th St. (Bklyn Army Terminal)   800-285-4000
Brooklyn, NY 11220   FAX 718-492-8711
Hours: 8:30-7 Mon-Fri   E-mail: sales@usballoon.com
www.usballoon.com
Lighted balloon fixtures, 3 sizes. RENTALS. CREDIT CARDS.

Wildfire, Inc. 310-755-6780
2908 Oregon Ct., Ste. G1   800-937-8065
Torrace, CA 90503   FAX 310-755-6781
Hours: 8-5 Mon-Fri   E-mail: sales@wildfirefx.com
www.wildfirefx.com
Manufacturer of long throw UV lighting fixtures. Complete UV visual effects
production services. P.O.s and CREDIT CARDS.

LIGHTING DESIGN SOFTWARE

Electronic Theatre Controls, Inc. (ETC) 800-688-4116
   630 Ninth Ave., Ste 1001(45th St)   212-397-8080
   NY, NY 10036   FAX 212-397-4340
   Hours: 9-5 Mon-Fri

   6640 Sunset Blvd., Ste 200   323-461-0216
   Los Angeles, CA 90028   FAX 323-461-7830
   Hours: 9:00-5:00 Mon-Fri

   3031 Plesant View   608-831-4116
   Middleton, WI 53562   FAX 608-836-1736
   Hours: 8-5 Mon-Fri

   3031 Pleasant View Rd.   608-831-4116
   Middleton, WI 53562   FAX 608-836-1736
   Hours: 8-5 Mon-Fri
   www.etcconnect.com
   Distributers of WYSIWYG, WYSICAD, WYSIPAPER and WYSILAB family of
   lighting design software manufactured by CAST Lighting.

John McKernon Software 908-387-1994
   2650 Belvidere Rd.
   Phillipsburg, NJ 08865
   Hours: by appt.
   www.mckernon.com
   Creates & distributes îLightwright,î the best program for lighting design
   paperwork and îBeamwright,î a simple and affordable utility that helps you
   choose the right light for every situation. Demo available. CREDIT CARDS.

Stage Research, Inc. 440-717-7510
   P.O. Box 670557   888-267-0859
   Northfield, OH 44067   FAX 888-668-0751
   Hours: 9-5 Mon-Fri   E-mail: info@stageresearch.com
   www.stageresearch.com
   Windows-based software tools for stage and studio lighting industry,
   including SFX & ShowBuilder as well as sound cards from Echo. See website
   for various demos and tours of their software. CREDIT CARDS.

Westside Systems 888-724-6203
   39 Farnham Ave # 43
   New Haven, CT 06515
   www.westsidesystems.com   E-mail: info@westsidesystems.com
   Developer and publisher of personal computer products for the
   entertainment industry. Virtual Light Lab, a desktop light lab and Cue to Cue,
   a lighting console disk translation service.

LIGHTING FIXTURES

Action Lighting, Inc. 406-586-5105
310 Ice Pond Rd.   800-248-0076
Bozeman, MT 59715   FAX 406-585-3078
Hours: 8-5 Mon-Fri closed 11:30-12:30 daily   E-mail: catalog@actionlighting.com
www.actionlighting.com
Bulbs of all kinds. Great catalog and website. Staff very helpful. Orders under $25 will be charged a small order fee of $7.50. CREDIT CARDS.

Art & Industrial Design 212-477-0116
50 Great Jones St. (4th Ave)   FAX 212-477-1420
NY, NY 10012
Hours: 10-5 Mon-Fri / 10-1 Sat   E-mail: info@aid20c.com
www.aid20c.com
20th-century and Art Deco furniture, furnishings, art and objects. Many original high-style works. Also collectibles, clocks and lighting fixtures. RENTALS. CREDIT CARDS.

Authentiques 212-675-2179
255 W 18th St. (7-8th Ave)
NY, NY 10011
Hours: 12-6 Wed-Sat / 1-6 Sun or by appt.   E-mail: fab.stuff@verizon.net
www.fab-stuff.com
1950s to 70s small props and lamps. Wonderful selection of lighting fixtures and antique Christmas decorations.

Bowery Lighting Corp 212-941-8244
148 Bowery (Grand St)   866-418-9673
NY, NY 10013   FAX 212-226-7046
Hours: 9:30-6 Daily
www.lightingnewyork.com
General range of lighting fixtures at good prices. RENTALS. CREDIT CARDS.

Braswell Galleries 203-327-5101
1 Muller Ave.   203-357-0753
Norwalk, CT 06851   FAX 203-846-0617
Hours: 10:30-5 Mon-Sat / 11-5 Sun   E-mail: kathy@braswellgalleries.com
www.braswellgalleries.com
Wide range of furniture and furnishings, paintings, chandeliers, lighting, artwork, glassware and china. Rugs from many time periods and also unique items such as a x-ray machine from 1930-50. Animal heads, rowing scull and more. Rentals as well as sales at very reasonable prices. RENTALS.

City Barn Antiques 718-855-8566
145 Front St. (Jay-Pearl St)
Brooklyn, NY 11201
Hours: 12-6 Daily   E-mail: citybarn@aol.com
1930-1960 modern furniture, lighting accessories. Specializing in vintage Heywood-Wakefield. Also Herman Miller, Knoll. RENTALS.

City Knickerbocker, Inc. 212-586-3939
　　665 Eleventh Ave, 2nd Fl. (corner 48th)　　　　　　　FAX 212-262-2889
　　NY, NY 10019
　　Hours:　8:30-5　Mon-Fri　　　　　　　E-mail: info@cityknickerbocker.com
　　www.cityknickerbocker.cot
　　Convenient midtown location; The best stop for rental of antique and some
　　contemporary lighting fixtures and shades.　Lighting repair and rewiring.
　　Some halogen repairs. Nice people; see Ken or Scott.　RENTALS. CREDIT
　　CARDS.

Eclectic / Encore Properties, Inc. 212-645-8880
　　620 W 26th St., 4th Fl. (11-12th Ave)　　　　　　　FAX 212-243-6508
　　NY, NY 10001
　　Hours:　9-5　Mon-Fri / or by appt.　　　　　E-mail: props@eclecticprops.com
　　www.eclecticprops.com
　　Collection of period and antique lighting fixtures, antique chandeliers, table
　　lamps, wall sconces, standing lamps including many classics from the 50s
　　60s and 70s.　A full-service prop rental company. Can request rental items
　　thru online catalog.　RENTALS. CREDIT CARDS.

Eighth Avenue Lighting, Inc. 212-279-1323
　　545 Eighth Ave. (37-38th St)　　　　　　　　　　FAX 212-279-1324
　　NY, NY 10018
　　Hours:　9-6 Mon-Sat
　　Electrical supplies, lighting fixtures, halogen lamps, track lights, novelty
　　lights, paper lanterns, and a full line of light bulbs.　CREDIT CARDS.

Elizabeth Street Gallery, Inc. 212-941-4800
　　209 Elizabeth St. (Spring-Prince St.)　　　　　　　FAX 212-274-0057
　　NY, NY 10012
　　Hours:　10-5 Mon-Fri　call for appt.　　　E-mail: info@elizabethstreetgallery.com
　　www.elizabethstreetgallery.com
　　French, English and American stone and marble fireplaces.　17th-19th century
　　garden statuary and furniture; columns, pilasters and keystones. Also studio
　　collection of reproductions based on historical designs. RENTALS.　CREDIT
　　CARDS.

Gallery 532 203-858-1432
　　50 John St. (John Street Antiques) (Manhattan-Market)　　　203-324-4677
　　Stamford, CT 06902
　　Hours: 10:30-5:30 Daily　　　　　　　　　　E-mail: gallery532@aol.com
　　Early 20th century (1900-1920) furniture, lighting fixtures and other decorative
　　arts. Currently selling at John St. Antiques. Very helpful. RENTALS.　CREDIT
　　CARDS.

Home Depot 800-553-3199
　　550 Hamilton Ave.(16-17th St)　　　　　　　　　　　718-832-8553
　　Brooklyn, NY 11232
　　Hours:　6-12pm Mon-Sat / 8-9pm Sun

　　124-04 31st Ave.(College Point Blvd)　　　　　　　　718-661-4608
　　Flushing, NY 11354　　　　　　　　　　　　　　FAX 718-670-3437
　　Hours:　6-11pm Mon-Sat / 7-9pm Sun

ATAC

Home Depot (cont.) 212-929-9571
40 W 23rd St.(5-6th Ave)
NY, NY 10010
Hours: 7-9pm Mon-Sat / 8-7 Sun

980 Third Ave.(58-59th St)   212-888-1512
NY, NY 10022
Hours: 7-9pm Mon-Sat / 8-7 Sun

50-10 Northern Blvd.(50th St-Newtown Rd)   718-278-9031
Long Island City, NY 11101
Hours: 6-11pm Mon-Sat / 8-9pm Sun
www.homedepot.com
Hardware, tools, lumber, plumbing supplies, gardening supplies, electrical
and lighting supplies. Windows, doors and cabinets. Queens and Brooklyn
locations open 24-hrs. for those emergency needs (less crowded then, too.)
Check web for additional locations. CREDIT CARDS.

Howard Kaplan Designs 646-443-7170
240 E 60th St. (2nd-3rd St)   FAX 646-443-7174
NY, NY 10022
Hours: 10-5:30 Mon-Fri   E-mail: hkaplandesigns@aol.com
www.howardkaplandesigns.com
French and English formal and country antiques and reproductions; also
lighting fixtures and vintage telephones. RENTALS. CREDIT CARDS.

Hugo, Ltd. 212-750-6877
233 E 59th St. (2nd-3rd Ave)   FAX 212-750-7346
NY, NY 10022
Hours: 10-5 Tue-Fri / weekends by appt.
A source for the largest collection of authentic 19th century lamps and
chandeliers, hand restored to museum level. Consultations. RENTALS.

Karl Barry Studio 718-596-1419
265 Douglas St. (Nevins-3rd Ave)
Brooklyn, NY 11217
Hours: by appt. only   E-mail: karlbarry@aol.com
www.karlbarrystudio.com
Arts and Crafts style of lighting fixtures, beautiful stuff. Mostly custom but
has some stock pieces. CREDIT CARDS.

Lee's Art Shop & Studio 212-247-0110
220 W 57th St. (B'way-7th Ave)   FAX 212-581-7023
NY, NY 10019
Hours: 9-7:30 Mon-Fri / 10-7 Sat / 11-6 Sun   E-mail: info@leesartshop.com
www.leesartshop.com
Contemporary, upscale and avant garde lighting, mostly halogen. Also stocks
fans. Expensive. Repairs and RENTALS available . CREDIT CARDS.

Lehman's 330-857-5757
One Leham Cr. / P.O. Box 270   888-438-5346
Kidron, OH 44636   FAX 888-780-4975
Hours; 8-5:30 Mon-Sat / Thurs til 8   E-mail: GetLehmans@aol.com
www.lehmans.com
Housewares, oil lamps, cast-iron cookery, wood cook stoves, homestead tools. Rustic old-fashioned stuff. Non-electric Amish products. Plus, all those old-fashioned health and beauty products, canning supplies, food and laundry supplies. Great catalog ($10 including shipping) or shop online. CREDIT CARDS.

Light Curves / Joan Nicole 845-434-5081
10 Rockview Lane   845-978-7653
Loch Sheldrake, NY 12759   FAX 845-434-5081
Hours: By appt., 24-hr. answering mach.   E-mail: lightcurves@gmail.com
Exquisite custom stained glass, tiffany style, leaded, painted glass, fused glass and mosaic. Also lighting fixtures, glass sculpture and jewelry, folding screens, windows, etc.

Lighting by Gregory 212-226-1276
158 Bowery (Delancey-Broome St)   800-807-1826
NY, NY 10012   FAX 212-226-2705
Hours: 9-5:30 Daily   E-mail: customerservice@lightingbygregory.com
www.lightingbygregory.com
Good selection track lighting, contemporary and high-tech lamps. RENTALS. CREDIT CARDS.

Lost City Arts 212-375-0500
18 Cooper Sq. (5th St)   FAX 212-375-9342
NY, NY 10012
Hours: 10-6 Mon,-Fri / 12-6 Sat-Sun   E-mail: lostcityarts@yahoo.com
www.lostcityarts.com
Unusual lighting fixtures, lamps, illuminated clocks, etc. RENTALS. CREDIT CARDS.

Lowe's 718-249-1151
118 Second Ave. (9th-12th St)   800-445-6337
Brooklyn, NY 11215   FAX 718-249-1154
Hours: 5-12 Mon-Sun
www.lowes.com
Big-box home improvement store that carries gardening supplies, kitchen cabinets, lighting fixtures, tools, lumber and much more. Check website for other locations. CREDIT CARDS.

Nowell's Lighting 415-332-4933
615 Irwin St. (Lincoln-Anderson Dr)   FAX 415-332-4936
San Raphael, CA 94961
Hours: 9:30-5 Tue-Sat   E-mail: sales@nowellslighting.com
www.nowellslighting.com
Reproduction and antique Victorian and Edwardian fixtures and shades; custom work. Rewiring and repairs, including halogens.

The Prop Company / Kaplan and Associates 212-691-7767
111 W 19th St., 8th Fl. (6-7th Ave)   FAX 212-727-3055
NY, NY 10011
Hours: 9-5 Mon-Fri   E-mail: propcompany@yahoo.com
Some contemporary, antique and designer fixtures and lamps for the home and office. Contact Maxine Kaplan. RENTALS.

Recycling the Past 609-660-9790
381 N. Main St.   FAX 609-660-0878
Barnegat, NJ 08005
Hours: 10-5 Tue-Sun / by appt.   E-mail: contact@gmail.com
www.recyclingthepast.com
Architectural salvage and antiques. Vintage tile, statuary, iron fencing, doors, garden items and other funky finds. Inventory changes, check web-site for new items daily. RENTALS. CREDIT CARDS.

Red Barn Antiques 413-528-3230
72 Main St.   FAX 413-528-6751
South Egremont, MA 01258
Hours: 10-5 daily   E-mail: redbarn@bcn.net
www.antiquejunction.com/redbarn
Antique lighting fixtures, some furniture and accessories. Repairs and restoration, including halogen. Speak to John or Mary Walther. CREDIT CARDS.

Remains Lighting 212-675-8051
130 W 28th St. (6-7th Ave)   FAX 212-675-8052
NY, NY 10001
Hours: 9-6 Mon-Fri   E-mail: mail@remains.com
www.remains.com
Vintage and antique lighting fixtures, sconces, etc. RENTALS. CREDIT CARDS.

Retro-Modern 212-674-0530
28 E 10th St. (B'way-University)
NY, NY 10003
Hours: 10-6 Mon-Fri / or by appt.
Mostly Art Deco and Modern light fixtures (1910-1960). RENTALS.

Roland Antiques Gallery, Inc. 212-260-2000
74 E 11th St. (University-Broadway)   FAX 212-260-2778
NY, NY 10003
Hours: 10-5 Mon-Fri   E-mail: info@rolandantiques.com
www.rolandantiques.com
18th, 19th and early 20th century furniture, paintings, early antique lighting, bric-a-brac; wholesaler. RENTALS. CREDIT CARDS.

SLD Lighting 212-245-4155
318 W 47th St. (8-9th Ave)   800-245-6630
NY, NY 10036   FAX 212-956-6537
Hours: 9-5:30 Mon-Wed, Fri / 9-6:30 Thurs   E-mail: sales@sldlighting.com
www.sldlighting.com
Stocking distributor of major lighting/sound manufacturers and specialty items. Retail store and mail order department. Full-line catalog available. Shipping worldwide. RENTALS. CREDIT CARDS.

Victorian Trading Company 800-700-2035
15600 W 99th St.   913-438-3995
Lenexa, KS 66219   FAX 913-438-5225
Hours: 24 on website
www.victoriantradingco.com
Mail order company with a selection of reproduction Victorian lamps, shades
and candles. Great website. CREDIT CARDS.

Weiss & Biheller 212-979-6990
116 E 16th St., 9th Fl. (Park-Irving Pl)   888-296-8919
NY, NY 10003   FAX 212-979-8283
Hours: 9-4:45 Mon-Fri
www.weissandbiheller.com
Large stock of chandeliers, sconces, lamp parts, also crystal trimmings.
Wholesale only. $50 min.

Zero to Sixties 212-925-0932
354 Broadway (Franklin)
NY, NY 10013
Hours: 11-6 Mon-Fri   E-mail: genie354@bellatlantic.net
19th-and 20th-century furniture, furnishings, art, lighting and accessories.
Unusual items. RENTALS. CREDIT CARDS.

LINENS
See also: ANTIQUES: All Headings
                PROP RENTAL HOUSES

ABC Carpet & Home Co., Inc. 212-473-3000
888 Broadway(19th St)   FAX 212-777-3713
NY, NY 10003
Hours: 10-8 Mon - Fri / 10-7 Sat / 11-6:30 Sun

1055 Bronx River Ave.(Bruckner Blvd) Outlet   718-842-8772
NY, NY 10472   FAX 718-812-6905
Hours: 10-7 Mon - Fri / 10-7 Sat / 11-6 Sun
www.abccarpet.com
Large selection of sheets, towels, spreads, pillows, tablecloths and
accessories. Pricey. RENTALS. CREDIT CARDS.

April Cornell 888-332-7745
87 Church St. (83rd-84th St)
Burlington, VT 05401
Hours: 8-6 Mon-Fri
www.aprilcornell.com
Interesting selection of pillows, bedspreads, window treatments, throw rugs;
also ceramics and clothing. RENTALS. CREDIT CARDS.

Bed, Bath and Beyond . . . . .1-800-Go Beyond
620 Sixth Ave.(18th St)   212-255-3550
NY, NY 10011   FAX 212-229-1040
Hours: 8-9 Daily

410 E 61st St.(1st Ave)   646-215-4702
NY, NY 10010   FAX 646-215-4713
Hours: 9-9 Daily

Bed, Bath and Beyond (cont.) . . . . .1-800-Go Beyond
1932 Broadway (64-65th St)   917-441-9391
NY, NY 10023
Hours: 9-10 Daily
www.bedbathandbeyond.com
A department store for bedroom, bathroom and kitchen: as well as seasonal.
Visit the website for other locations across the USA. CREDIT CARDS.

Boutross Imports 718-965-0070
209 25th St. (4th Ave)   800-227-7781
Brooklyn, NY 11232   FAX 718-965-9837
Hours: 9-5 Mon-Fri   E-mail: boutross@boutross.com
www.boutross.com
Wholesaler of fancy linens and laces; also damask and linen table cloths.
Catalog, will ship; see Mike. CREDIT CARDS.

Eldridge Textile Co. 732-544-4500
22 Meridian Rd. # 3   800-635-4399
Eatontown, NJ 07724   FAX 732-544-4555
Hours: 9:30-6 Mon-Fri   E-mail: custserv@eldridgetextile.com
www.eldridgetextile.com
Sheets, bedding, towels, tablecloths and custom window treatments. $3
refundable charge for catalog. Will ship. Catalog available online. CREDIT
CARDS.

Katonah Image, Inc. 914-232-0961
22 Woodsbridge Rd.   FAX 914-232-3944
Katonah, NY 10536
Hours: 9-6 Mon-Fri / 9-5 Sat
Vintage linens, quilts, chenilles, tablecloths, bark cloth, lace textiles and
more. RENTALS. CREDIT CARDS.

La Terrine 877-837-7463
Hours: 10-5:30 Mon-Sat   212-988-3366
1024 Lexington Ave.(73rd St)   FAX 212-249-5846
NY, NY 10021
Hours: 10-5:30 Mon-Sat

280 Columbus Ave.   212-362-2122
NY, NY 10023
Hours: 11-7 Mon-Sat / 12-6 Sun   E-mail: info@laterrinedirect.com
www.laterrinedirect.com
Tabletop ceramics, linens, glassware. Will ship. Speak to Marsha Goldstein or
Yvette Goddard. RENTALS. CREDIT CARDS.

Laytner's Linen & Home 800-690-7200
2270 Broadway(82nd-83rd St)   212-724-0180
NY, NY 10024   FAX 212-769-0620
Hours: 10-8 Mon-Sat / 11-7 Sun

237 E 86th St.(2nd-3rd Ave)   212-996-4439
NY, NY 10028
Hours: 10-8 Mon-Sat / 11-7 Sun

Laytner's Linen & Home (cont.) 800-690-7200
72-10 Austin St.   718-793-0003
Forest Hills, NY 11375
Hours: 10:30-7:30 Mon-Sat / 11-6 Sun

794 Union St.   718-622-0300
Park Slope, NY 11215
Hours: 10-7:30 Mon-Sat / 11-7 Sun   E-mail: sales@laytners.com
www.laytners.com
Nice selection of bedding, towels, bath rugs, shower curtains, accessories;
will ship. Catalog. Online shopping. CREDIT CARDS.

M & A Decorators 212-226-3910
294 Grand St. (Eldridge & Allen)   FAX 212-334-5273
NY, NY 10002
Hours: 9:30-6 Sun-Thurs / 9:30-4 Fri / Closed Sat
Blinds, fine fabrics, upholstery, bed coverings, window designs, imported
tablecloths. CREDIT CARDS.

The Prop Company / Kaplan and Associates 212-691-7767
111 W 19th St., 8th Fl. (6-7th Ave)   FAX 212-727-3055
NY, NY 10011
Hours: 9-5 Mon-Fri   E-mail: propcompany@yahoo.com
Beautiful selection of contemporary and antique table linens, tapestries,
quilts, blankets, pillows, lace panels, fabrics, pure white to vibrant colors.
Contact Maxine Kaplan.

Ruth Fischl ....Linens 212-273-9710
141 W 28th St. (6-7th Ave)   Hardgoods 212-967-2493
NY, NY 10001   FAX 212-273-9718
Hours: 9-5 Mon-Thurs / 9-3 Fri   E-mail: ruthfischl@hotmail.com
www.ruthfischl.com
Excellent selection of rental linens, iron works, tables, candelabras, etc.
Purchase available. Open to trade by appointment. RENTALS.

Sunham & Co. (USA), Inc. 212-695-1218
308 Fifth Ave. (31st-32nd St)   FAX 212-947-4793
NY, NY 10001
Hours: 9-5:30 Mon-Fri   E-mail: info@sunham.com
www.sunham.com
Embroidered tablecloths and handkerchiefs, lace tablecloths. Bedding: quilts,
comforters and pillows.

Superior Drapery 201-343-3300
385 Prospect Ave.   800-274+0505
Hackensack, NJ 07601   FAX 201-343-0602
Hours: 8:30-5 Mon-Fri   E-mail: paul@superiordrapery.com
www.superiordrapery.com
Custom tablecloths and napkins in stock colors, rush orders, good prices; see
Laurie.

Table Wraps, Ltd. 516-334-8833
666 Cantiague Rock Rd.   FAX 516-334-6853
Jericho, NY 11753
Hours: 9-5 Mon-Fri   E-mail: staff@tablewraps.com
www.tablewraps.com
Party cloths; prints, solids, laces, satins and lamÈs. Located 45 mins. from NYC. RENTALS. CREDIT CARDS.

The Tablecloth Co., Inc. 800-227-5251
514 Totowa Ave.   973-942-1555
Paterson, NJ 07522   FAX 973-942-3092
Hours: 8-5 Mon-Fri   E-mail: info@tablecloth.com
www.tablecloth.com
Excellent service and great selection. CREDIT CARDS.

The Terrence Conran Shop 212-755-9079
888 Broadway Lower Level (18-19th St)   FAX 212-755-3989
NY, NY 10003
Hours: 11-8 Mon-Fri / 10-7 Sat / 12-6 Sun
                    E-mail: terenceconranshop@conranusa.com
www.conranusa.com
Designer furniture, household, bedding and bath, textiles and hardware. Very nice people. Will do rentals to film and television. CREDIT CARDS.

Yankee Linen Service 973-278-1225
63 2nd Ave.   FAX 973-278-5145
Paterson, NJ 07514
Hours: 8-5:30 Mon-Fri
www.yankeelinen.com
Yankee Linen can provide you with many different services from table linens, uniforms, floor mats, restroom supplies, and much more. Delivery. RENTALS. CREDIT CARDS.

LUGGAGE & HANDBAGS

Lup / Reel Jewelry 212-924-5588
1133 Broadway, Ste. 1314 (25-26th St)   FAX 212-924-2002
NY, NY 10010
Hours: By Appt.   E-mail: jessica@luprocks.com
www.luprocks.com
Fashion jewelry and watches from over 100 top designers. Jewelry cleared with designers for use in TV, film and print product placement. Diamonds, pearls, colored gemstones, platinum and gold available for use. Watches, Handbags, Shoes & Sunglasses. No credit cards.

The Prop Company / Kaplan and Associates 212-691-7767
111 W 19th St. 8th Fl. (6-7th Ave)   FAX 212-727-3055
NY, NY 10011
Hours: 9-5 Mon-Fri   E-mail: propcompany@yahoo.com
Contemporary tabletop, decorative accessories, antiques, ephemera and furniture. A nice collection of linens. RENTALS.

The Village Tannery 212-979-0013
7 Great Jones St.(B-way-Lafayette)
NY, NY 10012   FAX 212-473-9317
Hours: 11-7 Daily

173 Bleecker St.(Macdougal & Sullivan)   212-673-5444
NY, NY 10012
Hours: 11-11 Mon-Thrus / 11-1am Fri-Sat / 11-11 Sun
Unique line of bags-handbags, briefcases, suitcases and saddlebags.
Luggage and handbag repair. Specializes in repairing vintage luggage. All
repairs carry a lifetime guarantee. CREDIT CARDS.

LUGGAGE, HANDBAGS & LEATHER REPAIR

Altman Luggage 212-254-7275
135 Orchard St. (Delancey-Rivington St)   800-372-3377
NY, NY 10002   FAX 212-254-7663
Hours: 9-6 Sun-Thurs / 9-3 Fri   E-mail: info@altmanluggage.com
www.altmanluggage.com
Luggage, trunks, business cases, backpacks and travel accessories. RENTALS.
CREDIT CARDS.

T. Anthony Ltd. 212-750-9797
445 Park Ave. (56th St)   800-722-2406
NY, NY 10022   FAX 212-486-1184
Hours: 9:30-6 Mon-Fri / 10-6 Sat   E-mail: customerservice@tanthony.com
www.tanthony.com
Selection of fine luggage. RENTALS. CREDIT CARDS.

Crouch & Fitzgerald 212-755-5888
400 Madison Ave. (48th St)   800-6-CROUCH
NY, NY 10017   FAX 212-832-6461
Hours: 9-6 Mon-Fri/ 11-6 Sat   E-mail: kevin@crouchandfitzgerald.com
www.crouchandfitzgerald.com
Luggage, expensive. CREDIT CARDS.

The Leather Solution . . . . .800-GO HIDEY
2870 Milburn Ave.   516-223-3340
Baldwin, NY 11510   FAX 516-223-3748
Hours: 9-3 Mon-Fri   E-mail: info@leathersolutions.com
www.leathersolutions.com
Formerly Total Leather Care. Repair and restoration of leather furniture. See
website for other locations

Modern Leather Goods & Zipper Service 212-947-7770
2 W 32nd St., 4th Fl. (B'way-5th Ave)   212-279-3263
NY, NY 10001   FAX 212-967-3463
Hours: 8:30-4:45 Mon-Fri / 8:30-1 Sat
www.modernleathergoods.com
Repairs of luggage, briefcases; zipper repair for bags, luggage and clothing.
CREDIT CARDS.

Moormend Luggage Shop 212-289-3978
1228 Madison Ave. (88-89th St)   FAX 212-289-2302
NY, NY 10128
Hours: 9-6 Mon-Fri / 9-5 Sat
Luggage, trunks, leather goods. CREDIT CARDS.

Ohio Travel Bag 440-498-1955
6481 Davis Industrial Pkwy.   800-800-1941
Solon, OH 44139   FAX 440-498-9811
Hours: 8-5 Mon-Fri   E-mail: info@ohiotravelbag.com
www.ohiotravelbag.com
Wholesale buckles and hardware for leatherwork; catalog.

Superior Leather Restorers 212-889-7211
141 Lexington Ave. (29th St.)   FAX 212-447-5141
NY, NY 10016
Hours: 10-6 Mon-Fri / 10-3 Sat   E-mail: fixit@superiorleathernyc.com
www.superiorleathernyc.com
Repairs of leather clothing, luggage, etc. CREDIT CARDS.

The Village Tannery 212-979-0013
7 Great Jones St. (B-way-Lafayette)   FAX 212-473-9317
NY, NY 10012
Hours: 11-7 Daily

173 Bleecker St. (Macdougal & Sullivan)   212-673-5444
NY, NY 10012
Hours: 11-11 Mon-Thrus / 11-1am Fri-Sat / 11-11 Sun
Unique line of bags-handbags, briefcases, suitcases and saddlebags.
Luggage and handbag repair. Specializes in repairing vintage luggage. All
repairs carry a lifetime guarantee. CREDIT CARDS.

LUMBER

City Lumber 888-290-CITY
550 W 37th St. (10-11th Ave)   212-244-3743
NY, NY 10018   FAX 212-695-1710
Hours: 6-5 Mon- Fri

49-47 31st St.   718-937-6300
Long Island City, NY 11100   FAX 718-937-9387
Hours: 6-5 Mon-Fri   E-mail: rspodek@citylumber.net
www.citylumber.net
Lumber and building materials, including fire-retardant lumber.

Dykes Lumber 718-893-2127
1777 West Farms Rd.   FAX 718-991-4739
Bronx, NY 10460
Hours: 7:30-5 Mon-Fri

348 W 44th St. (8-9th Ave)   212-582-1930
NY, NY 10036   FAX 212-265-6735
Hours: 7:30-5 Mon-Fri / 8-1 Sat

Dykes Lumber (cont.) 718-784-3920
    26-16 Jackson Ave. (Near Queens Plaza)   FAX 718-361-5906
    Long Island City, NY 11101
    Hours: 7:30-5 Mon-Fri / 8-1 Sat

    1899 Park Ave. (Main Yard and General Offices)   201-867-0391
    Weehawken, NJ 07087   FAX 201-867-1674
    Hours: 7:30-5 Mon-Fri / 8-1 Sat

    555 Rt. 17   201-327-1300
    Ramsey, NJ 07446   FAX 201-327-1635
    Hours: 7:30-5 Mon, Tue, Wed, Fri / 7:30-7 Thurs / 8-4 Sat

    167 Sixth St. (2-3rd Ave)   718-624-3350
    Brooklyn, NY 11215   FAX 718-596-9233
    Hours: 7:30-5 Mon-Fri / 8-1 Sat

    8 Saw Mill River Rd.   914-347-1400
    Hawthorne, NY 10532   FAX 914-347-7150
    Hours: 7:30-5 Mon-Fri / 8-4 Sat   E-mail: info@dykeslumber.com
    www.dykeslumber.com
    General lumber and plywood; some hardwood; mouldings and millwork.
    Wood or styro beams. Catalog available, also online catalog. Delivery.
    CREDIT CARDS.

Feldman Lumber 718-786-7777
    1281 Metropolitan Ave.   FAX 718-472-3575
    Brooklyn, NY 11222
    Hours: 7-3:30 Mon-Fri / pick up by 2pm

    692 Thomas Boyland St. (Bumont)   718-498-6600
    Brooklyn, NY 11212   FAX 718-922-1189
    Hours: 7-5 Mon-Fri / pick up by 4:30pm / 7-12:30 Sat

    58-30 57th St.   718-418-7777
    Maspeth, NY 11378   FAX 718-472-3575
    Hours: 7-5 Mon-Fri
    Large orders at good prices; will deliver. CREDIT CARDS.

Home Depot 800-553-3199
    550 Hamilton Ave. (16-17th St)   718-832-8553
    Brooklyn, NY 11232
    Hours: 6-12pm Mon-Sat / 8-9pm Sun

    124-04 31st Ave. (College Point Blvd)   718-661-4608
    Flushing, NY 11354   FAX 718-670-3437
    Hours: 6-11pm Mon-Sat / 7-9pm Sun

    40 W 23rd St. (5-6th Ave)   212-929-9571
    NY, NY 10010
    Hours: 7-9pm Mon-Sat / 8-7 Sun

    980 Third Ave. (58-59th St)   212-888-1512
    NY, NY 10022
    Hours: 7-9pm Mon-Sat / 8-7 Sun

Home Depot (cont.) 800-553-3199
  50-10 Northern Blvd.(50th St-Newtown Rd)   718-278-9031
Long Island City, NY 11101
Hours: 6-11pm Mon-Sat / 8-9pm Sun
www.homedepot.com
*Hardware, tools, lumber, plumbing supplies, gardening supplies, electrical
and lighting supplies. Windows, doors and cabinets. Queens and Brooklyn
locations open 24-hrs. for those emergency needs (less crowded then, too.)
Check web for additional locations. CREDIT CARDS.*

Kamco Supply 718-768-1234
  80 21st St. (3rd Ave)   FAX 718-788-8607
Brooklyn, NY 11232
Hours: 7-5 Mon-Fri

  153 Tenth Ave. (19th St)   212-736-7350
NY, NY 10011   FAX 212-564-6436
Hours: 6-5 Mon-Fri / 7-12 Sat
www.kamco.com
*Large selection of lumber and supplies at good prices. Next-day delivery.
CREDIT CARDS.*

LeNobel Lumber Co., Inc. 212-246-0150
  38-20 Review Ave.   718-784-5230
Long Island City, NY 11101   FAX 718-784-1422
Hours: 8-5 Mon-Fri / (closed for lunch 12-1) Pick-up until 3:30
www.lenoblelumber.com   E-mail: website.lenoble@att.net
*Doors, plywood, laminates, mouldings, masonite, millwork, windows,
Sonotube. Cutting 1-3:30 pm. Delivery. Cash, certified check or accounts only.*

Lowe's 718-249-1151
  118 Second Ave. (9th-12th St)   800-445-6337
Brooklyn, NY 11215   FAX 718-249-1154
Hours: 5-12 Mon-Sun
www.lowes.com
*Big-box home improvement store that carries gardening supplies, kitchen
cabinets, lighting fixtures, tools, lumber and much more. Check website for
other locations. CREDIT CARDS.*

Lumber Boys 212-683-0410
  698 Second Ave. (38th St)   FAX 212-683-0412
NY, NY 10016
Hours: 7:30-4:30 Mon-Fri / 8:30-3 Sat
www.lumberboys.com
Lumber cut to size. CREDIT CARDS.

Lumberland Hardware 212-696-0022
  368 Third Ave. (29th St)   FAX 212-481-9223
NY, NY 10016
Hours: 9-7 Mon-Sat
*Wooden spindles, hardwood, some decorative hardware, mouldings and
power tools; same day delivery for orders received by 1 pm. CREDIT CARDS.*

M. Fine Lumber 718-381-5200
1301 Metropolitan Ave.   FAX 718-366-8907
Brooklyn, NY 11237
Hours: 8-5 Mon-Fri / pick-up by 4 pm   E-mail: merritt@mfinelumber.com
www.mfinelumber.com
Lumber and plywood. Large selection of recycled and used lumber. Antique
heart pine and used douglas fir. Heavy timber. Will ship overseas. CREDIT
CARDS.

Metropolitan Lumber & Hardware 718-898-2100
108-56 Roosevelt Ave. (108-111th St)   FAX 718-898-3026
Corona, NY 11368
Hours: 7-7 Mon-Fri / 8-6 Sat / 9-4:30 Sun

175 Spring St. (Thompson St-W B'way)   212-966-3466
NY, NY 10012   FAX 212-941-1453
Hours: 8-5:45 Mon-Fri / 8-4:45 Sat / 10-4 Sun

617 Eleventh Ave. (46-47th St)   212-246-9090
NY, NY 10036   212-262-3856
Hours: 6-6 Mon-Fri / 7:30-4 Sat / 10-4 Sun   FAX 212-765-2142
www.themetlumber.com
Hardwoods, plywood, hand and power tools, doors, windows, laminates,
mouldings. Complete building center. Free delivery on orders over $100.
Lumber yard closes one hour before showroom. CREDIT CARDS.

Midtown Lumber 212-675-2230
276 W 25th St. (7-8th Ave)   FAX 212-675-2642
NY, NY 10001
Hours: 7-4:30 Mon-Fri
Prop kit supplies, mouldings, hardwood flooring, tileboard, glass block,
doors, hardware and laminates; lumber cut to size. Contact Mike. CREDIT
CARDS.

Mike's Lumber Store, Inc..........................212-595-8884
254 W 88th St. (B'way-West End Ave)   FAX 212-874-6921
NY, NY 10024
Hours: 8-6 Mon-Fri / 8-5 Sat
Formicas, some hardware, unfinished furniture, doors, stain, mouldings.
CREDIT CARDS.

Miron Building Supply 718-497-1111
268 Johnson Ave. (near Bushwick)   FAX 718-366-0357
Brooklyn, NY 11206
Hours: 7-5 Mon-Fri / 7-2 Sat
Hardwood, mouldings, good prices. Will deliver to Manhattan; pick-ups until
2:30. No credit cards.

Prince Lumber Co., Inc. 212-777-1150
404 W 15th St. (9-10th Aves)   FAX 646-638-3539
NY, NY 10011
Hours: 7-4:30 Mon-Fri / 7:30-1:30 Sat
www.princelumber.com
Lumber, laminates, plywood, mouldings, doors, windows. Pleasant, good
service. Free delivery with $300 order. Delivery to the outer boroughs with
minimal charge. Also hardware and supplies. CREDIT CARDS.

Rosenzweig Lumber Corp. 718-585-8050
    801 E 135th St. (near Bruckner Blvd)   800-228-7674
    Bronx, NY 10454   FAX 718-292-8611
    Hours: 7-4 Mon-Fri / 9:30-4 pick-ups   E-mail: admin@rosenzweiglumber.com
    www.rosenzweiglumber.com

Good selection hardwoods, veneers, plywood, lumber and mouldings; good prices, prompt next day delivery. Catalog. CREDIT CARDS.

Tulnoy Lumber 718-901-1700
    1620 Webster Ave. (173rd St)   800-899-5833
    Bronx, NY 10457   FAX 718-229-8920
    Hours: 7-5 Mon-Fri   E-mail: sales@tulnoylumber.com
    www.tulnoylumber.com

Lumber, plywood and mouldings, laminates and paper products in stock. Contact Peter Tulchin.

MACHINISTS & MACHINISTS' TOOLS

McMaster-Carr Supply Co. 609-259-8900
    200 New Canton Way   FAX 609-259-3575
    Robbinsville, NJ 08691
    Hours: 24-hrs. / 7 days   E-mail: nj.sales@mcmaster.com
    www.mcmaster.com
    Top quality items, esp. hardware. A vast selection of even the hard-to-find stuff. Most items available for next day delivery to NYC via UPS. Great catalog. CREDIT CARDS.

MSC Industrial Supply Co. 717-865-5888
    100 MSC Dr.   800-645-7270
    Jonestown, PA 17038   FAX 717-861-5810
    Hours: 7-5 Mon-Fri   E-mail: branchhbu@mscdirect.com
    www.mscdirect.com
    Mail order machine tools; drills, reamers, cutters, etc.; great catalog, $25 minimum. Extensive hardware selection. Good one stop shop for large machines and tools. Competitive prices. Also good source for transmission parts. Order by 4 pm and get items delivered next day. Several depots across US. CREDIT CARDS.

Travers Tool Co. 718-886-7200
    PO Box 541550, 128-15 26th Ave. (Ulmer)   800-221-0270
    Flushing, NY 11354   FAX 800-722-0703
    Hours: 8-5 Mon-Fri   E-mail: ideas@travers.com
    www.travers.com
    Drill bits, chuck keys, clamps, sanding belts, more. 1130-page catalog! CREDIT CARDS.

Victor Machinery Exchange 718-366-9293
    56 Bogart St.   800-723-5359
    Brooklyn, NY 11206   FAX 718-366-7026
    Hours: 8:15-4:15 Mon-Fri   E-mail: sales@victornet.com
    www.victornet.com
    Tool room equipment, vises, micrometers, etc. CREDIT CARDS.

M

MAGAZINES & COMIC BOOKS
See also: BOOKSTORES

Forbidden Planet 212-473-1576
    840 Broadway (13th St)   (office) 212-475-6161
    NY, NY 10003
    Hours: 10-10 Sun-Tue / 9-12am Wed, 10-12am Thur-Sat
    www.fpnyc.com   E-mail: jeff@fpnyc.com
    Current special effects magazines, fantasy comic books. CREDIT CARDS.

Holmes and Meier 201-833-2270
    P.O. Box 943 (Maiden Ln)   FAX 201-833-2272
    Teaneck, NJ 07666
    Hours: 9-5 Mon-Fri   E-mail: info@holmesandmeier.com
    www.holmesandmeier.com
    Books and periodicals of scholarly interest, including costume design. CREDIT CARDS.

MAGAZINES & COMIC BOOKS

Hotaling News Agency 212-974-9419
630 W 52nd St. (11-12th Ave)   Cell 732-861-1058
NY, NY 10019
Hours: 3:30am-11:30am Mon-Fri   E-mail: hotalinginc@aol.com
In business since 1905! Good selection of current out-of-town newspapers.
Will ship. CREDIT CARDS.

Old Paper World 603-456-3338
Rt. 103 Box 246   FAX 603-456-3903
Warner, NH 03278
Hours: by appt. call ahead   E-mail: oldpaperwrld@conknet.com
Thousands of old paper collectibles, books, photographs, magazines, maps,
sheet music. Very helpful.

MAGIC SUPPLIES & NOVELTIES

Abracadabra 212-627-5194
19 W 21st St. (5-6th Ave)   FAX 212-627-7435
NY, NY 10001
Hours: 11-7 Mon-Sat / 12-5 Sun
www.abracadabrasuperstore.com
Magic tricks and illusions, gags and novelties. Catalog available online.
CREDIT CARDS.

Frank Bee Stores, Inc. 718-823-9792
3435 E Tremont Ave. (Bruckner Blvd)   877-937-2652
Bronx, NY 10465   FAX 718-824-2979
Hours: 9-6 Mon-Sat / until 7 Fri / 9-3 Sun   E-mail: frankiebe@aol.com
www.costumeman.com
Wide selection of Halloween and mascot costumes, make-up, wigs, magic
supplies. Volume discount. RENTALS. CREDIT CARDS.

Gamblers General Store 702-382-9903
800 S. Main St.   (outside NV) 800-322-2447
Las Vegas, NV 89101   FAX 702-366-0329
Hours: 9-6 Daily   E-mail: ggs@lasvegas.net
www.gamblersgeneralstore.com
The world's largest gambling superstore. Located just minutes from the
famous Las Vegas Strip, they host over 5000 gambling items in their 30,000
sq. ft. warehouse. Custom prize wheels, poker chips and cards. Must visit
website to see all they carry. Shop online or call for catalog. RENTALS
available for large productions. CREDIT CARDS.

Gothic Renaissance 212-780-9558
110 Fourth Ave. (11-12th St)   FAX 212-780-9560
NY, NY 10003
Hours: 11-8 Mon-Sat / 12-7 Sun   E-mail: gothicrenaissance@gmail.com
www.gothicrenaissance.com
Everything from the Gothic / Renaissance era. Modern with a Goth bend,
Victorian costumes. Wonderful selection of Goth and glam corsets and
masks. Small occult section. CREDIT CARDS.

GreatBigStuff.com 800-773-8832
　128 Patriot Dr., Units 8,9, and 10　　　　　　FAX 206-337-1725
　Middletown, DE 19709
　Hours: 9:30-6 Mon-Fri　　　　　　E-mail: service@greatbigstuff.com
　www.greatbigstuff.com
　Just as the name says, this website carries just about everything oversized.
　Rulers, pencils, alarm clocks, food items, bottles, baby items, game pieces
　and much, much more. Be sure to check out their website for other COOL
　items. CREDIT CARDS.

Halloween Adventure 212-673-4546
　104 Fourth Ave. (11-12th St)　　　　　　FAX 212-358-0927
　NY, NY 10003
　Hours: 11-8 Mon-Sat / 12-7 Sun
　www.newyorkcostumes.com
　The masters of masquerade with the city's largest selection of costumes,
　masks, wigs, magic supplies and theatrical make-up, plus custom fangs, f/x
　kits and much more. CREDIT CARDS.

Martinka & Co., Inc. 201-444-7576
　85 Godwin Ave.　　　　　　　　FAX 201-444-7576
　Midland Park, NJ 07432
　Hours: 10-5 Mon-Fri / 10-4 Sat　　　　E-mail: magic@martinka.com
　www.martinka.com
　Magicians headquarters carrying items for both beginners and professionals.
　Shop online or visit their store. RENTALS. CREDIT CARDS.

Oriental Trading Company, Inc. 800-875-8480
　4206 S. 108th St.　　　　　　　　402-331-6800
　Omaha, NE 68137　　　　　　FAX 402-331-3873
　Hours: 24-hr. online catalog service
　www.orientaltrading.com
　Thousands of small toys, novelties and party supplies for every occasion.
　Catalog available. CREDIT CARDS thru Paypal.

Paper Magic Group 800-278-4085
　PO Box 977　　　　　　　　　　570-961-3863
　Scranton, PA 18501　　　　FAX 800-648-7772 570-207-7825
　Hours: 8:30-5 Mon-Fri　　　　E-mail: orders@papermagic.com
　www.papermagic.com
　Rubber latex masks; inexpensive. Also carries wonderful selection of seasonal
　decorations. Catalog available. CREDIT CARDS.

Prank Place 860-761-7235
　206 Murphy Rd.　　　　　　　　800-901-1163
　Hartford, CT 06114　　　　　　FAX 800-717-8963
　Hours: 8:30-5 Mon-Fri / 24-hr web-site　　E-mail: help@prankplace.com
　www.prankplace.com
　Unique collection of outrageous pranks, t-shirts, practical jokes, and gag
　gifts. Prank Place offers the web's largest collection of funny novelties, gag
　gifts, and more. Visit web-site for many funny items. CREDIT CARDS.

M

ShinDigZ by Stumps 260-723-5171
101 Carrol Rd.   800-314-8736
South Whitley, IN 46787   FAX 260-723-6976
Hours: 7-9 Mon-Fri   E-mail: csr@chindigz.com
www.shindigZ.com

One of the most complete party supply superstores found on the web. Very
helpful with party suggestions. Prom theme props, fabrics, balloons, crepe
papers (up to 4" wide), seamless papers in 23 colors, float supplies and
novelties. Custom printing for invitations, glasses, etc. Quick delivery.
Catalog. CREDIT CARDS.

Tannen's Magic 212-929-4500
45 W 34th St., Ste. 608 (5-6th Ave)   FAX 212-929-4565
NY, NY 10001
Hours: 10-5 Mon-Fri / 10-4 Sat-Sun / Thurs tull 7pm
www.tannens.com

One of the most complete magic dealers in the country. Flash powder, flash
paper; will assist with complicated tricks; consulting service available.
Catalog. CREDIT CARDS.

MAKE-UP SUPPLIES

425 Enterprises Ltd. 516-223-4030
200 E Sunrise Hwy. (Meadowbrook Pkwy)   516-223-0772
Freeport, NY 11520   FAX 516-223-0348
Hours: 9-5:30 Mon-Fri / 11-3:30 Sun   E-mail: info@beautyprops.com
www.beautyprops.com

Lighted mobile make-up mirrors. Large variety of make-up chairs. See Scott.
RENTALS. CREDIT CARDS.

Abracadabra 212-627-5194
19 W 21st St. (5-6th Ave)   FAX 212-627-7435
NY, NY 10001
Hours: 11-7 Mon-Sat / 12-5 Sun
www.abracadabrasuperstore.com

Full line of theatrical make-up. Professional equipment. Wholesale and retail.
Some minimums apply. Catalog available online. CREDIT CARDS.

ADM Tronics 201-767-6040
224 Pegasus Ave.   FAX 201-784-0620
Northvale, NJ 07647
Hours: 9-5 Mon-Fri   E-mail: sales@admtronics.com
www.admtronics.com

Specializes in non-toxic waterbased adhesives, coatings and additives
suitable for make-up.

Alcone N.Y.C. 800-466-7446
5-45 49th Ave. (Mail Order Whse)(5th St-Vernon Blvd)   718-361-8373
Long Island City, NY 11101   FAX 718-729-8296
Hours: 9-5 Mon-Fri

M

Alcone N.Y.C. (cont.) 800-466-7446
  322 W 49th St.(8-9th Aves)   212-757-3734
  NY, NY 10019
  Hours: 11-6 Mon-Sat
  www.alconeco.com
  Theatrical make-up, stage blood, latex, foam latex. Theatrical supply house.
  Catalog. CREDIT CARDS.

Ben Nye Co. 310-839-1984
  3655 LeNawee Ave.   FAX 310-839-2640
  Los Angeles, CA 90016
  Hours: 8-4:30 Mon-Fri
  www.bennyemakeup.com
  Theatrical make-up kits. Catalog. Available through Alcone.

Costume World 800 258-0333
  950 S Federal Hwy.   954-428-6266
  Deerfield Beach, FL 33441   FAX 954-428-4959
  Hours: 10-7 Mon-Fri / 10-6 Sat
  www.costumeworld.com
  Show packages for all major musicals. Will do small rentals. Store locations
  in Pittsburg, Dallas and headquarters in Deerfield Beach that specialize in
  Halloween rentals, make-up and wig supplies. 55,000 square feet of
  costumes. Costume plots available. RENTALS. CREDIT CARDS.

D.R. Wigs 416-429-1402
  48 Coleridge Ave.   416-816-2564
  Toronto, Ontario, Canada M4C 4H5   FAX 416-429-1402
  Hours: by Appt.   E-mail: drwigs@sympatico.ca
  www.dawnbrides.com
  Licensed hairstylist, make-up artist and custom wig builder for film and
  theatre. Owns over 800 stock wigs for rentals. Can provide crew for make-
  up and hairstylists for large or small productions. RENTALS. PayPal.

Halloween Adventure 212-673-4546
  104 Fourth Ave. (11-12th St)   FAX 212-358-0927
  NY, NY 10003
  Hours: 11-8 Mon-Sat / 12-7 Sun
  www.newyorkcostumes.com
  The masters of masquerade with the city's largest selection of costumes,
  masks, wigs, magic supplies and theatrical make-up, plus custom fangs, f/x
  kits and much more. CREDIT CARDS.

Hosmer Dorrance Corp. 408-379-5151
  561 Division St.   FAX 408-379-5263
  Campbell, CA 95008
  Hours: 7:30-4:30 Mon-Fri
  www.hosmer.com
  Manufacturer of prosthetic body parts. Prosthetic making supplies; latex and
  pigments; catalog.

The Make-Up Center Ltd. 212-977-9494
  Hours: 10-6 / Thurs until 7 /10-5 Sat
  www.make-up-center.com
  Make-up and supplies, many brands; stage blood. Mail order only. CREDIT
  CARDS.

M

Mehron, Inc. 845-426-1700
    100 Red School House Rd., Bldg C   FAX 845-426-1515
    Spring Valley, NY 10977
    Hours: 9-5 Mon-Fri   E-mail: info@mehron.com
    www.mehron.com
    Theatrical make-up and kits. Catalog. CREDIT CARDS.

Ricky's 212-769-3678
    112 W 72nd St. (Amst-Col)
    NY, NY 10024
    Hours: 9-10 Mon-Fri / 10-9 Sat / 10-8 Sun   FAX 212-769-0320

    1189 First Ave.(Corner of 64th & 1st Ave)   212-879-8361
    NY, NY 10021
    Hours: 10-9 Mon-Sun   FAX 212-879-8359

    332 W 57th St.(8-9th Aves)   212-247-8010
    NY, NY 10019
    Hours: 9-9 Mon-Fri / 10-9 Sat / 9-8 Sun   FAX 212-247-8011

    44 E 8th St.(Corner of Greene St)   212-254-5247
    NY, NY 10003
    Hours: 10-9 Mon-Sun   FAX 212-254-6523

    466 Sixth Ave.(11-12th St)   212-924-3401
    NY, NY 10011
    Hours: 9-10 Mon-Sat / 10-10 Sun   FAX 212-924-3404

    590 Broadway(Prince-Houston St)   212-226-5552
    NY, NY 10012
    Hours: 9-10 Mon-Sat / 10-8 Sun   FAX 212-226-5595

    267 W 23rd St.(7-8th Ave)   212-206-0234
    New York, NY 10011   FAX 212-206-0379
    Hours: 9-11 Mon-Sat / 10-10 Sun   E-mail: info@rickysnyc.com
    www.rickysnyc.com
    Way beyond your average drug / cosmetic store. Ricky's is truly an
    experience specializing in haircare products, wigs, make-up and some stores
    have salons in them. During Halloween all stores carry costume supplies.
    Several locations carry costume supplies year round. Check the website for
    salon locations. Ricky's is adding additional stores, keep checking website
    for their locations. CREDIT CARDS.

Spotlight Costumes, LLC 412-381-7733
    1503 E Carson St. (S 16th St)   800-256-8645
    Pittsburgh, PA 15203   FAX 412-381-0260
    Hours: 10-6 Mon-Sat / 12-9 (October)   E-mail: info@spotlightcostumes.com
    www.spotlightcostumes.com
    Costume rental and construction. In-house design services available. Also
    wigs, masks and make-up. RENTALS. CREDIT CARDS.

M

Temptu Marketing, Inc. 212-675-4000
   26 W 17th St. #503 (5-6th Ave)   800-972-9682
   NY, NY 10011   FAX 212-675-4075
   Hours: 9:30-6 Mon-Fri   E-mail: sales@temptu.com
   www.temptu.com
   Make-up and novelties, tattoos, beauty mark kits and stage blood. Fast service. Catalog. CREDIT CARDS.

Zeller International, Ltd. 607-363-7792
   15261 Highway 30   FAX 607-363-2071
   Downsville, NY 13755
   Hours: 9-5 Mon-Fri   E-mail: contact@zeller-int.com
   www.zeller-int.com
   Safe, specialty chemicals used by make-up and FX people. Mold-making and casting materials. Flame retardent products. CREDIT CARDS.

MANNEQUINS

Bernstein Display 212-683-2406
   151 W 25th St.   718-237-2215
   NY, NY 10001   FAX 718-237-5922
   Hours: 9-5 Mon-Fri   E-mail: solutions@bernsteindisplay.com
   www.bernsteindisplay.com
   Mannequins, great selection of display fixtures, rolling racks, hangers, garment bags, 3-fold mirrors and clothes steamers. Catalog. Will ship. RENTALS. CREDIT CARDS.

Frank Glover Productions, Inc. 212-242-8344
   138 W 25th St., 4th Fl. (6-7th Ave)   FAX 212-242-8551
   NY, NY 10001
   Hours: 9-5 Mon-Fri   E-mail: info@frankgloverproductions.com
   www.frankgloverproductions.com
   New and reconditioned mannequins. Repair/refurbishing and spraying services available. Download inventory PDF file from website. Factory located in Jersey City. Sales and RENTALS.

M

Goldsmith Mannequins 212-366-9040
   601 W 26th St. Ste 350 (10-11th Ave)   FAX 212-366-9048
   NY, NY 10001
   Hours: 9-4 Mon-Fri / Showroom by Appt.   E-mail: info@goldsmith-inc.com
   www.goldsmith-inc.com
   Manufacturer of mannequins, forms, accessories fixtures and furniture. Visual merchandising. Wig heads. Free catalog. Will ship. RENTALS.

Katonah Image, Inc. 914-232-0961
   22 Woodsbridge Rd.   FAX 914-232-3944
   Katonah, NY 10536
   Hours: 9-6 Mon-Fri / 9-5 Sat
   Photo lab with antiques, memorabilia and collectibles. RENTALS. CREDIT CARDS.

Mannequin Madness 866-444-1752
97-02 Springfield Blvd.
Queens, NY 11429
Hours: by appt. only   E-mail: sales@mannequinmadness.com
www.mannequinmadness.com
Mannequins for rent or sale. They carry a wide range of high-fashion, athletic and dressmaker mannequins from different manufactures. They deliver all over Manhattan. Other offices located in California and Las Vegas. Specializing in recycling mannequins. Rent dress forms with collapsible shoulders by the week, reasonable prices. RENTALS. CREDIT CARDS.

Pucci Manikins 212-633-0452
44 W 18th St., 12th Fl. (5-6th Ave)   FAX 212-633-1058
NY, NY 10011
Hours: 9-5 Mon-Fri by appt.   E-mail: info@ralphpucci.net
www.ralphpucci.net
Mannequins and interior furnishings.

Studio Eis 718-797-4561
55 Washington St., Ste. 400 (Washington)   FAX 718-797-4562
Brooklyn, NY 11201
Hours: 9-5 Mon-Fri   E-mail: info@studioeis.com
www.studioeis.com
Custom life-cast figures for museums and display.

Travel Auto Bag Co., Inc. 212-840-0025
264 W 40th St. (7-8th Ave)   (Outside NY) 800-840-0095
NY, NY 10018   FAX: 212-302-8267
Hours: 9-4:30 Mon-Fri   E-mail: info@travelautobag.com
www.travelautobag.com
All types of garment bags, collapsible rolling racks, steamers, hangers, mannequins and display fixtures. Not a store, they will mail anywhere, free delivery within garment district or you can pick up order. Shop using the website. Staff is nice and knowledgeable. CREDIT CARDS.

MAPS

Argosy Book Stores, Inc. 212-753-4455
116 E 59th St. (Park-Lex Ave)   FAX 212-593-4784
NY, NY 10022
Hours: 10-6 Mon-Fri / 10-5 Sat (Sept-April)   E-mail: argosy@argosybooks.com
www.argosybooks.com
Maps, prints, some out-of print books. Phone orders welcome. CREDIT CARDS.

The Complete Traveller Antiquarian 212-685-9007
199 Madison Ave. (35th St)   FAX 212-481-3253
NY, NY 10016
Hours: 9:30-6:30 Mon-Fri / 10-6 Sat / 12-5 Sun   E-mail: info@ctrarebooks.com
www.ctrarebooks.com
Antique maps, childrens collectible, out-of-print and rare collectible books and accessories. CREDIT CARDS.

M

Hagstrom Travel Center 212-398-1222
51 W 43rd St. (5-6th Ave)   FAX 212-398-9856
NY, NY 10036
Hours: 8:30-6 Mon-Fri / 10:30-4:30 Sat   E-mail: midtown@hagstrommap.com
www.hagstrommap.com
Wide selection of national and foreign maps, topographical maps, globes and travel books. CREDIT CARDS.

Map and Latitudes Travel Store 952-927-9061
4811 Excelsior Blvd.   FAX 952-927-9163
St Louis Park, MN 55416
Hours: 10-6 Mon-Thurs / 10-5 Fri-Sat   E-mail: info@latitudesmapstore.com
www.latitudesmapstore.com
World atlases, wall maps, map software, laminating, mounting and framing. Travel books, globes, world clocks and outdoor maps. View website for other travel related accessories. CREDIT CARDS.

New York Nautical Instrument & Service Corp. 212-962-4522
158 Duane St. (W Bway-Hudson)   FAX 212-406-8420
NY, NY 10013
Hours: 9-5 Mon-Fri   E-mail: sales@newyorknautical.com
www.newyorknautical.com
Star and nautical maps of the world; nautical instruments and their repair. Phone orders welcome. RENTALS. CREDIT CARDS.

Old Paper World 603-456-3338
Rt. 103 Box 246   FAX 603-456-3903
Warner, NH 03278
Hours: by appt. call ahead   E-mail: oldpaperwrld@conknet.com
Thousands of old paper collectibles, books, photographs, magazines, maps, sheet music. Very helpful.

Pageant Book & Print Shop 212-674-5296
PO Box 1081, Canal St. Station / 69 E 4th St.
NY, NY 10013
Hours: 12-8 Tue-Sat / 1-7 Sun   E-mail: info@pageantbooks.com
www.pageantbooks.com
Rents books by subject area, by the foot. Also many maps; see Shirley Solomon. RENTALS. CREDIT CARDS.

Rand McNally & Co. 800-275-7263
9855 Woods Dr.   847-329-8100
Skokie, IL 60077   FAX 800-934-3479
Hours: 8-5:30 Mon-Fri   E-mail: store@randmcnally.com
www.randmcnally.com
Up-to-date Rand McNally maps, topographical maps, guide books and travel accessories.   Phone orders welcome. CREDIT CARDS.

M

MARBLE

A & R Asta Ltd. 212-750-3364
1152 Second Ave. (60-61st St)   FAX 212-751-5418
NY, NY 10021
Hours: 9:30-5 Mon-Fri / Weekends by appt. only   E-mail: asta1152@aol.com
Custom marble cutting for tables, sinks, fireplaces, antique fireplace
accessories and marble statuary. Fireplace installation. Contact Vincent.
RENTALS.

Acme Marble Works, Inc. 718-788-0527
160 17th St. (3rd-4th Ave)   718-965-3560
Brooklyn, NY 11215   FAX 718-788-0528
Hours: 7-3 Mon-Fri
Large selection of marble, custom work and cutting.

Alcamo Marble Works, Inc. 212-255-5224
541 W 22nd St. (10-11th Ave)   FAX 212-255-4060
NY, NY 10011
Hours: 8-4:30 Mon-Fri
www.alcamomarbleworksinc.com
Marble and granite. See Francesca. RENTALS. No credit cards.

Appia Marble & Granite 718-745-5309
824 62nd St. (8th Ave)   FAX 718-680-7481
Brooklyn, NY 11220
Hours: 9-5 Mon-Fri / 9-2 Sat (Call to confirm closing time)
www.appiamarblegranite.com   E-mail: questions@appiamarblegranite.com
Stone fabricator and installer for kitchen, bath, flooring, fireplace and
commercial projects. They have a large selection of granite, marble, slate and
limestone slabs and tiles. Samples are available to borrow. Friendly,
knowledgeable and fast service.

Bergen Bluestone Co., Inc. 908-237-2680
30 Copper Penny Rd.   FAX 908-237-2681
Flemington, NJ 08822
Hours: 7:30-4:30 Mon-Fri / 8-1 Sat
Natural stone suppliers and contractors. Carries marble, granite, limestone,
slate, sandstone, quartzite, landscaping stones, boulders, petrified wood.
CREDIT CARDS.

The Compleat Sculptor, Inc. 212-243-6074
90 Vandam St. (Hudson-Greenwich)   800-9-SCULPT
NY, NY 10013   FAX 212-243-6374
Hours: 9-6 Mon, Thurs-Sat / 9-8 Tue-Wed   E-mail: tcs@sculpt.com
www.sculpt.com
Carries complete line of sculpture materials including; clay, wood, wax,
sculpting tools, alabaster, marble, mold-making and casting materials, books,
videos, pedestals and bases. Friendly and knowledgeable help. Catalog.
Technical support line (212) 367-7561. CREDIT CARDS.

M

Empire State Marble Mfg. Corp. 212-534-2307
   207 E 110th St. (2nd-3rd Ave)   FAX 212-534-7795
   NY, NY 10029
   Hours: 7:30-3:30 Mon-Fri
   Will cut to size. Also sells tile. RENTALS. No credit cards.

Marble Modes 718-539-1334
   15-25 130th St. (20th Ave)   800-826-MODS
   College Point, NY 11356   FAX 718-353-8564
   Hours: 9-4 Mon-Fri / 8-12 Sat   E-mail: sales@marblemodes.com
   www.marblemodes.com
   Marble fabrication and repair; sells about 130 varieties of marble. CREDIT CARDS.

New York Marble Works, Inc. 212-929-1817
   24 W 23rd St., 2nd Fl. (5-6th Ave)   FAX 212-929-6698
   NY, NY 10010-5200
   Hours: 9-6 Mon-Fri
   www.newyorkmarble.com
   Sells marble cut to size. No credit cards.

Quarry Tile Marble & Granite 212-679-8889
   132 Lexington (28-29th St)   FAX 212-889-1364
   NY, NY 10016
   Hours: 9-5 Mon-Fri / 11-3:30 Sat   E-mail: quarrytile@aol.com
   www.qtmg.net
   Contractor who sells ceramic tile, marble and granite. Excellent selection, samples available. CREDIT CARDS.

MARINE EQUIPMENT

M

Arrangements, Inc. Marine Division 914-238-1300
   301 Roaring Brook Rd. (Saw Mill River Pkwy)   FAX 914-238-9776
   Chappaqua, NY 10514
   Hours: 9-5 Mon-Fri / or by appt.
   100's of ship models, ranging in size from 1' to 7', all types of vessels, cased or uncased, will ship or deliver. Contact Gabriel Rosenfeld. RENTALS.

Defender Industries, Inc. 800-628-8225
   42 Great Neck Rd.   860-701-3420
   Waterford, CT 06385   FAX 800-654-1616
   Hours: 8-6 Mon-Fri / 9-5 Sat / 9-3 Sun (June-Aug) E-mail: orders@defender.com
   www.defender.com
   Extensive stock of marine supplies: boat hardware, sailcloth, epoxies, polyester gel, coat release, fiberglass supplies and more. Catalog. $25 minimum. Phone orders. CREDIT CARDS.

New York Nautical Instrument & Service Corp. 212-962-4522
   158 Duane St. (W Bway-Hudson)   FAX 212-406-8420
   NY, NY 10013
   Hours: 9-5 Mon-Fri   E-mail: sales@newyorknautical.com
   www.newyorknautical.com
   Star and nautical maps of the world; nautical instruments and their repair. Phone orders welcome. RENTALS. CREDIT CARDS.

Sea Shell World / Cyber Island Shops, Inc. 888-515-3103
4600 Cecile Drive   407-787-3362
Kissimmee, FL 34746   FAX 407-396-2242
Hours: 10-6 Mon-Fri   E-mail: customerservice@seashellworld.com
www.seashellworld.com
Shells, sea glass, books also authentic and replica nautical items & props.
Quick delivery service. Catalog. CREDIT CARDS.

Seattle Fabrics 206-525-0670
8702 Aurora Ave. N (N 87th St)   866-925-0670
Seattle, WA 98103   FAX 206-525-0779
Hours: 9-6 Mon-Sat   E-mail: seattlefabrics@msn.com
www.seattlefabrics.com
Outdoor and recreational fabric & hardware. Specialty fabrics, webbing,
thread and zippers; neoprene and closed cell foam. Patterns for outdoor and
sports attire; equestrian, tents and backpacks. Fabric samples available.
CREDIT CARDS.

West Marine 212-594-6065
12 W 37th St. (5-6th Ave)   800-BOATING
NY, NY 10018   FAX 212-594-0721
Hours: 9-7 Mon-Wed, Fri / 9-8 Thurs / 9-4 Sat-Sun
www.westmarine.com
Everything for the sail and power boat; fishing, scuba and marine equipment.
Bungee cord in various thicknesses by the foot. Catalog available. Formerly
Goldberg's Marine RENTALS. CREDIT CARDS.

MEDICAL & SCIENTIFIC SUPPLIES: DENTAL

American ReSource Medical 201-833-1550
324 W Englewood Ave.   973-742-6622
Teaneck, NJ 7666   FAX 201-833-1575
Hours: 9-5 Mon-Fri   E-mail: arme@optonline.net

463 Grand St.   973-742-6622
Patterson, NJ 7505
Hours: 9-5 Mon-Fri
One of the largest inventory of medical props outside Los Angeles. Extensive
experience in all areas of the field. RENTALS.

Belmont Equipment 732-469-5000
101 Belmont Dr.   800-223-1192
Somerset, NJ 8873   FAX 800-280-7504
Hours: 9-5 Mon-Fri or by appt.   E-mail: rswain@belmontequip.com
www.belmontequip.com
Manufacturer of dental office equipment.

Huntington Dental Supply / Rubenstein Dental Equip. Corp. . .718-275-2583
67-09 Main St. (Melbourne)   FAX 718-275-7768
Flushing, NY 11367
Hours: 8:30-5 Mon-Fri / 8:30-2 Sat   E-mail: dental@huntingtondental.com
Dental tools, equipment and supplies, alginate. Catalog. CREDIT CARDS.

MEDICAL & SCIENTIFIC SUPPLIES: HOSPITAL

Aimes, Inc. 718-993-4400
2417 Third Ave.   718-993-4401
Bronx, NY 10451   FAX 718-993-4260
Hours: 9-5 Mon-Fri or by appt.   E-mail: doctorprops@aol.com
www.aimesmedical.com
Formerly American International Medical Equipment. Lab and hospital
equipment, CTscan, MRIs, hospital rooms, wheelchairs, etc. RENTALS.
CREDIT CARDS.

Alatheia Prosthetics 877-252-8434
504 Grants Ferry Rd.   601-919-2113
Brandon, MS 39047   FAX 877-REHAB-YOU
Hours: by appt.   E-mail: info@dermatos.com
www.alathera.com
Custom prosthetic silicone skins and coverings. . Serves medical industry
primarily. Can do very life-like replications of all body parts. Custom projects
welcome. Expensive.

American ReSource Medical 201-833-1550
324 W Englewood Ave.   973-742-6622
Teaneck, NJ 7666   FAX 201-833-1575
Hours: 9-5 Mon-Fri   E-mail: arme@optonline.net

463 Grand St.   973-742-6622
Patterson, NJ 7505
Hours: 9-5 Mon-Fri
One of the largest inventory of medical props outside Los Angeles. Extensive
experience in all areas of the field. RENTALS.

Apria Health Care 718-358-8854
109-05 14th Ave.   800-294-2275
College Point, NY 11356   FAX 718-358-7946 / 0734
Hours: 8:30-9 Mon-Fri
www.apria.com
New and used medical equipment. Time and patience needed to find the
good stuff. Pick-up and delivery. RENTALS. CREDIT CARDS.

Chelsea Mobility and Medical Equipment 212-255-5522
327 Eighth Ave. (25-26th St)   800-249-1188
NY, NY 10001   FAX 212-255-4686
Hours: 9-6 Mon-Fri / 11-4 Sat   E-mail: info@surgicaldepot.biz
www.surgicaldepot.biz
Everything for the sickroom. Beds to blood pressure kits. Many styles of
walkers, canes and crutches. Power lift recliner chairs. Speak with Paul
Lieberman. Catalog. Sales and RENTALS. CREDIT CARDS.

Cinema World Studios 718-389-9800
220 Dupont St. (Provost)   FAX 718-389-9897
Greenpoint, NY 11122
Hours: 9-7 Mon-Fri by appt.   E-mail: cinemaworldfd@verizon.net
www.cinemaworldstudios.com
Complete medical equipment and consultation. RENTALS.

M

Falk Surgical Corp. 212-744-8080
259 E 72nd St. (2nd Ave)   FAX 212-737-1521
NY, NY 10021
Hours: 9-7:30 Mon-Fri / 9-5 Sat / 10-3 Sun
Orthopedic and sickroom equipment. RENTALS. CREDIT CARDS.

Gem Wheelchair & Scooter Service .718-969-8600
176-39 Union Tpke. (Utopia Pkwy)   800-WHEELSUSA
Flushing, NY 11366   FAX 718-969-8300
Hours: 9-4:45 Mon-Fri / 9-2 Sat   E-mail: info@wheelchairsusa.com
*New and used wheelchairs (some vintage) and 3-wheel scooters. Wheelchair
retreading and repairs. Helpful. RENTALS. CREDIT CARDS.*

New England Orthotic & Prothetic Systems 212-682-9313
235 E 38th St. (2nd-3rd Ave)   888-551-8588
NY, NY 10016   FAX 212-682-9318
Hours: 9-5 Mon-Fri   E-mail: nyc@neops.com
www.neops.com
*Surgical supports, braces, back supports, pillows, wheelchairs, walkers.
CREDIT CARDS.*

Medical Solutions 732-905-5400
315B 4th St.   877-463-5818
Lakewood, NJ 8701   FAX 800-661-6999
Hours: 9-5 Mon-Thurs / 9-2 Fri   E-mail: info@4mdmedical.com
www.4mdmedical.com
*Good selection of medical props and supplies. Clinical room furniture as well
as new diagnostic equipment. All items are new and for sale. CREDIT
CARDS.*

Prime Care Medical Supplies, Inc. 631-447-0093
25 Corporate Dr.   FAX 631-447-0148
Holtsville, NY 11742
Hours: 9-5 Mon-Fri   E-mail: primecare@optonline.net
www.primecaremed.com
*A complete provider of home medical equipment. Hospital beds, bathroom
safety equipment wheelchairs, oxygen equipment and supplies. Free delivery
and pick-up. Medical consultations available. Contact Peter Amico.
RENTALS. CREDIT CARDS.*

Sammons Preston 800-323-5547
1000 Remington Blvd., Ste. 210   630-378-6000
Bolingbrook, IL 60440   FAX 630-378-6010
Hours: WEB 24-hrs.   E-mail: sp@patterson-medical.com
www.sammonspreston.com
Thermoplastic (Roylan), Velcroô and miscellaneous post-op therapy items.

Zee Medical 800-942-1805
931-C Conklin St.   516-249-4678
Farmingdale, NY 11735   FAX 516-249-4826
Hours: 8-5 Mon-Fri   E-mail: zeenewyork@zeemedical.com
www.zeemedical.com
*Nationwide supplier of industrial first aid and safety equipment. Gloves,
respirators, first aid supplies, safety training and evaluation. CREDIT CARDS.*

MEDICAL & SCIENTIFIC SUPPLIES: LABORATORY

American ReSource Medical 201-833-1550
　324 W Englewood Ave. 　　　　　　　　　　　　973-742-6622
　Teaneck, NJ 7666 　　　　　　　　　　　　FAX 201-833-1575
　Hours: 9-5 Mon-Fri 　　　　　　　　　E-mail: arme@optonline.net

　463 Grand St. 　　　　　　　　　　　　　　　973-742-6622
　Patterson, NJ 7505
　Hours: 9-5 Mon-Fri
　One of the largest inventory of medical props outside Los Angeles. Extensive experience in all areas of the field. RENTALS.

Anatomical Chart Co. 847-679-4700
　4711 Golf Road, Ste. 650 　　　　　　　　　　800-621-7500
　Skokie, IL 60076 　　　　　　　　　　　　FAX 847-674-0211
　Hours: 8:30-5 Mon-Fri 　　　　　E-mail: accinfo@anatomical.com
　www.anatomical.com
　Biological and scientific products; skeletons, skulls, anatomical charts; catalog. RENTALS. CREDIT CARDS.

Carolina Biological Supply 800-334-5551
　2700 York Rd. 　　　　　　　　　　　　　　336-584-0381
　Burlington, NC 27215 　　　　　　　　　FAX 800-222-7112
　Hours: 8-5 Mon-Fri / Open until 8 for orders　　E-mail: carolina@carolina.com
　www.carolina.com
　Lab equipment and supplies. Human and animal anatomical parts, charts, skulls, bones, skeletons; great catalog available; good prices and helpful service. Phone orders. CREDIT CARDS.

Caswell-Massey Co. Ltd. 212-755-2254
　518 Lexington Ave. (48th St) 　　　　　　　　800-326-0500
　NY, NY 10017 　　　　　　　　　　　　FAX 212-888-4915
　Hours: 9-7 Mon-Fri / 10-6 Sat / 9-5 Sun
　www.caswell-massey.com
　Antique apothecary bottles, soaps, talc, hair and body care items. For catalog call 800-326-0500. CREDIT CARDS.

Chelsea Mobility and Medical Equipment 212-255-5522
　327 Eighth Ave. (25-26th St) 　　　　　　　　800-249-1188
　NY, NY 10001 　　　　　　　　　　　　FAX 212-255-4686
　Hours: 9-6 Mon-Fri / 11-4 Sat 　　　E-mail: info@surgicaldepot.biz
　www.surgicaldepot.biz
　Surgical supplies & lab equipment. Speak with Paul Lieberman. Catalog. Sales & RENTALS. CREDIT CARDS.

Cole Parmer Instrument Co. 800-323-4340
　625 E Bunker Ct. 　　　　　　　　　　　FAX 847-247-2929
　Vernon Hills, IL 60061
　Hours: 7-7 Mon-Fri 　　　　　　　　E-mail: info@coleparmer.com
　www.coleparmer.com
　Supply house for lab and scientific equipment; good selection of plastic test tubes and vials; catalog, rush orders. CREDIT CARDS.

M

Edmund Scientific Co. 800-728-6999
60 Pearce Ave.   FAX 800-828-3299
Tonawanda, NY 14150
Hours: 8-8 Mon-Fri / 8-5 Office Hours   E-mail: scientifics@edsci.com
www.scientificsonline.com
Lab equipment, optics, microscopes, pumps, scientific toys and more;
catalog. Occasional rentals. CREDIT CARDS.

Hitech Trader 609-518-9100
136 Hulme St. / P.O. Box 58
Mount Holly, NJ 8060
Hours: 9-5 Mon-Fri / and by appt.
Used laboratory equipment, scientific equipment: glassware to
instrumentations and benches. Semiconductors and production equipment.
Consultations, searches. Sales and RENTALS. CREDIT CARDS.

Maxilla and Mandible Ltd. 212-724-6173
451 Columbus Ave. (81st-82nd St)   FAX 212-721-1073
NY, NY 10024
Hours: 11-7 Mon-Sat
www.maxillaandmandible.com
Human and animal skulls, bones, skins, horns, fossils and seashells. Phone
orders welcome. RENTALS. CREDIT CARDS.

Omaha Vaccine Co. 800-367-4444
11143 Mockingbird Dr.   FAX 800-242-9447
Omaha, NE 68137
Hours: 7-7 Mon-Fri / 8-2 Sat   E-mail: catalogs@omahavaccine.com
www.omahavaccine.com
Oversized medical equipment, giant syringes, etc.; catalog. Also veterinary
and animal care supplies. CREDIT CARDS.

P.C.I. Scientific 973-244-9002
41 Plymouth St.
Fairfield, NJ 7004
Hours: 8:30-5 Mon-Fri
www.pciscientific.com
Lab and scientific supplies. Very helpful. Also carry vacuum chambers.
Contact Larry Delaney. CREDIT CARDS.

MEMORABILIA

Art & Industrial Design 212-477-0116
50 Great Jones St. (4th Ave)   FAX 212-477-1420
NY, NY 10012
Hours: 10-5 Mon-Fri / 10-1 Sat   E-mail: info@aid20c.com
www.aid20c.com
20th-century designer and art deco furniture for all settings. Period prints and
posters, art and collectibles. RENTALS. CREDIT CARDS.

Authentiques 212-675-2179
255 W 18th St. (7-8th Ave)
NY, NY 10011
Hours: 12-6 Wed-Sat / 1-6 Sun or by appt.   E-mail: fab.stuff@verizon.net
www.fab-stuff.com
1950s to 70s small props and lamps. Wonderful selection of lighting fixtures and antique Christmas decorations.

Early Halloween 212-691-2933
130 W 25th St., 11th Fl. (6-7th Ave)   FAX 212-243-1499
NY, NY 10001
Hours: by appt. only   E-mail: earlyhalloween@aol.com
www.earlyhalloween.com
Vintage clothing, hats, shoes and accessories. Also vintage luggage and memorabilia. RENTAL only.

Gargoyles LTD 215-629-1700
120 N Third St.   FAX 215-592-8441
Philadelphia, PA 19106
Hours: 9-5:30 Tue-Fri / 11-6 Sat   E-mail: gargoylesltd@yahoo.com
www.gargoylesltd.com
Theme decor for restaurants. Country and period advertising memorabilia, period advertising mirrors, English and American antiques, Sports memorabilia and scale models. RENTALS. CREDIT CARDS.

Gaslight Advertising Archives, Inc. 631-462-4444
17 Bernard Ln.   FAX 631-462-7394
Commack, NY 11725
Hours: 9-5 Mon-Fri   E-mail: gaslight@earthlink.net
www.gaslightarchives.com
Authentic old print ads back to the 1880s. Over a million ads, all subjects, products and companies. RENTALS.

Katonah Image, Inc. 914-232-0961
22 Woodsbridge Rd.   FAX 914-232-3944
Katonah, NY 10536
Hours: 9-6 Mon-Fri / 9-5 Sat
Photo lab with antiques, memorabilia and collectibles. RENTALS. CREDIT CARDS.

Lost City Arts 212-375-0500
18 Cooper Sq. (5th St)   FAX 212-375-9342
NY, NY 10012
Hours: 10-6 Mon,-Fri / 12-6 Sat-Sun   E-mail: lostcityarts@yahoo.com
www.lostcityarts.com
Good selection of memorabilia, advertising clocks, antique toys and collectibles. RENTALS. CREDIT CARDS.

Love Saves the Day 215-862-1399
1 South Main St. (7th St)
New Hope, PA 18938
Hours: 11-7 Daily
Vintage clothing, toys, props. Phone orders. CREDIT CARDS.

M

New York Mets Clubhouse Shops 212-768-9534
11 W 42nd St.(5-6th Ave)
NY, NY 10036
Hours: 10-6:30 Mon-Sat / 11-5 Sun

Roosevelt Field Mall # 1141(Old Country Road-Meadow Brook Pkwy)
Garden City, NY 11530   516-248-1931
Hours: 9:30-9:30 Mon-Sat / 11-7 Sun
www.sportsavenue.com
Wonderful selection of NY Mets memorabilia. No Checks. CREDIT CARDS.

OFFSTAGE DESIGN 845-265-0078
28 Lane Gate Rd. (Rt 9)   914-522-0283
Cold Spring, NY 10516   FAX 845-265-2322
Hours: by appt.   E-mail: denise@offstagedesign.com
www.offstagedesign.com
Paper memorabilia is our speciality. Household labels, containers, photos,
documents, postal, certificates, catalogs and everything ephemera. Contact
Denise Grillo or Denny Clark. Member ATAC.

Old Paper World 603-456-3338
Rt. 103 Box 246   FAX 603-456-3903
Warner, NH 03278
Hours: by appt. call ahead   E-mail: oldpaperwrld@conknet.com
Thousands of old paper collectibles, books, photographs, magazines, maps,
sheet music. Very helpful.

The Prop Company / Kaplan and Associates 212-691-7767
111 W 19th St., 8th Fl. (6-7th Ave)   FAX 212-727-3055
NY, NY 10011
Hours: 9-5 Mon-Fri   E-mail: propcompany@yahoo.com
Postcards, pens, books, sheet music, prints, photographs, tins, maps,
advertising, letters, memorabilia from the 18th to the 20th Century. Contact
Maxine Kaplan.

Props for Today 212-244-9600
330 W 34th St. (8-9th Ave)   FAX 212-244-1053
NY, NY 10001
Hours: 8:30-5 Mon-Fri   E-mail: info@propsfortoday.com
www.propsfortoday.com
Bulk mail and files. Calendars, certificates, diplomas, menus, hotel items,
food labels and more. RENTALS. CREDIT CARDS.

Geno Sartori 212-691-9776
440 W 24th St. #4B (mailing only)
NY, NY 10011
Hours: by appt.   E-mail: genosar@aol.com
Formerly Brandon Memorabilia. Large collection of paper embellishments
consisting of gold embossed paper borders, color cutouts of florals, animals
and figures, etc.

Spink Smythe 800-622-1880
3100 Monticello Ave.   972-788-2100
Dallas, TX 75205   FAX 972-788-2788
Hours: by appt. only

M

Spink Smythe (cont.) 800-622-1880
    145 W 57th St., 18th FL   212-262-8400
    NY, NY 10019   FAX 212-262-8484
    Hours: by appt. only   E-mail: Malberti@smytheonline.com
    www.spinksmythe.com
    Antique paper material. Stocks, bonds, autographs, historic documents, bank notes and coins, currency and ancient coins.

WinCraft 800-533-8006
    1124 W Fifth St.   507-452-4765
    Winona, MN 55987   FAX 507-453-0690
    Hours: 24-hrs. by web / 9-5 Mon-Fri Corporate Office
    www.wincraft.com   E-mail: contact@wincraft.com
    WinCraft is a recognized leader in retail licensed and promotional products. You can provide your customer with collectible and home decor products from NFL, NHL, NBA, NASCAR, NCAA, Olympics not to mention they have over 300 licenses. They offer licensed products for every retail selling season, hot market, and major event. CREDIT CARDS.

Yellow Shed Antiques 845-628-0362
    PO Box 706, 571 Rt 6   FAX 845-628-2777
    Mahopac, NY 10541
    Hours: 10-5 Wed-Sun
    China, crystal, silver items, memorabilia, quilts, jewelry, posters and prints. 1 hr. from Manhattan. 8,000 sq. ft. of decorative accessories. Contact Mark or Patty. RENTALS. CREDIT CARDS.

MEMORABILIA: THEATRE & FILM

Broadway New York.com 212-944-4133
    1535 Broadway (46th St)   (mail order) 800-223-1320
    NY, NY 10036
    Hours: 9-11 Daily   E-mail: orders@broadwaynewyork.com
    www.broadwaynewyork.com
    Broadway show t-shirts, posters; New York souvenirs. CREDIT CARDS.

Colony Records 212-265-2050
    1619 Broadway (49th St)   FAX 212-956-6009
    NY, NY 10019
    Hours: 9:30-1am Mon-Sat / 10-midnight Sun   E-mail: colony1@aol.com
    www.colonymusic.com
    Large selection of sheet music, records, CDs; will ship anywhere. Out-of-print LPs, nostalgia, movie, Broadway posters, rock-related toys and autographs. Best selection of Karaoke music in Manhattan. CREDIT CARDS.

Encore at Bella Sorella 352-242-5142
    763 W. Montrose St.   FAX 352-243-9744
    Clermont, FL 34711
    Hours: 10-6 Mon-Fri   E-mail: encoreatbella@ymail.com
    Antiques and collectables. CREDIT CARDS.

M

Love Saves the Day 215-862-1399
1 South Main St. (7th St)
New Hope, PA 18938
Hours: 11-7 Daily
Vintage clothing, toys, props. Phone orders. CREDIT CARDS.

Movie Star News 212-620-8160
134 W 18th St. (6-7th Ave)   FAX 212-727-0634
NY, NY 10011
Hours: 10:30-6:30 Mon-Fri / 10:30-4:30 Sat   E-mail: kramermsn@yahoo.com
www.moviestarnews.com
Movie posters and stills; color and B&W portraits, scenes from movies.
Catalog $10. Contact Ira. CREDIT CARDS.

Jerry Ohlinger's Movie Material Store, Inc. 212-989-0869
253 W 35th St. (7-8th Ave)   FAX 212-989-1660
NY, NY 10001
Hours: 11-7 Mon-Sat   E-mail: jomms@aol.com
www.moviematerials.com
8x10s, film stills, movie posters. Can be difficult, but he really knows his
business. RENTALS. CREDIT CARDS.

Triton Galleries, Inc. 212-765-2472
630 Ninth Ave., Ste 808 (44-45th St)   800-626-6674
NY, NY 10036   FAX 212-956-6179
Hours: 10-6 Mon-Sat / 1-6 Sun   E-mail: info@tritongallery.com
www.tritongallery.com
Good collection of Broadway posters, some foreign theatre and film posters;
picture and poster framing. CREDIT CARDS.

MERCHANDISING & PROMOTION

George Fenmore, Inc. 212-977-4140
250 W 54th St. Rm 712 (B'way-8th Ave)   FAX 212-977-4404
NY, NY 10019
Hours: 9-5 Mon-Fri
Prop promotion for plays, TV and video.

Platinum Guild International USA 949-760-8279
620 Newport Center Dr.   FAX 949-760-8780
Newport Beach, CA 92660
Hours: 8:30-5 Mon-Fri
www.preciousplatinum.com
Will loan platinum jewelry for film, photo shoots, television and theatre. Can
make referrals to NYC jewelry retailers for product placement.

MESSENGER SERVICES

Dependable Transport & Messenger Services 212-594-1300
    240 W 37th St., 7th FL (7-8th Ave)   212-594-0320
    NY, NY 10018   FAX 212-594-4375
    Hours: 9-6 Mon-Fri   E-mail: gary@dependablemessengers.com
    www.dependablemessengers.com
    Bonded parking garages, truck parking, storage, temporary and production
    office rentals. RENTALS. CREDIT CARDS.

Prop Transport, Inc. 212-957-4004
    630 Ninth Ave # 309 (44-45th St)   FAX 212-957-6569
    NY, NY 10036
    Hours: available 24 hours   E-mail: proptrucks@aol.com
    www.proptransport.com
    Local trucking service geared to the film industry; reliable. Storage space
    available. AMEX CREDIT CARD ONLY.

METALS & FOILS

Alufoil Products Co., Inc. 631-231-4141
    PO Box 11023, 135 Oser Ave., Ste 3   FAX 631-231-1435
    Hauppauge, NY 11788
    Hours: 8-5 Mon-Fri   E-mail: sales@alufoil.com
    www.alufoil.com
    Manufacturer of plain and colored foils; foil papers and boards; catalog.
    Some minimums. CREDIT CARDS.

CREATIVE METAL WORKS, INC. / STEPHEN MCMAHON 631-537-9501
    172 Butter Lane   FAX 631-537-4669
    Bridgehampton, NY 11932
    Hours: by Appt.   E-mail: mail@creativemetalworksinc.com
    www.creativemetalworksinc.com
    Creative Metal Works crafts fine architectural elements from all types of
    metals, including: stainless steel, steel mesh, galvanized steel, brushed steel,
    bronze, brass, nickel, copper, aluminum and titanium. Custom metal projects
    range from architecural elements, railings and canopies, to sculpture,
    hardware, decorative lighting,and fixtures. Member ATAC.

Grand Brass Lamp Parts, Inc. 212-226-2567
    51 Railroad Ave.   FAX 212-226-2573
    West Haven, CT 06516
    Hours: 9-4 Mon-Fri   E-mail: sales@grandbrass.com
    www.grandbrass.com
    Decorative brass trims, lamp bases, globes, chimneys. RENTALS. CREDIT
    CARDS.

Hadco Aluminum & Metal Corp. 718-291-8060
    104-20 Merrick Blvd. (Liberty-104th Ave)   800-221-0344
    Jamaica, NY 11433   FAX 718-291-8388
    Hours: 8:30-5 Mon-Fri
    www.hadco-metal.com
    Aluminum plate, rod, tubes, sheets, etc. Catalog. No minimum. Deliveries.
    No Checks. CREDIT CARDS.

M

McNichols 732-846-8333
2 Home News Row   800-237-3820
New Brunswick, NJ 08901   FAX 732-846-5555
Hours: 8-5 Mon-Fri   E-mail: newbrunswick.sales@mcnichols.com
www.mcnichols.com
All types of expanded and perforated metal, wire cloth and grating. Excellent prices and fast service. Catalog. CREDIT CARDS.

Metalliferrous 212-944-0909
34 W 46th St., 2nd FL (5-6th Ave)   888-944-0909
NY, NY 10036   FAX 212-944-0644
Hours: 8:30-6 Mon-Fri / 10-3 Sat   E-mail: info@metalliferous.com
www.metalliferous.com
Metal findings. Jewelry-making supplies, tools and books. Brass screening and stamped metal pieces. CREDIT CARDS.

New Amsterdam Metalworks, LLC 718-472-9775
67 Jefferson St.   FAX 718-707-9687
Brooklyn, NY 11206
Hours: 8-6 Mon-Fri   E-mail: newamsterdammetalworks@gmail.com
www.amsterdammetalworks.com
Custom metal work and machining. Large and small jobs accepted. Brass, stainless, ironwork, copper etc.

Rapid Steel Supply Corp. 718-392-9500
4963 30th St.   FAX 718-392-9515
Long Island City, NY 11101
Hours: 8-5 Mon-Fri
www.rapidsteel.us
Full selection of steel, excellent prices. Will deliver small quantities. Next day delivery available. Speak with Roy. CREDIT CARDS.

Triboro Iron Works 718-361-9600
38-30 31st St. (39th Ave)   718-361-9611
Long Island City, NY 11101   FAX 718-361-5422
Hours: 8-5 Mon-Fri
Steel and iron in small quantities. No credit cards.

Unique Aluminum Extrusion. LLC 732-271-1160
333 Cedar Ave.   800-218-6004
Middlesex, NJ 08846   FAX 732-271-8327
Hours: 7:30-4 Mon-Fri   E-mail: info@unalext.com
www.unalext.com
Aluminum extruder and drawn product fabricator. No credit cards.

MILLINERY SUPPLIES

Beacon Adhesives 914-699-3405
125 MacQuesten Pkwy. South   FAX 914-699-2783
Mt. Vernon, NY 10550
Hours: 8:30-4:30 Mon-Fri   E-mail: davidmesh@cs.com
www.beacon1.com
Manufacturers of millinery adhesives and lacquers. $50 minimum.

Fred's Hat Block . . . .
  Philadelphia, PA
  Hours: 24 hour website E-mail: fjraab@verizon.net
  http://users.erols.com/fjraab/
  Wooden hat blocks, spinners, stands and risers. Great prices. Will do custom shapes.

Judith M. Millinery Supply 877-499-4407
  104 S. Detroit St. 260-499-4407
  LaGrange, IN 46761 FAX 260-499-3477
  Hours: 9-6 Mon-Fri E-mail: info@judithm.com
  www.judithm.com
  *Full selection of millinery supplies for online shopping or fax in orders only.
  Buckrum, visorboard, hat blocks, strip straw, straw and felt bodies, grograins,
  hatpins, sizing, horsehair, books and videos - they have everything in some
  form. Usually a little more expensive than other places, but they carry hard
  to find items. Easy to work with - ships quickly, happy to help. They have a
  lot of instructional info on their website and offer classes. CREDIT CARDS.*

Kingform Cap Co., Inc. 516-822-2501
  121 New South Rd. FAX 516-822-2536
  Hicksville, NY 11801
  Hours: 8-4 Mon-Fri (Fri close at 12)
  www.kingformcap.com
  Bontex, peaks and more.

Manny's Millinery Supply Co. 212-840-2235
  26 W 38th St. (5-6th Ave) FAX 212-944-0178
  NY, NY 10018
  Hours: 11-6 Tue-Thurs / 11-4:30 Fri E-mail: info@mannys-millinery.com
  www.mannys-millinery.com
  *Manny's will be staying open, however they are streamlining their inventory.
  Limited quantities of straw and felt bodies. Visit website or call for updated
  information. Large selection of flowers, tubular horsehair braid, veiling, and
  feathers. Shop online. Be sure to call before dropping by store. CREDIT
  CARDS.*

Pattern Studio 513-821-4287
  P.O. Box 15874
  Cincinnati, OH 45215
  Hours: 24 hr website E-mail: pstudio@patternstudio.com
  www.patternstudio.com
  *Good selection of buckrum frames (hard to find these days!) Also patterns
  for hats and gloves. Glove making kits. Online store only. Minimum order
  $10. CREDIT CARDS.*

Tinsel Trading 212-730-1030
  1 W 37th St. (5-6th Ave) FAX 212-768-8823
  NY, NY 10018
  Hours: 9:45-5:30 Mon-Fri / 11-5 some Sat (call first)
  www.tinseltrading.com E-mail: sales@tinseltrading.com
  *Gold mesh fabrics, metallic and antique trims, vintage flowers, fruit stamens,
  buttons, fringes, cords, tassels, horsehair, ribbons, etc. Also upholstery gimps
  and trims. $75 minimum order for shipping. CREDIT CARDS.*

M

Washington Millinery Supply 301-963-4444
  8645 Ziggy Lane   FAX 301-963-8402
  Gathersburg, MD 20877
  Hours: 9-5 Mon-Fri
  Millinery supplies, cape net; wholesale. CREDIT CARDS.

Zeeman Corp. 908-281-0881
  5 Jill Ct., Bldg. 14, Unit 2 (7-8th Ave)   800-884-7928
  Hillsborough, NJ 08844   FAX 908-281-5259
  Hours: 9-5 Mon-Fri   E-mail: papajoel44@aol.com
  www.zeemancorp.com
  Buckram, adhesives, sizing, grosgrain and other ribbons, wire, cape net. See
  online catalog. No minimum.

MOTORS & MECHANICAL COMPONENTS

Beardslee Transmission Equip. Co. 718-784-4100
  27-22 Jackson Ave. (42nd-43rd St)   FAX 718-784-4106
  Long Island City, NY 11101
  Hours: 7-4:30 Mon-Fri
  Gear boxes, belts, ball bearings, maintenance items. CREDIT CARDS.

Casters, Wheels and Industrial Handling 631-650-0500
  8 Engineers Ln. (Pinelawn Rd)   800-645-8450
  Farmingdale, NY 11735   FAX 631-650-0501
  Hours: 8-5 Mon-Fri
  www.cwih.com
  Specialize in casters and hand trucks; catalog available. CREDIT CARDS.

Edmund Scientific Co. 800-728-6999
  60 Pearce Ave.   FAX 800-828-3299
  Tonawanda, NY 14150
  Hours: 8-8 Mon-Fri / 8-5 Office Hours   E-mail: scientifics@edsci.com
  www.scientificsonline.com
  Fine catalog; hobby motors, magnets, lasers, kaleidoscopes, mirrors, strobes,
  etc. CREDIT CARDS.

Grainger, Div. of W.W. Grainger, Inc. 888-361-8649
  150 Varick St.(Spring-Vandam St)   212-629-5660
  NY, NY 10013   FAX 212-465-2677
  Hours: 7-5 Mon-Fri

  619 W 54th St. FL1(11-12th Ave)   212-629-5660
  NY, NY 10019   FAX 212-629-5816
  Hours: 7-5 Mon-Fri

  815 Third Ave.(27-28th St)   718-499-1500
  Brooklyn, NY 11232   FAX 718-894-0167
  Hours: 7-5 Mon-Fri
  www.grainger.com
  Wholesale only. Dayton motors, bearings; catalog. CREDIT CARDS.

M

Herbach & Rademan Co. Corporation 856-802-0422
353 Crider Ave.   (orders only) 800-848-8001
Moorestown, NJ 08057   FAX 856-802-0465
Hours: 8-5 Mon-Fri / 1-4 Daily (pick-up hours only) E-mail: sales@herbach.com
www.herbach.com
Surplus motors, fans, electrics, lenses, etc. Minimums: $25 cash, C.O.D.; $50
open account; $500 international. CREDIT CARDS.

Micro-Mo Electronics, Inc. 800-807-9166
14881 Evergreen Ave.   FAX 727-572-7763
Clearwater, FL 33762
Hours: 8:30-5 Mon-Fri   E-mail: info@micromo.com
www.micromo.com
Services PM motors and gearheads; encoders, tachs at list prices. No credit
cards.

North Side Power Transmission Corp. 718-782-5800
309 Morgan Ave. (Metropolitan & Sharon)   800-822-6116
Brooklyn, NY 11211   FAX 718-782-1757
Hours: 8-5 Mon-Fri   E-mail: sales@nsptcorp.com
Gears, bearings, transmissions, small mechanicals. CREDIT CARDS.

Northern Tool and Equipment 952-894-9510
2800 Southcross Dr. W   FAX 952-894-1020
Burnsville, MN 55306
Hours: 24 hours daily (catalog sales)
www.northerntool.com
Generators, compressors, air tools, winches, accessories; catalog. CREDIT
CARDS.

Pic Design 800-243-6125
PO Box 1004, 86 Benson Rd.   203-758-8272
Middlebury, CT 06762   FAX 203-758-8271
Hours: 8-5 Mon-Fri   E-mail: sales@pic-design.com
www.pic-design.com
Stock mail order precision mechanical components; ask for catalog. CREDIT
CARDS.

Sava Industries, Inc. 973-835-0882
PO Box 30, 4 N Corporate Dr.   FAX 973-835-0877
Riverdale, NJ 07457
Hours: 8-5 Mon-Fri
www.savacable.com
Aircraft cable, fittings, small ball bearing pulleys; minimum order applies; ask
for catalog #14. No credit cards.

Siegal Brothers 718-387-0300
880 Meeker Ave. (Varick St)   FAX 718-387-1874
Brooklyn, NY 11222
Hours: 6-5 Mon-Fri
www.siegelbros.com
Large selection of tools, Crosby clamps, motors. CREDIT CARDS.

M

Small Parts, Inc. 305-558-1038
15901 SW 29th St., Ste. 201   800-220-4242
Miramar, FL 33027   FAX 800-423-9009
Hours: 8-7 Mon-Fri   E-mail: parts@smallparts.com
www.smallparts.com
Great selection of parts, mechanical components, tools; catalog #11. CREDIT CARDS.

Stock Drive Products 516-328-3300
2101 Jericho Trpk. / P.O. Box 5416   800-819-8900
New Hyde Park, NY 11040   FAX 516-326-8827
Hours: 8:30-5 Mon-Fri   E-mail: sdp-sisupport@sdp-si.com
www.sdp-si.com
Invaluable catalog of mechanical components, gears, rack and pinions, timing belts, etc. CREDIT CARDS.

United Staging & Rigging 203-416-5380
250 Fifth St.   FAX 203-416-5387
Bridgeport, CT 06607
Hours: 8:30-4:30 Mon-Fri

96 Commerce Way   781-376-9180
Canton, MA 01801   FAX 781-376-9185
Hours: 8-5 Mon-Fri
www.unitedstaging.com
CM Motors, Stageright staging, roofs, Genie lifts, soft goods, truss, rugging. Large RENTALS inventory. Contact Doug Frawley (CT) or Jon Sharpe (MA).

M

MOULDINGS
See also: LUMBER
                  ARCHITECTURAL ELEMENTS

American Wood Column Corp. 718-782-3163
913 Grand St. (Bushwick-Morgan Ave)   FAX 718-387-9099
Brooklyn, NY 11211
Hours: 8-4:30 Mon-Fri
www.americanwoodcolumn.com
All types of wood turnings, columns, pedestals and mouldings. Brochure. Will ship worldwide. Speak with Tom Lupo.

Bendix Mouldings 800-526-0240
90 Dayton Ave., Ste 4, Bldg. 5-A 2nd FL   973-473-4780
Passaic, NJ 07055   FAX 973-473-4785
Hours: 8:15-4 Mon-Fri   E-mail: exec@bendixarchitectural.com
www.bendixarchitectural.com
Mouldings and ornaments from three departments: finished frames, length mouldings for framers and ornamental or decorative mouldings; catalog available. Flexmold can be special ordered. CREDIT CARDS.

Cellofoam, Inc. 800-288-7663
16 Baron Park Rd.   800-332-3626
Fredericksburg, VA 22405   FAX   540-899-5429
Hours: 8-5 Mon-Fri   E-mail: info@cellofoam.com
www.cellofoam.com
*EPS foam & styrofoam mouldings, cornices, columns & capitals. Lightweight
& cost effective. CREDIT CARDS.*

Center Lumber Company 973-742-8300
85 Fulton St.   FAX 973-742-8303
Paterson, NJ 07509
Hours: 7:30-5 Mon-Fri   E-mail: astrid.frank@centerlumber.com
*Great selection of custom mouldings, with many profiles not seen in the
regular catalogs. You'll need some lead time, but definitely worth it.*

M.L. Condon Co., Inc. 914-946-4111
250 Ferris Ave.   FAX 914-946-3779
White Plains, NY 10603
Hours: 8-4:30 Mon-Fri
*Hardwood lumber, hardwood and marine plywood and mouldings; planing
and ripping facilities; deliveries. Good prices, no minimum. Good quality.
Catalog. No credit cards.*

Constantines Wood Center of Florida, Inc. 954-561-1716
1040 E Oakland Park Blvd.   800-443-9667
Ft. Lauderdale, FL 33334   FAX 954-565-8149
Hours: 8:-5:30 Mon-Fri / 9-3 Sat
www.constantines.com
*Wood mouldings, woodworking tools, exotic woods. Good products, good
service. See online catalog. CREDIT CARDS.*

The Decorators Supply Co. 773-847-6300
3610 S Morgan St.   FAX 773-847-6357
Chicago, IL 60609
Hours: 7:45-4 Mon-Fri CST   E-mail: info@decoratorssupply.com
www.decoratorssupply.com
*Over 16,000 repro ornaments for exteriors, interiors and furniture. Capitals
and brackets. Complete set of 5 catalogs, $25. Min. order $40. No credit
cards.*

Dykes Lumber 718-893-2127
1777 West Farms Rd.   FAX 718-991-4739
Bronx, NY 10460
Hours: 7:30-5 Mon-Fri

348 W 44th St.(8-9th Ave)   212-582-1930
NY, NY 10036   FAX 212-265-6735
Hours: 7:30-5 Mon-Fri / 8-1 Sat

167 Sixth St.(2-3rd Ave)   718-624-3350
Brooklyn, NY 11215   FAX 718-596-9233
Hours: 7:30-5 Mon-Fri / 8-1 Sat

26-16 Jackson Ave.(Near Queens Plaza)   718-784-3920
Long Island City, NY 11101   FAX 718-361-5906
Hours: 7:30-5 Mon-Fri / 8-1 Sat

M

Dykes Lumber (cont.) 201-867-0391
1899 Park Ave. (Main Yard and General Offices)   FAX 201-867-1674
Weehawken, NJ 07087
Hours: 7:30-5 Mon-Fri / 8-1 Sat

555 Rt. 17   201-327-1300
Ramsey, NJ 07446   FAX 201-327-1635
Hours: 7:30-5 Mon, Tue, Wed, Fri / 7:30-7 Thurs / 8-4 Sat

284 Rt. 59   845-357-6000
Tallman, NY 10982   FAX 845-368-4797
Hours: 7:30-5 Mon-Fri / 8-1 Sat

8 Saw Mill River Rd.   914-347-1400
Hawthorne, NY 10532   FAX 914-347-7150
Hours: 7:30-5 Mon-Fri / 8-4 Sat   E-mail: info@dykeslumber.com
www.dykeslumber.com
*Lumber, styro and wood beams; large moulding catalog. **CREDIT CARDS.***

Flex Moulding 201-487-8080
16 E Lafayette St.   800-307-3357
Hackensack, NJ 07601   FAX 201-487-6637
Hours: 8:30-5 Mon-Fri   E-mail: info@flexiblemoulding.com
www.flexiblemoulding.com
Flexible and rigid mouldings; selection of decorative ornaments; contact Miguel. Catalog viewable online.

Glaziers Hardware Products 718-361-0555
25-07 36th Ave. (Crescent St)   FAX 718-361-0762
Long Island City, NY 11106
Hours: 8-4:30 Mon-Fri
www.glaziershardware.com
*Mouldings, accessories, tools for the mirror, glass, storefront and picture framing industries. Carries suction grips for handling glass. Browse products online. **CREDIT CARDS.***

Home Depot 800-553-3199
550 Hamilton Ave. (16-17th St)   718-832-8553
Brooklyn, NY 11232
Hours: 6-12pm Mon-Sat / 8-9pm Sun

124-04 31st Ave. (College Point Blvd)   718-661-4608
Flushing, NY 11354   FAX 718-670-3437
Hours: 6-11pm Mon-Sat / 7-9pm Sun

40 W 23rd St. (5-6th Ave)   212-929-9571
NY, NY 10010
Hours: 7-9pm Mon-Sat / 8-7 Sun

980 Third Ave. (58-59th St)   212-888-1512
NY, NY 10022
Hours: 7-9pm Mon-Sat / 8-7 Sun

M

Home Depot (cont.) 800-553-3199
50-10 Northern Blvd. (50th St-Newtown Rd) 718-278-9031
Long Island City, NY 11101
Hours: 6-11pm Mon-Sat / 8-9pm Sun
www.homedepot.com
Hardware, tools, lumber, plumbing supplies, gardening supplies, electrical
and lighting supplies. Windows, doors and cabinets. Queens and Brooklyn
locations open 24-hrs. for those emergency needs (less crowded then, too.)
Check web for additional locations. CREDIT CARDS.

LeNobel Lumber Co., Inc. 212-246-0150
38-20 Review Ave. 718-784-5230
Long Island City, NY 11101 FAX 718-784-1422
Hours: 8-5 Mon-Fri / (closed for lunch 12-1) Pick-up until 3:30
www.lenoblelumber.com E-mail: website.lenoble@att.net
Doors, plywood, laminates, mouldings, masonite, millwork, windows,
Sonotube. Cutting 1-3:30 pm. Delivery. Cash, certified check or accounts only.

Lumberland Hardware 212-696-0022
368 Third Ave. (29th St) FAX 212-481-9223
NY, NY 10016
Hours: 9-7 Mon-Sat
Wooden spindles, hardwood, some decorative hardware, mouldings and
power tools; same day delivery for orders received by 1 pm. CREDIT CARDS.

Metropolitan Lumber & Hardware .718-898-2100
108-56 Roosevelt Ave. (108-111th St) FAX 718-898-3026
Corona, NY 11368
Hours: 7-7 Mon-Fri / 8-6 Sat / 9-4:30 Sun

175 Spring St. (Thompson St-W B'way) 212-966-3466
NY, NY 10012 FAX 212-941-1453
Hours: 8-5:45 Mon-Fri / 8-4:45 Sat / 10-4 Sun

617 Eleventh Ave. (46-47th St) 212-246-9090
NY, NY 10036 212-262-3856
Hours: 6-6 Mon-Fri / 7:30-4 Sat / 10-4 Sun FAX 212-765-2142
www.themetlumber.com
Hardwoods, plywood, hand and power tools, doors, windows, laminates,
mouldings. Complete building center. Free delivery on orders over $100.
Lumber yard closes one hour before showroom. CREDIT CARDS.

Midtown Lumber 212-675-2230
276 W 25th St. (7-8th Ave) FAX 212-675-2642
NY, NY 10001
Hours: 7-4:30 Mon-Fri
Prop kit supplies, mouldings, hardwood flooring, tileboard, glass block,
doors, hardware and laminates; lumber cut to size. Contact Mike. CREDIT
CARDS.

Mike's Lumber Store, Inc. 212-595-8884
254 W 88th St. (B'way-West End Ave) FAX 212-874-6921
NY, NY 10024
Hours: 8-6 Mon-Fri / 8-5 Sat
Formicas, some hardware, unfinished furniture, doors, stain, mouldings.
CREDIT CARDS.

M

Miron Building Supply 718-497-1111
268 Johnson Ave. (near Bushwick) FAX 718-366-0357
Brooklyn, NY 11206
Hours: 7-5 Mon-Fri / 7-2 Sat
Hardwood, mouldings, good prices. Will deliver to Manhattan; pick-ups until 2:30. No credit cards.

New York Metal 718-726-5151
19-40 45th St. 800-483-7553
Astoria, NY 11105 718-726-3453
Hours: 8-4 Mon-Fri E-mail: larson@newyorkmetal.com
www.newyorkmetal.com
Aluminum and stainless steel mouldings. Custom extruded aluminum shapes, whatever purpose, however complex or intricate the configuration. Visit web address for other locations. CREDIT CARDS.

Prince Lumber Co., Inc. 212-777-1150
404 W 15th St. (9-10th Aves) FAX 646-638-3539
NY, NY 10011
Hours: 7-4:30 Mon-Fri / 7:30-1:30 Sat
www.princelumber.com
Lumber, laminates, plywood, mouldings, doors, windows. Pleasant, good service. Free delivery with $300 order. Delivery to the outer boroughs with minimal charge. Also hardware and supplies. CREDIT CARDS.

Rosenzweig Lumber Corp. 718-585-8050
801 E 135th St. (near Bruckner Blvd) 800-228-7674
Bronx, NY 10454 FAX 718-292-8611
Hours: 7-4 Mon-Fri / 9:30-4 pick-ups E-mail: admin@rosenzweiglumber.com
www.rosenzweiglumber.com
Good selection hardwoods, veneers, plywood, lumber and mouldings; good prices, prompt next day delivery. Catalog. CREDIT CARDS.

Traditional Lines 212-627-3555
143 W 21st St. (6-7th Ave) FAX 212-645-8158
NY, NY 10011
Hours: 8:30-5 Mon-Fri E-mail: restore@tradititionalalline.com
www.traditionalline.com
Historical restoration, interiors. Will also fabricate paneling, fireplaces, moulding and hardware.

Tulnoy Lumber 718-901-1700
1620 Webster Ave. (173rd St) 800-899-5833
Bronx, NY 10457 FAX 718-229-8920
Hours: 7-5 Mon-Fri E-mail: sales@tulnoylumber.com
www.tulnoylumber.com
Large stock of mouldings. Contact Peter Tulchin. Call for new catalog.

J. P. Weaver Co. 818-500-1740
941 Air Way FAX 818-500-1798
Glendale, CA 91201
Hours: 8:30-4 Mon-Fri by appt. only E-mail: info@jpweaver.com
www.jpweaver.com
Composition ornament capitals and brackets. Catalog is clear and in scale. Technical help over the phone. Contact Mayra Gomez. CREDIT CARDS.

M

Wilson Art 866-455-8297
  250 Karin (19th Ave)   516-935-6980
  Hicksville, NY 11801   FAX 516-935-6875
  Hours: 8-4:30 Mon-Fri
  www.wilsonart.com
  Stocks a large variety of aluminum and stainless steel mouldings, including
  counter edging, price tag, angles, nosing, bars, channels; Wilsonart Laminet.
  $50 minimum on deliveries; catalog. CREDIT CARDS.

Yale Picture Frame Corp. 718-788-6200
  770 Fifth Ave. (27-28th St)   (outside NY) 800-331-YALE
  Brooklyn, NY 11232   FAX 718-788-5852
  Hours: 8-5 Mon-Thur / 8-3 Fri / 11-3 Sun
  www.yalepf.com
  Wide selection of picture frame mouldings, all styles and widths. Catalog.
  Will ship. CREDIT CARDS.

MOVING & TRANSPORT

Anthony Augliera 203-937-9080
  34 Hamilton St.   FAX 203-937-0140
  West Haven, CT 6516
  Hours: 8:30-5 Mon-Fri   E-mail: info@augliera.com
  www.augliera.com
  Interstate theatrical haulers, moving and storage. CREDIT CARDS.

Clark Transfer 800-488-7585
  800-A Paxton St.   717-238-0801
  Harrisburg, PA 17104   FAX 717-238-4865
  Hours: 8-5 Mon-Fri   E-mail: tawna@clarktransfer.com
  www.clarktransfer.com
  Theatrical transportation services. Contact Tawna.

Van Gogh Movers 718-832-6313
  4210 Second Ave.   212-226-0500
  Brooklyn, NY 11232   FAX 718-832-2760
  Hours: 9-5 Mon-Fri
  www.vangoghmovers.com
  Interstate and international moving; commercial or residential; also fine art
  crating.

Walton Hauling & Warehouse Corp. 212-246-8685
  609 W 46th St. (11-12th Ave)   FAX 212-586-4628
  NY, NY 10036
  Hours: 7-4:30 Mon-Fri   E-mail: walton609@aol.com
  www.waltonhauling.com
  115-plus year-old theatrical hauling company; local, some storage.

M

MUSICAL INSTRUMENTS

Accordion-O-Rama 732-727-7715
236 N Stevens Ave. (27-28th St)
South Amboy, NJ 08879
Hours: 10-5:30 Tue-Fri / 11-3 Sat / or by appt.
www.accordion-o-rama.com   E-mail: info@accordion-o-rama.com
New and reconditioned accordions and concertinas. Also repairs. RENTALS.
CREDIT CARDS.

Sam Ash Music Stores 212-719-2299
160 W 48th St. (6-7th Ave)   FAX 212-302-1388
NY, NY 10036
Hours: 10-8 Mon-Sat / 12-6 Sun   www.samashmusic.com
Guitars, amps, wind and string instruments; repair. Sheet music. Call or check
website for other locations. RENTALS. CREDIT CARDS.

Ayers Percussion 212-582-8410
410 W 47th St. (9-10th Ave)   FAX 212-586-0862
NY, NY 10036
Hours: 9-5 Mon-Fri / or by appt   www.ayerspercussion.com.
Acoustic percussion; will custom build; repairs; very helpful. Will ship.
RENTALS. CREDIT CARDS.

Jon Baltimore Music, Inc. 212-840-7165
151 W 46th St., 2nd FL (7th Ave)   FAX 212-575-7835
NY, NY 10036
Hours: 9-6 Mon-Fri / 10-6 Sat   E-mail: info@jonbaltimoremusic.com
www.jonbaltimoremusic.com
Repairs and sales of musical instruments. RENTALS. CREDIT CARDS.

Beethoven Pianos 212-765-7300
232 W 58th St. (B'way-7th Ave)   800-241-0001
NY, NY 10019   FAX 212-765-6544
Hours: 9-8 Mon-Sat /12-5 Sun   E-mail: info@beethovenpianos.com
www.beethovenpianos.com
Piano and organ rentals, sales, restoring, tuning, rebuilding, refinishing,
storage and moving. Ask for Carl. RENTALS. CREDIT CARDS.

Carroll Musical Instrument Rental 212-868-4120
625 W 55th St., 6th Fl. (11-12th Ave)   FAX 212-868-4126
NY, NY 10019
Hours: 96- Mon-Fri / 9-5 Sat   E-mail: irent@carrollmusic.com
www.carrollmusic.com
Large stock instruments, stands, etc. RENTALS ONLY. Rehearsal studio
space available. Three floors of rental space. CREDIT CARDS.

Drummers World, Inc. 212-840-3057
151 W 46th St. (B'way-6th Ave)   FAX 212-391-1185
NY, NY 10036
Hours: 10-6 Mon-Fri / 10-4 Sat   E-mail: info@drummersworld.com
www.drummersworld.com
Anything dealing with percussion and/or sound effects; the familiar and the
unusual. Very helpful, will order; see Barry. Catalog available. Photography
rentals only. CREDIT CARDS.

M

Guitar Center, Inc. 212-463-7500
25 W 14th St. (5-6th Ave)   FAX 212-463-7592
NY, NY 10011
Hours: 10-9 Mon-Fri / 10-8 Sat / 11-7 Sun   E-mail: mlahey@guitarcenter.com
www.guitarcenter.com
Guitars, musical instruments, audio, lighting and sound equipment for the
professional and hobbyist. Music lessons and accessories. Over 60 stores
nationwide. Check web address for local vendors. RENTALS. CREDIT
CARDS.

Lark in the Morning Musique Shoppe 877-964-5569
18791 N. Hwy # 1   707-964-5569
Fort Bragg, CA 95437   FAX 707-964-1979
Hours: 8-5 Mon-Sat   E-mail: support@larkinam.com
www.larkinthemorning.com
They offer an interesting selection of the many items that you find in their
mail order catalog, from harps to early wind instruments to African
percussion, books, recordings, and videos. Catalog. CREDIT CARDS.

Mandolin Brothers LTD 718-981-8585
629 Forest Ave. (Oakland Ave)   718-981-3226
Staten Island, NY 10310   FAX 718-816-4416
Hours: 10-6 Mon-Sat   E-mail: mandolin@mandoweb.com
www.mandolinbrothers.com
Everything from late 19th century Appalachian open-back banjos to 1920s
Gibson mandolins. Largest dealer of new and used American fretted
instuments. Quality repairs. Some RENTALS. CREDIT CARDS.

Music Inn 212-243-5715
169 W 4th St. (6-7th Ave)
NY, NY 10014
Hours: 11-7 Mon-Sat   E-mail: musicinn@nyc.rr.com
Antique, ethnic, standard musical instruments. Also ethnic artifacts and
jewelry. Will ship. RENTALS. CREDIT CARDS.

Pioneer Piano Corp. 212-586-3718
NY, NY 10019   800-746-6407
Hours: call for appt. only   FAX 212-586-3719
www.pioneerpiano.com
Pianos. Pioneer no longer has showroom, but still has pianos for sale. Call
for appointment. CREDIT CARDS.

Pro Piano 212-206-8794
85 Jane St. (Washington-Greenwich St)   800-367-0777
NY, NY 10014   FAX 212-633-1207
Hours: 9-5 Mon-Fri / 10-4 Sat   E-mail: info-ny@propiano.com
www.propiano.com
Pianos. Check website for info on office in San Francisco. Purchase or
RENTALS. CREDIT CARDS.

M

Rayburn Musical Instruments 212-541-6236
44 W 62nd St. (Columbus Ave)   FAX 212-541-6630
NY, NY 10023
Hours: 10-6 Mon-Sat   E-mail: rayburnmusicny@gmail.com
www.rayburn.com
Musical instruments, accessories and repairs. Will ship. RENTALS. CREDIT CARDS.

Steinway & Sons 212-246-1100
109 W 57th St. (6-7th Ave)   800-366-1853
NY, NY 10019   FAX 212-397-4621
Hours: 8-5 Mon-Fri   E-mail: info@steinway.com
www.steinway.com
The legend continues: sales, tuning, restoration; will buy used Steinways. Speak to Betsy Hirsch. RENTALS. CREDIT CARDS.

Studio Instrument Rentals 212-627-4900
520 W 25th St. (Rehearsal Studios) (10-11th Ave)   FAX 212-627-7032
NY, NY 10001
Hours: 8-7 Mon-Fri   E-mail: info@sir-usa.com
www.sir-usa.com
Large selection of instruments. Rehearsal studios. See website for locations throughout USA. RENTALS. CREDIT CARDS.

Total Piano and Organ Rental 212-868-4120
625 W 55th St., 6th FL (11-12th Ave)   FAX 212-868-4126
NY, NY 10019
Hours: 8-8 Mon-Fri / 9-5 Sat / 9-5 Sun   E-mail: irent@carrolmusic.com
www.carrollmusic.com
All types of pianos and organs. RENTALS. CREDIT CARDS.

Matt Umanov Guitars 212-675-2157
273 Bleecker St. (6-7th Ave)   FAX 212-727-8404
NY, NY 10014
Hours: 11-7 Mon-Sat / 12-6 Sun
www.umanovguitars.com
New and used guitars, amps, effects, repairs. RENTALS for photo shoots only. CREDIT CARDS.

Universal Musical Instrument Co. 212-254-6917
732 Broadway (8th-Waverly Pl)   FAX 516-593-2397
NY, NY 10003
Hours: 9-2 Mon-Fri / 10-1 Sat (closed Sat Apr.-Aug.)
                              E-mail: universalmusic@aol.com
All types of instruments and accessories including finger cymbals, castanets and sheet music. RENTALS. CREDIT CARDS.

Worldtone Dance 212-691-1934
230 Seventh Ave., 2nd Fl. (23rd-24th St)   866-WTD-SHOES
NY, NY 10011   FAX 212-691-2554
Hours: 11-7 Mon-Wed / 11-8 Thurs-Sat / 12-6 Sun   E-mail: info@wtdance.com
www.worldtonedance.com
Castanets, finger cymbals, (zils) flamenco videos. CREDIT CARDS.

M

NEON
See also: SIGNS & LETTERS

Artkraft Strauss Sign Corp. 212-265-5155
1776 Broadway # 1600   FAX 212-265-5262
NY, NY 10019
Hours: 9-5 Mon-Fri   E-mail: info@artkraft.com
www.artkraft.com
Custom signs; metal, wood, neon and computerized. They do many of the
large displays in Times Square. Will do the small jobs, too.

Every Thing Neon 512-719-4400
2305 Donley Dr., Ste 116   800-719-NEON
Austin, TX 78758   FAX 512-719-4490
Hours: 9-6 Mon-Fri   E-mail: sales@everythingneon.com
www.everything-neon.com
Just as the name implies, Every Thing Neon has it. Business, Beer, Sports
Bar and even Neon Sculptures. Great website. Custom work as well as
stock items. CREDIT CARDS.

Krypton Neon 718-728-4450
5-51 47th Ave (34-35th St)   FAX 718-728-7206
Long Island City, NY 11101
Hours: by appt.   E-mail: krypton@neonshop.com
www.neonshop.com
Custom manufacturer of neon art, stage effects, designs, lighting and neon
signs. Has supplied neon to numerous Broadway shows.

Let There Be Neon, Inc. 212-226-4883
38 White St. (Church-B'way)   FAX 212-431-6731
NY, NY 10013
Hours: 9-5 Mon-Fri   E-mail: info@lettherebeneon.com
www.lettherebeneon.com
Custom and stock neon; speak to Phillip or Jeff. RENTALS. CREDIT CARDS.

Manhattan Neon Sign Corp. 212-714-0430
640 W 28th St.   FAX 212-947-3906
NY, NY 10001
Hours: 9-5 Mon-Fri / or by appt.   E-mail: sales@manhattanneon.com
www.manhattanneon.com
Custom-made neon and rentals, 3-D props and displays, large-format full-
color graphics, LED moving message signs and vinyl signs, cut acrylic, wood
metal and foam. Contact Peter.

Midtown Sign Services 212-736-3838
1040 45th St. (10-11th Ave)   800-322-7274
Long Island City, NY 11101   FAX 212-629-0455
Hours: by appt.   E-mail: midtown01@aol.com
Stock and custom neon, name brand and generic. RENTALS.

Sign Expo 212-925-8585
102 Franklin St.   FAX 212-680-0195
NY, NY 10013
Hours: 9-5:30 Mon-Fri   E-mail: signs@signexpo.com
www.signexpo.com
Banners, awnings, signs, letters, neon.

N-O

Super Neon Lights Co. 718-236-5667
  7813 16th Ave. (78-79th St)   FAX 718-236-6101
  Brooklyn, NY 11214
  Hours: 8-5 Mon-Fri
  Neon signs; good work, good prices.

NETS

Sterling Net 973-783-9800
  18 Label St.   800-342-0316
  Montclair, NJ 07042   FAX 973-783-9808
  Hours: 9-5 Mon-Fri   E-mail: info@sterlingnets.com
  www.sterlingnets.com
  Theatrical, decorative, agricultural, fishing, cargo nets; bulk and custom.

NEWSPAPERS

Baumwell Graphics, Inc. 704-814-4550
  8923 Providence Estates Ct.   888-266-7246
  Charlotte, NC 28270
  Hours: 9-6 Mon-Fri   E-mail: clyde@chromatype.com
  www.chromatype.com
  *Custom replicas of current and back-dated newspapers, magazines, and fake
  money. Custom transfers. Reasonably priced. Contact Clyde Baumwell.
  CREDIT CARDS.*

Dependable Delivery, Inc. 212-586-5552
  360 W 52nd St. (8-9th Ave)   FAX 212-582-2629
  NY, NY 10019
  Hours: 7-3:30 Mon-Fri   E-mail: info@dependabledel.com
  www.dependabledel.com
  *Back issues of NYC newspapers, previous 6 months only. All current issues of
  U.S. and foreign newspapers. CREDIT CARDS.*

The Hand Prop Room LP 323-931-1534
  5700 Venice Blvd. (Venice & Curson)   FAX 323-931-2145
  Los Angeles, CA 90019
  Hours: 7-7 Mon-Fri   E-mail: info@hpr.com
  www.hpr.com
  *Full printing and graphics service; newspapers, license plates, IDs, "Greeked"
  product labels. CREDIT CARDS.*

Earl Hays Press 818-765-0700
  10707 Sherman Way   FAX 818-765-5245
  Sun Valley, CA 91352
  Hours: 8-4:30 Mon-Fri   E-mail: ehp@la.twcbc.com
  *Period repro newspapers, books, diplomas; also license plates,
  "Greeked"product labels, etc. RENTAL of money bills and police dept. mug
  books.*

Historic Newspaper Archives 732-381-2332
1592 Hart St.   800-221-3221
Rahway, NJ 07065   FAX 732-381-2699
Hours: 9-5 Mon-Fri or leave message
www.historicnewspaper.com
Back-dated newspapers, 1880-1989, from major USA cities; catalog available.
Original papers available for gift items. CREDIT CARDS.

Hotaling News Agency 212-974-9419
630 W 52nd St. (11-12th Ave)   Cell 732-861-1058
NY, NY 10019
Hours: 3:30am-11:30am Mon-Fri   E-mail: hotalinginc@aol.com
In business since 1905! Good selection of current out-of-town newspapers.
Will ship. CREDIT CARDS.

Revolution Graphics & Design 212-741-7122
Pier 40, Ground floor (West St)   FAX 212-633-6101
NY, NY 10014
Hours: 8:30-5 Mon-Fri   E-mail: bob@revolutiongraphics.com
www.revolutiongraphics.com
Graphics and signage for the entertainment industry. CREDIT CARDS.

NOTIONS: GENERAL

AGH Trim Source 212-643-7300
229 W 36th St., 4th Fl. (7th Ave)   800-THE-TRIM
NY, NY 10018   FAX 212-268-3488
Hours: 9-5 Mon-Fri   E-mail: sales@aghtrimsource.com
www.aghtrimsource.com
Zippers, thread, trim, seam binding, elastic, horsehair, hook and loop
fasteners, boning. $250 minimum order. CREDIT CARDS.

Arrow Wholesale Co. 508-753-5830
28 Water St. (Mercer St)   800-452-6310
Worcester, MA 01604   FAX 508-753-5316
Hours: 9-6 Mon-Fri   E-mail: info@arrowonthenet.com
www.arrowonthenet.com
Wholesale party supplies; also seasonal merchandise, stationery, school
supplies and props.

Atlanta Thread & Supply Co. 770-389-9115
695 Red Oak Rd.   800-847-1001
Stockbridge, GA 30281   FAX 800-298-0403
Hours: 8:15-5:30 Mon-Fri   E-mail: awootton@atlantathread.com
www.atlantathread.com
Wide selection of notions and sewing supplies from industrial machines to
home irons to needles and pins. Very helpful staff. Shipping and phone orders
available. Online catalog. CREDIT CARDS.

N-O

C-Thru Ruler Co. 860-243-0303
6 Britton Dr.   800-243-8419
Bloomfield, CT 06002   FAX 860-243-1856
Hours: 8:30-5 Mon-Fri   E-mail: thecrew@cthruruler.com
www.cthruruler.com
C-Thru plastic rulers. Scrapbooking supplies, custom designed rulers, printed cards, diecut cards and more.

The City Quilter 212-807-0390
133 W 25th St. (6-7th Ave)   FAX 212-807-9451
NY, NY 10001
Hours: 11-7 Tue-Fri / 10-6 Sat / 11-5 Sun   E-mail: info@cityquilter.com
www.cityquilter.com
Wonderful selection of quilting needles, pins, basters and wide range of threads, including cotton, rayon, silk and metallic. CREDIT CARDS.

Clotilde LLC 800-772-2891
P.O Box 7500   800-545-4002
Big Sandy, TX 75755   FAX 573-754-5290
Hours: 7-9 Mon-Fri / 7-5 Sat / 9-5 Sun
www.Clotilde.com
Mail order source for sewing notions, threads, books and scissors. Wholesale or retail. Catalog. CREDIT CARDS.

Design Craft Fabric Corp. 847-904-7000
2230 Ridge Dr.   800-755-1010
Glenview, IL 60025   FAX 847-904-7102
Hours: 8:30-5 Mon-Fri   E-mail: dcinfo@design-craft.com
www.design-craft.com
Foam-backed fabrics, 60" wide loop weave fabric. Wholesale.

Gizmo Notion Corp. 212-477-2773
160 First Ave. (9-10th St)   FAX 212-463-0301
NY, NY 10009
Hours: 11-7 Mon-Fri / 12-7Sat   E-mail: gizmocorp@aol.com
Patterns, buttons, thread, zippers, etc. Also sewing machines. Contact Rosa or Hossein. No credit cards.

Greenberg & Hammer, Inc. 212-246-2835
535 Eighth Ave. 6th Fl. North (36-37th St)   800-955-5135
NY, NY 10018   FAX 212-765-8475
Hours: 9-5 Mon-Fri   E-mail: greenberghammer1@cs.com
www.greenberg-hammer.com
Enormous selection of sewing notions, sewing tools and wardrobe kit supplies; phone and mail orders; see Frank. CREDIT CARDS.

Howard Notion & Trimming Co. 718-482-6666
2127 Borden Ave.   FAX 718-482-7660
Long Island City, NY 11101
Hours: 8-5 Mon-Thurs / 8-3 Fri
General notions wholesaler.

N-O

Kreinik Mfg. Co., Inc. 800-537-2166
  1708 Gihon Rd.   304-422-8900
  Parkersburg, WV 26102   FAX 304-428-4326
  Hours: 8:30-5 Mon-Fri
  www.kreinik.com
  Needles, metallic and silk threads, etc.; catalog available.

Levitt Industrial Textile, Inc. 516-933-7553
  PO Box 7150, 70 E Old Country Rd.   800-548-0097
  Hicksville, NY 11801   FAX 516-933-7554
  Hours: 9-5 Mon-Fri   E-mail: sales@levitttextiles.com
  www.levitttextiles.com
  VELCRO brand hook and loop fasteners in tape, coins, felt display plaques
  and cloth for immediate delivery; speak to Ken Kantner. CREDIT CARDS.

Oshman 212-226-7448
  88 Eldridge St. (Hester-Grand St)   FAX 212-226-7889
  NY, NY 10002
  Hours: 9-4 Sun-Fri
  www.oshmanbrothers.com
  Tailors supplies and trimmings. Wholesaler, jobber in textile linings and
  supplies.

Richard the Thread / Roy Cooper 310-837-4997
  10405 Washington Blvd.   800-473-4997
  Culver City, CA 90222   FAX 310-836-4996
  Hours: 7-4 Mon-Fri   E-mail: info@richardthethread.com
  www.richardthethread.com
  Specializes in hard-to-find items; silk dress shields; catalog, mail and phone
  orders. UPS-CODs and CREDIT CARDS.

Seattle Fabrics 206-525-0670
  8702 Aurora Ave. N (N 87th St)   866-925-0670
  Seattle, WA 98103   FAX 206-525-0779
  Hours: 9-6 Mon-Sat   E-mail: seattlefabrics@msn.com
  www.seattlefabrics.com
  Outdoor and recreational fabric & hardware. Specialty fabrics, webbing,
  thread and zippers; neoprene and closed cell foam. Patterns for outdoor and
  sports attire; equestrian, tents and backpacks. Fabric samples available.
  CREDIT CARDS.

Sew Right 718-468-5858
  223-20 Union Tpke.   FAX 718-468-5909
  Bayside, NY 11364
  Hours: 10-6 Tue-Fri / 10-5 Sat / 11-4 Sun   E-mail: info@sewright.com
  www.sewright.com
  Sales and service of home sewing machines and sergers. Offering sewing
  classes and notions. Speak to Harvey. RENTALS. CREDIT CARDS.

N-O

The Sewing Outlet 718-899-1900
40-48 82nd St. (Roosevelt Ave)   866-707-1739
Jackson Heights, NY 11372
Hours: 8:30-5:30 Mon-Fri / 9:30-5 Sat   E-mail: info@thesewingoutlet.com
www.thesewingoutlet.com
Sewing machine and supplies. Baby Lock dealer. NY's best resource for all your sewing, embroidery and software needs for all brands of sewing machines. CREDIT CARDS.

Siska, Inc. 201-794-1124
8 Rosol Ln. Ext.   800-393-5381
Saddle Brook, NJ 07663   FAX 201-794-8147
Hours: 8-5 Mon-Fri   E-mail: sales@siska.com
www.siska.com
Eyelets, grommets, washers, rivets and setting tools in stock. Accept orders of any size. Samples on request. Large selection. Will ship anywhere. CREDIT CARDS.

Sposabella Lace 212-354-4729
252 W 40th St. (7-8th Ave)   FAX 212-391-4208
NY, NY 10018
Hours: 9:15-6 Mon-Fri / 9:15-5 Sat   E-mail: sposabellalace@aol.com
www.sposabellalace.com
Notions, trimmings, novelties; wholesale and retail. CREDIT CARDS.

Steinlauf & Stoller, Inc. 212-869-0321
239 W 39th St. (7-8th Ave)   877-869-0321
NY, NY 10018   FAX 212-302-4465
Hours: 8-5:30 Mon-Fri   E-mail: steinlauf@rcn.com
www.steinlaufandstoller.com
One of the most complete suppliers of sewing notions, sewing tools, cleaning supplies, wardrobe kit supplies. CREDIT CARDS.

Studio Trimming 212-564-0265
327 W 36th St., 11th Fl. (8-9th Ave)   FAX 212-564-6262
NY, NY 10018
Hours: 8-5 Mon-Fri   E-mail: metrotrimming@gmail.com
www.metrotrimmingcorp.com
Tubular pipings, trimmings, bias flowers, passementerie loops and frogs.

Textol Systems, Inc. 201-935-1220
435 Meadow Lane   800-624-8746
Carlstadt, NJ 07072   FAX 201-935-1824
Hours: 8-5 Mon-Fri   E-mail: sales@textol.com
www.textol.com
Drapery supplies and velcro just about any way you need it. Super nice service. CREDIT CARDS.

Top Trimmings 212-302-2999
228 W 39th St. (7-8th Aves)
NY, NY 10018
Hours: 9-7 Mon-Fri / 10-6 Sat / 11-5 Sun   E-mail: toptrimming@yahoo.com
www.toptrimming.com
Wholesale and retail. Custom productions. Sequins, beads, feathers, ribbons, stones, buckles, chains novelties, findings and more. Sewing supplies, thread, yarn and tools. CREDIT CARDS.

V & V Thread & Supplies Corp 212-971-0701
320 W 37th St.   FAX 212-967-5257
NY, NY 10018
Hours: 9-5 Mon-Fri
Zipper, hanger tape, draw cord, thread, etc. Nice people.

NOTIONS: BONES, BONING, HOOPWIRE

Farthingales 310-392-1787
3306 Pico Blvd(West of Santa Monica Freeway)
Santa Monica, CA 90404
Hours: by appt. only   E-mail: sales@farthingalesla.com
www.farthingalesla.com
North America's largest source for costume corset fabrics, bones, zigzag wire,
wiggle bones and busks. Hoopsteel, crinoline, tutu net and stiff period shirt
interfacing. Grommets, hooks and eyes, buckles, garters and historic sewing
patterns. Dyable silks and cottons. View website for new products and
ordering, no telephone orders. Los Angeles location only carries corsets.
CREDIT CARDS.

Finebrand 323-588-3228
3720 S Santa Fe Ave.   FAX 323-588-4835
Los Angeles, CA 90058
Hours: 7-3:30 Mon-Fri   E-mail: info@finebrand.net
www.finebrand.net
Flat and spiral boning. Bust pads, bra cups, straps, hooks, garters elastic,
Velcroô and trimmings. $25 minimum. Call for catalog.

Nathanís Boning Co. 212-244-4781
302 W 37th St., 4th Fl. (8-9th Ave)   FAX 212-244-4784
NY, NY 10018
Hours: 8:30-5:30 Mon-Thurs / 8:30-5 Fri
Feather and spring steel boning, tutu wire in buckram.

Patriarche & Bell, Inc. 973-824-8297
98 Parkhurst St.   212-242-4400
Newark, NJ 7114   FAX 973-824-8298
Hours: 9-5 Mon-Fri
Hoop and spring steel.

N-O

NOTIONS: BUTTONS, BUCKLES, GROMMETS

Albest Metal Stamping Corp. 718-388-6000
1 Kent Ave. (N 13-N 14th St)   FAX 718-388-0404
Brooklyn, NY 11211
Hours: 8-5 Mon-Thurs / 8-1 Fri   E-mail: info@albest.com
www.albest.com
Leading manufacturer of metal and plastic hardware. Carries full line of Eisen
products. Buckles, clips, military spec. hardware, rings, snap hooks, studs,
nailheads, settings. CREDIT CARDS.

Archangel Antiques 212-260-9313
334 E 9th St. (1st-2nd Ave)
NY, NY 10003
Hours: 1-7 Tue-Sun or by appt.
www.archangelantiquesnyc.com
Unbelievable selection of vintage buttons, cufflinks and eyeglasses; jewelry,
vintage clothing, collectibles, small furnishings, cigarette cases, etc.
Reasonably priced, very helpful. RENTALS.

Arlene Novelty Corp. 212-921-5711
263 W 38th St. (7th-B'way)   FAX 212-302-1759
NY, NY 10001
Hours: 9-5 Mon-Fri
Plastic-covered buttons. No credit cards.

Botani Trimming, Inc. 212-224-3222
263 W 36th St. (7-8th Ave)   FAX 212-244-3363
NY, NY 10018
Hours: 9-6 Mon-Fri   E-mail: botaniusa@botaniusa.com
www.botaniusa.com
Amazing selection of buckles, buttons and all sorts of D-rings, magnetic
snaps. Some notions. Good quantity. CREDIT CARDS

C & C Metal Products 201-569-7300
456 Nordhoff Place (7-8th Ave)   FAX 201-569-4112
Englewood, NJ 07631
Hours: 8-5 Mon-Fri or by appt.   E-mail: sales@ccmetal.com
www.ccmetal.com
Wholesale only; metal buttons, buckles, nailheads, jewelry findings &
rhinestones; large catalog available to volume purchasers. CREDIT CARDS.

Fastex, Div. of Illinois Tool Works 847-299-2222
195 Algonquin Rd.   FAX 847-390-6183
Des Plaines, IL 60016
Hours: 8-4:45 Mon-Fri
www.itw-fastex.com
Grommets, rivets, fasteners of all kinds in plastic; wholesale large orders;
catalog. This main office will refer you on to your local retailer.

Greenberg & Hammer, Inc. 212-246-2835
535 Eighth Ave. 6th Fl. North (36-37th St)   800-955-5135
NY, NY 10018   FAX 212-765-8475
Hours: 9-5 Mon-Fri   E-mail: greenberghammer1@cs.com
www.greenberg-hammer.com
Enormous selection of sewing notions including grommets, grommet kits,
snaps, snap tape, buttons, etc.; phone and mail orders; see Frank. CREDIT
CARDS.

N-O

Grommet Mart 973-278-4100
80 George St.   800-923-1022
Paterson, NJ 07503   FAX 973-278-4101
Hours: 8-6 Mon-Fri   E-mail: info@grommetmart.com
www.grommetmart.com
Attaching machines, hand tools grommets & dies, curtain grommets, jean accessories, button covers, snaps, tubular rivets, plastic & metal hardware. Wide selection of items. Their highly trained staff can help you choose the correct fastener and/or machine to complete your job. CREDIT CARDS.

Guardian Rivet & Fastener 631-585-4400
35 Carlough Rd. Unit 1A   800-865-3687
Bohemia, NY 11716   FAX 631-585-4683
Hours: 8:30-5 Mon-Fri   E-mail: guardianr@aol.com
www.guardianrivet.com
Wholesale rivets and fasteners.

Joyce Trimming, Inc. 212-719-3110
109 W 38th St. (Bway-7th Ave)   800-719-7133
NY, NY 10018   FAX 212-719-3091
Hours: 9-6 Mon-Fri   E-mail: info@ejoyce.com
www.ejoyce.com
Broad selection of rhinestones, bandings, buttons, beads, trimmings and accessories. Heat transfer motifs in crystal and metal studs. Visit website to view selections. CREDIT CARDS.

Maxant Button & Supply, Inc. 770-460-2227
155 Carnes Dr.   866-462-9268
Fayetteville, GA 30214   FAX 770-460-8863
Hours: 7-5:30 Mon-Thurs   E-mail: maxantbuttonandsupply.com
www.maxantbuttonandsupply.com
Coverable buttons, belt hooks, belting, applied fasteners and hardware. CREDIT CARDS.

Quest Outfitters 800-359-6931
4919 Hubner Cr.   941-923-5006
Sarasota, FL 34241   FAX 941-923-4246
Hours: 8-4 Mon-Fri   E-mail: info@questoutfitters.com
www.questoutfitters.com
Trademark fabrics in poly and nylon, fleece coated fabrics, neoprene and foam meshes. Roll goods insulated fabrics. Zippers, plastic buckles. CREDIT CARDS.

Richard the Thread / Roy Cooper 310-837-4997
10405 Washington Blvd.   800-473-4997
Culver City, CA 90222   FAX 310-836-4996
Hours: 7-4 Mon-Fri   E-mail: info@richardthethread.com
www.richardthethread.com
Whopper poppers, #4 and #6 hooks and bars, zig-zag wire; specializes in hard to find items; catalog, mail and phone orders. UPS-CODs and CREDIT CARDS.

N-O

Seattle Fabrics 206-525-0670
8702 Aurora Ave. N (N 87th St)   866-925-0670
Seattle, WA 98103   FAX 206-525-0779
Hours: 9-6 Mon-Sat   E-mail: seattlefabrics@msn.com
www.seattlefabrics.com
Outdoor and recreational fabric & hardware. Specialty fabrics, webbing, thread and zippers; neoprene and closed cell foam. Patterns for outdoor and sports attire; equestrian, tents and backpacks. Fabric samples available. CREDIT CARDS.

Siska, Inc. 201-794-1124
8 Rosol Ln. Ext.   800-393-5381
Saddle Brook, NJ 07663   FAX 201-794-8147
Hours: 8-5 Mon-Fri   E-mail: sales@siska.com
www.siska.com
Eyelets, grommets, washers, rivets and setting tools in stock. Accept orders of any size. Samples on request. Large selection. Will ship anywhere. CREDIT CARDS.

Steinlauf & Stoller, Inc. 212-869-0321
239 W 39th St. (7-8th Ave)   877-869-0321
NY, NY 10018   FAX 212-302-4465
Hours: 8-5:30 Mon-Fri   E-mail: steinlauf@rcn.com
www.steinlaufandstoller.com
One of the most complete suppliers of sewing notions including eyelets, grommets, eyelet and grommet kits, snaps, snap tape, buttons, hook & eye and metal goods. CREDIT CARDS.

Stimpson Co., Inc. 631-472-2000
900 Sylvan Ave.   877-765-0748
Bayport, NY 11705   FAX 631-472-2425
Hours: 8:30-4:45 Mon-Fri
www.stimpsonco.com
Grommets, snaps, rivets. Catalog.

Tender Buttons 212-758-7004
143 E 62nd St. (Lex-3rd Ave)   (office) 212-980-3540
NY, NY 10065   FAX 212-319-8474
Hours: 10:30-6 Mon-Fri /10:30-5:30 Sat
Beautiful antique and modern buttons, buckles; antique cufflinks.

Top Trimmings 212-302-2999
228 W 39th St. (7-8th Aves)
NY, NY 10018
Hours: 9-7 Mon-Fri / 10-6 Sat / 11-5 Sun   E-mail: toptrimming@yahoo.com
www.toptrimming.com
Wholesale and retail. Custom productions. Sequins, beads, feathers, ribbons, stones, buckles, chains novelties, findings and more. Sewing supplies, thread, yarn and tools. CREDIT CARDS.

Vardhman, Inc. 212-840-6950
269 W 39th St. (7-8th Ave)   FAX 212-840-5056
NY, NY 10018
Hours: 10-6:30 Mon-Fri / 11-5:30 Sat
www.vardhmaninc.com
Nice selection of buttons, trimmings, knittings, yarn and accessories.

N-O

Wooden Buttons 212 354-7591
    260 West 39th St., 3rd Fl. (7-8th Ave)   FAX 212 354-8291
    NY, NY 10018
    Hours: 9-5 Mon-Fri   E-mail: info@woodbuttons.com
    www.woodbuttons.com
    Wooden beads, buttons, buckles; wholesale. Catalog available online.
    CREDIT CARDS.

NOTIONS: ELASTIC

American Cord & Webbing Co., Inc. .401-762-5500
    88 Century Dr.   FAX 401-762-5514
    Woonsocket, RI 02895
    Hours: 8-5 Mon-Fri   E-mail: dsmith@acw1.com
    www.acw1.com
    Elastic cord; also webbing tape, binding; $150 minimum. Catalog with
    samples available. CREDIT CARDS.

Greenberg & Hammer, Inc. 212-246-2835
    535 Eighth Ave. 6th Fl. North (36-37th St)   800-955-5135
    NY, NY 10018   FAX 212-765-8475
    Hours: 9-5 Mon-Fri   E-mail: greenberghammer1@cs.com
    www.greenberg-hammer.com
    Enormous selections of sewing notions including elastic in a variety of
    widths; phone and mail orders; see Frank. CREDIT CARDS.

Steinlauf & Stoller, Inc. 212-869-0321
    239 W 39th St. (7-8th Ave)   877-869-0321
    NY, NY 10018   FAX 212-302-4465
    Hours: 8-5:30 Mon-Fri   E-mail: steinlauf@rcn.com
    www.steinlaufandstoller.com
    One of the most complete suppliers of sewing notions including elastic in a
    variety of widths; flat, cord, horsehair, non-roll, etc. CREDIT CARDS.

N-O

NOTIONS: NEEDLES & PINS

Colonial Needle Co. 914-946-7474
    74 Westmorland Ave.   800-9-NEEDLE
    White Plains, NY 10606   FAX 914-946-7002
    Hours: 9-5 Mon-Fri   E-mail: jim@colonialneedle.com
    www.colonialneedle.com
    Hand sewing, gloves and lacing needles; wholesale. CREDIT CARDS.

Diamond Needle 201-507-1771
    60 Commerce Rd. (6-7th Ave)   800-221-5818
    Carlstadt, NJ 07072   FAX 201-507-1715
    Hours: 9-5 Mon-Fri   E-mail: info@diamondneedle.com
    www.diamondneedle.com
    Industrial or domestic: shears and machine feet. CREDIT CARDS.

NOTIONS: THREAD

American & Efird, Inc. 800-453-5128
22 American St. (29-30th St)   704-827-4311
Mt. Holly, NC 28120   FAX 704-827-0974
Hours: 8:30-5 Mon-Fri   E-mail: northamerica.homepage@amefird.com
www.amefird.com
Manufacturer of nylon thread, industrial threads.

Criterion Thread Co. 718-464-4200
217-44 98th Ave   800-695-0080
Queens Village, NY 11429   FAX 718-464-3310
Hours: 8-5 Mon-Fri   E-mail: info@cthread.com
www.cthread.com
Silk, cotton, nylon, metalic, synthetic, sewing and embroidery threads; also notions.

Greenberg & Hammer, Inc. 212-246-2835
535 Eighth Ave. 6th Fl. North (36-37th St)   800-955-5135
NY, NY 10018   FAX 212-765-8475
Hours: 9-5 Mon-Fri   E-mail: greenberghammer1@cs.com
www.greenberg-hammer.com
Enormous selections of sewing notions including spools, tubes and cones of threads of all kinds; phone and mail orders; see Frank. CREDIT CARDS.

La Lame, Inc. 212-921-9770
132 W 36th St., 11th Fl. (5-6th Ave)   FAX 212-302-4359
NY, NY 10018
Hours: 9-5 Mon-Fri   E-mail: edschneer@lalame.com
www.lalame.com
Lumi thread-metallic for Merrow machines. CREDIT CARDS.

Steinlauf & Stoller, Inc. 212-869-0321
239 W 39th St. (7-8th Ave)   877-869-0321
NY, NY 10018   FAX 212-302-4465
Hours: 8-5:30 Mon-Fri   E-mail: steinlauf@rcn.com
www.steinlaufandstoller.com
One of the most complete suppliers of sewing notions including, cotton, poly, poly blend, nylon and silk thread. CREDIT CARDS.

N-O

OCCULT PARAPHERNALIA

Enchantments, Inc. 212-228-4394
    424 E 9th St. (1st-A Ave)
    NY, NY 10003
    Hours: 1-9 Mon, Wed-Sun
    www.enchantmentsincnyc.com
    Books, herbs, oils, incense, crystal balls, robes, jewelry and occult
    paraphernalia. Mail order. CREDIT CARDS.

OFFICE SUPPLIES & STATIONERY

7th Avenue Stationers 212-695-4900
    210 W 35th St., 2nd Fl. (7-8th Ave)   800-320-5735
    NY, NY 10001   FAX 212-643-0480
    Hours: 9-5:30 Mon-Fri   E-mail: info@7thavenuecollector.com
    www.pensandgifts.com
    Art, drafting, graphics, office supplies and stationery. CREDIT CARDS.

Arthur Brown International Pen Shop 212-575-5555
    2 W 45th St. (5-6th Ave)   800-772-PENS
    NY, NY 10036   FAX 212-575-5825
    Hours: 9-6:15 Mon-Fri / 10-6 Sat   E-mail: penshop@artbrown.com
    www.artbrown.com
    Stationery, Ink and refills, desk sets and ink pens. CREDIT CARDS.

Julius Blumberg, Inc. 212-431-5000
    62 White St. (B'way-Church St)   800-529-6278
    NY, NY 10013   FAX 800-561-9018
    Hours:8:45-5:45 Mon-Fri   E-mail: weborders@blumberg.com
    www.blumberg.com
    Main store; all legal forms on file; purchase by the sheet or pad. Speak to Bob
    Blumberg for large orders. CREDIT CARDS.

Central Time Clock, Inc. 718-784-4900
    5-23 50th Ave.   800-556-3504
    Long Island City, NY 11101   FAX 718-742-9491
    Hours: 8-5 Mon-Fri   E-mail: info@centraltimeclock.com
    www.centraltimeclock.com
    Timeclocks, supplies, sales and service. All makes and models; digital,
    biometric hand readers and stock broker timestamps. Timecards and racks.
    Contact Hal. RENTALS. CREDIT CARDS.

The Container Store 800-266-8246
    629 Sixth Ave.(18-19th St)   212-366-4200
    NY, NY 10011
    Hours: 9-9 Mon-Sat / 10-8 Sun

    725 Lexington Ave.(58-59th St)   212-366-4200
    NY, NY 10022
    Hours: 9-9 Mon-Sat / 10-8 Sun
    www.containerstore.com
    For all your organizational needs; bins, files, boxes, metro shelving and closet
    organizers. The Container Store has everything. Contact the website or toll-
    free number for other locations. CREDIT CARDS.

N-O

Flynn Stationers 212-339-8700
55 E 59th St. (Madison-Park)   FAX 212-355-3738
NY, NY 10022
Hours: 9-5:15 Mon-Fri   E-mail: customerservice@flynns.com
www.flynns.com
Large general store of stationery supplies with printing service, also fountain pens. CREDIT CARDS.

Fountain Pen Hospital/FPH Office Supplies 212-964-0580
10 Warren St. (B'way-Church St)   800-253-7367
NY, NY 10007   FAX 212-227-5916
Hours: 7:45-5:30 Mon-Fri   E-mail: info@fountainpenhospital.com
www.fountainpenhospital.com
Sells fountain and calligraphy pens and repairs. Vintage fountain pens. Online shopping. CREDIT CARDS.

Goes Lithographing Company 800-349-6700
42 W 61st. St.   FAX 773-684-2065
Chicago, IL 60621
Hours: 9-5 Mon-Fri / Website 24-hrs.   E-mail: sales@goeslitho.com
www.goeslitho.com
Excellent selection of blank stock certificates, bland borders, awards and corporation supplies. Sold in bundles 10 to 100. CREDIT CARDS.

Il Papiro 212-288-9330
1021 Lexington Ave. (73rd-74th St)   FAX 212-570-1587
NY, NY 10021
Hours: 10-6 Mon-Fri / 10-5:30 Sat
www.ilpapirofirenze.it
Marbled papers and Italian stationery items; expensive. CREDIT CARDS.

Jam Envelope & Paper Co. / Hudson Envelope Co. 212-473-6666
135 Third Ave. (14th St.)   FAX 212-473-7300
NY, NY 10003
Hours: 8:30-8 Mon-thrus / 8:30-7 Fri / 10-6 Sat-Sun
www.jampaper.com   E-mail: info@jampaper.com
All sizes and colors of envelopes, paper, pens, notebooks, journals and rubber stamps. Also gift-wrap bags and boxes, shredded papers and other gift-wrapping needs. Low prices. CREDIT CARDS.

Joseph Meyer Office Supplies, Inc. .212-226-1657
48 Howard St.
NY, NY 10013
Hours: 9-5 Mon-Fri
www.biggestbook.com
Good selection of stationery and office supplies. Experience with production companies. Rush orders no problem.

New York Stationery 212-243-4222
474-A Sixth Ave. (11-12th St)   FAX 212-727-9424
NY, NY 10011
Hours: 9-8 Mon-Fri / 10-8 Sat / 11-8 Sun
Stationery, rubber stamps, small leather goods and desk calendars. CREDIT CARDS.

Office Depot 888-GO-DEPOT
   1441 Broadway (40th-41st St)   212-764-2465
   NY, NY 10018
   Hours: 9-9 Mon-Sat / 10-6 Sun
   www.officedepot.com
   Discount office supplies, desk accessories, computer equipment, telephones
   and office furniture. Catalog. Call 888-GO-DEPOT for other locations.
   CREDIT CARDS.

Paper Presentation 212-463-7035
   23 W 18th St. (5-6th Ave)   1-800-PAPER-01
   NY, NY 10011   FAX 212-463-7022
   Hours: 9-7 Mon-Fri, 11-6 Sat-Sun   E-mail: info@paperpresentation.com
   www.paperpresentation.com
   Excellent assortment of papers, stamps, embossing supplies, cards, office
   supplies and stationery. Catalog. CREDIT CARDS.

Park Heights Stationers Copy Center 718-398-0202
   164 Park Pl. (Flatbush-7th Ave)   FAX 718-622-3860
   Brooklyn, NY 11217
   Hours: 9-7:30 Mon-Fri / 10-7:30 Sat / 12-5 Sun
   Copy service, color, B&W; commercial stationer, stationery supplies.

Staples, Inc. 212-997-4446
   1065 Sixth Ave.(40th-41st St)   FAX 212-997-3918
   NY, NY 10018
   Hours: 7-9 Mon-Fri / 9-6 Sat / 11-6 Sun

   776 Eighth Ave., 2nd Fl.(46-47th St)   212-265-4550
   NY, NY 10036   FAX 212-265-4395
   Hours: 7-8 Mon-Fri / 9-6 Sat / 12-5 Sun

   57 W 57th St.(6th Ave)   212-308-0335
   NY, NY 10019   FAX 212-308-0567
   Hours: 7-8 Mon-Fri / 9-6 Sat / 12-5 Sun

   699 Sixth Ave.(22nd-23rd St)   212-675-5698
   NY, NY 10017   FAX 212-675-5749
   Hours: 7-8 Mon-Fri / 9-6 Sat / 12-7 Sun

   575 Lexington Ave.(51st-52nd St)   212-644-2118
   NY, NY 10022   FAX 212-644-3095
   Hours: 7-7 Mon-Fri / 9-6 Sat / 11-5 Sun

   5 Union Sq. W(16-17th St)   212-929-6323
   NY, NY 10003   FAX 212-929-5457
   Hours: 7-10 Mon-Fri / 9-9 Sat-Sun

   2248 Broadway(80th-81st St)   212-712-9617
   NY, NY 10024   FAX 212-712-9635
   Hours: 7-9 Mon-Fri / 9-9 Sat / 11-9 Sun

   1293-1311 Broadway(Herold Sq. 34th & B-way) 212-564-8580
   NY, NY 10001   FAX 212-564-8661
   Hours: 7-8 Mon-Fri / 9-6 Sat / 12-5 Sun

N-O

Staples, Inc. (cont.) 646-227-0585
    535 Fifth Ave.(44-45th St)   FAX 646-227-0573
    NY, NY 10017
    Hours: 7-8 Mon-Fri / 9-6 Sat / 11-6 Sun

    217 Broadway(Vesey-Barclay)   212-346-9624
    NY, NY 10007   FAX 212-346-9633
    Hours: 7-7 Mon-Fri / 9-6 Sat / 12-5 Sun
    www.staples.com
    Discount office supplies, furniture, desk accessories. Very well stocked.
    Catalog available. Call 800 number for additional locations. CREDIT CARDS.

Victorian Trading Company 800-700-2035
    15600 W 99th St.   913-438-3995
    Lenexa, KS 66219   FAX 913-438-5225
    Hours: 24 on website
    www.victoriantradingco.com
    Mail order company with a nice selections of Victorian stationery, holiday
    cards, rubber stamps, stickers, ornaments and fine art prints. Great website.
    CREDIT CARDS.

N-O

PACKING MATERIALS

Abbot & Abbot Box Corp. 718-392-2600
　37-11 10th St. (37-38th Ave)　　　　　　　　　　　　　　　800-377-0037
　Long Island City, NY 11101　　　　　　　　　　　　FAX 718-392-8439
　Hours: 8-5 Mon-Fri　　　　　　　　　E-mail: crates@abbotbox.com
　www.abbotbox.com
　Wooden boxes, crates, crating, pallets and skids, packing supplies, cartons,
　bubble wrap and foam. Since 1888 NY's most complete source for all crating
　and box requirements. P.O.s accepted. No credit cards.

Atlantic Paper Products 212-674-4400
　4916 Maspeth Ave.　　　　　　　　　　　　　　　　FAX 718-386-1434
　Maspeth, NY 11378
　Hours: 7-3 Mon-Fri　　　　　　　　　　E-mail: ATL4916@aol.com
　www.atlanticpaperproducts.com
　Full-service paper distributor supplying a complete line of retail packaging,
　shipping, janitorial and food service items. Family owned for over 50 years.
　Custom design and printing available. CREDIT CARDS.

Atlas Materials 718-875-1162
　116 King St. (Van Brunt)　　　　　　　　　　　　　FAX 718-875-1163
　Brooklyn, NY 11231
　Hours: 8-3 Mon-Fri　　　　　　　　　E-mail: info@atlasmaterials.com
　www.atlasmaterials.com
　Excelsior, ethafoam. Shredded papers available in 8 different colors and
　packing materials. AB foam. Paper catalog available. CREDIT CARDS.

Better-Pak Container Co. 888-904-0202
　675 Dell Rd.　　　　　　　　　　　　　　　　　　FAX 201-804-0787
　Carlstadt, NJ 07072
　Hours: 5-3 Mon-Fri　　　　　　　E-mail: brian.betterpak@gmail.com
　www.betterpak.com
　Corrugated boxes. CREDIT CARDS.

Cellofoam, Inc. 800-288-7663
　16 Baron Park Rd.　　　　　　　　　　　　　　　　　　800-332-3626
　Fredericksburg, VA 22405　　　　　　　　　　　　FAX 540-899-5429
　Hours: 8-5 Mon-Fri　　　　　　　　　E-mail: info@cellofoam.com
　www.cellofoam.com
　Excelsior wood shavings, foam rubber, ethafoam and polystyrene. Catalog.
　$35 minimum phone order. CREDIT CARDS.

Dura-Foam Products, Inc. 718-894-2488
　63-02 59th Ave.　　　　　　　　　　　　　　　　　FAX 718-894-2493
　Maspeth, NY 11378
　Hours: 8-4:30 Mon-Fri　　　　　　E-mail: durafoaminc@yahoo.com
　Large selection of flexible and rigid urethane foam, foam rubber, beads and
　wrapping materials.

P

DuraLast Products Corp. 901-323-8448
  580 Tillman, Ste. 5   888-323-8448
  Memphis, TN 38112   FAX 901-323-8442
  Hours: 8-4:30 Mon-Fri   E-mail: nathan@duralast.com
  www.duralast.com
  Rubberized hog hair media, a natural fiber used to create various special effects; sound effects construction, sound dampening, rain making, etc. Available in various sizes and thicknesses. Also air conditioner filters. CREDIT CARDS.

Falcon Supply Co. 732-396-8200
  55 Randolph Ave.   800-356-TAPE
  Avenel, NJ 07001   FAX 732-396-9642
  Hours: 8:30-5 Mon-Fri   E-mail: info@falconsupply.com
  www.falconsupply.com
  Tape, staples and staplers, packing lists, boxes, all packing material needs. Janitorial supplies. Great website. Can arrange to p/u order from warehouse. CREDIT CARDS.

Hybrid Cases 631-563-1181
  1121-20 Lincoln Ave.   800-343-1433
  Holbrook, NY 11741   FAX 631-563-1390
  Hours: 10-8 Mon-Fri
  www.hybridcases.com
  Transit cases, flight cases, airline transit approved. Custom-made and standard sizes available.

International Tape Products Co., Inc. 888-748-9312
  901 Murray Rd. / P.O. Box 376   FAX 973-599-0220
  E. Hanover, NJ 07936
  Hours: 8-5 Mon-Fri   E-mail: fpinfo@fidelitypaper.com
  www.fidelitypaper.com
  Distributors of all major brands; gaffers, spike, glo, dance floor and double-sided. Also offers special tape conversions services and special application tapes. No minimum. CREDIT CARDS.

Robert Karp Container Corp. 201-200-1151
  134 Garfield Ave. Unit D (11-12th Ave)   FAX 201-200-1168
  Jersey City, NJ 07305
  Hours: 7-4 Mon-Fri   E-mail: forboxes@aol.com
  Corrugated boxes and sheets, twine, tape, tissue, kraft paper, jiffy bags, bubble-pak; large or small orders. Free delivery. AMEX Only.

Movers Supply House, Inc. 718-671-1200
  1476 E 222nd St. (Baychester Ave)   800-432-1MSH
  Bronx,, NY 10469   FAX 718-379-4403
  Hours: 8-5 Mon-Fri
  www.moversupply.com
  Packing blankets, loading straps, hampers, j-bars; good prices; will ship COD. CREDIT CARDS.

National Van Equipment Co., Inc. 718-784-4433
    38-20 Review Ave.   FAX 718-784-4660
    Long Island City, NY 11101
    Hours: 9-4:30 Mon-Fri
    Formerly Canvas Specialty Co. Packing blankets, webbing, and canvas.
    CREDIT CARDS.

Prime Packaging Corp. 718-417-3000
    1290 Metropolitan Ave.   FAX 718-417-3348
    Brooklyn, NY 11237
    Hours: 7:30-5 Mon-Thurs / 7:30-1 Fri
    www.primepackaging.com
    Corrugated boxes, extra heavy and double wall cartons, special sizes made to
    order. Shipping and packaging supplies. Catalog. CREDIT CARDS.

Snow Craft Co., Inc. 516-739-1399
    200 Fulton Ave.   FAX 516-739-1637
    Garden City Park, NY 11040
    Hours: 9-5 Mon-Fri
    Foam, will cut to size; other foams and packing materials; delivery is extra.
    $150 minimum. CREDIT CARDS.

Supplies Unlimited 718-937-5004
    45-40 21st St. (45th Rd - 46th Ave)   800-339-7190
    Long Island City, NY 11101   FAX 718-482-1118
    Hours: 8-4:30 Mon-Fri   E-mail: sales@wesupplyit.com
    www.wesupplyit.com
    Janitorial supplies; Dustmops, brooms, mopping equipment and packing
    supplies; bubblewrap, kraft paper, foam peanuts, cartons, tape, etc. CREDIT
    CARDS.

Technical Library Services, Inc./ TALAS 212-219-0770
    330 Morgan Ave.   FAX 212-219-0735
    Brooklyn, NY 11211
    Hours: 9-5:30 Mon-Fri
    www.talasonline.com
    Acid-free tissue for costume packing. Presentation boxes.

Tomar Industries 732-780-2200
    300 Commerce Dr.   FAX 732-780-4123
    Freehold, NJ 07728
    Hours: 9-5 Mon-Fri   E-mail: tfieldjr@tomarind.com
    www.tomarind.com
    Gaffers, duct, many types of pressure-sensitive tapes. Honeycomb paper
    products. Janitorial supplies, safety equipment and adhesives. A 3-M dealer.
    CREDIT CARDS.

P

PAINTS & DYES: BRONZING POWDER & LEAFING SUPPLIES

Crescent Bronze Powder Co., Inc. 920-230-3270
3321 County Rd. A   800-445-6810
OshKosh, WI 54901   FAX 920-231-8085
Hours: 8-4 Mon-Fri   E-mail: mary@crescentbronze.us
www.crescentbronze.us

A full spectrum of bronzing powders and liquids, pearlescent and fluorescent paint, metallic paints, aerosol paint; color cards and price lists available. 1 lb. minimum.

Epstein's Paint Center 212-265-3960
822 Tenth Ave. (54-55th St)   800-464-3432
NY, NY 10019   FAX 212-765-8841
Hours: 8-5:30 Mon-Fri / 8:30-3 Sat   E-mail: sales@epsteinspaint.com
www.epsteinspaint.com

Bronzing powders, theatrical paint supplies. CREDIT CARDS.

Lee's Art Shop & Studio 212-247-0110
220 W 57th St. (B'way-7th Ave)   FAX 212-581-7023
NY, NY 10019
Hours: 9-7:30 Mon-Fri / 10-7 Sat / 11-6 Sun   E-mail: info@leesartshop.com
www.leesartshop.com

Leafing supplies; drafting, framing, drawing and painting supplies. No phone orders. CREDIT CARDS.

New York Central Art Supply, Inc. 212-473-7705
62 Third Ave. (10-11th St)   800-950-6111
NY, NY 10003   FAX 212-475-2513
Hours: 8:30-6:15 Mon-Sat   E-mail: sales@nycentralart.com
www.nycentralart.com

Bronzing powders; gold, silver and metal leafs, dry pigments, sizing, agate burnishers, patinas and glitter. Accepts phone orders. CREDIT CARDS.

Pearl Paint / World's Largest Creative Resource 800-451-7327
308 Canal St.(B'way-Church St)   212-431-7932
NY, NY 10013   (mail order) 800-221-6845
Hours: 9-7 Mon-Fri / 10-7 Sat / 10-6 Sun   FAX 212-431-6798

42 Lispenard St. (Craft & Home Center)(B'way-Church St)   212-226-3717
NY, NY 10013   800-221-6845
Hours: 9-7 Mon-Fri / 10-7 Sat / 10-6 Sun

776 Rt. 17 N   201-447-0300
Paramus, NJ 07652   FAX 201-447-4012
Hours: 10-9 Mon-Sat

1033 E Oakland Park Blvd.(Corp. Office)   954-567-9678
Ft. Lauderdale, FL 33334
www.pearlpaint.com

Dutch metal, silver, copper and gold leaf; bronzing powders and liquids at very good prices; catalog. Online shopping available. CREDIT CARDS.

Sepp Leaf Products, Inc. 212-683-2840
   381 Park Ave. S, Rm 1301 (27th St)   800-971-7377
   NY, NY 10016   FAX 212-725-0308
   Hours: 9-5 Mon-Fri   E-mail: sales@seppleaf.com
   www.seppleaf.com
   German and Italian gold leaf, imitation leaf in rolls and sheets; list of
   products available. CREDIT CARDS.

United States Bronze Powders 908-782-5454
   408 US Hwy 202   FAX 908-782-3489
   Flemington, NJ 08822
   Hours: 9-5 Mon-Fri
   www.usbronzepowders.com
   Wholesale; minimum order $100.

Wolf Paints, S. Wolf Div. of Janovic Plaza 212-245-3241
   771 Ninth Ave. (51st-52nd St)   FAX 212-974-0591
   NY, NY 10019
   Hours: 7:30-6:30 Mon-Fri / 9-6 Sat / 11-5 Sun
   Bronzing powders, dyes, brushes; house and theatrical paints. CREDIT
   CARDS.

PAINTS & DYES: FABRIC

ALJO Mfg. Co. 212-226-2878
   49 Walker St. (B'way-Church)   866-293-8913
   NY, NY 10013   FAX 212-274-9616
   Hours: 8:30-6 Mon-Fri / 10:30-4:30 Sat   E-mail: sales@aljodye.com
   www.aljodye.com
   Direct, disperse, fiber-reactive, acid, basic and vat dyes; chemicals and
   auxiliary agents for dying. Neon pigment dyes. CREDIT CARDS.

Arrow Wholesale Co. 508-753-5830
   28 Water St. (Mercer St)   800-452-6310
   Worcester, MA 01604   FAX 508-753-5316
   Hours: 9-6 Mon-Fri   E-mail: info@arrowonthenet.com
   www.arrowonthenet.com
   Rit and Tintex by the dozen.

Createx Colors / Colorcraft 860-653-5505
   14 Airport Park Rd.   800-243-2712
   East Granby, CT 06026   FAX 860-653-0643
   Hours: 8:30-5 Mon-Fri   E-mail: customerservice@createxcolors.com
   www.createxcolors.com
   Manufacturer of Createx, a heat-set fabric paint; non-toxic water-based dyes;
   catalog. CREDIT CARDS.

W. Cushing & Co. 207-967-3711
   PO Box 351, 21 North St.   800-626-7847
   Kennebunkport, ME 04046   FAX 207-967-8682
   Hours: 9-4 Mon-Fri   E-mail: orders@wcushing.com
   www.wcushing.com
   Manufacturer of dyes and dispersing agents; also rug-hooking supplies.
   CREDIT CARDS.

Dharma Trading Co. . . . .(store) 415-456-1211
1604 Fourth St.   (mail order) 800-542-5227
San Rafael, CA 94901   FAX 415-456-8747
Hours: 10-6 Mon-Sat / 12-5 Sun   E-mail: catalog@dharmatrading.com
www.dharmatrading.com
Textile art supplies; dyes, fabrics, tools, books; catalog; mail and phone orders. CREDIT CARDS.

Dixon Ticonderoga 800-824-9430
195 International Pkwy.   407-829-9000
Heathrow, FL 32746   FAX 800-232-9396
Hours: 8:30-5 Mon-Fri
www.dixonticonderoga.com
Accolite colors, Prang textile paints. Markers, chalk, adhesives, clay. Wholesale.

Ivy Imports 301-474-7347
6806 Trexler Rd.   FAX 301-441-2395
Lanham, MD 20706
Hours: 10-5 Mon-Fri   E-mail: spin@silkpainter.org
www.silkpainters.org
Fabric paints, dyes, resists and all associated products; books, instructional materials and seminars. Networking newsletter "Silkworm" available for $18 (6 issues). CREDIT CARDS.

New York Central Art Supply, Inc. 212-473-7705
62 Third Ave. (10-11th St)   800-950-6111
NY, NY 10003   FAX 212-475-2513
Hours: 8:30-6:15 Mon-Sat   E-mail: sales@nycentralart.com
www.nycentralart.com
Silk dyes, rocion dyes for natural fabrics, glitter, puffy, slick and spatter fabric paints, batik supplies. Accepts phone orders. CREDIT CARDS.

PRO Chemical & Dye, Inc. 508-676-3838
PO Box 14   800-228-9393 Orders only
Somerset, MA 02726   FAX 508-676-3980
Hours: 24 hour phone service. / 8:30-5 Mon-Fri
www.prochemical.com   E-mail: promail@prochemical.com
Dyes for cotton, linen, silk, rayon and synthetic fibers. Cold water dyes, wide range of colors. Fabric paints: seta color and profab textile paints. Offer workshops, lectures and demo service available. Very informative website. CREDIT CARDS.

Rit Dye / Phoenix Brands LLC 317-231-8044
PO Box 21070, 1437 W Morris St.   866-794-0800
Indianapolis, IN 46221   FAX 317-231-8050
Hours: 8-4 Mon-Fri
www.ritdye.com
Quantity packing for the industry. Minimum 20 dozen boxes. Info and color card on request. Pro-line bulk dyes in 5 & 45 pound containers. No credit cards.

Rupert, Gibbon, & Spider, Inc. 800-442-0455
PO Box 425   707-433-9577
Healdsburg, CA 95448   FAX 707-433-4906
Hours: 8-5 Mon-Fri   E-mail: service@jacquardproducts.com
www.jacquardproducts.com
Fabric paints & dyes, economical full sizes, novelty paints, metallics,
flourescents, sparkles. Catalog. COD. CREDIT CARDS.

Screen Process Supplies Mfg. Co. 510-235-8330
530 MacDonald Ave.   925-899-3846
Richmond, CA 94801
Hours: 9:30-4 Tue-Fri
Cotton and silk dyes, silkscreening equipment and manuals; catalog
available. CREDIT CARDS.

Spectra Colors Corp. 201-997-0606
25 Rizzolo Rd.   800-527-8588
Kearny, NJ 07032   FAX 800-635-1811
Hours: 8:30-5 Mon-Fri   E-mail: dyes@spectracolors.com
www.spectracolors.com
Direct, disperse, acid dyes; 24-hrs. to pick-up. No credit cards.

PAINTS & DYES: HOUSEHOLD

American Home Hardware 212-765-7356
590 Ninth Ave. (42-43rd St)   FAX 212-757-7045
NY, NY 10036
Hours: 8-7 Mon-Fri / 8:30-6 Sat / 8:30-4 Sun
General neighborhood hardware and housewares store. They carry Benjamin
Moore paints, moving supplies and wardrobe boxes. Very nice to deal with.
CREDIT CARDS.

Epstein's Paint Center 212-265-3960
822 Tenth Ave. (54-55th St)   800-464-3432
NY, NY 10019   FAX 212-765-8841
Hours: 8-5:30 Mon-Fri / 8:30-3 Sat   E-mail: sales@epsteinspaint.com
www.epsteinspaint.com
Household and theatrical paints, rollers, brushes and roller patterns, etc.
CREDIT CARDS.

Janovic Plaza 212-772-1400
888 Lexington Ave.(66th St)   FAX 212-794-2913
NY, NY 10021
Hours: 7-7 Mon-Fri / 8-6 Sat / 11-5 Sun

1555 Third Ave.(87th St)   212-289-6300
NY, NY 10128   FAX 212-289-6831
Hours: 7-6:30 Mon-Fri / 9-6 Sat / 11-5 Sun

159 W 72nd St.(Amsterdam-Columbus Ave)   212-595-2500
NY, NY 10023   FAX 212-724-7846
Hours: 7:30-6:30 Mon-Fri / 9-6 Sat / 11-5 Sun

P

Janovic Plaza (cont.) 212-627-1100
    161 Sixth Ave.(Spring St)   FAX 212-924-7641
    NY, NY 10013
    Hours: 7:30-6:30 Mon-Fri / 9-6 Sat / 11-5 Sun

    215 Seventh Ave.(22nd-23rd St)   212-645-5454
    NY, NY 10011   FAX 212-691-1504
    Hours: 7:30-6:30 Mon-Fri / 9-6 Sat / 11-5 Sun

    2680 Broadway(102nd St)   212-531-2300
    NY, NY 10025   FAX 212-932-3476
    Hours: 7:30-6:30 Mon-Fri / 9-6 Sat / 11-5 Sun

    292 Third Ave.(22nd-23rd St)   212-777-3030
    NY, NY 10010   FAX 212-253-0985
    Hours: 7:30-6:30 Mon-Fri / 9-6 Sat / 11-5 Sun

    80 Fourth Ave.(10th St)   212-477-6930
    NY, NY 10003   FAX 212-254-4628
    Hours: 7:30-6:30 Mon-Fri / 9-6 Sat / 11-5 Sun

    30-35 Thompson Ave.(Van Dam & Queens Blvd)   347-418-3480
    Long Island City, NY 11101   Orders 718-392-3999
    Hours: 7-6 Mon-Fri / 8-4 Sat   FAX 718-784-4564
    www.janovic.com
    Household paints and paint supplies; tile, home decorating center; catalog on paint products. Very good prices. See website for other locations. CREDIT CARDS.

Pearl Paint / World's Largest Creative Resource 800-451-7327
    308 Canal St.(B'way-Church St)   212-431-7932
    NY, NY 10013   (mail order) 800-221-6845
    Hours: 9-7 Mon-Fri / 10-7 Sat / 10-6 Sun   FAX 212-431-6798

    42 Lispenard St. (Craft & Home Center)(B'way-Church St)   212-226-3717
    NY, NY 10013   800-221-6845
    Hours: 9-7 Mon-Fri / 10-7 Sat / 10-6 Sun

    776 Rt. 17 N   201-447-0300
    Paramus, NJ 07652   FAX 201-447-4012
    Hours: 10-9 Mon-Sat

    1033 E Oakland Park Blvd.(Corp. Office)   954-567-9678
    Ft. Lauderdale, FL 33334
    www.pearlpaint.com
    Large selection of household paints; fluorescent and wrinkle spray paint; also art supplies; catalog. Very good prices. Online shopping available. CREDIT CARDS.

Pintchik Home Hardware and Decorating Center 718-783-3333
    478 Bergen St. (Flatbush Ave)   FAX 718-857-7932
    Brooklyn, NY 11217
    Hours: 7:30-6:50 Mon-Fri / 8:30-5:50 Sat / 9-5:50 Sun
    Extensive selection of different brands of household paints, including an inexpensive house brand. Also floorings and wallcoverings. CREDIT CARDS.

P

Wolf Paints, S. Wolf Div. of Janovic Plaza 212-245-3241
   771 Ninth Ave. (51st-52nd St)   FAX 212-974-0591
   NY, NY 10019
   Hours: 7:30-6:30 Mon-Fri / 9-6 Sat / 11-5 Sun
   Household and theatrical paints; roller patterns. CREDIT CARDS.

PAINTS & DYES: SCENIC

ALJO Mfg. Co. 212-226-2878
   49 Walker St. (B'way-Church)   866-293-8913
   NY, NY 10013   FAX 212-274-9616
   Hours: 8:30-6 Mon-Fri / 10:30-4:30 Sat   E-mail: sales@aljodye.com
   www.aljodye.com
   ALJO scenic aniline dyes and Lockwood transparent wood dyes and stains.
   CREDIT CARDS.

Epstein's Paint Center 212-265-3960
   822 Tenth Ave. (54-55th St)   800-464-3432
   NY, NY 10019   FAX 212-765-8841
   Hours: 8-5:30 Mon-Fri / 8:30-3 Sat   E-mail: sales@epsteinspaint.com
   www.epsteinspaint.com
   A major supplier of scenic supplies; paints, dyes, brushes and expendables to
   the television, film and theatrical businesses of NYC. Computer matching of
   color. CREDIT CARDS.

Gordon Brush Manufacturing 800-950-7950
   6247 Randolph St.   323-724-7777
   Commerce, CA 90040   FAX 323-724-1111
   Hours: 7:30-4:30 Mon-Fri   E-mail: web@gordonbrush.com
   www.gordonbrush.com
   Commercial and artist brushes for all applications. Good prices.
   Comprehensive online catalog.   CREDIT CARDS.

Mann Brothers 323-936-5168
   757 N La Brea Ave. (Melrose-Sunset)   FAX 323-936-1980
   Los Angeles, CA 90038
   Hours: 6-5 Mon-Fri / 7-3 Sat   E-mail: info@mannbrothers.com
   www.mannbrothers.com
   Scenic paint supplier. Venitian plaster, gold leafs, beeswax, etc. Spray
   equipment and tolls. Download catalog or shop online. CREDIT CARDS.

P

Mutual Hardware Corp. 718-361-2480
   36-27 Vernon Blvd. (Vernon Blvd)   866-361-2480
   Long Island City, NY 11106   FAX 718-786-9591
   Hours: 8:30-4:30 Mon-Fri
   www.mutualhardware.com
   Scenic supplies and Flo-paint; catalog available. Contact John or Sal.

Production Advantage, Inc. 802-651-6915
P.O. Box 1700   800-424-99914
Williston, VT 05495   FAX 877-424-9991
Hours: 8:30-6 Mon-Fri   E-mail: sales@proadv.com
www.proadv.com

Catalog sales of hardware, lighting, rigging, scenic material, soft goods, sound equipment and expendables to the entertainment industry. All major brands carried. Catalog. CREDIT CARDS.

Rosco Laboratories, Inc. 203-708-8900
52 Harbor View Ave.   800-ROSCONY
Stamford, CT 06902   FAX 203-708-8919
Hours: 9-5 Mon-Fri   E-mail: info@rosco.com
www.rosco.com

Wide variety of scenic paints, coatings & adhesives to meet diverse needs. Flameproofing. Brochures.

Rose Brand 800-223-1624
FAX 800-594-7424

4 Emerson Lane(15-16th St)   800-223-1624
Secaucus, NJ 07094   201-809-1730
Hours: 8-5 Mon-Fri   FAX 201-809-1851

10616 Lanark St.   800-360-5056
Sun City, CA 91352   818-505-6290
Hours: 8-5 Mon-Fri   FAX 818-505-6293
www.rosebrand.com   E-mail: sales@rosebrand.com

Rosco, Artist Choice scenic paints. Complete scenic art supplies: shop papers, brushes, buckets, rollers, specialty scenic tools, metallic paint additives, gilding supplies, specialty coatings, adhesives, synthetic Venetian plaster, flame retardants. Catalog. Call or fax for catalog. CREDIT CARDS.

Sculptural Arts Coating, Inc. 800-743-0379
2912 Baltic Ave.   336-379-7652
Greensboro, NC 27406   FAX 336-379-7653
Hours: 9-5 Mon-Fri
www.sculpturalarts.com

Distributor of Artist's Choice paints, a new non-toxic water-based scenic paint with 30 colors. Very extendible. Also Sculpt or Coat and Plastic Varnish. Product brochure. CREDIT CARDS.

T J Ronan Paint Corp. 718-292-1100
749 E 135th St. (Willow Ave)   800-247-6626
Bronx, NY 10454   FAX 718-292-0406
Hours: 8-4:30 Mon-Fri   E-mail: info@ronanpaints.com
www.ronanpaints.com

First choice in sign finishing since 1889. Great selection of Aquacote (water-based enamal paints) used for sign painting, etc. CREDIT CARDS.

P

Wildfire, Inc. 310-755-6780
2908 Oregon Ct., Ste. G1   800-937-8065
Torrance, CA 90503   FAX 310-755-6781
Hours: 8-5 Mon-Fri   E-mail: sales@wildfirefx.com
www.wildfirefx.com
Manufacture, special effects paints and scenic work. Full-service scenic shop. P.O.s and CREDIT CARDS.

Wolf Paints, S. Wolf Div. of Janovic Plaza 212-245-3241
771 Ninth Ave. (51st-52nd St)   FAX 212-974-0591
NY, NY 10019
Hours: 7:30-6:30 Mon-Fri / 9-6 Sat / 11-5 Sun
Theatrical paint and dyes, clear latex, brushes; delivery. CREDIT CARDS.

PAINTS & DYES: SPECIALIZED

American Auto Body Supplies 718-463-7400
153-27 Barclay Ave. (Murray)   FAX 718-463-9388
Flushing, NY 11355
Hours: 8-5 Mon-Fri / 8-12:30 Sat.
Auto lacquer, urethane and enamel. CREDIT CARDS.

Chrome Everything, Inc. 718-325-4840
3530 Noell Ave (Boston Rd - Hollers Ave)   347-255-7101
Bronx, NY 10475   FAX 718-325-6510
Hours: 10-6 Mon-Fri   E-mail: racerx1200ccW@aol.com
www.chromeverything.com
Spray chrome any solid materials including leather, vinyl and all foams.

The Compleat Sculptor, Inc. 212-243-6074
90 Vandam St. (Hudson-Greenwich)   800-9-SCULPT
NY, NY 10013   FAX 212-243-6374
Hours: 9-6 Mon, Thurs-Sat / 9-8 Tue-Wed   E-mail: tcs@sculpt.com
www.sculpt.com
Carries complete line of sculpture materials including; clay, wood, wax, sculpting tools, alabaster, marble, mold-making and casting materials, books, videos, pedestals and bases. Friendly and knowledgeable help. Catalog. Technical support line (212) 367-7561. CREDIT CARDS.

Day-Glo Color Corp. 216-391-7070
4515 St. Clair Ave.   800-4DAYGLO
Cleveland, OH 44107   FAX 216-391-7751
Hours: 8:30-5 Mon-Fri   E-mail: dayglo@dayglo.com
www.dayglo.com
Carries Day-Glo flourescent colors in dry pigment and dispersible bases, water and oil. CREDIT CARDS.

P

Jurgen Industries, Inc. 800-735-7248
17461 147th St,. SE, Ste. 13   360-794-7886
Monroe, WA 98272   FAX 360-794-9825
Hours: 9-4 Mon-Thurs / 9-3 Fri   E-mail: sales@jurgeninc.com
www.jurgenindustries.com (Wholesale) www.glassgiftsforless.com (retail)
Glass stain color designed for simulated itiffany" glass. Also have synthetic
non-toxic product for stained glass production. First order $75 minimum.
CREDIT CARDS.

Kremer Pigments, Inc. 212-219-2394
247 W 29th St. (7-8th Ave)   800-995-5501
NY, NY 10001   FAX 212-219-2395
Hours: 11-6:30 Mon-Sat   E-mail: info@kremer-pigmente.de
www.kremer-pigmente.com
Deals with pigments only. Great source for pure pigments, pigment supplies
and books. RENTALS. CREDIT CARDS.

Old-Fashioned Milk Paint Co. 978-448-6336
436 Main St.   866-350-6455
Groton, MA 01450   FAX 978-448-2754
Hours: 9-5 Mon-Fri
www.milkpaint.com
Dry powder milk-based paint; natural earth colors. Brochure. CREDIT CARDS.

Pearl Paint / World's Largest Creative Resource 800-451-7327
                                            www.pearlpaint.com
308 Canal St.(B'way-Church St)   212-431-7932
NY, NY 10013   (mail order) 800-221-6845
Hours: 9-7 Mon-Fri / 10-7 Sat / 10-6 Sun   FAX 212-431-6798

42 Lispenard St. (Craft & Home Center)(B'way-Church St)   212-226-3717
NY, NY 10013   800-221-6845
Hours: 9-7 Mon-Fri / 10-7 Sat / 10-6 Sun

776 Rt. 17 N   201-447-0300
Paramus, NJ 07652   FAX 201-447-4012
Hours: 10-9 Mon-Sat

1033 E Oakland Park Blvd.(Corp. Office)   954-567-9678
Ft. Lauderdale, FL 33334
www.pearlpaint.com
Stained glass paints; also great selection of art supplies at very good prices;
catalog. Online shopping available. CREDIT CARDS.

S & G Auto Body Supplies 718-388-5151
172 Graham Ave. (Montrose)   718-384-8196
Brooklyn, NY 11206   FAX 718-384-6213
Hours: 8-4 Mon-Fri / 8-3 Sat
Good selection of metalflake and candy apple lacquer paints. CREDIT CARDS.

P

Shannon Luminous Materials, Inc. 714-550-9931
    304A N Townsend St.   800-543-4485
    Santa Ana, CA 92703   FAX 714-550-9938
    Hours: 8-12 Mon-Fri
    www.blacklite.com
    Blacklight reactive chalks, paints, crayons, etc. Brochure. $25 minimum. No
    credit cards.

The Silk Trading Co. 323-954-9280
    360 South La Brea Ave.   888-SILK-302
    Los Angeles, CA 90036   FAX 323-954-8024
    Hours: 9-6 Mon-Fri / 9-5 Sat
    www.silktrading.com
    Decorate without modesty. Wonderful selection of drapery and upholstery
    fabrics. Custom drapes, upholstery and decorator's paints. Some trims and
    tassels. CREDIT CARDS.

United Mineral & Chemical Corp. 201-507-3300
    1100 Valley Brook Ave.   800-777-0505
    Lindhurst, NJ 07071   FAX 201-507-1506
    Hours: 9-5 Mon-Fri   E-mail: inquries@umccorp.com
    www.umccorp.com
    UV phosphorous colors. A line of pigments that are white in natural light but
    can change to a vibrant spectrum mural in black light. Expensive. CREDIT
    CARDS.

PAPER & FOAMBOARD PRODUCTS

Alcan Composites 877-424-9860
    3480 Taylorsville Highway (Hwy 90)   800-626-3365
    Statesville, NC 28625
    Hours: 8-5 Mon-Fri   E-mail: info.usa@alcan.com
    www.gatorfoam.com
    Manufacturer of Gatorfoam and Gatorboard; available in 4'x8' sheets; 5
    thicknesses from 3/16 to 1 1/2"; wholesale only.

Chicago Watermark Company 212-600-1260
    Address omitted for security purposes   888-292-8376
    NY, NY 10018
    Hours: 9-5 Mon-Fri   E-mail: Don@chicagowatermark.com
    www.chicagowatermark.com
    Manufacturer of private watermarks for fine stationery and security papers.
    More than 40 different paper colors and 12 different paper textures. CREDIT
    CARDS.

Dymalon, Inc. 410-686-7711
    9100 Yellow Brick Rd., Ste D   FAX 410-686-7743
    Baltimore, MD 21237
    Hours: 8:30-5:30 Mon-Fri   E-mail: rjnee@verizon.net
    www.dymalon.com
    Excellent selection of wood grain contact papers, mattes, enamels, marbles,
    frosts, transparents, metallics and more. 17.5" wide, some up to 35". Foam
    tapes and all kinds of Velcro, including dual lock. Quick and friendly service.
    CREDIT CARDS.

P

Historical Document Co. 215-533-4500
2555 Orthodox St.   888-700-7265
Philadelphia, PA 19137   FAX 215-533-9319
Hours: 8:30-4:30 Mon-Fri   E-mail: info@histdocs.com
www.histdocs.com
Replicas of historical documents and currency. Quill pens. Good friendly and helpful people.

Kate's Paperie 800-809-9880
1282 Third Ave.(73rd-74th St)   212-396-3670
NY, NY 10021
Hours: 10-7 Mon-Fri / 11-6 Sat-Sun

8 W 13th St.(5-6th Ave)   212-633-0570
NY, NY 10011
Hours: 10-7:30 Mon-Fri / 10-6 Sat / 12-6 Sun

140 W 57th St.(6-7th Ave)   212-459-0700
NY, NY 10019
Hours: 9:30-8 Mon-Fri / 10-7 Sat / 11-7 Sun

125 Greenwich Ave.(Lewis St)   203-861-0025
Greenwich, CT 06830   FAX 203-861-0194
Hours: 10-6 Mon-Fri / 10-6 Sat / 12-5 Sun

72 Spring St.(Crosby-Lafayette St)   212-941-9816
NY, NY 10012
Hours: 10-8 Mon-Sat / 11-7 Sun
www.katespaperie.com
Good selection of handmade paper, journals, photo albums, pens, gift wrap, picture frames. Custom printing and business services. Easy to use website. CREDIT CARDS.

LeNobel Lumber Co., Inc. 212-246-0150
38-20 Review Ave.   718-784-5230
Long Island City, NY 11101   FAX 718-784-1422
Hours: 8-5 Mon-Fri / (closed for lunch 12-1) Pick-up until 3:30
www.lenoblelumber.com   E-mail: website.lenoble@att.net
Sonotube, Gatorboard; also masonite, Formica, plywood, etc.

Paper Presentation 212-463-7035
23 W 18th St. (5-6th Ave)   1-800-PAPER-01
NY, NY 10011   FAX 212-463-7022
Hours: 9-7 Mon-Fri, 11-6 Sat-Sun   E-mail: info@paperpresentation.com
www.paperpresentation.com
Excellent assortment of papers, stamps, embossing supplies, cards, office supplies and stationery. Catalog. CREDIT CARDS.

Pregis Corp. 203-288-7722
458 Sacket Point Rd.   800-834-9441
North Haven, CT 06473   FAX 203-248-6580
Hours: 8-5 Mon-Fri
www.pregis.com
International Company which are producers of Hexacomb panels, polystyrene foam sheets, food packing. No credit cards.

P

Rose Brand 800-223-1624
                                               FAX 800-594-7424

4 Emerson Lane(15-16th St)   800-223-1624
Secaucus, NJ 07094   201-809-1730
Hours: 8-5 Mon-Fri   FAX 201-809-1851

10616 Lanark St.   800-360-5056
Sun City, CA 91352   818-505-6290
Hours: 8-5 Mon-Fri   FAX 818-505-6293
www.rosebrand.com   E-mail: sales@rosebrand.com
Bogus, semi-wax, kraft, tough back, pre-gridded kraft, clear vinyl, contour building Forms-smooth surfaced, sturdy building forms. Call or fax for catalog. CREDIT CARDS.

Geno Sartori 212-691-9776
440 W 24th St. #4B (mailing only)
NY, NY 10011
Hours: by appt.   E-mail: genosar@aol.com
Formerly Brandon Memorabilia. Large collection of paper embellishments consisting of gold embossed paper borders, color cutouts of florals, animals and figures, etc.

ShinDigZ by Stumps 260-723-5171
101 Carrol Rd.   800-314-8736
South Whitley, IN 46787   FAX 260-723-6976
Hours: 7-9 Mon-Fri   E-mail: csr@chindigz.com
www.shindigZ.com
One of the most complete party supply superstores found on the web. Very helpful with party suggestions. Prom theme props, fabrics, balloons, crepe papers (up to 4" wide), seamless papers in 23 colors, float supplies and novelties. Custom printing for invitations, glasses, etc. Quick delivery. Catalog. CREDIT CARDS.

Sonoco Products Co. (Tubes & Cores) 843-339-3008
125 E Laurens Ave.   (sales) 800-377-2692
Hartsville, SC 29550   FAX 843-383-3394
Hours: 24-hrs. 7 days a week
www.sonoco.com
Sonotube, spiral tubes and cores. Brochures available on each product. Will ship. No credit cards.

Superior Giftwrap 812-949-2477
P.O. Box 458   812-949-2479
Floyd-Knobs, IN 47119
Hours: 8-5 Mon-Fri   E-mail: info@superiorgiftwrap.com
www.superiorgiftwrap.com
All your giftwrapping needs available at their website. Ribbon, giftwrap paper, tissue, bags, apparel boxes, gift tying yarns, bows and industrial paper cutters. Quick and courteous service. CREDIT CARDS.

P

Superior Specialties, Inc. 800-666-2545
2517 N Casaloma Dr. / P.O. Box 7170   920-560-6262
Appleton, WI 54912   FAX 920-727-3115
Hours: 8-5 Mon-Fri   E-mail: backgrounds@superspec.com
www.superspec.com

Comprehensive line of roll paper products. Spray adhesives, fake snow, photographic supplies. Catalog. CREDIT CARDS.

Superior Studio Specilities 800-354-3049
401 N Western Ave.   312-850-9016
Chicago, IL 60612   FAX 312-850-9026
Hours: 8:30-5 Mon-Fri   Email: chicago@superiorstudio.com

2239 S Yates Ave   323-278-0100
Commerce, CA 90040   FAX 323-278-0111
Hours: 8:30-5 Mon-Fri   Email: la@superiorstudio.com
www.superiorstudio.com

Seamless papers, fake food, wire mannequin frames, foam boards and cutting supplies. CREDIT CARDS.

Supply One 718-392-7400
58-51 Maspeth Ave.   FAX 718-361-2733
Maspeth, NY 11378
Hours: 8-5 Mon-Fri   E-mail: info-newyork@supplyone.com
www.supplyone.com

Hot glue by 25lb. carton or more; phone and fax orders delivered. Kraft paper. Packing materials and janitorial supplies. Adhesives and glues, staples and staple guns. Contact Katie Singh @ X230. CREDIT CARDS.

Theatrical Services & Supplies, Inc. 631-873-4790
415 Oser Ave.   FAX 631-873-4795
Hauppauge, NY 11788
Hours: 7-5 Mon-Fri   E-mail: sales@gotheatrical.com
www.gotheatrical.com

Honeycomb air-Lite panels, kraft finishes, 1/2"-1" thick. Catalog avalable. Shipping. Also theatrical supplies. CREDIT CARDS.

Tulnoy Lumber 718-901-1700
1620 Webster Ave. (173rd St)   800-899-5833
Bronx, NY 10457   FAX 718-229-8920
Hours: 7-5 Mon-Fri   E-mail: sales@tulnoylumber.com
www.tulnoylumber.com

Good stock of Gatorboard, Foamcore, Foam-X, Sonotube, bouyancy billets, polystyrene and 3 lb. pink and blue foam. Contact Peter Tulchin.

Village Supplies, Ltd. 708-824-1402
P.O. Box 605   FAX 708-824-1410
Oak Lawn, IL 60803
Hours: website 24-hrs.
www.artstuff.net

Art supplies, drafting and graphic supplies, modeling and casting, Pantone products, imaging, industrial lettering and laminating. Presentation papers, business furnishings and office supplies. Great website. $15 minimum order. CREDIT CARDS.

P

Wilma's Egg Art 765-284-6327
  5100 Southwest St.
  Muncie, IN 47307
  Hours: 10-6 Mon-Fri / Web 24-hrs.   E-mail: wilmaseggart@yahoo.com
  www.wilmaseggart.com
  This company has many varieties of art supplies for crafts as well as anything
  you would need for egg art. Miniature figurines, metal findings, paper cuts,
  pens, tools, adhesives and instructional videos and books. CREDIT CARDS.

PARKING GARAGES, BONDED

Dependable Transport & Messenger Services 212-594-1300
  240 W 37th St., 7th FL (7-8th Ave)   212-594-0320
  NY, NY 10018   FAX 212-594-4375
  Hours: 9-6 Mon-Fri   E-mail: gary@dependablemessengers.com
  www.dependablemessengers.com
  Bonded parking garages, truck parking, storage, temporary and production
  office rentals. RENTALS. CREDIT CARDS.

PARTY GOODS

Arenson Office Furnishings, Inc.. 212-633-2400
  1115 Broadway, 6th Fl. (24-25th St)   FAX 212-633-2777
  NY, NY 10010
  Hours: 8:30-5:30 Mon-Fri / or by appt.
  www.aof.com
  Folding chairs and tables, coat racks, etc. In-depth variety and inventory. Long
  and short-term rentals. Same day delivery. RENTALS.

Birthday Bakers / Party Makers 212-288-7112
  195 E 76th St. (3rd-Lex Ave)   888-321-PARTY
  NY, NY 10021   FAX 212-628-3084
  Hours: 10-5:30 Mon-Fri   E-mail: lindakaye@partymakers.com
  www.partymakers.com
  Cakes in all sizes and shapes for events and personal celebrations. 4-foot
  pop-out cake with optional edible layer serves up to 100. Expensive. Contact
  Linda Kaye. CREDIT CARDS.

Broadway Famous Party Rentals 718-821-4000
  134 Morgan Ave. (Meserole)   212-269-2666
  Brooklyn, NY 11237   FAX 718-821-4362
  Hours: 9-5 Mon-Fri
  www.broadwayfamous.com
  Party rental items: A-Z. Many patterns and colors of table linens; phone
  orders for delivery. Brochures avalable. RENTALS. CREDIT CARDS.

Classic Party Rentals 212-752-7661
  336 W 37th St., 2nd FL (showroom)(8-9th Ave)   FAX 212-752-0150
  NY, NY 10018
  Hours: 9-5 Mon-Fri

P

Classic Party Rentals (cont.) 718-822-1930
2350 Lafayette Ave. (warehouse)(Cypress Ave)   FAX 718-822-4159
Bronx, NY 10473
Hours: 9-5 Mon-Fri / 9-3 Sat
www.classicpartyrentals.com
Full-service party rental equipment company. All items on display in showroom. Large selection of rental linens. Table-top decor, lounge furniture and tenting capabilities. Custom work available. Will work with film and TV set decorators. RENTALS. CREDIT CARDS.

Event Energizers Make Parties, LLC 516-861-6482
300 Jericho Quadrangle Ste. 240 W   866-272-9897
Jericho, NY 11753   FAX 516-861-1033
Hours: 8:30-7 Mon-Fri / 24-hr web   E-mail: john@eventenergizers.com
www.eventenergizers.makeparties.com
Full service party supply store. Themed parities a specialty. CREDIT CARDS.

Fancy That 212-957-0005
12 W 57th St., Ste. 1004-A   FAX 212-957-0392
NY, NY 10019
Hours: by appt.   E-mail: fancythatnyc@aol.com
One-stop shopping for custom invitations, calligraphy, place cards, table-top accessories, theme ideas and development. All budgets. CREDIT CARDS.

Oriental Trading Company, Inc. 800-875-8480
4206 S. 108th St.   402-331-6800
Omaha, NE 68137   FAX 402-331-3873
Hours: 24-hr. online catalog service
www.orientaltrading.com
Thousands of small toys, novelties and party supplies for every occasion. Catalog available. CREDIT CARDS thru Paypal.

Paper House 212-724-8085
269 Amsterdam Ave. (72nd-73rd St)
NY, NY 10023
Hours: 8:30-10 Mon-Fri / 9-10:30 Sat / 10-8:30 Sun
Giftwrap, cards, paper plates, napkins, streamers, party favors, etc. CREDIT CARDS.

Party Time, Div. Academy Chair Rental Co. 718-457-1122
82-33 Queens Blvd.   212-682-8838 / 877-865-1122
Elmhurst, NY 11373   FAX 718-426-4510
Hours: 9-5 Mon-Fri / 9-2 Sat   E-mail: info@partytimeofcourse.com
www.partytimeofcourse.com
Everything for party rentals; dance floors to napkins; frankfurter and ice cream wagons. RENTALS. CREDIT CARDS.

Remember our Balloons 973-316-8200
623 Eagle Rock Ave.   973-296-0872
West Orange, NJ 07052
Hours: by appt. 7 days a week   E-mail: robbie@balloonsbyrobbie.com
www.balloonsbyrobbie.com
One-stop shopping for all your decorating needs. From the very quirky to regular balloon columns, Robbie is the most unique balloon artist. Visit website to see all the fun fantastical shapes he has dreamed up for film and TV. CREDIT CARDS.

Ruth Fischl . . . . .Linens 212-273-9710
141 W 28th St. (6-7th Ave)   Hardgoods 212-967-2493
NY, NY 10001   FAX 212-273-9718
Hours: 9-5 Mon-Thurs / 9-3 Fri   E-mail: ruthfischl@hotmail.com
www.ruthfischl.com
Excellent selection of rental linens, iron works, tables, candelabras, etc.
Purchase available. Open to trade by appointment. RENTALS.

ShinDigZ by Stumps 260-723-5171
101 Carrol Rd.   800-314-8736
South Whitley, IN 46787   FAX 260-723-6976
Hours: 7-9 Mon-Fri   E-mail: csr@chindigz.com
www.shindigZ.com
One of the most complete party supply superstores found on the web. Very
helpful with party suggestions. Prom theme props, fabrics, balloons, crepe
papers (up to 4" wide), seamless papers in 23 colors, float supplies and
novelties. Custom printing for invitations, glasses, etc. Quick delivery.
Catalog. CREDIT CARDS.

Stamford Tent & Party Rental 203-324-6222
84 Lenox Ave.   FAX 203-316-5116
Stamford, CT 06906
Hours: 8:30-5 Mon-Fri / 9-4 Sat
www.stamfordtent.com
Tents, air-conditioners, dance floor, lighting, chairs, tables and all tableware.
Set up and break down. RENTALS. CREDIT CARDS.

PERSONAL PROTECTION EQUIPMENT & SUPPLIES
See also: HEALTH & SAFETY SERVICES in the appendix

3M Company . . . .(product info) 651-737-6501
3M Center   800-364-3577
St. Paul, MN 55144   FAX 800-713-6329
Hours: 7-6 Mon-Fri
www.3m.com
NIOSH approved respirators. Best line of paper masks available. Non-toxic
adhesives. Catalog available. Some minimums required; distributors of 3M
glues and respirators.

A&M Industrial Supply and Safety Equipment 732-574-1111
1414 Campbell St. (Foundry)   877-257-0708
Rahway, NJ 07105   FAX 732-574-2081
Hours: 8-5 Mon-Fri   E-mail: sales@am-ind.com
www.am-ind.com
3M and Pulmosan safety equipment, hard hats, steel-toed shoes, disposable
clothing, etc. Will ship small orders; COD. Fast. CREDIT CARDS.

P

AEARO Co. 800-327-3431
8001 Woodland Dr.   FAX 800-488-8007
Indianapolis, IN 46278
Hours: 8-5 Mon-Fri   E-mail: customer_service@aearo.com
www.aearo.com
NIOSH approved respirators for organic vapors, paint spray and dust. Also, eye and ear protection equipment and safety harnesses. Great website. Catalog available. No credit cards.

Alfa Associates 843-746-7745
145 LeHigh Ave.   732-634-5700
Lakewood, NJ 08701   FAX 843-746-7733
Hours: 8-5 Mon-Fri
www.alfainc.com
Non-asbestos mineral fiber textiles; also fiberglass fabrics. Catalog available.

ARTS, CRAFTS & THEATRE SAFETY / ACTS 212-777-0062
181 Thompson St. #23   Pager 888-642-6120
NY, NY 10012   FAX 212-777-0062
Hours: by appt.   E-mail: actsnyc@cs.com
www.artscraftstheatersafety.org
Contact Monona Rossol. Member ATAC.

Avox Systems 716-683-5100
225 Erie St.   FAX 716-681-1089
Lancaster, NY 14086
Hours: 8-4:30 Mon-Fri
www.avoxsys.com
Oxygen systems and masks for commercial and military aviation. Passenger and crew masks.

BioShield Healthy Living 505-438-3448
3005 S. St. Francis Ste. 2A   800-621-2591
Santa Fe, NM 87505   FAX 505-438-0199
Hours: 9-5 Mon-Fri / 10-3 Sat   E-mail: info@bioshieldpaint.com
www.bioshieldpaint.com
Carries environmentally friendly paints, wood finishes, pigments, hand cleaners. Catalog. CREDIT CARDS.

The Compleat Sculptor, Inc. 212-243-6074
90 Vandam St. (Hudson-Greenwich)   800-9-SCULPT
NY, NY 10013   FAX 212-243-6374
Hours: 9-6 Mon, Thurs-Sat / 9-8 Tue-Wed   E-mail: tcs@sculpt.com
www.sculpt.com
Carries complete line of sculpture materials including; clay, wood, wax, sculpting tools, alabaster, marble, mold-making and casting materials, books, videos, pedestals and bases. Friendly and knowledgeable help. Catalog. Technical support line (212) 367-7561. CREDIT CARDS.

Conney Safety Co. 800-528-7405
3202 Latham Dr.　　　　　　　　　　　　　　FAX 800-760-2975
Madison, WI 53713
Hours: 7-7 Mon-Fri　　　　　　　　E-mail: salesservice@conney.com
www.conney.com
Bulk or individual safety gear. Rubber gloves, barrier skin creams, face masks
and filters. Respirators, tape, lighting. Eveything related to safety. Catalog
available. Will ship. CREDIT CARDS.

Fibre-Metal Products Co. 610-459-5300
PO Box 248, Baltimore Pike (Rt. 1)　　　　　　　　800-523-7048
Concordville, PA 19331　　　　　　　　　　FAX 800-852-3261
Hours: 8-4:30 Mon-Fri　　　　　　　E-mail: sales@fibre-metal.com
www.fibre-metal.com
Hard hats manufacturer, welding safety. Catalog.

Honeywell Safety Products 800-430-4110
2000 Plainfield Pike　　　　　　　　　　　　401-943-4400
Cranston, RI 02921　　　　　　　　　　FAX 401-946-7560
Hours: 8-4:30 Mon-Fri　　　E-mail: dlhlhspmarketingdepartment@honeywell.com
www.northsafety.com
NIOSH approved respirators, sizes for men and women. Catalog available.

Lab Safety Supply Co. 800-356-0783
PO Box 1368　　　　　　　　　　　　　FAX 800-543-9910
Janesville, WI 53547
Hours: 6-9 Mon-Fri / web 24hrs　　　　　E-mail: custsvc@labsafety.com
www.labsafety.com
Safety equipment and supplies, 1,000 pg. catalog available. CREDIT CARDS.

Mine Safety Appliances Co. 412-967-3000
P.O. Box 426　　　　　　　　　　　　　　800-672-2222
Pittsburgh, PA 15230
Hours: 8-8 Mon-Fri　　　　　　　　　　E-mail: info@msanet.com
www.msanet.com
NIOSH approved respirators. Gloves, disposable clothing, goggles, etc. Will
ship any size order. Open account billing. Catalog. CREDIT CARDS.

O.K. Uniforms Co. 212-791-9789
253 Church St. (Franklin-Leonard)　　　　　　FAX 212-791-9795
NY, NY 10013
Hours: 9:45-5:45 Mon-Thurs / 9:45-2 Fri / 12-4 Sun
www.okuniform.com　　　　　　　　　E-mail: okuniform@gmail.com
Complete selection of uniforms and accessories for all service industries.
Name and logo emblems available. Sales only. CREDIT CARDS.

Safety Supplies Unlimited 866-787-2336
36-06 43rd Ave.　　　　　　　　　　　　FAX 718-389-6155
Long Island City, NY 11101
Hours: 8-5:30 Mon-Fri　　　　　E-mail: sales@safetysuppliesunlimited.com
www.safetysuppliesunlimited.com
Huge variety of personal safety equipment plus safety storage cans and
cabinets, first aid and burn kits, janitoral supplies, caution sighs, hazard tapes
& traffic cones. Great Catalog. CREDIT CARDS.

Sapsis Rigging 800-727-7471
233 N Lansdowne Ave.   215-228-0888
Lansdowne, PA 19050   FAX 215-228-1786
Hours: 8-4:30 Mon-Fri   E-mail: bill@sapsis-rigging.com
www.sapsis-rigging.com
Fall arrest equipment; theatrical rigging; fire curtains. Catalog.

Sara Glove Co. 203-263-8933
PO Box 350   (outside NY) 800-243-3570
Woodbury, CT 06798   FAX 203-263-8918
Hours: 8-1 Mon-Fri   E-mail: info@saraglove.com
www.saraglove.com
Many types and sizes of latex and neoprene gloves. Catalog. Shipping.
CREDIT CARDS.

Simon Supplies 516-694-3131
32 S Mall   FAX 516-694-3135
Plainview, NY 11803
Hours: 9-5 Mon-Fri   E-mail: induco@aol.com
3M respirators and safety equipment, minimum 1 box. All factory supplies;
phone orders, catalog. CREDIT CARDS.

Sperian Protective Gloves, USA 800-343-3411
900 Douglas Pike   716-668-2000
Smithfield, RI 02917   FAX 716-668-3224
Hours: 8:30-5 Mon-Fri   E-mail: information@sperianprotection.com
www.sperian.com
NIOSH approved respirators, eye, fall and body protection. Visit website for
other locations.

Tomar Industries 732-780-2200
300 Commerce Dr.   FAX 732-780-4123
Freehold, NJ 07728
Hours: 9-5 Mon-Fri   E-mail: tfieldjr@tomarind.com
www.tomarind.com
Gaffers, duct, many types of pressure-sensitive tapes. Honeycomb paper
products. Janitorial supplies, safety equipment and adhesives. A 3-M dealer.
CREDIT CARDS.

The Traffic Safety Store 800-429-9030
P.O. Box 1449   FAX: 610-701-9369
West Chester, PA 19380
Hours: 24-hr web-site   E-mail: contact@trafficsafetystore.com
www.trafficsafetystore.com
Traffic cones, barricades, barricade flashers, and parking lot blocks, reflective
tapes, traffic and construction signs, just to name a few, are ready for
immediate, same-day shipment. Speak to Kevin. CREDIT CARDS.

Van Alstine & Sons 518-237-1613
18 New Cortland St.   800-552-4962
Cohoes, NY 12047   FAX 518-237-0462
Hours: 8-5 Mon-Fri
www.vanalstineinc.com
3M charcoal filter masks, organic vapors cartridges for respirators.

P

PET SUPPLIES
See also: TROPICAL FISH & AQUARIUMS

American Kennels 212-838-8460
    798 Lexington Ave. (61st St)   FAX 212-750-5519
    NY, NY 10021
    Hours: 10-7 Mon-Sat / 12-6 Sun   E-mail: americankennels@msn.com
    www.americankennels.com
    Basic neighborhood pet supply store.

Aquarium Design 845-352-1640
    80 Red Schoolhouse Rd. #217
    Chestnut Ridge, NY 10977
    Hours: by appt. (24 hour emergency service)
    www.aquariumdesign.com   E-mail: fishdoc@aquariumdesign.com
    Design, manufacture, install and maintain aquarium systems.

JB Wholesale Pet Supplies, Inc. 201-405-0042
    347 Rampo Valley Rd.   800-526-0388
    Oakland, NJ 07436   FAX 800-788-5055
    Hours: 9-8 Mon-Fri / 9-6 Sat / 11-4 Sun
    www.jbpet.com
    Pet supplies, breeding items, grooming and show equipment. Visit website for other loctions. CREDIT CARDS.

Omaha Vaccine Co. 800-367-4444
    11143 Mockingbird Dr.   FAX 800-242-9447
    Omaha, NE 68137
    Hours: 7-7 Mon-Fri / 8-2 Sat   E-mail: catalogs@omahavaccine.com
    www.omahavaccine.com
    Veterinary and animal care supplies; good source for oversized medical equipment. CREDIT CARDS.

Petland Discounts 866-687-3600
    132 Nassau St.(Ann-Beekman St)   212-964-1821
    NY, NY 10038   FAX 212-587-3076
    Hours: 9-7 Mon-Fri / 10-6 Sat / 11-5 Sun

    2708 Broadway(103rd-104th St)   212-222-8851
    NY, NY 10025
    Hours: 9-9 Mon-Fri / 10-7 Sat / 11-6 Sun

    312 W 23rd St.(8-9th Ave)   212-366-0512
    NY, NY 10011
    Hours: 9-9 Mon-Fri / 10-7 Sat / 11-6 Sun

    304 E 86th St.(1st-2nd Ave)   212-472-1655
    NY, NY 10028
    Hours: 10-9 Mon-Fri / 10-6 Sat / 11-6 Sun

    530 E 14th St.(Ave A&B)   212-228-1363
    NY, NY 10003
    Hours: 10-8 Mon-Fri / 10-7 Sat / 11-5 Sun

P

Petland Discounts (cont.) 212-459-9562
734 Ninth Ave.(49-50th St)
NY, NY 10019
Hours: 9-7 Mon-Sat / 11-5 Sun

137 W 72nd St.(B-way-Col)   212-875-9785
NY, NY 10023
Hours: 9-9 Mon-Fri / 10-7 Sat / 10-6 Sun   E-mail: info@petlanddiscounts.com
www.petlanddiscounts.com
Good selection of pet supplies; birds, fish, small animals. 110 Stores in NY,
NJ & CT. See website for other locations. CREDIT CARDS.

PEWTER ITEMS

Macy's Department Store 212-695-4400
151 W 34th St. (B'way-7th Ave)
NY, NY 10001
Hours: 10-9:30 Mon-Sat / 11-8 Sun
www.macys.com
Pewter located in Colonial Shop on 8th Fl. Store hours vary by season.
CREDIT CARDS.

The Prop Company / Kaplan and Associates 212-691-7767
111 W 19th St., 8th Fl. (6-7th Ave)   FAX 212-727-3055
NY, NY 10011
Hours: 9-5 Mon-Fri   E-mail: propcompany@yahoo.com
Contemporary tabletop, decorative accessories, antiques, ephemera and
furniture. A nice collection of linens. RENTALS.

PHOTOGRAPHIC EQUIPMENT

B & H Photo & Video 212-444-6615
420 Ninth Ave. (33rd-34th St)   800-606-6969
NY, NY 10001   FAX 212-239-7759
Hours: 9-7 Mon-Thurs / 9-1 Fri / 10-5 Sun
www.bhphotovideo.com
Good prices on film, photographic equipment and accessories. Also
binoculars, telescopes, microscopes and security camera equipment. Catalog
available. CREDIT CARDS.

Calumet 212-989-8500
22 W 22nd St. (5-6th Ave)   800-225-8638
NY, NY 10011   FAX 212-627-9088
Hours: 8:30-5:30 Mon-Fri / 9-5:30 Sat
www.calumetphoto.com
A full-service professional photograph shop. Cameras, photo shoot
equipment and expendables to presentation supplies. Shipping. RENTALS.
CREDIT CARDS.

Century Business Solutions and Photo Products 800-767-0777
P.O. Box 2100   FAX 800-786-7939
Santa Fe Springs, CA 90670
Hours: 6-5 Mon-Fri   E-mail: info@centurybusinesssolutions.com
www.centurybusinesssolutions.com
Plastic sleeves for slides and photos; quick mail order service. Catalog.
CREDIT CARDS.

Hello World Communications 212-243-8800
118 W 22nd St. (6-7th Ave)   FAX 212-691-6961
NY, NY 10011
Hours: 8-7 Mon-Fri / 9-6 Sat   E-mail: elronyo@msn.com
www.hwc.tv
Hello World Communications offers audio/digital video production tools and
postproduction services. Rentals include; audio, video, lighting,
computer/video projector, office equipment, cellular phone and two-way
radio (walkie-talkie). RENTALS. CREDIT CARDS.

The Lens & Repro Equipment Corp. .212-675-1900
33 W 17th St., 5th Fl. (5-6th Ave)   FAX 212-989-5018
NY, NY 10011
Hours: 8:30-5:30 Mon-Fri
www.lensandrepo.com
Retail supplier of prop cameras (still and movie), flash bulbs, etc. Period and
modern equipment for sale. Ship nationally. Brochure available.

Olden Camera 212-725-1234
1263 Broadway, 4th Fl. (32nd St)   FAX 212-725-1325
NY, NY 10001
Hours: 8-5 Mon-Thurs / 8-2 Fri
Photographic equipment. Some older camera styles; knowledgeable staff.
RENTALS. CREDIT CARDS.

Willoughby Konica Imaging 212-564-1600
298 Fifth Ave. (30th-31st St)   800-378-1898
NY, NY 10001   FAX 212-564-1608
Hours: 9:30-7 Sun-Thurs / 9:30-2 Fri   E-mail: sales@willoughbys.com
www.willoughbys.com
Camera equipment and accessories; while-you-wait print processing. Repairs.
RENTALS. CREDIT CARDS.

PHOTOGRAPHIC EQUIPMENT: REPAIR

Panorama Camera 212-563-1651
124 W 30th St., Ste 305 (6-7th Ave)   FAX 212-643-8796
NY, NY 10001
Hours: 9:30-5:30 Mon-Fri
Camera repairs. CREDIT CARDS.

Photo Tech Repair Service 212-673-8400
110 E 13th St. (3rd-4th Ave)   FAX 212-673-8451
NY, NY 10003
Hours: 8-6 Mon-Fri / 10-3 Sat pick or drop off only
www.phototech.com   E-mail: service@phototech.com
Photo equipment repair. Polaroid repair. CREDIT CARDS.

PHOTOGRAPHIC EQUIPMENT: USED & ANTIQUE

Eclectic / Encore Properties, Inc. 212-645-8880
620 W 26th St., 4th Fl. (11-12th Ave)   FAX 212-243-6508
NY, NY 10001
Hours: 9-5 Mon-Fri / or by appt.   E-mail: props@eclecticprops.com
www.eclecticprops.com
*All periods of professional and hobby cameras. Mitchel Cameras and their
supporting lighting equipment. Can request rental items thru online catalog.
RENTALS. CREDIT CARDS.*

The Lens & Repro Equipment Corp. 212-675-1900
33 W 17th St., 5th Fl. (5-6th Ave)   FAX 212-989-5018
NY, NY 10011
Hours: 8:30-5:30 Mon-Fri
www.lensandrepo.com
*Retail supplier of prop cameras (still and movie), flash bulbs, etc. Period and
modern equipment for sale. Ship nationally. Brochure available.*

PHOTOGRAPHIC SERVICES

291 Digital 212-697-2434
227 E 45th St. (2nd-3rd Ave)   800-683-2656
NY, NY 10017   FAX 212-697-0989
Hours: 9-5 Mon-Fri   E-mail: info@219digital.com
www.219digital.com / www.printint.com
*Quality custom printing. Rush service. Largest printed size 6' x 20'. Larger
work processed with seams. CREDIT CARDS.*

Ace Video & Props 718-392-1100
37-24 24th St., Ste. 106 (Houston & West St)   212-206-1475
Long Island City, NY 11101   FAX 718-392-1155
Hours: 10-6 Mon-Fri / 10-2 Sat by appt.
                       E-mail: acevideorentals@gmail.com / acepropsnyc@gmail.com
www.aceprops.com
*Convert video images and other computer data images into files suitable for
photographic output or for inclusion in electronic publishing. RENTALS.
CREDIT CARDS.*

Duggal Visual Solutions . . . .(Retail) 212-941-7000
    29 W 23th St. (5-6th Ave)   (Corp. Proj) 212-924-8100
    NY, NY 10011   FAX 212-486-1399
    Hours: 8-10 Mon-Fri / 9-6 Sat-Sun   E-mail: info@duggal.com
    www.duggal.com
    Large format graphics, vehicle wraps, mounting and liminations. Fast service on slides; photo murals, cibachromes, studio rental. Rush service. CREDIT CARDS.

Fokus, Inc. 908-241-3311
    136B Market St.   FAX 908-241-0090
    Kenilworth, NJ 07033
    Hours: 8:30-5:30 Mon-Fri   E-mail: information@fokusinc.com
    www.fokusinc.com
    Digital c-prints, transparencies from digital files.

Image King 212-867-4747
    227 E 45th St., 11th FL
    NY, NY 10017
    Hours: 24 hour service   E-mail: inform@imagekingvs.com
    www.imagekingvs.com
    Will print photos in sepia tone; B&W, color prints, slides. Offset printing up to 50" x 120". Rush service. CREDIT CARDS.

PIPE & TUBING

Canal Rubber Supply Co. 212-226-7339
    329 Canal St. (Greene St)   800-444-6483
    NY, NY 10013   FAX 212-219-3754
    Hours: 9-4:45 Mon-Fri / 9-3:45 Sat
    www.canalrubber.com
    Latex and rubber tubing, ventilation and vacuum hoses, dental dams, also air and water. CREDIT CARDS.

Fleischer Tube Distributing Corp. 631-968-8822
    71 Saxon Ave.   866-968-8822
    Bay Shore, NY 11706   FAX 631-968-5032
    Hours: 8:30-5 Mon-Fri   E-mail: sales@fleischertube.com
    www.fleischertube.com
    Any kind of metal tube, including thin wall, bar stock, structural shapes and sheet and plate; will deliver. CREDIT CARDS.

P

PLASTIC: FABRICATION

Accurate Plastics 914-476-0700
    18 Morris Pl.   800-431-2274
    Yonkers, NY 10705   FAX 914-476-0533
    Hours: 8-5:30 Mon-Fri
    www.acculam.com
    Plexiglass fabrication. No credit cards.

Ain Plastics, Inc. 914-668-6800
   60 Fullerton Ave.   800-431-2451
   Yonkers, NY 10704   FAX 914-668-8820
   Hours: 8-5 Mon-Fri   E-mail: tmxainad@aol.com
   www.ainplastics.com
   Plastic items, sheets, rods, tubes, film. Catalog. NIOSH approved respirators.
   Gloves, disposable clothing, goggles, etc. Will ship any size order. Sintra.
   Open account billing. CREDIT CARDS.

Fantasy Plastics 718-855-5520
   295 Third Ave.   FAX 718-855-7552
   Brooklyn, NY 11215
   Hours: 8-4:30 Mon-Fri
   www.fantasyplastics.com
   Plastic, Sintra, Lexan, plexi tubes, rods and sheets. Custom orders accepted.

Just Plastics 212-569-8500
   250 Dyckman St. (at B'way)   FAX 212-569-6970
   NY, NY 10034
   Hours: 7:30-4 Mon-Fri   E-mail: info@justplastics.com
   www.justplastics.com
   Furniture, lighting, museum and retail display cases and much more. Visit
   their website to see many other possibilities for your needs. Quality custom
   work; contact Lois. CREDIT CARDS.

Plexability Ltd. 914-665-3700
   229 Washington St. (S Columbus-S Fulton)   FAX 914-668-4044
   Mount Vernon, NY 10553
   Hours: by appt.   E-mail: plexability@aol.com
   www.plexability.com
   Lucite furnishings and props. Custom fabricators. RENTALS.

Saldarini & Pucci, Inc. 718-852-1656
   219 Westminister Rd. (Beverly Blvd)   FAX 718-852-1656
   Brooklyn, NY 11218
   Hours: 9-6 Mon-Fri   E-mail: paylessplastering@netscape.net
   Casting, mold-making, Established in 1925. Flexible resins. Also Plastic
   contracting and sculpting. No credit cards.

T & T Plastic Land 212-925-6376
   315 Church St. (Walker & Lispenard St)   FAX 212-274-9885
   NY, NY 10013
   Hours: 9:30-6 Mon-Sat   E-mail: info@ttplasticland.com
   www.ttplasticland.com
   Plastic cuts while you wait. Same day service. Custom fabrications,
   displays, frames and pedestals. Lucite, sintra, vinyl, lexan, mylar domes and
   casting resins. CREDIT CARDS.

Trengove Studios, Inc. 212-268-0020
   60 W 22nd St., 2nd FL (7-8th Ave)   800-366-2857
   NY, NY 10010   FAX 212-268-0030
   Hours: call for appt. 9-5 Mon-Fri   E-mail: info@trengovestudios.com
   www.trengovestudios.com
   Custom and stock props for wonderful ice and water effects, acrylic props.
   Brochure available. CREDIT CARDS.

P

PLASTIC: ITEMS

Ain Plastics, Inc. 914-668-6800
    60 Fullerton Ave.   800-431-2451
    Yonkers, NY 10704   FAX 914-668-8820
    Hours: 8-5 Mon-Fri   E-mail: tmxainad@aol.com
    www.ainplastics.com
    Plastic items, sheets, rods, tubes, film. Catalog. NIOSH approved respirators.
    Gloves, disposable clothing, goggles, etc. Will ship any size order. Sintra.
    Open account billing. CREDIT CARDS.

The Container Store 800-266-8246
    629 Sixth Ave.(18-19th St)   212-366-4200
    NY, NY 10011
    Hours: 9-9 Mon-Sat / 10-8 Sun

    725 Lexington Ave.(58-59th St)   212-366-4200
    NY, NY 10022
    Hours: 9-9 Mon-Sat / 10-8 Sun
    www.containerstore.com
    For all your organizational needs; bins, files, boxes, metro shelving and closet
    organizers. The Container Store has everything. Contact the website or toll-
    free number for other locations. CREDIT CARDS.

Outwater Plastics 888-688-9283
    24 River Rd.   201-498-8750
    Bogota, NJ 07603   FAX 800-888-3315
    Hours: 8:30-5 Mon-Fri
    www.outwater.com
    Decorative trim, tubing, frames, boxes in plastic. Good catalogs. $25 min.
    CREDIT CARDS.

Plexability Ltd. 914-665-3700
    229 Washington St. (S Columbus-S Fulton)   FAX 914-668-4044
    Mount Vernon, NY 10553
    Hours: by appt.   E-mail: plexability@aol.com
    www.plexability.com
    Lucite furnishings and props. Custom fabricators. RENTALS.

Plexi-Craft Quality Products Corp. 212-924-3244
    30-02 48th Ave. (30th Place-48th Ave)   800-24-PLEXI
    Long Island City, NY 11101   FAX 212-924-3508
    Hours: 9:30-5 Mon-Fri   E-mail: craft@plexi-craft.com
    www.plexi-craft.com
    Lucite furniture and accessories. One day RENTALS. CREDIT CARDS.

The Set Shop 212-255-3500
    36 W 20th St. (5-6th Ave)   800-422-7831
    NY, NY 10011   FAX 212-229-9600
    Hours: 8:30-6 Mon-Fri   E-mail: info@setshop.com
    www.setshop.com
    Ten types of ice cubes and shards, large selection of acrylic sheets. Custom
    fabrication available. CREDIT CARDS.

P

Trengove Studios, Inc. 212-268-0020
60 W 22nd St., 2nd FL (7-8th Ave)   800-366-2857
NY, NY 10010   FAX 212-268-0030
Hours: call for appt. 9-5 Mon-Fri   E-mail: info@trengovestudios.com
www.trengovestudios.com
Custom and stock props for wonderful ice and water effects, acrylic props.
Stock purchase of fake ice. Brochure available. CREDIT CARDS.

PLASTIC: SHEETS, TUBES, RODS & SHAPES

Accurate Plastics 914-476-0700
18 Morris Pl.   800-431-2274
Yonkers, NY 10705   FAX 914-476-0533
Hours: 8-5:30 Mon-Fri
www.acculam.com
Plexi sheets, tubes, rods. No credit cards.

Ain Plastics, Inc. 914-668-6800
60 Fullerton Ave.   800-431-2451
Yonkers, NY 10704   FAX 914-668-8820
Hours: 8-5 Mon-Fri   E-mail: tmxainad@aol.com
www.ainplastics.com
Plastic items, sheets, rods, tubes, film. Catalog. NIOSH approved respirators.
Gloves, disposable clothing, goggles, etc. Will ship any size order. Sintra.
Open account billing. CREDIT CARDS.

American Foam Technologies, Inc. 304-497-3000
Box 317 H   (Plant) 304-647-5439
Lewisburg, WV 24901   FAX 304-497-3001
Hours: 8-5 Mon-Fri   E-mail: don@americanfoamtech.com
www.americanfoamtech.com
Sells balsa-foam, a plastic product that carves like butter and paints like
wood.

Apex Plastic Industries, Inc. 800-APEX-INC
1400 Greenleaf Ave.
Elk Grove Village, IL 60007
Hours: 8-5 Mon-Fri   E-mail: info@apexplasticinc.com
www.apexplasticinc.com
Very large selection of vinyl, plastic and mylar sheets and films. Prisms,
marble, cracked ice. Vinyl ribbon, full rolls 40+ and wider. Will ship. CREDIT
CARDS.

E & T Plastics Mfg. Co., Inc. 718-729-6226
45-45 37th St. (Queens Blvd)   800-221-9555
Long Island City, NY 11101   FAX 718-392-6277
Hours: 9-5 Mon-Fri   E-mail: info@e-tplastics.com
www.e-tplastics.com
Plexi, acrylic, acetate, Lexan, Teflon, mylar, polystyrene, vacuumforming.
Locations in several states, visit website. CREDIT CARDS.

P

Fantasy Plastics 718-855-5520
  295 Third Ave.   FAX 718-855-7552
  Brooklyn, NY 11215
  Hours: 8-4:30 Mon-Fri
  www.fantasyplastics.com
  Plastic, Sintra, Lexan, plexi tubes, rods and sheets. Custom orders accepted.

Franklin Fibre-Lamitex Corp.........................302-652-3621
  PO Box 1768, 903 E 13th St.   800-233-9739
  Wilmington, DE 19899   FAX 302-571-9754
  Hours: 8-5 Mon-Fri   E-mail: info@franklinfibre.com
  www.franklinfibre.com
  Nylon stocks, coils, sheets, tubes; acetate, Lexan, Teflon, mylar. $50 min.
  Catalog.

Kamco Supply 718-768-1234
  80 21st St.(3rd Ave)   FAX 718-788-8607
  Brooklyn, NY 11232   FAX 718-788-8607
  Hours: 7-5 Mon-Fri

  153 Tenth Ave.(19th St)   212-736-7350
  NY, NY 10011   FAX 212-564-6436
  Hours: 6-5 Mon-Fri / 7-12 Sat
  www.kamco.com
  Sheet plastic. Good stock, reasonable prices. No minimum. Brochure
  available. CREDIT CARDS.

Laird Plastics 516-334-1124
  123 Frost St., Unit 2   800-873-8421
  Westbury, NY 11590   FAX 516-334-6928
  Hours: 8-5 Mon-Fri   E-mail: corporate@lairdplastics.com
  www.lairdplastics.com
  Latex tubing, Teflon, nylon, plexi, Lexan, acetate. Online product catalog, list
  of other locations on website. CREDIT CARDS.

Plastic-Craft Product Corp.........................845-358-3010
  744 W Nyack Rd.   800-627-3010
  West Nyack, NY 10994   FAX 845-358-3007
  Hours: 8-5 Mon-Fri   E-mail: info@plastic-craft.com
  www.plastic-craft.com
  Plastic sheets, rods and tubes; laminates, adhesives. For custom designs,
  contact Mark. CREDIT CARDS.

T & T Plastic Land 212-925-6376
  315 Church St. (Walker & Lispenard St)   FAX 212-274-9885
  NY, NY 10013
  Hours: 9:30-6 Mon-Sat   E-mail: info@ttplasticland.com
  www.ttplasticland.com
  Plastic cuts while you wait. Same day service. Custom fabrications,
  displays, frames and pedestals. Lucite, sintra, vinyl, lexan, mylar domes and
  casting resins. CREDIT CARDS.

ATAC

WFR / Aquaplast Corporation 800-526-5247
30 Lawlins Pk.   201-891-1042
Wyckoff, NJ 07481   FAX 201-891-2329
Hours: 8:30-5 Mon-Fri   E-mail: sales@q-fx.com
www.wfr-aquaplast.com
WFR / Aquaplast manufacturers and distributes low temperature
thermoplastics for use in the various medical and theatrical applications.
Various sizes of solid and perforated sheets, rods and pellets available. Mail
order. CREDIT CARDS.

PLATING & METAL FINISHES

Anacoat Corporation 718-361-1740
45-12 Vernon Blvd.   FAX 718-392-1842
Long Island City, NY 11101
Hours: 6-4 Mon-Thurs / 6-12 Fri
Anodizing. Catalog. No credit cards.

Atlantic Retinning and Metal Refinishing, Inc. 732-531-1221
260 Overbrook Ave.   NYC 212-244-4896
Oakhurst, NJ 07755
Hours: 9-5 Mon-Fri
www.retinning.com
Retinning and polishing and some repairs; see James Gibbons. No credit
cards.

Columbia Interiors 212-725-5250
162 E 33rd St. Frnt. (Lex-3rd Ave)   FAX 212-685-4496
NY, NY 10016
Hours: 10-5 Mon-Sat
Brass and silver plating. CREDIT CARDS.

Hygrade Polishing & Plating Co. 718-392-4082
22-07 41st Ave. (22nd St)   FAX 718-472-4117
Long Island City, NY 11101
Hours: 7-3 Mon-Fri / 8-12 Sat   E-mail: mbyers@hygradeplating.com
www.hygradeplating.com
Nickel, chrome, brass, gold, copper, bronze, antique finishing on all materials.
Working with Broadway for over 40 years. Rush work done, reliable. CREDIT
CARDS.

T & M Plating Co., Inc. 212-967-1110
357 W 36th St., 7th Fl. (8-9th Ave)   FAX 212-967-8912
NY, NY 10001
Hours: 8:30-5 Mon-Thurs / 8:30-3 Fri   E-mail: tandmplating@aol.com
Metal plating and finishing. Good variety of finishes. $50 minimum. No credit
cards.

PLUMBING SUPPLIES & FIXTURES

A.F. Supply 212-243-5400
    22 W 21st St., 5th Fl. (5-6th Ave)   800-366-2284
    NY, NY 10010   FAX 212-243-2403
    Hours: 9-5 Mon-Fri Appointment recommended.   E-mail: info@afnewyork.com
    www.afsupply.com / www.afnewyork.com
    Large showroom of bath fixtures, shower enclosures, faucets, sinks, etc.
    RENTALS. CREDIT CARDS.

Davis & Warshow, Inc. 718-937-9500
    57-22 48th St.   FAX 718-472-1892
    Maspeth, NY 11378
    Hours: 9-5 Mon-Fri / 10-3 Sat

    518-520 W 37th St.(10-11th Ave)   212-247-7710
    NY, NY 10018   FAX 212-977-3169
    Hours: 8:30-6--5Mon-Fri / 8-12 Sat

    75 Ludlow St.(Grand-Broome)   212-533-4800
    NY, NY 10002   FAX 212-477-0345
    Hours: 8:30-6:30 Mon-Fri

    207 E 119th St.(2nd-3rd Ave)   212-369-2000
    NY, NY 10035   FAX 212-860-8285
    Hours: 6:30-5 Mon-Fri
    www.daviswarshow.com
    Kohler, American Standard, Kallista and European imported bath and kitchen
    fixtures. RENTALS. CREDIT CARDS.

Decoware, Inc. 718-871-1212
    944 McDonald Ave. (Ave F-18th Ave)   877-871-1212
    Brooklyn, NY 11218   FAX 718-972-3277
    Hours: 9:30-5:30 Mon-Wed / 9:30-6:30 Thurs / 9:30-11:30 Fri / 10-4:30 Sun
    www.decow.com   E-mail: sales@decow.com
    Large selection of decorative hardware and plumbing fixtures. Delivery
    service available. CREDIT CARDS.

Greenwich Village Plumbers Supply 212-254-9450
    223 W 28th St. (7-8th Ave)   FAX 212-353-3801
    NY, NY 10001
    Hours: 7-4:30 Mon-Fri   E-mail: sales@gvps.net
    www.gvps.net
    Basic plumbing supplies, wholesale and retail. CREDIT CARDS.

P.E. Guerin 212-243-5270
    23 Jane St. (Greenwich-8th Ave)   FAX 212-727-2290
    NY, NY 10014
    Hours: 10-4 Mon-Fri by appt   E-mail: peguerin@aol.com
    www.peguerin.com
    Wonderful hardware and bathroom fixtures, primarily custom with a 4-8
    week delivery; catalog; expensive. CREDIT CARDS.

Home Depot 800-553-3199
550 Hamilton Ave.(16-17th St)   718-832-8553
Brooklyn, NY 11232
Hours: 6-12pm Mon-Sat / 8-9pm Sun

124-04 31st Ave.(College Point Blvd)   718-661-4608
Flushing, NY 11354   FAX 718-670-3437
Hours: 6-11pm Mon-Sat / 7-9pm Sun

40 W 23rd St.(5-6th Ave)   212-929-9571
NY, NY 10010
Hours: 7-9pm Mon-Sat / 8-7 Sun

980 Third Ave.(58-59th St)   212-888-1512
NY, NY 10022
Hours: 7-9pm Mon-Sat / 8-7 Sun

50-10 Northern Blvd.(50th St-Newtown Rd)   718-278-9031
Long Island City, NY 11101
Hours: 6-11pm Mon-Sat / 8-9pm Sun
www.homedepot.com
Plumbing supplies. Queens and Brooklyn location open 24 hours for those emergency needs. New Brooklyn store near Battery Tunnel. Many other locations. CREDIT CARDS.

Leesam Kitchen & Bath 212-243-6482
501 Seventh Ave. (37th St)   FAX 212-243-6494
NY, NY 10011
Hours: By appts. only   E-mail: leesammyc@aol.com
Sinks, toilets, bathtubs, shower doors, vanities, faucets, cabinets. RENTALS. CREDIT CARDS.

Lowe's 718-249-1151
118 Second Ave. (9th-12th St)   800-445-6337
Brooklyn, NY 11215   FAX 718-249-1154
Hours: 5-12 Mon-Sun
www.lowes.com
Big-box home improvement store that carries gardening supplies, kitchen cabinets, lighting fixtures, tools, lumber and much more. Check website for other locations. CREDIT CARDS.

New York Replacements Parts 212-534-0818
1456 Lexington Ave. (94th St)   FAX 212-410-5783
NY, NY 10128
Hours: 8-5 Mon-Fri / 9-6 Mon-Fri (Showroom)   E-mail: nyrpmike@hotmail.com
www.nyrpcorp.com
Repro faucet and plumbing parts: bring in sample for reproduction. CREDIT CARDS.

Simon's Hardware 212-532-9220
421 Third Ave. (29-30th St)   888-274-6667
NY, NY 10016   FAX 212-725-3609
Hours: 8-5:30 Mon-Fri / 8-7 Thurs / 10-6 Sat
www.simons-hardware.com   E-mail: sercice@simons-hardware.com
Bathroom fixtures, accessories, decorative hardware, faucets; get there early in the morning for better service. Catalog. Expensive. CREDIT CARDS.

Smolka Co., Inc. 212-686-2300
  231 E 33rd St. (2nd-3rd Ave)   FAX 212-686-2308
  NY, NY 10016
  Hours: 10-6 Mon-Tue, Wed / 10-7 Thurs / 10-5 Fri
  www.smolka.com
  Bathroom fixtures and accessories; expensive. RENTALS. CREDIT CARDS.

Solco Industries 212-243-7575
  209 W 18th St. (7-8th Ave)   FAX 212-924-0217
  NY, NY 10011
  Hours: 7-5 Mon-Fri
  www.solco.com
  Wholesale/retail plumbing supplies. CREDIT CARDS.

George Taylor Specialties 212-226-5369
  76 Franklin St. (Church-B'way)   FAX 212-274-9487
  NY, NY 10013
  Hours: 7:30-5 Mon-Thurs / 7:30-4 Fri   E-mail: gtspec@aol.com
  Porcelain knobs and reproduction faucets; obsolete parts replaced, repaired and/or reproduced. Full machine shop. RENTALS. CREDIT CARDS.

Sherle Wagner International, Inc. 212-758-3300
  300 E 62nd St. (Park Ave)   FAX 212-207-8010
  NY, NY 10065
  Hours: 9:30-5:30 Mon-Fri   E-mail: custserv@sherlewagner.com
  www.sherlewagner.com
  Bathroom fixtures and hardware; wall surfaces, tiles and custom tiles. Expensive. Check website for additional locations outside of NYC. RENTALS. CREDIT CARDS.

Waterworks 212-371-9266
  225 E 57th St. (2nd & 3rd Ave)   800-899-6757
  NY, NY 10022   FAX 212-371-9263
  Hours: 9-6 Mon-Fri / 11-5 Sat   E-mail: info@waterworks.com
  www.waterworks.com
  Huge selection of bathroom fixtures, tubs and accessories; towels, robes, bath soaps, oils and beads. Check website for additional locations. CREDIT CARDS.

POLICE EQUIPMENT

F & J Police Equipment 718-665-4535
  378 E 161st St. (Melrose)   FAX 718-292-8455
  Bronx, NY 10451
  Hours: 9-6 Mon-Fri / 9-4 Sat   E-mail: info@fjuniforms.com
  www.fjuniforms.com
  Uniforms, guns, shoes, bulletproof vests, everything. CREDIT CARDS.

P

Frank's Sport Shop . . . .(Store) 718-299-9628
    430 E Tremont Ave. (Park Ave)   (Office) 212-945-0020
    Bronx, NY 10457   FAX 718-583-1652
    Hours: 9-8 Mon-Fri / 9-6 Sat   E-mail: info@frankssports.com
    www.frankssports.com
    Guns, ammo, bulletproof vests, handcuffs, night sticks and all accessories.
    Carries uniforms for security, fireman, EMS, police and traffic. Also silk-
    screening and embroidery. RENTALS. CREDIT CARDS.

Reef Industries, Inc. 713-507-4251
    9209 Almeda Genoa Rd.   800-231-6074
    Houston, TX 77075   FAX 713-507-4295
    Hours: 7-5 Mon-Fri   E-mail: ri@reefindustries.com
    www.reefindustries.com
    Yellow barricade ribbon; "Crime Scene," "Do Not Cross," etc.; brochure
    available. Also manufacture "roll-a-sign" custom laminated signs for events.
    See website for details. CREDIT CARDS.

B. Schlesinger & Sons, Inc. 212-206-8022
    249 W 18th St. (7-8th Ave)   FAX 212-206-8559
    NY, NY 10011
    Hours: 9:30-6 Mon-Thurs / 9:30-5 Fri   E-mail: schlesin
eruniforms@verizon.net
    www.schlesinguniforms.com
    Handcuffs, nightsticks, police and security guard uniforms, accessories. No
    rentals. Phone orders OK. CREDIT CARDS.

Smith & Warren Co. 914-948-4619
    127 Oakley Ave.   FAX 914-948-1627
    White Plains, NY 10601
    Hours: 8-4:30 Mon-Fri   E-mail: contact@smithwarren.com
    www.smithwarren.com
    Badges only. CREDIT CARDS.

Some's Uniforms 201-843-1199
    314 Main St. (East Berry St)   FAX 201-843-3014
    Hackensack, NJ 07601
    Hours: 9-5 Mon-Fri / 9-1 Sat   E-mail: someunif@somes.com
    www.somes.com
    Police uniforms, nightsticks, handcuffs, holsters. Also firefighters uniforms
    and equipment. Catalog. Phone orders. CREDIT CARDS.

POSTERS & PRINTS

Argosy Book Stores, Inc. 212-753-4455
    116 E 59th St. (Park-Lex Ave)   FAX 212-593-4784
    NY, NY 10022
    Hours: 10-6 Mon-Fri / 10-5 Sat (Sept-April)   E-mail: argosy@argosybooks.com
    www.argosybooks.com
    Prints, maps, out-of-print books. CREDIT CARDS.

Art & Industrial Design 212-477-0116
50 Great Jones St. (4th Ave)   FAX 212-477-1420
NY, NY 10012
Hours: 10-5 Mon-Fri / 10-1 Sat   E-mail: info@aid20c.com
www.aid20c.com
11,000-sq-ft. showroom of 20th-century designer and art deco furniture for all settings. Period prints and posters, art and collectibles. RENTALS. CREDIT CARDS.

Gaslight Advertising Archives, Inc. 631-462-4444
17 Bernard Ln.   FAX 631-462-7394
Commack, NY 11725
Hours: 9-5 Mon-Fri   E-mail: gaslight@earthlink.net
www.gaslightarchives.com
Authentic old print ads back to the 1880s. Over a million ads, all subjects, products and companies. RENTALS.

George Glazer Gallery 212-535-5706
28 E 72nd St., Ste. 3A (Park-Madison Ave)   FAX 212-658-9512
NY, NY 10021
Hours: by appt. only   E-mail: worldglobe@georgeglazer.com
www.georgeglazer.com
A fine and extensive collection of antique terrestrial and celestial globes; floor-standing, table and miniature. Armillary spheres and orreries. Also atlases, maps, antique prints and photographs. Free catalog upon request. Part of inventory on website. Contact for use of web images. RENTALS.

Phyllis Lucas Gallery 212-755-1516
981 Second Ave. (52nd St)
NY, NY 10022
Hours: 10-5 Mon-Fri / 2-5 Sat-Sun   E-mail: mlucas@phyllislucasgallery.com
www.phyllislucasgallery.com
Framed and unframed prints; specializes in 30s, circus, travel and movie posters. RENTALS. AMEX.

New York Graphic Society 800-677-6947
129 Glover Ave.   203-847-2000
Norwalk, CT 06850   FAX 203-846-2105
Hours: 9-6 Mon-Fri
www.nygs.com
Large catalog of fine art posters; phone orders taken; will ship UPS. CREDIT CARDS.

Old Print Shop 212-683-3950
150 Lexington Ave. (29-30th St)   FAX 212-779-8040
NY, NY 10016
Hours: 9-5 Mon-Fri / Seasonal hours call first   E-mail: info@oldprintshop.com
www.oldprintshop.com
19th and 20th century American prints. 18th and 19th century maps. No rentals. CREDIT CARDS.

P

Pace Prints 212-421-3237
32 E 57th St., 3rd Fl. (Park-Madison Ave) showroom   877-440-PACE
NY, NY 10022   FAX 212-832-5162
Hours: 9:30-5:30 Tue-Fri / 10-5 Sat   E-mail: info@paceprints.com
www.paceprints.com
Contemporary fine art posters and prints.

Pageant Book & Print Shop 212-674-5296
PO Box 1081, Canal St. Station / 69 E 4th St.
NY, NY 10013
Hours: 12-8 Tue-Sat / 1-7 Sun   E-mail: info@pageantbooks.com
www.pageantbooks.com
Books and prints; see Shirley Solomon. RENTALS. CREDIT CARDS.

Paris Fine Custom Framing 212-873-5602
323 Amsterdam Ave. (75-76th St)   FAX 212-877-4122
NY, NY 10023
Hours: 11-7 Mon-Sat / 12-6 Sun
www.parisframemakers.com
Custom framing, lithographs, serigraphs and photographs. CREDIT CARDS.

J. Pocker & Son, Inc. 800-838-4588
135 E 63rd St. (Lexington-Park Ave)   212-838-5488
NY, NY 10065   FAX 212-750-2053
Hours: 9-5:30 Mon-Fri / 10-5:30 Sat   E-mail: info@jpocker.com
www.jpocker.com
Good stock of posters, prints; custom orders ship within two weeks. Framing service available. RENTALS. CREDIT CARDS.

Print Finders 888-997-6783
50 N. Eighth St.   800-455-3955
St. Genevieve, MO 63670   FAX 877-883-8946
Hours: 7-5 Mon-Fri   E-mail: prints@printfinders.com
www.printfinders.com
Mail and phone order print finding service. Access to over 50,000 prints and posters; very helpful. CREDIT CARDS.

Ro Gallery 718-937-0901
47-15 36th St. (47th Ave)   800-888-1063
Long Island City, NY 11101   FAX 718-937-1206
Hours: 11-7 Mon-Fri by appt. only   E-mail: art@rogallery.com
www.rogallery.com
Paintings, prints and posters. 3,000 images on hand. All manner of subjects. Will ship. RENTALS. CREDIT CARDS.

Star Magic 212-988-0300
301 E 78th St. (office) (1st-2nd Ave)
NY, NY 10021
Hours: 11-7 Daily 24-hr. Web   E-mail: star@starmagic.com
www.starmagic.com
Space-related items such as fiber optic lamps, lava lamps plasma balls, special effect LED lighting. Also science kits games and puzzles. Internet only web address. Local p/u in New York City. CREDIT CARDS.

POTTERY & GREENWARE

Ceramic Supply, Inc. 973-340-3005
  7 Rt. 46 W   800-723-7264
  Lodi, NJ 07644   FAX 973-340-0089
  Hours: 9-5 Mon-Fri   E-mail: orders@eceramicsupply.com
  www.7ceramic.com
  Ceramic materials and supplies, potter's plaster and casting plaster. CREDIT CARDS.

The Clay Pot 718-788-6564
  162 Seventh Ave. (Garfield-1st St)   (catalog) 800-989-3579
  Brooklyn, NY 11215   FAX 718-965-1138
  Hours: 11-7:30 Mon-Fri / 10:30-7 Sat / 12-6 Sun   E-mail: info@clay-pot.com
  www.clay-pot.com
  A "pottery gallery" featuring a number of quality potters; glass, jewelry and wooden crafts. RENTALS. CREDIT CARDS.

Claycraft Planters Company, Inc. 888-566-8522
  1 Highland Industrial Park Dr.   FAX 914-734-1982
  Peekskill, NY 10566
  Hours: 9-5 Mon-Fri   E-mail: claycraftplanters@gmail.com
  www.claycraft.com
  Fiberglass planters with real metals or color bonded into the material. Reproduction of historical styles to contemporary items. Also fountains and other garden decor. CREDIT CARDS.

Earthworks & Artisans 212-873-5220
  206 W 80th St. Basement (B'way & Amst)
  NY, NY 10024
  Hours: 1-7 Tue-Fri / 12-6 Sat & Sun
  www.earthworksandartisans.com
  Nice pottery pieces: bowls, vases, mugs, tea sets; also gives pottery classes. Some rentals. CREDIT CARDS.

Jamali Garden & Hardware Supplies, Inc. 212-244-4025
  149 W 28th St. (6-7th Ave)   212-594-5265
  NY, NY 10001   FAX 212-967-8196
  Hours: 6:30-5 Mon-Sat
  www.jamaligarden.com
  Hardware, garden supplies and floral supplies. Complete line of potting soil and fertilizers. Great selection of pottery from around the world and unique containers. CREDIT CARDS.

Lexington Gardens 212-861-4390
  1011 Lexington Ave. (72nd-73rd St)   FAX 212-988-0943
  NY, NY 10021
  Hours: 10- 6 Mon-Fri / 11-5 Sat   E-mail: inquiry@lexingtongardensnyc.com
  www.lexingtongardensnyc.com
  Wonderful antique iron furniture. Also has oversized garden pots from China and Vietnam in various glazes. Selected rentals on the antiques. CREDIT CARDS.

P

Mud, Sweat & Tears 212-974-9121
654 Tenth Ave. (46th St)
NY, NY 10036
Hours: 11-8 Mon-Fri / 12-7 Sat & Sun
www.mudsweat-tears.com
Nice gift selection and classes. CREDIT CARDS.

Supermud Pottery 212-865-9190
2744 Broadway, 2nd Fl. (105-106th St)
NY, NY 10025
Hours: 12-4 Tues-Fri / 12-3:30 Sat-Sun
www.supermudpotterystudio.com
Pottery, also classes available. CREDIT CARDS.

PRINTING SERVICES

Allied Reproductions 212-255-2472
121 Varick St., 9 FL (Dominick St)   FAX 212-255-2305
NY, NY 10013
Hours: 8-midnight Mon-Fri   E-mail: info@allied-print.com
www.allied-print.com
Offset printing, good service, inexpensive, volume laser printing. Print prop media materials. Mac and PC output.

Atlantic Blue Print Co., Inc. 212-755-3388
575 Madison Ave. (57th St)   FAX 212-751-5598
NY, NY 10022
Hours: 8:30-5 Mon-Fri (machines stop at 4:30)
www.atlanticblueprint.com
Blueprinting, offset, photocopies, including color Xerox. PC-based AutoCad along with printing and plotting. Pick-up and delivery if you have a charge account.

Atlantic Paper Products 212-674-4400
4916 Maspeth Ave.   FAX 718-386-1434
Maspeth, NY 11378
Hours: 7-3 Mon-Fri   E-mail: ATL4916@aol.com
www.atlanticpaperproducts.com
Full-service paper distributor supplying a complete line of retail packaging, shipping, janitorial and food service items. Family owned for over 50 years. Custom design and printing available. CREDIT CARDS.

BPI Reprographics 212-686-2436
295 Madison Ave.(41st St)
NY, NY 10017   FAX 212-532-8397
Hours: 7:30-6 Mon-Fri

11 Broadway, 9th FL(Morris-Beaver)   212-514-8010
NY, NY 10006   FAX 212-514-0838
Hours: 9-8 Mon-Fri

P

BPI Reprographics (cont.) 212-777-1110
   853 Broadway, 5th FL (Administrative Offices)   FAX 212-777-0880
   NY, NY 10003
   Hours: Administrative Offices Only   E-mail: info@bpirepro.com
   www.bpirepro.com
   Blue prints, B&W and color copying, photo stats, etc. Mac and IBM plotting.
   CREDIT CARDS.

Hart Multi-Copy, Inc. 212-704-0556
   555 Eighth Ave (37-38th St)   FAX 212-704-0003
   NY, NY 10018
   Hours: 9-5 Mon-Fri   E-mail: brett@hartrepro.com
   www.hartrepro.com
   Photocopying, offset printing, typesetting. Plotting from Mac-based.

Modern Postcard 800-959-8365
   1675 Faraday Ave.   760-431-7084
   Carlsbad, CA 92008   FAX 760-268-1700
   Hours: 8-5 Mon-Fri
   www.modernpostcard.com
   Promotional color postcards at great prices. Call the 800# for samples and
   ordering information. A variety of sizes and formats available. CREDIT CARDS.

ShinDigZ by Stumps 260-723-5171
   101 Carrol Rd.   800-314-8736
   South Whitley, IN 46787   FAX 260-723-6976
   Hours: 7-9 Mon-Fri   E-mail: csr@chindigz.com
   www.shindigZ.com
   One of the most complete party supply superstores found on the web. Very
   helpful with party suggestions. Prom theme props, fabrics, balloons, crepe
   papers (up to 4" wide), seamless papers in 23 colors, float supplies and
   novelties. Custom printing for invitations, glasses, etc. Quick delivery.
   Catalog. CREDIT CARDS.

PRODUCTION MANAGEMENT & TECHNICAL SERVICES

Access Event Services 800-823-5515
   322 Seaman St.   FAX 732-246-4456
   New Brunswick, NJ 08901
   Hours: 24-hr operation, call when you need us   E-mail: ed@8008235515.com
   www.redcarpetarrivals.com
   Event industries red carpet arrivals production company. Offering top notch
   equipment, bright 4K searchlights, street heat for heating your arrivals area,
   security services and crowd control. Unparalleled customer service and
   attention to every last detail. Last minute can do attitude. CREDIT CARDS.

P

Pook Diemont & Ohl, Inc. 718-402-2677
701 E 132nd St. (Cypress-Willow)   FAX 718-402-2859
Bronx, NY 10454-
Hours: 7-5 Mon-Fri   E-mail: info@pdoinc.com
www.pdoinc.com
Design/build company for theatre, TV and architectural environments
equipment systems. Scope includes new construction and renovation of
rigging systems, stage machinery, drapery and track, lighting and sound
systems.

PROMOTIONAL MATERIALS

Abat Printed Novelties 516-616-7201
121 Lakeville Rd.   800-807-9871
New Hyde Park, NY 11040   FAX 516-616-7223
Hours: 9-5 Mon-Fri   E-mail: sales@apnpromotions.com
www.apnpromotions.com
Advertising buttons, mugs, sashes, banners, badges, etc.; quick custom
service; will do small quantities. CREDIT CARDS.

Green Mountain Graphics 718-472-3377
21-10 44th Dr. (21st & 23rd St)   FAX 718-472-4040
Long Island City, NY 11101
Hours: 8:30-5 Mon-Fri   E-mail: sales@gm-graphics.com
www.gm-graphics.com
In-house manufacturers of engraved and silkscreened signs and promotional
products awards; also vinyl graphics. Suppliers of all kinds of signs including
cast bronze, faux cast bronze, etched, banners, etc. Also, blackboards and
bulletin boards. Convenient location to all L.I.C. soundstages. Catalogs and
rush service available. CREDIT CARDS.

Lup / Reel Jewelry 212-924-5588
1133 Broadway, Ste. 1314 (25-26th St)   FAX 212-924-2002
NY, NY 10010
Hours: By Appt.   E-mail: jessica@luprocks.com
www.luprocks.com
Fashion jewelry and watches from over 100 top designers. Jewelry cleared
with designers for use in TV, film and print product placement. Diamonds,
pearls, colored gemstones, platinum and gold available for use. Watches,
handbags, shoes & sunglasses.   No CREDIT CARDS.

Modern Postcard 800-959-8365
1675 Faraday Ave.   760-431-7084
Carlsbad, CA 92008   FAX 760-268-1700
Hours: 8-5 Mon-Fri
www.modernpostcard.com
Promotional color postcards at great prices. Call the 800# for samples and
ordering information. A variety of sizes and formats available. CREDIT CARDS.

Promote Your Team 866-913-0303
9704 Gunston Cove Rd., Unit A 703-372-5972
Lorton, VA 22079 . . . . FAX 703-372-1946
Hours: 24 on website . . . . E-mail: sales@promoteyourteam.com
www.promoteyourteam.com
Promotional mugs, pennants, poms and shakers, spirit towels and the all favorite Thunder Stix. Imprint and engraving optional. Can order items without printing. Fast and friendly service. Speak to Dan. CREDIT CARDS.

Quality Foam Designs 574-293-5547
2600 S Nappanee St. . . . . FAX 574-294-6283
Elkhart, IN 46517
Hours: 8-5 M-F . . . . E-mail: info@centuryfoam.com
www.qualityfoamdesigns.com
This helpful friendly company sells stock and custom novelty foam products. Made from safe toy spec foam. Imprinting available as well as color matching foam for large quantity jobs. Speak to Sandy. CREDIT CARDS.

The Queensboro Shirt Co. 910-251-1251
1400 Marstellar St. 800-847-4478
Wilmington, NC 28401 . . . . FAX 910-251-7771
Hours: 8-6 Mon-Fri . . . . E-mail: service@queensboro.com
www.queensboro.com
Quantity purchase of cotton polos, sweatshirts, jackets and golf towels; many sizes and several colors; will embroider your logo; catalog. CREDIT CARDS.

T-Gallery Corp. 212-420-9261
108 MacDougal St. (W 4th - Bleecker St.) 877-420-9261
NY, NY 10012
Hours: 12-10pm Daily . . . . E-mail: tshirts@teeshirtgallery.com
www.teeshirtgallery.com
Custom t-shirts using iron-on transfer paper within 15 minutes. You can email or bring a digital image file. Large selection of t-shirt styles for men, women and children. CREDIT CARDS.

T-Shirt Express 212-874-4464
209 W 80th St. (B'way-Amst Ave) 800-292-1562
NY, NY 10024 . . . . FAX 212-874-3740
Hours: 8-5 Mon-Fri / 9:30-3:30 Sat . . . E-mail: hp2@nyc.rr.com
www.tshirtexpress.com; www.printballoons.com
Custom screen printing, embroidery, heat transfers on all apparel. Latex and mylar balloons. No minimum. Speak to Harvey. CREDIT CARDS.

WinCraft 800-533-8006
1124 W Fifth St. 507-452-4765
Winona, MN 55987 . . . . FAX 507-453-0690
Hours: 24-hrs. by web / 9-5 Mon-Fri Corporate Office
www.wincraft.com . . . . E-mail: contact@wincraft.com
WinCraft is a recognized leader in retail licensed and promotional products. You can provide your customer with collectible and home decor products from NFL, NHL, NBA, NASCAR, NCAA, Olympics not to mention they have over 300 licenses. They offer licensed products for every retail selling season, hot market, and major event. CREDIT CARDS.

P

PROP & MODEL SHOPS

ABS Art Effects LLC 315-422-5825
110 Dorset Road
Syracuse, NY 13210
Hours: by appt.   E-mail: andrewbenepe@gmail.com
*Custom design and fabrication of representational sculpture, high end props
and environments in a wide range of materials for film, TV, stage & print; fast
turn-around.*

Acme Stimuli Design & Production .212-465-1071
889 Broadway   212-465-1071
NY, NY 10001
Hours: by appt.

2640 Rt. 214   845-688-5107
Lanesville, NY 12450
Hours: by appt.   E-mail: stimuli7@hvc.rr.com
www.acmestimuli.com
Prop design and fabrication; sculpture; mold-making. Contact Marc Rubin.

Bargsten Studios / ICBA, Inc. 201-420-8680
50 Dey St., Ste. 4404   FAX 201-792-5776
Jersey City, NJ 07306
Hours: 9-6 Mon-Fri   E-mail: bargsten@mindspring.com
*SPFX shop, props; also involved in film production, scenery and retail display.
Design services available.*

Baumwell Graphics, Inc. 704-814-4550
8923 Providence Estates Ct.   888-266-7246
Charlotte, NC 28270
Hours: 9-6 Mon-Fri   E-mail: clyde@chromatype.com
www.chromatype.com
*Custom graphic props: newspapers, magazines, fake money, credit cards, etc.
Contact Clyde Baumwell. CREDIT CARDS.*

Benjamin-Lee, Inc. 212-473-5422
893 Broadway, 3rd Fl. (19-20th St)   FAX 212-473-4761
NY, NY 10003
Hours: 9-5:30 Mon-Fri   E-mail: lcrimi@benjaminlee.com
www.benjaminlee.com
*Full-service design, management and consulting firm. Professional services
in special effects, design construction, specialized painting and sculpting.
Tradeshows and special promotional events.*

Brooklyn Model Works, Inc. 718-834-1944
60 Washington Ave. (Park-Flushing)   FAX 718-596-8934
Brooklyn, NY 11205
Hours: by appt.   E-mail: info@brooklynmodelworks.com
www.brooklynmodelworks.com
Experienced and reliable.

P

Capital Scenic, Inc. 845-429-4800
55 Railroad Ave. # 3C (Route 9W)   FAX 845-429-2138
Garnerville, NY 10923
Hours: 8-4 Mon-Fri   E-mail: capitalscenic@gmail.com
www.capitalscenic.com
Stunt furniture: modification, reinforcement and upholstery of antiques for stage. Scenic storage and maintenance. Scenic and prop rentals. Contact Richard or Neil.

Tom Carroll Scenery, Inc. 201-432-9047
25 Pollock Ave.   FAX 201-434-1146
Jersey City, NJ 07305
Hours: 8-4 Mon-Fri   E-mail: tcarrollscenery@comcast.net
www.tomcarrollscenery.com
Custom scenery and props for theater, TV, film and industrials. Licensed to issue flameproof certificates.

COMP 24 212-627-4000
127 W 30th St., 4th Fl. (6-7th Ave)   800-848-7716
NY, NY 10001   FAX 212-627-4287
Hours: 8-8 Mon-Fri
www.comp24.com
The largest packaging prototype facility in the world, specializing in color correct comps for advertising. Digital direct proofing and silkscreening; transfers; banners to bus wraps.

Constructive Display 718-237-3131
499 Van Brunt St.   FAX 718-237-4182
Brooklyn, NY 11231
Hours: 8:30-5 Mon-Fri
www.constructivedisplay.com
Set, prop, exhibit and special events design and construction.

Suzanne Couture Modelmaking 212-714-9310
227 W 29th St. (10-11th Ave)   FAX 212-714-0759
NY, NY 10001
www.suzannecouturemodelmaking.com
Miniature to oversized custom props, sets and costumes. Design and fabrication. Brochure, portfolio and reel available upon request.

Creative Engineering 718-937-5292
5-50 54th Ave. (Vernon Blvd)   347-386-6623
Long Island City, NY 11101   FAX 718-937-1271
Hours: 9-5 Mon-Fri   E-mail: creeng@aol.com
www.creativeengineeringinc.com
Custom scenery, props, metal fabrication anf fine furniture construction. If you can dream it, they can build it. RENTALS. CREDIT CARDS.

P

CREATIVE METAL WORKS, INC. / STEPHEN MCMAHON 631-537-9501
172 Butter Lane   FAX 631-537-4669
Bridgehampton, NY 11932
Hours: by Appt.   E-mail: mail@creativemetalworksinc.com
www.creativemetalworksinc.com
Creative Metal Works crafts fine architectural elements from all types of metals, including: stainless steel, steel mesh, galvanized steel, brushed steel, bronze, brass, nickel, copper, aluminum and titanium. Custom metal projects range from architecural elements, railings, and canopies, to sculpture, hardware, decorative lighting, and fixtures. Member ATAC.

John Creech Design & Production 718-237-1144
129 Van Brunt St. (President-Carroll St)   FAX 718-237-4133
Brooklyn, NY 11231
Hours: 8-6 Mon-Fri   E-mail: shop@jcdp.biz
www.webuildeverything.com
Custom scenery, props and special effects for theatre, film, television and display.

DUNHAM STUDIOS 518-494-3930
10 Dunham's Loop   FAX 518-494-3688
Pottersville, NY 12860
Hours: 9-5 Mon-Fri   E-mail: clarke@dunhamstudios.com
www.dunhamstudios.com
All category member USA Local #829. Designer of scenery, lighting & projections for Broadway, International Opera and national television. 2 Tony, 5 Drama Desk Nominations; Maharam Award, Jefferson Award. Custom design and fabrication of exxibits, architectural models and store interiors. Specializing in historically accurate and fantasy model railroads for museums and corporations. Also custom large format printing, murals, props and cut vinyl signs. Member ATAC.

Eastern Tabletop Manufacturing Company, Inc. 718-522-4142
1943 Pitkin Ave.   888-422-4142
Brooklyn, NY 11207   FAX 718-522-4155
Hours: 9-5 Mon-Thurs / 9-1 Fri / 24-hr website
                  E-mail: sales@easterntabletop.com
www.easterntabletop.com
Since 1950, Eastern Tabletop Manufacturing Co., Inc. has been dedicated to manufacturing and designing Silver Plated Holloware and Chafing Dishes for the food service industry. Trays, beverage servers and cover-ups. Now good selection of bars, high end carts and pidiums. Visit website for collection.

Dan Folkus/Visual Syntax Productions 856-939-3116
91 Harding Ave.
Runnemede, NJ 08078
Hours: 9-6 Mon-Fri   E-mail: folkus@visual-syntax.com
www.visual-syntax.com
Murals, models, sculpture, props, puppets, exhibit design. Computer graphics.

Geppetto, Inc. 718-398-9792
201 46th St. 2nd FL   FAX 718-622-2991
Brooklyn, NY 11220
Hours: 9-5 Mon-Fri   E-mail: gepstudios@aol.com
www.geppettostudios.com
Custom construction of soft sculpture props and costumes, foam rubber
masks, foam props and 3-D illustrations. Contact Scott, brochure available.

The Group Y! A Mark Yurkiw Company 646-873-0050
180 Cross Hwy.
Westport, CT 06880
Hours: by appt.   E-mail: mark@think3-D.com
www.think3-D.com
3-D design and fabrication for all media, events and exhibits.

Ice Fantasies, Inc. 800-NICE-ICE
220 Plymouth St., Ste. 5A   718-852-4895
Brooklyn, NY 11201   FAX 718-852-0434
Hours: 10-6 Tue-Sat   E-mail: fishman5@mac.com
www.icefantasies.com
Custom ice props, ice sculpture, snow making. Sound stage and set
experience, live TV and photography. CREDIT CARDS.

Martin Izquierdo Studio 212-807-9757
118 W 22nd St., 9th Fl. (6-7th Ave) FAX 212-366-5249
NY, NY 10011
Hours: 9-7 Mon-Fri   E-mail: izquierdostudio@gmail.com
www.izquierdostudio.com
Full-service custom work for theater, film, commercials, display and video. No
rentals.

JERARD STUDIO, INC. 718-852-4128
481 Van Brunt St., Ste. 11D (Beard St) FAX 718-852-2408
Brooklyn, NY 11231
Hours: 9-6 Mon-Fri   E-mail: mary@jerardstudio.com
www.jerardstudio.com
Custom design and fabrication of props and scenery; action props, puppets,
custom furniture, sculpture and structural costumes. Member ATAC.

JOSEPH GOURLEY 646-281-2040
567 Flushing Ave. Apt 505
Brooklyn, NY 11206
Hours: by appt.   E-mail: josephmgourley@yahoo.com
www.jmgtheadesign.com
Scenic and lighting designer. Drafting and 3-D Modeling as well as
modelmaking. Member ATAC.

Microform Models, Inc. 508-485-9333
158 Winter St.   877-489-3011
Marlborough, MA 01752
Hours: 8-4:30 Mon-Fri E-mail: greatservice@microformmodels.com
www.microformmodels.com
Cast metal furniture, props, trees, etc.; great selection in 1/4", some 1/2"
chairs, inexpensive. Phone orders. Shipping. Catalog with actual size photos.
CREDIT CARDS.

OFFSTAGE DESIGN 845-265-0078
28 Lane Gate Rd. (Rt 9)   914-522-0283
Cold Spring, NY 10516   FAX 845-265-2322
Hours: by appt.   E-mail: denise@offstagedesign.com
www.offstagedesign.com
Custom stage and trick furniture built, any period. Set pieces, window displays, upholstery, crafts and shopping services. Ephemera a specialty. Contact Denise Grillo or Denny Clark. Member ATAC.

Carl Paolino Studios 917-957-7305
3801 23rd Ave.   917-282-4756
Astoria, NY 11105   FAX (same)
Hours: by appt. only   E-mail: cpseffects@aol.com
www.paolinostudios.com
Contact Carl Paolino or Scott Sliger.

Bill Rybak / 3D Design & Fabrication 917-929-9124
59 South St.
Highland, NY 12528
Hours: by appt.   E-mail: billrybak@yahoo.com
www.billrybak.com
Custom design and fabrication of props, displays, showroom interiors, models and sculpture. Digital props and models imaging.

The Spoon Group 732-499-9370
970 New Brunswick Ave., Bldg I   FAX 732-574-8899
Rahway, NJ 07065
Hours: 8-5:30 Mon-Fri   E-mail: srobert@thespoongroup.com
www.thespoongroup.com
Roadboxes, gondolas, tech tables, wig ovens, hampers, rehearsal scenery and furniture. Production props fabrication, special effects for theatre, film and television. RENTALS. CREDIT CARDS.

Studio Eis 718-797-4561
55 Washington St., Ste. 400 (Washington)   FAX 718-797-4562
Brooklyn, NY 11201
Hours: 9-5 Mon-Fri   E-mail: info@studioeis.com
www.studioeis.com
Custom life-cast figures for museums and display.

Trengove Studios, Inc. 212-268-0020
60 W 22nd St., 2nd FL (7-8th Ave)   800-366-2857
NY, NY 10010   FAX 212-268-0030
Hours: call for appt. 9-5 Mon-Fri E-mail: info@trengovestudios.com
www.trengovestudios.com
Brochure and product sheet available. Great custom work in glass and acrylic. Stock purchase of fake ice. CREDIT CARDS.

VonErickson 347-239-6976
69 1st Ave., # 10
NY, NY 10003
Hours: By Appt.   E-mail: peter@vonerickson.com
www.vonerickson.com
Design and fabrication of custom props for print, TV, and theatre. Furniture and lamps. High quality, reasonably priced. CREDIT CARDS.

P

PROP & SCENIC CRAFTSPEOPLE

Aki-ology Design, Inc. 212-533-1694
140 Second Ave., Ste. 402   FAX 212-475-5737
NY, NY 10003
Hours: by appt.
Full-service scene shop. From art direction to set dressing.

NADINE CHARLSEN 212-307-0035
344 W 49th St. Apt 2D (8-9th Ave)   (cell) 917-656-1313
NY, NY 10019
Hours: by appt.   E-mail: nadinelc@nyc.rr.com
www.nadinepaints.com
Scenic design and painting. Research services available. AEA Stage Manager.
Member ATAC.

MARGARET CUSACK 718-237-0145
124 Hoyt St. (Dean St)   718-909-4402
Brooklyn, NY 11217   FAX 718-237-0145
Hours: by appt.   E-mail: cusackart@aol.com
www.margaretcusack.com
Unique stitched artwork, samplers, soft sculpture, quilted hangings, portraits
and props that have warmed up the images of clients from AT&T to Aunt
Millie's Spaghetti Sauce. Member ATAC.

Dan Folkus/Visual Syntax Productions 856-939-3116
91 Harding Ave.
Runnemede, NJ 08078
Hours: 9-6 Mon-Fri   E-mail: folkus@visual-syntax.com
www.visual-syntax.com
Murals, models, sculpture, props, puppets, exhibit design. Computer
graphics.

Nicole Gaignat 860-798-6121
3948 59th St., # 2 (Roosevelt)
Woodside, NY 11377
Hours: By appt. only   E-mail: nicoleprops@gmail.com
www.coroflot.com/nicoleprops
Freelance artisan in fabrication or acquiring props for theatre and window
display merchandising. Good skills from fake food to paper to softgoods.
Prop Master, prop artisan and sculptor.

DEBORAH GLASSBERG 973-429-2904
53 Spring St.   (cell) 973-930-4878
Bloomfield, NJ 07003
Hours: please callE-mail: debglassberg@earthlink.net / deb.glassberg@gmail.com
www.flickr.com/photos/debglassberg
Scenic sculpture, model building, upholstery, puppets and masks. Member
ATAC.

P

PROP & SCENIC CRAFTSPEOPLE

STOCKTON HALL 917-627-7847
615 E 14th St Apt 4B (B-C Ave)   (Agent) 212-255-3325
NY, NY 10009   FAX 212-217-2883
Hours: By Appt.   E-mail: stocktonhall@mac.com
www.stocktonhall.com / www.1plus1mgmt.com
Prop stylist, set designer, sculptor for fashion advertising and editorial,
events, theatre, television and film. Represented by 1 Plus 1 Management.
Member ATAC.

KATE DALE 718-253-1044
1375 Ocean Ave. (Ave I-H)   212-799-5000 X 214
Brooklyn, NY 11230
Hours: by appt.   E-mail: kdale@juilliard.edu
Soft goods, upholstery, prop and costume crafts. Resident Prop Master for
The Juilliard School. Member ATAC.

Linda LaBelle / The Yarn Tree 718-384-3793
347 Bedford Ave.   718-384-8030
Brooklyn, NY 11211   FAX (same)
Hours: 4-8 Mon-Thurs / 12-7 Sat-Sun / or by appt. E-mail: info@theyarntree.com
www.theyarntree.com
Costume design and construction, design and construction of soft props.
Custom handwoven fabrics, handknits and fabric painting.

JERRY L. MARSHALL, PROPS & TURNED OBJECTS 917-364-5015
415 W 55th St. # 3-A (9-10th Ave)
NY, NY 10019
Hours: by appt. only   E-mail: jlmars.nyc@mac.com
Broadway Propman, show supervision, shopping, fabrication and painting.
Member IATSE Local 1, United Scenic Artists Local 829. Member ATAC.

MICHAEL SMANKO / PRISM PROPS 732-382-9727
1015 Richard Blvd.
Rahway, NJ 07065
Hours: by Appt.
www.prismprops.com
Broadway Production propman & prop stylist. Prop supervision, shopping,
fabrication, upholstery, painting and finishes, prop construction, SPFX. 35
year IATSE member. BA Fine Arts, MFA Theater Design. Member ATAC.

Parrish Relics 781-438-1497
P O Box 80039
Stoneham, MA 02180
Hours: by appt.   E-mail: jen@parrishrelics.com
www.parrishrelics.com
Historical replicas, accessories and jewelry props. Lightweight museum
quality crown; medieval to Victorian. Design specialists. Visit website to
order. CREDIT CARDS.

P

Perfection Electricks 718-383-1155
1155 Manhattan Ave. (Commercial St)   FAX 718-383-1157
Brooklyn, NY 11222
Hours: 8:30-4:30 Mon-Fri   E-mail: marty@perfectionelectricks.com
www.perfectionelectricks.com
A custom electronics manufacturer specializing in game show equipment,
custom control devices and technology support for artists. Talk to Marty.
RENTALS.

Cornell H. Riggs 570-470-0936
530 Gravity Rd.   FAX 570-937-3569
Lake Ariel, PA 18436
Hours: by appt.   E-mail: creator@Art2specs.com
www.Art2specs.com
Scenery, prop construction, sculpture and furniture design.

Sean P. McArdle / Hero Props 646-734-2198
18 Bridge St. # 1A
Brooklyn, NY 11201
Hours: by appt.   E-mail: sean@heropropsnyc.com
www.heropropsnyc.com
Prop design and management. Carpentry, welding, turning, casting molding,
upholstery, costume crafts, model making and furniture construction.
Computer graphics design and desktop publishing.

Sets and Effects, LLC. 646-315-0785
1239 DeKalb Ave. (Dekalb - Evergreen)
Brooklyn, NY 11221
Hours: 8-9pm Mon - Fri   E-mail: davdjones@setsandeffects.com
www.setsandeffects.com
Sets, scenic shop for fashion, film, print, commercial, event, music, and
television. Specialty props.

Manju Shandler Design 917-826-3588
Hours: by appt.   E-mail: manju@nyc.rr.com
www.manjushandler.com
Specializing in costume design and building of foam sculptured costumes,
puppets, masks and props.

Jenny Stanjeski 917-405-9656
454 Ft. Washington Ave. 67B
NY, NY 10033
Hours: by appt (24-hr. voice mail)
Scenic charge, prop painting, carving, art reproduction.

Superior Studio Specilities 800-354-3049
401 N Western Ave.   312-850-9016
Chicago, IL 60612   FAX 312-850-9026
Hours: 8:30-5 Mon-Fri   Email: chicago@superiorstudio.com

2239 S Yates Ave   323-278-0100
Commerce, CA 90040   FAX 323-278-0111
Hours: 8:30-5 Mon-Fri   Email: la@superiorstudio.com
www.superiorstudio.com
Seamless papers, fake food, wire mannequin frames, foam boards and
cutting supplies. CREDIT CARDS.

P

ATAC

VonErickson 347-239-6976
69 1st Ave., # 10
NY, NY 10003
Hours: By Appt.   E-mail: peter@vonerickson.com
www.vonerickson.com
Design and fabrication of custom props for print, TV, and theatre. Furniture and lamps. High quality, reasonably priced. CREDIT CARDS.

PROP & SCENIC CRAFTSPEOPLE: MODEL MAKING

Cimmelli, Inc. 845-735-2090
16 Walter St.   845-735-4693
Pearl River, NY 10965   FAX 845-735-1643
Hours: 8:30-5:30 Mon-Fri / Sat by appt.
www.cimmellisfx.com
Masks, sculpture, puppets, props, models, rigs and special effects. Large variety of turntables available for rental use. Custom sculpture for any application. RENTALS.

DUNHAM STUDIOS 518-494-3930
10 Dunham's Loop   FAX 518-494-3688
Pottersville, NY 12860
Hours: 9-5 Mon-Fri   E-mail: clarke@dunhamstudios.com
www.dunhamstudios.com
All category member USA Local #829 Designer of scenery, lighting & projections for Broadway, International Opera and national television. 2 Tony, 5 Drama Desk Nominations; Maharam Award, Jefferson Award. Custom design and fabrication of exxibits, architectural models and store interiors. Specializing in historically accurate and fantasy model railroads for museums and corporations. Also custom large format printing, murals, props and cut vinyl signs. Member ATAC.

JAMES FENG 718-499-1601
221 Eighth Ave. (2nd St)
Brooklyn, NY 11215
Hours: by appt.
Scenery and models; designed, built and painted. Art direction.

Elizabeth Goodall 212-645-9480
78 Bedford St. (Barrow)   FAX 212-645-7789
NY, NY 10014
Hours: by appt.   E-mail: lizgoodall@aol.com
Model making for commercials and print; illustration.

Zoe Morsette 718-784-8894
43-01 21st St., Studio 224A   917-733-1731
Long Island City, NY 11101
Hours: by appt.
Rigid and soft sculpture for print, TV, film and stage. Also model railroad scenery.

P

Daniel Oates 860-364-5775
25 Millerton Rd.   FAX 860-364-6008
Sharon, CT 06059
Hours: 10-7 Mon-Fri   E-mail: daniel@danieloates.com
www.danieloates.com
Sculptor, modelmaker, propmaker with 16 years experience in a large variety of materials. Virtual 3D renderingand modelmaking using Lightwave 3D.

Carl Paolino Studios 917-957-7305
3801 23rd Ave.   917-282-4756
Astoria, NY 11105   FAX (same)
Hours: by appt. only   E-mail: cpseffects@aol.com
www.paolinostudios.com
Clay animation figures, mechanical puppets, specialty props. Speak to Carl.

BILL RYBAK / 3D DESIGN & FABRICATION 917-929-9124
59 South St.
Highland, NY 12528
Hours: by appt.   E-mail: billrybak@yahoo.com
www.billrybak.com
Custom design and fabrication of props, displays, showroom interiors, models and sculpture. Digital props and models imaging.

SPS EFFECTS, LLC / SUSAN PITOCCHi 917-519-5805
262 N 6th St., Apt 3
Brooklyn, NY 11211

96 Academy St.   845-292-6942
Liberty, NY 12754   FAX 845-292-6342
Hours: by appt.   E-mail: spitocchi@earthlink.net
www.spseffects.com
Custom fabrication of props, costumes and sculptures in materials including foam, fabric, wood, leather, plastics and casting materials.   Member IATSE Local 52. Member ATAC.

PROP & SCENIC CRAFTSPEOPLE: MOLD MAKING

Acme Stimuli Design & Production 212-465-1071
889 Broadway
NY, NY 10001
Hours: by appt.

2640 Rt. 214   845-688-5107
Lanesville, NY 12450
Hours: by appt.   E-mail: stimuli7@hvc.rr.com
www.acmestimuli.com
Moldmaking including fiberglass and vacuumform. Contact Marc Rubin.

RANDY CARFAGNO PRODUCTIONS 212-947-0302
347 W 39th St. #7E (8-9th Ave)   FAX 212-947-2941
NY, NY 10018
Hours: by appt.   E-mail: randycarfagnoproductions@gmail.com
www.randycarfagnoproductions.com
Waste molds to ultracal plasters; latex rubber molds. Member ATAC.

James Glass Studio 718-596-6463
20 Jay St., Ste. 734 (Plymouth St)   FAX Same
Brooklyn, NY 11201
Hours: by appt.   E-mail: jamesglassstudio@earthlink.net
www.jamesglassstudio.com
Custom sculpting studio, casting in 3D glass, stone and metal. Established
glass studio for 20 years.

MICHAEL SMANKO / PRISM PROPS 732-382-9727
1015 Richard Blvd.
Rahway, NJ 07065
Hours: by appt.
www.prismprops.com
Broadway Production propman & prop stylist. Prop supervision, shopping,
fabrication, upholstery, painting and finishes, prop construction, SPFX. 35
year IATSE member. BA Fine Arts, MFA Theater Design. Member ATAC.

Carl Paolino Studios 917-957-7305
3801 23rd Ave.   917-282-4756
Astoria, NY 11105   FAX (same)
Hours: by appt. only   E-mail: cpseffects@aol.com
www.paolinostudios.com
Clay animation figures, mechanical puppets, specialty props. Speak to Carl.

Julie Prince 212-486-9249
141 E 56th St. #9G (Lex-3rd Ave)   818-353-4525
NY, NY 10022   FAX (same)
Hours: by appt.   E-mail: portraicast@aol.com
www.portraicast.com
Life-casting; masks, sculptures and fragments; also props. In California call
818-353-4525.

Studio Eis 718-797-4561
55 Washington St., Ste. 400 (Washington)   FAX 718-797-4562
Brooklyn, NY 11201
Hours: 9-5 Mon-Fri   E-mail: info@studioeis.com
www.studioeis.com
Custom life-cast figures for museums and display.

PROP & SCENIC CRAFTSPEOPLE: PROP & SCENIC CRAFTS

ABS Art Effects LLC 315-422-5825
110 Dorset Road
Syracuse, NY 13210
Hours: by appt.   E-mail: andrewbenepe@gmail.com
Custom design and fabrication of representational sculpture, high-end props
and environments in a wide range of materials for film, TV, stage & print; fast
turnaround.

Daniel J. Aronson 212-544-0366
NY, NY 10040
Hours: by appt.
Design & construction of props and scenery; property master, art director for
media productions.

CHRIS BOBIN 646-742-0630
347 Fifth Ave., Rm 1102 (34-35th St)   917-683-5239
NY, NY 10016
Hours: by appt.   E-mail: chris@chrisbobin.com
www.chrisbobin.com
Sewn solutions for props; quilting, applique and embroidery. Member ATAC.

RANDY CARFAGNO PRODUCTIONS 212-947-0302
347 W 39th St. #7E (8-9th Ave)   FAX 212-947-2941
NY, NY 10018
Hours: by appt.   E-mail: randycarfagnoproductions@gmail.com
www.randycarfagnoproductions.com
Puppets, mascots, papier mache and vacuumform masks. All types of character hats. Oversized puppets and shoes. Member SAG, ATAC.

NADINE CHARLSEN 212-307-0035
344 W 49th St. Apt 2D (8-9th Ave)   (cell) 917-656-1313
NY, NY 10019
Hours: by appt.   E-mail: nadinelc@nyc.rr.com
www.nadinepaints.com
Research and design of sets, lights and props. Macintosh computer graphics. AEA Stage Manager. Member ATAC.

CINAF DESIGNS 212-501-9090
48 Fairway St.   917-796-4641
Bloomfield, NJ 07003   FAX 973-320-4493
Hours: by appt.   E-mail: cinaf@aol.com
www.cinafdesigns.com
Costume crafts, costume painting and distressing. Drapery and upholstery. Props for puppets. Prop and model builder. Member IATSE Local 1, 829 & Local 52. Member ATAC.

Suzanne Couture Modelmaking 212-714-9310
227 W 29th St. (10-11th Ave)   FAX 212-714-0759
NY, NY 10001
www.suzannecouturemodelmaking.com
Miniature to oversized custom props, sets and costumes. Design and fabrication. Brochure, portfolio and reel available upon request.

Sal Denaro / Motion by Design 917-596-5537
335 Court St. # 28   212-560-2507
Brooklyn, NY 11231   FAX 718-228-4840
Hours: by appt.   E-mail: salmotion@yahoo.com
www.saldenaro.com
Puppet creator/designer and toy model sculptor; stop motion models, foam latex and mold-making.

Stephen Edelstein 212-666-9198
771 West End Ave. #4C (97th St)
NY, NY 10025
Hours: by appt.   E-mail: UnclStevie@aol.com
Computer graphics, digital and underwater photography

JAMES FENG 718-499-1601
221 Eighth Ave. (2nd St)
Brooklyn, NY 11215
Hours: by appt.
Scenery and models; designed, built and painted. Art direction.

KEEN GAT 917-674-1477
225 Park Place # 5E
Brooklyn, NY 11238
Hours: by appt.　　　　　　　　　E-mail: keen@goosegirl.com
www.goosegirl.com
Digital prototypes, mold-making, sourceing and planning. Member ATAC.

Elizabeth Goodall 212-645-9480
78 Bedford St. (Barrow)　　　　　　　　　FAX 212-645-7789
NY, NY 10014
Hours: by appt.　　　　　　　　　E-mail: lizgoodall@aol.com
Prop and model making, sculpting, scenic painting, faux finishing, illustration. Local 829 scenic painter.

Louise Grafton 609-921-1919
229 Hartly Ave.
Princeton, NJ 08540
Hours: by appt.　　　　　　　　　E-mail: legraft@hotmail.com
Props, set and costume pieces, soft goods, circus and clown props. Also upholstery done in her studio.

JUNG K. GRIFFIN 718-391-0009
4316 42nd St. #3R　　　　　　　　　(cell) 646-498-4251
Sunnyside, NY 11104　　　　　　　　　FAX 718-391-0009
Hours: by appt.　　　　　　　　　E-mail: jgriffin95@aol.com
Props artisan, sculpture, crafts, carpentry, soft goods, upholstery. Member ATAC.

SUZANNE HAYDEN 413-259-1275
184 Wendell Rd.
Shutesbury, MA 01072　　　　　　　　　E-mail: shayden@mtholyoke.edu
Property crafts. Member ATAC.

Warren Jorgenson 914-699-5054
219 Watchung Ter.　　　　　　　　　914-882-7676
Scotch Plains, NJ 07076　　　　　　　　　FAX 914-667-4100
Hours: by appt.　　　　　　　　　E-mail: warrenj@att.net
www.artistsguildusa.com
A guild of scenic artist for film, television and restaurant themes. Contact Warren Jorgenson or their website for other information. All artists are members United Scenic Artists, Local 829.

Danielle Leon / Faultless Faux 718-832-2743
PO Box 1285 (Murray Hill Station)　　　　　　　　　305-781-6349
NY, NY 10156
Hours: by appt.　　　　　　　　　E-mail: faultlessfaux@att.net
Prop construction, shopping and styling; faux finishes; historical prop research.

JENNIE MARINO / MOONBOOTS PRODUCTIONS, INC. 845-359-6262
44 Slocum Ave.   Cell 845-642-0158
Tappan, NY 10983   FAX 845-680-6124
Hours: by appt.   E-mail: jenfx@aol.com
Special FX make-up, prosthetics, creatures. Prototypes maquettes and prop
fabrication. Masks in foam and cast latex; resin. Mechanical masks, dummies.
Hand, rod, mechanical & full body puppet design and fabrication. Member
ATAC.

JERRY L. MARSHALL, PROPS & TURNED OBJECTS 917-364-5015
415 W 55th St. # 3-A (9-10th Ave)
NY, NY 10019
Hours: by appt. only   E-mail: jlmars.nyc@mac.com
Broadway Propman, show supervision, shopping, fabrication and painting.
Member IATSE Local 1, United Scenic Artists Local 829. Member ATAC.

MONIQUE WALKER . . . . .Cell 732-740-5207
41 Oak St.
Keyport, NJ 07735
Hours: by appt.   E-mail: mqwalk@yahoo.com
Day or hourly shopping, coordinator, consulting. Call for appointment.
Member ATAC.

Zoe Morsette 718-784-8894
43-01 21st St., Studio 224A   917-733-1731
Long Island City, NY 11101
Hours: by appt.
Rigid and soft sculpture for print, TV, film and stage. Also model railroad
scenery.

Carl Paolino Studios 917-957-7305
3801 23rd Ave.   917-282-4756
Astoria, NY 11105   FAX (same)
Hours: by appt. only   E-mail: cpseffects@aol.com
www.paolinostudios.com
Clay animation figures, mechanical puppets, specialty props. Speak to Carl.

Robin Lu Payne 720-810-2102
3305 W 98th Ave. Unit B
Westminister, CO 80031   E-mail: paynerl@aol.com
Prop craftsperson, sculptor.

Julie Prince 212-486-9249
141 E 56th St. #9G (Lex-3rd Ave)   818-353-4525
NY, NY 10022   FAX (same)
Hours: by appt.   E-mail: portraicast@aol.com
www.portraicast.com
Life-casting; masks, sculptures and fragments; also props. In California call
818-353-4525.

Donald Recklies 718-768-9036
420 Fourth Ave. #1   FAX (same)
Brooklyn, NY 11215
Hours: by appt.   E-mail: recklies@earthlink.net
Costume and prop lighting effects.

P

BILL RYBAK / 3D DESIGN & FABRICATION 917-929-9124
59 South St.
Highland, NY 12528
Hours: by appt.　　　　　　　　　　　E-mail: billrybak@yahoo.com
www.billrybak.com
Custom design and fabrication of props, displays, showroom interiors,
models and sculpture. Digital props and models imaging.

Catherine Schmitt 201-573-9150
7 Ethridge Pl.
Park Ridge, NJ 07656
Hours: by appt.　　　　　　　　　E-mail: cschmitt@schmittsculpture.com
www.schmittsculpture.com
Sculpture and soft sculpture, custom props and costumes, display figures.

Sean P. McArdle / Hero Props 646-734-2198
18 Bridge St. # 1A
Brooklyn, NY 11201
Hours: by appt.　　　　　　　　　　E-mail: sean@heropropsnyc.com
www.heropropsnyc.com
Prop design and management. Carpentry, welding, turning, casting molding,
upholstery, costume crafts, model making and furniture construction.
Computer graphics design and desktop publishing.

LISA SHAFTEL / SHAFTEL S2DO 508-879-7772
24 Warren Rd.　　　　　　　　　　　　　　　(Cell) 617-755-1240
Framingham, MA 01702　　　　　　　　　　　　　　FAX (same)
Hours: 9-6 Mon-Fri　　　　　　　　E-mail: shaftels2do@verizon.net
www.s2do.com
Scenic designer and scenic artist, art direction, illustration, storyboards,
character design, CAD drafting and Photoshop. Puppet design and
fabrication, prop fabrication no rentals. Member USA Local 829, IATSE Local
481, and the Graphic Artist Guild. Member ATAC.

SPS EFFECTS, LLC / SUSAN PITOCCHI 917-519-5805
262 N 6th St., Apt 3
Brooklyn, NY 11211

96 Academy St.　　　　　　　　　　　　　　　845-292-6942
Liberty, NY 12754　　　　　　　　　　　　　FAX 845-292-6342
Hours: by appt.　　　　　　　　　　　　　FAX 845-292-6342
www.spseffects.com　　　　　　　　E-mail: spitocchi@earthlink.net
Custom fabrication of props, costumes and sculptures in materials including
foam, fabric, wood, leather, plastics and casting materials.   Member IATSE
Local 52. Member ATAC.

MARI TOBITA 212-254-8614
235 E 10th St., Apt 4D　　　　　　　　　　　　(cell) 917-304-5280
NY, NY 10003　　　　　　　　　　　　　　　　FAX 212-254-8614
Hours: by appt.　　　　　　　　　　E-mail: maritobita@aol.com
Theatrical masks, puppets, wooden marionettes, sculpture, props and
costume crafts. Member USA Local 829. Member ATAC.

PROP & SCENIC CRAFTSPEOPLE: SCENIC PAINTING

Gillian Bradshaw-Smith 214-948-8472
311 N Winnetka Ave.
Dallas, TX 75208
Hours: by appt.   E-mail: gillbs@swbell.net
www.gillianbradshaw-smith.net
Set Design and scenic painting. Custom murals, floorcloths and drops.
Speak to Gillian Bradshaw-Smith.

NADINE CHARLSEN 212-307-0035
344 W 49th St. Apt 2D (8-9th Ave)   (cell) 917-656-1313
NY, NY 10019
Hours: by appt.   E-mail: nadinelc@nyc.rr.com
www.nadinepaints.com
Scenic artist, muralist. Research and design of sets, lights and props.
Macintosh computer graphics. AEA Stage Manager. Member ATAC.

EILEEN CONNOR 212-421-4805
300 E 54th St. #25C   917-841-6482
NY, NY 10022
Hours: by appt.
Fabric and costume painting, scenic painting, murals, faux finishes, gilding,
crafts. Member ATAC.

Sal Denaro / Motion by Design 917-596-5537
335 Court St. # 28   212-560-2507
Brooklyn, NY 11231   FAX 718-228-4840
Hours: by appt.   E-mail: salmotion@yahoo.com
www.saldenaro.com
Puppet creator/designer and toy model sculptor; stop motion models, foam
latex and mold-making.

JAMES FENG 718-499-1601
221 Eighth Ave. (2nd St)
Brooklyn, NY 11215
Hours: by appt.
Scenery and models; designed, built and painted. Art direction.

Elizabeth Goodall 212-645-9480
78 Bedford St. (Barrow)   FAX 212-645-7789
NY, NY 10014
Hours: by appt.   E-mail: lizgoodall@aol.com
Scenic painting for film & theatre; also sculpting and illustration. Local 829
scenic painter.

LOUISE HUNNICUTT & ASSOCIATES, INC. 718-599-7777
119 N 11th St. #5A (Bedford-Berry)   (cell) 917-885-8088
Brooklyn, NY 11211
Hours: by appt.   E-mail: lshnyc@earthlink.com
www.louisehunnicutt.com / www.lshnyc.com
Specializing in hand-painted signage and murals. Italian plaster interiors:
residental and commercial. Member United Scenic Artist 829, Scenic Artist.
Member ATAC.

P

JERARD STUDIO, INC. 718-852-4128
481 Van Brunt St., Ste. 11D (Beard St)   FAX 718-852-2408
Brooklyn, NY 11231
Hours: 9-6 Mon-Fri   E-mail: mary@jerardstudio.com
www.jerardstudio.com
Custom backdrops, scenic painting, murals, decorative and faux finishes,
trompe l'oeil. Backpainted glass. Talk to Mary Therese Creede. Member
ATAC.

Warren Jorgenson 914-699-5054
219 Watchung Ter.   914-882-7676
Scotch Plains, NJ 07076   FAX 914-667-4100
Hours: by appt.   E-mail: warrenj@att.net
www.artistsguildusa.com
A guild of scenic artist for film, television and restaurant themes. Contact
Warren Jorgenson or their website for other information. All artists are
members United Scenic Artists, Local 829.

Danielle Leon / Faultless Faux 718-832-2743
PO Box 1285 (Murray Hill Station)   305-781-6349
NY, NY 10156
Hours: by appt.   E-mail: faultlessfaux@att.net
Specializing in faux finishes; also can create a period look on newer furniture.

JERRY L. MARSHALL, PROPS & TURNED OBJECTS 917-364-5015
415 W 55th St. # 3-A (9-10th Ave)
NY, NY 10019
Hours: by appt. only   E-mail: jlmars.nyc@mac.com
Broadway Propman, show supervision, shopping, fabrication and painting.
Member IATSE Local 1, United Scenic Artists Local 829. Member ATAC.

Jane Nelson Studios 212-431-4642
21 Howard St. (B'way-Lafayette St)
NY, NY 10013
Hours: by appt.   E-mail: janeynel@gmail.com
Custom painted backdrops, murals and sets. Rental stock available.
Member USA Local 829. RENTALS.

LINDA SKIPPER 212-864-3322
251 W 98th St. Apt 9B   (cell) 917-690-5812
NY, NY 10025   FAX 212-229-0935
Hours: by appt.   E-mail: linda@studio-etc.com
Scenic artist. Member ATAC.

Julie Sloane 917-604-4507
150 E 3rd St. #5E
NY, NY 10009
Hours: by appt.   E-mail: jbsloane@gmail.com
www.jsloanearts.com
Scenic painting, murals, antiquing. United Scenic Artist, Local 829.

Jessie Walker 212-675-7320
Hours: by appt   917-687-1042
Murals, faux and fantasy finishes, sculpture design. Member United Scenic
Local 829.

PROP & SCENIC CRAFTSPEOPLE: SCULPTURE

ABS Art Effects LLC 315-422-5825
110 Dorset Road
Syracuse, NY 13210
Hours: by appt.   E-mail: andrewbenepe@gmail.com
Custom sculpture in a wide range of materials for film, TV, stage and print;
any scale.

Acme Stimuli Design & Production .212-465-1071
889 Broadway
NY, NY 10001
Hours: by appt.

2640 Rt. 214   845-688-5107
Lanesville, NY 12450
Hours: by appt.
www.acmestimuli.com   E-mail: stimuli7@hvc.rr.com
Carved Styrofoam and most other media. Moldmaking; fiberglass;
vacuumform. Contact Marc Rubin.

Borem Studio 212-750-9066
231 E 50th St. # 2E (2nd & 3rd Aves)   917-334-4335
NY, NY 10022
Hours: by appt.   E-mail: hilda@inch.com
www.inch.com/~hilda
Creating environments, props and sculptures. They specialize in custom
fabrication, design and structural elements in a wide variety of materials for
film, TV, theatre and trade industries. Quick turnaround from a highly
experienced staff. Contact Hilda.

RANDY CARFAGNO PRODUCTIONS .212-947-0302
347 W 39th St. #7E (8-9th Ave)   FAX 212-947-2941
NY, NY 10018
Hours: by appt.   E-mail: randycarfagnoproductions@gmail.com
www.randycarfagnoproductions.com
Puppets, mascots, papier mache and vacuumform masks. All types of
character hats. Oversized puppets and shoes. Member SAG, ATAC.

Cimmelli, Inc. 845-735-2090
16 Walter St.   845-735-4693
Pearl River, NY 10965   FAX 845-735-1643
Hours: 8:30-5:30 Mon-Fri / Sat by appt.
www.cimmellisfx.com
Masks, sculpture, puppets, props, models, rigs and special effects. Large
variety of turntables available for rental use. Custom sculpture for any
application. RENTALS.

Costume Armour, Inc. 845-534-9120
PO Box 85, 2 Mill St.   FAX 845-534-8602
Cornwall, NY 12518
Hours: 8-4 Mon-Fri   E-mail: info@costumearmour.com
www.costumearmour.com
Sculpture, props, armor. RENTALS.

Daniel Oates 860-364-5775
25 Millerton Rd.   FAX 860-364-6008
Sharon, CT 06059
Hours: 10-7 Mon-Fri   E-mail: daniel@danieloates.com
www.danieloates.com
Sculptor, modelmaker, propmaker with 16 years experience in a large variety of materials. Virtual 3D renderingand modelmaking using Lightwave 3D.

Sal Denaro / Motion by Design 917-596-5537
335 Court St. # 28   212-560-2507
Brooklyn, NY 11231   FAX 718-228-4840
Hours: by appt.   E-mail: salmotion@yahoo.com
www.saldenaro.com
Puppet creator/designer and toy model sculptor; stop motion models, foam latex and mold-making.

Nicole Gaignat 860-798-6121
3948 59th St., # 2 (Roosevelt)
Woodside, NY 11377
Hours: By appt. only   E-mail: nicoleprops@gmail.com
www.coroflot.com/nicoleprops
Freelance artisan in fabrication or acquiring props for theatre and window display merchandising. Good skills from fake food to paper to softgoods. Prop Master, prop artisan and sculptor.

Elizabeth Goodall 212-645-9480
78 Bedford St. (Barrow)   FAX 212-645-7789
NY, NY 10014
Hours: by appt.   E-mail: lizgoodall@aol.com
Clay and foam sculpture including very small; 3-D illustration.

STOCKTON HALL 917-627-7847
615 E 14th St Apt 4B (B-C Ave)   (Agent) 212-255-3325
NY, NY 10009   FAX 212-217-2883
Hours: By Appt.   E-mail: stocktonhall@mac.com
www.stocktonhall.com / www.1plus1mgmt.com
Prop stylist, set designer, sculptor for fashion advertising and editorial, events, theatre, television and film. Represented by 1 Plus 1 Management. Member ATAC.

Yvette Helin Studio 718-389-8797
1205 Manhattan Ave., Unit 136 (New Town Creek)   Cell 917-617-5935
Brooklyn, NY 11222
Hours: 9-5 Mon-Fri, or by appt.   E-mail: yvette@yvettehelinstudio.com
www.yvettehelinstudio.com
Entertainment costume designer, maker. Specialty costumes.

JERARD STUDIO, INC. 718-852-4128
481 Van Brunt St., Ste. 11D (Beard St)   FAX 718-852-2408
Brooklyn, NY 11231
Hours: 9-6 Mon-Fri   E-mail: mary@jerardstudio.com
www.jerardstudio.com
Custom sculpture of all kinds, structural costumes and armatures, props and puppets. Talk to John Jerard. Member ATAC.

Gabriel Koren ....(studio) 718-625-1229
68 Jay St.   212-473-0891
Brooklyn, NY 11201
Hours: by appt.
Master sculptor. Life-sized figures in clay, plastiline, plaster, bronze.
Styrofoam carving for film, TV and theater. Member USA Local 829.

JERRY L. MARSHALL, PROPS & TURNED OBJECTS 917-364-5015
415 W 55th St. # 3-A (9-10th Ave)
NY, NY 10019
Hours: by appt. only   E-mail: jlmars.nyc@mac.com
Broadway Propman, show supervision, shopping, fabrication and painting.
Member IATSE Local 1, United Scenic Artists Local 829. Member ATAC.

Zoe Morsette 718-784-8894
43-01 21st St., Studio 224A   917-733-1731
Long Island City, NY 11101
Hours: by appt.
Rigid and soft sculpture for print, TV, film & stage. Also model railroad
scenery.

Carl Paolino Studios 917-957-7305
3801 23rd Ave.   917-282-4756
Astoria, NY 11105   FAX (same)
Hours: by appt. only   E-mail: cpseffects@aol.com
www.paolinostudios.com
Prosthetics, lifecasting, creature makeup. Speak to Carl.

Robin Lu Payne 720-810-2102
3305 W 98th Ave. Unit B
Westminister, CO 80031   E-mail: paynerl@aol.com
Prop craftsperson, sculptor.

BILL RYBAK / 3D DESIGN & FABRICATION 917-929-9124
59 South St.
Highland, NY 12528
Hours: by appt.   E-mail: billrybak@yahoo.com
www.billrybak.com
Custom design and fabrication of props, displays, showroom interiors,
models and sculpture. Digital props and models imaging.

Saldarini & Pucci, Inc. 718-852-1656
219 Westminister Rd. (Beverly Blvd)   FAX 718-852-1656
Brooklyn, NY 11218
Hours: 9-6 Mon-Fri   E-mail: paylessplastering@netscape.net
Casting, mold-making, Established in 1925. Flexible resins. Also Plastic
contracting and sculpting. No credit cards.

Catherine Schmitt 201-573-9150
7 Ethridge Pl.
Park Ridge, NJ 07656
Hours: by appt.   E-mail: cschmitt@schmittsculpture.com
www.schmittsculpture.com
Sculpture in clay, plaster, papier mache, etc. mold-making.

ATAC

JAMES SEFFENS 212-246-1453
405 W 44th St. (9-10th Ave)
New York, NY 10036
Hours: by appt.
www.jimseffens.com

E-mail: jim@jimseffens.com

Sculpture media - wood, paper-mache, plaster. Multiples and originals. Clay modeling and plaster molds. Masks, custom and studio collection. CREDIT CARDS. Member ATAC.

SPS EFFECTS, LLC / SUSAN PITOCCHI 917-519-5805
262 N 6th St., Apt 3
Brooklyn, NY 11211

96 Academy St.
Liberty, NY 12754
Hours: by appt.
www.spseffects.com

845-292-6942
FAX 845-292-6342
FAX 845-292-6342
E-mail: spitocchi@earthlink.net

Custom fabrication of props, costumes and sculptures in materials including foam, fabric, wood, leather, plastics and casting materials. Member IATSE Local 52. Member ATAC.

MARI TOBITA 212-254-8614
235 E 10th St., Apt 4D
NY, NY 10003
Hours: by appt.

(cell) 917-304-5280
FAX 212-254-8614
E-mail: maritobita@aol.com

Theatrical masks, puppets, wooden marionettes, sculpture, props and costume crafts. Member USA Local 829. Member ATAC.

PROP & SCENIC CRAFTSPEOPLE: SOFT GOODS

Anne Guay, Inc. 917-225-6550
689 Myrtle Ave. # 5-H (Spencer)
Brooklyn, NY 11205
Hours: By Appt.
www.anneguay.com

FAX 718-852-7589

E-mail: info@anneguay.com

Custom millinery, fashion accessories, costume crafts, soft goods for display, stage, print, TV and film. High-end draperies and fabric treatments. CREDIT CARDS.

CHRIS BOBIN 646-742-0630
347 Fifth Ave., Rm 1102 (34-35th St)
NY, NY 10016
Hours: by appt.
www.chrisbobin.com

917-683-5239

E-mail: chris@chrisbobin.com

Sewn solutions for props and illustrations; miniature and oversize-quilting, applique and embroidery. Member ATAC.

P

CINAF DESIGNS 212-501-9090
48 Fairway St.   917-796-4641
Bloomfield, NJ 07003   FAX 973-320-4493
Hours: by appt.   E-mail: cinaf@aol.com
www.cinafdesigns.com
Costume crafts, costume painting and distressing. Drapery and upholstery.
Props for puppets. Prop and model builder. Member IATSE Local 1, 829 &
Local 52. Member ATAC.

Contract Workroom / Janet Girard .718-782-6430
300 Morgan Ave. (Metropolitan-Grand St)   FAX 718-782-3805
Brooklyn, NY 11211
Hours: by appt.
Custom draperies, window treatments, upholstery, fabric tension structures;
quilting, soft sculpture, leather sculpture, fabric painting.

MARGARET CUSACK 718-237-0145
124 Hoyt St. (Dean St)   718-909-4402
Brooklyn, NY 11217   FAX 718-237-0145
Hours: by appt.   E-mail: cusackart@aol.com
www.margaretcusack.com
Unique stitched artwork, samplers, soft sculpture, quilted hangings, portraits
and props that have warmed up the images of clients from AT&T to Aunt
Millie's Spaghetti Sauce. Member ATAC.

Nicole Gaignat 860-798-6121
3948 59th St., # 2 (Roosevelt)
Woodside, NY 11377
Hours: By appt. only   E-mail: nicoleprops@gmail.com
www.coroflot.com/nicoleprops
Freelance artisan in fabrication or acquiring props for theatre and window
display merchandising. Good skills from fake food to paper to softgoods.
Prop Master, prop artisan and sculptor.

Louise Grafton 609-921-1919
229 Hartly Ave.
Princeton, NJ 08540
Hours: by appt.   E-mail: legraft@hotmail.com
Props, set and costume pieces, soft goods, circus and clown props. Also
upholstery done in her studio.

JUNG K. GRIFFIN 718-391-0009
4316 42nd St. #3R   (cell) 646-498-4251
Sunnyside, NY 11104   FAX 718-391-0009
Hours: by appt.   E-mail: jgriffin95@aol.com
Props artisan, sculpture, crafts, carpentry, soft goods, upholstery. Member
ATAC.

P

Yvette Helin Studio 718-389-8797
1205 Manhattan Ave., Unit 136 (New Town Creek)   Cell 917-617-5935
Brooklyn, NY 11222
Hours: 9-5 Mon-Fri, or by appt.   E-mail: yvette@yvettehelinstudio.com
www.yvettehelinstudio.com
Entertainment costume designer, maker. Specialty costumes.

MARIAN JEAN 'KILLER' HOSE, LLC 212-594-0990
307 W 38th St., Ste 1110 (8-9th Ave)   917-596-6405
NY, NY 10018   Fax 212-594-0990
Hours: by appt.   E-mail: oxoxkill@nyc.rr.com
www.myspace.com/oxoxkill
Custom costume crafts; sculptural wire framework, foam work, masks, millinery, wings, character costumes and soft goods. Member ATAC.

Martin Izquierdo Studio 212-807-9757
118 W 22nd St., 9th Fl. (6-7th Ave)   FAX 212-366-5249
NY, NY 10011
Hours: 9-7 Mon-Fri   E-mail: izquierdostudio@gmail.com
www.izquierdostudio.com
Full-service prop shop. Contact Jean Paul Nguyen.

AMANDA KLEIN 516-944-8447
3 Briarcliff Dr.   (cell) 516-606-6175
Port Washington, NY 11050   FAX 516-944-8447
Hours: by appt.   E-mail: amakle@optonline.net
Member USA Local 829, Costume Design. Soft goods. Member ATAC.

ARNOLD S. LEVINE, INC. 212-563-5830
555 Eighth Ave., Ste. # 2009 (37-38th St) FAX 212-563-5838
NY, NY 10018
Hours: 10-5:30 Mon-Fri / or by appt.   E-mail: aslevine@nyc.rr.com
www.asltheatricalmillinery.com
All types of soft goods for display, interiors and theatre. Member ATAC.

Zoe Morsette 718-784-8894
43-01 21st St., Studio 224A   917-733-1731
Long Island City, NY 11101
Hours: by appt.
Rigid and soft sculpture for print, TV, film and stage. Also model railroad scenery.

Ritta Bean Productions 646-361-8557
46-01 46th Ave. (5th Ave - Vernon Blvd)
Long Island City, NY 11101
Hours: by appt.   E-mail: rittabeanproductions@gmail.com
Specializing in custom fabricated interactive, portable, wearalble and functional props and accessories. Velcro, washable fabrics, durable construction, custom pattern, 3-D interactives.

Linda C. Schultz 212-222-0477
125 W 96th St. #6J (Columbus-Amsterdam Ave)
NY, NY 10025
Hours: by appt.
Soft goods (props), stylist.

Sally Thomas 718-797-4028
Brooklyn, NY 11201
Hours: by appt.   E-mail: sally@softworkstudio.com
www.softworkstudio.com
On-set sewing, costume construction and design. Miniature costumes for stop-motion, puppets and toys. Props and soft furnishings.

PROP RENTAL HOUSES

29th St. Marketplace / Chelsea Marketplace 212-594-8289
  245 W 29th St. (7-8th Ave)   FAX 212-967-6349
  NY, NY 10001
  Hours: 9-5:30 Mon-Fri / 9-12 Sat.   E-mail: info@chelseamarketplace.com
  www.chelseamarketplace.com
  A fine selection of table decor and accessories including candelabras,
  gazebos, specialty linens and containers for floral arrangements. Crystal,
  silver, gold and wrought iron. Visit website to view photos. RENTALS.
  CREDIT CARDS.

425 Enterprises Ltd. 516-223-4030
  200 E Sunrise Hwy. (Meadowbrook Pkwy)   516-223-0772
  Freeport, NY 11520   FAX 516-223-0348
  Hours: 9-5:30 Mon-Fri / 11-3:30 Sun   E-mail: info@beautyprops.com
  www.beautyprops.com
  A prop house specializing only in beauty/barber equipment and accessories.
  Barber chairs (1900s), flip top dryers (1960s), futuristic shampoo bowls for the
  year 2010. See Scot. RENTALS. CREDIT CARDS.

American ReSource Medical 201-833-1550
  324 W Englewood Ave.   973-742-6622
  Teaneck, NJ 07666   FAX 201-833-1575
  Hours: 9-5 Mon-Fri

  463 Grand St.   973-742-6622
  Patterson, NJ 07505
  Hours: 9-5 Mon-Fri   E-mail: arme@optonline.ne
  One of the largest inventory of medical props outside Los Angeles. Extensive
  experience in all areas of the field. RENTALS.

Anything But Costumes 908-788-1727
  111 Mine St.   FAX 908-237-1158
  Flemington, NJ 08822
  Hours: daily by appt.   E-mail: anythingbutcostumes@earthlink.net
  www.anythingbutcostumes.com
  Hand props, chandeliers, rugs, furniture. Will fax or e-mail photos. Deliveries
  available. RENTALS.

Arenson Prop Center 212-564-8383
  396 Tenth Ave. (31st-33rd St)   FAX 212-947-4856
  NY, NY 10001
  Hours: 9-5 Mon-Fri / or by appt.
  www.aof.com
  A full-service prop rental house with fine quality furniture for every room in
  the home as well as office. Lighting and accessories too. Buying service
  available. RENTALS. CREDIT CARDS.

P

Art & Industrial Design 212-477-0116
50 Great Jones St. (4th Ave)   FAX 212-477-1420
NY, NY 10012
Hours: 10-5 Mon-Fri / 10-1 Sat   E-mail: info@aid20c.com
www.aid20c.com
20th-century designer and art deco furniture for all settings. RENTALS.
CREDIT CARDS.

Bergen Office Furniture 212-366-6677
127 W 26th St. (6-7th Ave)   FAX 212-366-5779
NY, NY 10001
Hours: 9-5 Mon-Fri   E-mail: bergenup@aol.com
www.bergenofficefurniture.com
Specialize in vintage office furniture from 1920s-60s and contemporary office
furniture. Also has a furniture refinishing, upholstering and paint shop. Ask
for Ira. RENTALS.

Braswell Galleries 203-327-5101
1 Muller Ave.   203-357-0753
Norwalk, CT 06851   FAX 203-846-0617
Hours: 10:30-5 Mon-Sat / 11-5 Sun   E-mail: kathy@braswellgalleries.com
www.braswellgalleries.com
Wide range of furniture and furnishings, paintings, chandeliers, lighting,
artwork, glassware and china. Rugs from many time periods and also unique
items such as a x-ray machine from 1930-50. Animal heads, rowing scull and
more. Rentals as well as sales at very reasonable prices. RENTALS.

Bridge Furniture & Props 718-916-9706
126 Lombardy St., 2nd FL (Lompardy-Porter)   FAX 718-663-7130
Brooklyn, NY 11222
Hours: 8:30-5 Mon-Fri or by appt.   E-mail: matt@bridgeprops.com
www.bridgeprops.com
Modern and traditional furniture, lighting, decorative accessories and area
rugs. All items are photographed and indexed on their website. Speak to
Matt. RENTALS. CREDIT CARDS.

E. Buk, Antiques & Art 212-226-6891
151 Spring St., 2nd Fl. (Wooster-W.B'way)
NY, NY 10012
Hours: by appt.
www.ebuk.com
Specializing in mechanics, science and early technologies from late 18th to
20th century. Telescopes, globes, nautical, medical, scientific, industrial
objects, lighting and furniture. RENTALS.

Cinema World Studios 718-389-9800
220 Dupont St. (Provost)   FAX 718-389-9897
Greenpoint, NY 11122
Hours: 9-7 Mon-Fri by appt.   E-mail: cinemaworldfd@verizon.net
www.cinemaworldstudios.com
Complete medical equipment and consultation. RENTALS.

P

Computer Rent, Inc. 212-619-6363
225 Broadway (Barclay St)   800-872-2983
NY, NY 10007   FAX 212-619-6844
Hours: 9-6 Mon-Fri   E-mail: rentapcnow@aol.com
Computers, printers in all shapes and sizes; working or props. Can do custom configurations from large inventory. Rental of LCD panels, plasma screens, projectors. Willing to work with customers. RENTALS. CREDIT CARDS.

Concept Design Productions 626-932-0082
718 S. Primrose Ave.   800-846-0717
Monrovia, CA 91016   FAX 626-932-0072
Hours: 9-6 Mon-Fri   E-mail: info@conceptdesigninc.com
www.conceptdesigninc.com
Rental house for structural systems, props and scenic elements. Full sets and support services available. Check out their website for full listings. Also custom-built items. See James Leverton. RENTALS.

Cosmo Modern 718-302-4662
314 Wythe Ave. (Grand-S 1st)
Brooklyn, NY 11211
Hours: 11-6 Mon-Sun   E-mail: cosmomodern@mac.com
www.cosmomodern.com
Rental and sales of Mid Century modern and early 20th Century industrial furniture and lighting. Located in a 2,000 sq. ft. old industrial space, a unique location for photo and film shoots. Space is also for rent. Part prop shop, location and retail space. RENTALS. CREDIT CARDS.

Decorator Depot 914-771-7720
291 Tuckahoe Rd. (Suffolk - Clinton St)   716-908-9544
Yonkers, NY 10710
Hours: 8-4 Mon-Fri / or by appt.   E-mail: decoratordepot@gmail.com
www.thedecoratordepot.com
A full service prop rental house. Large collection of modern and antique furnishings, office furniture, decorative accessories, bulk paperwork and cleared art. Sales and RENTALS. CREDIT CARDS.

Early Halloween 212-691-2933
130 W 25th St., 11th Fl. (6-7th Ave)   FAX 212-243-1499
NY, NY 10001
Hours: by appt. only   E-mail: earlyhalloween@aol.com
www.earlyhalloween.com
Vintage luggage and memorabilia. Also vintage clothing, hats, shoes and accessories. RENTAL only.

Eclectic / Encore Properties, Inc. 212-645-8880
620 W 26th St., 4th Fl. (11-12th Ave)   FAX 212-243-6508
NY, NY 10001
Hours: 9-5 Mon-Fri / or by appt.   E-mail: props@eclecticprops.com
www.eclecticprops.com
A large and interesting collection. Many antiques and "character" items. A full-service prop rental company. Can request rental items thru online catalog. RENTALS. CREDIT CARDS.

P

Frankies Carnival Time 877-937-2652
   3437 E Tremont Ave. (Bruckner Blvd)   718-823-3033
   Bronx, NY 10465   FAX 718-824-2979
   Hours: 9-6 Mon-Sat / until 7 Fri / 9-3 Sun   E-mail: frankiebe@aol.com
   www.frankiescarnival.com
   Carnival games, booths, carts, fun house mirrors, inflatable rides, dunk tanks
   and bingo supplies. Hot dog carts, Cotton Candy and Popcorn machines.
   Tents, chairs, tables, etc. RENTALS. CREDIT CARDS.

Furniture Rental Associates 212-868-0300
   148 Madison Ave.   800-633-3748
   NY, NY 10016   FAX 212-594-5415
   Hours: 9-6 Mon-Fri or by appt.   E-mail: frarents@aol.com
   www.frarents.com
   Traditional, contemporary, modern and computer office furniture. Contact
   Randie Greenberg. RENTALS. CREDIT CARDS.

Gonzo Bros. 310-828-4989
   2834 Colorado Ave # 34   FAX 310-455-3360
   Santa Monica, CA 90404
   Hours: 9-6 Mon-Fri (PST)
   www.gonzobrothers.com
   2-D Flat People: audience cut-outs for crowd scenes. No credit cards.
   RENTALS.

Greenroom 212-625-1818
   270 Lafayette St., Ste. # 1303 (Prince-Houston)   FAX 212-219-9994
   NY, NY 10012
   Hours: by appt.   E-mail: jill@yourgreenroom.com
   www.yourgreenroom.com
   High-end furniture rental company that specializes in client greenrooms /
   lounge areas for commercial, film and television productions, and special
   events. They handle delivery, setup and design for clients. RENTALS.

The Hand Prop Room LP 323-931-1534
   5700 Venice Blvd. (Venice & Curson)   FAX 323-931-2145
   Los Angeles, CA 90019
   Hours: 7-7 Mon-Fri   E-mail: info@hpr.com
   www.hpr.com
   Full printing and graphics service; newspapers, license plates, IDs, "Greeked"
   product labels. CREDIT CARDS.

Howard's Visual Merchandise 978-768-7131
   165 Eastern Ave.   FAX 978-768-6386
   Essex, MA 01929
   Hours: by appt.   E-mail: info@howardsvm.com
   www.howardsvm.com
   Providing decor to theme restaurants, retail stores, the film industry, and
   amusement parks since 1981. Nautical, hunting, fishing, vintage sporting
   equipment, musical instruments etc. Large stock allows for multiples on
   many items. RENTALS. CREDIT CARDS.

P

 **PROP RENTAL HOUSES**

Katonah Image, Inc. 914-232-0961
  22 Woodsbridge Rd.   FAX 914-232-3944
  Katonah, NY 10536
  Hours: 9-6 Mon-Fri / 9-5 Sat
  Antiques, memorabilia and collectibles for rent or sale. RENTALS. CREDIT CARDS.

The Metropolitan Prop House 646-421-5128
  44-01 Eleventh St. (44th Rd)   FAX 718-392-8435
  Long Island City, NY 11101
  Hours: 9-6 Mon-Fri   E-mail: rental@metropolitanprops.com
  www.metropolitanprops.com
  European classic & modern furniture. Carpets, objects, distressed furniture, antiques, fabric, curtains, pillows, lamps, chandeliers, bikes and wooden ladders. RENTALS.

modprop 212-628-7582
  1044 Madison Ave. (79-80th St)
  NY, NY 10021
  Hours: 9-5 Mon-Fri   E-mail: info@modprop.com
  www.modprop.com
  Modern funiture prop rental house. Specializing in contemporary furniture, they rent anything from vintage automobiles, shooting locations to plates and glasses. Wide selections in superior condition. Speak to Stephen. RENTALS. CREDIT CARDS.

Paper Props Provider Co. 973-614-1170
  101 7th St.   973-485-1828
  Passaic, NJ 07055   FAX 973-614-1130
  Hours: 8-4 Mon-Fri
  www.advancepaper.net
  Rents generic office paper for props. Contact Jim DeMarco.

PM Amusements 914-937-1188
  36 Bush Ave.   FAX 914-939-8189
  Port Chester, NY 10573
  Hours: 9-5 Mon-Fri / 10-3 Sat
  www.pmamusements.com
  All types of amusement park and circus games, food booths. Including the popular Sumo Wrestlers, dunk machines, casino equipment, props and decor. RENTALS. CREDIT CARDS.

The Prop Company / Kaplan and Associates 212-691-7767
  111 W 19th St., 8th Fl. (6-7th Ave)   FAX 212-727-3055
  NY, NY 10011
  Hours: 9-5 Mon-Fri   E-mail: propcompany@yahoo.com
  Contemporary tabletop, decorative accessories, antiques, ephemera and furniture. A nice collection of linens. See Maxine Kaplan. RENTALS.

P

Prop Haus 646-638-9330
   147 W 25th St., 2nd Fl.   FAX 646-638-9329
   NY, NY 10001
   Hours: 9-5:30 Mon-Fri   E-mail: prophaus@verizon.net
   www.prophaus.net
   Prop rental house with loads of table-top items. China, glass, etc. Also
   antique luggage and bric-a-brac. Antique dining tables and chairs, and linens.
   RENTALS. CREDIT CARDS.

Props for Today 212-244-9600
   330 W 34th St. (8-9th Ave)   FAX 212-244-1053
   NY, NY 10001
   Hours: 8:30-5 Mon-Fri   E-mail: info@propsfortoday.com
   www.propsfortoday.com
   Full-service prop rental house with new and antique office furniture,
   accessories and general dressing. Bulk mail and file paper. RENTALS. CREDIT
   CARDS.

Props NYC 718-624-0842
   63 Flushing Ave, Unit 342 (Brooklyn Naval Yard)   FAX 718-624-0844
   Brooklyn, NY 11205
   Hours: 8-5 Mon-Fri   E-mail: info@gotprops.com
   www.gotprops.com
   Prop rental with mostly reproduction furniture and accessories. RENTALS.

Rent A Thing 845-628-9298
   Rt 6, Box 337   FAX 845-628-0390
   Baldwin Place, NY 10505
   Hours: 24 hours / leave message, will return call
   Props, costumes and antique cars and boats. Also many interesting sites for
   locating filming. Will help locate items. RENTALS.

RentQuest 212-243-4291
   568 Broadway Ste 507 (Prince)   FAX: 212-966-3295
   NY, NY 10012
   Hours: 9-6 Mon-Fri   E-mail: info@rentquestnyc.com
   www.rentquestnyc.com
   Full-service rental house offering a selection of custom made, high end
   lounge furniture, lighting, bars and other accessories essential to a successful
   event. They are able to customize their inventory to fit your needs. AMEX.
   RENTALS.

Ruth Fischl . . . . .Linens 212-273-9710
   141 W 28th St. (6-7th Ave)   Hardgoods 212-967-2493
   NY, NY 10001   FAX 212-273-9718
   Hours: 9-5 Mon-Thurs / 9-3 Fri   E-mail: ruthfischl@hotmail.com
   www.ruthfischl.com
   Excellent selection of rental linens, iron works, tables, candelabras, etc.
   Purchase available. Open to trade by appointment. RENTALS.

P

Showman Fabricators 718-935-9899
47-22 Pearson Place (Hamilton Ave-Bowne St)   FAX 718-855-9823
Long Island City, NY 11101
Hours: 7-5:30 Mon-Fri   E-mail: info@showfab.com
www.showfab.com
Showman stocks a wide array of scenic elements, backdrops and staging in its 40,000-sq ft warehouse. Great selection of Drapery, Airline seats and cockpits. Visit website to view most rental items.

State Supply Equipment & Props, Inc. 212-663-2300
1361 Amsterdam Ave. (126-128th St)   FAX 212-663-3802
NY, NY 10027
Hours: 8:30-5 Mon-Fri
www.statesupplyprops.com
Good source for many items, including coolers, canvas folding chairs, lockers, sterno, lamp oil, props, etc.; large stock. The ion set prop" shop.

Taylor Creative, Inc. 646-336-6808
150 W 28th St., Ste. 1001 (6-7th Aves)   888-245-4044
NY, NY 10001   FAX 646-336-6810
Hours: 9:30-5:30 Mon-Fri   E-mail: info@taylorcreativeinc.com
www.taylorcreativeinc.com
Prop rental company specializing in modern furniture. Their rentals are ideal for green rooms, photo shoots, product launches, press events and traveling tours. They also handle event productions from start to finish. RENTALS. CREDIT CARDS.

Toaster Central 212-744-3773
1427 York Ave. (76th St)
NY, NY 10021
Hours: by appt.   E-mail: pop@toastercentral.com
www.toastercentral.com
Working vintage toasters, small appliances, coffee pots, etc. from 1920 to present day. Great website, very helpful. Speak to Michael Sheafe. RENTALS. AMEX.

Ugly Luggage 718-384-0724
214 Bedford Ave.
Brooklyn, NY 11211
Hours: 1-8 Mon-Fri / 12-7 Sat-Sun (Call first, hours can vary)
www.uglyluggage.com
Antiques, furniture, collectibles and clothing. Ask for Jim Lanning. RENTALS. CREDIT CARDS.

P

PUPPETS & PUPPETRY

3-Design Studio, Inc. 212-627-1010
32 Leroy St.
NY, NY 10014
Hours: by appt.
Puppets for television and film, special effects, toy design and illustration.

ABS Art Effects LLC 315-422-5825
110 Dorset Road
Syracuse, NY 13210
Hours: by appt.   E-mail: andrewbenepe@gmail.com
Custom design, fabrication, rigging and articulation of live action puppets
and props for film, television and stage; any scale.

Anney Fresh Productions 917-838-3519
27 Olive St., # 8
Brooklyn, NY 11211
Hours: by appt.   E-mail: anney@anneyfresh.com
www.anneyfresh.com
Design and construction of puppets, costume characters, and props. Union
and non-union performer staffing and puppet wrangling.

RANDY CARFAGNO PRODUCTIONS .212-947-0302
347 W 39th St. #7E (8-9th Ave)   FAX 212-947-2941
NY, NY 10018
Hours: by appt.   E-mail: randycarfagnoproductions@gmail.com
www.randycarfagnoproductions.com
Professional puppeteer (SAG) for TV, film and stage. Puppet mascot building,
all types. Masks, sculpting, latex shoes, mold making, foam and wood
carving. Carved and patterned foam, fleece, furs, celastic, carved, jointed
wood marionettes.   Member ATAC.

Edward Christie 508-487-9457
7 Resolution Rd. / P.O. Box 472   646-483-7416
Truro, MA 02666   FAX same
Hours: by appt.   E-mail: egchristie@aol.com
Character design for puppets and mascots for TV, theater, film, commercial
and industrial.

Cimmelli, Inc. 845-735-2090
16 Walter St.   845-735-4693
Pearl River, NY 10965   FAX 845-735-1643
Hours: 8:30-5:30 Mon-Fri / Sat by appt.
www.cimmellisfx.com
Masks, sculpture, puppets, props, models, rigs and special effects. Large
variety of turntables available for rental use.   Custom sculpture for any
application. RENTALS.

Costumes and Creatures 612-378-2561
504 Malcolm Ave. SE, Ste. 200   FAX 612-378-2635
Minneapolis, MN 55414
Hours: 8-4:45 CST   E-mail: info@vee.com
www.vee.com
A division of VEE Corp., producer of Sesame Street Live Tours; specializing in
full body character and animal costumes; period garments, accessories, soft
props. Custom design and construction.

P

Daniel Oates 860-364-5775
   25 Millerton Rd.   FAX 860-364-6008
   Sharon, CT 06059
   Hours: 10-7 Mon-Fri   E-mail: daniel@danieloates.com
   www.danieloates.com
   Sculptor, modelmaker, propmaker with 16 years experience in a large variety
   of materials. Virtual 3D renderingand modelmaking using Lightwave 3D.

Sal Denaro / Motion by Design 917-596-5537
   335 Court St. # 28   212-560-2507
   Brooklyn, NY 11231   FAX 718-228-4840
   Hours: by appt.   E-mail: salmotion@yahoo.com
   www.saldenaro.com
   Puppet creator/designer and toy model sculptor; stop motion models, foam
   latex and mold-making.

Flexitoon Alliance 212-877-2757
   46 W 73rd St. #3A (CPW-Columbus Ave)
   NY, NY 10023
   Hours: by appt.   E-mail: craigmarin@flexitoon.com
   www.flexitoon.com
   Creators of flexible cartoon puppets. Speak to Craig Marin.

Dan Folkus/Visual Syntax Productions 856-939-3116
   91 Harding Ave.
   Runnemede, NJ 08078
   Hours: 9-6 Mon-Fri   E-mail: folkus@visual-syntax.com
   www.visual-syntax.com
   Murals, models, sculpture, props, puppets, exhibit design. Computer
   graphics.

Geppetto, Inc. 718-398-9792
   201 46th St. 2nd FL   FAX 718-622-2991
   Brooklyn, NY 11220
   Hours: 9-5 Mon-Fri   E-mail: gepstudios@aol.com
   www.geppettostudios.com
   Custom construction of soft sculpture puppets and character costumes,
   oversized foam props and window displays. Contact Scott; brochure
   available.

DEBORAH GLASSBERG 973-429-2904
   53 Spring St.   (cell) 973-930-4878
   Bloomfield, NJ 07003
   Hours: please callE-mail: debglassberg@earthlink.net / deb.glassberg@gmail.com
   www.flickr.com/photos/debglassberg
   Puppets, props and costume elements design and fabrication; many types:
   carved, cast, foam, masks, wire, wood, leather, reed. Scenic sculpture, props,
   models, soft goods. Also repairs and rebuilds. Member ATAC.

Yvette Helin Studio 718-389-8797
   1205 Manhattan Ave., Unit 136 (New Town Creek)   Cell 917-617-5935
   Brooklyn, NY 11222
   Hours: 9-5 Mon-Fri, or by appt.   E-mail: yvette@yvettehelinstudio.com
   www.yvettehelinstudio.com
   Entertainment costume designer, maker. Specialty costumes.

P

Hudson Vagabond Puppets 845-359-1006
PO Box 131   FAX 845-359-1008
Blauvelt, NY 10913
Hours: by appt.   E-mail: hvpuppets@prodigy.net
www.hvpuppets.org
Perform musicals with life-sized and oversized puppets for children's education programs. Less building of puppets.

JERARD STUDIO, INC. 718-852-4128
481 Van Brunt St., Ste. 11D (Beard St)   FAX 718-852-2408
Brooklyn, NY 11231
Hours: 9-6 Mon-Fri   E-mail: mary@jerardstudio.com
www.jerardstudio.com
Puppets and puppetry, structural costumes, masks and mechanics. Action props and engineering. Live action animation and animatronics. Member ATAC.

Ralph Lee 212-929-4777
55 Bethune St. # D405 (Bethune-Washington)
NY, NY 10014
Hours: by appt.   E-mail: info@mettawee.org
www.mettawee.org
Masks, larger-than-life puppets and costumes; wide range of materials.

JENNIE MARINO / MOONBOOTS PRODUCTIONS, INC. 845-359-6262
44 Slocum Ave.   Cell 845-642-0158
Tappan, NY 10983   FAX 845-680-6124
Hours: by appt.   E-mail: jenfx@aol.com
Hand, rod, mechanical and full body puppet design and fabriction. Also puppeteers and rents puppets. Member ATAC.

MULDER / MARTIN, INC. 610-807-9887
1606 Woodfield Dr.
Bethlehem, PA 18015
Hours: 8-6 Mon-Fri   E-mail: foam@rcn.com
Speciality costumes for theatre, opera, TV, industrials, sports and promotional events. The same reasonable and reliable service you have known for over 20 years. No rentals. Member ATAC.

Carl Paolino Studios 917-957-7305
3801 23rd Ave.   917-282-4756
Astoria, NY 11105   FAX (same)
Hours: by appt. only   E-mail: cpseffects@aol.com
www.paolinostudios.com
Mechanical & radio control puppets.

Paragon Props 866-859-5059
2342 Wyecroft Rd., Unite G-1   905-469-0061
Oakville, Ontario, Canada L6L 5N2   FAX 905-469-0062
Hours: 8-4:30 Mon-Fri   E-mail: sdiamond@paragonprops.com
www.paragonprops.com
Props, masks, puppets, special effects, etc. Visit website for photos.

P

Poko Puppets 860-342-2461
192 Thompson Hill Rd. (McDonald)   FAX 860-342-4642
Portland, CT 06480
Hours: by appt.   E-mail: info@pokopuppets.com
www.pokopuppets.com or www.puppetstuff.com
Puppets/props custom designed and created. Performances for commercials,
industrials and live shows. Larry Engler, Artistic Director. Workshops. See
website for other goodies. RENTALS. Paypal CREDIT CARDS.

Puppet Heap 201-222-1014
720 Monroe St. # C-202 (8th - Monroe)   201-683-7063
Hoboken, NJ 07030   FAX 201-222-0377
Hours: 10-7 Mon-Fri   E-mail: feedbag@puppetheap.com
www.puppetheap.com
Costumes, props and of course puppets. Whether in film, television, theater
or live events.

The Puppet People 518-393-2268
1236 Waverly Pl.
Schenectady, NY 12308
Hours: by appt.   E-mail: info@thepuppetpeople.org
www.thepuppetpeople.org
Custom or package shows; commercials, industrials; body puppet, marionette
construction.

The Puppet Works, Inc. 718-965-3391
338 Sixth Ave. (4th St)
Brooklyn, NY 11215
Hours: 9:30-3:30 daily   E-mail: puppetworks@verizon.net
www.puppetworks.org
Creates shows for touring schools; industrials, film, TV and workshops.
Primarily marionettes; theater on-site. Nicholas Coppola, Director. Check
website for performance schedules.

JODY SCHOFFNER 818-992-6574
24118 Philiprimm St.   (cell) 818-421-1736
Woodland Hills, CA 91367
Hours: by appt.   E-mail: sjodye@earthlink.net
Draper and puppet maker. Member ATAC.

LISA SHAFTEL / SHAFTEL S2DO .508-879-7772
24 Warren Rd.   (Cell) 617-755-1240
Framingham, MA 01702   FAX (same)
Hours: 9-6 Mon-Fri   E-mail: shaftels2do@verizon.net
www.s2do.com
Scenic designer and scenic artist, art direction, illustration, storyboards,
character design, CAD drafting and Photoshop. Puppet design and
fabrication, prop fabrication no rentals. Member USA Local 829, IATSE Local
481, and the Graphic Artist Guild. Member ATAC.

Manju Shandler Design 917-826-3588
Hours: by appt.   E-mail: manju@nyc.rr.com
www.manjushandler.com
Specializing in costume design and building of foam sculptured costumes,
puppets, masks and props.

MARI TOBITA 212-254-8614
   235 E 10th St., Apt 4D   (cell) 917-304-5280
   NY, NY 10003   FAX 212-254-8614
   Hours: by appt.   E-mail: maritobita@aol.com
Theatrical masks, puppets, wooden marionettes, sculpture, props and
costume crafts. Member USA Local 829. Member ATAC.

Vitoworld Productions 347-418-8622
   2268 28th St. # 2R
   Astoria, NY 11105
   Hours: by appt.   E-mail: vitoworld@yahoo.com
   www.vitoworldproductions.com
Puppets, mascot/character costumes, stilt walker costumes, large fantasy
type costumes and props.

P

QUILTS

The City Quilter 212-807-0390
133 W 25th St. (6-7th Ave)   FAX 212-807-9451
NY, NY 10001
Hours: 11-7 Tue-Fri / 10-6 Sat / 11-5 Sun   E-mail: info@cityquilter.com
www.cityquilter.com
Quilt making supplies, more than 2000 bolts of 100% cotton fabrics, batting,
etc. Books and classes. CREDIT CARDS.

Laura Fisher/ Antique Quilts & Americana 212-838-2596
305 E 61st St. (2nd Ave)   FAX 212-355-4403
NY, NY 10021
Hours: 11-4:30 Mon-Fri / or by appt.
www.laurafisherquilts.com
Quilts, American textiles, hooked rugs. Visit website for available stock.
RENTALS. CREDIT CARDS.

The Gazebo 770-632-7756
1427 Barberry Lane   800-998-7077
Peachtree City , GA 30269
Hours: 10-6 Mon-Sat   E-mail: response@thegazebo.com
www.thegazebo.com
Quilts, wicker furniture, rag rugs, pillows and country home furnishings;
Expensive. Customized handcrafted quilts. CREDIT CARDS.

Mike & Misha Pillow & Quilts, Inc. 212-260-7270
133 W 25th St. # 2W (6-7th Ave)
NY, NY 10001
Hours: By appt. only
Makes pillows and cushions.

Judith & James Milne, Inc. 212-472-0107
506 E 74th St., 2nd Fl. (York Ave)   FAX 212-472-1481
NY, NY 10021
Hours: 9:30-5:30 Mon-Fri / and by appt.   E-mail: milneinc@aol.com
www.milneantiques.com
Beautiful quilts; sales & rental; specializing in American country antiques.
RENTALS. CREDIT CARDS.

The Prop Company / Kaplan and Associates 212-691-7767
111 W 19th St., 8th Fl. (6-7th Ave)   FAX 212-727-3055
NY, NY 10011
Hours: 9-5 Mon-Fri   E-mail: propcompany@yahoo.com
Prop rental house with antique and vintage quilts and linens. RENTALS.

Q-R

Reproduction Fabrics.com 406-586-1775
205 Haggerty Ln., Ste. 190   800-380-4611
Bozeman, MT 59715   FAX 406-586-8847
Hours: 12-3 Mon-Fri / or by appt.   E-mail: staff@reproductionfabrics.com
www.reproductionfabrics.com
Excellent source for authentic reproduction cotton fabrics from 1775 to 1950;
including authentic linens, toiles, and feedsacks. Friendly staff will assist you
in your selections. Swatches available upon request. CREDIT CARDS.

Woodard & Greenstein 212-988-2906
506 E 74th St., 5th Fl. (York Ave)   800-332-7847
NY, NY 10021   FAX 212-734-9665
Hours: 10:30-6 Mon-Fri / Sat by appt.
www.woodardweave.com
Emphasis on quilts made between 1800-1940. Also has repro American rag rugs and some vintage outdoor furniture including cast-iron benches and urns. RENTALS. CREDIT CARDS.

Yellow Shed Antiques 845-628-0362
PO Box 706, 571 Rt 6   FAX 845-628-2777
Mahopac, NY 10541
Hours: 10-5 Wed-Sun
Lovely selection of antique & vintage quilts. RENTALS. CREDIT CARDS.

Q-R

RATTAN, REED, RAFFIA, WILLOW & BAMBOO

Bamboo & Rattan Works, Inc. 732-370-0220
470 Oberlin Ave. S   FAX 732-905-8386
Lakewood, NJ 08701
Hours: 8:30-4 Mon-Fri   E-mail: bambooman1@aol.com
www.bambooandrattan.com
Wholesale rattan, matting, bamboo and caning. CREDIT CARDS.

William Cahill / Roof Thatching & Bamboo 513-772-4974
PO Box 62054   FAX 513-772-6313
Cincinnati, OH 45262
Hours: by appt.   E-mail: info@roofthatch.com
www.roofthatch.com
*Specializing in custom roof thatching for interior and exterior themes and
displays. Bamboo and Eucalyptus poles.*

Charles H. Demarest, Inc. 973-492-1414
PO Box 238   FAX 973-838-6538
Bloomingdale, NJ 07403
Hours: 9-5 Mon-Fri   E-mail: demaralon@aol.com
www.tonkincane.com
Bamboo poles, decorative matting, raffia.

Corner House Antiques 413-229-6627
599 Sheffield Plain Rd., Rt 7   FAX 413-229-6627
Sheffield, MA 01257
Hours: open most days 10-5 (call first)
www.americanantiquewicker.com   E-mail: tetro@americanantiquewicker.com
*Specializes in antique wicker furniture. Also general selection of antiques
and country accessories including bamboo. See Kathleen or Thomas Tetro.
RENTALS.*

Frank's Cane and Rush Supply 714-847-0707
7252 Heil Ave. (Gothard St)   FAX 714-843-5645
Huntington Beach, CA 92647
Hours: 8-4 Mon-Fri   E-mail: mfrank@franksupply.com
www.franksupply.com
*Retail and wholesale caning and basketry supplies; huge stock. Products can
be viewed online. Will ship UPS/CODs fast. CREDIT CARDS.*

Inter-Mares Trading Co., Inc. 631-957-3467
PO Box 617, 1064 Rt.109 (Wellwood Ave)   800-229-2263
Lindenhurst, NY 11757   FAX 631-957-1005
Hours: 9-5 Mon-Fri   E-mail: canefish@aol.com
www.canefish.com
*Distributors of rattan, bamboo poles, thatching, reed, cane; full rolls, bales;
also natural grass skirts. Some brochures. Will ship. CREDIT CARDS.*

Peerless Rattan 877-611-2263
687 Miller Rd.
Plainwell, MI 49080
Hours: 9-5 Mon-Fri   E-mail: sales@peerlessrattan.com
www.peerlessrattan.com
Rattan, reed and caning supplies. Catalog.

Q-R

RECORDS, TAPES & CDs

H.H. Perkins, Inc. 203-787-1123
222 Universal Dr. South   800-462-6660
North Haven, CT 06473   FAX 203-787-1161
Hours: 9-5 Mon-Fri / 9-12 Sat   E-mail: caryl@hhperkins.com
www.hhperkins.com
Basketry, home decor products, baskets and bamboo. Seat weaving
supplies; catalog, will ship worldwide UPS/COD. CREDIT CARDS.

RECORDS, TAPES & CDs

Colony Records 212-265-2050
1619 Broadway (49th St)   FAX 212-956-6009
NY, NY 10019
Hours: 9:30-1am Mon-Sat / 10-midnight Sun   E-mail: colony1@aol.com
www.colonymusic.com
Large selection of sheet music, records, CDs; will ship anywhere. Out-of-print
LPs, nostalgia, movie, Broadway posters, rock-related toys and autographs.
Best selection of Karaoke music in Manhattan. CREDIT CARDS.

F.y.e. / for your entertainment 800-818-1941
5717 Myrtle Ave.   718-366-0204
Ridgewood, NY 11385
www.fye.com
Full line of CDs, videos and DVDs, videogames, PSP Movies and much more.
Visit website for other locations. CREDIT CARDS.

Footlight Records 888-627-3993
P.O. Box 496
Georgetown, CT 06829
Hours: 12-5 Sun-Fri   E-mail: info@footlight.com
www.footlight.com
Out-of-print, Broadway, film soundtracks, jazz, rock. Bought and sold. Internet
store only! $10 minimum order. CREDIT CARDS.

House of Oldies 212-243-0500
35 Carmine St. (6th Ave-Bleecker St)   FAX 212-989-1697
NY, NY 10014
Hours: 10-5 Tue-Sat   E-mail: rabramson@houseofoldies.com
www.houseofoldies.com
Large selection of rock ën' roll, 45s, 78s, 33s and beyond: catalog available.
CREDIT CARDS.

Tower Records . . . . .NONE
Internet orders only
Hours: 24-hr. Web Orders
www.tower.com
Good selection; extensive classical, jazz, soundtrack, original casts, electronic,
foreign, popular, 45s, tape and video. Internet only. CREDIT CARDS.

RELIGIOUS GOODS

American Bible Society Bookstore 212-408-1200
1865 Broadway (61st St)   866-895-4448
NY, NY 10023   FAX 212-408-1264
Hours: 11-7 Mon-Fri   E-mail: info@americanbible.org
www.americanbible.org
King James Bibles. Foreign languages. Music, CDs, scholarly materials,
children's books.

Carol J. Phipps 812-265-2124
2246 Shawnee Dr. #1
Madison, IN 47250
Hours: by appt.   E-mail: cjphipps_servo@msn.com
www.caroljphipps.com
Original artwork and photography designed and produced celebrating the
arts and the Creator. RENTALS.

Eclectic / Encore Properties, Inc. 212-645-8880
620 W 26th St., 4th Fl. (11-12th Ave)   FAX 212-243-6508
NY, NY 10001
Hours: 9-5 Mon-Fri / or by appt.   E-mail: props@eclecticprops.com
www.eclecticprops.com
History for rent. Selection of older styles and the unusual. Can request rental
items thru online catalog. RENTALS. CREDIT CARDS.

Holy Land Art Co., Inc. 201-666-6604
12 Sullivan St.   800-334-3621
Westwood, NJ 07675   FAX: 201-666-6069
Hours: 8-5:30 Mon-Fri   E-mail: info@holylandartcompany.com
www.holylandartcompany.com
Clerical clothing, vestment materials. Church furnishings, altar furniture,
pews, benches, statues, candlesticks, etc. Shop online. CREDIT CARDS.

Patrick Baker & Sons 860-628-5566
1650 West St.   FAX 860-620-1671
Southington, CT 06489
Hours: 9:30-5:30 Mon-Fri / 10-3 Sat   E-mail: dkowalik@patrickbaker.com
www.churchgoods.com
Religious supplies, church furnishings, candle supplies and church renovation
advice. CREDIT CARDS.

Weisburg Religious Articles 212-674-1770
45 Essex St., # 1 (Grand-Hester St)
NY, NY 10002
Hours: 9:30-5 Sun-Thurs / 9:30-3 Fri
Conservative Jewish religious items. RENTALS.

Q-R

RESTORATION & CONSERVATION

Glass Restorations 212-517-3287
    1597 York Ave. (84-85th St)   FAX (same)
    NY, NY 10028
    Hours: 10:30-6 Mon-Fri
    Cuts, grinds and repairs chipped or scratched glass; also repairs broken glass; polishes. Speak to Gus. No credit cards.

Julius Lowy Frame & Restoring Co., Inc. 212-861-8585
    223 E 80th St. (2nd-3rd Ave)   FAX 212-988-0443
    NY, NY 10021
    Hours: 9-5:30 Mon-Fri
    www.lowyonline.com
    Restoration of oil on canvas, artwork on paper, gold leaf and antique frames. CREDIT CARDS.

Poor Richard's Restoration Studio 973-783-5333
    101 Walnut St. (N Willow-Walnut Conor)
    Montclair, NJ 07042
    Hours: by appt.   E-mail: rickford99@yahoo.com
    www.rickford.com
    Antique restoration, conservation and repair of wood, metals, ceramics, paper, clocks, crystal, photographs, mirror resilvering, gold and silver leafing. CREDIT CARDS.

Rambusch 201-333-2525
    160 Cornelison Ave (Montgomery)   212-675-0400
    Jersey City, NJ 07304   FAX 201-433-3355
    Hours: by appt.   E-mail: info@rambusch.com
    www.rambusch.com
    Stained glass and church lighting fixture restoration. No credit cards.

Traditional Lines 212-627-3555
    143 W 21st St. (6-7th Ave)   FAX 212-645-8158
    NY, NY 10011
    Hours: 8:30-5 Mon-Fri   E-mail: restore@tradititionalalline.com
    www.traditionalline.com
    Historical restoration, interiors. Will also fabricate paneling, fireplaces, moulding and hardware.

REWEAVERS

The French-American Re-Weavers Co. 212-765-4670
    119 W 57th St. Rm 1406 (6-7th Ave)
    NY, NY 10019
    Hours: 10-4 Mon-Fri / 11-2 Sat (call first)
    Reweaving of damaged clothing and costumes.

Alice Zotta 212-840-7657
    2 W 45th St. #1701 (5th Ave)
    NY, NY 10036
    Hours: 8-6 Mon-Fri
    Reweaving; personal service.

Q-R

RIDING EQUIPMENT

Country Supply 800-637-6721
P.O. Box 369   FAX 888-262-3655
Louisiana, MO 63353
Hours: 9-5 Mon-Fri / orders 24 Hours a day
                          E-mail: customercare@countrysupply.com
www.countrysupply.com
Horse tack and equipment, various diameters of cotton rope, whips; catalog available; prompt service. CREDIT CARDS.

Manhattan Saddlery 212-673-1400
117 E 24th St. (Park-Lex Ave)   877-673-1400
NY, NY 10010   FAX 212-473-0128
Hours: 10-6 Mon-Sat (Thurs until 7)   E-mail: mike@manhattansaddlery.com
www.manhattansaddlery.com
Traditional equestrain clothing, tack and equipment. Very knowledgable staff. CREDIT CARDS.

The Old Habit 800-813-0515
PO Box 726   540-364-2999
Marshall, VA 20116   540-364-2490
Hours: 10-5 Mon-Sat / 12-4 Sun   E-mail: oldhabit@oldhabit.com
www.oldhabit.com
Fairly hunted (slightly used) riding equipment from England. Boots, clothing, saddles, flasks, crops, riding antiques, stuffed foxes and other fox hunting accoutrements. RENTALS. CREDIT CARDS.

RIGGING EQUIPMENT
See also: THEATRICAL HARDWARE

J.R. Clancy, Inc. 315-451-3440
7041 Interstate Island Rd.   800-836-1885
Syracuse,, NY 13209   FAX 315-451-1766
Hours: 8-5:30 Mon-Fri   E-mail: inquiries@jrclancy.com
www.jrclancy.com
Rigging equipment, stage and rigging hardware, winches; price list available. Catalog. CREDIT CARDS.

Columbus McKinnon Corp. / Theatrical Products Division 800-888-0985
140 John James Audubon   716-689-5400
Amherst, NY 14228   FAX 716-689-5644
Hours: 8-5:30 Mon-Fri
www.cmworks.com
Manufacturer of Lodestar chain hoists, CM theatrical shackles, wire rope clips for lifting and assorted rigging products. Catalog.

Fehr Bros. Industries, Inc. . . . .(out of NY) 800-431-3095
895 Kings Highway   845-246-9525
Saugerties, NY 12477   FAX 845-246-3330
Hours: 8-5 Mon-Fri   E-mail: stage@fehr.com
www.stageriggingonline.com
Stage rigging supplies, fall arresting equipment, motor control systems. $50 minimum. Online catalog. CREDIT CARDS.

I. Weiss and Sons, Inc. 718-706-8139
2-07 Borden Ave. (Vernon-Jackson Ave)   888-325-7192
Long Island City, NY 11101   FAX 718-482-9410
Hours: 8-5:30 Mon-Fri   E-mail: info@iweiss.com
www.iweiss.com
Cycs, scrims, rain curtains and hardware.

Mutual Hardware Corp. 718-361-2480
36-27 Vernon Blvd. (Vernon Blvd)   866-361-2480
Long Island City, NY 11106   FAX 718-786-9591
Hours: 8:30-4:30 Mon-Fri
www.mutualhardware.com
*Complete stage hardware, rigging supplies, casters, catalog. Contact John or
Sal.*

Pook Diemont & Ohl, Inc. 718-402-2677
701 E 132nd St. (Cypress-Willow)   FAX 718-402-2859
Bronx, NY 10454
Hours: 7-5 Mon-Fri   E-mail: info@pdoinc.com
www.pdoinc.com
*Design/build company for theatre, TV and architectural environments
equipment systems. Scope includes new construction and renovation of
rigging systems, stage machinery, drapery and track, lighting and sound
systems.*

Production Advantage, Inc. 802-651-6915
P.O. Box 1700   800-424-99914
Williston, VT 05495   FAX 877-424-9991
Hours: 8:30-6 Mon-Fri   E-mail: sales@proadv.com
www.proadv.com
*Catalog sales of hardware, lighting, rigging, scenic material, soft goods,
sound equipment and expendables to the entertainment industry. All major
brands carried. Catalog. CREDIT CARDS.*

Sapsis Rigging 800-727-7471
233 N Lansdowne Ave.   215-228-0888
Lansdowne, PA 19050   FAX 215-228-1786
Hours: 8-4:30 Mon-Fri   E-mail: bill@sapsis-rigging.com
www.sapsis-rigging.com
*Theatrical rigging; fall arrest equipment; counterweight, hemp-winch
systems; fire curtains, draperies, turntables, etc. Catalog.*

Siegal Brothers 718-387-0300
880 Meeker Ave. (Varick St)   FAX 718-387-1874
Brooklyn, NY 11222
Hours: 6-5 Mon-Fri
www.siegelbros.com
Large selection of tools, Crosby clamps, motors. CREDIT CARDS.

Q-R

Tomcat USA, Inc. 432-694-7070
2160 Commerce   FAX   432-689-3805
Midland, TX 79703
Hours: 8-5 Mon-Fri   E-mail: info@tomcatusa.com
www.tomcatglobal.com
Engineering and manufacturing of custom and standard trussing, lighting support and roof systems. Has full line of rigging accessories, custom cable assemblies, chain hoists, motions controls. CREDIT CARDS.

United Staging & Rigging 203-416-5380
250 Fifth St.   FAX   203-416-5387
Bridgeport, CT 06607
Hours: 8:30-4:30 Mon-Fri

96 Commerce Way   781-376-9180
Canton, MA 01801   FAX   781-376-9185
Hours: 8-5 Mon-Fri
www.unitedstaging.com
CM Motors, Stageright staging, roofs, Genie lifts, soft goods, truss, rugging. Large RENTALS inventory. Contact Doug Frawley (CT) or Jon Sharpe (MA).

ROCKS & MINERALS

American Museum of Natural History - Earth & Planetary Sciences
79th St. & Central Park West   212-769-5390
NY, NY 10024   FAX   212-769-5339
Hours: 10-5:45 Sun-Thurs / 10-8:45 Fri-Sat
www.amnh.org/rose
Consultation and some rentals; contact physical science division at Rose Center for Earth and Space. Call for Museum hours. RENTALS.

Astro Gallery 212-889-9000
185 Madison Ave. (34th St)   FAX   212-689-4016
NY, NY 10016
Hours: 10-7 Mon-Sat / Thurs til 8 / 11-6 Sun   E-mail: info@astrogallery.com
www.astrogallery.com
Rocks, gems, polished stones and crystals. RENTALS. CREDIT CARDS.

Star Magic 212-988-0300
301 E 78th St. (office) (1st-2nd Ave)
NY, NY 10021
Hours: 11-7 Daily   24-hr. Web   E-mail: star@starmagic.com
www.starmagic.com
Other-worldly gemstones and minerals, space age & crystal jewelry; books, guides and charts. CREDIT CARDS.

Q-R

RUBBER STAMPS

A.C. Moore 201-902-0377
400 Mill Creek Dr. (Mill Creek Mall Area)
Secaucus, NJ 07094
Hours: 99 Mon-Fri / 9-8 Sat-Sun
www.acmoore.com
Chain based craft supply store. General crafts, art materials & framing, yarn and needlecrafts, wedding supplies and more. Visit website for other 95 locations across the USA. CREDIT CARDS.

American Marking System 212-227-1877
121 Fulton St., 2nd FL (Nassau-Williams St)   800-782-6766
NY, NY 10038   FAX 212-619-9137
Hours: 8-4Mon-Fri   E-mail: krengel@ams-stamps.com
www.ams-stamps.com
Rubber stamps, reasonable prices; next day service. CREDIT CARDS.

Jam Envelope & Paper Co. / Hudson Envelope Co. 212-473-6666
135 Third Ave. (14th St.)   FAX 212-473-7300
NY, NY 10003
Hours: 8:30-8 Mon-thrus / 8:30-7 Fri / 10-6 Sat-Sun
www.jampaper.com   E-mail: info@jampaper.com
All sizes and colors of envelopes, paper, pens, notebooks, journals and rubber stamps. Also gift-wrap bags and boxes, shredded papers and other gift-wrapping needs. Low prices. CREDIT CARDS.

New York Stationery 212-243-4222
474-A Sixth Ave. (11-12th St)   FAX 212-727-9424
NY, NY 10011
Hours: 9-8 Mon-Fri / 10-8 Sat / 11-8 Sun
Stationery, rubber stamps, small leather goods and desk calendars. CREDIT CARDS.

Rubber Stamps, Inc. 212-675-1180
11 W 25th St. (5-6th Ave)   FAX 212-675-3849
NY, NY 10010
Hours: 7:30-4:30 Mon-Fri   E-mail: sales@rubberstampsinc.com
www.rubberstampsinc.com
Some stock, mostly custom work. CREDIT CARDS.

SCALES

All Care Business Machine, Inc. 212-431-3200
 184 Bowery (Spring-Delancy St)   866-431-3200
 NY, NY 10012   FAX 212-219-1744
 Hours: 8-5 Mon-Fri / 9-4 Sat   E-mail: info@acbm-inc.com
 www.acbm-inc.com
 New and used cash registers, restaurant equipment and safes. RENTAL.
 CREDIT CARDS.

Arlyn Scales 516-593-4465
 59 Second St.   800-645-4301
 East Rockaway, NY 11518   FAX 516-593-4607
 Hours: 9-5 Mon-Fri   E-mail: sales@arlynscales.com
 www.arlynscales.com
 Excellent selection of oversized scales and regular scales for any possible
 use. Call to discuss your weighing requirements with their highly trained
 sales staff. RENTALS. CREDIT CARDS.

Detecto & Precision Scales 201-944-3888
 240 Grand Ave.   800-972-2537
 Leonia, NJ 07605   FAX 201-944-3808
 Hours: 8:30-4:30 Mon-Fri E-mail: precisinscales@verizon.net
 Scales for every weighing need. RENTALS. CREDIT CARDS.

Samuel Underberg, Inc. 718-363-0787
 1784 Atlantic Ave. (Utica)   FAX 718-363-0786
 Brooklyn, NY 11213
 Hours: 8-4 Mon-Fri
 Complete supplies for food stores and butcher shops. Shopping carts, scales,
 baskets, platters, utensils and knives, pans and trays, price markers, paper
 cutters, plastic dividers for deli cases, blackboards and numbered ticket
 dispensers. RENTALS.

SCENIC SHOPS
See also: BACKDROPS

Acadia Scenic, Inc. 201-653-8889
 PO Box 197, 130 Bay St.   FAX 201-653-4717
 Jersey City, NJ 07302
 Hours: 7:30-5 Mon-Fri
 Full-service non-union shop. See David Lawson.

Acme Stimuli Design & Production .212-465-1071
 889 Broadway
 NY, NY 10001
 Hours: by appt.

 2640 Rt. 214   845-688-5107
 Lanesville, NY 12450
 Hours: by appt.   E-mail: stimuli7@hvc.rr.com
 www.acmestimuli.com
 Prop design and fabrication; sculpture; mold-making. Contact Marc Rubin.

S-T

ATAC

Adirondack Studio 518-638-8000
439 County Rt 45   FAX 518-761-3362
Argyle, NY 12809
Hours: 9-5 Mon-Fri
www.adirondackscenic.com
Sets, props, soft goods, lighting equipment. RENTALS.

Aki-ology Design, Inc. 212-533-1694
140 Second Ave., Ste. 402   FAX 212-475-5737
NY, NY 10003
Hours: by appt.
Full-service scene shop. From art direction to set dressing.

Blackthorn Scenic Studio, Inc. 845-267-5405
612 Corporate Way   FAX 845-267-5407
Valley Cottage, NY 10989
Hours: 8-4:30 Mon-Fri   E-mail: postmaster@blackthornscenic.com
www.blackthornscenic.com
Blackthorn Scenic Studio is committed to producing quality professional theatrical scenery for a variety of clients of varying sizes and budgets.

SHARON BRAUNSTEIN / INFINITE DIMENSIONS 404-872-3762
393 Fifth St. #2   770-670-7725
Atlanta, GA 30308
Hours: by appt.   E-mail: sharonjb@att.net
www.id3group.com
Scene shop. Corporate retail, museums, permanent installations. Member ATAC.

Broderson Backdrops 212-925-9392
873 Broadway Studio 603 (18th St)   FAX 212-473-6464
NY, NY 10003
Hours: 9-5 Mon-Fri   E-mail: info@brodersonbackdrops.com
www.brodersonbackdrops.com
Specializing in construction for photographers and small commercial shoots. Also has stock backdrops.

BTL Productions 201-943-4190
815 Fairview Ave., Unit 11 (Tracey Ave)   FAX 201-943-4191
Fairview, NJ 07022
Hours: 9-5 Mon-Fri   www.bltprod.com
Full service production company providing project management, design (scenic, lighting and sound.) Fabrication and installation. Extensive experience in fashion shows and special / corporate events as well as theatre and television. They will help you design or realize your design. Custom logos and backdrops. RENTALS.

Capital Scenic, Inc. 845-429-4800
55 Railroad Ave. # 3C (Route 9W)   FAX 845-429-2138
Garnerville, NY 10923
Hours: 8-4 Mon-Fri   E-mail: capitalscenic@gmail.com
www.capitalscenic.com
Design, engineering and construction for theatre, industrials and special events. Stunt furniture: modification, reinforcement and upholstery of antiques for stage. Scenic storage and maintenance. Scenic and prop rentals. Contact Richard or Neil.

S-T

Tom Carroll Scenery, Inc. 201-432-9047
25 Pollock Ave.   FAX 201-434-1146
Jersey City, NJ 07305
Hours: 8-4 Mon-Fri   E-mail: tcarrollscenery@comcast.net
www.tomcarrollscenery.com
*Custom scenery and props for theater, TV, film and industrials. Licensed to
issue flameproof certificates.*

Center Line Studios, Inc. 845-534-7143
2 Mill St. Box 510   FAX 845-534-4560
Cornwall, NY 12518
Hours: 8-5 Mon-Fri   E-mail: sgray@centerlinestudios.com
www.centerlinestudios.com
*A full-service union scene shop specializing in steel and aluminum
fabrication. Ask for Roger Gray. CREDIT CARDS.*

Chalkline Studios 954-454-8336
7015 River Club Dr. (3rd Ave)   Cell 305-546-9998
Bradenton, FL 34202   FAX (same)
Hours: by appt.   E-mail: info@chalklinestudios.com
www.chalklinestudios.com
*Non-union paint shop. Custom drops, scenery, murals and props. Rental
space available daily or weekly.*

COBALT STUDIOS 845-583-7025
134 Royce Rd.   FAX 845-583-7025
White Lake, NY 12786
Hours: 8-5 Mon-Fri   E-mail: mail@colbaltstudios.net
www.cobaltstudios.net
*Cobalt Studios paints custom backdrops and rents backdrops to the
entertainment and exhibit industries. Scenic art training and seminars
available. RENTALS. CREDIT CARDS. Member ATAC.*

Concept Design Productions 626-932-0082
718 S. Primrose Ave.   800-846-0717
Monrovia, CA 91016   FAX 626-932-0072
Hours: 9-6 Mon-Fri   E-mail: info@conceptdesigninc.com
www.conceptdesigninc.com
*Rental house for structural systems, props and scenic elements. Full sets
and support services available. Check out their website for full listings. Also
custom-built items. See James Leverton. RENTALS.*

Constructive Display 718-237-3131
499 Van Brunt St.   FAX 718-237-4182
Brooklyn, NY 11231
Hours: 8:30-5 Mon-Fri
www.constructivedisplay.com
Set, prop, exhibit and special events design and construction.

Creative Engineering 718-937-5292
5-50 54th Ave. (Vernon Blvd)   347-386-6623
Long Island City, NY 11101   FAX 718-937-1271
Hours: 9-5 Mon-Fri   E-mail: creeng@aol.com
www.creativeengineeringinc.com
*Custom scenery, props, metal fabrication anf fine furniture construction. If
you can dream it, they can build it. RENTALS. CREDIT CARDS.*

S-T

CREATIVE METAL WORKS, INC. / STEPHEN MCMAHON 631-537-9501
172 Butter Lane   FAX 631-537-4669
Bridgehampton, NY 11932
Hours: by Appt.   E-mail: mail@creativemetalworksinc.com
www.creativemetalworksinc.com
Creative Metal Works crafts fine architectural elements from all types of
metals, including: stainless steel, steel mesh, galvanized steel, brushed steel,
bronze, brass, nickel, copper, aluminum and titanium. Custom metal projects
range from architecural elements, railings, and canopies, to sculpture,
hardware, decorative lighting, and fixtures. Member ATAC.

John Creech Design & Production 718-237-1144
129 Van Brunt St. (President-Carroll St)   FAX 718-237-4133
Brooklyn, NY 11231
Hours: 8-6 Mon-Fri   E-mail: shop@jcdp.biz
www.webuildeverything.com
Custom scenery, props and special effects for theatre, film, television and
display.

Daddy-O Productions, Inc. 718-625-2135
Brooklyn Navy Yard, Bldg 280, Ste. 821   917-453-3083
Brooklyn, NY 11205
Hours: 8-5 Mon-Fri   E-mail: info@daddy-o.com
www.daddy-o.net
Full-service fabrication/design shop for scenery and props. Some rentals.

F & D Scene Changes Ltd. 403-233-7633
2b. 803-24 Avenue SE   FAX 403-266-7597
Calgary, Alberta, Canada T2G 1P5
Hours: 7-5 Mon-Fri   E-mail: info@fdscenechanges.com
www.fdscenechanges.com
Full-service scenic shop. Metal work, fiberglass and scenic painting.

Global Scenic Services 203-334-2130
46 Brookfield Ave. (Exit 32)   FAX 203-333-3077
Bridgeport, CT 06610
Hours: 7:30-4 Mon-Fri   E-mail: wkatz@globalscenicservices.com
www.globalscenicservices.com
Full-service union shop, fabrication and rigging. RENTALS.

Gotham Scenic 201-868-1007
71 West Side Ave. (W Houston-West St)   212-741-3399
North Bergen, NY 07047   FAX 201-868-1367
Hours: 8-5 Mon-Fri
www.gothamscenic.com
Full-service union scene shop. Specializes in theatre, TV, displays and
exhibits. High quality and competitive pricing. Talk to John Prisco.

Hudson Scenic Studio 914-375-0900
130 Fernbrook St.   FAX 914-378-9134
Yonkers, NY 10705
Hours: 8-5:30 Mon-Fri   E-mail: info@hudsonscenic.com
www.hudsonscenic.com
Union scene shop. Primarily custom work. Speak to Neil Mazzella.

S-T

JERARD STUDIO, INC. 718-852-4128
481 Van Brunt St., Ste. 11D (Beard St)   FAX 718-852-2408
Brooklyn, NY 11231
Hours: 9-6 Mon-Fri   E-mail: mary@jerardstudio.com
www.jerardstudio.com
Sculpture, props and scenery to order. Murals, backdrops, decorative and faux finishes, trompe l'oeil, back-painted glass. Member ATAC.

Kadan Productions, Inc. 212-674-7080
3200 Liberty Ave., Bldg 3 (Paterson Plank Rd)   FAX 212-674-7244
North Bergen, NJ 07047
Hours: 9-6 Mon-Fri
www.kadaninc.com
Full-service staging, lighting, audio/video, set construction and design company. Extensive experience in fashion, corporate conventions and special events. Can provide video graphics and slide projection. Will design or make any part of your design happen.

MICHAEL SMANKO / PRISM PROPS 732-382-9727
1015 Richard Blvd.
Rahway, NJ 07065
Hours: by Appt.
www.prismprops.com
Broadway Production propman & prop stylist. Prop supervision, shopping, fabrication, upholstery, painting and finishes, prop construction, SPFX. 35 year IATSE member. BA Fine Arts, MFA Theater Design. Member ATAC.

PRG 201-758-4000
539 Temple Hill Rd.   845-567-5700
New Windsor, NY 12553   FAX 845-567-5800
Hours: 8-6 Mon-Fri

7777 West Side Ave.   201-758-4000
North Bergen, NJ 07047   FAX 201-758-4312
Hours: 8-6 Mon-Fri

250 E Sandford Blvd.   914-662-3540
Mt. Vernon, NY 10550   FAX 914-668-6844
Hours: 8-6 Mon-Fri

9111 Sunland Blvd.   818-252-2600
Sun Valley, CA 91352   818-262-3983
Hours: 8-6 Mon- Fri   FAX 818-252-2620

6050 S Valley View Blvd.   702-942-4774
Las Vegas, NV 89118   702-942-4774
Hours: 8-6 Mon-Fri   FAX 702-942-4772

2480 Tedlo St.   905-270-9050
Mississauga, ON L5A 3V3   FAX 905-270-2590
Hours: 8-6 Mon-Fri

1902 Cypress Lake Dr., Ste 100   407-855-8060
Orlando, FL 32837   FAX 407-855-8059
Hours: 8-6 Mon-Fri

S-T

PRG (cont.) 615-834-3190
8351 Eastgate Blvd.   FAX 615-834-3192
Mount Juliette, TN 37122
Hours: 8-6 Mon-Fri

8617 Ambassador Row Ste. 120   214-630-1963
Dallas, TX 75247   FAX 214-630-5867
Hours: 8-6 Mon-Fri

11801 E. 33rd Ave., Ste. D   303-341-4848
Aurora, CO 80010   FAX 702-942-4623
Hours: 8-6 Mon-Fri   E-mail: prg.com
www.prg.com
Custom scenic construction, scenic painting, mechanized set, special effects,
automated rigging systems, slow motion control. RENTALS.

Cornell H. Riggs 570-470-0936
530 Gravity Rd.   FAX 570-937-3569
Lake Ariel, PA 18436
Hours: by appt.   E-mail: creator@Art2specs.com
www.Art2specs.com
Scenery, prop construction, sculpture and furniture design.

Scenic Art Studios, Inc. 845-534-5300
2 Mill St.   FAX 845-534-5394
Cornwall, NY 12518
Hours: 8-4 Mon-Fri   E-mail: laurieatsas@aol.com
www.scenicartstudios.com
United Scenic Artists, Local 829 paint shop serving the Broadway community.
Contact Joe Forbes.

Sets and Effects, LLC. 646-315-0785
1239 DeKalb Ave. (Dekalb - Evergreen)
Brooklyn, NY 11221
Hours: 8-9pm Mon - Fri   E-mail: davdjones@setsandeffects.com
www.setsandeffects.com
Sets, scenic shop for fashion, film, print, commercial, event, music, and
television. Specialty props.

Showman Fabricators 718-935-9899
47-22 Pearson Place (Hamilton Ave-Bowne St)   FAX 718-855-9823
Long Island City, NY 11101
Hours: 7-5:30 Mon-Fri   E-mail: info@showfab.com
www.showfab.com
Platform and flat rental, Gusmer Tech spray foam, computer routing. Storage
space available.

Stiegelbauer Assoc., Inc. 718-624-0835
Brooklyn Navy Yard, Bldg 20 (Cumberland-Flushing)   FAX 718-624-0844
Brooklyn, NY 11201
Hours: 7-2:30 Mon-Fri   E-mail: stiegassoc@aol.com
Union shop: TV, theatrical and industrial set construction. Also props and
special effects. Contact Steve Paone. RENTALS.

S-T

Surface Studio 212-244-6107
242 W 30th St., Ste. 1203 (7-8th Ave)   FAX 212-244-8522
NY, NY 10001
Hours: 9-5 Mon-Thurs / 9-3:30 Fri
www.surfacestudio.com
Tabletop surfaces in a variety of styles, sizes and materials, including wood,
patinated copper, iron, zinc, aluminum and colored cement. RENTALS.

Tulnoy Lumber 718-901-1700
1620 Webster Ave. (173rd St)   800-899-5833
Bronx, NY 10457   FAX 718-229-8920
Hours: 7-5 Mon-Fri   E-mail: sales@tulnoylumber.com
www.tulnoylumber.com
Architectural and scenic design elements available in lightweight vacuum-
formed vinyl plastic. Any piece can be custom made to your own design.

UV/FX Scenic Productions, Inc. 310-821-2657
171 Pier Ave.   FAX 310-392-6817
Santa Monica, CA 90405
Hours: 9-5 Mon-Fri   E-mail: richard@uvfx.com
www.uvfx.com
UV/FX provides innovative custom ultraviolet scenic effects, products and
services to a variety of industries. Visit website for demo of various projects.

Wildfire, Inc. 310-755-6780
2908 Oregon Ct., Ste. G1   800-937-8065
Torrance, CA 90503   FAX 310-755-6781
Hours: 8-5 Mon-Fri   E-mail: sales@wildfirefx.com
www.wildfirefx.com
Manufacture, special effects paints and scenic work. Full-service scenic shop.
P.O.s and CREDIT CARDS.

SCISSORS

Gingher, Inc. 800-446-4437
322-D Edwardia Dr.   336-292-6237
Greensboro, NC 27409   FAX 336-292-6250
Hours: 8:15-5 Mon-Fri   E-mail: gingherinfo@gingher.com
www.gingher.com
Manufacturers of fine scissors and shears. Discount to costumers, price list
available. Online catalog. Sharpening service of Ginghers only - they come
back like new. See details on website.

Japan Woodworker 510-521-1810
1731 Clement Ave.   800-537-7820
Alameda, CA 94501   FAX 510-521-1864
Hours: 9-5 Mon-Sat   E-mail: support@japanwoodworker.com
www.japanwoodworker.com
Importer of Japanese tools, shears, scissors, planes, saws, chisels, punches
and stencil knives. Catalog available. CREDIT CARDS.

S-T

SCISSORS

Henry Westpfal & Co. 212-563-5990
   115 W 25th St. (6-7th Ave)   FAX 212-563-5068
   NY, NY 10001
   Hours: 9:30-6 Mon-Fri
   Scissors, cutlery and blades sharpened; also leather working tools and
   sewing supplies. Distributors of Swiss Army knives. Sells scissors, knives.
   Business checks and CREDIT CARDS.

SEASHELLS

Maxilla and Mandible Ltd. 212-724-6173
   451 Columbus Ave. (81st-82nd St)   FAX 212-721-1073
   NY, NY 10024
   Hours: 11-7 Mon-Sat
   www.maxillaandmandible.com
   Seashells, human and animal skulls, bones, fossils, skins and horns. Phone
   orders accepted. CREDIT CARDS.

Sea Shell World / Cyber Island Shops, Inc. 888-515-3103
   4600 Cecile Drive   407-787-3362
   Kissimmee, FL 34746   FAX 407-396-2242
   Hours: 10-6 Mon-Fri   E-mail: customerservice@seashellworld.com
   www.seashellworld.com
   Shells, sea glass, books also authentic and replica nautical items & props.
   Quick delivery service. Catalog. CREDIT CARDS.

SEWING MACHINES & DRESS FORMS

American Trading / D.B.A. Spacesaver Hdwr. 212-691-3666
   125 Oak St. (6-7th Ave)   FAX 212-989-7468
   Clifton, NJ 07014
   Hours: 8:30-5 Mon-Fri   E-mail: spacesaverny@aol.com
   Industrial and domestic machines. Repairs. No longer have store, but will do
   pick-up and delivery. CREDIT CARDS.

Atlanta Thread & Supply Co. 770-389-9115
   695 Red Oak Rd.   800-847-1001
   Stockbridge, GA 30281   FAX 800-298-0403
   Hours: 8:15-5:30 Mon-Fri   E-mail: awootton@atlantathread.com
   www.atlantathread.com
   Wide selection of notions and sewing supplies from industrial machines to
   home irons to needles and pins. Very helpful staff. Shipping and phone orders
   available. Online catalog. CREDIT CARDS.

The City Quilter 212-807-0390
   133 W 25th St. (6-7th Ave)   FAX 212-807-9451
   NY, NY 10001
   Hours: 11-7 Tue-Fri / 10-6 Sat / 11-5 Sun   E-mail: info@cityquilter.com
   www.cityquilter.com
   Authorized Bernina location. Call for appointment to view machines. Speak
   to Cathy. CREDIT CARDS.

S-T

Crown Machine Service 212-663-8968
2792 Broadway (at 108th St)   212-663-9325
NY, NY 10025
Hours: 9-6 Mon-Fri / 9-5 Sat
Sales and service on home sewing machines. Will do in-home service. Trade-ins and used machines bought. Also, vacuum and electronics repair and sales. CREDIT CARDS.

Diamond Needle 201-507-1771
60 Commerce Rd. (6-7th Ave)   800-221-5818
Carlstadt, NJ 07072   FAX 201-507-1715
Hours: 9-5 Mon-Fri   E-mail: info@diamondneedle.com
www.diamondneedle.com
Industrial or domestic: shears and machine feet. CREDIT CARDS.

Fox Sewing Machine, Inc. 212-594-2438
307 W 38th St. (8-9th Ave)
NY, NY 10018
Hours: 9-6 Mon-Fri
Sewing machine sales, rental, repair, new and used dress and coat forms; steam irons, cutting machines, factory supplies. RENTALS.

Garment Center Sewing Machine, Inc. 212-279-8774
1332 Coney Island Ave. (7-8th Ave)   FAX 212-564-1463
Brooklyn, NY 11230
Hours: 8-5:30 Mon-Fri
Used machines and dress forms, factory supplies. Scissors sharpened. CREDIT CARDS.

Gizmo Notion Corp. 212-477-2773
160 First Ave. (9-10th St)   FAX 212-463-0301
NY, NY 10009
Hours: 11-7 Mon-Fri / 12-7Sat   E-mail: gizmocorp@aol.com
New and rebuilt sewing machines as well as parts and supplies. Contact Rosa or Hossein. No credit cards.

Harwitt Industries 516-623-9787
61 Main St. (6-7th Ave)   516-242-1869
Freeport, NY 11520   FAX 516-623-9784
Hours: 8:30-4:30 Mon-Fri   E-mail: harwittind@aol.com
Many industrial machines used in the garment business; Merrow machines and supplies. Also pattern-making supplies. RENTALS. CREDIT CARDS.

Hecht Sewing Machine & Motor Co., Inc. 212-563-5950
304 W 38th St. (8-9th Ave)
NY, NY 10018
Hours: 9-5 Mon-Fri
Machine sales and service. Lamps, oil, belting and industrial factory antiques. RENTALS.

S-T

S. Hoffman Sewing Center 718-851-1776
5516 Thirteenth Ave. (55-56th St)   800-246-2086
Brooklyn, NY 11219
Hours: 10-6 Mon-Fri / 10-5 Sun
Most types; industrial, Merrow and household sewing machine repair; CREDIT CARDS.

Merrow Sales Corp. 800-431-6677
502 Bedford St.   FAX 508-689-4098
Fall River, MA 02720
Hours: 8-5 Mon-Fri   E-mail: info@merrow.com
www.merrow.com
Merrow machines; service, parts, needles. No Credit Cards.

Ronis Bros. 516-887-5266
39 Harriet Pl.   FAX 516-887-5288
Lynbrook, NY 11563
Hours: 8-4:30 Mon-Fri
www.ronis.com
Manufacturers of Royal forms; dress and accessory forms. Very helpful.
CREDIT CARDS.

Sew Right 718-468-5858
223-20 Union Tpke.   FAX 718-468-5909
Bayside, NY 11364
Hours: 10-6 Tue-Fri / 10-5 Sat / 11-4 Sun   E-mail: info@sewright.com
www.sewright.com
Sales and service of home sewing machines and sergers. Offering sewing
classes and notions. Speak to Harvey. RENTALS. CREDIT CARDS.

The Sewing Outlet 718-899-1900
40-48 82nd St. (Roosevelt Ave)   866-707-1739
Jackson Heights, NY 11372
Hours: 8:30-5:30 Mon-Fri / 9:30-5 Sat   E-mail: info@thesewingoutlet.com
www.thesewingoutlet.com
Sewing machine and supplies. Baby Lock dealer. NY's best resource for all
your sewing, embroidery and software needs for all brands of sewing
machines. CREDIT CARDS.

Superior Model Forms Co. 212-947-3633
12 W 25th St. (6-7th Ave)   FAX 212-633-0491
NY, NY 10001
Hours: 9-6 Mon-Fri   E-mail: info@superiormodel.com
www.superiormodel.com
Dress forms.

Wolf Forms Co., Inc. 201-567-6556
PO Box 510, 17 Van Nostrand Ave.
Englewood, NJ 07631
Hours: 9:30-4 Mon, Wed-Thurs / 9-3 Fri
www.wolfform.com
The very best custom dress forms, full body forms and the small "student
scale"forms. No stock. Large or small orders.

S-T

SHEET MUSIC

Sam Ash Music Stores 212-719-2299
160 W 48th St. (6-7th Ave)   FAX 212-302-1388
NY, NY 10036
Hours: 10-8 Mon-Sat / 12-6 Sun
www.samashmusic.com
Guitars, amps, wind and string instruments; repair. Sheet music. Call or check
website for other locations. RENTALS. CREDIT CARDS.

Colony Records 212-265-2050
1619 Broadway (49th St)   FAX 212-956-6009
NY, NY 10019
Hours: 9:30-1am Mon-Sat / 10-midnight Sun   E-mail: colony1@aol.com
www.colonymusic.com
Large selection of sheet music, records, CDs; will ship anywhere. Out-of-print
LPs, nostalgia, movie, Broadway posters, rock-related toys and autographs.
Best selection of Karaoke music in Manhattan. CREDIT CARDS.

Frank Music Co. 212-582-1999
244 W 54th St., 10th Fl. (B'way-8th Ave)   FAX 212-582-6125
NY, NY 10019
Hours: 11-5 Mon-Fri   E-mail: heidirogers@frankmusiccompany.com
www.frankmusiccompany.com
Printed classical sheet music. Heidi Rogers, owner. CERDIT CARDS.

Music Theatre International 212-541-4684
421 W 54th St., 2nd Fl. (9-10th Ave)   FAX 212-397-4684
NY, NY 10019
Hours: 9-6 Mon-Fri   E-mail: licensing@mtishows.com
www.mtishows.com
Mail order catalog of musical scores. RENTALS only.

Joseph Patelson Music House .212-582-5840
160 W 56th St. (6-7th Ave)   FAX 212-246-5633
NY, NY 10019
Hours: 9-6 Mon-Wed, Fri-Sat / 9-7 Thurs / 12-5 Sun   E-mail: info@patelson.com
www.patelson.com
Large selection of sheet music, scores, opera libretti, books. CREDIT CARDS.

Rogers & Hammerstein Organization 212-541-6600
229 W 28th St., 11th FL (40th St)   FAX 212-586-6155
NY, NY 10001
Hours: 9:30-5:30 Mon-Fri   E-mail: editor@rhn.com
www.rnh.com
Catalog available of musicals for production. Information on how to get
rights to produce, etc. RENTALS.

S-T

SHELVING & LOCKERS

Able Steel Equipment Corp. 718-361-9240
50-02 23rd St. (50th Ave)   FAX 718-937-5742
Long Island City, NY 11101
Hours: 8-4 Mon-Fri   E-mail: ablesteel@aol.com
www.ablesteelequipment.com
New and used lockers and steel shelving. Nice people. RENTALS. No credit cards.

Allracks Industry, Inc. 212-244-1069
361 W 36th St. (8-9th Ave)   FAX 212-279-3879
NY, NY 10018
Hours: 8:30-4:30 Mon-Fri   E-mail: info@allracks.net
www.allracks.net
Shelving, garment racks. CREDIT CARDS.

The Container Store 800-266-8246
629 Sixth Ave.(18-19th St)   212-366-4200
NY, NY 10011
Hours: 9-9 Mon-Sat / 10-8 Sun

725 Lexington Ave.(58-59th St)   212-366-4200
NY, NY 10022
Hours: 9-9 Mon-Sat / 10-8 Sun
www.containerstore.com
For all your organizational needs; bins, files, boxes, metro shelving and closet organizers. The Container Store has everything. Contact the website or toll-free number for other locations. CREDIT CARDS.

New York Store Fixture Company 914-591-1100
145 Palisade St. Ste. 249 (Broome-Delancey)   800-336-8353
Dobbs Ferry, NY 10522   FAX 914-591-1070
Hours: by appt.   E-mail: info@nystorefixture.com
www.nystorefixture.com
Distributor of Metro Shelving and components. Black and chrome in stock, 11 more colors as special order. New and used display cases. Catalog. Some rentals. CREDIT CARDS.

Rehab Vintage 323-935-8438
7609 Beverly Blvd.   800-668-1020
Los Angeles, CA 90036   FAX 323-935-7338
Hours: 10-6 Mon-Fri / 12-5 Sat   E-mail: inforehabvintage.net
www.rehabvintage.net
Vintage American steel furniture. Old steel locks, lockers, tables, cabinets, shelving, etc. Great selection of office furnishings. Expensive. CREDIT CARDS.

SHIPPING

See also: MOVING & TRANSPORT
MESSENGER SERVICES

Federal Express 800-GO-FEDEX
560 W 42nd St. (10-11th Ave)   800-463-3339
NY, NY 10036
Hours: 9-9 Mon-Fri / 9-6 Sat (call for latest pickup in your area)
www.fedex.com
Overnight and 2-day delivery nationwide; international service; door to door
service or will accept packages and hold for pick-up at offices. Over 30
locations in NYC. Free catalog available. 150 lb. limit, maximum size;
130"girth or 108"long. Excellent tracking system. CREDIT CARDS.

Greyhound Package Service 212-971-6300
625 Eighth Ave. Port Authority (Ninth Ave at 41st St) Cust. Serv.   212-971-6325
NY, NY 10018
Hours: 7-7:30 Mon-Fri / 24-hr website
www.shipgreyhound.com
Inexpensive shipping by bus, check for size limitations. See web address for
other locations.

United Parcel Service 800-742-5877
1514 Broadway (11th Ave)   646-366-8867
NY, NY 10036
Hours: 10-10 Mon-Sat / 11-9 Sun
www.ups.com
Overnight, 2-day, or guaranteed 5-day service.

SHOE ALTERATION, REPAIR & DRESSINGS

Angelus Shoe Polish Company 562-229-0521
13500 Excelsior Dr.   800-722-4848
Santa Fe Springs, CA 90670   FAX 562-229-0702
Hours: WEB 24-hrs.   E-mail: paul@angelusshoepolish.com
www.angelusshoepolish.com
Manufacturer of Angelus brand shoe polishes. Many varieties available.
Leather dye, paints and water-based paints. Check website for color charts
and products. CREDIT CARDS.

Drago Shoe Repair 212-799-0559
2214 Broadway (78-79th St)
NY, NY 10024
Hours: 8-7 Mon-Sat
Shoe repair.

East Village Shoe Repair 212-529-8339
1 St. Marks Pl. (2nd-3rd Ave)   FAX 212-375-8770
NY, NY 10003
Hours: 12:30-8 Daily   E-mail: eastvillage.custom@verizon.net
http://home1.gte.net/vze6z7id
Custom shoe and sneaker design. Air-brushing designs on sneakers and
clothing. Shoe and sneaker repairs. Novelty sneakers for sale and trade.
CREDIT CARDS.

S-T

Kaufman Shoe Repair Supplies, Inc. 212-777-1700
346 Lafayette St. (Bond-Bleecker St)   FAX 212-777-1747
NY, NY 10012
Hours: 6:30-2 Sun-Fri
Shoe making, repair and supplies; crepe soles, dance rubber, sole materials, leather, Barge, Magix, elastic and lacings. Mostly wholesale, will not sell in small quantities. CREDIT CARDS.

Toscana 212-799-1940
2348 Broadway (85-86th St)
NY, NY 10024
Hours: 7:30-7 Mon-Fri / 9-6:30 Sat
Shoe repairs. Nice and fast service.

Vasili Shoe Repair 212-581-2491
255 W 51st St. (8th-B'way)
NY, NY 10019
Hours: 8-6 Mon-Sat   E-mail: samvasili@att.net
Located near the theatre district, they do lots of work for all the Broadway shows, Radio City Music Hall, etc.

SHOES & BOOTS
See also: CLOTHING: Accessories
     CLOTHING: Uniforms

Albright 212-977-7350
62 Cooper Sq. (6-7th Ave)   212-375-1465
NY, NY 10003
Hours: By appt. only
www.albrightnyc.com
Over 4000 sq. ft. of top designer collections shoes and accessories. As the name implies, especially strong in shoes. Contact Irene Albright. RENTALS. CREDIT CARDS.

Ballroom Dance Shoppe 952-476-0058
3403 Kilmer Lane N.   877-888-9436
Plymouth, MN 55441   FAX 763-541-7448
Hours: 11-3 Mon-Fri E-mail: mconstantine@celebritydanceshoes.com
www.celebritydanceshoes.com
Custom made dance and street shoes and boots. Will work from your designs. Contact Chrysana Constantine.

Capezio Dance-Theatre Shop 212-245-2130
1650 Broadway, 2nd Fl. (B-way-7th Ave) FAX 212-245-2235
NY, NY 10019
Hours: 10-7 Mon-Sat / 12-5 Sun   E-mail: store1@balletmakers.com
www.capeziodance.com
Can accommodate stock and special order shoes. Pete Ktenas does taps, dance rubbers, heel braces on premises. Very helpful and knowledgeable. Ask for David Shaffer. CREDIT CARDS.

S-T

Capezio at 69th 212-586-5140
201 Amsterdam Ave. (69th St)   FAX 212-262-1747
NY, NY 10019
Hours: 10-7 Mon-Fri / 10-6 Sat / 12-5 Sun
www.capezio57stnyc@balletmakers.com / www.capeziodance.com
Outfitters for dance, fitness and special events; dance footwear, bodywear and accessories. Also videos, records, books and teaching materials. Catalogs available. CREDIT CARDS.

Catskill Mountain Moccasins 845-679-7302
PO Box 294   FAX 845-810-0477
Woodstock, NY 12498
Hours: 9-9 daily   E-mail: mark@catskillmoccasins.com
www.catskillmoccasins.com
Custom footwear made of leather or exotic skins, ankle to knee high, any period or design. Will travel for fittings. CREDIT CARDS.

Church's English Shoes Ltd. 212-758-5200
689 Madison Ave. (62nd St)   FAX 212-758-2559
NY, NY 10017
Hours: 10-6 Mon-Fri / 10-6 Sat / 12-5 Sun
High-quality men's dress and sport shoes, classic styles. Phone and mail orders. CREDIT CARDS.

Claro Shoes 718-875-2981
312 Livingston St.   FAX 718-625-1580
Brooklyn, NY 11217
Hours: 9:30-6 Mon-Wed, Sat / 9:30-7 Thurs-Fri
www.clarotallandwide.com
Women's large size shoes. CREDIT CARDS.

Clown Shoes & Props, Inc. 352-324-3256
23313 S Dewey Robbins Rd.
Howey In The Hills, FL 34737
Hours: by appt.   E-mail: clownshoe@earthlink.net
www.clownshoesandprops.com
Custom-made clown shoes and props; custom magic props. Will also make fitted lace-up boots (similar to wrestlers' shoes) stitched to a plate of leather that make great inserts for character shoes. Reasonable prices, friendly service. P.O.s accepted. CREDIT CARDS.

Cowboy Boot Hospital 212-941-9532
396 Broome St. (Mulberr7-LaFayette St)
NY, NY 10013
Hours: 9-6 Mon-Fri / 10-6 Sat
High quality custom and one-of-a-kind cowboy boots. Vintage designs a la Roy Rogers. Fast shoe repair. Very friendly and helpful. See Jim Babchek, boot maker.

S-T

East Village Shoe Repair 212-529-8339
  1 St. Marks Pl. (2nd-3rd Ave)   FAX 212-375-8770
  NY, NY 10003
  Hours: 12:30-8 7 Days   E-mail: eastvillage.custom@verizon.net
  http://home1.gte.net/vze6z7id
  Custom shoe and sneaker design. Air-brushing designs on sneakers and
  clothing. Shoe and sneaker repairs. Novelty sneakers for sale and trade.
  CREDIT CARDS.

Peter Fox Shoes 212-431-7426
  151 First Ave., #172 (W B-way-Sullivan)
  NY, NY 10003
  Hours: by appt.   E-mail: info@peterfox.com
  www.peterfoxshoes.com
   Exclusive online sales and service. Superb Italian-made high-top lace-up
  boots and shoes with Louis heel, leather and satin covered. Mail shoes to be
  dyed. CREDIT CARDS.

Freed of London Ltd. 866-693-7333
  21-01 44th Ave. 3rd FL   FAX   718-729-8086
  Long Island City, NY 11101
  Hours: 9-5 Mon-thurs / 9-3 Fri   E-mail: info@freedusa.com
  www.freedusa.com
  Specializes in dance shoes, also makes custom period shoes. Shop online or
  to find a location near you. CREDIT CARDS.

GREAT NORTHERN BOOT CO. /
MONTANA LEATHERWORKS, LTD 406-862-9129
  185 Reservoir Rd.
  Whitefish, MT 59937
  Hours: by appt. (June-Aug)

  47 Green St.(Broome-Grand St)   212-431-4015
  NY, NY 10013
  Hours: by appt. (Sept-May)
  Custom shoes and boots. Contact Sharlot Battin. Member ATAC.

Grishko 800-474-7454
  241 King Manor Dr., Ste. D   FAX 610-239-6441
  King of Prussia, PA 19406
  Hours: 10-6 Mon-Fri   E-mail: info@grishko.com
  www.grishko.com
  High quality custom designed shoes and boots for men, women and dance.
  Also nice selection of dancewear and gifts. Good website. CREDIT CARDS.

Handmade Shoes / Frederick Longtin 902-532-2233
  Box 141, Granville Ferry   FAX 902-532-2991
  Nova Scotia, CAN B0S 1K0
  Hours: by appt.   E-mail: fred@handmadeshoes.ca
  Custom boots, shoes, sandals, dance footwear for theatre; contact Fred.
  Federal Express next day shipping.

S-T

Harry's 212-874-2035
   2299 Broadway (at 83rd St)   FAX 212-874-7616
   NY, NY 10024
   Hours: 10-7:45 Mon, Thurs / 10-6:45 Tue-Wed, Fri-Sat / 11-6 Sun
   www.harrys-shoes.com
   Large selection of men's and women's contemporary footwear. Some lace-up
   boots. CREDIT CARDS.

J.C. Theatrical & Custom Footwear 212-529-1125
   890 Broadway, 5th Fl. (19th St)
   NY, NY 10003
   Hours: 10-4 Mon-Fri
   Excellent work, especially on one-of-a-kind items. See Jacob Citerer.

LaDuca Shoes 212-586-2079
   319 W 47th St. (8th Ave)   FAX 212-586-2658
   New York, NY 10036
   Hours: 10:30-6:30 Mon-Fri / 11-6:30 Sat / 12-5 Sun
   www.laducashoes.com   E-mail: info@laducashoes.com
   Custom shoes/books, custom stock shoes and shoes for Broadway, stage,
   film concert as well as street wear for fashion. CREDIT CARDS.

Louis Birns & Sons, Ltd. 518-690-7141
   6 Charles Blvd.   800-533-3023
   Guilderland, NY 12084   FAX 518-690-7142
   Hours: 8-5 Mon-Fri   E-mail: lbssons@vuno.com
   Wholesale to the shoe and leather repair trades. Pre-cut leather soles, half
   soles and heels. Lacings, leather dyes and glues, shoemaker supplies.
   CREDIT CARDS.

Menkes 212-541-8401
   250 W 54th St., 8th Fl. (B'way-8th Ave)   877-227-5460
   NY, NY 10019   FAX 212-541-7409
   Hours: 11-6 Mon-Sat   E-mail: menkesny@verizon.net
   www.menkes.es
   Flamenco shoes, clothing and accessories. Spanish combs, bullfighter
   apparel. Castanets.

Michael Salem Boutique 212-697-0644
   300 E 46th St., 2nd Fl. (2nd Ave)   917-412-9739
   NY, NY 10017
   Hours: by appt only 24/7   E-mail: msaleminc@msn.com
   www.michaelsalem.com
   Complete line of ladies' clothing for men, including shoes and wigs. CREDIT
   CARDS.

Shrader Bootmaker 707-527-5026
   898 Irwin Ln.
   Santa Rosa, CA 95401
   Hours: by appt. only   E-mail: john@shraderbootmaker.com
   www.shraderbootmaker.com
   Specializing in custom-made theatrical boots (especially "bucket boots") and
   period footwear. Flyer available.

S-T

SHOES & BOOTS

T-O-Dey Custom Made Shoes 212-683-6300
9 E 38th St., 7th Fl. (5th & Mad)   FAX 212-683-3445
NY, NY 10016
Hours: by appt.   E-mail: todeyco@aol.com
www.todeyshoes.com
Custom-made shoes for theatre and dance.

Tall Size Shoes 212-736-2060
32 W 39th St. (5-6th Ave)   FAX 212-594-0310
NY, NY 10019
Hours: 9:30-6 Mon-Wed, Sat / 9:30-7 Thurs-Fri
www.clarotallandwide.com
Women's large sizes. Mail and phone orders. CREDIT CARDS.

Worldtone Dance 212-691-1934
230 Seventh Ave., 2nd Fl. (23rd-24th St)   866-WTD-SHOES
NY, NY 10011   FAX 212-691-2554
Hours: 11-7 Mon-Wed / 11-8 Thurs-Sat / 12-6 Sun   E-mail: info@wtdance.com
www.worldtonedance.com
*Dance shoes: Ballroom, character, flamenco, tap and jazz. Also dance
recordings, books, videos, castanets and zils. CREDIT CARDS.*

SIGNS & LETTERS
See also: FLAGS & BANNERS
            NEON
            SILKSCREENING

Ace Banner, Flag & Graphics Co. .212-620-9111
107 W 27th St. (6th Ave)   800-675-9112
NY, NY 10011   FAX 212-463-9128
Hours: 7:30-4 Mon-Fri   E-mail: service@acebanner.com
www.acebanner.com / www.acebannershop.com
*Foreign and domestic flags; custom banners; screen-printing. CREDIT
CARDS.*

Active Signs 212-564-9696
59 W 28th St., FL 2 (6th-Bway)   FAX 212-643-1852
NY, NY 10001
Hours: 8-5 Mon-Fri   E-mail: activesigns@verizon.net
www.activesignsinc.net
*All types: Handpainted and vinyl letters and logos. Speak to Frank Soldo.
Rush service, works with film industry.*

Alpha Engraving Co. 212-247-5266
254 W 51 St. (B'way-8th Ave)   FAX 212-247-2014
NY, NY 10019
Hours: 9-6 Mon-Thurs / 9-4 Fri   E-mail: salesinfo@alphaengraving.com
www.alphaengraving.com
Metal and plastic engraved signs, also name tags.

S-T

 **ATAC**

Ancient Art 212-662-2571
336 W 95th St. (Riverside)   800-675-4653
NY, NY 10025   FAX 212-865-5766
Hours: by appt.   E-mail: email@ancientartny.com
www.ancientartny.com
Gold leaf lettering and sign painting.

Artkraft Strauss Sign Corp. 212-265-5155
1776 Broadway # 1600   FAX 212-265-5262
NY, NY 10019
Hours: 9-5 Mon-Fri   E-mail: info@artkraft.com
www.artkraft.com
*Custom signs; metal, wood, neon and computerized. They do many of the
large displays in Times Square. Will do the small jobs, too.*

Bernard Maisner Calligraphy and Hand-Lettering Studio 212-477-6776
56 Mount St.   732-899-9858
Bayhead, NJ 08742   FAX 732-899-9859
Hours: by appt. only   E-mail: bernard@bernardmaisner.com
www.bernardmaisner.com
*Creative hand-lettering and calligraphy, also professional hand model for live
writing for TV and film.*

Big Apple Sign Corp. 212-629-3650
247 W 35th St. (7-8th Ave)   877-244-2775
NY, NY 10001   FAX 212-629-4954
Hours: 9-5:30 Mon-Fri   E-mail: amir@bigapplegroup.com
www.bigapplegroup.com
Full-service sign company; 24-hr. service available. CREDIT CARDS.

Brushfire Studio 860-518-4046
46 Hatch St.
New Britain, CT 06053
Hours: by appt.
*Union-made signs, banners and murals, lettering, airbrush and pictorials.
Works with students in painting murals and airbrushing. Contact Mike
Alewitz.*

Bulletin Boards & Directory Products, Inc. 914-248-8008
2986 Navajo St.   FAX 914-248-5150
Yorktown Heights, NY 10598
Hours: 9-4:30 Mon-Fri
*Mfg. of directory boards, engraved nameplates, vinyl letters, chalkboards, etc.
Catalog. Contact Charles Kranz.*

Green Mountain Graphics 718-472-3377
21-10 44th Dr. (21st & 23rd St)   FAX 718-472-4040
Long Island City, NY 11101
Hours: 8:30-5 Mon-Fri   E-mail: sales@gm-graphics.com
www.gm-graphics.com
*In-house manufacturers of engraved and silkscreened signs and promotional
products awards; also vinyl graphics. Suppliers of all kinds of signs including
cast bronze, faux cast bronze, etched, banners, etc. Also, blackboards and
bulletin boards. Convenient location to all L.I.C. soundstages. Catalogs and
rush service available. CREDIT CARDS.*

S-T

ATAC

Katonah Image, Inc. 914-232-0961
22 Woodsbridge Rd.   FAX 914-232-3944
Katonah, NY 10536
Hours: 9-6 Mon-Fri / 9-5 Sat
Photo lab with antiques, memorabilia and collectibles. RENTALS. CREDIT CARDS.

L & M Architecutral Graphics, Inc. 973-575-7665
20 Montesano Rd.   FAX 973-575-6709
Fairfield, NJ 07004
Hours: 9-5 Mon-Fri   E-mail: info@lmsigns.com
www.lmsigns.com
Custom architectural signs in any material.

Main Attractions 732-225-3500
85 Newfield Ave. (Raritan Ctr Pkwy)   800-394-3500
Edison, NJ 08837   732-225-2110
Hours: 9:30-5 Mon-Fri   E-mail: events@mainattractions.com
www.mainattractions.com
Special events contractors; specializing in custom tent rentals, restroom trailers, decor, portable staging, lighting and the production of displays and signage. Visit website to see the full spectrum of their products. RENTALS. CREDIT CARDS.

Manhattan Neon Sign Corp. 212-714-0430
640 W 28th St.   FAX 212-947-3906
NY, NY 10001
Hours: 9-5 Mon-Fri / or by appt.   E-mail: sales@manhattanneon.com
www.manhattanneon.com
Custom-made neon and rentals, 3-D props and displays, large-format full-color graphics, LED moving message signs and vinyl signs, cut acrylic, wood metal and foam. Contact Peter.

Maven Graphics, Inc. 516-741-6412
274 Jericho Turnpike   FAX 516-741-6482
Mineola, NY 11501
Hours: 9-5 Mon-Fri   E-mail: mavengraphics@aol.com
Prop signage, banners vinyl transfers and printing on vinyl. Can do on-site mounting. Personal service, super friendly and helpful. Associated with Variety Scenic Studios. Member USA Local 829.

National Flag & Display Co., Inc. 212-462-4000
22 W 21st St., 7th Fl. (5-6th St)   FAX 212-462-2624
NY, NY 10010
Hours: 9-5:30 Mon-Fri / eves. & weekends by appt.
www.nationalflag.com   E-mail: hsiegel@nationalflag.com
Manufacturers of banners, flags, backdrops and wall murals. Applique, silkscreen, inkjet, dye-sublimation and electrostatic full-color printing. Rush orders. RENTALS. CREDIT CARDS.

S-T

Scott Sign System 800-237-9447
PO Box 1047   941-355-5171
Tallevast, FL 34270   FAX 941-351-1787
Hours: 8-6 Mon-Thurs / 8-5 Fri   E-mail: quote@scottsigns.com
www.scottsigns.com
Plexiglas, plastic foam, gypsum letters in many styles and thicknesses,
custom repro of logos, graphics and ABCs. Catalog available. CREDIT CARDS.

Sign Design of New York 718-392-0779
33-26 Northern Blvd.   FAX 718-937-6935
Long Island City, NY 11101
Hours: 9-6 Mon-Fri   E-mail: info@sdgny.com
www.sdgny.com
Manufacturer of all types of custom signage and visual display materials.
Services from design to installations. CREDIT CARDS.

Sign Expo 212-925-8585
102 Franklin St.   FAX 212-680-0195
NY, NY 10013
Hours: 9-5:30 Mon-Fri   E-mail: signs@signexpo.com
www.signexpo.com
Awnings, signs, neon, banners, silkscreen, lettering, materials. RENTALS.
CREDIT CARDS.

Specialty Sign Co., Inc. 212-243-8521
54 W 21st St., 2nd Fl. (5-6th Ave.)   800-394-3433
NY, NY 10010   FAX 212-243-6457
Hours: 9-5 Mon-Fri   E-mail: sales@specialtysigns.com
www.specialtysigns.com
Stock signs and custom work and name tags. Rush orders. CREDIT CARDS.

Sweetbryar Calligraphics 845-679-7335
31 Overlook Dr.
Woodstock, NY 12498
Hours: 10-6 Mon-Sat / by appt. only   E-mail: bryarcalli@aol.com
www.sweetbryar.com
Calligraphy and sign painting, air brushing, hand lettering, logos, banners,
posters (all custom), menus. On location if necessary.

SILKSCREENING
See also: ART SUPPLIES
              SIGNS & LETTERS

Ace Banner, Flag & Graphics Co. .212-620-9111
107 W 27th St. (6th Ave)   800-675-9112
NY, NY 10011   FAX 212-463-9128
Hours: 7:30-4 Mon-Fri   E-mail: service@acebanner.com
www.acebanner.com / www.acebannershop.com
Foreign and domestic flags; custom banners; screen-printing. CREDIT
CARDS.

S-T

Ambassador Arts 718-482-8208
43-01 22nd St., 2nd Fl.   FAX 718-482-8656
Long Island City, NY 11101
Hours: 9-5 Mon-Fri
Does large screening art and signs on plexi, wood, etc. No credit cards.

Artisan Silkscreen & Embroidery 718-526-0600
179-10 93rd Ave. (6-7th Ave)   FAX 718-526-5700
Jamaica, NY 11433
Hours:9-5 Mon-Thurs / 9-3 Fri   E-mail: info@artisansilkscreen.com
www.artisansilkscreen.com
Custom silkscreening, t-shirts, jackets, etc., yours or theirs; also posters,
signs, etc. Catalog available. CREDIT CARDS.

Dye-Namix, Inc. 212-941-6642
151 Grand St. 2nd FL   FAX 212-941-7407
NY, NY 10013
Hours: 9:30-6 Mon-Fri / or by appt.   E-mail: info@dyenamix.com
www.dyenamix.com
Creative dyeing, painting and silkscreening of samples, yardages and
garments for the fashion, theatre and film industries. Contact Raylene
Marasco for project estimates. No credit cards.

Frank's Sport Shop . . . .(Store) 718-299-9628
430 E Tremont Ave. (Park Ave)   (Office) 212-945-0020
Bronx, NY 10457   FAX 718-583-1652
Hours: 9-8 Mon-Fri / 9-6 Sat   E-mail: info@frankssports.com
www.frankssports.com
Silkscreening and embroidery on premise; hats, t-shirts, jackets,etc. Rush
orders available. CREDIT CARDS.

GENE MIGNOLA, INC. 718-858-8902
610 Smith Street (3rd Fl)   FAX 718-858-8667
Brooklyn, NY 11231
Hours: 9-5 Mon-Fri   E-mail: GM5919@aol.com
Custom dyeing and silkscreening. Call before stopping by. Member ATAC.

Green Mountain Graphics 718-472-3377
21-10 44th Dr. (21st & 23rd St)   FAX 718-472-4040
Long Island City, NY 11101
Hours: 8:30-5 Mon-Fri   E-mail: sales@gm-graphics.com
www.gm-graphics.com
In-house manufacturers of engraved and silkscreened signs and promotional
products awards; also vinyl graphics. Suppliers of all kinds of signs including
cast bronze, faux cast bronze, etched, banners, etc. Also, blackboards and
bulletin boards. Convenient location to all L.I.C. soundstages. Catalogs and
rush service available. CREDIT CARDS.

Ideal 718-252-5090
1816 Flatbush Ave.(Avenue K)   FAX 718-692-0492
Brooklyn, NY 11210
Hours: 9-7:30 Mon-Fri / 10-7 Sat / 11-6 Sun

S-T

Ideal (cont.) 718-239-4010
  1575 Unionport Rd.
  Bronx, NY 10462
  Hours: 10-7 Mon-Sat / 10:30-5:30 Sun
  www.idealuniform.com
  Custom silkscreening and embroidery on hats, t-shirts, jackets, bags, etc.
  Our merchandise or yours. CREDIT CARDS.

Martin Izquierdo Studio 212-807-9757
  118 W 22nd St., 9th Fl. (6-7th Ave)   FAX 212-366-5249
  NY, NY 10011
  Hours: 9-7 Mon-Fri   E-mail: izquierdostudio@gmail.com
  www.izquierdostudio.com
  Custom work; full-service costume and prop shop. Contact Jean Paul
  Nguyen.

Maven Graphics, Inc. 516-741-6412
  274 Jericho Turnpike   FAX 516-741-6482
  Mineola, NY 11501
  Hours: 9-5 Mon-Fri   E-mail: mavengraphics@aol.com
  Prop signage, banners vinyl transfers and printing on vinyl. Can do on-site
  mounting. Personal service, super friendly and helpful. Associated with
  Variety Scenic Studios. Member USA Local 829.

Standard Screen Supply Co. 212-627-2727
  121 Varick St., 2nd Fl. (Dominic-Broome St)   800-221-2697
  NY, NY 10013   FAX 212-627-2770
  Hours: 8-5:30 Mon-Fri   E-mail: info@standardscreen.com
  www.standardscreen.com
  Custom silkscreens; supplies. Wholesale and retail. Very helpful. CREDIT
  CARDS.

SILVER ITEMS

See also: ANTIQUES: All Headings
            DEPARTMENT STORES
            PARTY GOODS
            PROP RENTAL HOUSES

Classic Party Rentals 212-752-7661
  336 W 37th St., 2nd FL (showroom)(8-9th Ave)   FAX 212-752-0150
  NY, NY 10018
  Hours: 9-5 Mon-Fri

  2350 Lafayette Ave. (warehouse)(Cypress Ave)   718-822-1930
  Bronx, NY 10473   FAX 718-822-4159
  Hours: 9-5 Mon-Fri / 9-3 Sat
  www.classicpartyrentals.com
  Silverware, candelabras, chafing dishes, coffee pots, etc. RENTALS. CREDIT
  CARDS.

Columbia Interiors 212-725-5250
  162 E 33rd St. Frnt. (Lex-3rd Ave)   FAX 212-685-4496
  NY, NY 10016
  Hours: 10-5 Mon-Sat
  Silversmiths. Brass and silver plating. See Matthew. CREDIT CARDS.

S-T

Michael C. Fina Co. 212-557-2500
545 Fifth Ave. (45th St)   800-289-3462
NY, NY 10017   FAX 212-557-3862
Hours: 11-8 Mon-Thurs / 10-7 Fri / 10-6 Sat / 11-6 Sun
www.michaelcfina.com
Silver, silverware, china, crystal and jewelry. Good prices. Catalog and online shopping available. CREDIT CARDS.

Jean's Silversmiths 212-575-0723
16 W 45th St. (5th Ave)   866-575-1100
NY, NY 10036   FAX 212-921-0991
Hours: 9-4:45 Mon-Fri   E-mail: jeans@jeanssilversmiths.com
www.jeanssilversmith.com
Large selection of tea sets, candelabras, etc. Expensive. Go early in the day. RENTALS. CREDIT CARDS.

Georg Jensen Silversmiths 212-759-6457
687 Madison Ave. (61-62nd St)   FAX 212-355-1529
NY, NY 10065
Hours: 10-6 Mon-Sat / 12-5 Sun
www.georgjensen.com
Modern design sterling silver, stainless flatware, barware and gifts. Sterling silver and 18 carat jewelry and watches. Catalog. Contact Martha Palhno. RENTALS. CREDIT CARDS.

Props for Today 212-244-9600
330 W 34th St. (8-9th Ave)   FAX 212-244-1053
NY, NY 10001
Hours: 8:30-5 Mon-Fri   E-mail: info@propsfortoday.com
www.propsfortoday.com
Full-service prop rental house. Large selection of serving pieces and flatware from all periods. RENTALS. CREDIT CARDS.

R & P Kassai 212-302-7010
14 W 45th St., 4th FL (5-6th Ave)   917-885-2925
NY, NY 10036   FAX 212-302-3763
Hours: 9-5 Mon-Fri   E-mail: orders@kassai.com
www.kassai.com
Antique silver company that has items for rent from all periods; 17th Century to present. They can help you with any period and selecting the right pieces for your needs. RENTALS.

Regency Service Carts, Inc. 718-855-8304
337-361 Carroll St. (Hoyt-Bond St)   FAX 718-834-8507
Brooklyn, NY 11231
Hours: 8-5 Mon-Fri   E-mail: regeastny@aol.com
www.regencynylv.com
Silver-plated tabletop items, chaffing dishes, domes and dessert carts, room service carts, holloware; catalog. Wonderful website. RENTALS.

S-T

SMOKING ACCESSORIES & SUPPLIES

Arnold Tobacco Shop 212-697-1477
268 Newton Rd.   800-591-4545
Plainview, NY 11803   FAX 516-767-3692
Hours: 9-4 Mon-Fri   E-mail: info@arnoldstobacco.com
www.arnoldstobacco.com
Pipes, tobacco, cigars, lighters and pipe repairs. CREDIT CARDS.

Barclay-Rex Pipe Shop 888-378-6222
570 Lexington Ave.   212-888-1015
NY, NY 10022   FAX 212-980-3741
Hours: 8-6:30 Mon-Fri (til 7:30 Thurs-Fri) / 9:30-5:30 Sat

75 Broad St.(B'way)   212-962-3355
NY, NY 10038   FAX 212-962-3372
Hours: 8-6 Mon-Fri

70 E 42nd St.(Park Ave)   212-692-9680
NY, NY 10017
Hours: 8-6:30 Mon-Fri / 9:30-5:30 Sat   E-mail: info@barclayrex.com
www.barclayrex.com
Pipes, cigars, tobacco, humidors, repairs. CREDIT CARDS.

De La Concha 212-757-3167
1390 Sixth Ave. (56-57th St)   888-CIGAR-04
NY, NY 10019   FAX 212-333-3162
Hours: 9:30-8 Mon-Fri / 11-7 Sat / 12-6 Sun
www.delaconcha.com
Cigars, cigarettes, pipes, tobacco; imported and domestic.

Alfred Dunhill of London 212-753-9292
545 Madison Ave. (54-55th St)   FAX 212-980-2959
NY, NY 10022
Hours: 10-6:30 Mon-Sat / 12-5 Sun
www.alfreddunhill.com
Pipes, cigars, tobacco, humidors. Expensive. See website for other locations.
CREDIT CARDS.

J R Tobacco Corp. 800-564-3576
2589 Eric Lane
Burlington, NC 27215
Hours: View website for hours
www.jrcigars.com
Large selection of cigars, pipe tobacco, lighters, etc. Great website. CREDIT
CARDS.

Mantiques Modern, Ltd. 212-206-1494
146 W 22nd St. (6-7th Ave)   FAX 212-355-4403
NY, NY 10022
Hours: 10:30-6:30 Mon-Fri / 11-7 Sat-Sun   E-mail: info@mantiquesmodern.com
www.mantiquesmodern.com
Fine antique smoking accessories, furniture, desk dressing, sporting goods
and canes. Visit website. RENTALS. CREDIT CARDS.

S-T

SMOKING ACCESSORIES & SUPPLIES

Nat Sherman 212-764-4175
   489 Fifth Ave. (42nd St)   800-692-4427
   NY, NY 10110   FAX 212-764-5134
   Hours: 10-8 Mon-Fri
   www.natsherman.com
   Large selection cigars, cigarettes, tobacco. CREDIT CARDS.

SOUND & COMMUNICATION EQUIPMENT
For consumer & household equipment, see AUDIO& VIDEO EQUIPMENT

AAA Communications 973-808-8888
   15 Riverside Dr.   800-WALKIES
   Pine Brook, NJ 07058   FAX 973-808-8588
   Hours: 9-5 Mon-Fri   E-mail: jackie@aaacomm.com
   www.aaacom.com
   Wrap around head mics, two way radios. Repeaters, temporary phone systems. Additional offices in CA and GA. RENTALS. CREDIT CARDS.

Ace Video & Props 718-392-1100
   37-24 24th St., Ste. 106 (Houston & West St)   212-206-1475
   Long Island City, NY 11101   FAX 718-392-1155
   Hours: 10-6 Mon-Fri / 10-2 Sat by appt.
         E-mail: acevideorentals@gmail.com / acepropsnyc@gmail.com
   www.aceprops.com
   P.A. systems; working & non-working electronic and A/V equipment. RENTALS. CREDIT CARDS.

BTL Productions 201-943-4190
   815 Fairview Ave., Unit 11 (Tracey Ave)   FAX 201-943-4191
   Fairview, NJ 07022
   Hours: 9-5 Mon-Fri
   www.bltprod.com
   Full service production company providing project management, design (scenic, lighting and sound.) Fabrication and installation. Extensive experience in fashion shows and special / corporate events as well as theatre and television. the will help you design or realize your design. Custom logos and backdrops. RENTALS.

CP Communications, Inc. 914-345-9292
   200 Clearbrook Rd.   800-762-4254
   Elmsford, NY 10523   FAX 914-345-9222
   Hours: 8-6 Mon-Fri
   www.cpcomms.com
   Communication and RF-related equipment rentals and sales. Intercom systems, wireless mics and headsets, walkie-talkies, cellular telephones. Contact Michael Mason. RENTALS. CREDIT CARDS.

S-T

Goddard Design Co. 718-599-0170
51 Nassau Ave. FAX 718-599-0172
Brooklyn, NY 11222
Hours: 10-6 Mon-Fri E-mail: sales@goddarddesign.com
www.goddarddesign.com
Designers and manufacturers. of theatrical electronics. DMX test equipment
512 and distribution , intercom systems, scenery mechanization controllers.
DMX or RDM Consulting.

Ins & Outs, Inc. 845-256-0899
60 Jansen Rd. FAX 845-256-1484
New Paltz, NY 12561
Hours: 9-5 Mon-Fri / after hours by appt. E-mail: sfxone@aol.com
www.insandoutssound.com
Pro Audio rental house. Design and installation. Theatre, live music,
corporate. Sales and RENTALS.

Kadan Productions, Inc. 212-674-7080
3200 Liberty Ave., Bldg 3 (Paterson Plank Rd) FAX 212-674-7244
North Bergen, NJ 07047
Hours: 9-6 Mon-Fri
www.kadaninc.com
Full-service staging, lighting, audio/video, set construction and design
company. Extensive experience in fashion, corporate conventions and special
events. Can provide video graphics and slide projection. Will design or make
any part of your design happen.

Masque Sound & Recording Corp. .800-307-8666
21 E Union Ave. FAX 201-939-4704
East Rutherford, NJ 07073
Hours: 9-5 Mon-Fri E-mail: NE-sales@masquesound.com
www.masquesound.com
Rentals of sound and recording equipment for industrials and corporate
theatre. Contact Walter Yurgel, Dennis Short or Scott Kalata. RENTALS.
CREDIT CARDS.

Musson Theatrical 800-THEATER
890 Walsh Ave. 408-986-0210
Santa Clara, CA 95050 FAX 408-986-9552
Hours: 8:30-5:30 Mon-Fri / 10-2 Sat E-mail: info@musson.com
www.musson.com
Great West Coast full-service supply for lighting and sound. Very
knowledgable and helpful. Contact Bob Smay. RENTALS.

One Dream Light & Sound Corp. 718-433-3030
36-15 48th Ave. FAX 718-433-1389
Long Island City, NY 11101
Hours: 10-6 Mon-Fri
www.onedreamsound.com
Provides sound equipment rentals, design and consulting services for
theatrical, industrial and private live functions. Sells gear and provides labor.
Lighting and staging. RENTALS. CREDIT CARDS.

S-T

PRG 201-758-4000
539 Temple Hill Rd.   845-567-5700
New Windsor, NY 12553   FAX 845-567-5800
Hours: 8-6 Mon-Fri

7777 West Side Ave.   201-758-4000
North Bergen, NJ 07047   FAX 201-758-4312
Hours: 8-6 Mon-Fri

250 E Sandford Blvd.   914-662-3540
Mt. Vernon, NY 10550   FAX 914-668-6844
Hours: 8-6 Mon-Fri

9111 Sunland Blvd.   818-252-2600
Sun Valley, CA 91352   818-262-3983
Hours: 8-6 Mon- Fri   FAX 818-252-2620

6050 S Valley View Blvd.   702-942-4774
Las Vegas, NV 89118   702-942-4774
Hours: 8-6 Mon-Fri   FAX 702-942-4772

2480 Tedlo St.   905-270-9050
Mississauga, ON L5A 3V3   FAX 905-270-2590
Hours: 8-6 Mon-Fri

1902 Cypress Lake Dr., Ste 100   407-855-8060
Orlando, FL 32837   FAX 407-855-8059
Hours: 8-6 Mon-Fri

8351 Eastgate Blvd.   615-834-3190
Mount Juliette, TN 37122   FAX 615-834-3192
Hours: 8-6 Mon-Fri

8617 Ambassador Row Ste. 120   214-630-1963
Dallas, TX 75247   FAX 214-630-5867
Hours: 8-6 Mon-Fri

11801 E. 33rd Ave., Ste. D   303-341-4848
Aurora, CO 80010   FAX 702-942-4623
Hours: 8-6 Mon-Fri   E-mail: prg.com
www.prg.com

A premier audio reinforcement company known for innovation, reliability and service. Experienced in the Broadway market, theatrical touring, corporate theatre and special events. RENTALS.

ProMix, Inc. / PRG 914-662-3540
250 E Sandford Blvd.   FAX 914-662-3731
Mt. Vernon, NY 10550
Hours: 9-5 Mon-Fri
www.prg.com

Provider of sound equipment rentals, design and consulting services for theatrical, industrial and private functions. Tour packages available. RENTALS. CREDIT CARDS.

See Factor Industry, Inc. 718-784-4200
    37-11 30th St. (37th Ave)   FAX 718-784-0617
    Long Island City, NY 11101
    Hours: 9-5 Mon-Fri
    www.seefactor.com
    Sound and lighting rental company. Complete production services and personnel available for any event. RENTALS.

Sound Associates, Inc. 212-757-5679
    424 W 45th St. (9-10th Ave)   888-772-7686
    NY, NY 10036   FAX 212-265-1250
    Hours: 10-5:30 Mon-Fri   E-mail: newyork@soundassociates.com
    www.soundassociates.com
    Full sound shop; mail and phone orders. See website for additional US locations. RENTALS. CREDIT CARDS.

Wits End Productions 212-242-9400
    547 W 49th St.   212-757-4545
    NY, NY 10019   FAX 212-242-1797
    Hours: 24-hr. service   E-mail: tvgully@aol.com
    www.witsendnyc.com
    Excellent company to handle all your production needs for film and photography shoots. They have expendible kits you can rent that contain EVERYTHING you could possibly need for any situation. Rent their trucks full of expendables and you even get a truck driver experienced to assist in any and all your needs. If they don't have what you need, they will buy it. Just added to their stock are mole fans, ladders, 600W generators and much much more. Visit their website to view their extensive RENTALS. CREDIT CARDS.

SPECIAL EFFECTS SERVICES

Alfonso's Breakaway Glass 818-768-7402
    8070 San Fernando Rd.   866-768-7402
    Sun Valley, CA 91352   FAX 818-767-6969
    Hours: 7-5:30 Mon-Fri E-mail: info@alfonsosbreakawayglass.com
    www.alfonsosbreakawayglass.com
    Great selection of breakaways. Just about anything you can think of, they have it. Catalog. CREDIT CARDS.

Daniel J. Aronson 212-544-0366
    NY, NY 10040
    Hours: by appt.
    Mechanical rigging and props; smoke, fog and rain atmospheric effects.

Artistry in Motion 818-994-7388
    15101 Keswick St.   FAX 818-994-7688
    Van Nuys, CA 91405
    Hours: 9-6 Mon-Fri   E-mail: confetti@artistryinmotion.com
    www.artistryinmotion.com
    Best in the industry for confetti cannons and confetti. Custom designing for each event. CREDIT CARDS.

S-T

Auto Props 973-470-9354
8 Lexington Ave.   FAX 973-591-1835
Wallington, NJ 07057
Hours: by appt.   E-mail: 57gasser@comcast.net
www.autoprops-waterworks.com
Automobiles and trucks of all types and periods, including Harley Davidson motorcycles. Stunt rigging; wet downs, water effects, water trucks, scuba; garage facilities. Ask about other effects. Talk to Ken Maletsky. RENTALS. CREDIT CARDS.

BMI Supply 518-793-6706
571 Queensbury Ave.   800-836-0524
Queensbury, NY 12804   FAX 518-793-6181
Hours: 8-6 Mon-Fri   E-mail: bminy@bmisupply.com
www.bmisupply.com
A full-line theatrical supply house and on-site contractor. Retail and wholesale at everyday wholesale prices. Special effects. Sales only. CREDIT CARDS.

Brooklyn Model Works, Inc. 718-834-1944
60 Washington Ave. (Park-Flushing)   FAX 718-596-8934
Brooklyn, NY 11205
Hours: by appt.   E-mail: info@brooklynmodelworks.com
www.brooklynmodelworks.com
Experienced and reliable.

Fred Buchholz/Acme Special Effects .212-874-7700
202 W 88th St. # 7 (B'way-Amst)   Cell: 917-549-1896
NY, NY 10024   FAX 212-874-4107
Hours: by appt.   E-mail: fred@acmespecialeffects.com
www.acmespecialeffects.com
Special effects, props, rigging and pyrotechnics for film, theatre, video; props incorporating light.

Cimmelli, Inc. 845-735-2090
16 Walter St.   845-735-4693
Pearl River, NY 10965   FAX 845-735-1643
Hours: 8:30-5:30 Mon-Fri / Sat by appt.
www.cimmellisfx.com
Licensed pyrotech, various special effects available. Rigging, models and turntables. RENTALS.

John Creech Design & Production 718-237-1144
129 Van Brunt St. (President-Carroll St)   FAX 718-237-4133
Brooklyn, NY 11231
Hours: 8-6 Mon-Fri   E-mail: shop@jcdp.biz
www.webuildeverything.com
Custom scenery, props and special effects for theatre, film, television and display.

S-T

DuraLast Products Corp. 901-323-8448
  580 Tillman, Ste. 5   888-323-8448
  Memphis, TN 38112   FAX 901-323-8442
  Hours: 8-4:30 Mon-Fri   E-mail: nathan@duralast.com
  www.duralast.com
  **Rubberized hog hair media, a natural fiber used to create various special
  effects; sound effects construction, sound dampening, rain making, etc.
  Available in various sizes and thicknesses. Also air conditioner filters.
  CREDIT CARDS.**

EFEX Rentals 718-505-9465
  5805 52nd Ave. (43rd Ave)   FAX 718-505-9631
  Woodside, NY 11377
  Hours: 8:30-5:30 Mon-Fri   E-mail: efexrentals@verizon.net
  www.efexrentals.com
  **Major distributors of many different types of fog machines, fog juice; also
  turntables and rigging. RENTALS.**

Fireworks by Grucci 631-286-0088
  1 Grucci Ln.   FAX 631-286-9036
  Brookhaven, NY 11719
  Hours: 9-6 Mon-Fri   E-mail: pbutler@grucci.com
  www.grucci.com
  The legendary family fireworks company. Training seminars.

J&M Special Effects 718-875-0140
  524 Sackett St.   FAX 718-596-8329
  Brooklyn, NY 11217
  Hours: 9-4 Mon-Fri by appt.   E-mail: info@jmfx.net
  www.jmfx.net
  **Full-service special effects shop; design, construction, rental, sales of
  equipment and supplies. Speak to Greg Meeh. RENTALS.**

Peter Kunz Co., Inc. 845-687-0400
  55 Creek Rd.   (cell) 914-388-4387
  Highfalls, NY 12440   FAX 845-687-0579
  Hours: 8:30-5:30 Mon-Fri
  **Pyrotechnics, atmospherics, electro-mechanical effects. Model making.
  RENTALS.**

Luna Tech, Inc. / Utratech 256-725-4224
  148 Moon Dr.   FAX 256-725-4811
  Owens Cross Road, AL 35763
  Hours: 9-5 Mon-Fri   E-mail: pyropak@aol.com
  www.pyropak.com
  Atmospheric, pyrotechnic devices; Pyropak brand. DISCOVER Only.

Michael Maniatis 212-620-0398
  48 W 22nd St. (5-6th Ave)   FAX 212-620-4281
  NY, NY 10010
  Hours: 9-5 Mon-Fri   E-mail: effects@nyc.rr.com
  www.effects4film.com
  **Special props, custom casting and reproduction, vacuumforming, remote
  control, electrical/mechanical effects.**

S-T

MICHAEL SMANKO / PRISM PROPS 732-382-9727
1015 Richard Blvd.
Rahway, NJ 07065
Hours: by Appt.
www.prismprops.com
Broadway Production propman & prop stylist. Prop supervision, shopping, fabrication, upholstery, painting and finishes, prop construction, SPFX. 35 year IATSE member. BA Fine Arts, MFA Theater Design. Member ATAC.

Carl Paolino Studios 917-957-7305
3801 23rd Ave.   917-282-4756
Astoria, NY 11105   FAX (same)
Hours: by appt. only   E-mail: cpseffects@aol.com
www.paolinostudios.com
Prosthetics, lifecasting, creature makeup. Speak to Carl.

Paragon Props 866-859-5059
2342 Wyecroft Rd., Unite G-1   905-469-0061
Oakville, Ontario, Canada L6L 5N2   FAX 905-469-0062
Hours: 8-4:30 Mon-Fri   E-mail: sdiamond@paragonprops.com
www.paragonprops.com
Props, masks, puppets, special effects, etc. Visit website for photos.

SFX Design, Inc. 817-599-0800
2500 I-20 E   FAX 817-599-0496
Weatherford, TX 76087
Hours: 8-4 Mon-Fri   E-mail: info@sfxdesigninc.com
www.sfxdesigninc.com
Stock and custom gobos. Decorative and fighting swords, handguns, rifles, machine guns; any period, able to fire blanks. Breakaway resin to mold your own bottles, glass, panes, etc. Fog-Master machines and Aquafog component; also cobweb system. Pyrotechnics and miniature pneumatics, blood effects, atmospherics; custom projects. Great website. Catalog. No credit cards.

Special F/X, Inc. 732-469-0519
PO Box 293   FAX 732-469-1294
South Bound Brook, NJ 08880
Hours: 10-5 Mon-Fri   E-mail: sales@aerotechnic.com
www.aerotechnic.com
Manufacturer air and CO2 cannons, stramers and confetti. Consultant for special effects users. Sell special effects books, electronic devices and aerotechnics products. Mail order only. CREDIT CARDS.

Stiegelbauer Assoc., Inc. 718-624-0835
Brooklyn Navy Yard, Bldg 20 (Cumberland-Flushing)   FAX 718-624-0844
Brooklyn, NY 11201
Hours: 7-2:30 Mon-Fri   E-mail: stiegassoc@aol.com
Union shop: TV, theatrical and industrial set construction. Also props and special effects. Contact Steve Paone. RENTALS.

S-T

Trengove Studios, Inc. 212-268-0020
60 W 22nd St., 2nd FL (7-8th Ave)   800-366-2857
NY, NY 10010   FAX 212-268-0030
Hours: call for appt. 9-5 Mon-Fri   E-mail: info@trengovestudios.com
www.trengovestudios.com
Brochure and product sheet available. Breakaways, fog, plastics fabrication.
Wonderful water and ice effects. CREDIT CARDS.

Wellington Enterprises 845-429-3377
PO Box 315, 55 Railroad Ave. Bldg 3-D   FAX 845-429-3765
Garnerville, NY 10923
Hours: 7-5:30 Mon-Thurs.   E-mail: bill@wellingtonent.com
www.wellingtonent.com
Custom magicians illusions, levitations, productions and transformation;
contact Bill Schmelk.

Zeller International, Ltd. 607-363-7792
15261 Highway 30   FAX 607-363-2071
Downsville, NY 13755
Hours: 9-5 Mon-Fri   E-mail: contact@zeller-int.com
www.zeller-int.com
Casting materials, flameproofing, fog, make-up supplies, breakaways and
atmospherics. Some minimums apply. Contact Carla Zelaschi. Catalog.
CREDIT CARDS.

Zenith Pyrotechnology 631-242-2110
25 W Jefryn Blvd., Ste. C   FAX 631-242-2125
Deer Park, NY 11729
Hours: 9-4 Mon-Fri   info@zenithpyro.com
www.zenithpyro.com
Full-line pyrotechnical company for all kinds of special effects. Custom
shows for film, TV and concerts.

SPONGES

J. Racenstein Co. 201-809-1680
74 Henry St.   800-221-3748
Secaucus, NJ 07094   FAX 201-348-1385
Hours: 8:30-4:30 Mon-Fri   E-mail: helpdesk@jracenstein.com
www.jracenstein.com
Natural Mediterranean sponges and synthetics. Window cleaning and
janitorial supplies. Ladders, harnesses, and safety equipment. Extra cool
website. CREDIT CARDS.

Supply Plus, Inc. / Optisource 973-481-4800
35 Martin Luther King Blvd.   800-724-5106
Newark, NJ 07104   FAX 973-481-7775
Hours: 9-5 Mon-Thurs / 9-3 Fri   E-mail: s.neustein@opti-source.net
www.opti-source.net
Natural and synthetic sponges. Janitor supplies. $200 minimum.

S-T

SPORTING GOODS

American Baton Co. 608-754-2238
PO Box 266, 300 S Wright Rd.   FAX 608-754-1986
Janesville, WI 53547
Hours: 8-5 Mon-Fri (closed for lunch)   E-mail: baton@americanbaton.com
www.americanbaton.com
All types of batons, accessories and cases. Catalog available. Shipping.
CREDIT CARDS.

Blatt Bowling & Billiard Corp. 212-674-8855
809 Broadway (11-12th St)   800-252-8855
NY, NY 10003   FAX 212-598-4514
Hours: 9-6 Mon-Fri / 10-4 Sat   E-mail: info@blattbilliards.com
www.blattbilliards.com
All types bowling and billiard supplies, tables. RENTALS. CREDIT CARDS.

BQ Sports, Inc. 718-349-3528
601 Manhattan Ave. (Nassau - Driggs)   FAX 718-389-0143
Brooklyn, NY 11040
Hours: 10:30-7:30 Mon-Sat   E-mail: gmax907@msn.com
Custom logo design, embroidery, screen printing, chenille work. CREDIT
CARDS.

Brigade Quartermasters, Ltd. / Ira Green, Inc. 800-663-7487
177 Georga Ave.   800-228-7344
Providence, RI 02905   FAX 800-738-8522
Hours: 8-4:30 Mon-Sat   E-mail: critter @iragreen.com
www.brigadequartermasters.com
Combat, SWAT uniforms and accessories; survival, camping, climbing,
hunting and expedition gear, outdoor action gear. Online catalog. No rentals.
CREDIT CARDS.

Gerry Cosby & Co., Inc. 212-563-6464
1110 Penn Plaza (31st St Between 6-7th Ave)   877-563-6464
NY, NY 10001   FAX 212-967-0876
Hours: 9:30-6 Mon-Fri   E-mail: gemsg@aol.com
www.cosbysports.com
Athletic outfitters for official sport uniforms. Phone orders. See Patty or Herb.
RENTAL on equipment only. CREDIT CARDS.

Cougar Sports, Inc. 914-693-8877
917 Saw Mill River Rd.   FAX 914-693-9453
Ardsley, NY 10502
Hours: 10-6 Tue-Wed, Fri-Sat / 10-8 Thurs
Archery equipment, arrows made to size; darts; also scuba diving gear. Will
ship. CREDIT CARDS.

Cran Barry 781-586-0111
330C Lynnway   800-992-2021
Lynn, MA 01903
Hours: 8:30-5 Mon-Fri   E-mail: service@cranbarry.com
www.cranbarry.com
Cheerleading clothes and pom-poms, field hockey and lacrosse equipment.
Also custom warm-ups and letter jackets. Will ship. CREDIT CARDS.

S-T

Eastern Mountain Sports 212-966-8730
530 Broadway (Prince-Spring St)
NY, NY 10012
Hours: 10-9 Mon-Fri / 10-8 Sat / 12-6 Sun
www.ems.com
Camping equipment; sleeping bags, tents, clothing, outdoor gear. Check website for other locations. RENTALS on equipment only. CREDIT CARDS.

Everlast Sporting Goods Mfg. 888-863-8375
P.O. Box 219318
Kansas City, MO 64121
Hours: 8-9pm Mon-Thurs / 8-7 Fri / 9-5 Sat
www.everlastboxing.com
Mostly boxing equipment, also aerobic and exercise equipment. Great website, shopping available online. CREDIT CARDS.

Frank's Sport Shop . . . .(Store) 718-299-9628
430 E Tremont Ave. (Park Ave)   (Office) 212-945-0020
Bronx, NY 10457   FAX 718-583-1652
Hours: 9-8 Mon-Fri / 9-6 Sat   E-mail: info@frankssports.com
www.frankssports.com
Silk-screening and embroidery on premise. Uniforms for work or sports. NYC municipal uniforms. Rush orders available. CREDIT CARDS.

Gym Source 212-688-4222
40 E 52nd St. (Park-Madison Ave)   Sales 212-688-6933
NY, NY 10022   FAX 212-750-2886
Hours: 9-7 Mon-Fri / 10-6 Sat / 12-5 Sun
www.gymsource.com
Rentals and sales of exercise equipment. Visit web address for other locations. RENTALS. CREDIT CARDS.

J. C. P. Precision Bowling 631-582-5450
200 Oval Dr.   FAX 631-582-5875
Central Islip, NY 11722
Hours: 8:30-5 Mon-Fri   E-mail: jcpbowling@att.net
www.jcpbowling.com
Bowling equipment, used and refurbished shoes, balls, parts and supplies. RENTALS. CREDIT CARDS.

K-Mart 212-760-1188
250 W 34th St.(7-8th Ave)
NY, NY 10019
Hours: 8-10 Mon-Thurs / 9-10 Fri-Sun

770 Broadway(8th St)   212-673-1540
NY, NY 10003-9535
Hours: 8-10 Daily
www.kmart.com
Sporting goods, camping gear, household goods. P.O.s. CREDIT CARDS.

S-T

Levy's Sports Center 201-861-7100
6116 Bergenline Ave., 2nd Fl.   FAX 201-861-8836
West New York, NJ 07093
Hours: 10-6 Mon-Fri / 10-3 Sat   E-mail: levysports@verizon.net
Complete athletic equipment and clothing. Also custom pads and matting.
Will ship. CREDIT CARDS.

Modell's 866-835-9129
1293 Broadway(Herald Sq)   212-244-4544
NY, NY 10001   FAX 212-594-1696
Hours: 9-9 Mon-Sat / 11-8 Sun

234 W 42nd St.(7-8th Ave)   212-764-7030
NY, NY 10017
Hours: 8-12am Mon-Thurs / 8-1am Fri-Sat / 9-1 Sun

1535 Third Ave.(86th St)   212-996-3800
NY, NY 10028
Hours: 9-9 Mon-Sat / 10-8 Sun
www.modells.com
Discount sporting goods and camping equipment. See website for additional
locations. CREDIT CARDS.

New York Kayak Company 212-924-1327
Pier 40, Southside (W Houston & West St)   800-KAYAK99
New York, NY 10014   FAX 212-924--0814
Hours: 10-6 Mon-Thurs / 10-5 Fri-Sat   E-mail: randall@nykayak.com
www.nykayak.com
Full-service sea kayak center featuring world-class instruction, guides, sea
kayaks, folding kayaks, all kayak gear, clothing and accessories. RENTALS.
CREDIT CARDS.

Paragon Sporting Goods Co. 212-255-8889
867 Broadway (18th St)   800-961-3030
NY, NY 10003
Hours: 10-8 Mon-Sat / 11-7 Sun   E-mail: info@paragonsports.com
www.paragonsports.com
Very large store; excellent selection of sporting goods, camping, hiking and
climbing gear. Never tell them you work in the industry, salespeople become
impolite. CREDIT CARDS.

Scuba Network 212-750-9160
669 Lexington(55-56th St)
NY, NY 10022
Hours: 10:30-7 Mon-Tue & Thurs / 10:30-8 Wed & Fri / Sat 10:30-6 / 12-5 Sun

655 Sixth Ave.(19-20th St)   212-243-2988
NY, NY 10010
Hours: 11-8 Mon-Fri / Sat 11-6 / 12-5 Sun

294 Fifth Ave   212-993-6166
NY, NY 10001
Hours: 11-8 Mon-Fri / 11-6 Sat / 12-5 Sun   E-mail: info@scubanetwork.com
www.scubanetwork.com
One of Manhattan's complete scuba shops. Visit the website for other
locations in NJ and FL. RENTALS. CREDIT CARDS.

S-T

Seating Solutions 631-845-0449
60 Austin Blvd.   888-959-7328
Commack, NY 11725   FAX 631-845-0470
Hours: 8:30-5 Mon-Fri / leave message   E-mail: rental@sitonthis.com
www.sitonthis.com
Seating systems, recreational props, boxing rings, etc. Bleachers and risers.
Playground equipment and trampolines. RENTALS.

Seattle Fabrics 206-525-0670
8702 Aurora Ave. N (N 87th St)   866-925-0670
Seattle, WA 98103   FAX 206-525-0779
Hours: 9-6 Mon-Sat   E-mail: seattlefabrics@msn.com
www.seattlefabrics.com
Outdoor and recreational fabric & hardware. Specialty fabrics, webbing,
thread and zippers; neoprene and closed cell foam. Patterns for outdoor and
sports attire; equestrian, tents and backpacks. Fabric samples available.
CREDIT CARDS.

Soccer Sport Supply Co. 212-427-6050
1745 First Ave. (90-91st St)   800-223-1010
NY, NY 10128   FAX 212-427-8769
Hours: 10-6 Mon-Fri / 10-4 Sat   E-mail: soccersport@verizon.net
www.homeofscoccer.com
Good selection of anything related to soccer. CREDIT CARDS.

Sports Equipment Specialists LLC 607-865-8128
15 East St. (Grizwald St)   607-865-8556
Walton, NY 13856   FAX 607-865-8128
Hours: 7-10 Mon-Fri   E-mail: gymnastics@stny.rr.com
Sales and rentals of all gymnastics related equipment including matting and
Olympic apparatus. RENTALS. CREDIT CARDS.

Tent & Trails 212-227-1760
21 Park Pl. (Church-B'way)   800-237-1760
NY, NY 10007   FAX 212-267-0488
Hours: 9:30-6 Mon-Wed & Sat / 9:30-7 Thurs-Fri / 12-6 Sun
www.tenttrails.com   E-mail: jamie@tenttrails.com
Large selection camping and climbing equipment, backpacks, sleeping bags,
clothing, accessories and camping foods. Knowledgeable staff. Tent RENTALS.
CREDIT CARDS.

Urban Angler 212-689-6400
206 Fifth Ave., 3rd FL (25-26th St)   800-255-5488
NY, NY 10010   FAX 212-689-6410
Hours: 10-6 Mon-Tue, Thurs-Fri / 10-7 Wed / 10-5 Sat
www.urbanangler.com
The source for everything fly fishing. CREDIT CARDS.

Weiss & Mahoney 212-675-1915
142 Fifth Ave. (19th St)   FAX 212-633-8573
NY, NY 10011
Hours: 9-6:30 Mon-Fri / 9-5 Sat
www.weissmahoney.com
Inexpensive military clothing and surplus goods; shoes, medals, camping
attire and equipment. No rentals. CREDIT CARDS.

S-T

SPORTING GOODS

WinCraft 800-533-8006
1124 W Fifth St.   507-452-4765
Winona, MN 55987   FAX 507-453-0690
Hours: 24-hrs. by web / 9-5 Mon-Fri Corporate Office
www.wincraft.com   E-mail: contact@wincraft.com
WinCraft is a recognized leader in retail licensed and promotional products. You can provide your customer with collectible and home decor products from NFL, NHL, NBA, NASCAR, NCAA, Olympics not to mention they have over 300 licenses. They offer licensed products for every retail selling season, hot market, and major event. CREDIT CARDS.

SPRINGS, SPRING STEEL & WIRE

Lee Spring Co. 718-236-2222
140 58th St., Unit 3-C (1st-2nd Ave)   888-777-4647
Brooklyn, NY 11220   FAX 888-426-6655
Hours: 8-5 Mon-Fri   E-mail: sales@leespring.com
www.leespring.com
Stock and custom order springs. Catalog. See website for other locations. CREDIT CARDS.

Modern International Wire 732-696-9100
145 Cliffwood Ave. (35th Ave)   800-322-WIRE
Cliffwood, NJ 07721   FAX 732-696-9111
Hours: 9-5 Mon-Fri   E-mail: rstein@moderninternational.com
www.moderninternational.com
All types of wire. $100 minimum. CREDIT CARDS.

Paramount Wire Co., Inc. 973-672-0500
2-8 Central Ave.   FAX 973-674-0727
East Orange, NJ 07018
Hours: 9-5 Mon-Fri
www.parawire.com
Millinery, piano, ribbon wire, cotton and rayon covered wire, paper stakes. $100 minimum.

Weico Wire & Cable 631-254-2970
161 Rodeo Dr.   FAX 631-245-2099
Edgewood, NY 11717
Hours: 9-5 Mon-Fri   E-mail: info@weicowire.com
www.weicowire.com
Carries tungsten wire, piano wire, heat shrinkable tubing, as well as a largest inventory of wire in the industry. Call or shop online only. CREDIT CARDS.

STATUARY

Art for Media 212-431-0607
84 Walker St. (B'way-Lafayette St)   212-431-3828
NY, NY 10013   FAX 212-219-0183
Hours: by appt.   E-mail: media4art@att.net
Rents art for film, TV, photography and corporations. We specialize in contempory paintings, drawings, sculpture and photography. Sale and fabrication available. RENTALS.

S-T

Eclectic / Encore Properties, Inc. 212-645-8880
620 W 26th St., 4th Fl. (11-12th Ave)   FAX 212-243-6508
NY, NY 10001
Hours: 9-5 Mon-Fri / or by appt.   E-mail: props@eclecticprops.com
www.eclecticprops.com
Large selection of bronzes, garden statuary and Blackamoors. Can request rental items thru online catalog. RENTALS. CREDIT CARDS.

Elizabeth Street Gallery, Inc. 212-941-4800
209 Elizabeth St. (Spring-Prince St.)   FAX 212-274-0057
NY, NY 10012
Hours: 10-5 Mon-Fri call for appt.   E-mail: info@elizabethstreetgallery.com
www.elizabethstreetgallery.com
Garden statuary and furniture, architectural elements. RENTALS. CREDIT CARDS.

F.A.S.T. Corp. 608-269-7110
PO Box 258, 14177 County Hwy Q   FAX 608-269-7514
Sparta, WI 54656
Hours: 8-5 Mon-Fri   E-mail: info@fastkorp.com
www.fastkorp.com
Manufacturers of all types and sizes of fiberglass animals, statuary and fountains. Catalog available. RENTALS. CREDIT CARDS.

Film Art 323-461-4900
5241 Melrose Ave.   888-858-7107
Hollywood, CA 90038   FAX 323-461-4959
Hours: 9-5 Mon-Fri   E-mail: info@filmartla.com
www.filmartla.com
Film Art is your answer to finding painting, sculpture, posters, prints and photography. Rents and sells the artwork of over 300 established artists. All artwork comes with a copyright license. Online art research available.

Florentine Craftsmen, Inc. 718-937-7632
46-24 28th St. (Skillman-47th Ave)   800-971-7600
Long Island City, NY 11101   FAX 718-937-9858
Hours: 8-4:30 Mon-Fri   E-mail: info@florentinecraftsmen.com
www.florentinecraftsmen.com
Outdoor statuary, fountains, garden furniture. Expensive. Download catalog from website. Contact Bill Reany. RENTALS. CREDIT CARDS.

Blaine Kern Artists, Inc. / Mardi Gras World 504-361-7821
1380 Port of New Orleans Pl.   800-362-8213
New Orleans, LA 70130   FAX 504-558-1865
Hours: 8-5 Mon-Fri   E-mail: sabine@martigrasworld.com
www.mardigrasworld.com
Custom and stock. Extensive inventory from 47 years of Mardi Gras Parade floats; papier mache, fiberglass props, figures, statuary, masks. Brochure available. Tours of facilities as well as workshops on mask making. P.O.s accepted. Beautiful website. RENTALS. CREDIT CARDS.

S-T

Kenneth Lynch & Sons 203-264-2831
114 Willenbrock   FAX 203-264-2833
Oxford, CT 06478
Hours: 8:30-5 Mon-Fri   E-mail: info@klynchandsons.com
www.klynchandsons.com
Statuary in lead, bronze and stone, topiary frames, fountains, planters, benches, weathervanes, made to order. No stock. Catalog $15.

Plaster Galaxy 718-769-8500
2756 Coney Island Ave. (Ave Y)   917-353-5754
Brooklyn, NY 11235   FAX 718-368-3430
Hours: 11-7 daily   E-mail: plastergalaxy@yahoo.com
www.jimmyplastercreations.com
Stock and custom columns, pedestals, etc. in plaster; also plaster statuary and figurines. CREDIT CARDS.

Recycling the Past 609-660-9790
381 N. Main St.   FAX 609-660-0878
Barnegat, NJ 08005
Hours: 10-5 Tue-Sun / by appt.   E-mail: contact@gmail.com
www.recyclingthepast.com
Architectural salvage and antiques. Vintage tile, statuary, iron fencing, doors, garden items and other funky finds. Inventory changes, check web-site for new items daily. RENTALS. CREDIT CARDS.

Sculpture House Casting 212-645-9430
155 W 26th St. (6-7th Ave)   888-374-8665
NY, NY 10001   FAX 212-645-3717
Hours: 8-5:30 Mon-Fri / 10-3 Sat / call for Summer hoursE-mail:
orders@sculptshop.com
www.sculptshop.com
Plaster and metal statuary including busts, casting and sculpting tools, supplies and materials. CREDIT CARDS.

STORAGE

Dependable Transport & Messenger Services 212-594-1300
240 W 37th St., 7th FL (7-8th Ave)   212-594-0320
NY, NY 10018   FAX 212-594-4375
Hours: 9-6 Mon-Fri   E-mail: gary@dependablemessengers.com
www.dependablemessengers.com
Bonded parking garages, truck parking, storage, temporary and production office rentals. RENTALS. CREDIT CARDS.

Network Transportation Systems, Inc. 908-689-4000
35 Brown St.   FAX 908-689-6025
Washington, NJ 07882
Hours: 8:30-5 Mon-Fri
Trucking and warehousing for scenery, lighting and trade shows. No Credit Cards.

S-T

Prop Transport, Inc. 212-957-4004
630 Ninth Ave # 309 (44-45th St)   FAX 212-957-6569
NY, NY 10036
Hours: available 24 hours   E-mail: proptrucks@aol.com
www.proptransport.com
Local trucking service geared to the film industry; reliable. Storage space
available. AMEX CREDIT CARD ONLY.

Showman Fabricators 718-935-9899
47-22 Pearson Place (Hamilton Ave-Bowne St)   FAX 718-855-9823
Long Island City, NY 11101
Hours: 7-5:30 Mon-Fri   E-mail: info@showfab.com
www.showfab.com
Platform and flat rental, Gusmer Tech spray foam, computer routing. Storage
space available.

Stiegelbauer Assoc., Inc. 718-624-0835
Brooklyn Navy Yard, Bldg 20 (Cumberland-Flushing)   FAX 718-624-0844
Brooklyn, NY 11201
Hours: 7-2:30 Mon-Fri   E-mail: stiegassoc@aol.com
Union scenic shop; storage rental available; contact Mike.

Walton Hauling & Warehouse Corp. .212-246-8685
609 W 46th St. (11-12th Ave)   FAX 212-586-4628
NY, NY 10036
Hours: 7-4:30 Mon-Fri   E-mail: walton609@aol.com
www.waltonhauling.com
115-plus year-old theatrical hauling company; local, some storage.

S-T

The professional trade association for artists and craftspeople working in theatre, film, television and advertising

ATAC Membership 2010-11

Sharlot Battin
 Montana Leatherworks
Chris Bobin
Sharon Braunstein
Randy Carfagno
Nadine Charlsen
Eileen Connor
Mary Creede
Margaret Cusack
Cindy Anita Fain
 CINAF Designs
James Feng
Keen Gat
Deborah R. Glassberg
Rodney Gordon
Joseph Gourley
Corrinna Griffin
Jung K. Griffin
Denise Grillo
 Offstage Design
Stockton Hall
Karen Hart
Suzanne Hayden

Marian Jean "Killer" Hose
J. Michelle Hill
Louise Hunnicutt
John Jerard
 Jerard Studio
Joni Johns
Jan Kastendieck
Rachel Keebler
 Cobalt Studios
Amanda Klein
Arnold S. Levine
 Arnold S. Levine, Inc.
Janet Linville
Jeanne Marino
 Moonboots Productions
Jerry Marshall
Betsey McKearnan
Gene Mignola
 Gene Mignola, Inc.
Mary Mulder
 Mulder / Martin, Inc.
Susan Pitocchi
Elizabeth Popeil

Adele Recklies
Monona Rossol
 Arts, Crafts, & Theatre
 Safety (A.C.T.S.)
Bill Rybak
Jody Schoffner
James R. Seffens
Lisa Shaftel
 Shaftel S2DO
Stanley Allen Sherman
 Mask Arts Company
Linda Skipper
Michael Smanko
 Prism Prips
Sarah Timberlake
 Timberlake Studios
Mari Tobita
US Institute for Theatre
 Tech. (USITT)
Monique Walker
Anne-Marie Wright
John Yavroyan
 Yavroyan & Nelsen, LTD

For membership information visit our website at
www.ATACBIZ.com
Email: info@ATACBIZ.com
Or drop us a line at:

ATAC Membership Application
Anne-Marie Wright
280 Third St. Apt # 1
Jersey City, NJ 07302-2759

S-T

TAPE, ADHESIVE

Dymalon, Inc. 410-686-7711
9100 Yellow Brick Rd., Ste D   FAX 410-686-7743
Baltimore, MD 21237
Hours: 8:30-5:30 Mon-Fri   E-mail: rjnee@verizon.net
www.dymalon.com
Excellent selection of wood grain contact papers, mattes, enamels, marbles, frosts, transparents, metallics and more. 17.5" wide, some up to 35". Foam tapes and all kinds of Velcro, including dual lock. Quick and friendly service. CREDIT CARDS.

Hollywood Rentals Production Services 800-233-7830
19731 Nordhoff St.   FAX 818-407-7875
Northridge, CA 91324
Hours: 8-6 Mon-Fri / mobile car for 24-hr. service
www.hollywoodrentals.com
Fuller's earth, glue, tape and other studio supplies. Will deliver. CREDIT CARDS.

International Tape Products Co., Inc. 888-748-9312
901 Murray Rd. / P.O. Box 376   FAX 973-599-0220
E. Hanover, NJ 07936
Hours: 8-5 Mon-Fri   E-mail: fpinfo@fidelitypaper.com
www.fidelitypaper.com
Distributors of all major brands; gaffers, spike, glo, dance floor and double-sided. Also offers special tape conversions services and special application tapes. No minimum. CREDIT CARDS.

Numax, Inc. 800-842-4230
1073 Rte 94, Unit 11   845-674-9060
New Windsor, NY 12553   FAX 845-562-1145
Hours: 8-5 Mon-Fri (Close at 4:30 on Fridays in summer)
www.numax.com
High-and low-tack tapes, hot melt glues and applicators. Catalog. No minimum. CREDIT CARDS.

Production Advantage, Inc. 802-651-6915
P.O. Box 1700   800-424-99914
Williston, VT 05495   FAX 877-424-9991
Hours: 8:30-6 Mon-Fri   E-mail: sales@proadv.com
www.proadv.com
Catalog sales of hardware, lighting, rigging, scenic material, soft goods, sound equipment and expendables to the entertainment industry. All major brands carried. Catalog. CREDIT CARDS.

Rose Brand 800-223-1624
        FAX 800-594-7424

4 Emerson Lane(15-16th St)   800-223-1624
Secaucus, NJ 07094   201-809-1730
Hours: 8-5 Mon-Fri   FAX 201-809-1851

S-T

Rose Brand (cont.) 800-223-1624
10616 Lanark St.   800-360-5056
Sun City, CA 91352   818-505-6290
Hours: 8-5 Mon-Fri   FAX 818-505-6293
www.rosebrand.com   E-mail: sales@rosebrand.com
Complete selection of tapes. Custom widths, decorative tapes available. Pro tape, Permacel, show tape, clear adhesive gaffers'. Call or fax for catalog. ***CREDIT CARDS.***

The Set Shop 212-255-3500
36 W 20th St. (5-6th Ave)   800-422-7831
NY, NY 10011   FAX 212-229-9600
Hours: 8:30-6 Mon-Fri   E-mail: info@setshop.com
www.setshop.com
Four types and strengths of spray adhesives and 50 different kinds of tape. ***CREDIT CARDS.***

TAXIDERMISTS & TAXIDERMY SUPPLIES

BIW Taxidermy World 203-634-1953
113 Broad St.   800-929-5844
Meriden, CT 06450
Hours: 9-5 Mon-Fri (closed Wed)   E-mail: taxidermyworld@att.net
www.taxidermyworld.com
Custom taxidermy from wolves to raccoons. Mounted animals and birds. Also teaches taxidermy and wood carvings. Contact Brian McGray. ***RENTALS.*** ***CREDIT CARDS.***

McKenzie Taxidermy Supply 800-279-7985
PO Box 480   704-279-7985
Granite Quarry, NC 28072   FAX 704-279-8958
Hours: 8-8 Mon-Fri   E-mail: taxidermy@mckenziesp.com
www.mckenziesp.com
Mail order. Great catalog - taxidermy forms, mounts, reference materials, respirators, modeling and casting supplies. Skulls. Technical assistance 8-5 Mon-Fri. ***CREDIT CARDS.***

E. J. Morgan 201-933-0284
539 Jefferson St.
Carlstadt, NJ 07072
Hours: 9-5 Mon-Fri
Custom taxidermy. Talk to Josh. ***RENTALS.***

G. Schoepfer, Inc. 203-250-7794
460 Cook-Hill Rd.   orders only 800-875-6939
Cheshire, CT 06410   FAX 203-250-7796
Hours: 8-4:30 Mon-Fri   E-mail: schoepferseyes@aol.com
www.schopferseyes.com
Glass eyes for dolls, decoys and animals. Catalog. $25 minimum. ***CREDIT CARDS.***

S-T

VanDyke's 605-796-4425
39771 SD Hwy 34
Woonsocket, SD 57385
Hours: 8-6 Mon-Fri / 9-3 Sat
www.vandykes.com
800-787-3355
FAX 605-796-4085
E-mail: restoration@cabelas.com

Taxidermy supplies. 24-hr. order with live operators. Great catalog. Very
pleasant to deal with. CREDIT CARDS.

Westchester Taxidermy Quality Mounts 845-228-0780
4 Meads Ct.
Carmel, NY 10512
Hours: by appt.

Over 700 animals and birds mounted They no longer carry taxidermy
supplies or offer taxidermy services. RENTALS.

TELEPHONES

Ace Video & Props 718-392-1100
37-24 24th St., Ste. 106 (Houston & West St)
Long Island City, NY 11101
Hours: 10-6 Mon-Fri / 10-2 Sat by appt.
212-206-1475
FAX 718-392-1155
E-mail: acevideorentals@gmail.com / acepropsnyc@gmail.com
www.aceprops.com

Telephones, fax machines, answering machines. RENTALS. CREDIT CARDS.

CEI, Inc. (Custom Electronics Industries) 563-382-5659
PO Box 51
Decorah, IA 52101
Hours: 10-6 Mon-Fri
www.tele-q.com
E-mail: mail@tele-q.com

Tele-Q telephone ringing system works with any single-line phone. For
brochure and information contact Bruce Larson or Robert Campbell. CREDIT
CARDS.

Chicago Old Telephone 800-843-1320
10 Binnington Ct.
Kingston, Ontario, Canada K7M 853
Hours: 9-5:30 Mon-Fri
www.chicagooldtelephone.com
613-548-7712
FAX 613-548-7036
E-mail: sales@chicagooldtelephone.com

Working antique telephones; brochure, publications on history and styles of
telephones. RENTALS. CREDIT CARDS.

Payphone Warehouse / Artemis & Jenny USA, Inc. 800-988-9056
610 S Marengo Ave.
Alhambra, CA 91803
Hours: 8-4:30 Mon-Fri
www.vending-usa.com
626-281-8069
FAX: 626-821-9685

Large selection of payphones at low cost. Will sell wholesale if purchasing
quantity. Many overseas-type payphones. Also, vending machines. Contact
Johnson. Very nice and helpful. CREDIT CARDS.

S-T

Phoneco- Old Telephones 608-582-4124
PO Box 70, 19813 E Mill Rd.   FAX 608-582-4593
Galesville, WI 54630
Hours: 9-5 Mon-Fri / (will take calls until 9 pm)   E-mail: phonecoinc@aol.com
www.phonecoinc.com
Antique and repro telephones; will ship UPS; contact Mary. Catalog.
RENTALS. CREDIT CARDS.

Waves 212-273-9616
40 W 25th St., Gallery 107 (in the Antiques Showplace)   FAX 201-461-7121
NY, NY 10001
Hours: 11-5 Wed-Sun   E-mail: wavesllc@gmail.com
www.wavesllc.com
Vintage telephones, radios, 78s, Victrolas. RENTALS. CREDIT CARDS.

TELESCOPES & BINOCULARS

Clairmont-Nichols, Inc. 212-758-2346
1016 First Ave. (56th St)   FAX 212-750-3583
NY, NY 10022
Hours: 9-6 Mon-Fri / (Tue & Thurs until 7) / 9-5 Sat   E-mail: cno56@aol.com
Good quality; repairs, sales and RENTALS. CREDIT CARDS.

Star Magic 212-988-0300
301 E 78th St. (office) (1st-2nd Ave)
NY, NY 10021
Hours: 11-7 Daily 24-hr. Web   E-mail: star@starmagic.com
www.starmagic.com
Telescopes, star maps and finders, astronomy-related books and posters.
CREDIT CARDS.

Tower Optical 203-866-4535
PO Box 251 / 275 East Ave.   FAX 203-866-2467
South Norwalk, CT 06856
Hours: 8-5 Mon-Fri
www.toweropticalco.com
Maintains and owns many coin-operated binoculars in the NYC area.
RENTALS.

THEATRICAL HARDWARE
See also: RIGGING EQUIPMENT

Automatic Devices Co. 610-797-6000
2121 S 12th St.   800-360-2321
Allentown, PA 18103   FAX 610-797-4088
Hours: 8-5 Mon-Fri   E-mail: info@automaticdevices.com
www.automaticdevices.com
Manufactures curtain tracks and motors, stage hardware; call for local dealer.
Also interior and hospital applications.

S-T

BMI Supply 518-793-6706
   571 Queensbury Ave.   800-836-0524
   Queensbury, NY 12804   FAX 518-793-6181
   Hours: 8-6 Mon-Fri   E-mail: bminy@bmisupply.com
   www.bmisupply.com
   A full-line theatrical supply house and on-site contractor. Retail and wholesale at everyday wholesale prices. Special effects. Sales only. CREDIT CARDS.

Chicago Canvas & Supply Co. 773-478-5700
   3719 W. Lawrence Ave.   FAX 773-588-3139
   Chicago, IL 60625
   Hours: 8-4 Mon-Fri Closed 12-1 daily   E-mail: email@chicagocanvas.com
   www.chicagocanvas.com
   Chicago's leading theatrical supply house. Hardware, curtain track, fabrics, expendables; gaffers tape, drop cloths, velcro, scenic supplies, Deca dyes, artist's canvas as well as muslin. CREDIT CARDS.

I. Weiss and Sons, Inc. 718-706-8139
   2-07 Borden Ave. (Vernon-Jackson Ave)   888-325-7192
   Long Island City, NY 11101   FAX 718-482-9410
   Hours: 8-5:30 Mon-Fri   E-mail: info@iweiss.com
   www.iweiss.com
   90 years in the theatrical business supplying drapery track & rigging. Catalog.

Kee Safety 716-896-4949
   100 Stradtman St.   800-851-5181
   Buffalo, NY 14206   FAX 716-896-5696
   Hours: 8-5:30 Mon-Fri   E-mail: info@keesafety.com
   www.keesafety.com
   Manufacturers of Kee Klamps; use with 1/2" to 2i"pipe. Catalog. CREDIT CARDS.

Mutual Hardware Corp. 718-361-2480
   36-27 Vernon Blvd. (Vernon Blvd)   866-361-2480
   Long Island City, NY 11106   FAX 718-786-9591
   Hours: 8:30-4:30 Mon-Fri
   www.mutualhardware.com
   Complete stage hardware, rigging supplies, casters, catalog. Contact John or Sal.

Oasis/Stage Werks 801-363-0364
   249 Rio Grande St.   FAX 801-575-7121
   Salt Lake City, UT 84101
   Hours: 9-6 Mon-Fri
   www.oasis-stage.com
   Largest stock in the Intermountain West. Featuring ETC, Altman, Lycian, Rosco, GAM, American DJ Supply, Anchor Tapes, LE Nelson Sales, Osram Sylvania and Ushio America. RENTALS. CREDIT CARDS.

S-T

Pfeifer Corp. 516-873-2033
288 E Jericho Turnpike   800-645-5544
Mineola, NY 11501   FAX 516-873-3695
Hours: 8:30-4:45 Mon-Fri   E-mail: info@pfeifercaster.com
www.pfeifercaster.com
Theatrical hardware, great selection of casters, dollies and handtrucks.
Catalog. CREDIT CARDS.

Pook Diemont & Ohl, Inc. 718-402-2677
701 E 132nd St. (Cypress-Willow)   FAX 718-402-2859
Bronx, NY 10454
Hours: 7-5 Mon-Fri   E-mail: info@pdoinc.com
www.pdoinc.com
Design/build company for theatre, TV and architectural environments
equipment systems. Scope includes new construction and renovation of
rigging systems, stage machinery, drapery and track, lighting and sound
systems.

Production Advantage, Inc. 802-651-6915
P.O. Box 1700   800-424-99914
Williston, VT 05495   FAX 877-424-9991
Hours: 8:30-6 Mon-Fri   E-mail: sales@proadv.com
www.proadv.com
Catalog sales of hardware, lighting, rigging, scenic material, soft goods,
sound equipment and expendables to the entertainment industry. All major
brands carried. Catalog. CREDIT CARDS.

Reynolds Drapery Service, Inc. 315-845-8632
7440 Main St.   FAX 315-845-8645
Newport, NY 13416
Hours: 8-4 Mon-Fri   E-mail: rynldpry@ntc.net.com
Curtain tracks, rigging; drapery mfg. and maintenance. No credit cards.

Rose Brand 800-223-1624
                                                          FAX 800-594-7424

4 Emerson Lane(15-16th St)   800-223-1624
Secaucus, NJ 07094   201-809-1730
Hours: 8-5 Mon-Fri   FAX 201-809-1851

10616 Lanark St.   800-360-5056
Sun City, CA 91352   818-505-6290
Hours: 8-5 Mon-Fri   FAX 818-505-6293
www.rosebrand.com   E-mail: sales@rosebrand.com
Stocking suppliers of ADC track. Rigging, theatrical hardware, scenic
supplies, tapes. Call or fax for catalog. CREDIT CARDS.

South Co 610-459-4000
210 N Brinton Lake Rd.   FAX 610-459-4012
Concordville, PA 19331
Hours: 8-5 Mon-Thurs / 8-4:30 Fri   E-mail: info@southco.com
www.southco.com
Case hardware, roto-locks, screw buttons. Catalog. CREDIT CARDS.

S-T

THEATRICAL SUPPLY HOUSES

BMI Supply 518-793-6706
571 Queensbury Ave.   800-836-0524
Queensbury, NY 12804   FAX 518-793-6181
Hours: 8-6 Mon-Fri   E-mail: bminy@bmisupply.com
www.bmisupply.com
A full-line theatrical supply house and on-site contractor. Retail and wholesale at everyday wholesale prices. Special effects. Sales only. CREDIT CARDS.

Chicago Canvas & Supply Co. 773-478-5700
3719 W. Lawrence Ave.   FAX 773-588-3139
Chicago, IL 60625
Hours: 8-4 Mon-Fri Closed 12-1 daily   E-mail: email@chicagocanvas.com
www.chicagocanvas.com
Chicago's leading theatrical supply house. Hardware, curtain track, fabrics, expendables; gaffers tape, drop cloths, velcro, scenic supplies, Deca dyes, artist's canvas as well as muslin. CREDIT CARDS.

Limelight Productions, Inc. 413-243-4950
471 Pleasant St.   800-243-4950
Lee, MA 01238   FAX 413-243-4993, 800-243-4951
Hours: 9-5 Mon-Fri
www.limelightproductions.com
Custom theatrical curtains. Authorized service for Rosco foggers, ETC dimming and control and Strong followspots. Catalog. CREDIT CARDS.

Norcostco, Inc. 973-575-3503
333A Rt. 46 W   800-220-6940
Fairfield, NJ 07004   FAX 973-575-2563
Hours: 9:30-6 Mon-Fri / 10-5 Sat (Winter)   E-mail: newjersey@norcostco.com
www.norcostco.com
Theatrical supply house, including costumes. Catalog. RENTALS. CREDIT CARDS.

Oasis/Stage Werks 801-363-0364
249 Rio Grande St.   FAX 801-575-7121
Salt Lake City, UT 84101
Hours: 9-6 Mon-Fri
www.oasis-stage.com
Largest stock in the Intermountain West. Featuring ETC, Altman, Lycian, Rosco, GAM, American DJ Supply, Anchor Tapes, LE Nelson Sales, Osram Sylvania and Ushio America. RENTALS. CREDIT CARDS.

Production Advantage, Inc. 802-651-6915
P.O. Box 1700   800-424-99914
Williston, VT 05495   FAX 877-424-9991
Hours: 8:30-6 Mon-Fri   E-mail: sales@proadv.com
www.proadv.com
Catalog sales of hardware, lighting, rigging, scenic material, soft goods, sound equipment and expendables to the entertainment industry. All major brands carried. Catalog. CREDIT CARDS.

S-T

Theatrical Services & Supplies, Inc. .631-873-4790
415 Oser Ave.   FAX 631-873-4795
Hauppauge, NY 11788
Hours: 7-5 Mon-Fri   E-mail: sales@gotheatrical.com
www.gotheatrical.com
Theatrical supplies, air-lite panels, will ship. CREDIT CARDS.

Tobins Lake Studios, Inc. 810-229-6666
7030 Whitmore Lake Rd.   888-719-0300
Brighton, MI 48116   FAX 810-229-0221
Hours: 9-5 Mon-Fri   E-mail: studio@tobinslake.com
www.tobinslake.com
*Theatrical supply house, including rental of backdrops and fog machines,
paint, hardware, vacuumformed architectural detail and ornaments. Catalog.
CREDIT CARDS.*

United Staging & Rigging 203-416-5380
250 Fifth St.   FAX 203-416-5387
Bridgeport, CT 06607
Hours: 8:30-4:30 Mon-Fri

96 Commerce Way   781-376-9180
Canton, MA 01801   FAX 781-376-9185
Hours: 8-5 Mon-Fri
www.unitedstaging.com
*Sales, rentals, installations. CM Motors, Stageright staging, stage roofs, soft
goods, truss, Genie lifts, riging, pipe & drape. Large RENTALS inventory.
Contact Doug Frawley (CT) or Jon Sharpe (MA).*

Vadar Productions 954-978-8442
1300 W McNab Rd.   800-221-9511
Fort Lauderdale, FL 33309   FAX 954-978-8446
Hours: 9-5 Mon-Fri   E-mail: info@avadar.com
www.avadar.com
*Scenic supplies and lighting equipment, stage hardware, fabric and draperies,
tapes, fire retardant specialities. Catalog available.*

Wits End Productions 212-242-9400
547 W 49th St.   212-757-4545
NY, NY 10019   FAX 212-242-1797
Hours: 24-hr. service   E-mail: tvgully@aol.com
www.witsendnyc.com
*Excellent company to handle all your production needs for film and
photography shoots. They have expendible kits you can rent that contain
EVERYTHING you could possibly need for any situation. Rent their trucks full
of expendables and you even get a truck driver experienced to assist in any
and all your needs. If they don't have what you need, they will buy it. Just
added to their stock are mole fans, ladders, 600W generators and much much
more. Visit their website to view their extensive RENTALS. CREDIT CARDS.*

S-T

THRIFT SHOPS

Cancer Care Thrift Shop 212-879-9868
1480 Third Ave. (83-84th St)   FAX 212-717-7184
NY, NY 10028
Hours: 11-6 Mon-Fri / Wed-Thurs until 7 / 11-4:30 Sat / 12-5 Sun
www.cancercare.org
*Mostly clothing, some jewelry, linens, picture frames, knick-knacks. CREDIT
CARDS.*

City Opera Thrift Shop 212-684-5344
222 E 23rd St. (2nd-3rd Ave)   FAX 212-684-5345
NY, NY 10010
Hours: 10-7 Mon-Fri/ 10-6 Sat / 12-5 Sun
www.nycopera.com/support/thrift.aspx
*Clothing, furniture, carpets, silver items, jewelry, knick-knacks. CREDIT
CARDS.*

Enamoo 718-624-0175
109 Smith St. (Pacific & Atlantic Aves.)
Brooklyn, NY 11201
Hours: 11-7 Mon-Sun
*This is not your grandmother's antiques store. Eclectic housewares ranging
anywhere from handmade German cuckoo clocks to Korean ceramic
dishware. Best known for their Brooklyn T-shirt lines. Phone orders
accepted. CREDIT CARDS.*

Housing Works Thrift Shops . . . . .212-366-0820 (Donations)
143 W 17th St.(6-7th Ave)   718-838-5050 (Store)
NY, NY 10011   FAX 212-691-8892
Hours: 10-7 Mon-Fri / 10-6 Sat / 12-5 Sun

202 E 77th St.(2nd-3rd Ave)   212-772-8461
NY, NY 10021
Hours: 11-7 Mon-Fri / 10-6 Sat / 12-5 Sun

157 E 23rd St.(Lexington-3rd Ave)   212-529-5955
NY, NY 10010
Hours: 10-7 Mon-Fri / 10-6 Sat / 12-5 Sun

306 Columbus Ave.(74-75th St)   212-579-7566
NY, NY 10023
Hours: 11-7 Mon-Fri / 10-6 Sat / 12-5 Sun
www.housingworks.org
*Furniture, clothing, housewares and luggage. Some designer goods.
Constantly changing inventory. See web address for other locations.*

Memorial Sloan-Kettering Thrift Shop 212-535-1250
1440 Third Ave. (82nd St)   FAX 212-737-9746
NY, NY 10028
Hours: 10-5:20 Mon-Fri / 11-4:45 Sat   E-mail: askienaa@mske.org
www.mskcc.org
Limited selection; furniture, clothing, books, knick-knacks. CREDIT CARDS.

S-T

THRIFT SHOPS

Salvation Army Store . . . . .www.satruck.com
436 Atlantic Ave.(Bond-Nevins St)   718-834-1562
Brooklyn, NY 11217
Hours: 10-5:30 Mon-Sat

536 W 46th St.(10-11th Ave)   212-757-2311
NY, NY 10036
Hours: 9-5:30 Mon-Sat
Large selection of men's and women's clothing, very large supply of
sweaters, knick-knacks, china and some furniture. Visit website for other
locations nation and worldwide.

Spence-Chapin Thrift Shop 212-369-0300
410 E. 92nd St. (83-84nd St)   FAX 212-794-2384
NY, NY 10128
Hours: 10:30-6:15 Mon-Fri / 10:30-6 Sat / 12-5 Sun
www.spence-chapin.org
Mostly clothing, some books, magazines, furniture, bric-a-brac.

Stuyvesant Square Thrift Shop 212-831-1830
1704 Second Ave. (88-89th St)
NY, NY 10028
Hours: 10-8 Mon-Sat / 10-7:30 Sun
Two floors of clothing at great prices and well organized. Some jewelry,
furniture, knick-knacks, etc. The place to go for "no budget" projects. CREDIT
CARDS.

Ugly Luggage 718-384-0724
214 Bedford Ave.
Brooklyn, NY 11211
Hours: 1-8 Mon-Fri / 12-7 Sat-Sun (Call first, hours can vary)
www.uglyluggage.com
Antiques, furniture, collectibles and clothing. Ask for Jim Lanning. RENTALS.
CREDIT CARDS.

TILE, BRICKS & COBBLESTONES

Appia Marble & Granite 718-745-5309
824 62nd St. (8th Ave)   FAX 718-680-7481
Brooklyn, NY 11220
Hours: 9-5 Mon-Fri / 9-2 Sat (Call to confirm closing time)
www.appiamarblegranite.com   E-mail: questions@appiamarblegranite.com
Stone fabricator and installer for kitchen, bath, flooring, fireplace and
commercial projects. They have a large selection of granite, marble, slate and
limestone slabs and tiles. Samples are available to borrow. Friendly,
knowledgeable and fast service.

Bella Tile Co. Inc. 212-475-2909
178 First Ave. (11th St)   FAX 212-475-2499
NY, NY 10009
Hours: 10-6 Mon-Tu3 / 10-7 Wed / 10-6 Thur-Fri / 10-4 Sat
www.bellatilenyc.com
American Olean dealer. Tools for the trade. Fast service, samples available.
Warehouse location: 408 E 11th St, NYC. CREDIT CARDS.

S-T

Bergen Bluestone Co., Inc. 908-237-2680
30 Copper Penny Rd.   FAX   908-237-2681
Flemington, NJ 08822
Hours: 7:30-4:30 Mon-Fri / 8-1 Sat
Natural stone suppliers and contractors. Carries marble, granite, limestone, slate, sandstone, quartzite, landscaping stones, boulders, petrified wood. CREDIT CARDS.

Bergen Tile Corp. 516-249-9100
330 Conklin Street (Dean-Bergen St)   866-789-4850
Farmingdale, NY 11735   FAX   718-638-9787
Hours: 7:30-6 Mon-Sat / 11-5 Sun   E-mail: request@bergentile.com
www.bergentile.com
Ceramic and vinyl tiles, linoleum, carpet and carpet tiles. Tools and materials. Small delivery charge. CREDIT CARDS.

Country Floors 212-627-8300
15 E 16th St. (Univ Pl-5th Ave)   FAX 212-242-1604
NY, NY 10003
Hours: 9-5 Mon-Fri   E-mail: info@countryfloors.com
www.countryfloors.com
Handpainted tiles, large selection of terra cotta tiles. CREDIT CARDS.

Ideal Tile 212-759-2339
405 E 51st St. (1st Ave)   FAX 212-826-0391
NY, NY 10022
Hours: 9-5 Mon-Fri / 10-3 Sat
www.idealtile.com
Italian ceramic tile importers. Tools and materials. CREDIT CARDS.

Italian Tile Import Corp. 201-796-0722
410 Market St.   FAX 201-796-2313
Elmwood Park, NJ 07407
Hours: 8:30-5 Mon-Fri / (Thurs until 6) / 9-2 Sat
Ceramic tile by the square foot; reasonably priced, good quality. Tools and materials. CREDIT CARDS.

New York Builders Supply Corp 212-564-5050
460 W 128th St. (Amsterdam Ave)   FAX 212-564-6355
NY, NY 10027
Hours: 7-3 Mon-Fri
www.newyorkbbuilderssupply.com
Bricks, cinderblocks, sand and plaster. Ask for Arthur Gold.

Paris Ceramics 212-644-2782
150 E 58th St., 7th Fl. (3rd-Lexington Ave)   FAX 212-644-2785
NY, NY 10155
Hours: 9-5 Mon-Fri   E-mail: newyork@parisceramicsusa.com
www.parisceramicsusa.com
Antique limestone and terra-cotta tiles, custom mosiacs and handpainted ceramic tiles. Will do custom work, CREDIT CARDS.

S-T

Quarry Tile Marble & Granite 212-679-8889
132 Lexington (28-29th St)   FAX 212-889-1364
NY, NY 10016
Hours: 9-5 Mon-Fri / 11-3:30 Sat   E-mail: quarrytile@aol.com
www.qtmg.net
Contractor who sells ceramic tile, marble and granite. Excellent selection,
samples available. CREDIT CARDS.

Vedovato Bros. 212-534-2854
246 E 116th St. (2nd Ave)   FAX 212-996-6506
NY, NY 10029
Hours: 8-1 Mon-Fri / 9-2 Sat   www.vedovatobrothers.com
Good selection of ceramic tiles, including mosaics. Tools and materials.
Contact George or Bob.

TOOLS

Abbey Rent-All 718-428-0400
203-16 Northern Blvd.   718-428-0146
Bayside, NY 11361
Hours: 8-5:30 Tue-Sat / 7:30-5:30 Mon   FAX 718-428-0404

301 S Broadway(Rt. 107)   516-681-1323
Hicksville, NY 11801   FAX 516-681-1326
Hours: 7:30-5 Mon-Sat   E-mail: abbeyrent@aol.com
Power tools. RENTAL. CREDIT CARDS.

B & N Hardware 212-242-1136
12 W 19th St. (5-6th Ave)   FAX 212-255-3973
NY, NY 10011
Hours: 8-5 Mon-Fri / 9-2 Sat
Good selection of hardware, tools, paint. Ask for Dave. CREDIT CARDS.

Best Hardware & Mill Supply, Inc. 516 354-0529
406 Jericho Tpke. (Sycamore-Lewis Ave)   FAX 516-354-1908
Floral Park, NY 11010
Hours: 7:30-5:30 Mon-Thurs / 7:30-7 Fri / 8-5 Sat / 10-2:30 Sun
Cobalt drill bits, milling supplies, tools, case-hardened bolts, hardware.
CREDIT CARDS.

C-Thru Ruler Co. 860-243-0303
6 Britton Dr.   800-243-8419
Bloomfield, CT 06002   FAX 860-243-1856
Hours: 8:30-5 Mon-Fri   E-mail: thecrew@cthruruler.com
www.cthruruler.com
C-Thru plastic rulers. Scrapbooking supplies, custom designed rulers, printed
cards, diecut cards and more.

Carter, Milchman & Frank 718-361-2300
28-10 37th Ave. (29th St)   FAX 718-937-5671
Long Island City, NY 11101
Hours: 6-5 Mon-Fri   E-mail: sales@cmftool.com
www.cmftool.com
Large power tools, repair parts for tools. CREDIT CARDS.

Constantines Wood Center of Florida, Inc. 954-561-1716
 1040 E Oakland Park Blvd.   800-443-9667
 Ft. Lauderdale, FL 33334   FAX 954-565-8149
 Hours: 8:-5:30 Mon-Fri / 9-3 Sat
 www.constantines.com
 Fine woodworking tools; hardwoods, veneers. Good products, good service.
 See online catalog. CREDIT CARDS.

Enkay Trading Co., Inc. 718-272-5570
 660 Atkins Ave. (Stanley-Workman)   866-310-8650
 Brooklyn, NY 11208   FAX 718-272-1520
 Hours: 8-4 Mon-Thur / 8-3:30 Fri   E-mail: enkay@erols.com
 www.enkayproducts.com
 Polishing equipment, drill bits, files, rotary files; imported and domestic tools;
 minimum order $150. Wholesale mail order only.

Forrest Manufacturing Co., Inc. 800-733-7111
 457 River Rd.   973-473-5236
 Clifton, NJ 07014   FAX 973-471-3333
 Hours: 9-5 Mon-Fri   E-mail: sales@forrestblades.com
 www.forrestblades.com
 The finest circular saw blades on the market. Expensive, but worth it.
 Duraline A.T. or Woodworker 1 for acrylic cuts. Also sell dado sets. Sharpening
 services. Online shopping. Very nice people. CREDIT CARDS.

Garden Hardware & Supply Co. 212-247-2888
 701 Tenth Ave. (47-48th St)   FAX 212-247-2859
 NY, NY 10036
 Hours: 8:30-5 Mon-Fri / 8:30-2 Sat
 Known as "Broadway's Hardware Store," this icon carries a large selection of
 "to the trade" hardware and supplies. Don't be surprised with the dis-
 organization of the store, Bobby can help you find just about anything.
 CREDIT CARDS.

Glaziers Hardware Products 718-361-0555
 25-07 36th Ave. (Crescent St)   FAX 718-361-0762
 Long Island City, NY 11106
 Hours: 8-4:30 Mon-Fri   www.glaziershardware.com
 Mouldings, accessories, tools for the mirror, glass, storefront and picture
 framing industries. Carries suction grips for handling glass. Browse products
 online. CREDIT CARDS.

Grainger, Div. of W.W. Grainger, Inc. 888-361-8649
 150 Varick St.(Spring-Vandam St)   212-629-5660
 NY, NY 10013   FAX 212-465-2677
 Hours: 7-5 Mon-Fri

 619 W 54th St. Fl1(11-12th Ave)   212-629-5660
 NY, NY 10019   FAX 212-629-5816
 Hours: 7-5 Mon-Fri

 815 Third Ave.(27-28th St)   718-499-1500
 Brooklyn, NY 11232   FAX 718-894-0167
 Hours: 7-5 Mon-Fri
 www.grainger.com
 Wide selection of hand and power tools, tool boxes, chests. Large catalog.
 Wholesale only. CREDIT CARDS.

S-T

H.T. Sales 212-265-0747
718 Tenth Ave. (49-50th St.)   877-HARDWARE
NY, NY 10019   FAX 212-262-0150
Hours: 7:30-4:30 Mon-Fri   E-mail: henry@htsalescompany.com
www.htsalescompany.com
Hand and power tools. CREDIT CARDS.

Home Depot 800-553-3199
550 Hamilton Ave.(16-17th St)   718-832-8553
Brooklyn, NY 11232
Hours: 6-12pm Mon-Sat / 8-9pm Sun

124-04 31st Ave.(College Point Blvd)   718-661-4608
Flushing, NY 11354   FAX 718-670-3437
Hours: 6-11pm Mon-Sat / 7-9pm Sun

40 W 23rd St.(5-6th Ave)   212-929-9571
NY, NY 10010
Hours: 7-9pm Mon-Sat / 8-7 Sun

980 Third Ave.(58-59th St)   212-888-1512
NY, NY 10022
Hours: 7-9pm Mon-Sat / 8-7 Sun

50-10 Northern Blvd.(50th St-Newtown Rd)   718-278-9031
Long Island City, NY 11101
Hours: 6-11pm Mon-Sat / 8-9pm Sun
www.homedepot.com
*Hardware, tools, lumber, plumbing supplies, gardening supplies, electrical
and lighting supplies. Windows, doors and cabinets. Queens and Brooklyn
locations open 24-hrs. for those emergency needs (less crowded then, too.)
Check web for additional locations. CREDIT CARDS.*

HomeFront Hardware 212-545-1447
202 E 29th St. (2nd-3rd Aves)   FAX 212-545-0092
NY, NY 10016
Hours: 24-hr Daily
www.homefronthardware.com
Hardware, housewares and tool rentals. CREDIT CARDS.

Japan Woodworker 510-521-1810
1731 Clement Ave.   800-537-7820
Alameda, CA 94501   FAX 510-521-1864
Hours: 9-5 Mon-Sat   E-mail: support@japanwoodworker.com
www.japanwoodworker.com
*Importer of Japanese tools, shears, scissors, planes, saws, chisels, punches
and stencil knives. Catalog available. CREDIT CARDS.*

S-T

Lehman's 330-857-5757
One Leham Cr. / P.O. Box 270   888-438-5346
Kidron, OH 44636   FAX 888-780-4975
Hours; 8-5:30 Mon-Sat / Thurs til 8   E-mail: GetLehmans@aol.com
www.lehmans.com
Housewares, oil lamps, cast-iron cookery, wood cook stoves, homestead tools. Rustic old-fashioned stuff. Non-electric Amish products. Plus, all those old-fashioned health and beauty products, canning supplies, food and laundry supplies. Great catalog ($10 including shipping) or shop online. CREDIT CARDS.

Lowe's 718-249-1151
118 Second Ave. (9th-12th St)   800-445-6337
Brooklyn, NY 11215   FAX 718-249-1154
Hours: 5-12 Mon-Sun
www.lowes.com
Big-box home improvement store that carries gardening supplies, kitchen cabinets, lighting fixtures, tools, lumber and much more. Check website for other locations. CREDIT CARDS.

McMaster-Carr Supply Co. 609-259-8900
200 New Canton Way   FAX 609-259-3575
Robbinsville, NJ 08691
Hours: 24-hrs. / 7 days   E-mail: nj.sales@mcmaster.com
www.mcmaster.com
Top quality items, esp. hardware. A vast selection of even the hard-to-find stuff. Most items available for next day delivery to NYC via UPS. Great catalog. CREDIT CARDS.

Microflame, Inc. / Azure Moon Trading Corp. 603-627-5699
8817 S. 71st East Ave.   877-638-6724
Tulsa, OK 74133   FAX 603-471-3845
Hours: 8:30-4:30 Mon-Thurs   E-mail: info@azuremoon.com
www.microflame.com
Miniature butane torches. CREDIT CARDS.

MSC Industrial Supply Co. 717-865-5888
100 MSC Dr.   800-645-7270
Jonestown, PA 17038   FAX 717-861-5810
Hours: 7-5 Mon-Fri   E-mail: branchhbu@mscdirect.com
www.mscdirect.com
Mail order machine tools; drills, reamers, cutters, etc.; great catalog, $25 minimum. Extensive hardware selection. Good one stop shop for large machines and tools. Competitive prices. Also good source for transmission parts. Order by 4 pm and get items delivered next day. Several depots across US. CREDIT CARDS.

New Hippodrome Hardware 212-840-2791
23 W 45th St. (5-6th Ave)   FAX 212-302-3306
NY, NY 10036
Hours: 8-5:30 Mon-Fri / 9-2 Sat
Dremel accessories, hardware, Black & Decker, Stanley, Keys made. CREDIT CARDS.

S-T

Northeast Equipment 973-256-2040
1190 Route 23 S   FAX 973-256-1766
Cedar Grove, NJ 07009
Hours: Seasonal hours, call first
Outdoor power equipment. Power generators, large garden equipment, blowers, supplies. RENTALS. CREDIT CARDS.

Numax, Inc. 800-842-4230
1073 Rte 94, Unit 11   845-674-9060
New Windsor, NY 12553   FAX 845-562-1145
Hours: 8-5 Mon-Fri (Close at 4:30 on Fridays in summer)
www.numax.com
East Coast distributor of Duo-Fast products. Staplers, nailers, tackers (air and electric); tapes and adhesives; hot melt glue guns. Phone orders. No minimum. CREDIT CARDS.

Rudolph Bass, Inc. 212-226-4000
45 Halladay St. (Carterett)   201-433-3800
Jersey City, NJ 07304   FAX 201-433-6853
Hours: 8-4 Mon-Fri   E-mail: rbassmachy@aol.com
www.rudolphbassinc.net
Specialty is large power tools, including parts and maintenance. CREDIT CARDS.

Seven Corners Hardware 800-328-0457
216 W 7th St.   651-224-4859
St. Paul, MN 55102   FAX 651-224-8263
Hours: 7-5:30 Mon-Fri / 8-3 Sat   E-mail: sevencorner@aol.com
www.7corners.com
Very good prices on power and hand tools; catalog. CREDIT CARDS.

Sid's Hardware 718-875-2259
345 Jay St. (Myrtle-Willoughby St)   FAX 718-852-3369
Brooklyn, NY 11201
Hours: 8-6:15 Mon-Fri / 8-5:45 Sat / 10-4:45 Sun
www.sidshardware.com   E-mail: info@sidshardware.com
Large selection of general and household hardware, power tools and household supplies. CREDIT CARDS.

Siegel Brothers 718-387-0300
880 Meeker Ave. (Varick St)   FAX 718-387-1874
Brooklyn, NY 11222
Hours: 6-5 Mon-Fri
www.siegelbros.com
Large selection of tools, Crosby clamps, motors. CREDIT CARDS.

S-T

Sprotzer Tools & Hardware Co., Inc. 718-349-2580
2743 Jackson Ave.
Long Island City, NY 11101
Hours: 8-5 Mon-Fri
Wholesale supplier of hand tools and cutting tools. Phone orders accepted.

Travers Tool Co. 718-886-7200
  PO Box 541550, 128-15 26th Ave. (Ulmer)   800-221-0270
  Flushing, NY 11354   FAX 800-722-0703
  Hours: 8-5 Mon-Fri   E-mail: ideas@travers.com
  www.travers.com
  Drill bits, chuck keys, clamps, sanding belts, more. 1130-page catalog! CREDIT
  CARDS.

Vercesi Hardware 212-475-1883
  152 E 23rd St. (3rd-Lex Ave)   FAX 212-979-8482
  NY, NY 10010
  Hours: 8-7 Mon-Fri / 9-7 Sat / 12-5 Sun   E-mail: acehardwarestore@gmail.com
  www.vercesihardware.com
  A wonderfully stocked general hardware store. Electrical and plumbing parts.
  Housewares, paints, appliances and window blinds. Accounts welcome. Note
  the late hours. CREDIT CARDS.

The Garrett Wade Co., Inc. 212-807-1155
  233 Spring St., 3rd Fl.   800-221-2942
  NY, NY 10013   FAX 212-255-8552
  Hours: 9-5 Mon-Fri
  www.garrettwade.com
  Fine woodworking tools from all countries; small selection of solid brass
  furniture hardware; also a few antique tools for the collector. Catalog. CREDIT
  CARDS.

Woodcraft Supply Corp. . . . .(orders) 800-225-1153
  1177 Roseman Ave. (PO Box 1686)   (customer service) 800-535-4482
  Parkersburg, WV 26102   FAX 304-428-8271
  Hours: 8-5 Mon-Fri Cust. Service / 8:30-9 Mon-Fri Technical Advice
  www.woodcraft.com   E-mail: custserv@woodcraft.com
  Excellent selection of quality tools, some hardware. Catalog. CREDIT CARDS.

TOYS & GAMES

Ambassador Toys 415-759-8697
  186 W Portal Ave.   FAX 415-566-8081
  San Francisco, CA 94127
  Hours: 9-7 Daily   E-mail: customerservice@ambassadortoys.com
  www.ambassadortoys.com
  Award winning toy store offering quality toys from around the world. Visit
  website for selection. Will ship worldwide. CREDIT CARDS.

Arrow Wholesale Co. 508-753-5830
  28 Water St. (Mercer St)   800-452-6310
  Worcester, MA 01604   FAX 508-753-5316
  Hours: 9-6 Mon-Fri   E-mail: info@arrowonthenet.com
  www.arrowonthenet.com
  Toys wholesale; also seasonal merchandise, stationery, school supplies &
  props. Mom & Pop "5 and Dimeî"treasures.

S-T

The Children's General Store 212-426-4479
168 E 91st St.
NY, NY 10128
Hours: 10-6 Mon-Sat / 11-5 Sun
Overall good store for basic children's toys, books, stuffed animals and those hard-to-find old-fashioned wooden toys. CREDIT CARDS.

Classic Toys 267-687-3673
2138 E Cumberland St.   215-909-5081
Philadelphia, PA 19125
Hours: 12-6 Mon-Fri
www.classictoysnyc.com
Large selection of old and new die-cast metal vehicles and toy soldiers; stuffed animal and play sets. Former store location in the West Village of NYC. Online based orders only. CREDIT CARDS.

The Compleat Strategist 212-685-3880
11 E 33rd St. (Madison-5th Ave)   FAX 212-685-2123
NY, NY 10016
Hours: 10:30-6 Mon-Sat / Thurs until 9
www.thecompleatstrategist.com
Games, role playing, card games. Visit web address for other locations. CREDIT CARDS.

Creative Toymakers / Toys 2 Wish 4 860-228-3102
93 Mill Plain Rd.(Teacher - Parent Store)   203-794-0577
Danbury, CT 06811   FAX 203-798-9854
Hours: 10-6 Mon-Fri / 10-5 Sat

127 Main St.   860-657-8697
Hebron, CT 06248   FAX 860-228-5272
Hours: 10-6 Mon-Sat / 12-4 Sun   E-mail: info@toys2wish4.com
www.toys2wish4.com
Dolls and doll furniture; also general and educational toys. Two hours from Manhattan.

Eclectic / Encore Properties, Inc. 212-645-8880
620 W 26th St., 4th Fl. (11-12th Ave)   FAX 212-243-6508
NY, NY 10001
Hours: 9-5 Mon-Fri / or by appt.   E-mail: props@eclecticprops.com
www.eclecticprops.com
History for rent. Selection of older styles and the unusual. Can request rental items thru online catalog. RENTALS. CREDIT CARDS.

Rita Ford Music Boxes, Inc. 212-535-6717
                                                                908-377-3225
New Providence, NJ 07974   FAX 212-772-0992
Hours: 9-5 Mon-Sat
www.ritafordmusicboxes.com
All kinds of music boxes, antique and new, jewelry boxes and hand painted eggs; repairs. Shopping online only. CREDIT CARDS.

S-T

Fun Antiques 917-837-6499
2024 E Everly Rd.   212-838-0730
Shorewood, WI 53211
Hours: 24-hrs. on call   E-mail: george@funantiques.net
www.funantiques.net
Large selection of antique and not-so-antique toys and games. Contact
George. Ebay Store: funantiquesnyc. RENTALS. CREDIT CARDS.

Gamblers General Store 702-382-9903
800 S. Main St.   (outside NV) 800-322-2447
Las Vegas, NV 89101   FAX 702-366-0329
Hours: 9-6 Daily   E-mail: ggs@lasvegas.net
www.gamblersgeneralstore.com
The world's largest gambling superstore. Located just minutes from the
famous Las Vegas Strip, they host over 5000 gambling items in their 30,000
sq. ft. warehouse. Custom prize wheels, poker chips and cards. Must visit
web-site to see all they carry. Shop online or call for catalog. RENTALS
available for large productions. CREDIT CARDS.

Games & Names 212-769-2514
302 W 78th St. (Riverside-W End Ave)   FAX call first
NY, NY 10024
Hours: by appt.   E-mail: bridgeproof@yahoo.com
Vintage games and playing cards, boards, board games, playing pieces, dice
and related graphics. Customized games for parties and promotions.

GreatBigStuff.com 800-773-8832
128 Patriot Dr., Units 8,9, and 10   FAX 206-337-1725
Middletown, DE 19709
Hours: 9:30-6 Mon-Fri   E-mail: service@greatbigstuff.com
www.greatbigstuff.com
Just as the name says, this website carries just about everything oversized.
Rulers, pencils, alarm clocks, food items, bottles, baby items, game pieces
and much, much more. Be sure to check out their website for other COOL
items. CREDIT CARDS.

Kidding Around 212-645-6337
60 W 15th St. (5-6th Ave)   877-543-2768
NY, NY 10011
Hours: 10-7 Mon-Sat / 11-6 Sun   www.kiddingaround.us
Great selection of toys and games. Many educational toys and designer baby
items. CREDIT CARDS.

Oriental Trading Company, Inc. 800-875-8480
4206 S. 108th St.   402-331-6800
Omaha, NE 68137   FAX 402-331-3873
Hours: 24-hr. online catalog service
www.orientaltrading.com
Thousands of small toys, novelties and party supplies for every occasion.
Catalog available. CREDIT CARDS thru Paypal.

S-T

Paladin Amusements, Inc. 908-464-0826
9 Maple Ave.   800-699-8552
Berkeley Heights, NJ 07922   FAX 908-464-3661
www.paladinamusements.com   E-mail: paladin@paladinamusements.com
Rental of Carnival games, trailers, tents, rides, speedball, hi-striker and other
carnival and amusement equipment. Sales of carnival and boardwalk-type
prizes and merchandise. RENTALS.

Penny Whistle Toys 212-873-9090
448 Columbus Ave.(81st-82nd St)
NY, NY 10024
Hours: 10-6 Sun-Thurs / 10-7 Fri-Sat

72 Westchester Ave.   914-764-8699
Pound Ridge, NY 10576
Hours: 10-7 Mon-Fri / 10-5 Sat / 10-4 Sun
www.pwtoys.com
Interesting selection of quality toys (some European), games, books and
tapes. RENTALS for photo shoots. CREDIT CARDS.

pucciManuli 484-466-2067
66 W. Stratford Ave.   FAX 484-466-2437
Lansdowne, PA 19050
Hours: 8-6 Mon-Fri   E-mail: info@puccimanuli.com
www.puccimanuli.com
High-end, individually handcrafted toys, games, kaleidoscopes and
playthings made by artisans from around the world. A true treat for all
craftspeople. RENTALS. CREDIT CARDS.

The Rocking Horse Shop . . . .+44 (0)1759-368737
Fangfoss   FAX +44 (0)1759-368-194
York, England, YO41 5JH
Hours: 9-4 Mon-Sat (Great Britain)   E-mail: info@rockinghorse.co.uk
www.rockinghorse.co.uk
Everything you need to carve a rocking horse. Bridles, saddles, glass eyes,
real horsehair and artificial manes and tails, rocking hardware, plans, full kits.
Also "The Rocking Horse Maker," a wonderful book on the art of carving. Full
color catalog. CREDIT CARDS.

Star Magic 212-988-0300
301 E 78th St. (office) (1st-2nd Ave)
NY, NY 10021
Hours: 11-7 Daily 24-hr. Web   E-mail: star@starmagic.com
www.starmagic.com
Space-related items such as fiber optic lamps, lava lamps, plasma balls,
special effect LED lighting. Also science kits games and puzzles. CREDIT
CARDS.

Toys R' Us 800-869-7787
1514 Broadway (44th at Times Square)
NY, NY 10001
Hours: 10-10 Mon-Sat / 11-8 Sun
www.toysrus.com
World's largest toy store, located in the heart of Times Square. 110,000
square feet of toys, including a ferris wheel and kid friendly-cafe. CREDIT
CARDS.

S-T

Village Chess Shop 212-475-9580
   230 Thompson St. (Bleecker-W 3rd St)   FAX 212-995-9192
   NY, NY 10012
   Hours: 11-12 daily   E-mail: info@chess-shop.com
   www.chess-shop.com
   Chess sets, books, boards; can also play here for $1 an hour. RENTALS.
   CREDIT CARDS.

Western Spirit 800-976-9287
   395 Broadway (Walker)   212-343-1476
   NY, NY 10013   FAX 212-343-0257
   Hours: 10:30-7:30 Mon-Fri / 11-8 Sat-Sun   E-mail: iwesternspiritj@yahoo.com
   www.westernspiritny.com
   Largest Western shop in NYC. Native American art, crafts, jewelry, pottery,
   leathercraft and headdresses. Western clothing in men's, women's and
   children's sizes. Toys. CREDIT CARDS.

TRIMMINGS: GENERAL

Artistic Ribbon & Novelty Co. 212-255-4224
   22 W 21st St. (5-6th Ave)   FAX 212-645-6589
   NY, NY 10010
   Hours: 9-5 Mon-Fri   E-mail: info@artisticribbon.com
   www.artisticribbon.com
   Satin, grosgrain, velvet, poly ribbon; washable, flame retardant.

S. Axelrod Co., Inc. 212-594-3022
   7 W 30th St., 2nd Fl. (5th-B'way)   FAX 212-947-3787
   NY, NY 10001
   Hours: 9-5 Mon-Fri   E-mail: sales@axelrodco.com
   www.axelrodco.com
   Decorative trims, rhinestones, metal findings and moving eyes for dolls.
   CREDIT CARDS.

B&Q Trimmings 212-398-0988
   210 W 38th St. (7-8th Aves)   FAX 212-869-2899
   NY, NY 10018
   Hours: 10-6 Mon-Sat   E-mail: info@shinetrim.com
   www.shinetrim.com
   Specializing in beaded and sequined trimming and appliques as well as
   feathers, rhinestones, iron-on embroideries, satin ribbon, lace, fancy buttons,
   gloves and more. CREDIT CARDS.

Beads World, Inc. 212-302-1199
   1384 Broadway (37-38th St)   FAX 212-302-2330
   NY, NY 10018
   Hours: 9-7 Mon-Fri / 10-6 Sat-Sun   E-mail: beadsworld@aol.com
   www.beadsworldusa.com
   Beads, trimmings, chains and findings. Wholesale and retail. CREDIT CARDS.

S-T

Berwick Offray 800-344-5533
350 Clark Dr.
Bud Lake, NJ 07828
Hours: Phone calls only
www.offray.com
Wholesale ribbons; satin, grosgrain, velvet, etc.; woven-edge, craft and floral ribbons. Catalog available.

C & C Metal Products 201-569-7300
456 Nordhoff Place (7-8th Ave)   FAX 201-569-4112
Englewood, NJ 07631
Hours: 8-5 Mon-Fri or by appt.   E-mail: sales@ccmetal.com
www.ccmetal.com
Wholesale only; metal buttons, buckles, nailheads, jewelry findings & rhinestones; large catalog available to volume purchasers. CREDIT CARDS.

Daytona Trimmings Co. 212-354-1713
251 W 39th St. (7-8th Ave)   FAX 212-391-0716
NY, NY 10018
Hours: 9-6:30 Mon-Fri / 9:30-5:20 Sat   E-mail: daytrim@worldnet.att.net
Ric-rac, braids, laces, scarves, emblems, shoulder pads; wholesale. CREDIT CARDS.

Douglas and Sturgess / Artstuf.com 888-278-7883
730 Bryant St.   510-235-8411
San Francisco, CA 94107   FAX 510-235-4211
Hours: 8:30-5 Mon-Wed, Fri / 8:30-8 Thurs
www.artstuf.com
Distributors of metallic beaded mesh (MBM); acetate beads fastened to a polyester mesh and coated with a variety of metallic and non-metallic finishes.

Farber Trimming Corp. 212-967-6540
149 W 36th St. 9th FL (B-way-7th Ave)   800-223-2702
NY, NY 10001   FAX 212-967-7455
Hours: 9-5 Mon-Fri   E--mail: info@farberbraid.com
www.farberbraid.com
Wholesale. Metallic braids and trims, cords, rickrack etc.. Online orders only. Speak to Glen or Mark.

Fred Frankel & Sons, Inc. 212-840-0810
19 W 38th St. (5-6th Ave)   FAX 212-391-1214
NY, NY 10018
Hours: 8:30-4:30 Mon-Fri   E-mail: info@fredfrankel.com
www.fredfrankel.com
Wholesale only. Loose rhinestones, rhinestone bandings, pearl, beaded and sequined trims and motifs. Catalog available online. All orders must be placed first then pick up. Best price in town for Swarovski heat sets.CREDIT CARDS.

S-T

Gelberg Braid Co., Inc. 212-730-1121
231 W 39th St., FL 8 (7-8th Ave)   FAX 212-840-7474
NY, NY 10018
Hours: 9-5 Mon-Fri   E-mail: custserv@gelbergbraid.com
www.gelbergbraid.com
Manufacturer of dress trimmings, braids, tassels, cords, braided buttons.
Shop online, however this is a 36 yd / $250 minimum. Download current
catalog for references. Their trimmings are available for retail purchases at at
Calico Corners. Speak to Irwin. CREDIT CARDS.

Ginsburg Trim LLC 212-244-4539
242 W 38th St. (7-8th Ave)   800-929-2529
NY, NY 10018   FAX 212-921-2014
Hours: 9-5 Mon-Fri
www.ginstrim.com
Washable ribbons, velvet, grosgrain, satin, jacquard and braids. Catalog.
Some trims available online. CREDIT CARDS.

Elliot Greene & Co., Inc. 212-391-9075
37 W 37th St. (5-6th Ave)   FAX 212-391-9079
NY, NY 10018
Hours: 9-4 Mon-Fri   E-mail: egbeads@juno.com
www.egbeads.com
Rhinestones, spangles, jewels, beads, pearls, beaded trims.

Grey Owl Indian Crafts 732-389-4626
15 Meridian Rd.   (orders) 800-487-2376
Eatontown, NJ 07724   FAX 732-389-4629
Hours: 9-5 Mon-Fri   E-mail: sales@greyowlcrafts.com
www.greyowlcrafts.com
Indian beads, feathers, kits; catalog. CREDIT CARDS.

Hai's Trimming Co. 212-764-2166
242 W 38th St. (7-8th Ave)   FAX (same)
NY, NY 10018
Hours: 10-6 Mon-Fri / 10-5 Sat
All kinds of trims; bridal accessories. Good stock of heat fix and glue on
rhinestones, ribbons, buttons, etc. Beaded trims and feathers. Vinyl repair
glues and adhesives that stick vinyl to vinyl. CREDIT CARDS.

Hyman Hendler & Sons 212-840-8393
21 W 38th St. (5-6th Ave)   FAX 212-704-4237
NY, NY 10018
Hours: 9-5 Mon-Fri / Sat by appt.
www.hymanhendler.com
Quality ribbons; grosgrain, satin, all types; some drapery, upholstery, antique
trims. CREDIT CARDS.

Jay Notions & Novelties, Inc. 212-921-0440
22 W 38th St. (5-6th Ave)   888-529-8746
NY, NY 10018   FAX 212-575-2620
Hours: 8:30-5 Mon-Fri   E-mail: custserv@jaytrim.com
www.jaytrim.com
Wholesale ribbon, braid, trim. CREDIT CARDS.

S-T

Joyce Trimming, Inc. 212-719-3110
109 W 38th St. (Bway-7th Ave)   800-719-7133
NY, NY 10018   FAX 212-719-3091
Hours: 9-6 Mon-Fri   E-mail: info@ejoyce.com
www.ejoyce.com
Broad selection of rhinestones, bandings, buttons, beads, trimmings and
accessories. Heat transfer motifs in crystal and metal studs. Visit website to
view selections. CREDIT CARDS.

Kahaner Co., Inc. 516-766-6363
3405 Ocean Ave.   FAX 516-766-7238
Oceanside, NY 11572
Hours: 9-5 Mon-Fri   E-mail: ktrimsales@aol.com
www.sequins4u.com
Trims, especially rhinestone, sequin and beaded. Catalog available. CREDIT
CARDS.

La Lame, Inc. 212-921-9770
132 W 36th St., 11th Fl. (5-6th Ave)   FAX 212-302-4359
NY, NY 10018
Hours: 9-5 Mon-Fri   E-mail: edschneer@lalame.com
www.lalame.com
Selection of metallic laces, braids and cords is excellent. Many ecclestical
trims. CREDIT CARDS.

M & J Trimmings . . . . .1-800-9MJ TRIM
1008 Sixth Ave. (37-38th St)   212-204-9595
NY, NY 10018   FAX 212-704-8090
Hours: 9-8 Mon-Fri / 10-6 Sat / 12-6 Sun   E-mail: info@mjtrim.com
www.mjtrim.com
Pricey; ribbons, buttons, buckles, frogs, beads, rhinestones, handbag handles
and Swarovski heatsets. CREDIT CARDS.

Margola Import Corp 212-695-1115
48 W 37th St. (5-6th Ave)   FAX 212-594-0071
NY, NY 10018
Hours: 8:30-6 Mon-Fri / 10-4 Sat
www.margola.com
Rhinestones, beads, rosemontees, pearls, beaded and embroidered trims.
View catalog online. Contact them for minimum ordering requirements.
CREDIT CARDS.

May Art 203-637-8366
PO Box 478   FAX 203-637-5285
Riverside, CT 06878
Hours: 9-5 Mon-Fri   E-mail: sales@mayarts.com
www.mayarts.com
Sells beautiful imported French organdy silk ribbons and flowers. Wholesale.
Minimum order $100.

S-T

Mayer Import Co., Inc. 212-391-3831
25 W 37th St. (5-6th Ave)   FAX 212-768-9183
NY, NY 10018
Hours: 8:30-4:30 Mon-Fri   E-mail: store@mayerimport.com
www.mayerimport.com
Jewels, pearls, cameos, trade beads, faceted plastic domes, etc. Catalog
available.

Metro Trimming Corp. 212-564-7966
327 W 36th St., 10th Fl. (8-9th Aves)   FAX 212-564-6262
New York, NY 10018
Hours: 8-4 Mon-Fri
Custom bindings, piping, flat bias cording, fringing, ruffling etc. Talk to Gary
and Jay. $75 minimum. Fast quick service.

Metropolitan Impex, Inc. 516-374-2296
775 Bryant St. (35-36th St)   FAX 516-374-2298
Woodmere, NY 11598
Hours: 9-6 Mon-Sat   E-mail: trims1@aol.com
Good selection of general trimmings; feathers, laces, beads, etc. CREDIT
CARDS.

Mokuba 212-869-8900
55 W 39th St. (5-6th Ave)
NY, NY 10018
Hours: 9-5 Mon-Fri
Over 3,500 square feet of decorative ribbons and trims. Every fabric, shape,
size and color imaginable; stretchable faux fur trims, braided leathers and
washable fake suedes. Bugle-beaded tassle ribbons. Company based in
Japan and has more than 43,000 items. CREDIT CARDS.

Novelty Pom Pom Co. 212-391-9175
247 W 37th St.,11th Fl. (7-8th Ave)   FAX 212-575-9688
NY, NY 10018
Hours: 8:30-5 Mon-Fri
Manufacturers of pompoms, tassels, braids, fringe, piping, cords, frogs,
passementeries; wholesale or retail. Speak to John.

Ornamental Beads 303-567-2222
5712 W. 38th Ave.   800-876-6762
Wheat Ridge, CO 80212   FAX 303-567-4245
Hours: 10-6 Mon-Sat / 12/4 Sun   E-mail: orna@ornabead.com
www.ornabead.com
Jewelry findings and supplies, new and antique stones and beads. Costume
jewelry. 40 years in business. Used by many Broadway shows.

Owl Mills 732-942-8025
500 James St. Unit 11   FAX 732-907-2621
Lakewood, NJ 08701
Hours: 9-5 Mon-Fri   E-mail: owlmills@gmail.com
www.owlmills.com
Silk organza, sheers, nets, linens. Popular plain and metallic braids, ribbons
and cord trims imported from Europe. Swatching. No credit cards.

S-T

Penn & Fletcher, Inc. 212-239-6868
21-07 41st Ave., 5th Fl.   FAX 212-239-6914
Long Island City, NY 11101
Hours: 9-5 Mon-Fri   E-mail: mail@pennandfletcher.com
www.pennandfletcher.com
Fine quality trims and lace; also beading and embroidery serrvices. Contact
Ernie Smith for information. CREDIT CARDS.

Penn Braid & Trimming Co. 718-361-1900
P.O. Box 211   FAX 516-681-2313
Jericho, NY 11753
Hours: 8-5 Mon-Fri   E-mail: pntrimming@aol.com
Metallic trims, edging braid, fringe, soutache, embroidered motifs, hood
cords.

Pirates Treasure Cove 813-677-1137
6212 E Kracker Ave.   FAX 813-671-2915
Gibsonton, FL 33534
Hours: 9-5 Mon-Sat   E-mail: piratestreasurecove@ij.net
www.piratestreasurecove.webs.com
Sequins, jewels, trims and fabrics. Good prices, will ship anywhere, fast
service. Catalog available. CREDIT CARDS.

Roth International 212-840-1945
13 W 38th St. (5-6th Ave)   FAX 212-391-1033
NY, NY 10018
Hours: 9-5 Mon-Fri   E-mail: rothimport@verizon.net
www.rothinternational.net
Sequin and beaded applique, sequins and rhinestones by the yard, metallic
braids and cords, beaded fringe; wholesaler, large orders only.

So-Good, Inc. 212-398-0236
28 W 38th St. (5-6th Ave)   FAX 212-768-1325
NY, NY 10018
Hours: 9-5 Mon-Fri
Ribbons, braid and piping.

Studio Trimming 212-564-0265
327 W 36th St., 11th Fl. (8-9th Ave)   FAX 212-564-6262
NY, NY 10018
Hours: 8-5 Mon-Fri   E-mail: metrotrimming@gmail.com
www.metrotrimmingcorp.com
Tubular pipings, trimmings, bias flowers, passementerie loops and frogs.

Tinsel Trading 212-730-1030
1 W 37th St. (5-6th Ave)   FAX 212-768-8823
NY, NY 10018
Hours: 9:45-5:30 Mon-Fri / 11-5 some Sat (call first)
www.tinseltrading.com   E-mail: sales@tinseltrading.com
Trims, tassels, fringes, etc. Specializing in vintage metallics. CREDIT CARDS.

S-T

Toho Shoji, Inc. 212-868-7465
990 Sixth Ave. (36-37th St)   212-868-7466
NY, NY 10018   FAX 212-868-7464
Hours: 9-7 Mon-Fri / 10-6 Sat / 10-5 Sun   E-mail: toho@tohoshoji-ny.com
www.tohoshoji-ny.com
Large selection of beads, buttons, chains, jewelry components and findings
in a well-lighted shop. Wholesale and retail. CREDIT CARDS.

Trims de Carnival 212-730-2774
40 W 38th St.   212-730-2775
NY, NY 10018   FAX 212-730-0153
Hours: 9:30-5:30 Mon-Fri
Beaded Appliques, trims and fringes. Beautiful selection, very nice service.
CREDIT CARDS.

TRIMMINGS: FLOWERS

AA Feather Company / Gettinger Feathers 212-695-9470
16 W 36th St., FL 8 (5-6th Ave)   FAX 212-695-9471
NY, NY 10018
Hours: 9-5 Mon, Wed-Thurs / 9-1 Fri   E-mail: gettfeath@aol.com
www.gettingerfeather.com
Colorful feathers and boas, silk flowers, etc.

Cinderella Flower & Feather Corporation 212-564-2929
48 W 37th St. (5-6th Ave)   FAX 212-594-0071
NY, NY 10018
Hours: 9-6 Mon-Fri / 10-4 Sat   E-mail: cinderella@margola.com
Fancy feathers, boas, flowers, fruit. Merged with Margola Corporation.
CREDIT CARDS.

Dulken & Derrick, Inc. 212-929-3614
(5-6th Ave)   FAX 212-929-8078
NY, NY 10010
Hours: by appt. only   E-mail: info@dulkenandderrick.com
www.flowersinthecity.com
Beautiful silk and fancy flowers; will custom-make. Sales thru website or by
special appt. only. CREDIT CARDS.

Manny's Millinery Supply Co. 212-840-2235
26 W 38th St. (5-6th Ave)   FAX 212-944-0178
NY, NY 10018
Hours: 11-6 Tue-Thurs / 11-4:30 Fri   E-mail: info@mannys-millinery.com
www.mannys-millinery.com
Manny's will be staying open, however they are streamlining their inventory.
Limited quantities of straw and felt bodies. Visit website or call for updated
information. Large selection of flowers, tubular horsehair braid, veiling, and
feathers. Shop online. Be sure to call before dropping by store. CREDIT
CARDS.

S-T

M&S Schmalberg 212-244-2090
242 W 36th St. 7th Fl. (7-8th Ave)   212-244-2091
NY, NY 10018   FAX 212-244-2097
Hours: 9-4:30 Mon-Fri   E-mail: customfabricflowers@verizon.net
www.customfabricflowers.com
Custom flowers to your specifications, has some fabrics in stock. Nice selection of stock in various colors. Hundreds of tools and dies to choose from, anything from petal, leaf to a complete flower. Any size; will work with you on styles and shapes. Brochure. Contact Debra or Warren Brand.

TRIMMINGS: LACE & LACE MOTIFS

B&Q Trimmings 212-398-0988
210 W 38th St. (7-8th Ave)   FAX 212-869-2899
NY, NY 10018
Hours: 10-6 Mon-Sat   E-mail: info@shinetrim.com
www.shinetrim.com
Specializing in beaded and sequined trimming and appliques as well as feathers, rhinestones, iron-on embroideries, satin ribbon, lace, fancy buttons, gloves and more. CREDIT CARDS.

Novik Sales 516-599-8678
84 Atlantic Ave.   FAX 516-599-8696
Lynbrook, NY 11563
Hours: 10-5 Mon-Fri / Call first
Lace motifs and yardage; net, tulle, maline, marquisette; wholesale only, must order from sample books.

Penn & Fletcher, Inc. 212-239-6868
21-07 41st Ave., 5th Fl.   FAX 212-239-6914
Long Island City, NY 11101
Hours: 9-5 Mon-Fri   E-mail: mail@pennandfletcher.com
www.pennandfletcher.com
High quality laces and trims; also beading and embroidery services. Contact Ernie Smith for information. CREDIT CARDS.

Sposabella Lace 212-354-4729
252 W 40th St. (7-8th Ave)   FAX 212-391-4208
NY, NY 10018
Hours: 9:15-6 Mon-Fri / 9:15-5 Sat   E-mail: sposabellalace@aol.com
www.sposabellalace.com
Notions, trimmings, novelties; wholesale and retail. CREDIT CARDS.

TRIMMINGS: UPHOLSTERY & DRAPERY

S-T

Brimar, Inc. 847-247-0100
28250 Ballard Dr.   800-274-1205
Lake Forest, IL 60045   FAX 847-247-9270
Hours: 8-4:30 Mon-Fri   E-mail: brimar@brimarinc.com
www.brimarinc.com
Variety of tassels, cords and trimmings for draperies and upholstery, wired ribbons and metallics. $25 minimum with $10 handling fee. Catalogs for individual collections. CREDIT CARDS.

Brunschwig & Fils, Inc. 212-838-7878
979 Third Ave., 12th FL (58-59th St)   FAX 212-838-5611
NY, NY 10022
Hours: 9-5 Mon-Fri   E-mail: newyork@brunschwig.com
www.brunschwig.com
Decorator house, to the trade only; traditional American and European trims,
fabric, wallpaper; expensive. Account required.

BZI Distributors 212-966-6690
314 Grand St. (Basement level of Harry Zarin) (Allen-Grand St.)FAX 212-966-8962
NY, NY 10002
Hours: 9-6 Sun-Fri / 10-6 Sat
www.zarinfabrics.com
Vertical and mini-blinds, many styles of curtain rods and hardware.
Trimmings, upholstery supplies, foam rubber. Contact David or Gerry. $25
minimum on CREDIT CARDS.

Clarence House 212-752-2890
979 Third Ave., Ste. 205   800-221-4704
NY, NY 10022   FAX 212-755-3314
Hours: 9-5 Mon- Fri   E-mail: info@clarencehouse.com
www.clarencehouse.com
To the trade, account required. Expensive but unique European tassels &
trims. Some stock but allow plenty of time. CREDIT CARDS.

Greentex Upholstery Supplies 212-206-8585
236 W 26th St. (7-8th Ave)   800-762-8303
NY, NY 10001   FAX 212-206-6671
Hours: 8-3:30 Mon-Thurs / 8-1 Fri   E-mail: info@greentexinc.com
www.greentexinc.com
Upholstery supply house; simple selection in good quantities. No Credit
Cards.

Hai's Trimming Co. 212-764-2166
242 W 38th St. (7-8th Ave)   FAX (same)
NY, NY 10018
Hours: 10-6 Mon-Fri / 10-5 Sat
All kinds of trims; bridal accessories. Good stock of heat fix and glue on
rhinestones, ribbons, buttons, etc. Beaded trims and feathers. Vinyl repair
glues and adhesives that stick vinyl to vinyl. CREDIT CARDS.

I. Weiss and Sons, Inc. 718-706-8139
2-07 Borden Ave. (Vernon-Jackson Ave)   888-325-7192
Long Island City, NY 11101   FAX 718-482-9410
Hours: 8-5:30 Mon-Fri   E-mail: info@iweiss.com
www.iweiss.com
Custom manufacturer of stage curtains. Trims to match. Custom appliques,
tassels, rope, fringe, etc. Also scenic fabrics and flameproofing.

S-T

Kravet Fabrics 800-645-9068
979 Third Ave., Ste. 324(58-59th St) (D&D Building)   212-421-6363
NY, NY 10022   FAX 212-751-7196
Hours: 9-5 Mon-Fri

200 Lexington Ave., 4th Fl.   212-725-0340
NY, NY 10016   FAX 212-684-7350
Hours: 9-5 Mon-Fri

225 Central Ave. S   516-293-2000
Bethpage, NY 11714   FAX 516-293-2737
Hours: 10-4 Mon-Fri
www.kravet.com
To the trade, account required. Mostly to order, some stock, fringe, braid, gimp, tassels.

M & J Trimmings . . . . .1-800-9MJ TRIM
1008 Sixth Ave. (37-38th St)   212-204-9595
NY, NY 10018   FAX 212-704-8090
Hours: 9-8 Mon-Fri / 10-6 Sat / 12-6 Sun   E-mail: info@mjtrim.com
www.mjtrim.com
Pricey; ribbons, buttons, buckles, frogs, beads, rhinestones, handbag handles and Swarovski heatsets. CREDIT CARDS.

Tinsel Trading 212-730-1030
1 W 37th St. (5-6th Ave)   FAX 212-768-8823
NY, NY 10018
Hours: 9:45-5:30 Mon-Fri / 11-5 some Sat (call first)
www.tinseltrading.com   E-mail: sales@tinseltrading.com
Gold mesh fabrics, metallic and antique trims, vintage flowers, fruit stamens, buttons, fringes, cords, tassels, horsehair, ribbons, etc. Also upholstery gimps and trims. $75 minimum order for shipping. CREDIT CARDS.

TROPHIES & ENGRAVERS

Alpha Engraving Co. 212-247-5266
254 W 51 St. (B'way-8th Ave)   FAX 212-247-2014
NY, NY 10019
Hours: 9-6 Mon-Thurs / 9-4 Fri   E-mail: salesinfo@alphaengraving.com
www.alphaengraving.com
Engraves trophies, awards; metal and plastic engraved signs; name tags.

Atlantic Trophy Co. 212-684-6020
866 Ave. of the Americas, 3rd Fl. (30th-31st St)   FAX 212-689-2665
NY, NY 10001
Hours: 9-4:30 Mon-Fri   E-mail: info@atlantictrophy.com
www.atlantictrophy.com
Custom trophies and engraving; plaques and signage. Friendly and funny in a Bronx kind of way. RENTALS. CREDIT CARDS.

S-T

ATAC

Green Mountain Graphics 718-472-3377
21-10 44th Dr. (21st & 23rd St)   FAX 718-472-4040
Long Island City, NY 11101
Hours: 8:30-5 Mon-Fri   E-mail: sales@gm-graphics.com
www.gm-graphics.com
In-house manufacturers of engraved and silkscreened signs and promotional products awards; also vinyl graphics. Suppliers of all kinds of signs including cast bronze, faux cast bronze, etched, banners, etc. Also, blackboards and bulletin boards. Convenient location to all L.I.C. soundstages. Catalogs and rush service available. CREDIT CARDS.

Kraus & Sons, Inc. 212-620-0408
261 W 35th St. (7-8th Ave)   FAX 212-924-4081
NY, NY 10001
Hours: 9-5 Mon-Fri   E-mail: info@krausbanners.com
www.krausbanners.com
Custom trophies and ribbons, also flags and banners. No credit cards.

RV Awards 800-979-9755
8902 N Marathon Dr.   520-742-3265
Tucson, AZ 85704   FAX 520-877-9824
Hours: 9-5 Mon-Fri   E-mail: info@rvawardsaz.com
www.rvawardsaz.com
More than 100 styles of custom award ribbons, rosettes and equestrian ribbons, badges and sashes. More than 30 colors to choose from. Also wide variety of trophies and plaques. Fast and friendly service. Speak with Kathy or Janet. CREDIT CARDS.

Truart Stryppman Engraving 201-867-7445
705 27th St. (Summit Ave)
Union City, NJ 07087
Hours: 9-5 Mon-Fri
www.truart.com
Dimensionally precise figurative brass engraving.

TROPICAL FISH & AQUARIUMS

Aquarium Design 845-352-1640
80 Red Schoolhouse Rd. #217
Chestnut Ridge, NY 10977
Hours: by appt. (24 hour emergency service)
www.aquariumdesign.com   E-mail: fishdoc@aquariumdesign.com
Design, manufacture, install and maintain aquarium systems.

Aquarius Aquariums 212-749-4970
214 Riverside Dr. Ste. 612 (93-94th St)   (page) 917-556-7058
NY, NY 10025   FAX 212-749-0601
Hours: by appt.   E-mail: info@aquariusaquariums.com
www.aquariusaquariums.com
Acrylic and glass, salt and fresh water aquarium design and installation.

S-T

Berkel Marine 718-937-1133
41-12 Ditmars Blvd. (40th Rd)   800-775-4237
Astoria, NY 11105   FAX 718-937-5187
Hours: 10-5 Mon-Fri / 11-6 Sat   E-mail: berkelnewyork@compuserve.com
Custom aquarium systems installed and maintained. Will setup and take down for commercial shoots or film. Near all LIC Sound Stages. CREDIT CARDS.

Petland Discounts 866-687-3600
132 Nassau St.(Ann-Beekman St)   212-964-1821
NY, NY 10038   FAX 212-587-3076
Hours: 9-7 Mon-Fri / 10-6 Sat / 11-5 Sun

2708 Broadway(103rd-104th St)   212-222-8851
NY, NY 10025
Hours: 9-9 Mon-Fri / 10-7 Sat / 11-6 Sun

312 W 23rd St.(8-9th Ave)   212-366-0512
NY, NY 10011
Hours: 9-9 Mon-Fri / 10-7 Sat / 11-6 Sun

304 E 86th St.(1st-2nd Ave)   212-472-1655
NY, NY 10028
Hours: 10-9 Mon-Fri / 10-6 Sat / 11-6 Sun

530 E 14th St.(Ave A&B)   212-228-1363
NY, NY 10003
Hours: 10-8 Mon-Fri / 10-7 Sat / 11-5 Sun

734 Ninth Ave.(49-50th St)   212-459-9562
NY, NY 10019
Hours: 9-7 Mon-Sat / 11-5 Sun

137 W 72nd St.(B-way-Col)   212-875-9785
NY, NY 10023
Hours: 9-9 Mon-Fri / 10-7 Sat / 10-6 Sun   E-mail: info@petlanddiscounts.com
www.petlanddiscounts.com
Good selection of pet supplies; birds, fish, small animals. 110 Stores in NY, NJ & CT. See website for other locations. CREDIT CARDS.

TURNTABLES

Cimmelli, Inc. 845-735-2090
16 Walter St.   845-735-4693
Pearl River, NY 10965   FAX 845-735-1643
Hours: 8:30-5:30 Mon-Fri / Sat by appt.
www.cimmellisfx.com
Masks, sculpture, puppets, props, models, rigs and special effects. Large variety of turntables available for rental use. Custom sculpture for any application. RENTALS.

S-T

EFEX Rentals 718-505-9465
5805 52nd Ave. (43rd Ave)   FAX 718-505-9631
Woodside, NY 11377
Hours: 8:30-5:30 Mon-Fri   E-mail: efexrentals@verizon.net
www.efexrentals.com
Distributors of many types of fog machines and fog juice; also special effects materials; snow, breakaways, turntables and rigging. Catalog available. P.O.s accepted. RENTALS.

J M Turntables 212-777-1465
873 Broadway # 700 (18th St)   917-836-7009
NY, NY 10003   FAX 866-316-5822
Hours: by appt.   E-mail: jeffreymeyer@mac.com
www.jmturntables.com
Widest selection of turntables for the film industry in the NY metropolitan area. RENTALS.

Mechanical Displays, Inc. 718-258-5588
4420 Farragut Rd. (E 45th St)   FAX 718-258-6202
Brooklyn, NY 11203
Hours: 8-4:30 Mon-Fri   E-mail: info@mechanicaldisplays.com
www.mechanicaldisplays.com
Stock and custom animated figures with simple or pneumatic mechanisms; also turntables. See Lou Nasti for photos and price list. P.O.s accepted. No credit cards.

Sapsis Rigging 800-727-7471
233 N Lansdowne Ave.   215-228-0888
Lansdowne, PA 19050   FAX 215-228-1786
Hours: 8-4:30 Mon-Fri   E-mail: bill@sapsis-rigging.com
www.sapsis-rigging.com
Theatrical rigging; fall arrest equipment; counterweight, hemp-winch systems; fire curtains, draperies, turntables, etc. Catalog.

TWINES & CORDAGE

American Cord & Webbing Co., Inc. .401-762-5500
88 Century Dr.   FAX 401-762-5514
Woonsocket, RI 02895
Hours: 8-5 Mon-Fri   E-mail: dsmith@acw1.com
www.acw1.com
Wholesale cotton, jute, webbing, tape, binding, elastic cord and webbing. 100 yard or 500 piece minimum. Catalog with samples available. CREDIT CARDS.

Hartford Cordage & Twine Co. 800-235-6610
1866 NW 54th Ave.   FAX 203-874-1253
Margate, FL 33063
Hours: 8-7 Mon-Fri   E-mail: mikegreen@theatrerope.com
www.theatrerope.com
Wholesale hemp, black trick line, sash cord, aircraft cable. No minimum.

S-T

William Usdan & Sons 973-844-9988
140 Little St.   FAX 973-844-9909
Bellville, NJ 07109
Hours: 8-4:30 Mon-Fri   E-mail: sales@wm-usdan.com
www.wm-usdan.com
Poly cordage.

S-T

UMBRELLAS & CANES

Peerless Umbrella 973-578-4900
427 Ferry St.   FAX 973-578-2626
Newark, NJ 07105
Hours: 8:30-5:30 Mon-Fri   E-mail: peter@peerlessumbrella.com
www.peerlessumbrella.com
Made to order umbrellas. Northeast representative: Peter Hiatrides.

Rain or Shine 212-741-9650
45 E 45th St. (Madison & Vanderbilt)   FAX 201-224-4410
NY, NY 10017
Hours: 10-6 Mon-Sat   E-mail: Peggylevee30@aol.com
www.rainorshine.biz
Specialty retail umbrellas, parasols and walking canes. CREDIT CARDS.

Zip Jack Custom Umbrellas 914-592-2000
141 S Central Ave. (Route 9A)   FAX 914-592-3023
Elmsford, NY 10523
Hours: 9-4:30 Mon-Sat   E-mail: sales@zipjack.com
www.zipjack.com
*Custom work including huge market umbrellas and bases. Catalog. CREDIT
CARDS.*

UPHOLSTERERS

Brent Porter Fabrications & Interiors Ltd. 212-594-5323
260 W 35th St. #403 (7-8th Ave)   (cell) 917-880-5961
NY, NY 10001   FAX 212-594-5099
Hours: 9-5 Mon-Fri   E-mail: bpfabrications@msn.com
*Experienced theatrical and film upholstery and soft goods. Quick service,
reasonable prices.*

DFB Sales 718-729-8310
21-07 Borden Ave. (Bordon-21st St)   800-433-4546
Long Island City, NY 11101   FAX 718-706-0526
Hours: 9-5 Mon-Fri   E-mail: dfb@dfbsales.com
www.dfbsales.com
Upholstery & slipcovers for film, TV and theatre. Fast.

Economy Foam & Futons 212-475-4800
56 8th St. (5-6th Ave)   FAX 212-475-2727
NY, NY 10011
Hours: 10-7 Mon-Thurs / Fri call for hours / 10:30-6 Sun
                        E-mail: sales@economyfoamandfutons.com
www.economyfoamandfutons.com
*Batting by the bag or roll; foam rubber sheets, shapes; pillows; vinyl fabrics;
futons. Custom pillow and pad covering. CREDIT CARDS.*

U-Z

Fishman's Fabrics 312-922-7250
1101 S Desplaines St.   FAX 312-922-7402
Chicago, IL 60607
Hours: 9-5 Mon-Fri / 10-4 Sat   E-mail: info@fishmansfabrics.com
www.fishmansfabrics.com
All kinds of fabrics; in store and mail order. Specializing in designer and bridal fabrics. Custom reupholstery and drapery available. P.O.s and CREDIT CARDS.

Furniture Rental Associates 212-868-0300
148 Madison Ave.   800-633-3748
NY, NY 10016   FAX 212-594-5415
Hours: 9-6 Mon-Fri or by appt.   E-mail: frarents@aol.com
www.frarents.com
Full-service office furniture rentals: traditional, contemporary, modern and computer office furniture. Same day service. Reupholstery and refinishing. Contact Randie Greenberg. RENTALS. CREDIT CARDS.

Louise Grafton 609-921-1919
229 Hartly Ave.
Princeton, NJ 08540
Hours: by appt.   E-mail: legraft@hotmail.com
Props, set and costume pieces, soft goods, circus and clown props. Also upholstery done in her studio.

JUNG K. GRIFFIN 718-391-0009
4316 42nd St. #3R   (cell) 646-498-4251
Sunnyside, NY 11104   FAX 718-391-0009
Hours: by appt.   E-mail: jgriffin95@aol.com
Props artisan, sculpture, crafts, carpentry, soft goods, upholstery. Member ATAC.

M & A Decorators 212-226-3910
294 Grand St. (Eldridge & Allen)   FAX 212-334-5273
NY, NY 10002
Hours: 9:30-6 Sun-Thurs / 9:30-4 Fri / Closed Sat
Blinds, fine fabrics, upholstery, bed coverings, window designs, imported tablecloths. CREDIT CARDS.

Marc Tash Interiors 212-385-2253
2483 65th St. (24th Ave-Dayhill Rd)   718-336-3326 or 800-MARC TASH
Brooklyn, NY 11204
Hours: by appt.   E-mail: info@marctashinteriors.com
www.marctashinteriors.com
Custom drapery and window treatments. Re-upholstery and slipcovers. Complete design service and installation. Wood blinds, Roman and balloon shades, valances and cornices. Marc will pick up and deliver items for re-upholstery. CREDIT CARDS.

MICHAEL SMANKO / PRISM PROPS .732-382-9727
1015 Richard Blvd.
Rahway, NJ 07065
Hours: by Appt.
www.prismprops.com
Broadway Production propman & prop stylist. Prop supervision, shopping, fabrication, upholstery, painting and finishes, prop construction, SPFX. 35 year IATSE member. BA Fine Arts, MFA Theater Design. Member ATAC.

OFFSTAGE DESIGN 845-265-0078
28 Lane Gate Rd. (Rt 9)   914-522-0283
Cold Spring, NY 10516   FAX 845-265-2322
Hours: by appt.   E-mail: denise@offstagedesign.com
www.offstagedesign.com
Full-service prop shop. Furniture built, upholstery, crafts and shopping services. Period paper and products. Window displays. Contact Denise Grillo or Denny Clark. Member ATAC.

Pretty Decorating & Upholstering 212-674-1310
417 E 6th St. (2nd St)
NY, NY 10009
Hours: by appt.
Fast service, upholstery, slipcovers and draperies. Sewing classes. Reasonable rates.

Roy Rudin Decorators, Inc. 718-786-7267
5024 46th St.   718-786-8352
Woodside, NY 11377   FAX 718-786-8408
Hours: 9-5 Mon-Fri   E-mail: dan46te@earthlink.net
Experienced theatrical and film upholstery and soft goods.

The Silk Trading Co. 323-954-9280
360 South La Brea Ave.   888-SILK-302
Los Angeles, CA 90036   FAX 323-954-8024
Hours: 9-6 Mon-Fri / 9-5 Sat
www.silktrading.com
Decorate without modesty. Wonderful selection of drapery and upholstery fabrics. Custom drapes, upholstery and decorator's paints. Some trims and tassels. CREDIT CARDS.

WolfHome 800-220-1893
936 Broadway (22nd St)   646-602-3246
NY, NY 10010   FAX 212-254-7105
Hours: 10-7 Mon-Sat / 11-6:30 Sun
www.wolfhome-ny.com
Beautiful high-end fabrics. Large selection of embroidered silks. Some ready made pillows, drapes and curtains. Interior goods and furniture made to order, shades and window treatments, reupholstery service. They have their own mills and can custom weave and color. Workroom on premises for custom work. Fast deadlines no problem. Very helpful and willing to accommodate entertainment business needs. CREDIT CARDS.

U-Z

UPHOLSTERY TOOLS & SUPPLIES

Albany Foam and Supply, Inc. 800-235-0888
1355 Broadway   518-433-7000
Albany, NY 12204   FAX 518-433-8638
Hours: 8-5 Mon-Fri   E-mail: sales@ausinc.com
www.ausinc.net
Extensive stock of every imaginable upholstery supply including caning, adhesives, dacron, down, foam rubber, webbing, swivel bases and cleaners. Free freight on all orders of $75 or more. Catalog.

American Cord & Webbing Co., Inc. 401-762-5500
88 Century Dr.   FAX 401-762-5514
Woonsocket, RI 02895
Hours: 8-5 Mon-Fri   E-mail: dsmith@acw1.com
www.acw1.com
Webbing, binding, cotton, jute, elastic webbing. Wholesale. Catalog with samples available. CREDIT CARDS.

BZI Distributors 212-966-6690
314 Grand St. (Basement level of Harry Zarin) (Allen-Grand St.)FAX 212-966-8962
NY, NY 10002
Hours: 9-6 Sun-Fri / 10-6 Sat
www.zarinfabrics.com
Major upholstery supply house, also trimmings and foam rubber. $25 minimum on CREDIT CARDS.

Greentex Upholstery Supplies 212-206-8585
236 W 26th St. (7-8th Ave)   800-762-8303
NY, NY 10001   FAX 212-206-6671
Hours: 8-3:30 Mon-Thurs / 8-1 Fri   E-mail: info@greentexinc.com
www.greentexinc.com
Upholstery needles, tacks, staples, snap tape, hook & loop tape, trims and webbing. Catalog. No credit cards.

National Webbing Products 516-346-4636
77 Second Ave.   800-886-6060
Garden City Park, NY 11040   FAX 516-346-4366
Hours: 8-5 Mon-Fri   E-mail: info@nationalwebbing.com
www.nationalwebbing.com
Nylon, cotton, elastic and polypropylene webbings. Some minimums. Catalog. No credit cards.

C.S. Osborne Tools 973-483-3232
125 Jersey St.   FAX 973-484-3621
Harrison, NJ 07029
Hours: 8-4:30 Mon-Fri   E-mail: cso@csosborne.com
www.csosborne.com
Tools for upholstery; specialty pins, curved and ballpoint needles. Catalog available.

U-Z

VACUUMFORMING & VACUUMFORM PANELS

E & T Plastics Mfg. Co., Inc. 718-729-6226
45-45 37th St. (Queens Blvd)   800-221-9555
Long Island City, NY 11101   FAX 718-392-6277
Hours: 9-5 Mon-Fri   E-mail: info@e-tplastics.com
www.e-tplastics.com
Plexi, acrylic, acetate, Lexan, Teflon, mylar, polystyrene, vacuumforming.
Locations in several states, visit website. CREDIT CARDS.

Global Effects, Inc. 818-503-9273
7115 Laurel Canyon Blvd.   FAX 818-503-9459
N. Hollywood, CA 91605
Hours: by appt.   E-mail: chris@globaleffects.com
www.globaleffects.com
Higy Quality replicas of NASA Space Suits and fabrication of armour,
vacuumforming, etc. Leather masks, creature suits, ventilated walk-around
costumes. Medieval: armour, weapons, jewelry. Very pleasant to deal with.
RENTALS. CREDIT CARDS.

Historic Arms & Armor 760-789-2299
17228 Voorhes Ln.   FAX 760-789-6644
Ramona, CA 92065
Hours: 9-6 Mon-Fri, by appt.   E-mail: info@historicenterprises.com
www.historicenterprises.com
Ancient Greek to vacuumform sci-fi armor. Specializes in medieval and
renaissance. RENTALS.

Prop Masters, Inc. 818-846-3915
272 Empire Ave   FAX 818-846-1278
Burbank, CA 91504
Hours: 9-5 Mon-Fri
www.propmastersinc.com
Armor, robots and vacuumforming. Contact Henry.

Provost Displays, Inc. 800-555-3772
501 W Washington St., 2nd Fl.   610-279-3970
Norristown, PA 19401   FAX 610-279-3968
Hours: 8-5:30 Mon-Thurs   E-mail: toprovost@verizon.net
www.provostdisplays.com
Vacuumformed architectural & scenic panels. Manufacturers of
GIANTFORMEô; flame and weatherproof vacuumformed plastic decorative
panels up to 4' x 12'. Custom molds made to order. Free shipping to NY and
NJ areas. Catalog of stock designs available. CREDIT CARDS.

Tobins Lake Studios, Inc. 810-229-6666
7030 Whitmore Lake Rd.   888-719-0300
Brighton, MI 48116   FAX 810-229-0221
Hours: 9-5 Mon-Fri   E-mail: studio@tobinslake.com
www.tobinslake.com
Vacuumformed armor and helmets, columns, mantels, windows, ornamental
detail, pay phones. Catalog available. CREDIT CARDS.

U-Z

VACUUMFORMING & VACUUMFORM PANELS

Tulnoy Lumber 718-901-1700
1620 Webster Ave. (173rd St)   800-899-5833
Bronx, NY 10457   FAX 718-229-8920
Hours: 7-5 Mon-Fri   E-mail: sales@tulnoylumber.com
www.tulnoylumber.com

Architectural and scenic design elements available in lightweight vacuum-formed vinyl plastic. Any piece can be custom made to your own design.

VENDING MACHINES

W. Chorney Antiques 203-387-9707
42 Morris St. (Westville Section)   FAX 203-387-9707
Hamden, CT 06515
Hours: call for information   E-mail: w.chorney@juno.com

Antique jukeboxes, including diner remotes; period cigarette, pinball, gumball, vending and soda fountains; radios, kitchen equipment and bar items. Antique office furniture and accessories. 90 mins. from Manhattan. Will search for items; speak to Wayne. RENTALS. AMEX.

Jukebox Classics & Vintage Slot Machines 718-833-8455
36 72nd St.   FAX 718-833-0560
Brooklyn, NY 11209
Hours: by appt. only

Jukeboxes and coin operated antiques. Will help locate unusual items. Speak to John. RENTALS. CREDIT CARDS.

Payphone Warehouse / Artemis & Jenny USA, Inc. 800-988-9056
610 S Marengo Ave.   626-281-8069
Alhambra, CA 91803   FAX: 626-821-9685
Hours: 8-4:30 Mon-Fri
www.vending-usa.com

Large selection of payphones at low cost. Will sell wholesale if purchasing quantity. Many overseas-type payphones. Also, vending machines. Contact Johnson. Very nice and helpful. CREDIT CARDS.

U-Z

WALL COVERINGS

ABC Carpet & Home Co., Inc. 212-473-3000
888 Broadway(19th St)   FAX 212-777-3713
NY, NY 10003
Hours: 10-8 Mon - Fri / 10-7 Sat / 11-6:30 Sun

    1055 Bronx River Ave.(Bruckner Blvd) Outlet   718-842-8772
    NY, NY 10472   FAX 718-812-6905
    Hours: 10-7 Mon - Fri / 10-7 Sat / 11-6 Sun
    www.abccarpet.com
Reproduction vintage wall coverings and borders from the 40s-50s. CREDIT CARDS.

Aywon Chalkboard, Inc., DBA The Cork Store 718-853-2300
P.O. Box 280088 (Ocean Pkwy-Coney Island Ave)   FAX 718-238-0684
Brooklyn, NY 11228
Hours: 8-4 Mon-Thurs / 8-12 Fri   www.aywon.com
Fabric and wallcoverings in coordinating patterns. Speak to Mr. Pines. CREDIT CARDS.

Bradbury & Bradbury Wallpaper 707-746-1900
940 Tyler St. Studio 12   FAX 707-745-9417
Benicia, CA 94510
Hours: 9-5 Mon-Fri   E-mail: info@bradbury.com
www.bradbury.com
Manufacturer of handprinted wallpapers of 19th century designs. Online catalog.

Brunschwig & Fils, Inc. 212-838-7878
979 Third Ave., 12th FL (58-59th St)   FAX 212-838-5611
NY, NY 10022
Hours: 9-5 Mon-Fri   E-mail: newyork@brunschwig.com
www.brunschwig.com
To the trade, account required. Traditional American and European styles. Expensive.

Clarence House 212-752-2890
979 Third Ave., Ste. 205   800-221-4704
NY, NY 10022   FAX 212-755-3314
Hours: 9-5 Mon- Fri   E-mail: info@clarencehouse.com
www.clarencehouse.com
To the trade, account required. Wallpaper repros of traditional and historical patterns; some fabrics and trimmings. Expensive. CREDIT CARDS.

Design Tex 800-221-1540
200 Varick St., 8th Fl.   212-886-8200
NY, NY 10014   FAX 212-886-8219
Hours: 9-5 Mon-Fri

    979 Third Ave., Ste. 232(D&D Bldg. 59th St)   212-752-2535
    NY, NY 10022   FAX 212-838-5668
    Hour: 9-5 Mon-Fri
    www.designtexgroup.com
Vinyl, textile, and acoustical wallcovering, rugs, digital panels, and upholstery fabrics. See website for other showroom locations or call 800-221-1540.

U-Z

Donghia Textiles 212-935-3713
   979 Third Ave. Ste. 613   FAX 212-935-9707
   NY, NY 10022
   Hours: 9-5 Mon-Fri   E-mail: mail@donghia.com
   www.donghia.com
   *To the trade, account required. Contemporary patterns, floral and paisley
   wallcoverings and fabrics; custom furniture. Expensive. See website for other
   locations.*

Dymalon, Inc. 410-686-7711
   9100 Yellow Brick Rd., Ste D   FAX 410-686-7743
   Baltimore, MD 21237
   Hours: 8:30-5:30 Mon-Fri   E-mail: rjnee@verizon.net
   www.dymalon.com
   *Excellent selection of wood grain contact papers, mattes, enamels, marbles,
   frosts, transparents, metallics and more. 17.5" wide, some up to 35". Foam
   tapes and all kinds of Velcro, including dual lock. Quick and friendly service.
   CREDIT CARDS.*

Epstein's Paint Center 212-265-3960
   822 Tenth Ave. (54-55th St)   800-464-3432
   NY, NY 10019   FAX 212-765-8841
   Hours: 8-5:30 Mon-Fri / 8:30-3 Sat   E-mail: sales@epsteinspaint.com
   www.epsteinspaint.com
   *Many styles of blinds and shades, custom service within 24-hrs. Also large
   stock of floor coverings, wallpaper, scenic/household paints, tints and dyes.
   See Marty. CREDIT CARDS.*

Janovic Plaza 212-772-1400
   888 Lexington Ave.(66th St)   FAX 212-794-2913
   NY, NY 10021
   Hours: 7-7 Mon-Fri / 8-6 Sat / 11-5 Sun

   1555 Third Ave.(87th St)   212-289-6300
   NY, NY 10128   FAX 212-289-6831
   Hours: 7-6:30 Mon-Fri / 9-6 Sat / 11-5 Sun

   159 W 72nd St.(Amsterdam-Columbus Ave)   212-595-2500
   NY, NY 10023   FAX 212-724-7846
   Hours: 7:30-6:30 Mon-Fri / 9-6 Sat / 11-5 Sun

   161 Sixth Ave.(Spring St)   212-627-1100
   NY, NY 10013   FAX 212-924-7641
   Hours: 7:30-6:30 Mon-Fri / 9-6 Sat / 11-5 Sun

   215 Seventh Ave.(22nd-23rd St)   212-645-5454
   NY, NY 10011   FAX 212-691-1504
   Hours: 7:30-6:30 Mon-Fri / 9-6 Sat / 11-5 Sun

   2680 Broadway(102nd St)   212-531-2300
   NY, NY 10025   FAX 212-932-3476
   Hours: 7:30-6:30 Mon-Fri / 9-6 Sat / 11-5 Sun

   292 Third Ave.(22nd-23rd St)   212-777-3030
   NY, NY 10010   FAX 212-253-0985
   Hours: 7:30-6:30 Mon-Fri / 9-6 Sat / 11-5 Sun

Janovic Plaza (cont.) 212-477-6930
80 Fourth Ave.(10th St)   FAX 212-254-4628
NY, NY 10003
Hours: 7:30-6:30 Mon-Fri / 9-6 Sat / 11-5 Sun

30-35 Thompson Ave.(Van Dam & Queens Blvd)   347-418-3480
Long Island City, NY 11101   Orders 718-392-3999
Hours: 7-6 Mon-Fri / 8-4 Sat   FAX 718-784-4564
www.janovic.com
Home decorating center; wallpaper including Anaglypta wallpapers, paint
and supplies. CREDIT CARDS.

Marimekko Store 212-628-8400
1262 Third Ave. (72nd-73rd St)   800-527-0624
NY, NY 10021   FAX 212-628-2814
Hours: 10-7 Mon-Sat / 12-5 Sun   E-mail: info@kiitosmariemekko.com
www.kiitosmarimekko.com
Stylish contemporary fabrics, Wallpaper and large scale prints. Pricey.
CREDIT CARDS.

Arthur Sanderson & Sons 212-319-7220
979 Third Ave. (58-59th St)   FAX 212-593-6184
NY, NY 10022
Hours: 9-5 Mon-Fri   E-mail: sales@zoffany.com
www.sanderson-uk.com
To the trade. William Morris, arts and crafts wall covering and decorator
fabrics. Expensive.

F. Schumacher & Co (showroom) 212-415-3900
979 Third Ave., Ste. 832 (59th St)   800-523-1200
NY, NY 10022   FAX 212-415-3907
Hours: 9-5 Mon-Fri
www.fsco.com
To the trade, account required. Large collection Victorian wallpapers and
matching fabrics.

Secondhand Rose 212-393-9002
230 Fifth Ave. (W B'way-Church St)   FAX 212-393-9084
NY, NY 10001
Hours: 10-6 Mon-Fri /Weekends by appt.   E-mail: shroseltd@aol.com
www.secondhandrose.com
Period wallpaper, linoleum and fabrics. Good selection. Contact Suzanne
Lipschutz. CREDIT CARDS.

Wolf Paints, S. Wolf Div. of Janovic Plaza 212-245-3241
771 Ninth Ave. (51st-52nd St)   FAX 212-974-0591
NY, NY 10019
Hours: 7:30-6:30 Mon-Fri / 9-6 Sat / 11-5 Sun
Wallpapers including Anaglypta wallpapers, blinds, fabrics, upstairs; also
paints and supplies. CREDIT CARDS.

U-Z

WALL COVERINGS

Wolf-Gordon Wallcovering, Inc. 800-347-0550
   33-00 47th Ave.(33-34th St) offices   718-391-4800
   Long Island City, NY 11101   FAX 718-361-1090
   Hours: 8:30-7 Mon-Fri

   979 Third Ave., Rm 413(58-59th St) Showroom   212-319-6800
   NY, NY 10022
   Hours: 9:30-4:30 Mon-Fri

   8687 Melrose Ave., Ste BM5(N Sweetzer & N Harper Ave)   310-652-1914
   Los Angeles, CA 90069
   Hours: 9-4 Mon-Fri

   200 World Trade Ctr.(Merchandise Mart # 10-61)   312-755-1892
   Chicago, IL 60654
   Hours: 9-5 Mon-Fri   E-mail: info@wolf-gordon.com
   www.wolf-gordon.com
   Wallcoverings: vinyl, cork, acoustical, wood veneers, paperbacked fabric; at showroom. To the trade, account required. CREDIT CARDS.

WEDDINGS

Artistry in Motion 818-994-7388
   15101 Keswick St.   FAX 818-994-7688
   Van Nuys, CA 91405
   Hours: 9-6 Mon-Fri   E-mail: confetti@artistryinmotion.com
   www.artistryinmotion.com
   Best in the industry for confetti cannons and confetti. Custom designing for each event. CREDIT CARDS.

Oriental Trading Company, Inc. 800-875-8480
   4206 S. 108th St.   402-331-6800
   Omaha, NE 68137   FAX 402-331-3873
   Hours: 24-hr. online catalog service
   www.orientaltrading.com
   Thousands of small toys, novelties and party supplies for every occasion. Catalog available. CREDIT CARDS thru Paypal.

Props for Today 212-244-9600
   330 W 34th St. (8-9th Ave)   FAX 212-244-1053
   NY, NY 10001
   Hours: 8:30-5 Mon-Fri   E-mail: info@propsfortoday.com
   www.propsfortoday.com
   Full-service prop rental house with party planning service available. Large selection of china and glassware. RENTALS. CREDIT CARDS.

Ernest Winzer 718-294-2400
   1828 Cedar Ave. (179th-Major Deegan)   877-WINZER1
   Bronx, NY 10453   FAX 718-294-2729
   Hours: 6:30-5 Mon-Fri, Radio Dispatch 24-hrs. E-mail: borntoclean@yahoo.com
   www.ernestwinzer.com
   Wedding cleaning & bridal gown preservation.

U-Z

WELDERS & SPOT WELDERS

Acme Stimuli Design & Production 212-465-1071
889 Broadway
NY, NY 10001
Hours: by appt.

2640 Rt. 214   845-688-5107
Lanesville, NY 12450
Hours: by appt.   E-mail: stimuli7@hvc.rr.com
www.acmestimuli.com
Welding and metal fabrication; armatures. Contact Marc Rubin.

Creative Metal Works, Inc. / Stephen McMahon 631-537-9501
172 Butter Lane   FAX 631-537-4669
Bridgehampton, NY 11932
Hours: by Appt.   E-mail: mail@creativemetalworksinc.com
www.creativemetalworksinc.com
Creative Metal Works crafts fine architectural elements from all types of metals, including: stainless steel, steel mesh, galvanized steel, brushed steel, bronze, brass, nickel, copper, aluminum and titanium. Custom metal projects range from architecural elements, railings, and canopies, to sculpture, hardware, decorative lighting, and fixtures. Member ATAC.

Ferra Designs 718-852-8629
63 Flushing Ave. Unit 135, Brooklyn Navy Yard Bldg. 275 Ste. 101
(Flushing-Cumberland)   917-439-3057
Brooklyn, NY 11205   FAX 718-852-5940
Hours: 9-5 Mon-Fri   E-mail: info@ferradesigns.com
www.ferradesigns.com
Custom metal fabrication, specializing in traditional and contemporary metalwork. Ferra Designs can design and develop the entire project or fabricate from blueprints. Waterjet cutting is also available for metal, stone, glass and plastics. CNC Machining, contact for quotes.

Kern/Rockenfield, Inc. 718-230-7878
178 Classon Ave.   FAX 718-230-5652
Brooklyn, NY 11205
Hours: 8-5 Mon-Fri   E-mail: jkern@kernrock.com
www.kernrock.com
Custom metalwork, welding, bending, shaping in aluminum, steel, brass and other metals. Very helpful; willing to try anything.

WELDING SUPPLIES

American Compressed Gasses 718-392-9800
3452 Laurel Hill Blvd.   FAX 718-937-1218
Maspeth, NY 11378
Hours: 8-4 Mon-Fri
Full range of supplies, gasses (including helium), torches, rods, etc. CREDIT CARDS.

U-Z

WELDING SUPPLIES

ATAC

Awisco 718-786-7788
55-15 43rd St.   800-834-1925
Maspeth, NY 11378   FAX 718-361-1855
Hours: 7-5:30 Mon-Fri / 8-12 Sat   E-mail: sales@awisco.com
www.awisco.com

Tools, supplies, machine rentals and repairs. Competitive prices. See website
for other locations in NY and NJ. CREDIT CARDS.

McKinney Welding Supply 212-246-4390
535 W 52nd St. (10-11th Ave)   FAX 212-582-3105
NY, NY 10019
Hours: 7-4:30 Mon-Fri   E-mail: sales@mckinneynyc.com
www.mckinneynyc.com

New dept. will carry sheet metal, rebar, welding rods, flux, oxy-acetylene
torches and finishing tools. Helium; industrial, medical and specialty gases.
CREDIT CARDS.

T.W. Smith Welding Supply 718-388-7417
885 Meeker Ave. (Bridgewater-Varick St)   FAX 718-388-8943
Brooklyn, NY 11222
Hours: 7:30-4:30 Mon-Fri   E-mail: info@twsmith.com
www.twsmith.com

Soldering and welding supplies, propane tanks and regulators, will buy back
empties. Also Helium and balloon attachments. Deposit required.

Zibitt Associates, Ltd. 516-764-7694
3353 Bayfield Blvd.   FAX 516-678-9446
Oceanside, NY 11572
Hours: 9-5 Mon-Fri   E-mail: azibitt@optonline.net
Welding and industrial supplies, abrasive wheels, grinding wheels, nuts and
bolts. PO's accepted.

WINE & BREWING SUPPLIES

Sommer Cork Company 800-242-0808
259 W 61st St.   630-852-8500
Westmont, IL 60559   FAX 630-852-8502
Hours:9-4:30 Mon-Fri   E-mail: info@sommercork.com
www.sommercork.com

Cork stoppers and bulletin board cork. No credit cards.

Williams Brewing 800-759-6025
2088 Burroughs Ave.   510-895-2739
San Leandro, CA 94577   FAX 510-895-2745
Hours: 8-5 Mon-Fri
www.williamsbrewing.com

Beer-making supplies only. Large catalog available. $20 minimum on CREDIT
CARDS.

U-Z

 **ATAC**

WINE & BREWING SUPPLIES

Wine Enthusiast 800-356-8466
333 Worth Bedford Rd.   FAX 800-833-8466
Mt, Kisco, NY 10549
Hours: 9-6 Mon-Fri / 10-5 Sat (showroom) / 24-hour phone orders
www.wineenthusiast.com   E-mail: custserv@wineenthusiast.com
Catalog of wine racks, cellars and accessories. CREDIT CARDS.

The professional trade association for artists and craftspeople working in theatre, film, television and advertising

ATAC Membership 2010-11

Sharlot Battin
　Montana Leatherworks
Chris Bobin
Sharon Braunstein
Randy Carfagno
Nadine Charlsen
Eileen Connor
Mary Creede
Margaret Cusack
Cindy Anita Fain
　CINAF Designs
James Feng
Keen Gat
Deborah R. Glassberg
Rodney Gordon
Joseph Gourley
Corrinna Griffin
Jung K. Griffin
Denise Grillo
　Offstage Design
Stockton Hall
Karen Hart
Suzanne Hayden

Marian Jean "Killer" Hose
J. Michelle Hill
Louise Hunnicutt
John Jerard
　Jerard Studio
Joni Johns
Jan Kastendieck
Rachel Keebler
　Cobalt Studios
Amanda Klein
Arnold S. Levine
　Arnold S. Levine, Inc.
Janet Linville
Jeanne Marino
　Moonboots Productions
Jerry Marshall
Betsey McKearnan
Gene Mignola
　Gene Mignola, Inc.
Mary Mulder
　Mulder / Martin, Inc.
Susan Pitocchi
Elizabeth Popeil

Adele Recklies
Monona Rossol
　Arts, Crafts, & Theatre
　Safety (A.C.T.S.)
Bill Rybak
Jody Schoffner
James R. Seffens
Lisa Shaftel
　Shaftel S2DO
Stanley Allen Sherman
　Mask Arts Company
Linda Skipper
Michael Smanko
　Prism Prips
Sarah Timberlake
　Timberlake Studios
Mari Tobita
US Institute for Theatre
　Tech. (USITT)
Monique Walker
Anne-Marie Wright
John Yavroyan
　Yavroyan & Nelsen, LTD

For membership information visit our website at
www.ATACBIZ.com
Email: info@ATACBIZ.com
Or drop us a line at:

ATAC Membership Application
Anne-Marie Wright
280 Third St. Apt # 1
Jersey City, NJ 07302-2759

YARN,WEAVING, KNITTING & NEEDLECRAFT SUPPLIES

W. Cushing & Co. 207-967-3711
PO Box 351, 21 North St.   800-626-7847
Kennebunkport, ME 04046   FAX 207-967-8682
Hours: 9-4 Mon-Fri   E-mail: orders@wcushing.com
www.wcushing.com
Manufacturer of dyes and dispersing agents; also rug-hooking supplies.
CREDIT CARDS.

Gotta Knit 212-989-3030
14 E 34th St., 5th FL (5th-Mad Ave)
NY, NY 10016
Hours: 11-6 Mon, Wed, Fri / 11-7 Tue, Thur / 11-4 Sat-Sun
www.gottaknit.net
Large selection of yarns, supplies and tools for knitting and needlecrafts.
Custom pattern writing: based on your own measurements. Visit website to
sign up for promotions. CREDIT CARDS.

Habu 212-239-3546
135 W 29th St., Ste. 804 (7-8th Ave)   FAX 212-239-4173
NY, NY 10001
Hours: 10-6 Mon-Sat   E-mail: habu@habutextiles.com
www.habutextiles.com
Simple Japanese and American handwoven fabrics of natural materials. Yarns
are hand dyed with natural dyes. Visit website for catalog information.

Linda LaBelle / The Yarn Tree 718-384-3793
347 Bedford Ave.   718-384-8030
Brooklyn, NY 11211   FAX (same)
Hours: 4-8 Mon-Thurs / 12-7 Sat-Sun / or by appt.
www.theyarntree.com   E-mail: info@theyarntree.com
Costume design and construction, design and construction of soft props.
Custom handwoven fabrics, handknits and fabric painting.

Lion Brand Yarn . . . .(orders) 800-258-YARN
135 Kero Rd.   (cust. service) 800-661-7551
Carlstadt, NJ 07072   FAX 212-627-8154
Hours: (cust service) 9-4 Mon-Fri / (orders) 24-hrs.
www.lionbrand.com
Mail order knitting yarns, patterns and accessories. Catalog and color cards
available. CREDIT CARDS.

P & S Textile 212-226-1534
359 Broadway (Franklin-Leonard St)   212-226-1572
NY, NY 10013   FAX 212-343-1838
Hours: 9:30-6:30 Mon-Thurs / 9:30-3 Fri / 11-5:30 Sun
Fabrics, patterns, notions & trimmings and yarn, needles and how-to books.
Wide selection and great prices. CREDIT CARDS.

U-Z

Purl SoHo 212-420-8796
459 Broome St. (Mercer-Greene) 800-597-7875
NY, NY 10013
Hours: 12-7 Mon-Fri / 12-6 Sat-Sun E-mail: customerservice@purlsoho.com
www.purlsoho.com
Carefully selected fibers, from cotton, bamboo, silk and linen to warm alpaca, merino, and cashmere. Friendly atmosphere. Visit web address to view broad selections. CREDIT CARDS.

School Products 212-679-3516
1201 Broadway, Ste. 301 (28-29th St)
NY, NY 10001
Hours: 9:30-6:30 Mon-Fri / 10-3:30 Sat E-mail: info@schoolproducts.com
www.schoolproducts.com
Wide selection of yarn for hand or machine knitting and weaving. Also pattern books, weaving looms and Brother knitting machines. CREDIT CARDS.

Silk City Fibers . . . .(orders) 800-899-7455
155 Oxford St. 973-942-1100
Paterson, NJ 07522 FAX 973-942-8110
Hours: 9-5 Mon-Fri E-mail: inquiry@silkcityfibers.com
www.silkcityfibers.com
A wholesale and retail mail order source for a large stock of hand and machine yarns, including Sunray yarns. Color cards available. They have a warehouse outlet at the same address. CREDIT CARDS.

Smiley's Yarn 718-849-9873
92-03 Jamacia Ave. 718-847-2185
Woodhaven, NY 11421
Hours: 10-5:30 Mon-Tue, Thurs-Sat / Closed Wed & Sun
www.smileysyarns.com
Smileys Yarns offers premium quality knitting yarns and crochet yarns. Name brand yarns include: Bernat, Patons, Lion Brand, Red Heart and more, all at discount prices of up to 50% off retail. Visit website. CREDIT CARDS.

Straw Into Gold / Crystal Palace Yarn 510-237-9988
160 23rd St.
Richmond, CA 94804
Hours: see website
www.straw.com
Wholesale only. Natural fibers and hair, spinning supplies, yarn. Write for catalog. Check website for shops in particular areas.

Top Trimmings 212-302-2999
228 W 39th St. (7-8th Aves)
NY, NY 10018
Hours: 9-7 Mon-Fri / 10-6 Sat / 11-5 Sun E-mail: toptrimming@yahoo.com
www.toptrimming.com
Wholesale and retail. Custom productions. Sequins, beads, feathers, ribbons, stones, buckles, chains novelties, findings and more. Sewing supplies, thread, yarn and tools. CREDIT CARDS.

U-Z

Vardhman, Inc. 212-840-6950
269 W 39th St. (7-8th Ave)   FAX 212-840-5056
NY, NY 10018
Hours: 10-6:30 Mon-Fri / 11-5:30 Sat
www.vardhmaninc.com
Nice selection of buttons, trimmings, knittings, yarn and accessories.

Webs, Division of Valley Fibers Corp. 800-367-9327
75 Service Center Rd. (Service Center)   413-584-2225
Northampton, MA 01060   FAX 413-584-1603
Hours: 10-5:30 Mon-Sat / Thurs until 8pm   E-mail: webs@yarn.com
www.yarn.com
*Mail order source for hand and machine yarns with frequent sales. Color
cards available. Online shopping available. CREDIT CARDS.*

John Wilde & Bro., Inc. 215-482-8800
PO Box 4662, 3737 Main St.   FAX 215-482-8210
Philadelphia, PA 19127
Hours: 8:30-4:30 Mon-Fri   E-mail: info@wildeyarns.com
www.wildeyarns.com
Wool yarns and carded wools; mail order only. Catalog available.

Erica Wilson Needle Works 508-228-9881
25 Main St. (63rd-64th St)   800-973-7422
Nantucket, MA 02554
Hours: 10-6 Mon-Fri / 10-3 Sat
www.ericawilson.com
*Appleton yarns, all needlecraft supplies, books, kits and best of all, advice.
No knitting yarns however. Will finish pillows.*

The Woolgathering 212-734-4747
318 E 84th St. (1st-2nd Ave)
NY, NY 10028
Hours: 10:30-6 Wed-Fri / 10:30-5 Sat / 12-5 Sun
www.thewoolgathering.com   E-mail: info@thewoolgathering.com
*Don't expect friendly service, but they do have a nice selection of hand-
knitting yarns.*

Yarn Company 212-787-7878
2274 Broadway, 2nd Fl. (81st-82nd St)   888-YARNCOI
NY, NY 10024   FAX 212-595-6998
Hours: 12-6 Tue-Sat / 12-8 Wed
www.theyarnco.com
Yarn, designer patterns, workshops. CREDIT CARDS.

The Yarn Tree 718-384-8030
347 Bedford Ave. (S 4th St)
Brooklyn, NY 11211
Hours: 4-9 Mon-Thurs / 12-7 Sat-Sun   E-mail: info@theyarntree.com
www.theyarntree.com
*Yarn - natural fibers only including hand dyed yarns, organic yarns and yarns
dyed with natural dyes! Knitting supplies, classes in all levels of knitting, as
well as felting and spinning. The shop also carries handknit and handwoven
items for sale.*

U-Z

NOTES

U-Z

www.entertainmentsourcebook.com

DESIGN RESOURCES

American Museum of Natural History Library 212-769-5400
    79th St. & Central Park West   FAX 212-769-5009
    NY, NY 10024
    Hours: 11-4 Tue-Fri   E-mail: libref@amnh.org
    www.library.amnh.org
    Photographic collection: 500,000 black and white; 60,000 slides.

Americas Society 212-249-8950
    680 Park Ave. (68-69th St)   FAX 212-249-1880
    NY, NY 10021
    Hours: 12-6 Tue-Sun   E-mail: inforequest@as-coa.org
    www.americas-society.org
    Important resource for art and literature of Latin America, Canada and the
    Caribbean. Library has artbooks, monographs, magazines and an archive of
    slides on 4000 artists from the Americas Gallery.

Anthology Film Archives: Library 212-505-5181
    32 Second Ave. (2nd St)   FAX 212-477-2714
    NY, NY 10003
    Hours: 10-6:30 Mon-Fri
    www.anthologyfilmarchives.org
    Films, stills, posters, books; also shows independent films.

ASSOCIATION OF THEATRICAL ARTISTS AND CRAFTSPEOPLE (ATAC) . . . . .
. 212-501-9090
    555 Eighth Ave. #2009 (mailing address) c/o Arnold S. Levine
    NY, NY 10018
    Hours: by appt.   E-mail: atacbiz@aol.com
    www.atacbiz.com
    Professional trade association for artists and craftspeople working in theater,
    film, television and advertising. ATAC creates a professional network through
    quarterly meetings, a membership directory and articles in the ATAC
    Quarterly. Compilers and editors of The Entertainment Sourcebook.

CINDY ANITA FAIN 212-501-9090
    48 Fairway St.   917-796-4641
    Bloomfield, NJ 07003   FAX 973-320-4493
    Hours: by appt.   E-mail: cinaf@aol.com
    www.cinafdesigns.com
    Cosume crafts, costume painting and distressing. Drapery and upholstery.
    Model building, props for puppets and speciality prop and crafts. Set
    decoration, prop shopping and photo styling. Member IATSE Local 1
    Stagehands, 52 Motion Pictures and 829 United Scenic Artists. Member
    ATAC.

Bard Graduate Center 212-501-3000
    18 W 86th St. (Columbus & CPW)   212-501-3035
    NY, NY 10024   FAX 212-501-3099
    Hours: 10-6 Mon-Thurs / 10-5 Fri / 12-5 Sat-Sun E-mail: reference@bgc.bard.edu
    www.bgc.bard.edu
    Library on decorative arts of all periods. Rotating exhibitions of decorative
    arts. When you call, ask for the librarian. Outside researchers must call for
    an appointment.

App

Marcella Beckwith 941-586-3282
5119 Lymbar Dr.
Houston, TX 77096
Hours: by appt.   E-mail: hmbeckwith@aol.com
Freelance costume and set designer for film, TV, theatre and print work.
Shopping and costume construction, crafts, millinery, painting and dyeing,
some scenic painting. Member USA Local 829.

The Brooklyn Museum: Art Reference Library and Wilbour Library of
Egyptology 718-501-6307
200 Eastern Pkwy. (Washington Ave)   FAX 718-501-6125
Brooklyn, NY 11238
Hours: 10-4:30 Wed-Fri   E-mail: library@brooklynmuseum.org
www.brooklynmuseum.org
Art and ethnology relating to American painting and sculpture, Asian art,
decorative arts, costumes and textiles. Fashion sketches: 1900-1950, leading
American designers in museum archives. Wilbour library has great references
on ancient Egypt.

NADINE CHARLSEN 212-307-0035
344 W 49th St. Apt 2D (8-9th Ave)   (cell) 917-656-1313
NY, NY 10019
Hours: by appt.   ,   E-mail: nadinelc@nyc.rr.com
www.nadinepaints.com   www.nadinedesigns.com
Research and design of sets, lights and props. Macintosh computer graphics.
AEA Stage Manager. Member ATAC.

Columbia University: Avery Architectural & Fine Arts Library . .212-854-3501
300 Avery Hall, Columbia University - 1172 Amsterdam Ave.
(B'way-116th St)
NY, NY 10027   FAX 212-854-8904
Hours: 9-11 Mon-Thurs / 9-9 Fri / 10-7 Sat / 12-10 Sun
www.columbia.edu
Architecture, archeology, city planning, housing, painting, sculpture,
decorative arts, graphic arts. Columbia ID required or contact Library
information office at 212-854-7309.

Cooper Hewitt Museum of Design: Library 212-849-8330
2 E 91st St. (5th Ave)   FAX 212-860-6339
NY, NY 10128
Hours: 9:30-5:30 Mon-Fri (by appt. only)   E-mail: libmail@si.edu
www.ndm.si.edu
Decorative arts and design books on textiles, wallpaper, early natural history,
architecture and interiors. The picture collection of 1,500,000 items filed by
category (available 1997). Appointment required. www.siris-libraries.si.edu
address will access the entire card catalog of The Smithsonian and all its
affiliated museums.

Corbis 212-777-6200
902 Broadway, 5th Fl. (20th-21st St)   800-260-0444
NY, NY 10010   FAX 212-358-9018
Hours: 9-5 Mon-Fri for research, by appt.   E-mail: sales@corbis.com
www.corbis.com
Collections of movie, theater, jazz, science and NY Daily Mirror; $75 minimum
research fee. News photo collection, UPI historical news images, fine arts
arrangement with Christies, images in London. CREDIT CARDS.

The Costume Society of America 800-CSA-9447
203 Towne Center Dr.   908-359-1471
Hillsborough, NJ 08844   FAX 908-359-7619
Hours: 8:30-4:30 Mon-Fri   E-mail: national.office@costumesocietyamerica.com
www.costumesocietyamerica.com
Referral service for the identification and conservation of costumes; various
publications, newsletter and journal; annual membership fee. Contact by
letter, website or e-mail for information.

Culver Pictures 718-752-9393
51-02 21st St.   FAX 718-752-9394
Long Island City, NY 11101
Hours: 9-5 Mon-Fri by appt.   E-mail: research@culverpictures.com
www.culverpictures.com
9,000,000 choice old photos, engravings, prints, movie stills, trade cards,
sheet music covers, old greeting cards, tintypes and glass plate negatives.
Leased for reproduction.

Dover Publications, Inc. 516-294-7000
31 E 2nd St.   FAX 516-742-6953
Mineola, NY 11501
Hours: 9-4:30 Mon-Fri   E-mail: rights@doverpublications.com
www.doverpublications.com
Mail order catalogs with a thorough collection of paperback books on fine
arts and crafts with many facsimile reproductions and excellent pictorial
archives. Order online or view web address for retail locations.

Fashion Institute of Technology, Museum @ FIT 212-217-4578
Seventh Ave. (27th St)   FAX 212-217-5978
NY, NY 10001
Hours: Gallery 12-8 Tue-Fri / 10-5 Sat   E-mail: museuminfo@fitnyc.edu
www.fitnyc.edu
Extensive collection of costumes and textile swatches. By becoming a
"design member," you have access to the online collection.

Fashion Institute of Technology: Library . . .(reference desk) 212-217-4400
Seventh Ave. (27th St)
NY, NY 10001
Hours: 8-12am Mon-Thurs / 8-6:30 Fri / 10-5 Sat / 12-9 Sun
www.fitnyc.edu/library
Fashion, textile and interior design books and magazines; also original
sketches by designers, historical and contemporary. Some printed and
electronic resources available by appt only. Library hours change by
semester, be sure to call for hours.

Fiber Works Sources 212-866-0386
P.O. Box 20128
NY, NY 10025
Hours: by appt only   E-mail: fwsllc@earthlink.net
Personal shopping service for costume designers specializing in fabric,
garments, notions and accessories. Speak to Bonnie. Bonnie can help you
access the resources of the NY Garment and Textile industry by researching
sources, scheduling appointments with suppliers and providing detailed
shopping itineraries.

App

Frick Art Reference Library 212-547-0641
10 E 71st St. (5th-Mad Ave)   FAX 212-879-2091
NY, NY 10021
Hours: 10-5 Mon-Fri / 9:30-1 Sat (Closed June-Aug in Summer)
www.frick.org   E-mail: library@frick.org
Paintings, drawings, sculpture and illuminated MSS of Western Europe and the USA from the 4th century AD to 1860. Over 400,000 classified study photographs. ID required for registration and access.

Getty Images 646-613-4000
75 Varick St.   800-462-4379
NY, NY 10013
Hours: 8-8 Mon-Fri   E-mail: sales@gettyimages.com
www.gettyimages.com
6 million color transparencies and B&W photos, CD-ROM contemporary and historical collection; large-format scenic transparencies. Agents in 30 key cities worldwide; charge for reproduction. Not for individual use, company authorization required.

KAREN HART 908-931-0998
Hours: by appt.   E-mail: tx2ny@aol.com
Costume design, construction and shopping services. Member ATAC

Huntington Free Library and Reading Room 718-829-7770
9 Westchester Sq. (Westchester Ave-E Tremont Ave)   FAX 718-829-4875
Bronx, NY 10461
Hours: 10-4 Mon-Fri by appt.   E-mail: hflib1@rmi.net
Turn of the century library specializing in Bronx history. The staff will photocopy while you wait for a small fee. Easily accessible via the IRT #6.

Information for Inspiration 212-777-0517
24 Fifth Ave., Ste. 1426 (9th St)
NY, NY 10011
Hours: by appt.   E-mail: debs245@hotmail.com
Pictorial researcher for all types of subject matter. Over 14 years of experience.

Lark Books 828-253-0467
67 Broadway
Asheville, NC 28801
Hours: 9-8:30 Mon-Fri / 24-hour customer service
www.larkbooks.com   E-mail: customerservice@larkbooks.com
Large variety of craft, beading, textiles, needlework fiberarts and books. Folkwear patterns. Catalog available.

Danielle Leon / Faultless Faux 718-832-2743
PO Box 1285 (Murray Hill Station)   305-781-6349
NY, NY 10156
Hours: by appt.   E-mail: faultlessfaux@att.net
Prop research for all media.

Lighting Associates 860-873-1910
PO Box 461
Moodus, CT 06469
Hours: 9-6 Mon-Fri   E-mail: info@lightingtemplates.com
www.lightingtemplates.com
Lighting, scenic design and furniture templates for theatrical and TV
designers; metric templates. Catalog available, phone orders. No credit cards.

Maximum Events & Designers 330-284-6239
1017 Camden Ave. SW
Canton, OH 44706
Hours: 8-6 Mon-Fri   E-mail: maxevntsdesigns@yahoo.com
Event planner, coordinator, designer, florist and party favors. RENTALS.
CREDIT CARDS.

The Metropolitan Museum of Art:
  Photograph and Slide Library 212-535-7710
1000 Fifth Ave. (82nd St)   FAX 212-472-2764
NY, NY 10028
Hours: 9:30-5:30 Tue-Thurs & Sun / 9:30-9 Fri-Sat
www.metmuseum.org   E-mail: communications@metmuseum.org
Extensive color and B&W slide and photograph collection covering history of
art; call for further information.

The Metropolitan Museum of Art:
  The Costume Institute Storage Collection 212-650-2663
1000 Fifth Ave. (82nd St)   FAX 212-570-3970
NY, NY 10028
Hours: by appt.
www.metmuseum.org
Excellent collection of costumes from 17th-20th centuries emphasizing haute
couture and regional clothing. Dennita Sewell, collections associate. Fashion
sketches (originals), photographs, books, some patterns, prints (fashion
plates) from late 16th through second half of 20th century.

Museum For African Art, Inc. 718-784-7700
36-01 43rd Ave., 3rd Fl. (Queens Blvd)   FAX 718-784-7718
Long Island City, NY 11101
Hours: 10-5 Mon, Thurs & Fri / 11-6 Sat-Sun   E-mail: museum@africanart.org
www.africanart.org
Good bookstore and giftshop.

The Museum of Modern Art Library .212-708-9400
11 W 53rd St. (5th Ave)   FAX 212-333-1122
NY, NY 10001
Hours: 10-5 Mon, Thurs-Fri by appt.   E-mail: info@moma.org
www.moma.org
Painting, sculpture, graphic arts, drawing, architecture, design, photography
and film from 1880s to present.

Museum of the City of New York 212-534-1672
1220 Fifth Ave. (103rd St)   (collection) FAX 212-534-5974
NY, NY 10029   (director) FAX 212-423-0758
Hours: 10-5 Wed-Sat / 12-5 Sun   E-mail: info@mcny.org
www.mcny.org
Extensive collection of 18th-20th century costumes and accessories.
Collection either made or purchased by New Yorkers.

National Museum of the American Indian .....(general info) 212-514-3700
1 Bowling Green   (resource center) 212-514-3799
NY, NY 10004
Hours: 10-5 Mon-Sat / Thurs til 8
www.americanindian.si.edu
Great bookstore and research center. All aspects of American Indian life and
art.

New York City Archives: Municipal Dept. ....212-NEW-YORK / 311
31 Chambers St. (Centre-Elk St)   212-788-8577
NY, NY 10007   FAX 718-935-6459
Hours: 9-4:30 Mon-Thurs / 9-1 Fri   E-mail: lgidlund@records.nyc.gov
www.nyc.gov/records
History of the five boroughs. Pictures of NYC from the turn-of-the-century to
present; also court dockets. Photocopy service available. Good for pictures of
specific neighborhoods. Collection now available online.

New York Public Library & Museum of the Performing Arts at Lincoln Center
212-870-1630
40 Lincoln Center Plaza (65th St)
NY, NY 10023
Hours: 12-8 Mon & Thurs / 11-6 Tue-Wed, Fri / 10-6 Sat
www.nypl.org
The most thorough selection of music books and scores, records, drama,
dance reference and circulating collections; also non-book materials including
videotape archives and specialized research collections, clippings, sketches,
etc.; photocopying service.

New York Public Library: Art & Picture Collection Mid-Manhattan Library
212-340-0877
455 Fifth Ave., 3rd Fl. (40th St)   FAX 212-576-0048
NY, NY 10016
Hours: 8-9 pm Mon-Thurs / 8-8 Fri / 10-6 Sat
www.nypl.org
5 million clippings from books and magazines (published from 1700s to date)
covering pictorial subjects of all areas and periods; free consultation. Have
coin photocopy machines. Materials are available to check-out with valid
library card.

New York Public Library: Schomburg Center for Research in Black Culture
212-491-2200
515 Malcolm X Blvd. (135th St)   FAX 212-491-6760
NY, NY 10037
Hours: 12-8 Mon-Wed / 11-6 Thurs-Fri / 10-6 Sat
www.nypl.org
General research and reference. Rare books, records, tapes, artifacts,
photographic and film archives and picture file.

App

New York Public Library: Mid Manhattan Library, Art & Picture Collection
212-340-0871
455 Fifth Ave., 3rd Fl. (39-40th St)
NY, NY 10016
Hours: 8-11 Mon-Thurs / 8-8 Fri / 10-6 Sat-Sun   E-mail: mmart@nypl.org
www.nypl.org
Books on visual and graphic arts, costume, textile design. Hard to get
through by phone.

The New York Times Pictures 212-556-1243
229 W 43rd St. (7-8th Ave)   800-698-4637
NY, NY 10036   FAX 212-556-5257
Hours: 9-5 Mon-Fri
www.newsday.com
Over 4 million photos from date of 1st publication: requests for specific
photos must be phoned in with date information, fees vary. If research is
required add $100 fee.

Yukinobu Okazaki 646-703-1443
244 W 16th St. Apt BRW (7-8th Ave)   FAX 212-989-9719
NY, NY 10011
Hours: by appt.   E-mail: surge67@earthlink.net
Scenic design and art direction.

Princeton Antiques and Bookfinding Librarians 609-344-1943
2917 Atlantic Ave.   FAX 609-344-1944
Atlantic City, NJ 08401
Hours: 8:30-5 Mon-Fri / 8-1 Sat   E-mail: princetn@earthlink.net
www.princetonantiques.com
24-hr. international search service, 250,000 titles in-stock and cataloged. Ship
worldwide. Also does RENTALS of antiques and books. CREDIT CARDS.

School of Visual Arts Library 212-592-2000
209 E. 23rd St. (Park-3rd Ave)   888-220-5782
NY, NY 10010   FAX 212-592-2655
Hours: 9-9 Mon-Thurs / 9-7 Fri / 10:30-5:30 Sat / 12-5 Sun
www.schoolofvisualarts.edu
Fine arts, art history, photography, film, graphic design: 30,000 pictures,
30,000 slides. Metro referral card required for non-students.

LISA SHAFTEL / SHAFTEL S2DO 508-879-7772
24 Warren Rd.   (Cell) 617-755-1240
Framingham, MA 01702   FAX (same)
Hours: 9-6 Mon-Fri   E-mail: shaftels2do@verizon.net
www.s2do.com
Scenic designer and scenic artist, art direction, illustration, storyboards,
character design, CAD drafting and Photoshop. Puppet design and
fabrication, prop fabrication no rentals. Member USA Local 829, IATSE Local
481, and the Graphic Artist Guild. Member ATAC.

App

Society for Creative Anachronism 408-263-9305
PO Box 360789   800-789-7486
Milpitas, CA 95036   FAX 408-263-0641
Hours: 9-4 Mon-Thur / mail order only   E-mail: membership#sca.org
www.sca.org
Contact group for artisans specializing in medieval costumes, weaponry, furniture, related props and publications. Mail order information.

South Street Seaport Museum 212-748-8600
12 Fulton St. (Fulton St)
NY, NY 10038
Hours: 10-6 Mon-Fri
www.southstreetseaportmuseum.org
Museum of South Street Seaport.

Vintage Pattern Lending Library 510-655-3091
869 Aileen St.   FAX 510-654-6442
Oakland, CA 94608
Hours 9-5 Mon-Fri / 24-hr web-site   E-mail: librarian@vpll.org
www.vpll.org
The Vintage Pattern Lending Library preserves, archives, and replicates historic fashion patterns from 1840 through 1950, vintage sewing publications, and fashion prints of the past. High quality, user-friendly print replications of our patterns and copies of our publications are available for purchase to our guests and purchase or loan to Library members. See web-site for membership information. CREDIT CARDS.

HEALTH & SAFETY SERVICES

ARTS, CRAFTS & THEATRE SAFETY / ACTS 212-777-0062
181 Thompson St. #23   Pager 888-642-6120
NY, NY 10012   FAX 212-777-0062
Hours: by appt.   E-mail: actsnyc@cs.com
www.artscraftstheatersafety.org
Contact Monona Rossol. Member ATAC.

Chemical Pollution Control, Inc. 631-586-0333
120 S 4th St.   FAX 631-586-0727
Bayshore, NY 11706
Hours: 8-5 Mon-Fri
Safe removal of old and unwanted toxic chemical waste. CREDIT CARDS.

Fehr Bros. Industries, Inc. . . . .(out of NY) 800-431-3095
895 Kings Highway   845-246-9525
Saugerties, NY 12477   FAX 845-246-3330
Hours: 8-5 Mon-Fri   E-mail: stage@fehr.com
www.stageriggingonline.com
Stage rigging supplies, fall arresting equipment, motor control systems. $50 minimum. Online catalog. CREDIT CARDS.

Incord 860-537-1414
   226 Upton Rd.   800-596-1066
   Colchester, CT 06415   FAX 860-537-7393
   Hours: 8-5 Mon-Fri   E-mail: netting@incord.com
   www.incord.com
   Stage netting, safety netting, rope and cargo nets. CREDIT CARDS.

Poison Control Center of NYC 800-222-1222
   NY, NY 10016   212-764-7667
   Hours: 24 hour phone service
   www.nyc.gov/health
   Very helpful with information. Keep phone number handy as the website is not easy to find phone numbers. Covers Metropolitan NYC region. This and the Rocky Mountain Center are the two most comprehensive poison control centers in the USA. For Spanish language call 212-836-3667

J. Racenstein Co. 201-809-1680
   74 Henry St.   800-221-3748
   Secaucus, NJ 07094   FAX 201-348-1385
   Hours: 8:30-4:30 Mon-Fri   E-mail: helpdesk@jracenstein.com
   www.jracenstein.com
   Natural Mediterranean sponges and synthetics. Window cleaning and janitorial supplies. Ladders, harnesses, and safety equipment. Extra cool website. CREDIT CARDS.

Radiac Research Corp. 718-963-2233
   261 Kent Ave. (Grand Ave)   800-640-7511
   Brooklyn, NY 11211   FAX 718-388-5107
   Hours: 8:30-4:30 Mon-Fri
   www.radiacenv.com
   Waste chemical disposal and radioactive disposal pick-up.

Rocky Mountain Poison and Drug Center 303-739-1127
   777 Bannok St. MC0180   800-222-1222
   Denver, CO 80204
   Hours: 24 hour phone service
   www.rmpdc.org
   RMPDC is designated regional poison control center for CO, MT, NV and ID by American Association of Poison Control Centers.

Safety Supplies Unlimited 866-787-2336
   36-06 43rd Ave.   FAX 718-389-6155
   Long Island City, NY 11101
   Hours: 8-5:30 Mon-Fri   E-mail: sales@safetysuppliesunlimited.com
   www.safetysuppliesunlimited.com
   Huge variety of personal safety equipment plus safety storage cans and cabinets, first aid and burn kits, janitoral supplies, caution sighs, hazard tapes & traffic cones. Great Catalog. CREDIT CARDS.

Triumvirate Environmental 718-274-3339
   42-14 19th Ave. (43rd St)   800-966-9282
   Astoria, NY 11105   FAX 718-726-7917
   Hours: 7-5 Mon-Fri   E-mail: contactus@triumvirate.com
   www.triumvirate.com
   Chemical waste disposal. CREDIT CARDS.

App

U.S. Department of Labor Occupational Safety and Health Assoc. (OSHA)
212-620-3200
201 Varick St. Rm 908
NY, NY 10014   FAX 212-620-4121
Hours: 8-4:30 Mon-Fri
www.osha.gov
OSHA information and regulations.

Zee Medical 800-942-1805
931-C Conklin St.   516-249-4678
Farmingdale, NY 11735   FAX 516-249-4826
Hours: 8-5 Mon-Fri   E-mail: zeenewyork@zeemedical.com
www.zeemedical.com
Nationwide supplier of industrial first aid and safety equipment. Gloves,
respirators, first aid supplies, safety training and evaluation. CREDIT CARDS.

ORGANIZATIONS, UNIONS & SUPPORT SERVICES

aboutsources 646-218-2538
50 W 40th St., 4th FL (5-6th Ave)
NY, NY 10018
Hours: by appt.   E-mail: sp@aboutsources.com
www.aboutsources.com
Business to business information provider for the fashion industry.

Actors' Equity Association 212-869-8530
165 W 46th St. (7th Ave)   FAX 212-719-9815
NY, NY 10036
Hours: 9:30-5:30 Mon-Fri (membership hours 10-4)
www.actorsequity.org
Union for actors and stage managers in legitimate theatre.

Advertising Photographers of America (APA) 212-807-0399
27 W 20th St. #601 (5-6th Ave)   FAX 212-727-8120
NY, NY 10011
Hours: 9:30-5:30 Mon-Fri   E-mail: ceo@apany.com
www.apany.com
APA is a professional trade association serving advertising photographers,
companies and individuals supplying the photography community. In
addition to the New York organization, there are chapters in other key cities.
Newsletter, business forms, information hotline, member discounts.

Alliance for the Arts 212-947-6340
330 W 42nd St. #1701 (8-9th Ave)   FAX 212-947-6416
NY, NY 10036
Hours: 9:30-5:30 Mon-Fri   E-mail: info@allianceforarts.org
www.allianceforarts.org
Publishes NYC Culture Guide and Calendar. A comprehensive guide to
museums, performance and exhibitions spaces, theatres, historic sights,
botanical gardens and zoos.

App

Alliance of Resident Theatres / ART/New York 212-244-6667
520 Eighth Ave., Ste. 319   FAX 212-714-1918
NY, NY 10018
Hours: 10-6 Mon-Fri   E-mail: questions@art-newyork.com
www.art-newyork.com
ART/New York serves over 190 of NYC's not-for-profit professional theatres.
The Alliance provides its members with services, skills and information to
help them survive and flourish. ART/New York also functions as an
information center for other artists, related professionals, students, the press,
funding sources and the general public. Publishes "Theatre Times" and a list
of Off-Off Broadway Theatres.

American Theatre Wing 212-765-0606
570 Seventh Ave. (B'way-8th Ave)   FAX 212-307-1910
NY, NY 10018
Hours: 9:30-5:30 Mon-Fri   E-mail: mailbox@americantheatrewing.org
www.americantheatrewing.org
Not for Profit. Provides educational services to the community through
"Working in Theatre"Seminars, The Hospital Show program, Introduction to
Broadway program, "Theatre in the School"and annual grants and
scholarships. Founders of the Tony Awards.

Central Opera Service / OPERA America 212-796-8620
330 Seventh Ave., 16th FL (28-29th St)   FAX 212-796-8633
NY, DCNY 10001
Hours: 9-6 Mon-Fri   E-mail: info@operaamerica.org
www.operaamerica.org
Maintains a library of books and periodicals and the most comprehensive
operatic and musical theatre archives in the United States. Research areas
include: repertory, performances, musical materials, translations, captions
and projections, scenery, costumes, props (rental, sale or exchange
opportunities), company statistics, annual opera and musical theatre
statistics for the United States.

Compu-Tab Services, Inc. 914-273-1220
84 Business Park Dr., Ste. 113   FAX 914-273-3883
Armonk, NY 10504
Hours: 9-5 Mon-Fri
Provides on going accounting services to not-for-profit organizations and
small businesses at a reduced fee.

The Costume Society of America 800-CSA-9447
203 Towne Center Dr.   908-359-1471
Hillsborough, NJ 08844   FAX 908-359-7619
Hours: 8:30-4:30 Mon-Fri   E-mail: national.office@costumesocietyamerica.com
www.costumesocietyamerica.com
National organization of people interested in all aspects of costume. Over
1500 members including; curators, historians, artists and designers,
librarians, entertainers, educators and students. Publishes DRESS, the annual
journal of the CSA, a quarterly newsletter and a number of scholarly
publications. Conducts symposia, study tours and grants for students and
researchers.

App

Dance Notation Bureau 212-571-7011
111 John St. Ste 704 (6-7th Ave)   FAX 212-571-7012
NY, NY 10038
Hours: 10-6 Mon-Fri / call first   E-mail: dnbinfo@dancenotation.org
www.dancenotation.org
A non-profit service organization for dance. Referral of certified dance notators, notation teachers and dance reconstructors. Library for members.

Dance Theatre Workshop . . . .(admin. office) 212-691-6500
219 W 19th St. (7-8th Ave)   (b.o.) 212-924-0077
NY, NY 10011   FAX 212-633-1974
Hours: Office 10-8 Mon-Fri / 12-8 Sat / 11-6 Sun   E-mail: dtw@dtw.org
www.dancetheatreworkshop.org
Publishes the Poor Dancer's Almanac, a survival manual for choreographers, dancers and management personnel. Non-profit organization. NY state dance force offering children and adult classes.

Director's Guild of America 212-581-0370
110 W 57th St. (6-7th Ave)   800-356-3754
NY, NY 10019   FAX 212-581-1441
Hours: 9-6 Mon-Fri
www.dga.org
National union representing film and television directors and assistant directors. See Website for offices in Chicago and Los Angeles.

Entertainment Services & Technology Association (ESTA) 212-244-1505
875 Sixth Ave., Ste. 1005 (31st St)   FAX 212-244-1502
NY, NY 10001
Hours: 9-6 Mon-Fri   E-mail: info@esta.org
www.esta.org
A professional trade association of dealers, manufacturers, distributors, production and service companies who supply the theatrical and live entertainment industries. Member services include: business insurance, credit reporting program, trade show promotion, industry surveys, seminars and development of technical standards.

Foundation Center 212-620-4230
79 Fifth Ave., 2nd Fl. (15-16th St)   800-424-9836
NY, NY 10003   FAX 212-807-3677
Hours: 10-5 Mon-Tue, Thurs & Fri / 10-8 Wed   E-mail: ajt@foundationcenter.org
www.foundationcenter.org
Clearinghouse for private funding information for non-profit groups and individuals. Reference library available. Free seminars. Field locations in Atlanta, Cleveland, DC, San Francisco.

Graphic Artists Guild 212-791-3400
32 Broadway Ste. 1114   FAX 212-791-0333
NY, NY 10004
Hours: 9-5 Tue-Thurs
www.graphicartistsguild.org / www.gag.org
Member service organization for graphic and commercial artists. Offers pricing scale and ethical guidelines. Dues are based on annual income.

IATSE Local 1 212-333-2500
320 W 46th St. (8-9th Ave)　　　　　　　　　800-745-0045
NY, NY 10036　　　　　　　　　　　　FAX 212-586-2437
Hours: 9:30-4:30 Mon-Fri
www.iatselocalone.org
Union representing stagehands for TV, theatre and the Javits Center. Local 1s
jurisdiction is Manhattan, Staten Island and the Bronx.

IATSE Local 4 718-252-8777
2917 Glenwood Rd. (Nostrand-Flatbush)　　　　FAX 718-421-5605
Brooklyn, NY 11210
Hours: 734 Mon-Fri
www.iatselocal4.org
Stagehands for Brooklyn and Queens - TV and theater..

IATSE Local 52 212-399-0980
326 W 48th St. (8-9th Ave)　　　　　　　　　FAX 212-315-1073
NY, NY 10036
Hours: 7:30-5:30 Mon-Fri
www.iatselocal52.org
Film local for New York City.

IATSE Local 764 212-957-3500
545 W 45th St., 2nd Fl. (10-11th Aves)　　(P&W Funds) 212-957-3900
NY, NY 10036　　　　　　　　　　　　　FAX 212-957-3232
Hours: 9-5:30 Mon-Fri　　　　　　E-mail: support@ia764.org
www.ia764.org
Theatrical wardrobe union covering film, television and Broadway.

IATSE Local 798 212-627-0660
152 W 24th St. (5-6th Ave)　　　　　　　　FAX 212-627-0664
NY, NY 10011
Hours: 8:30-5:30 Mon-Fri
www.798makeupandhair.com
Union representing hair and make-up artists for TV and film.

International Alliance of Theatrical Stage Employees (IATSE) .212-730-1770
1430 Broadway, 20th Fl. (37-38th St)　　　　FAX 212-730-7809
NY, NY 10018
Hours: 9-5 Mon-Fri
www.iatse-Intl.org
National office for union representing stagehands and motion picture
operators.

Krannert Center for the Performing Arts 217-333-6700
500 S Goodwin　　　　　　　　　　　　FAX 217-244-0810
Urbana, IL 61801-3741
www.krannertcenter.com　　　　E-mail: webmaster@kcpa.uiuc.edu
Performing arts center.

App

L.A. Trade Tech. . . . . .Bookstore 213-763-7210
400 W Washington Blvd.   Library 213-763-3958
Los Angeles, CA 90015
Hours: Bookstore 7:15-7 Mon-Thurs / 7:15-3 Fri / 8-12:30 Sat Library: 8-6:50
Mon-Thurs / 8-12:50 Fri / 9:30-1:30 Sat
www.http://college.lattc.edu/library/
Fashion Technical school: bookstore and library open to public for research.
Library has online research database.

Materials for the Arts Warehouse 718-729-3001
33-00 Northern Blvd., 3rd Fl. (32nd-34th St)   FAX 718-729-3941
Long Island City, NY 11101
Hours: 9-5 Mon-Fri / call for appt.   E-mail: info@mfta.org
www.mfta.org
Free goods and materials to legitimate NYC non-profit qualifying artists and
organizations. 10,000 sq. ft. warehouse of books, construction equipment,
furniture, fabric, etc. Joint project of the NYC Dept. of Cultural Affairs and
Sanitation's recycling program. Drop-offs: M, W, F 9-3. MUST BE PRE-
APPROVED.

BETSEY MCKEARNAN 413-298-4637
PO Box 1358
Stockbridge, MA 01262   E-mail: betseybowen@roadrunner.com
Education Chairperson - Berkshire Theatre Festival. Founding member ATAC.

Museum of Arts & Design 212-299-7777
2 Columbus Cr. (5-6th Ave)   FAX 212-299-7701
NY, NY 10019
Hours: 10-6 Mon-Wed, Fri-Sun / 10-8 Thurs   E-mail: info@madmuseum.org
www.madmuseum.org
Formerly the American Craft Museum. New location 2003.

NAPO-NY 212-439-1088
459 Columbus Ave., PMB 210
NY, NY 10024
www.napo-ny.net   E-mail: napo@napo-ny.net
National Association of Professional Organizers-Greater New York Chapter.
Professional association whose members specialize in business and personal
organizing, including corporate event planning and party planning.

National Alliance for Musical Theatre 212-714-6668
520 Eighth Ave., Ste. 301 (36-37th St)   FAX 212-714-0469
New York, NY 10018
Hours: 10-6 Mon-Fri   E-mail: info@namt.net
www.namt.org
National non-profit organization serving musical theatre producers and
presenters. Annual Festival of New Musicals in the fall. National set and
costume registry on website.

National Costumers Association, Inc. 317-351-1940
121 N Bosart Ave.   FAX 317-351-1941
Indianapolis, IN 46201
www.costumers.org   E-mail: office@costumers.org
*Organzation of costume rental businesses (shops and suppliers). Publishes
"Costumer Magazine,"Mary Lou Schultz, Editor. Can direct you to shop which
can fulfill your specific needs. Members in USA and Canada. LaMar Kerns
Secretary/Treasurer.*

National Endowment for the Arts 202-682-5400
1100 Pennsylvania Ave. NW
Washington, D.C. 20506
Hours: 9-5:30 Mon-Fri   E-mail: webmgr@atts.gov
www.nea.gov
*An independent federal agency that receives annual appropriations from
Congress from which it awards matching grants to non-profit, tax exempt
arts organizations of outstanding quality and fellowships to artists of
exceptional talent.*

New York City Department of Cultural Affairs 212-513-9300
31 Chambers St., 2nd FL (8-9th Ave)
NY, NY 10007
Hours: 9-5 Mon-Fri
www.nyc.gov/html/dcla
*Support of cultural institutions and activities through a variety of programs:
Materials for the arts, an arts apprenticeship program, a city gallery for group
art shows and a public works project providing personnel assistance for
cultural institutions.*

New York City Office of Film, Theater, & Broadcasting 212-489-6710
1697 Broadway, 6th Fl. (53rd St)   FAX 212-307-6237
NY, NY 10019
Hours: 9-4 Mon-Thurs / 9-3 Fri
www.nyc.gov/film
Mayor's office of film, theatre and broadcasting.

New York Foundation for the Arts 212-366-6900
20 Jay St., 7th FL   FAX 212-366-1778
Brooklyn, NY 11201
Hours: 9:30-5:00 Mon-Fri   E-mail: nyfainfo@nyfa.org
www.nyfa.org
*Formerly The Cultural Council Foundation. Fiscal management for non-profit
arts groups and city agencies. Now offering classified adds to post job
openings, services and events. See website www.nyfa.org/classifieds.*

NYCOSH 212-227-6440
116 John St., Ste. 604 (Pearl-Gold)   FAX 212-227-9854
NY, NY 10038
Hours: 9-6 Mon-Fri   E-mail: nycosh@nycosh.org
www.nycosh.org
*A technical and educational resource, NYCOSH is a non-profit organization
for workers in the theatrical trades. They deal with occupational safety and
health hazards on the job, supplying information regarding rights and
responsiblilties of employers and employees under the OSHA Act. Can
provide help with research. Publications.*

App

Puppeteers of America, Inc. 888-568-6235
26 Howard Ave.
New Haven, CT 06519
www.puppeteers.org   E-mail: membership@puppeteers.org
National non-profit corporation for professionals and amateurs. Sponsors
festivals, workshops and seminars. Maintains publications, advisory and
educational services and an endowment fund. Their audio-visual library is a
resource center with archives of recorded history; selections available for
borrowing by members. Contact Fred Thompson.

Puppetry Guild of Greater New York . . . . .Hotline 212-866-5156
PO Box 117
NY, NY 10116
Hours: by appt.   E-mail: ptrlws@nyc.rr.com
www.johnbaloney.com
Independent non-profit corporation chartered by Puppeteers of America.
Serves as a public awareness and support organization for amateurs,
professionals and educators in the New York area. Contact Peter Lewis.

Set Decorators Society of America SDSA 818-255-2425
71 Tujunga Ave. Ste # A   FAX 818-982-8597
Hollywood, CA 91605
Hours: 8-5 Mon-Fri   E-mail: sdsa@setdecorators.org
www.setdecorators.org
The Set Decorators Society of America, founded in 1993, is the only national
non-profit organization dedicated to the support of the past, present and
future of our profession. Members include qualified Set Decorators of Motion
Pictures and Television, including commercials and music videos, as well as
Business Members who provide furnishings, materials, and professional
services to our trade.

Society of Stage Directors and Choreographers (SSDC) 212-391-1070
1501 Broadway, Ste. 1701 (43-44th St)   800-541-5204
NY, NY 10036   FAX 212-302-6195
Hours: 10-6:20 Mon-Fri   E-mail: info@sdcweb.org
www.ssdc.org
Union representing stage directors and choreographers. Holds semiannual
meetings, publishes a monthly newsletter, "SSDC Notes" and, through the
SDC Foundation, gives awards, holds staged readings and roundtable
discussions and publishes a biannual journal.

Stage Manager's Association (SMA) . . . . .NONE
PO Box 275, Times Sq. Station
NY, NY 10108
Hours: Leave message   E-mail: info@stagemanagers.org
www.stagemanagers.org
An association for professional union and non-union stage managers.
Information and skill seminars given. Newsletter published with list of job
openings. Projects include "Operation Observation,"in which stage managers
observe their peers working backstage; also publishes The Stage Managers
Directory.

Support Services Alliance, Inc. 518-295-7966
PO Box 130 / 107 Prospect St.   (NY) 800-836-4SSA
Schoharie, NY 12157
Hours: 8:30-5 Mon-Thurs / 8:30-4 Fri   E-mail: info@ssamembers.com
www.ssamember.org
*Organization serving self-employed, small business and not-for-profit groups.
Offers group health insurance, disability and life insurance, rental cars, credit
union, discount prescription and vitamin service, travel agency, One-Write
bookkeeping system, Harvard medical newsletter and educational loans. Low
membership fee; bimonthly newsletter.*

The Broadway League 212-764-1122
226 W 47th St.,, 5th Fl. (B'way-8th Ave)   FAX 212-944-2136
NY, NY 10036
Hours: 9:30-5:30 Mon-Fri   E-mail: league@broadwayleague.org
www.broadwayleague.org
*The association for Broadway and regional promotors, producers and theatre
owners. Research and statistics on the professional theatre and a data bank
of technical specs on road houses.*

Theatre Communications Group (TCG) 212-609-5900
520 Eigth Ave., 24th Fl. (36-37st St)   FAX 212-609-5901
NY, NY 10018
Hours: 10-6 Mon-Fri   E-mail: tcg@tcg.org
www.tcg.org
*National organization for not-for-profit professional theatres. Provides nearly
30 centralized programs and services for theatre institutions and individuals.
Publishes American Theatre Magazine, several books and a directory of
member theatres.*

Theatre Development Fund (TDF) 212-912-9770
520 Eighth Ave. Ste 801 (36th St)   FAX 212-768-1563
NY, NY 10016
Hours: 10-6 Mon-Fri   E-mail: info@tdf.org
www.tdf.org
*An audience development organization supporting theatre, music and dance.
Administers the Costume Collection, TKTS booths and "Theatre Access
Project" for disabled individuals. Discount tickets available by mail for
qualifying individuals and groups (visit website or send stamped, self-
addressed envelope for information and application).*

Theatre Row Studios 212-714-2442
410 W 42nd St. (9-10th Ave)   FAX 212-714-2772
NY, NY 10036
Hours: 10-6 Mon-Fri   E-mail: erika@theatrerow.org
www.theatrerow.org
*Studio and office rental spaces. Stage door: 407 W 41st St. Talk to Erica or
Adam for booking matters.*

United Scenic Artists IATSE Local 829 (USA) 212-581-0300
29 W 38th St., 15th Fl. (5-6th Ave)   FAX 212-977-2011
NY, NY 10018
Hours: 9-5 Mon-Fri   E-mail: usa829@aol.com
www.usa829.org
*Union representing scenic artists, set, costume and lighting designers,
craftspeople, mural artists, diorama, model and display makers.*

App

UNITED STATES INSTITUTE FOR THEATRE TECHNOLOGY (USITT) . . . .
. 800-938-7488
315 South Crouse Ave., Ste. 200 315-463-6463
Syracuse, NY 13210 FAX 866-398-7488
Hours: 8:30-5:30 Mon-Fri E-mail: info@office.usitt.org
www.usitt.org
*The American Association of Design and Production Professionals in the
Performing Arts. Provides an active forum for the development and exchange
of practical and theoretical information through its quarterly journal, regular
newsletters, annual national conference and frequent regional meetings.
Member ATAC.*

PROFESSIONAL SERVICES

Carroll Musical Instrument Rental 212-868-4120
625 W 55th St., 6th Fl. (11-12th Ave) FAX 212-868-4126
NY, NY 10019
Hours: 96- Mon-Fri / 9-5 Sat E-mail: irent@carrollmusic.com
www.carrollmusic.com
*Large stock instruments, stands, etc. RENTALS ONLY. Rehearsal studio
space available. Three floors of rental space. Ressonable prices. CREDIT
CARDS.*

Compu-Tab Services, Inc. 914-273-1220
84 Business Park Dr., Ste. 113 FAX 914-273-3883
Armonk, NY 10504
Hours: 9-5 Mon-Fri
*Provides on going accounting services to not-for-profit organizations and
small businesses at a reduced fee.*

ELIZABETH POPIEL 917-374-1266
4761 Broadway 6-G (Thayer-Cumming St)
NY, NY 10034
Hours: by appt. E-mail: scenicdesigner@hotmail.com
Scenic Designer. Member ATAC.

Glick and Weintraub, P.C. 212-944-1501
1501 Broadway #2401 (43rd-44th St) FAX 212-768-0785
NY, NY 10036
Hours: by appt.
Attorney services.

John Kilgore Sound & Recording 212-245-4623
630 Ninth Ave. Rm 307 (44-45th St) FAX 212-262-4013
NY, NY 10036
Hours: 9-5 Mon-Fri / or by appt. E-mail: john@johnkilgore.com
www.johnkilgore.com
*Sound recording studio, sound effect recordings, music and post production.
Scoring for film, video and theatrical productions.*

JOSEPH GOURLEY 646-281-2040
567 Flushing Ave. Apt 505
Brooklyn, NY 11206
Hours: by appt.   E-mail: josephmgourley@yahoo.com
www.jmgtheadesign.com
Scenic and lighting designer. Drafting and 3-D Modeling as well as modelmaking. Member ATAC.

KATE DALE 718-253-1044
1375 Ocean Ave. (Ave I-H)   212-799-5000 X 214
Brooklyn, NY 11230
Hours: by appt.   E-mail: kdale@juilliard.edu
Soft goods, upholstery, prop and costume crafts. Resident Prop Master for The Juilliard School. Member ATAC.

JERRY L. MARSHALL, PROPS & TURNED OBJECTS 917-364-5015
415 W 55th St. # 3-A (9-10th Ave)
NY, NY 10019
Hours: by appt. only   E-mail: jlmars.nyc@mac.com
Broadway Propman, show supervision, shopping, fabrication and painting. Member IATSE Local 1, United Scenic Artists Local 829. Member ATAC.

MICHAEL SMANKO / PRISM PROPS 732-382-9727
1015 Richard Blvd.
Rahway, NJ 07065
Hours: by Appt.
www.prismprops.com
Broadway Production propman & prop stylist. Prop supervision, shopping, fabrication, upholstery, painting and finishes, prop construction, SPFX. 35 year IATSE member. BA Fine Arts, MFA Theater Design. Member ATAC.

Mobile Stage Network, Inc............................516-650-7200
119 Cabot St.   FAX 631-249-3409
West Babylon, NY 11709
Hours: 9:30-6 Mon-Fri   E-mail: info@mobilestagenetwork.com
www.mobilestagenetwork.com
Providing stages, platforms, mobile staging for indoor and outdoors. Many sizes and heights. CREDIT CARDS. RENTALS

NPI Production Services, Inc.........................818-566-7878
2550 Hollywood Way, Ste. 430 (Thornton Ave)   FAX 818-566-7881
Burbank, CA 91515
Hours: 9-5 Mon-Fri   E-mail: diego@npiproductionservices.com
www.npiproductionservices.com
Specializing in entertainment payroll services. They service union or non-union talent and crew in the USA or Canada.

Stage Research, Inc................................440-717-7510
P.O. Box 670557   888-267-0859
Northfield, OH 44067   FAX 888-668-0751
Hours: 9-5 Mon-Fri   E-mail: info@stageresearch.com
www.stageresearch.com
Windows-based software tools for stage and studio lighting industry, including SFX & ShowBuilder as well as sound cards from Echo. See website for various demos and tours of their software. CREDIT CARDS.

App

Theatre Projects 203-299-0830
25 Elizabeth St.   FAX 203-299-0835
S. Norwalk, CT 06854
Hours: 9-5 Mon-Fri
www.tpcworld.com
Advice on planning, design and technology for all types of new and restored cultural facilities.

Volunteer Lawyers for the Arts 212-319-2787
1 E 53rd St,. 6th Fl. / The Paley Bldg. (5th Ave)   FAX 212-752-6575
NY, NY 10022
Hours: 9:30-5 Mon-Fri / by appt.   E-mail: vlany@bway.com
www.vlany.org
Provides free legal assistance and information to individual artists and not-for-profit arts organizations with arts-related problems; library available.

Wits End Productions 212-242-9400
547 W 49th St.   212-757-4545
NY, NY 10019   FAX 212-242-1797
Hours: 24-hr. service   E-mail: tvgully@aol.com
www.witsendnyc.com
Excellent company to handle all your production needs for film and photography shoots. They have expendible kits you can rent that contain EVERYTHING you could possibly need for any situation. Rent their trucks full of expendables and you even get a truck driver experienced to assist in any and all your needs. If they don't have what you need, they will buy it. Just added to their stock are mole fans, ladders, 600W generators and much much more. Visit their website to view their extensive RENTALS. CREDIT CARDS.

YAVROYAN & NELSEN, INC. 212-921-0575
1501 Broadway, Ste. 1510 (43rd-44th St)   FAX 212-768-3661
NY, NY 10036
Hours: 10-6 Mon-Fri
Serving the tax and accounting needs of artists and craftspeople. Accountants for ATAC (Formerly The John Yavroyan Company). Member ATAC.

SOUND STAGES

CBS Broadcast Center: Newsroom 212-975-4321
524 W 57th St. (10-11th Ave)   FAX 212-975-9387
NY, NY 10019
Hours: 9-5 Mon-Fri / (facilities open 24-hrs.)   E-mail: webmail@cbs.com
www.cbs.com

Horvath Studios 212-463-0061
335 W 12th St. (Washington-Greenwich St)   (stage) 212-924-8492
NY, NY 10014   FAX 212-989-7570
Hours: 89-5:30 Mon-Fri   E-mail: contact@horvathstudios.com
www.horvathstudios.com

Kaufman-Astoria Studios 718-392-5600
   34-12 36th St. (34-35th Ave)   FAX 718-706-7733
   Astoria, NY 11106
   Hours: 8:30-6 Mon-Fri
   www.kaufmanastoria.com

Primus Studio 212-966-3803
   64 Wooster #3E   FAX 212-966-3803
   NY, NY 10012
   Hours: by appt.   E-mail: info@primusnyc.com
   www.primusnyc.com
   Rental studios built for the needs of the photographer. ***CREDIT CARDS.***

Silvercup Studios 718-906-2000
   42-22 22nd St.   FAX 718-906-2585
   Long Island City, NY 11101
   Hours: open 24-hrs.   E-mail: silvercup@silvercupstudios.com
   www.silvercupstudios.com

THEATRES: BROADWAY

Al Hirschfeld / Martin Beck Theatre . . . .(backstage) 212-245-9770
   302 W 45th St. (8-9th Ave)   (b.o.) 212-246-6386
   NY, NY 10036
   Hours: Box Office 10-8 Mon-Sat

Ambassador Theatre . . . .(b.o.) 212-239-6200
   215 W 49th St. (B'way-8th Ave)   (backstage) 212-664-9617
   NY, NY 10019

American Airlines / Roundabout 212-719-1300
   227 W 42nd St. (7-8th Ave)   (b.o.) 212-869-8400
   NY, NY 10036   FAX 212-869-8817
   www.roundabouttheatre.org
   Administration offices located at: 231 W 39th St. Ste 1200, NY, NY 10036.
   Member LORT (A+), (A+) and (B).

August Wilson Theatre / Virginia Theatre . . . .(backstage) 212-974-9853
   245 W 52nd St. (B'way-8th Ave)   (tix) 212-239-6200
   NY, NY 10019
   www.august-wilson-theatre.com

Belasco Theatre . . . .(backstage) 212-944-4103
   111 W 44th St. (B'way-6th Ave)   (tele-charge) 212-239-6200
   NY, NY 10036

Bernard B Jacobs / Royale Theatre . . . .(backstage) 212-391-8879
   242 W 45th St. (B'way-8th Ave)   (tele-charge) 212-239-6200
   NY, NY 10036

App

Biltmore Theatre / Samuel J. Friedman Theatre . .Telecharge - 212-239-6200
  261 West 47th St. (B'way-8th Ave)   212-399-3000
  NY, NY 10036
  www.mtc-nyc.org
  Operates under the auspices of Manhattan Theatre Club.

Booth Theatre . . . .(backstage) 212-391-8886
  222 W 45th St. (B'way-8th Ave)   (tele-charge) 212-239-6200
  NY, NY 10036
  Hours: 10-8

Broadhurst Theatre . . . .(backstage) 212-719-0693
  235 W 44th St. (B'way-8th Ave)   (tele-charge) 212-239-6200
  NY, NY 10036
  Hours: 10-8:30 Mon-Sat

Broadway Theatre . . . .(backstage) 212-664-9587
  1681 Broadway (53rd St)   (tele-charge) 212-239-6200
  NY, NY 10019
  Hours: 10-8 Mon-Sat / 12-6 Sun

Brooks Atkinson Theatre . . . .(backstage) 212-221-8955
  256 W 47th St. (B'way-8th Ave)   (b.o.) 212-719-4099
  NY, NY 10036
  Hours: 10-8 Mon-Sat / 12-6 Sun
  www.brooksatkinsontheater.com

Circle In The Square Theatre . . . .(backstage) 212-245-7304
  1633 Broadway on 50th St. (B'way-8th Ave)   (tele-charge) 212-239-6200
  (box office) 212-664-0983
  NY, NY 10019
  www.circle-in-the-square.com

City Center . . . .(backstage) 212-974-9833
  131 W 55th St. (6-7th Ave)   (admin. office) 212-247-0430
  NY, NY 10019   (tix) 212-581-1212
  Hours: 10-6 Mon-Fri (Admin. office)
  www.citycenter.org

Cort Theatre . . . .(backstage) 212-997-9776
  138 W 48th St. (6-7th Ave)   (tele-charge) 212-239-6200
  NY, NY 10036
  Hours: 10-8:30 Mon-Sat / 12-6 Sun
  www.cort-theatre.com

Ethel Barrymore Theatre . . . .(b.o.) 212-944-3847
  243 W 47th St. (B'way-8th Ave)
  NY, NY 10036
  Box Office Hours: 10-8:30

App

ATAC

Eugene O'Neill Theatre . . . .(backstage) 212-765-0490
230 W 49th St. (B'way-8th Ave)   (tele-charge) 212-239-6200
NY, NY 10019

Gerald Schoenfeld / Plymouth Theatre . . . .(backstage) 212-391-8878
236 W 45th St. (B'way-8th Ave)   (b.o.) 212-944-3880
NY, NY 10036   (tix) 212-239-6200

Gershwin Theatre (Uris) . . . .(backstage) 212-664-8473
222 W 51st St. (B'way-8th Ave)   (admin. office) 212-586-6510
NY, NY 10019
Hours: 10-8 Mon / 10-8:30 Tue-Sat / 12-6 Sun
www.gershwintheatre.com

Helen Hayes Theatre . . . .(backstage) 212-730-9197
240 W 44th St. (B'way-8th Ave)   (admin. office) 212-944-9450
NY, NY 10036   (telecharge) 212-239-6200
Hours: 10-6 Mon-Fri

Hilton Theatre / Ford Center for the Performing Arts . . . .
                                                           (backstage) 212-556-4750
213 W 42nd St.   (b.o.) 212-391-4810
NY, NY 10036
Hours: Box Office 10-8 Mon-Sat / 12-6 Sun
www.hiltontheatre.com

Imperial Theatre . . . .(backstage) 212-997-8843
249 W 45th St. (B'way-8th Ave)   (tele-charge) 212-239-6200
NY, NY 10036

John Golden Theatre . . . .(backstage) 212-764-0199
252 W 45th St. (B'way-8th Ave)   (tele-charge) 212-239-6200
NY, NY 10036
Hours: 10-8 Mon-Sat
www.johngoldentheatre.net

Lincoln Center Theatre 212-362-7600
150 W 65th St.   (tele-charge) 212-239-6200
NY, NY 10023   FAX 212-873-0761
www.lct.org   E-mail: info@lct.org
Member LORT (A+) and (B)

Mitzi E. Newhouse Theatre . . . .(admin. office) 212-362-7600
150 W 65th St. (Lincoln Center)   (tele-charge) 212-239-6200
NY, NY 10023
Hours: 9-11pm Mon-Fri
www.lct.org

Longacre Theatre . . . .(backstage) 212-974-9462
220 W 48th St. (B'way-8th Ave)   (tele-charge) 212-239-6200
NY, NY 10036
Hours: 10-8 Mon-Sat

App

Lunt/Fontanne Theatre . . . .(backstage) 212-997-8816
205 W 46th St. (B'way-8th Ave)   (b.o.) 212-575-9200
NY, NY 10036
Hours: 10-8 Mon-Sat / 12-6 Sun
www.luntfontainnetheatre.com

Lyceum Theatre . . . .(backstage) 212-997-9472
149 W 45th St. (6-7th Ave)   (tele-charge) 212-239-6200
NY, NY 10036
Hours: 10-8 Mon-Sat / 12-6 Sun

Majestic Theatre . . . .(backstage) 212-764-1750
245 W 44th St. (B'way-8th Ave)   (b.o.) 212-944-3877
NY, NY 10036
Hours: 10-8 Mon-Sat / 12-6 Sun
www.majestic-theatre.com

Manhattan Theatre Club . . . .(b.o.) 212-581-1212
131 W 55th St.(6-7th Ave) Stage I & II   (b.o.) 212-581-1212
NY, NY 10019
Hours: 12-8 Mon-Sun

311 W 43rd St., 8th FL(8-9th Ave) offices   212-399-3000
NY, NY 10036   FAX 212-399-4329
Hours: 10-6 Mon-Fri   E-mail: questions@mtc-nyc.org
www.mtc-nyc.org
Not-for-profit theatre organization. Resident Broadway theatre,The Friedman Theatre and City Center. Member LORT (A+), (B) and (D)

Marquis Theatre . . . .(backstage) 212-764-0182
1535 Broadway (45-46th St)   (b.o.) 212-382-0100
NY, NY 10036
Hours: 10-8 Mon-Sat / 12-6 Sun
www.marquistheatre.com

Minskoff Theatre . . . .(backstage) 212-840-9797
1515 Broadway (B'way-8th Ave)   (b.o.) 212-869-0550
NY, NY 10036
Hours: 10-8 Mon-Sat
www.minskoff-theater.com

Music Box Theatre . . . .(backstage) 212-997-8870
239 W 45th St. (B'way-8th Ave)   (tele-charge) 212-239-6200
NY, NY 10036

Nederlander Theatre . . . .(backstage) 212-221-9770
208 W 41st St. (7-8th Ave)   (b.o.) 212-921-8000
NY, NY 10036

Neil Simon Theatre . . . .(backstage) 212-974-9445
250 W 52nd St. (B'way-8th Ave)   (b.o.) 212-757-8646
NY, NY 10019

New Amsterdam Theatre 212-282-2900
   214 W 42nd St. (7-8th Ave)   (b.o.) 212-307-4100
   NY, NY 10036

New Apollo Theatre ....(backstage) 212-531-5329
   253 W 125th St. (7th-8th Ave)   (b.o.) 212-531-5305
   NY, NY 10027
   Hours: 10-6 Mon-Fri / 12-6 Sat
   www.apollotheatre.com
   Admin. Offices: 212-531-5300

Marquis Theatre ....(backstage) 212-764-0182
   1535 Broadway (45-46th St)   (b.o.) 212-382-0100
   NY, NY 10036
   Hours: 10-8 Mon-Sat / 12-6 Sun
   www.marquistheatre.com

Minskoff Theatre ....(backstage) 212-840-9797
   1515 Broadway (B'way-8th Ave)   (b.o.) 212-869-0550
   NY, NY 10036
   Hours: 10-8 Mon-Sat
   www.minskoff-theater.com

Music Box Theatre ....(backstage) 212-997-8870
   239 W 45th St. (B'way-8th Ave) (tele-charge) 212-239-6200
   NY, NY 10036

Nederlander Theatre ....(backstage) 212-221-9770
   208 W 41st St. (7-8th Ave)   (b.o.) 212-921-8000
   NY, NY 10036

Neil Simon Theatre ....(backstage) 212-974-9445
   250 W 52nd St. (B'way-8th Ave)   (b.o.) 212-757-8646
   NY, NY 10019

New Amsterdam Theatre 212-282-2900
   214 W 42nd St. (7-8th Ave)   (b.o.) 212-307-4100
   NY, NY 10036

New Apollo Theatre ....(backstage) 212-531-5329
   253 W 125th St. (7th-8th Ave)   (b.o.) 212-531-5305
   NY, NY 10027
   Hours: 10-6 Mon-Fri / 12-6 Sat
   www.apollotheatre.com
   Admin. Offices: 212-531-5300

App

New Victory Theater .... (tix) 212-239-6200
209 W 42nd St. (7-8th Ave)   646-223-3020
NY, NY 10036   FAX 646-562-0775
www.newvictory.org   E-mail: info@newvictory.org

New York State Theatre .... (backstage) 212-870-5500
20 Lincoln Ctr. (62nd-Columbus)   (b.o.) 212-870-5570
NY, NY 10023
www.nycballet.com   E-mail: clanders@nycballet.com

Palace Theatre .... (backstage) 212-221-9057
1564 Broadway (46-47th St)   (b.o.) 212-307-4747
NY, NY 10036
www.palacetheaternewyork.com

Radio City Music Hall .... (administration) 212-485-7000
1260 Sixth Ave. (50th St)   (ticketmaster) 212-307-7171
NY, NY 10020
Hours: 11:30-6 Mon-Sun   E-mail: feedback@radiocitythegarden.com
www.radiocity.com

Richard Rodgers Theatre .... (backstage) 212-997-9416
226 W 46th St. (B'way-8th Ave)   (b.o.) 212-221-1211
NY, NY 10036

Shubert Theatre .... (backstage) 212-764-0184
225 W 44th St. (B'way-8th Ave)   (tele-charge) 212-239-6200
NY, NY 10036
www.shubert-theatre.com

St. James Theatre .... (b.o.) 212-239-6200
246 W 44th St. (B'way-8th Ave)
NY, NY 10036

Studio 54 212-664-9400
254 W 54th St. (B'way-8th Ave)   (tele-charge) 212-239-6200
NY, NY 10019

Vivian Beaumont Theatre .... (backstage) 212-501-3100
150 W 65th St. (Lincoln Center)   212-362-7600 (admin. office)
NY, NY 10023   212-239-6200 (tix)
Hours: 10-8 Mon-Sat / 12-6 Sun

Walter Kerr Theatre .... (backstage) 212-664-9154
219 W 48th St. (B'way-8th Ave)   (tele-charge) 212-239-6200
NY, NY 10036
Hours: 10-8 Mon-Sat / 12-6 Sun
www.walterkerrtheatre.com

Winter Garden Theatre .... (backstage) 212-664-9608
1634 Broadway (50th-51st St)   (tele-charge) 212-239-6200
NY, NY 10019
www.wintergarden-theater.com

THEATRES: DANCE, CONCERT & OPERA

Alice Tully Hall . . . .(backstage) 212-875-5058
   1941 Broadway (Lincoln Center)   (admin. office) 212-875-5000
   NY, NY 10023   (b.o.) 212-875-5050
   www.lincolncenter.org   E-mail: athbo@lincolncenter.org

Avery Fisher Hall . . . .(backstage) 212-875-5016
   132 W 65th St. (Lincoln Center)   (admin. office) 212-875-5000
   NY, NY 10023   (b.o.) 212-875-5030
   www.lincolncenter.org

Bessie Schonberg Theatre (part of Dance Th. Workshop) . . . .
   . . . .(b.o.) 212-924-0077
   219 W 19th St. (7-8th Ave)   (admin. office) 212-691-6500
   NY, NY 10011
   Hours: 10-6 Mon-Fri   www.dtw.org
   Rental space and classes.

Brooklyn Academy of Music, Opera House . . .(admin. office) 718-636-4111
   30 Lafayette Ave. (Ashland-St. Felix)   (backstage) 718-636-4150
   Brooklyn, NY 11217   (prod. office) 718-636-4146 FAX 718-636-4179
   www.bam.org

Carnegie Hall . . . .(house mang.) 212-903-9605
   881 Seventh Ave. (57-56th St)   (admin. office) 212-903-9600
   NY, NY 10019   (b.o.) 212-247-7800 (bookings) 212-903-9710
   Hours: 9-6 Business Hours
   www.carnegiehall.org

Dance Theatre Workshop . . . .(admin. office) 212-691-6500
   219 W 19th St. (7-8th Ave)   (b.o.) 212-924-0077
   NY, NY 10011   FAX 212-633-1974
   Hours: Office 10-8 Mon-Fri / 12-8 Sat / 11-6 Sun   E-mail: dtw@dtw.org
   www.dancetheatreworkshop.org
   Publishes the Poor Dancer's Almanac, a survival manual for choreographers,
   dancers and management personnel. Non-profit organization. NY state
   dance force offering children and adult classes.

Florence Gould Hall (at the French Institute) . . . .(b.o.) 212-355-6160
   22 E 60th St. (Park-Madison Ave)   (admin.) 212-355-6100
   NY, NY 10022   FAX 212-355-6189
   Hours: 11-7 Tue / 12-7 Wed-Fri / 12-4 Sat   E-mail: wlaurent@fiaf.org
   www.fiaf.org

Jazz at Lincoln Center / Frederick P. Rose Hall 212-258-9800
   10 Columbus Circle, 5th Fl. (Columbus Cr)   212-258-9900
   NY, NY 10022
   Hours: 8-5 Mon-Fri
   www.jalc.org
   Mailing address: 33 W 60th St. 11th FL, NY, NY 10023.

App

Joyce Soho 212-431-9233
155 Mercer St. (Houston-Prince)   FAX 212-334-9025
NY, NY 10012
Hours: 10-10 Mon-Sun
www.joyce.org
Performance/rehearsal space.

The Joyce Theatre .... (co. mang.) 212-691-9638
175 Eighth Ave. (19th St)   (admin. office) 212-691-9740
NY, NY 10011   (b.o.) 212-242-0800 FAX 212-727-3658
Hours: 10-6 Mon-Fri   E-mail: staff@joyce.org
www.joyce.org

The Juilliard School 212-799-5000
60 Lincoln Center Plaza (66th St)   FAX 212-724-0263
NY, NY 10023
www.juilliard.edu

The Kaye Playhouse at Hunter College ...... (admin. office) 212-772-5207
695 Park Ave. (Hunter College Lex-Park Ave)   (b.o.) 212-772-4448
NY, NY 10065
Hours: 12-6 Mon-Sat (Box office)   E-mail: kayeinfo@hunter.cuny.edu
http://kayeplayhouse.hunter.cuny.edu
Production Office 212-650-3693, General Manager 212-772-4471

The Marymount Manhattan Theatre .... (theatre office) 212-774-0760
221 E 71st St. (2nd-3rd Ave)   (dance dept.) 212-517-0610
NY, NY 10021
Hours: 10-6 Mon-Fri   E-mail: tickets@mmm.edu
www.marymount.mmm.edu

Merkin Concert Hall / Kaufman Cultural Center .... (b.o.) 212-501-3330
129 W 67th St. (B'way-Amsterdam)   212-501-3340
NY, NY 10023   FAX 212-501-3317
Hours: 12-7 Sun-Thurs / 12/4 Fri
www.kaufman-center.org

The Metropolitan Opera .... (b.o.) 212-362-6000
Broadway at 65th St. (Lincoln Center)   (admin. office) 212-799-3100
NY, NY 10023
Hours: 10-8 Mon-Sat / 12-6 Sun
www.metopera.org

New York State Theatre .... (backstage) 212-870-5500
20 Lincoln Ctr. (62nd-Columbus)   (b.o.) 212-870-5570
NY, NY 10023
www.nycballet.com   E-mail: clanders@nycballet.com

Riverside Church 212-870-6877
490 Riverside Dr.   212-870-6700
NY, NY 10027   FAX 212-870-6800
www.theriversidechurchny.org

ATAC

St. Mark's Church in the Bowery, Ontological Theatre 212-533-4650
131 E 10th St. (2nd-3rd Ave)   (admin. office) 212-420-1916
NY, NY 10003
www.ontological.com   E-mail: info@ontological.com
Box office (theatremania) 212-352-3101.

Peter Norton Symphony Space .... (b.o.) 212-864-5400
2537 Broadway (95th St)   (admin. office) 212-864-1414
NY, NY 10025   FAX 212-932-3228
www.symphonyspace.org   E-mail: ssadmin@symphonyspace.org

Town Hall .... (b.o.) 212-840-2824
123 W 43rd St. (B'way-6th Ave)   (admin. office) 212-997-1003
NY, NY 10036   FAX 212-997-1929
www.the-townhall-nyc.org   E-mail: info@the-townhall-nyc.org
*Not just a road house. Town Hall offers production services and produces
many operas, dance, music, etc. Outreach program with public schools in NY
State.*

THEATRES: OTHER NEW YORK

The Acorn Theater 212-714-2442
410 W 42nd St. (9-10th Ave)   FAX 212-714-2772
NY, NY 10036
Hours: 10-6 Mon-Fri   E-mail: theatres@theatrerow.org
www.theatrerow.org
*Part of the Theatre Row Theatres. Off-Broadway rental houses. Seating
compacity 199. Stage door: 407 W 41st St.*

Acting Studio, Inc. 212-580-6600
244 W 54th St., 12th Fl. (CPW-Columbus)
NY, NY 10019
www.actingstudio.com   E-mail: actingstudioinc@yahoo.com
*Private acting school/studio offering classes for actors and directors in film
and theatre.*

The Actor's Studio 212-757-0870
432 W 44th St. (9-10th Ave)
NY, NY 10036
Hours: 10-6 Mon-Fri
www.theactorsstudio.org

Actors Playhouse .... (tix) 212-239-6200
100 Seventh Ave. S (Bleecker-Christopher St)
NY, NY 10014

AMAS Musical Theatre 212-563-2565
115 MacDougal St., Ste. 2B   FAX 212-239-8332
NY, NY 10012
www.amasmusical.org   E-mail: amas@amasmusical.org
*AMAS Musical Theatre is dedicated to bringing people of all races, colors,
creeds, and national origins together through the performing arts.*

App

American Place Theatre 212-594-4482
630 Ninth Ave., Ste 809 (44-45th St)   FAX 212-594-4208
NY, NY 10019
Hours: 9-5 Mon-Fri   E-mail: edu@americanplacetheatre.org
www.americanplacetheatre.org

American Theatre of Actors 212-581-3044
314 W 54th St. (8-9th Ave)
NY, NY 10019
www.appleboxdesign.com/ATA/ata.html

Astor Place Theatre 212-254-4370
434 Lafayette St. (Astor Pl-W 4th St)
NY, NY 10003
www.blueman.com
Manny Egregious - publicist, Blue Man Group 212-387-9415 x 320.

Atlantic Theater ....(tix) 212-279-4200
336 W 20th St. (9-10th Ave)   (office) 212-645-8015
NY, NY 10011   FAX 212-645-8755
www.atlantictheater.org
Administrative Office: 76 Ninth Ave Ste 537 (16th St) NY, NY 10011 (212) 691-5919

Beacon Theatre ....(b.o.) 212-465-6500
2124 Broadway (74th St)
NY, NY 10023
Hours: 11-7 Mon-Sat (b.o.)
www.beacontheatre.com

The Beckett Theater 212-714-2442
410 W 42nd St. (9-10th Ave)   FAX 212-714-2772
NY, NY 10036
Hours: 10-6 Mon-Fri
www.theatrerow.org
Part of the Theatre Row Theatres. Off-Broadway rental houses. Seating compacity 99. Stage door: 407 W 41st St.

Century Center ....(tix) 212-239-6200
111 E 15th St. (Union Square E)
NY, NY 10003
299 Seat house.

Cherry Lane Theatre ....(b.o.) 212-989-2020
38 Commerce St. (7th Ave-Hudson St)   FAX 212-989-2867
NY, NY 10014
Hours: 2-8 Tue-Fri / 2-9 Sat / 12-7 Sun
www.cherrylanetheatre.org
Tickets must be purchased in person. 212-239-6200 for telecharge tickets.

City Center ....(backstage) 212-974-9833
131 W 55th St. (6-7th Ave)   (admin. office) 212-247-0430
NY, NY 10019   (tix) 212-581-1212
Hours: 10-6 Mon-Fri (Admin. office)
www.citycenter.org

App

Classic Stage Co. (CSC Rep.) . . . .(b.o.) 212-677-4210
136 E 13th St. (3rd-4th Ave)   FAX 212-477-7504
NY, NY 10003
Hours: 10-6 Mon-Fri (Office) / 1-7 Mon-Sat (b.o.)   E-mail: info@classicstage.org
www.classicstage.org

The Clurman Theater 212-714-2442
410 W 42nd St. (9-10th Ave)   FAX 212-714-2772
NY, NY 10036
Hours: 10-6 Mon-Fri   E-mail: theatres@theatrerow.org
www.theatrerow.org
*Part of the Theatre Row Theatres. Off-Broadway rental houses. Seating
compacity 99. Stage door: 407 W 41st St.*

Douglas Fairbanks Theatre . . . .(b.o.) 212-239-4321
432 W 42nd St. (9-10th Ave)   (backstage) 212-239-4323
NY, NY 10036   (tix) 212-239-6200

Edison Theatre / The Supper Club 212-921-1940
240 W 47th St. (B'way-8th Ave)
NY, NY 10036

Ensemble Studio Theatre . . . .(admin. office) 212-247-4982
549 W 52nd St. (10-11th Ave)   FAX 212-664-0041
NY, NY 10019
Hours: 10-6 Mon-Fri
www.ensemblestudiotheatre.org
Developmental theater for new American plays.   Produces Octoberfest.

Forty Seventh Street Theatre
(Puerto Rican Traveling Theatre) . . . .(tix) 212-239-6200
304 W 47th St. (8-9th Ave)   (Admin) 212-354-1293
NY, NY 10036   FAX 212-307-6769
Hours: 10-6 Mon-Fri   E-mail: prtt@prtt.org
www.prtt.org

Grove Street Playhouse 212-581-8896
39 Grove St. (7th Ave)   212-741-6436
NY, NY 10014

Heckscher Theatre of Museo del Barrio . . . .(b.o.) 212-831-7949
1230 Fifth Ave. (104th St)   212-831-7272 Ext 132
NY, NY 10025   FAX 212-831-7927
Hours: Gallery 11-6 Wed-Sun   E-mail: info@elmuseo.org
www.elmuseo.org

Henry Street Settlement, Louis Abrons Art Center . . .212-598-0400 ext 215
466 Grand St. (Pitt-Willet)
NY, NY 10002
Hours: 8:30-5:30 Mon-Fri
www.henrystreet.org

App

Here Arts Center 212-647-0202
145 Ave. of the Americas (Spring St)   (b.o.) 212-647-0202
NY, NY 10013   FAX 212-647-0257
Hours: 10-6 Mon-Fri
www.here.org

INTAR 212-695-6134
P.O. Box 756   FAX 212-268-0102
NY, NY 10108
www.intartheatre.org

Irish Arts Center 212-757-3318
553 W 51st St. (10-11th St)   FAX 212-247-0930
NY, NY 10019
Hours: 10-6 Mon-Fri
www.irishartscenter.org

Irish Repertory Theatre . . . . .212-727-2737 Box O
132 W 22nd St. (6-7th Ave)   (office) 212-255-0270
NY, NY 10011   FAX 212-727-2232
www.irishrep.org

Jewish Repertory Theatre (JRT) 212-415-5550
1395 Lexington Ave. (91st-92nd St)   (B.O.) 917-606-8200
NY, NY 10128

Joseph Papp Public Theatre . . . .(b.o.) 212-260-2400
425 Lafayette St. (Astor Pl-W 4th St)
NY, NY 10003
Hours: 1-6 Sun-Mon / 1-7:30 Tue-Sat
www.publictheater.org

Joseph Papp Public Theatre /NYSF Delacorte Theatre . .(b.o.) 212-260-2400
Central Park (W 81st St Entrance)   (tele-charge) 212-239-6200
NY, NY 10023
Hours: 1-6 Sun-Mon / 1-7:30 Tue-Sat
www.publictheater.org

Julia Miles Theater / The Women's Project . . .(Admin. Office) 212-765-1706
424 W 55th St. (9-10th Ave)   (Theatre) 212-757-3900
NY, NY 10019   FAX 212-765-2024
www.womensproject.org   E-mail: info@womensproject.org
Rental space.

The Kirk Theater 212-714-2442
410 W 42nd St. (9-10th Ave)   FAX 212-714-2772
NY, NY 10036
Hours: 10-6 Mon-Fri   E-mail: theatres@theatrerow.org
www.theatrerow.org
Part of the Theatre Row Theatres. Off-Broadway rental houses. Seating
compacity 99. Stage door: 407 W 41st St.

La Mama ETC . . . .(b.o.) 212-475-7710
74A E 4th St. (Bowery-2nd Ave)　　　　　(admin. office) 212-254-6468
NY, NY 10003　　　　　　　　　　　　　　　　　FAX 212-254-7597
Hours: 10-10 Mon-Fri / 12-10 Sat-Sun　　　E-mail: web@lamama.org
www.lamama.org

Lamb's Theatre . . . .(b.o.) 212-575-0300 X21
130 W 44th St. (B'way-6th Ave)　　　　　　　　　　FAX 212-302-7847
NY, NY 10036
www.lambstheatre.org　　　　　　　　　E-mail: office@lambstheatre.org

The Lion Theater 212-714-2442
410 W 42nd St. (9-10th Ave)　　　　　　　　　(b.o.) 212-279-4200
NY, NY 10036　　　　　　　　　　　　　　　　　FAX 212-714-2772
Hours: 10-6 Mon-Fri　　　　　　　E-mail: theatres@theatrerow.org
www.theatrerow.org
Part of the Theatre Row Theatres. Off-Broadway rental houses. Seating
compacity 88. Stage door: 407 W 41st St.

Little Shubert Theatre 212-944-3700
422 W 42nd St. (9-10th Ave.)　　　　　　　Telecharge: 212-239-6200
NY, NY 10036
Hours: 10-6 Mon-Fri
www.shubert-theater.com
Recently opened by the Shubert Organization, this 499 seat Off-Broadway
theatre incorporates stadium seating and the stage and orchestra pit are
comparable in size to the dimensions of many Broadway theatres.

Lucille Lortel Theatre . . . .(b.o.) 212-279-4200
121 Christopher St. (Bleecker-Hudson St)　　(admin. office) 212-924-2817
NY, NY 10014　　　　　　　　　　　　　　　　Fax 212-989-0036
Hours: 10-6 Mon-Fri
www.lortel.org

Minetta Lane Theatre . . . .(b.o.) 212-307-4100
18 Minetta Ln. (6th Ave-MacDougal St)
NY, NY 10012
Hours: 1-6 Mon-Fri

Negro Ensemble Co . . . .(admin. office) 212-582-5860
303 W 42nd St. # 501 (8-9th Ave)　　　　　　　FAX 212-582-9639
NY, NY 10036
www.necinc.org　　　　　　　　　　　　　E-mail: info@necinc.org

New Dramatists 212-757-6960
424 W 44th St. (9-10th Ave)　　　　　　　　　FAX 212-265-4738
NY, NY 10036
www.newdramatists.org　　　　E-mail: newdramatists@newdramatists.org

New Federal Theatre 212-353-1176
292 Henry St.　　　　　　　　　　　　　　　FAX 212-353-1088
NY, NY 10002
www.newfederaltheatre.org　　　　　　　E-mail: newfederal@aol.com

App

New World Stages 646-871-1730
340 West 50th St. (8-9th Ave)   FAX 646-871-1733
NY, NY 10019
www.newworldstages.com   E-mail: info@newworldstages.com
**New Off-Broadway theatre complex opening Fall 2004. 5 new theatrical
spaces ranging in audience capacity from 199 to 499. For further information
call Tony Magner, General Manager.**

New York Theatre Workshop ....(backstage) 212-995-8367
79 E 4th St.   (b.o.) 212-460-5475
NY, NY 10003   (admin. office) 212-780-9037
Hours: 1-6 Tue-Sat
www.nytw.org

Ohio Theatre Space 212-966-4844
66 Wooster St. (Spring & Broome)   (b.o.) 212-966-9290
NY, NY 10012
www.alexeipro.com

Orpheum Theatre ....(b.o.) 212-477-2477
126 Second Ave, (7-8th St)
NY, NY 10003

Pearl Theatre Company ....(office) 212-505-3401
307 W 38th St., Ste 1805 (8-9th Ave)   (b.o.) 212-598-9802
NY, NY 10018   FAX 212-505-3404
www.pearltheatre.org   E-mail: info@pearltheatre.org

The Performing Garage ....(admin. office) 212-966-9796
33 Wooster St. (Grand-Broome St)   FAX 212-226-6576
NY, NY 10013
www.thewoostergroup.org   E-mail: mail@thewoostergroup.org
Mailing address: PO Box 654, Canal St Station, NYC, NY 10013.

Players Theatre ....(b.o.) 212-475-1237
115 MacDougal St. (W 3rd-Bleeker St)   (office) 212-475-1449
NY, NY 10012
Hours: varies by show   E-mail: theplayerstheatre@yahoo.com
www.theplayerstheatre.com
Theatre space for rent.

Playwrights Horizons ....(b.o.) 212-279-4200
416 W 42nd St. (9-10th Ave)   (admin. office) 212-564-1235
NY, NY 10036   FAX 212-594-0296
Hours: 10-6 Mon-Fri
www.playwrightshorizons.org

Primary Stages Co. ....(b.o.) 212-753-5959
59 E 59th St. (Park-Madison Ave)   (admin. office) 212-840-9705
NY, NY 10022   FAX 212-840-9725
Hours: 10-6 Mon-Fri   E-mail: info@primarystages.org
www.primarystages.com
Admin. Offices located at: 307 W 38th St. Ste 1510, NY, NY 10018

Puerto Rican Traveling Theatre Co., Inc. . . . . .(admin. office) 212-354-1293
    304 W 47th St. (8-9th Ave)   FAX 212-307-6769
    NY, NY 10036
    Hours: 10-6 Mon-Fri   E-mail: prtt@prtt.org
    www.prtt.org
    Mailing Address: 141 W 94th St., NY, NY 10025

Rattlestick Playwrights Theatre . . . .(admin. office) 212-627-2556
    224 Waverly Pl. (Perry-W 11th St)   FAX 630-839-8352
    NY, NY 10014
    www.rattlestick.org   E-mail: info@rattlestick.org

Second Stage . . . .(b.o.) 212-246-4422
    307 W 43rd St. (8th Ave)   (admin. office) 212-787-8302
    NY, NY 10036   FAX 212-397-7066
    Hours: 10-6 Mon-Fri   E-mail: info@2st.com
    www.2st.com

Snapple Theatre Center . . . .(b.o.) 212-921-7862
    1627 Broadway (50th St)
    NY, NY 10036

Soho Repertory Theatre . . . .(b.o.) 212-352-3101
    46 Walker St. (Church-B'way)   212-941-8632
    NY, NY 10013   FAX 212-941-7148
    www.sohorep.org   E-mail: sohorep@sohorep.org
    *Tickets available thru www.smarttix.com. Adminstration offices at 86
    Franklin St.. 4th Fl., NY, NY 10013.*

Theatre for the New City 212-254-1109
    155 First Ave. (9-10th St)   FAX 212-979-6570
    NY, NY 10003
    www.theatreforthenewcity.net

Theatreworks/ USA . . . .(admin. office) 212-647-1100
    151 W 26th St., 7th Fl. (6-7th Ave)   800-497-5007
    NY, NY 10001   FAX 212-924-5377
    Hours: 9-5 Mon-Fri   E-mail: info@theatreworksusa.org
    www.theatreworksusa.org

Tinker Auditorium at The French Institute 212-355-6100
    22 E 60th St. (Mad-5th Ave)   646-388-6601
    NY, NY 10022   FAX 212-935-4119
    Hours: Mon-Thurs 9-8 / Sat 9-5   E-mail: reception@fiaf.org
    www.fiaf.org
    *3 venues open for lecture / screening / presentation rental space. Newly
    opened Le Skyroom for receptions equipped with a fully functional kitchen
    for any type of catered event. Speak to Wendy Laurent at 646-388-6601.
    RENTAL.*

Tribeca Performing Arts Center . . . .(b.o.) 212-220-1460
    199 Chambers St. #S110C (Greenwich-W Side Hwy)   (Admin off.) 212-220-1459
    NY, NY 10007   FAX 212-732-2482
    www.tribecapac.org

App

Union Square Theatre ....(b.o.) 212-505-0700
100 E 17th St. (Park Ave S)   212-505-9021
NY, NY 10003   FAX 212-505-0709

Variety Arts ....(tix) 212-239-6200
110 Third Ave. (13-14th St)
NY, NY 10003

Vineyard Theatre 212-353-3366
108 E 15th St. (Park Ave S-Irving Pl)   (b.o.) 212-353-0303
NY, NY 10003   FAX 212-353-3803
www.vineyardtheatre.org   E-mail: boxoffice@vineyardtheatre.org

Vortex Theatre 212-206-1764
164 Eleventh Ave. (22-23rd St)   FAX 212-206-1765
NY, NY 10011
www.vortextheater.com

Westbeth Entertainment 212-691-2272
111 W 17th St., 3rd Fl. (6-7th Ave)   FAX 212-504-2680
NY, NY 10011
Hours: 10-6 Mon-Fri
www.westbethent.com
Producers of standpup comedy and Off-Broadway productions.

Westside Theatre 212-239-6200
407 W 43rd St. (9-10th Ave)
NY, NY 10036
www.westsidetheatre.com

Women's Interart Center 212-246-1050
549 W 52nd St. (10-11th Ave)
NY, NY 10019

The Zipper Theatre ....(Ticketmaster) 800-432-7250
336 W. 37th St. (8-9th Ave)   212-563-0480
NY, NY 10018

THEATRES: REGIONAL/LORT

A Contemporary Theatre 206-292-7660
Kreielsheimer Pl., 700 Union St.   (b.o.) 206-292-7676
Seattle, WA 98101   FAX 206-292-7670
Hours: b.o. 12-8 Tue-Sat (in performance) / 12-6 Tue-Sat (non performance)
www.acttheatre.org   E-mail: act@acttheatre.org
Member LORT (B), (C-2), and (TYA)

Actors Theatre Of Louisville 502-584-1265
316 W Main St.   (b.o.) 502-584-1205
Louisville, KY 40202   FAX 502-561-3300
www.actorstheatre.org   E-mail: mail@actorstheatre.org
Member LORT (C-1), (D) and (D)

Alabama Shakespeare Festival 334-271-5300
  1 Festival Dr.   (b.o.) 800-841-4ASF
  Montgomery, AL 36117   FAX 334-271-5348
  www.asf.net   E-mail: asfmail@mindspring.com
  Member LORT (C-1) and (D)

Alley Theatre 713-228-9341
  615 Texas Ave.   (b.o.) 713-228-8421
  Houston, TX 77002   FAX 713-222-6542
  Hours: Box Office 12-6 Mon-Sat   E-mail: webmaster@alleytheatre.org
  www.alleytheatre.org
  Member LORT (B) and (C-2)

Alliance Theatre Company 404-733-4650
  1280 Peachtree St. NE (Robert W. Woodruff Arts Center)   (b.o.) 404-733-5000
  Atlanta, GA 30309   FAX 404-733-4625
  www.alliancetheatre.org   E-mail: info@alliancethratre.com
  Member LORT (B), (D) and (TYA)

American Airlines / Roundabout 212-719-1300
  227 W 42nd St. (7-8th Ave)   (b.o.) 212-869-8400
  NY, NY 10036   FAX 212-869-8817
  www.roundabouttheatre.org
  Administration offices located at: 231 W 39th St. Ste 1200, NY, NY 10036.
  Member LORT (A+), (A+) and (B).

American Conservatory Theatre 415-834-3200
  30 Grant Ave., 6th Fl.   (b.o.) 415-749-2228
  San Francisco, CA 94108   FAX 415-834-3360
  Hours: 12-6 Tue-Sun
  www.act-sf.org
  Member LORT (A) and (D)

American Repertory Theatre 617-495-2668
  Loeb Drama Center, 64 Brattle St.   (b.o.) 617-547-8300
  Cambridge, MA 02138   FAX 617-495-1705
  www.amrep.org   E-mail: information@amrep.org
  Member LORT (B), (D), and (D)

Arden Theatre Company . . . .(b.o.) 215-922-1122
  40 N 2nd St.   FAX 215-922-7011
  Philadelphia, PA 19106
  Hours: 10-6 Mon-Sat
  www.ardentheatre.org
  Arcadia and Otto Hause Theatres. Member Lort (D) and (D)

Arena Stage 202-554-9066
  1101 6th St. SW   (b.o.) 202-488-3300
  Washington, DC 20024   FAX 202-488-4056
  www.arenastage.org   E-mail: info@arenastage.org
  Member LORT (B+), (B) and (D)

App

Arizona Theatre Company 602-256-6899
502 W Roosevelt St.   (b.o.) 602-256-6995
Phoenix, AZ 85003   FAX 602-256-7399
www.arizonatheatre.org   E-mail: atcphoenix@aztheatreco.org
Member LORT (B), (B) and (B)

Arkansas Repertory Theatre 501-378-0445
601 Main St.   (b.o.) 866-6THEREP
Little Rock, AR 72201
www.therep.org
Member Lort (D) and (D)

Asolo Theatre Company 941-351-9010
5555 N Tamiami Trl.   (b.o.) 941-351-8000
Sarasota, FL 34243   FAX 941-351-5796
www.asolo.org
Member LORT (C-1) and (D)

Barter Theatre . . . . .Box Office 276-628-2281
127 W Main St   Adm. Office 276-619-3300
Abingdon, VA 24210   FAX 276-619-3335
www.bartertheatre.com
Member LORT (D) and (D)

Berkeley Repertory Theatre 510-647-2900
2025 Addison St. (Shattuck Ave)   (b.o.) 510-647-2949
Berkeley, CA 94704   FAX 510-647-2976
www.berkeleyrep.org   E-mail: info@berkeleyrep.org
Member LORT (B), (B), and (TYA)

Berkshire Theatre Festival 413-298-5536
PO Box 797   (b.o.) 413-298-5576
Stockbridge, MA 01262   FAX 413-298-3368
www.berkshiretheatre.org   E-mail: info@berkshiretheatre.org
Member LORT (B)

Capital Repertory Company 518-462-4531
111 N Pearl St.   (b.o.) 518-445-SHOW
Albany, NY 12207   FAX 518-465-0213
www.capitalrep.org   E-mail: info@capitalrep.org
Member LORT (D)

Center Stage 410-986-4000
700 N Calvert St.   (b.o.) 410-332-0033
Baltimore, MD 21202
www.centerstage.org   E-mail: info@centerstage.org
Member LORT (B) and (C-2)

Center Theatre Group 213-628-2772
601 W Temple St
Los Angeles, CA 90012
www.centertheatregroup.org
Operates three venues; The Ahmanson Theatre, The Mark Taper Forum and
The Kirk Douglas Theatre. Member LORT (A) and (D)

Cincinnati Playhouse In The Park 800-582-3208
PO Box 6537   (b.o.) 513-421-3888
Cincinnati, OH 45206   TDD 513-345-2248
www.cincyplay.com   E-mail: administration@cincyplay.com
Member LORT (B+) and (D)

City Theatre Company 412-431-CITY
1300 Bingham Street
Pittsburgh, PA 15203
www.citytheatrecompany.org
Member LORT (D) and (D)

Clarence Brown Theatre 865-974-5161
206 McClung Tower   (Dept of Theatre) 865-974-6011
Knoxville, TN 37996   FAX 865-974-4867
www.clarencebrowntheatre.com   E-mail: cbt@utk.edu
Member LORT (D), (D) at the University of Tennessee.

The Cleveland Playhouse 800-278-ICPH
8500 Euclid Ave.   (b.o.) 216-795-7000
Cleveland, OH 44106   FAX 216-795-7005
Hours: 9-5 Mon-Fri (Admin. Offices)
www.clevelandplayhouse.com
Member LORT (C-1), (C-1), (C-2), (D) and (D)

Court Theatre 773-702-7005
5535 S Ellis Ave.   (b.o.) 773-753-4472
Chicago, IL 60637   FAX 773-834-1897
www.courttheatre.org   E-mail: info@courttheatre.org
Member LORT (D)

Dallas Theater Center 214-526-8210
3636 Turtle Creek Blvd.   (b.o.) 214-522-8499
Dallas, TX 75219   FAX 214-521-7666
Hours: 9-6 Mon-Fri   E-mail: comments@dallastheatercenter.org
www.dallastheatercenter.org
Member LORT (B) and (C-1)

Delaware Theatre Company 302-594-1104
200 Water St.   (b.o.) 302-594-1100
Wilmington, DE 19801   FAX 302-594-1107
www.delawaretheatre.org   E-mail: dtc@delawaretheatre.org
Member LORT (D)

Denver Center Theatre Company 303-893-4000
1101 13th St.   (b.o.) 303-893-4100
Denver, CO 80204   FAX 303-825-2117
www.denvercenter.org   E-mail: webmaster@dcpa.org
Member LORT (B), (C-2), (D) and (D)

Florida Stage . . . .(Admin) 561-585-3404
262 S Ocean Blvd   (b.o.) 800-514-3837
Manalapan, FL 33462   FAX 561-588-4708
www.floridastage.org   E-mail: subscriptions@floridastage.org
Member LORT (C-2)

App

Florida Studio Theatre 941-366-9017
1241 N Palm Ave   (b.o.) 941-366-9000
Sarasota, FL 34236
Hours: 9-6 Mon / 9-9 ue-Sat / 11-9 Sun   E-mail: info@floridastudiotheatre.org
www.floridastudiotheatre.org
Member LORT (D), (D)

Ford's Theatre . . . .(b.o.) 202-347-4833
511 10th St, NW (E St NW)   (Admin) 202-638-2941
Washington, DC 20004   FAX 202-347-6269
Hours: 10-6 Mon-Fri (Administrative Offices)
www.fordstheatre.org
Member LORT (B+) Free daily tours are available of this historic site, 9-5.

Geffen Playhouse / Audrey Skirball-Kenis Theatre 310-208-6500
10886 LeConte Ave.   (b.o.) 310-208-5454
Los Angeles, CA 90024   FAX 310-208-0341
Hours: (b.o.) 12-6 Mon-Sun   E-mail: boxoffice@geffenplayhouse.com
www.geffenplayhouse.com
Member LORT (B) and (D)

George Street Playhouse 732-846-2895
9 Livingston Ave.   (b.o.) 732-246-7717
New Brunswick, NJ 08901   FAX 732-247-9151
Hours: (Admin) 10-6 Mon-Fri   E-mail: boxoffice@georgestplayhouse.org
www.georgestplayhouse.org
Member LORT (C-2)

Georgia Shakespeare Festival 404-504-3400
4484 Peachtree Rd, NE   (b.o.) 404-264-0020
Atlanta, GA 30319   FAX 404-504-3414
www.gashakespeare.org
Member LORT (D)

Geva Theatre 585-232-1366
75 Woodbury Blvd.   (b.o.) 585-232-GEVA
Rochester, NY 14607   FAX 585-232-4031
Hours: (Admin) 8:30-5 Mon-Fri   E-mail: gevatalk@gevatheatre.org
www.gevatheatre.org
Member LORT (B) and (D)

Globe Theatres 619-231-1941
Box 122171   (b.o.) 619-234-5623
San Diego, CA 92112   FAX 619-231-5879
Hours: 9-5 Mon-Fri   E-mail: oldglobe@theoldglobe.org
www.theoldglobe.org
Old Globe, Lowel Davies & Cassius Carter Theaters. Member LORT (B), (B) and (D)

The Goodman Theatre 312-443-3811
170 N. Dearborn St.   (b.o.) 312-443-3800
Chicago, IL 60601   FAX 312-263-6004
www.goodman-theatre.org   E-mail: staff@goodman-theatre.org
Member LORT (B), and (D)

Goodspeed Opera House 860-873-8664
6 Main St.   (b.o.) 860-873-8668
East Haddam, CT 06423   FAX 860-873-2329
www.goodspeed.org   E-mail: info@goodspeed.org
Member LORT (B) and (D)

Great Lakes Theatre Festival 216-241-5490
1501 Euclid Ave., Ste. 300   (b.o.) 216-241-6000
Cleveland, OH 44115   FAX 216-241-6315
www.greatlakestheater.org   E-mail: mail@greatlakestheater.org
Member LORT (B)

The Guthrie Theatre 877-44STAGE
818 S 2nd St.   (b.o.) 612-377-2224
Minneapolis, MN 55415   FAX 612-347-1188
www.guthrietheater.org
Member LORT (A) and (D)

Hartford Stage Company 860-525-5601
50 Church St.   (b.o.) 860-527-5151
Hartford, CT 06103   FAX 860-244-6183
www.hartfordstage.org
Member LORT (B)

Huntington Theatre Company 617-266-7900
264 Huntington Ave.   (b.o.) 617-266-0800
Boston, MA 02115   FAX 617-421-9674
www.huntingtontheatre.org
Member LORT (B+) and (C-2)

Indiana Repertory Theatre 317-635-5277
140 W Washington St.   (b.o.) 317-635-5252
Indianapolis, IN 46204   FAX 317-236-0767
Hours: 10-6 Mon-Fri   E-mail: info@irtlive.com
www.indianarep.com
Member LORT (C-1), (D) and (TYA)

Intiman Theatre Company 206-269-1901
201 Mercer St. / PO Box 19760   (b.o.) 206-269-1900
Seattle, WA 98109   FAX 206-269-1928
www.intiman.org   E-mail: lisaf@intiman.org
Member LORT (C-2)

The Kansas City Repertory Theatre 816-235-2727
4949 Cherry St.   (b.o.) 816-235-2700
Kansas City, MO 64110   FAX 816-235-5508
Hours: 10-5 Mon-Fri   E-mail: info@kcrep.org
www.missourirep.org
***Member LORT (B) and (D) Admin. Office 4825 Troost Ave # 101 Kansas City,
MO 64110***

La Jolla Playhouse 858-550-1070
2910 La Jolla Village Dr. / PO Box 12039   (b.o.) 858-550-1010
La Jolla, CA 92039   FAX 858-550-1025
www.lajollaplayhouse.com   E-mail: information@ljp.org
Member LORT (B), (B) and (C-2)

App

Laguna Playhouse 949-497-2787
   PO Box 1747 / 606 Laguna Canyon Rd.   800-946-5556
   Laguna Beach, CA 92652   FAX 949-497-6948
   Hours: 10-8 Daily (Box Office)   E-mail: boxoffice@lagunaplayhouse.org
   www.lagunaplayhouse.org
   Member LORT (B)

Lincoln Center Theatre 212-362-7600
   150 W 65th St.   (tele-charge) 212-239-6200
   NY, NY 10023   FAX 212-873-0761
   www.lct.org   E-mail: info@lct.org
   Member LORT (A+) and (B)

Mitzi E. Newhouse Theatre . . . .(admin. office) 212-362-7600
   150 W 65th St. (Lincoln Center)   (tele-charge) 212-239-6200
   NY, NY 10023
   Hours: 9-11pm Mon-Fri
   www.lct.org

Long Wharf Theatre 203-787-4284
   222 Sargent Dr.   (b.o.) 203-787-4282 or 800-782-8497
   New Haven, CT 06511   FAX 203-776-2287
   Hours: 9-5:30 Mon-Fri Admin. Hours   E-mail: info@longwarf.org
   www.longwharf.org
   Member LORT (B) and (C2)

Maltz Jupiter Theatre 561-743-2666
   1001 E Indiantown Rd   (tickets) 561-575-2223
   Jupiter, FL 33477   FAX (tickets) 561-743-0107
   Hours: b.o. 10-6 Mon-Fri / 10-2 Sat
   www.jupitertheatre.org
   Member LORT (C-1)

Manhattan Theatre Club . . . .(b.o.) 212-581-1212
   131 W 55th St.(6-7th Ave) Stage I & II   (b.o.) 212-581-1212
   NY, NY 10019
   Hours: 12-8 Mon-Sun

   311 W 43rd St., 8th FL(8-9th Ave) offices   212-399-3000
   NY, NY 10036   FAX 212-399-4329
   Hours: 10-6 Mon-Fri   E-mail: questions@mtc-nyc.org
   www.mtc-nyc.org
   Not-for-profit theatre organization. Resident Broadway theatre, The Friedman
   Theatre and City Center. Member LORT (A+), (B) and (D)

McCarter Theatre 609-258-6500
   91 University Pl.   (b.o.) 609-258-2787
   Princeton, NJ 08540   FAX 609-497-0369
   Hours: 10-6 Mon-Fri / 11-6 Sat-Sun   E-mail: sales@mccarter.org
   www.mccarter.org
   Member LORT (B+) and (B)

App

Merrimack Repertory Theatre 978-654-7550
Liberty Hall, 50 E Merrimack St.   (b.o.) 978-654-4678
Lowell, MA 01852   FAX 978-654-7575
Hours: 12-6 Tue-Sat   E-mail: box_office@merrimackrep.org
www.merrimackrep.org
Member LORT (D)

Milwaukee Repertory Theatre 414-224-1761
108 E Wells St.   (b.o.) 414-224-9490
Milwaukee, WI 53202   FAX 414-224-9097
www.milwaukeerep.com   E-mail: mailrep@milwaukeerep.com
Member LORT (A), (B), (C-1), (D) and (D)

Northlight Theatre /
  North Shore Center for the Performing Arts . . . .
. 847-679-9501
9501 Skokie Blvd.   (b.o.) 847-673-6300
Skokie, IL 60077   FAX 847-679-1879
Hours: 10-6 mon-Fri / 12-5 Sat   www.northlight.org
Member LORT (C-2)

People's Light & Theatre Company .610-647-1900
39 Conestoga Rd.   (b.o.) 610-644-3500
Malvern, PA 19355   FAX 610-640-9521
Hours: 9-5 Mon-Fri (Admin. office)   E-mail: pltc@peopleslight.org
www.peopleslight.org
Member LORT (D) and (D)

Philadelphia Theatre Company 215-985-1400
230 Broad St., Ste 1105   (Admin. Office) 215-985-0420
Philadelphia, PA 19102   FAX 215-985-5800
Hours: 9:30-5:30 Mon-Fri   E-mail: info@phillytheatreco.com
www.philadelphiatheatrecompany.org
Member LORT (D).

Pittsburgh Public Theater . . . .(Admin. Off) 412-316-8200
621 Penn Ave.   (b.o.) 412-316-1600
Pittsburgh, PA 15222   FAX 412-316-8219
Hours: 9-5:30 Mon-Fri   E-mail: info@ppt.org
www.ppt.org
Member LORT (B)

Playmakers Repertory Company . . . .(b.o.) 919-962-PLAY
CB#3235 Center for Dramatic Art (UNC Campus)   (Admin) 919-962-2489
Chapel Hill, NC 27599   FAX 919-962-5791
Hours: 12-6 Mon-Fri / Plus 2 hrs prior to performanceE-mail:
prcboxoffice@unc.edu
www.playmakersrep.org
Member LORT (D)

Portland Center Stage . . . .(Admin) 503-445-3720
128 NW 11th Ave.   (b.o.) 503-445-3700
Portland, OR 97209   FAX 503-796-6509
www.pcs.org
Member LORT (B) and (C-2)

App

Portland Stage Company . . . .(Admin. Office) 207-774-1043
25A Forest Ave.   (b.o.) 207-774-0465
Portland, ME 04104   FAX 207-774-0576
Hours: 9:30-5:30 Mon-Fri   E-mail: info@portlandstage.org
www.portlandstage.com
Member LORT (D)

Prince Music Theater 215-972-1000
100 S Broad St   (b.o.) 215-569-9700
Philadelphia, PA 19103
www.princemusictheater.org   E-mail: info@princemusictheater.org
*Member LORT (CBA) Theatre Address: 1412 Chestnut St. Philadelphia, PA
19103.*

Repertory Theatre Of St. Louis 314-968-7340
130 Edgar Rd.   (b.o.) 314-968-4925
St. Louis, MO 63119   FAX 314-968-9638
Hours: 9-5 Mon-Fri (Admn. office)   E-mail: mail@repstl.org
www.repstl.org
Member LORT (B+), (D), (D) and (TYA)

Round House Theatre . . . .(b.o.) 240-644-1100
PO Box 30688   (Admin) 240-644-1099
Bethesda, MD 20824   240-644-1090
www.roundhousetheatre.org   E-mail: roundhouse@roundhousetheatre.org
Member LORT

San Jose Repertory Theatre 408-367-7255
101 Paseo de San Antonio   (b.o.) 408-367-7255
San Jose, CA 95113   FAX 408-367-7236
www.sjrep.com   E-mail: help@sjrep.com
Member LORT (B) and (TYA)

Seattle Repertory Theatre 206-443-2210
155 Mercer St.   (b.o.) 206-443-2222
Seattle, WA 98109   FAX 206-443-2379
Hours: 9-6 Tue-Fri
www.seattlerep.org
Member LORT (B+) and (D)

Shakespeare Theatre Company 202-547-3230
516 8th St. SE   (b.o.) 202-547-1122
Washington, DC 20003   FAX 202-608-6350
Hours: 9:30-5:30 Mon-Fri   E-mail: web_admin@shakespearetheatre.cog
www.shakespearetheatre.org
Member LORT (B+), (B+) and (D)

South Coast Repertory 714-708-5500
PO Box 2197, 655 Town Center Dr.   (b.o.) 714-708-5555
Costa Mesa, CA 92628   FAX 714-545-0391
www.scr.org   E-mail: theatre@scr.org
Member LORT (B), (C-2) and (TYA)

Studio Arena Theatre 716-856-8025
710 Main St.   (b.o.) 800-745-3000
Buffalo, NY 14202   FAX 716-847-1644
www.studioarena.org   E-mail: studio@pce.net
Member LORT (B)

Syracuse Stage 315-443-4008
820 E Genesee St.   (b.o.) 315-443-3275
Syracuse, NY 13210   FAX 315-443-1408
www.syracusestage.org   E-mail: syrstage@syr.edu
Member LORT (C1) and (D)

Theatre for a New Audience 212-229-2819
154 Christopher St., Ste. 3D   FAX 212-229-2911
NY, NY 10014
Hours: 10-6 Mon-Fri   E-mail: info@tfana.org
www.tfana.org
Member LORT (D)

TheatreWorks . . . .(b.o.) 650-463-1950
PO Box 50458
Pala Alto, CA 94303
www.theatreworks.org
Member LORT (B) and (C-2)

Trinity Repertory Company 401-521-1100
201 Washington St.   (b.o.) 401-351-4242
Providence, RI 02903   FAX 401-521-0447
Hours: 9-5 Mon-Fri   E-mail: info@trinityrep.com
www.trinityrep.com
Member LORT (B) and (D)

Virginia Stage Company 757-627-6988
254 Granby St.   (b.o.) 757-627-1234
Norfolk, VA 23510   FAX 757-628-5958
Hours: 9-5 Mon-Fri   E-mail: cbauman@vastage.com
www.vastage.com
Member LORT (D)

The Wilma Theater 215-893-9456
265 S Broad St.   (b.o.) 215-546-7824
Philadelphia, PA 19107   FAX 215-893-0895
www.wilmatheater.org   E-mail: info@wilmatheater.org
Member LORT (C-2)

Yale Repertory Theatre 203-432-1500
PO Box 208244, 1120 Chapel St.   (b.o.) 203-432-1234
New Haven, CT 06505   FAX 203-432-6423
Hours: 9-5 Mon-Fri (Office)   E-mail: yalerep@yale.edu
www.yalerep.org
Member LORT (D), (D) and (D)

App

WEB RESOURCES

aboutsources 646-218-2538
50 W 40th St., 4th FL (5-6th Ave)
NY, NY 10018
Hours: by appt.   E-mail: sp@aboutsources.com
www.aboutsources.com
Business to business information provider for the fashion industry.

American Association of Community Theatre 817-732-3177
1300 Gendy St.   866-687-2228
Ft Worth, TX 76107   FAX 817-732-3178
www.aact.org   E-mail: info@aact.org
Homepage of the American Association of Community Theatre.

American Theatre Wing 212-765-0606
570 Seventh Ave. (B'way-8th Ave)   FAX 212-307-1910
NY, NY 10018
Hours: 9:30-5:30 Mon-Fri   E-mail: mailbox@americantheatrewing.org
www.americantheatrewing.org
Homepage of American Theatre Wing featuring info on productions across the country.

Artist's Health Insurance Resource Center 800-798-8447
729 Seventh Ave., 10th Fl. (National Headquarters) The Actors Fund
NY, NY 10019
Hours: 11-7 Mon-Fri
www.actorsfund.org/ahirc
Website that provides information to artists about individual and small group health insurance options available in each state.

Backstage ....www.Backstage.com
Online version of weekly entertainment newspaper, including some tech job listings.

New York City Office of Film, Theater, & Broadcasting 212-489-6710
1697 Broadway, 6th Fl. (53rd St)   FAX 212-307-6237
NY, NY 10019
Hours: 9-4 Mon-Thurs / 9-3 Fri
www.nyc.gov/film
Mayor's office of film, theatre and broadcasting.

Playbill ....www.playbill.com
Homepage for Playbill magazine featuring info on theatre as well as some job listings. Sign up for a free membership to receive special offers on tickets and merchandise.

Theatre Development Fund (TDF) 212-912-9770
520 Eighth Ave. Ste 801 (36th St)   FAX 212-768-1563
NY, NY 10016
Hours: 10-6 Mon-Fri   E-mail: info@tdf.org
www.tdf.org
An audience development organization supporting theatre, music and dance. Administers the Costume Collection, TKTS booths and "Theatre Access Project" for disabled individuals. Discount tickets available by mail for qualifying individuals and groups (visit website or send stamped, self-addressed envelope for information and application).

Theatre Resources . . . . .www.wwar.com//perform.html
Theatre resource website featuring links to many other theatre, educational and design resource sites.

Variety Magazine . . . . .www.variety.com
360 Park Ave.
NY, NY 10010
Homepage for Variety magazine

App

NOTES

PRODUCT INDEX

ATAC

JOIN ATAC

ATAC creates a professional network through its quarterly meetings, newsletter, membership directory and web site. Since the nature of our work is often independent, many ATAC members find this network indispensable for tracking industry activities and finding new and exciting projects. Members get a listing and a link on the ATAC website, a listing in the members only *Yellow Book Membership Directory* and access to web posted job listings thru our web site.

Full Member
Open to those who have attained a high degree of expertise in their individual crafts. A minimum of two years professional experience is required.

Associate Member/Student
Open to those who have not worked professionally or have only limited experience.

Organizational Member
Open to nonprofit organizations such as colleges, universities, foundations, etc.

Sustaining Member
Open to commercial businesses, firms and establishments interested in supporting the purposes and ideal of ATAC.

Friends of ATAC
Open to patron of the arts who support ATAC's goals. A nonvoting contributor.

Write for a free membership brochure:
membership@atacbiz.com